Contents

Section 1

The Sociology of Race
by John Richardson and John Lambert

Chapter Four

Ethnicity 53

Chapter Five

Structure and Conflict 70

Bibliography 87

Section 2

The Sociology of Development

by Aidan Foster-Carter

Chapter Four

Urbanization

Chapter Five

Rural Development

Chapter Six

Population

Chapter Seven

Health

Chapter Eight

Education

Chapter Nine

Women and Development

Section 3

Urban Sociology
by Martin Slattery

Chapter Three

Urban Studies 265

Chapter Four

Urban Policy-Making: The Inner City 279

Section 4

The Sociology of Youth

by Simon Frith

Chapter One

Definitions

Chapter Two

The Concept of Youth Culture

Chapter Three

Chapter Four

Chapter Five

Chapter Six

Critiques of Sub-cultural Theory

Chapter Seven

The Future of Youth

Section 5

The Sociology of Mass Media
by David Glover

Chapter One

Media Effects

Chapter Two

Media Imagery and Representations

Chapter Three

The Structure and Organization of the Mass Media

Section 6

The Sociology of Knowledge

by David Glover and Sheelagh Strawbridge

Chapter One
Knowledge and Society

Chapter Two

Classical Perspectives on the Sociology of Knowledge

Chapter Six

**New Sociologies of Scientific Knowledge
and the Problem of Relativism**

Section 7

The Sociology of Health and Medicine
by Nicky Hart

Chapter One

Health and the Mythology of Medicine

Chapter Two

Human Health and Society

Chapter Five

Becoming Ill as a Social Process   598

Chapter Six

Medicine as an Institution of Social Control   615

Chapter Seven

The Power of Medicine in Society   630

Section 1

The Sociology of Race

John Richardson and John Lambert

Chapter One
Race and Sociology

This section is about the way sociologists have tried to come to terms with the nature and causes of those conflicts and problems that are termed 'race relations' problems. It would not have been written if there was not a widespread recognition that there are indeed severe race relations *problems*. For some, of course, such problems are the fault of, or caused by, racial or ethnic minorities. For others the problems are caused by racists and by racism.

An important task for sociology is to assess the significance of various explanations, and at the outset it may be useful to distinguish five traditions or perspectives, in order to locate sociology's special contribution.

Perspectives on Race

(1) The 'moral' approach. In this view, the problems associated with 'race' are reducible to fundamental moral issues. Racism is attributed to outright human wickedness, or to common human failings such as selfishness and ignorance. The appropriate solution, then, lies in critical soul-searching, appealing to nobler moral values, and in affirming the dignity and worth of all members of the one human race. Rather predictably, social scientists tend to dismiss this moral approach as 'naïve' and hoplessly abstract, but it is certainly true that race relations present urgent moral choices, and this means that the banishment of moral considerations would be misguided. However, it is far more informative to locate moral issues within specific social and historical contexts. Why, for example, does racial goodwill vary between societies and within one society over time? What are the obstacles (e.g. financial interests, power relationships) which stand in the way of inter-racial harmony? By asking these sorts of questions, the

sociologist reaches beyond abstract moral debate towards a more socially informed examination of the particular types of environments and interests which shape moral choices.

(2) The 'biological' approach. At its simplest, this approach assumes that prejudice against 'out-groups' is a more or less natural instinct, determined by some genetic code which supposedly enhances survival chances (e.g. by favouring people of similar appearance, the survival chances of the 'selfish gene' are improved). Furthermore, the social disadvantages of ethnic minorities are portrayed as a direct reflection of their innate inferiority (e.g. the poor educational results and low status jobs of minority groups are explained not by prejudice nor discrimination nor cultural dislocation, but by their allegedly inferior IQ levels or by some biologically-based inability to develop sophisticated cultures). However, as we will argue later in this chapter, the sociologist can safely ignore these discredited and highly misleading views. It is the social meanings of biological differences which matter, not the biological differences in themselves.

(3) The 'psychological' approach. Rather than describing prejudice as an inborn mechanism triggered off by the mere sight of people of different physical appearance, psychologists are far more likely to resort to explanations in terms of learning experiences, personality quirks, and the general psychological processes involved in attitude formation. Thus, certain high-risk personalities (subjected to unfortunate socialisation) may be especially predisposed towards bigotry; or perhaps prejudice has more general currency among small groups exposed to recurrent psychological frustrations (e.g. the frustration-aggression model, in which cumulative psychological frustrations result in a fund of aggression which may be displaced on to some 'safe' scapegoat group). As for social disadvantage, this can be explained by the direct discriminatory practices of the prejudiced, or by the demoralisation and lowered self-esteem of the victims of racism. Some of these psychological arguments undoubtedly illuminate important areas and dimensions in race relations.

(4) The 'cultural' approach. This approach also tackles 'attitudes', but from a sociological orientation which makes few references to personalities or mental processes. Instead, emphasis is placed upon the dynamics of 'cultural' allegiances and traditions, and the main interest lies in the social origins, functions and consequences of these cultural phenomena. In this model, cultural racism has its roots in the dim colonial past, but the racist stereotypes developed during that period are transmitted to succeeding generations as part of the general folk-lore, and it is by inculcating this cultural tradition that white people develop prejudices against blacks. Another, contemporary, version, explains racial friction as a form of 'ethnic conflict' sparked off by groups jealously guarding the integrity of their distinctive cultural identities. The 'ethnicity' approach, which we elaborate in Chapter 4, also allows that much racial disadvantage is not due to racialism pure and simple, but to wider cultural factors (lack of familiarity with British language and customs; voluntary segregation; continued ties with 'home' country).

(5) The 'structural' approach. This group of explanations traces the reasons for racism back to the major structural features and social processes of the dominant society. So the main source of racism is located not in the hearts and minds of people, nor in abstract cultural allegiances, but firmly in the principal structural arrangements of the society. If the social structure systematically generates sharp conflicts of material interests, or if it breeds cumulative social frustrations, then this is likely to fan the flames of racial prejudice (e.g. whites blame blacks for what in fact are structurally-created problems of unemployment, housing shortages, and so on). Moreover, racial minorities in Britain generally have insufficient power to compete successfully in the economic and political struggle for scarce resources, and therefore they constitute a disadvantaged section of the population. In these sorts of ways, the basic social structure (the key institutions, patterned social networks, and especially the stratification system) crucially affects the nature of race relations and the life chances of racial minorities.

This brief review of the major perspectives available for explaining problems and issues of race relations helps to establish a distinctive sociological approach, but clearly these perspectives cannot be rigidly separated, and in the chapters which follow we will explore aspects of their differences and of their overlap.

A particular set of complications arise from the broad sweep of structural and cultural explanations – the major concern of the sociologist. Although all structural approaches rely on structural 'strains' and 'tensions' as a clue to understanding race relations, this shared emphasis still accommodates an interesting diversity of detailed arguments. Some indication of this diversity is provided by Taylor (1982), who usefully describes the many explanations which can be used to make sense of the 'race riots' (or 'urban riots', since they included white participants) which broke out in such inner-city areas as Brixton, St. Pauls and Toxteth in the early 1980s. The British riots represent a fertile testing-ground for structural explanations, and Taylor shows that nearly all literature on riots refers to structural factors, usually broken down into long-term 'preconditions' (such as unemployment and urban deprivation) and the more immediate 'precipitants' of conflict (such as police ineptitude or heavy-handedness). Nevertheless, this still leaves a bewildering variety of specific explanations, in terms of such things as system malfunctions, underclass revolt, internal colonialism, political marginalisation, 'pressure-cooker' theories of violence, failures of policy initiatives, ecological defence, and several other accounts. Taylor wisely contends that no single 'factor' can adequately explain the outbreak of violence and the eruption of frustrations, but he also suggests that theoretical frameworks are valuable in arranging the relevant factors and in drawing out the underlying processes. And, as in so many other branches of sociology, the dominant sociological frameworks for this task are the familiar ones of functionalism and conflict theory.

Functionalism – or the 'order' model – depicts society as a more or less integrated and cohesive system in which consensus is ensured by cooperative relationships between the various sub-systems and by a unifying set of common norms and values. Social elements persist because they fulfil some function which contributes towards the overall stability and survival of the system, and this system therefore serves the interests of all members of society. The system tends to rest in a state of equilibrium in which the tensions between the component sub-systems are reduced to a minimum, but occasionally this equilibrium is disrupted, and in this event self-regulating processes will come into play to restore stability. The functionalist model lends itself readily to the study of race relations, and the immigrant-host model described in Chapter 2 is perhaps the most striking example: here a stable host society is temporarily disturbed by the confusing arrival of new elements (the immigrants) who do not share the same values, and consensus is presumably restored by the 'healing' process of resocial-isation and long-term structural integration. Thus, Schermerhorn (1970) states that the systems approach dwells on:

> the functions the ethnic group performs for the entire system, viewing the ethnic group itself as a sub-system gradually fitting into the entire society by a series of adaptive adjustments regulated by the norms and values of its institutions that eventually become internalised by members of the ethnic groups involved.

However, the equilibrium-restoring mechanisms may prove

inadequate or slow, and these system failures will then result in blocked opportunity structures, unfulfilled aspirations, and social discontent. So the British riots can be accommodated within this framework, in spite of its bias towards 'consensus' rather than 'conflict'. Indeed, Mason (1981) indicates a close affinity between functionalism and the 'liberal reformist' assumptions of the famous Scarman Report (1981) on the riots:

> These assumptions include a view of social life in which individuals compete with one another for access to scarce resources, making, as they do so, rational decisions on the basis of more or less complete or accurate information. Racial disadvantage occurs when the normal opportunities for free competition are distorted by obstacles arising from economic misfortune (recession, urban decay), failures of policy (often resulting from inadequate information, misjudgement, and so on), or mischief-making (by pathologically prejudiced individuals and right-wing propagandists, aided again by inadequate information, education or training).

Drawing on this image of a basically sound society acting in the long-term interests of everyone, the Scarman Report regarded piecemeal reforms as the appropriate solution: the state was obliged to intervene to remove unfortunate social and economic obstacles which temporarily stood in the way of a fair deal for individual members of the ethnic minorities. The proposed reforms included employment and housing measures, the promotion of racial harmony, and steps to eradicate racial prejudice in the police force. However, it is the basic notion of a consensual, even-handed society whose problems can be remedied by *ad hoc* adjustments which most significantly differentiates the functionalist model from conflict approaches.

For the conflict theorist, either the favoured reforms do not go far enough, or they are unlikely to be implemented anyway because of the basic conflicts of interests between socio-economic groups. The conflict image of society is one of a continuous struggle between dominant and subordinate groups whose divergent sectional interests create divisive conflicts rather than stability and consensus. Society is based on systematic exploitation which benefits the powerful groups at the expense of others, but the dominant groups manage to maintain control by means of coercion and ideological manipulation. Still, the major strains and fierce tensions – or 'contradictions' – which are generated by an unfair and oppressive system are likely to encourage organised protest and opposition. Only a fundamental structural transformation and a significant shift in the balance of power will remove the distress and exploitation of the disadvantaged groups, and there is little prospect of ruling groups voluntarily passing legislation which will make deep inroads into their privileges or adversely affect their material interests.

The Delusion of Race

Whatever sociological framework or explanatory perspective is adopted, there is an unavoidable truth to face:

> As a way of categorising people, race is based upon a delusion, because popular ideas about racial classification lack scientific validity and are moulded by political pressures rather than by evidence from biology. (Banton and Harwood, 1975.)

In the aftermath of World War II which had seen the slaughter of the holocaust justified by a doctrine of racial superiority and the linked quest for racial purity to promote a master race for world order, the World's scientists unambiguously stated that there was no scientific basis for the belief that one race was superior to another:

> Current biological knowledge does not permit us to impute cultural achievements to differences in genetic potential. Differences in the achievements of different peoples should be attributed solely to their cultural history. The peoples of the world today appear to possess equal biological potentialities for attaining any level of civilization. (UNESCO, 1967.)

But as we all know, the delusion, and actions based on it, persist worldwide. In the field of race relations, W. I. Thomas's famous sociological dictum has immediate relevance: if people define a situation as real, it is real in its social consequences. Thus, if white people actually believe that blacks are congenitally inferior and irredeemably primitive, then this attitude constitutes their social reality, and it will influence their subsequent behaviour towards blacks. Likewise, if Rastafarians believe that all whites are corrupt plotters in a sinister 'Babylonian conspiracy', then this may well have far-reaching consequences in their dealings with white people. So social attitudes and constructions of 'race' are not just interesting curiosities: they form the medium of exchange in daily interaction between the groups concerned. We need to examine the roots of the delusion.

The Doctrine of Racial Superiority

Banton (1977) notes how various nineteenth century thinkers were impressed both by the rapid advances in biology and zoology and by the tremendous technological achievements of Western European powers. Consequently, they became fascinated with the prospect of constructing taxonomies (classifications) of human beings which introduced a link between racial attributes and moral and cultural superiority. These writers did not always agree on important details, and so competing taxonomies were canvassed and fiercely debated, but beneath this surface rivalry there existed a shared set of assumptions which Banton calls the 'theory of racial typology'. This entailed the following propositions:

(1) Variations in the physical appearance of peoples indicate distinctive racial 'types' of a fixed, permanent kind.
(2) These racial 'types' develop markedly different cultures, since culture is decisively influenced by biological status.
(3) It is possible, therefore, to acknowledge the superiority of Europeans in general, and 'Aryans' in particular.
(4) Friction between nations or different racial groups is 'natural' insofar as it springs ultimately from biological sources.

Although these assertions have now been discredited or modified out of all recognition – at least as far as respectable science is concerned – they nevertheless survive as lingering components of 'commonsense' views: in particular, the notion of races as more or less fixed, mutually exclusive groups arranged in some hierarchy of superiority. The unsupportable nature of the doctrine of racial superiority can be demonstrated, however, if we pursue two basic questions:

(1) What is a 'race'?
(2) What is the relationship between biology and culture?

What is a Race?

Biologists and botanists generally find it useful to construct taxonomies which identify and arrange different species and their related sub-groups. Just as it is possible to distinguish plants and animals in this way, so attempts were made from the nineteenth century on to classify human beings according to physical and biological criteria. Inevitably this enterprise threw up a number of fanciful and crankish ideas (including the dangerously misleading theory of racial typology), but gradually a firmer understanding developed. Thus, it became clear that all human beings belong to a single species, in the sense that the various 'members' are potentially capable of producing fertile offspring if they mate with each other. But the members differ noticeably in physical appearance, and so the term 'race' has been adopted to denote a recognisable sub-division of the species. UNESCO, for example, has used the term to refer to groups of humanity showing well-developed and primarily heritable physical differences from other groups. For convenience, then, various 'physical markers' have been employed to map the boundaries between one race and another. No single physical feature is sufficiently sensitive for this purpose, but normally the working assumption is made that certain 'clusters' of physical characteristics – hair type, skin colour, nasal shape, lip form, etc. – permit reasonable demarcation. This assumption lies behind the familiar distinction between Mongoloid, Negroid and Caucasoid races (see Table 1).

Table 1.   Conventional taxonomy of phenotypical differences

Racial Group	Eyes	Hair	Skin	Face	Main location
Mongoloid	Black 'slanted'	Black straight	Yellow-reddish brown	Flat, high cheekbones, sparse beard	S & E Asia, N & S America Pacific
Negroid	Brown	Black tightly curled	Dark brown-black	Broad nose, wide nostrils, thick lips, sparse beard	Sub-Saharan African
Caucasoid	Light blue to dark brown	Straight, wavy, curly, balding more common	White to dark brown	Narrow nose thin lips, more facial hair	Europe, M. East N. Africa, India

Clearly, this classification is very broad and sweeping, and so it does not totally succeed in avoiding awkward cases (e.g. are Bushmen and aboriginals part of the Negroid group, or do they constitute a separate race?). This type of problem has led to the construction of yet further sub-groups within each racial division. In the Caucasoid group, for example, the distinction between 'whites' and 'Asian Indians' is obvious enough. But there is also a division between various European groups (Nordic, Alpine and Mediterranean). Nevertheless, subsequent modifications of this basic schema have not resulted in acceptably tidy groupings, and so the classification still remains no more than suggestive. Moreover, it has become increasingly apparent that there are more informative means of distinguishing between human groupings, in terms of the altogether more reliable methods of modern genetics.

The technical details of genetics are not important here – suffice to say that each human body consists of many thousands of genes which incorporate chemical codes in complex permutations and which account for the unique character of individuals. Modern knowledge in genetics casts considerable doubts on the validity and utility of the older taxonomics based on physical appearance. The relationship between *genotype* – the underlying genetic patterning of individuals and groups – and *phenotype* – the difference and patterns of physical appearance – is extraordinarily complex. In particular, the following three aspects should be noted:

(1) The older notion of 'race' referred to a few broad groups, distinguished by selected phenotypical differences. This has been replaced by the more sophisticated and flexible concept of numerous 'gene pools' or 'populations', each marked out by a characteristic 'genetic profile'. Thus, even within a relatively small geographical area, local populations may differ in the frequencies of certain genes. The patterns of genetic traits are determined by various factors: climate, physical environment, diet, genetic mutations which affect adaptation, genetic drift (selective migration), geographical barriers (seas, mountains, deserts) and social influences (mating and breeding patterns, and political forces like apartheid).

(2) Modern genetics shifts us away from the notion of static, permanent 'types' towards a much more fluid conception of human groupings. These groups are seen as part of a general evolutionary process in which change is occurring all the time. Genetic mutation, breeding and inter-breeding patterns, and changing environmental circumstances make it improbable that the genetic profile of a group will remain constant.

(3) The notion of 'pure' race is misleading in the extreme. Firstly, there is considerable diversity within any group, since its members do not share exactly the same genes. But even more importantly, there is considerable continuity and overlap between groups. The basic under-lying human genotype (e.g. genes which determine that we have two legs, a prehensible thumb, etc.) suggests that the differences are less striking than the similarities. Moreover, the differences which do exist typically relate not to the presence or absence of certain genes, but rather to the *statistical* frequencies of those genes in the populations being compared.

Biology and Culture

The other leading assertion in the theory of racial typology concerns the alleged link between biology and culture. Proponents of the doctrine argued that there was a strong causal connection, so that the biological level set limits on the cultural achievements of 'inferior' races and at the same time encouraged the relatively unhampered progress of 'superior' races. Such arguments tended to be presented in confident fashion, as if they were the irresistible conclusions of sound scientific research. It does not take a great stretch of the imagination to appreciate the social and political attractions of such ideas in the nineteenth century. They proved a useful rallying point for the British nation in its efforts to forge and consolidate an Empire; they acted as an inspiration to further cultural achievement, and they simultaneously legitimised imperial ventures (e.g. the Empire was seen as a 'civilising' mission to help 'backward' peoples). In this respect, the theory of racial typology was not so much a neutral scientific statement, but rather an integral part of an over-arching ideology which played an important role in a situation of social and political conflict. And this ideology gained strength by appearing not simply as a case of special pleading or political intrigue but as based on solid scientific 'fact', and this is what the proponents of the theory of racial typology promised to provide.

The motives of those scientists must be separated from the issue of the consequences and social effects of their writings, including the ways in which politicians adopted and used their ideas. Banton is surely correct in insisting that genuine scientific errors were made, and that in the nineteenth century context these racial ideas had a certain surface plausibility. For example, Darwin's evolutionary theory seemed to reinforce the notion of a biologically-based hierarchy of human types with each race representing successive 'stages' in evolutionary advancement. And even today we still find tentative advocates of the core ideas enshrined in the theory of racial typology. Belief in racial superiority of sorts still prevails – in a much more guarded and sophisticated form – in those 'scientific' theories (e.g. sociobiology) which contend that apparent racial differences in intelligence and social behaviour are ultimately attributable to biological causes. However, the champions of this line of reasoning have not been conspicuously successful in establishing their case. We can now look briefly at some of the reasons for their lack of success:

(1) Firstly, it is extremely difficult to identify the precise links between the biological level and socio-cultural phenomena. Given the immense complexity of genetic processes, it is perhaps not surprising

that the supposed biological causes tend to be assumed rather than convincingly demonstrated. Most commonly, the writers concerned start from rather broad socio-cultural differences, then proceed to speculate on some underlying, as yet unspecified, biological mechanisms which are presumably responsible for these differences. Now, it would be foolish to suggest that biology has no bearing on socio-cultural behaviour, but, with the exception of some biological abnormalities which result in low intelligence or bizarre behaviour, we would normally expect the linkages to be remote and indirect. The whole task becomes much more perplexing when a racial dimension is included, because then we would expect the proponents to show that socio-cultural patterns neatly, or even nearly, coincide with the lines of biologically-defined races. No such correspondence is demonstrable.

(2) Powerful explanations of social phenomena can be offered without resorting to biological 'reductionism' (explaining events at one level by referring to a 'lower', presumably more basic, level). Indeed, sociology is based on a firm recognition of the 'autonomy' of the social level, on the necessity of dealing with social events in their own terms. Unlike animals, human beings are not so rigidly bound to inbuilt instincts or innate biological triggers; on the contrary, human survival and progress is enhanced if cultural flexibility prevails. So, while biology is obviously important (we would not be recognisably 'human', or even exist, without our biology), it sets only rather broad limits on cultural development. To this extent, then, human beings are 'freed' from biological destiny. A clear illustration of this is the way in which a given 'race' can create quite contrasting 'cultures' in different geographical locations; likewise, members of separate biological 'races' may contribute to the development of a single 'culture' in a particular society. Therefore the complex social, political and historical manifestations of 'race' demand study in their own right, rather than being dismissed in favour of deterministic biological 'programmes'.

(3) The notion of 'cultural superiority' is highly problematic. What are the yardsticks by which we assess the relative merits of different cultures? People tend to judge these matters from an 'ethnocentric' viewpoint which predisposes them to value the 'familiar' and to disparage other cultures. What lent racial doctrines a certain credibility was the impressive technological spurt of Western European nations in recent centuries, but claims of 'progress' appear less convincing when we consider the subsequent problems of industrial pollution, personal alienation, and the possibility of nuclear warfare. The African pygmy or Mongolian herdsman is arguably in a more 'harmonious' relationship with his physical and human environment than is the

urban inhabitant of London or New York. However, the main point is that cultural achievements do not thereby demonstrate some 'innate' or permanent superiority, as a glance at history quickly reveals. For example, ethnocentric white Europeans tend to overlook proud African civilisations of the past, such as the Songhai, Ashanti and Zimbabwe empires, at a time when Europe was in the 'Dark Ages'. Also, Goldthorpe (1975) argues that, in 1600, an impartial observer would probably have rated China as the most 'developed' nation, with India and Arabia vying for second place. Plainly, the history of racial achievement resembles a see-saw, so it offers no compelling evidence for undisputed racial superiority.

The Intelligence Controversy

In spite of these telling points, the thorny debate about racial superiority gained fresh impetus in the late 1960s, and this time it focussed squarely on the issue of intelligence. In the United States the key figure was Jensen (1969), who argued that compensatory 'environmental' programmes to boost educational performance had failed dismally thereby suggesting the overriding importance of heredity. Meanwhile in Britain, Eysenck (1971) concluded that the research findings of psychometrics (the testing and measuring of mental capacities) indicated distinct racial differences in intellectual abilities. For example, in the USA the average IQ score of black groups lagged about fifteen points behind the average score of equivalent white groups. Although the 'hereditarian' views of Eysenck and Jensen soon came under fierce attack, opponents tended to be dismissed as rather utopian idealists whose liberal values prevented them from recognising the 'objective' evidence of 'hard-headed' scientists. However, the irony is that the most authoritative criticism emerged from within the scientific community itself, and it is the scientific credentials of the hereditarian arguments which have been shown to be suspect. The numerous methodological deficiences – poor research design, circumstantial evidence, tests of dubious validity, etc. – have been rehearsed elsewhere (Kamin, 1981) and need not detain us here. Still, it is important to note that the case of 'intelligence' definitely does *not* lend belated support to the doctrine of racial superiority.

First of all, it is perfectly obvious that members of a given 'race' are not confined to a narrow IQ band. Whatever IQ tests measure – and this is a matter of some controversy – it is nonetheless evident that members typically spread over the whole range of possible scores. Therefore the scores of different 'races' exhibit considerable overlap, and so the debate only concerns group averages (no one suggests that all – or even most – members of one group are superior to, or inferior to, the members of another group). Moreover, the weakness in crude hereditarian arguments is most clearly exposed when we examine the alleged link between biology and IQ. The debate between 'nature' and 'nurture' is perennial because, while everyone recognises the influence of heredity and of environment, there are no reliable means of assessing their *relative* contributions. Despite this major obstacle, the indefensible hereditarian argument over-confidently asserts that IQ tests are a valid measure of a 'fixed', 'intrinsic' ability which is largely genetically determined; and that this genetic determination suggests relatively unchangeable IQ differences between races. But already we have seen that 'races' themselves are not unchanging, and we have also noted that the IQ differences are of a small magnitude. Furthermore, environmental influences just cannot be assigned the minor role of simply 'topping-up' a given genetic potential. Even the most convinced environmentalists accept some underlying genetic contribution to intelligence, but they insist that intellectual development springs from the unique, dynamic *interaction* of genes and environment. Consequently, there is little way of knowing how a given individual or group would have turned out if environmental circumstances had been otherwise. John Rex (1973) has aptly pointed to the contrasts in the different environments of white and black in America and suggests that there can be no true comparison without an experiment in which:

> The peoples of Africa conquer, capture and enslave some millions of European and American whites, under conditions in which a very large proportion of the white population dies, in which the white culture is systematically destroyed, and in which, finally, a group of emancipated whites in 'good neighbourhoods' are then compared to their negro masters... the differences in the history of negroes and whites are a factor of immense significance, and... any statistical reasoning which leaves them out can reach no conclusions of any value whatever.

The Social Construction of Race

We have shown that, scientifically speaking, *race* (in the sense of 'gene pools') refers to clusters of biological characteristics which are changeable rather than unalterably fixed and which relate to gradually altering gene frequencies among diverse human groups rather than to clearly identifiable basic human types. We have shown, too, how the idea that there is a strong causal chain between the biological level and the sphere of socio-cultural behaviour is untenable. Science cannot give support to the idea that social characteristics and cultural forms are biologically programmed either in essential detail or in broad general sweep. There is no demonstrable genetic basis for cannibalism or for Christianity, for rising divorce rates, shifts in fashion of clothes or music, or for racial hatred. Social customs and patterns of behaviour are not pre-determined by rigid laws of nature incorporated in the genes, but emerge in the course of social interaction. Social reality is *socially* constructed.

So the sociologist can safely leave biology aside and concentrate on how race is socially constructed. Once people choose to attribute variable social meanings to physical differences and behave as if biology *did* fix attributes and abilities, then *that* becomes part of social reality. What people make of physical differences, the everyday or commonsense notions which influence them, constitutes the social meaning of race. The distinction that Banton (1974) draws between 'analytical' and 'folk' concepts of race is useful. Race, in the scientific or analytical sense, has limited relevance as a rough indicator of clusters of gene pools. But in this book we are primarily concerned with the 'folk' concept, the everyday attitudes regarding racial differences.

Far from being 'natural' or 'instinctive', these social attitudes to race tend to vary according to time and place. In some societies, at certain times, people are found to attach little weight to racial differences, while in other contexts we might find intense hostility and pronounced patterns of racial 'exclusion' and 'inclusion'.

But a sociology of race reaches beyond the description of relevant belief systems towards a search for the social factors which shape and condition those beliefs. It is not satisfactory to accept cultural beliefs as 'given' or simply 'there', as if they were plucked arbitrarily from thin air. Rather, we would expect that a society's 'culture' (its network of attitudes, values, meanings and ideologies) is connected in intimate ways which its 'structure' (the pattern of social institutions, productive arrangements and power relationships). The distinctive emphasis on the 'social construction of reality' allows that human beings have a genuinely active role in striving to create and sustain meanings and in generally asserting themselves in the world. Nevertheless, this creative work takes place within particular historical and structural contexts which tend to limit human choices and make certain types of cultural response and behaviour more likely than others. It is in this dynamic interplay – people creating 'social reality', and this social reality acting back on people – that the social construction of race can be located.

Therefore, if hostile racist attitudes are widespread in a society, then we might expect to discover something in the history or social structure of that society which predisposes people towards these attitudes. Perhaps internal conflict is so rife that it creates the need for racial 'scapegoats' to ease social tensions; or perhaps powerful groups are manipulating racial prejudices in order to weaken and exploit racial minorities for the purpose of economic gain. As Schermerhorn (1970) remarks, 'prejudice is a product of situations, historical situations, economic situations, political situations; it is not a little demon that emerges in people simply because they are depraved'. Of course, racial attitudes are not simply a direct automatic reflection of social situations: to a certain extent they gain momentum of their own, interacting with other cultural elements (e.g. political and religious ideologies) and acting back on and changing the structural reality itself. So culture and structure interact in complex and shifting ways, and it is unrealistic to expect an absolutely straightforward match between particular types of racial belief systems and distinctive types of social structure. Nevertheless, the social structure provides valuable clues to the source and consequences of racial hostility.

The sociology of race, then, entails the study of social consciousness, of inter-group behaviour and of social structure. By focussing attention on three sociologists' treatment of race in contemporary Britain we can discover the key elements in the search for a distinctive sociology of race: John Rex, a noted Weberian; Robert Miles, writing from a Marxist standpoint; and Michael Banton, writing from a more eclectic standpoint rooted in social anthropology and role theory, and closer perhaps to the British empirical tradition in social sciences.

John Rex's work represents the most developed attempt to demarcate a special domain of race relations entailing a distinct set of social phenomena. A persistent theme in his writings is the insistence that 'race' must be taken seriously as a social issue and as a sociological concept. Of course, Rex is fully aware that the social meanings of race contain numerous errors and falsehoods, but what matters is the human actor's point of view, and he recognises the ways in which subjective understandings of race translate themselves into objective consequences. However, he is at pains to stress that race problems are not solely a matter of mistaken ideas or false consciousness, and he does not believe that these problems will simply vanish if the errors are challenged. Alongside the subjective definitions, then, due attention must be paid to the underlying social structures which help create and sustain racial belief systems and racial tensions.

Rex's various studies underline his concern to develop a rigorous, theoretically informed definition of the appropriate subject matter for a sociology of race. He sees three necessary (but not sufficient) conditions for a fully fledged race relations situation, structure or problem. These are:

(1) A social situation in which at least two groups co-exist in a context of inequality and conflict.
(2) The boundaries between the groups are such that group categorization is on an ascriptive basis which limits movement between groups.
(3) The availability of *deterministic* belief systems which draw a causal link between group membership and social and cultural achievements, and in so doing provide a justification for discrimination. These belief systems may be systematic biological or theological doctrines, or may be current as 'folklore', 'proverbs', or 'superstition'. (Rex 1970.)

Each of these elements has a certain measure of independence, and each deserves special attention, but Rex is primarily interested in their interrelations. For Rex, the main task of a sociology of race is the detailed analysis, along comparative and historical lines, of the major types of race relations situations.

The sociological influence of Max Weber is very apparent in Rex's writing – his concern to focus on social meanings, an action frame of reference, his concern for comparative and historical work, but essentially his presentation of social order and structure arising out of *diverse* intergroup conflicts, among which those relating to production and the organising of the economy are important, but not necessarily paramount. Within that sociological framework there is room for a distinct sociology of race.

For Robert Miles, such an enterprise is quite misguided because 'race relations' is not a legitimate sphere of study. If race has that highly limited scientific validity to which we referred earlier, then for sociologists to treat it as an analytic concept with explanatory significance is a nonsense – and a dangerous nonsense, because it becomes part of the process whereby the error of race persists (Miles 1982).

Just as stratification theorists develop their own analytical concepts rather than relying on 'folk views' of class, so, Miles suggests, sociologists should abandon concepts like 'race' or 'race relations' and rely instead on more valid categories and concepts. Otherwise, they merely introduce misleading commonsense discourse into academic thought, and in so doing seem to bestow credibility on those flawed commonsense views. Also, the retention of terms like 'race' or 'race relations' seems to suggest that 'race' has some independent force: race becomes a causal factor in its own right, something with 'real', 'objective' status which influences and determines social events. Against this, Miles seeks to locate the delusion within an essentially Marxist framework where the organisation of production and its attendant class relations in capitalist society shape intergroup conflicts, including 'race' conflicts (and in Miles's work 'race' is always in inverted commas). Explanations of 'race and racism' are to be sought in the exploited role of migrant labour in the economies of advanced capitalist countries. It is the distinctive economic structure which shapes the social reality of intergroup conflicts, the violence and discrimination and politics of hate (the social significance of which Miles in no way seeks to deny). Miles recognises the existence of a set of beliefs about the inferiority of black races, and *'racism'* is the important concept he uses to characterise an ideology with potent implications for class struggle. Another author who writes from a Marxist standpoint is Stuart Hall, and he has written of racism as a prism which *mis*represents the pattern of class relations as race relations (Hall, 1978). Miles would seem to share this view, whilst also acknowledging as real what he calls a 'racialised fraction' of social class, due to the tendency for black migrant workers in Britain to be concentrated in certain kinds of work positions outside the mainstream of secure unionised and good status positions. The task for sociology, in Miles's view, is to reveal, behind the distortions and delusions, the class structure of society.

A much more provisional approach is favoured by Michael Banton (1977), who simply proposes that the sociology of race relations is distinguished by its 'tradition of enquiry'. Such a tradition incorporates sets of ideas of how to go about the task, what topics to investigate, and what methods to use. According to this recommendation, then, there is no need to erect rigid boundaries or impose authoritative definitions in advance – instead, the area of study is roughly mapped by the familiar preoccupations, of self-designated 'race relations' specialists. One such preoccupation, quite obviously, is the 'social construction of race', and another is the notion of 'inclusion-exclusion boundaries' between socially-defined racial groups. But the tradition of enquiry will gradually alter as knowledge progresses and new interests are added. Moreover, Banton does not wish to represent 'race relations' as a special ghetto requiring unique concepts or exclusive theories, and so he invites the sociologist of race to ransack adjoining sociological areas (minorities, stratification, culture, deviancy, religion, etc.). The attractiveness of Banton's conceptualisation lies in its flexibility and tolerance. Any insistence on a strict definition of the field runs the danger of raising unproductive controversies and prematurely closing off potentially valuable areas of exploration. But Banton's approach makes few dogmatic assumptions, and it allows us to leave open the question of whether 'objective' or 'subjective' factors are fundamental, and whether 'race' or 'class' is the main determinant of social action.

Each of these authors, we should note, root their analysis and argument in detailed study of social relations in contemporary Britain, and each contribution is distinctive. Where they differ is perhaps not so much over whether there is a 'field' there which deserves attention, but over their more specific theoretical allegiances. But it is out of such diversity and debate that the sociological understanding of race and race relations emerges.

Chapter Two

Britain: Hosts and Immigrants

Our main task in this chapter is to note some special features of the arrival into Britain of significant numbers of 'coloured' immigrants whose presence – or more correctly *the response* to whose presence – has prompted the current race relations situation. The recent immigration and its response created what became termed a 'numbers game' as commentators vied with each other for the most accurate claims and counter claims of the past, present and future size of the immigrant population. It proved a game of considerable complexity which generated much heat but little light – not least because of the difficulty of agreeing who were 'the immigrants'.

It needs only the briefest of surveys of British history to emphasise how our island history is punctuated with arrivals of peoples of diverse sorts. The early Roman invaders encountered a mixed population of Britons, Picts and Celts, and when the Romans finally withdrew from these shores in 410 A.D. the succeeding centuries witnessed a series of forays and scattered settlements by varied groups of Angles, Saxons, Jutes, Danes and Vikings. This diversity was significantly enhanced by the arrival of the Normans, who not only had a profound influence on the laws, language and manners of the country, but also established more active lines of contact and exchange with the rest of Europe. The subsequent development of trade links and political alliances helped ensure thereafter that the 'insularity' of the island was always partial and relative.

Among the varied groups of immigrants from about the seventeenth century, it was the Irish whose labour power contributed hugely to the industrial revolution. The still current term 'Navvy' derives from the gangs of workers, largely Irish, who laboured to construct the Navigation canals and later the railways. Irish migration swelled even

21

more when the harrowing potato famines of the mid-1840s led to a mass exodus. The 1851 census estimated that there were at least half a million Irish-born living in the ports and industrial areas of England, Scotland and Wales. Although the pace of Irish immigration slackened somewhat after this period, it continued at a steady level and even accelerated in the twentieth century.

Another important immigrant group to be considered are the Jews, who first arrived in England in the wake of the Norman conquest. Like the Irish, they were met by a great deal of initial hostility, and indeed in 1290 they were expelled from England, only to reappear about 400 years later when Cromwell allowed them back. From that date there was a relatively modest growth in the Jewish population in Britain until a sudden upsurge in the latter years of the nineteenth century when there was a rush of Jewish refugees fleeing persecution and pogroms in Russia and Eastern Europe. Although the United States was the final port of destination for many of them, a considerable number settled in London, and by the time of the First World War the total Jewish community was estimated at around a quarter of a million.

Contrary to popular belief, the presence of coloured people in Britain is not a recent phenomenon. Fryer (1984) documents how blacks (Africans and Asians) have been living in Britain for close on 500 years – longer, if we include those who accompanied the Roman armies – and they have been born in Britain since about 1505. Advances in ship-building and in navigational skills obviously facilitated long-distance population transfers, but black migration must also be located against the backcloth of the steady growth of world trade and the spectacular expansion of the British Empire. As Hall (1978) observes, Britain's relations with the peoples of the Caribbean and the Indian sub-continent did not begin in the post-war period: for many centuries the 'imperialist chain' has indissolubly linked the fate of the peasants and workers in the colonies to the fortunes and actions of the people on the British mainland. In India, for example, we can trace the tentative establishment of British trading posts in the early seventeenth century, the haphazard and sometimes violent expansion of control in the eighteenth century, and the final consolidation of British rule in the nineteenth century, when India became the 'jewel in the crown' of the Victorian Empire. The history of the British Raj certainly contains episodes of violence and conflict, but these were undoubtedly surpassed by the sheer brutality of the slave trade and the establishment of sugar plantations in the West Indies. The British did not 'invent' the slave trade – the Portuguese were the first to export Negro slaves from the West African coast, and there was a previous history of slaving on the

African continent – but they increasingly played a prominent role. There were early slave trading ventures by English seafarers in the sixteenth century, but it was the creation of sugar plantations in the West Indies from the mid-seventeenth century on which resulted in a massive increase in slave transportation. Black Africans became human 'commodities' to be exchanged within the 'triangular trade route': British merchants shipped manufactured goods which were exchanged for black slaves on the West Coast of Africa; these slaves were then transported to the West Indies where they would be sold, and the money used to purchase sugar (or sometimes tobacco, cotton or molasses) which was resold in Britain. Great profits were made for British merchants and plantation owners, but at the cost of immense human misery and a heavy toll in human lives.

Amidst the hustle and bustle of trade and empire, black communities began to develop in Britain itself and in the mid-eighteenth century it was estimated that perhaps 20,000 black people were settled in Britain. But the black population did not grow: repatriation was talked about and promoted; trade patterns tended to maintain a demand for black labour in the colonies; and if black manservants were a status symbol of the fashionable wealthy, black families were very few. It was the later rise in tempo of the industrialising process which brought more ships to British ports and the gradual development of coloured settlements. The Indian trade brought Sikh pedlars of cloth to ply their special trade; and a small elite of Indian businessmen and administrators came for training or education for themselves or their sons. If the elite get caricatured in the upper class novels and games of the Victorian and Edwardian periods, the experience of the others was frequently far from 'cricket'. Race riots were a feature of a number of poor towns in the immediate aftermath of World War 1 as concern about unemployment rose.

It was the Second World War which caused a significant increase in the numbers of coloured immigrants – the thousands of Indian and West Indian troops whose war service brought them through Britain to the various fronts in which they played so notable a part. After demobilization in 1945 it was estimated that some 10,000 blacks were resident in Britain. But it was the following years which were to witness the largest increases in Britain's coloured population.

New Commonwealth Migration

The 'Old Commonwealth' is a term which refers to the long-established dominions or self-governing territories of the British

Commonwealth – Australia, Canada, New Zealand – which have a largely, but not exclusively, white population. Those ex-colonies which gained formal independence during the period since the Second World War are generally described as the 'New Commonwealth' (or, after Pakistan's secession from the Commonwealth in 1973, as the 'New Commonwealth and Pakistan'). It is these New Commonwealth countries which have provided the bulk of 'coloured' immigrants to Britain in the post-war period. Although the black presence in Britain has a long history, the scale of new Commonwealth migration eclipses earlier settlements in size and significance, and some familiarity with the contours of this migration is necessary for a full understanding of race relations in modern Britain.

The original reasons for migration obviously vary according to the groups and individuals concerned. Some of these 'sending' areas already had a tradition of migration (there was a well-trodden path between the West Indian islands and the United States and Canada; the Sikhs from the Punjab had soldiered round the world; and East African Asians had uprooted themselves from the Gujerat and Punjab areas of India in the 1920s and 1930s). So in some respects the migration to Britain fitted into a longer tradition of mobility. But in addition there were new incentives which appeared. For example, the 1947 partition of India (into India, and West and East Pakistan) led to millions of people crossing the newly-created borders because of fears for their safety, and the ensuing upheaval provoked further migration. Political conflict was also a powerful impetus to migration much later, around the 1970s, when the 'Africanisation' polices in Kenya, Uganda and Malawi placed increasing restrictions on the rights of Asian groups in those countries. But a constant spur to migration during the period under review was undoubtedly the desire for economic betterment. Whether it was the chronic unemployment or poverty of the West Indies, or the increasing population pressure on the land in India, the economic conditions of the sending countries compared unfavourably with the opportunities created in post-war Britain. Indeed, post-war Britain suffered an acute labour shortage, and although it attempted to fill the gap with European workers, there were still labour vacancies in many industries. As living standards in Britain steadily improved, the native population were reluctant to fill unpopular jobs in heavy or dirty industries (foundries, factories), low-paid jobs (textiles, manual jobs in National Health Service), and jobs which required regular shift work (transport, services). So, although migrants were also recruited to higher-status vacancies (doctors, nurses), they could be regarded largely as a low-level 'replacement population' which ensured the viability of essential services and industries. This responsiveness to labour needs determined that the post-war migrants were largely re-located in the industrial and growth areas of the South East and the major conurbations of the Midlands, Yorkshire and Greater Manchester, but considerable numbers gravitated to the old 'Empire' ports like Glasgow and Bristol.

The first main 'coloured group' to come to Britain in the post-war period were West Indians. There are great distances and cultural differences between the various West Indian islands, and island affiliations have been perpetuated in Britain in terms of geographical settlement and social relationships. The great majority of West Indian migrants originate from Jamaica, but Barbados, St. Kitts and other smaller islands are also represented. The trickle of migrants started in the late 1940s, and the main period of migration was the 1950s and early 1960s, after which it consisted mainly of dependents of the 'primary' settlers. The sex ratio among West Indian migrants has always tended to be rather evenly balanced, unlike the pattern among Asian migrants.

Migrants from the Asian sub-continent started rather later, in the 1950s, and the usual pattern was for men to act as the pioneers. A considerable number of Asian migrants had no firm plans to settle permanently in Britain, preferring to keep their options open, but gradually throughout the 1960s and 1970s the men were joined by wives and dependents (although the Pakistani community in Britain still has a preponderance of males). A particular feature of the Asian pattern was the phenomenon of 'chain migration' whereby a local village or kin group would routinely sponsor a series of migrants who either replaced or joined earlier migrants. This chain migration did not apply, of course, to the later Asian refugees from East Africa, who tended to arrive as complete families, and for whom there was little prospect of a return to Africa. These East African Asians, on the whole, were more prosperous and better-educated than their counterparts from the Indian sub-continent, although the African governments dispossessed many of them of their wealth and valuables before leaving the country. The East African Asians usually had a better command of the English language, but in many other cultural and religious respects they resembled the groups from the sub-continent. Most Asian migrants originate (directly, or via East Africa) from certain specific localities: the Punjab areas of India and Pakistan; the Gujerat region of India; the Sylhet area of Bangladesh (formerly East Pakistan); and the Mirpur and Kashmir regions of Pakistan. There are important cultural and linguistic differences between these areas, and of course there are major religious groups which can be identified. Most Pakistani and Bangladeshi migrants are Muslims (the largest religious group among Asians in Britain); and although there are also Muslims among the 'Indian' groups, Indians tend to be either Hindus or Sikhs (a group which broke away from the caste system of Hinduism, and which is recognisable by distinctive turbans for men). Therefore, just as there is a pattern of island groupings among 'West Indians' in Britian, so we have to recognise the varied religious, cultural and linguistic affiliations of the 'Asian' population.

As we suggested above, New Commonwealth migration played a valuable role in helping solve the post-war labour shortage in Britain, and some hard-pressed industries and employers even took the step of recruiting directly in those overseas countries. Thus, the National Health Service, London Transport, and various textiles and foundry companies either appointed local recruiting agents or advertised widely in the New Commonwealth countries. However, only a minority of the migrants were recruited directly in this manner, and for the most part the migration process was unregulated and unplanned. But this was to change in the 1960s when increasingly restrictive legislation was passed which curtailed rights of entry. Layton-Henry (1984) notes that post-war New Commonwealth migration had neither been widely anticipated nor welcomed by key policy-makers and politicians, but in spite of public disquiet little was done about it. Then, in the early 1960s the Conservative Party changed its policy on immigration. Layton-Henry suggests various reasons for this: the Conservatives felt that racial tension could be avoided only if controls were introduced; there was grass-roots pressure for restrictions from local constituency associations: it was no longer felt that the numbers were so small as to make restriction unnecessary; Britain's application for EEC membership weakened commitment to 'Commonwealth'; and there was a strong feeling that controls would be electorally popular. Consequently, the 1962 Commonwealth Immigration Act was passed, marking a decisive shift in the rights of Commonwealth citizens. Although it is true that 'aliens' have always been subject to vetting procedures, the notion of Commonwealth membership had seemed to secure a general right of entry. Even when independent Commonwealth countries such as Canada started introducing their own 'citizenship', this entailed no basic departure, and the 1948 British Nationality Act had guaranteed the rights of entry to Britain for every 'subject' or person born within the Empire and Commonwealth. But now, in the 1962 Act, this principle was undermined as controls were introduced: Commonwealth citizens without a passport issued in Britain were subject to an employment voucher system, and the numbers of these vouchers was limited. Moreover, the succeeding years were to witness a further tightening of entry controls. In 1968 a Labour Government passed the Commonwealth Immigrants Act, a panic measure to prevent a feared influx of Kenyan Asians expelled from that land. Although these Kenyan Asians had United Kingdom passports, the unprecedented step was taken of denying them entry as of right, unless certain strict requirements were met (e.g. if they had been born in Britain, or had a very close connection in some specified way). This 'close connection' idea was perpetuated and extended in the controversial 'patrials' clause enshrined in the 1971 Immigration Act. By restricting entry rights to 'patrials' (those born in Britain, or with a parent or grandparent born here, or adopted or naturalised in this country), this Act put a virtual end to all new 'coloured' immigration: most New Commonwealth migrants thereafter have entered under much the same controlled conditions as 'aliens', or else they have been dependents of already established primary settlers. Although a new British Nationality Act was passed in 1981, this was essentially a 'tidying-up' exercise (with several controversial elements) and the 1971 Act remains the working basis of present law.

Immigration laws are a highly complicated matter, and there are various loopholes, exemption clauses, and provisions for discretionary procedures and appeals. Sometimes the guidelines have been interpreted in a benevolent and liberal fashion – for example, large numbers of Kenyan Asians were eventually allowed to enter the country, in spite of the 1968 Act. However, a reasonable case can be made that the laws have been racist in their assumptions and intentions, and the main concern apparently has been to reduce *coloured* immigration while leaving white immigration relatively unrestricted. The 1971 Act, for example, actually made entry easier for many citizens of Old Commonwealth countries who had previously been subject to the voucher system, and the patrials clause seems a thinly disguised attempt to distinguish between white and black migrants. Moore (1975) has been especially critical of the laws, which he regards as flagrantly racist both in their basic conditions and in the discretionary practices which have accompanied them (e.g. applicants being callously treated by Embassy officials and immigration officers). In Moore's opinion, immigration laws involve a pernicious 'numbers game' which stigmatises blacks by defining them as a 'problem' whose numbers must be limited. Far from improving race relations, they reduce the security of those already settled (will their dependents be allowed in?, will there be moves to repatriation?), and encourage racist groups to make even greater demands. The passage of anti-discrimination legislation (e.g. the Race Relations Act of 1965, 1968 and 1971) therefore does not remove the damage done by immigration laws which brand coloured migrants as undesirable intruders.

The Numbers Game

Moore's suspicions about the 'numbers game' are shared by many commentators. Much of the politics of race has assumed that there is a tolerable number, beyond which some new set of difficulties inevitably develops: limit the numbers, send some home, and the problem recedes.

However, the 'numbers game' was played without reliable figures on the size of the coloured population. There was a tendency for many whites to wildly exaggerate its size, fearing they would be swamped by a massive influx of immigrants. Also, in the increasingly hostile world of

Table 2.   Ethnic Composition 1981

Ethnic Group	No. '000	%
White – born in Britain	48,335	90.0
White – born in Irish Republic	924	2.0
White – born in New Commonwealth Countries	446	1.0
White – born in Rest of the World or unstated or not known country	1,209	2.0
White sub-total	50,915	95.0
West Indian/Guyanese – Carribean born	463	0.90
– UK born	40	0.07
– born elsewhere	15	0.03
West Indian sub-total	519	1.0
Indian/Pakistan/Bangladesh – born there	831	1.54
– African born	164	0.35
– UK born	20	0.04
– born elsewhere	38	0.07
'Asian' sub-total	1,054	2.0
Other (including African, Arab and Chinese) – born abroad	327	0.52
– UK born	42	0.07
'Other' sub-total	369	0.6
Mixed ethnic origin – born abroad	135	0.25
– UK born	99	0.15
'Mixed' sub-total	234	0.4
Ethnic group not stated	608	1.0
All Ethnic groups	53,697	100

(Reproduced with the permission of the Controller of Her Majesty's Stationery Office)

racial politics, minorities were worried about the use to which data on their numbers might be put. Such data are necessary, however, in order to establish whether coloured people are receiving a fair deal in such fields as education, jobs and housing. By the late 1970s, more reliable data on the ethnic composition of Britain began to emerge.

The 1981 Census did not include any special 'ethnic' question but it did ask respondents about birthplace. This census data shows that only about 3 out of every 100 households is headed by someone born in a New Commonwealth country (*Social Trends*, 1984). A more informative source is the *Labour Force Survey* based on data gained by interviewing a nationally and regionally representative sample of heads of households. The 1981 survey asked respondents to select the ethnic group to which they considered they, and the members of their household, belonged. *Social Trends* (1983) summarises this data as shown in Table 2.

This table reveals some interesting details. The first thing to note is the modest size of the non-British born and of the non-white population. Secondly, perhaps, is the evidence that coloured immigrants from the New Commonwealth and their families are outnumbered by families whose heads were born in other countries in Europe or elsewhere – by no means are all 'immigrants' 'coloured'. Thirdly, the tables bring out the *diversity* of the non-British born.

Ballard, in a recent article based on more detailed analysis of census data stresses that:

> Each of these groups has very different demographic characteristics. The Caribbeans, for instance, have the strongest local roots. Exactly half are now British born while at the other extreme only a quarter of the Bangladeshis are British in that sense. But the 1981 census shows, just as did all previous ones, that non-European immigrants are outnumbered by Europeans. The categories 'immigrant' and 'non-European' are in no sense synonymous, whatever popular usage may assume.
>
> Indeed, now that the minorities are an integral part of British society, a preoccupation with immigration is largely irrelevant. Attention is much more appropriately focussed on the minorities' local characteristics, and on their difference from or similarities with the remainder of the population. (Ballard, 1983.)

He goes on to emphasise the quite different age structures of the different groups and their differences from the age structure of the total population:

If you look at these figures overall, what do they tell you about Britain's minority populations? Most strikingly – that we can expect a steady process of growth in the coming years, regardless of any attempt to tighten yet further the screws of immigration control. That growth will occur for two reasons. As the population ages, so the number of people in the more elderly (and at present, rather empty) age slots will increase. Then there is the high birthrate in certain sections of the minority population, especially among Pakistanis and Bangladeshis. As long as this continues, it will fuel growth.

But even here we must retain a due sense of proportion. Estimates for the year 2000 do not anticipate that the population descended from the New Commonwealth migration of the '60s and '70s will then comprise more than 6 per cent of the population. Finally, it should be remembered that Britain exports population as well as importing migrants. In fact, over the last twenty or thirty years we more typically lose population through net migration (so much for fears of becoming overcrowded!). And by no means all of the emigrants from these isles are white; in fact, in some years we have lost more migrants to the West Indies than we have gained. In 1980, Britain accepted 30,000 migrants from the New Commonwealth (mostly dependants of previously settled kin folk) but exported 15,000 in return.

The Immigrant-Host Model

The steady flow of New Commonwealth migrants into post-war Britain sparked off numerous public controversies and media debates about where it was all heading. The British people, it was claimed, were troubled and uneasy at the prospect of fresh waves of migrants introducing 'alien' cultures, competing with the native population for jobs, and imposing heavy burdens on the social services. More liberal commentators, on the other hand, voiced anxieties about the welfare of the migrants themselves, and it was feared that racial prejudice would damage their morale and limit their social and economic opportunities. In the debates that emerged in the 1950s and 1960s, politicians and policy-makers, social scientists and journalists struggled to understand the key issues and predict the likely outcome. Different positions were adopted, ranging from outright hostility to the newcomers through to an enthusiastic welcome for their cultural and economic contributions, but it is possible to argue that there was a particular 'model' or frame-work of assumptions which tended to dominate the debates. In social science circles this was referred to as the '*immigrant-host*' model, but it is important to remember that the same sets of assumptions appeared in more 'popular' form, in the pages of newspapers and in general political discussion. The social science groundwork for the immigrant-host model had been performed earlier in the century by Robert Park (1950), a leading figure in the inter-war 'Chicago school' of sociologists. Park often resorted to analogies between 'social' and 'biological' phenomena, and he sometimes explained racial antipathy as a more or less spontaneous expression of deep-seated 'instincts'. Nevertheless, as a pioneer of 'social interactionism', Park also laid great stress on social relationships and social processes, and he is some-times credited as the first writer to set out theoretical guidelines for a sociology of race relations. So, in spite of certain inconsistencies and omissions in his own wide-ranging writings, he undoubtedly inspired interest in the sociology of race generally, and more specifically in the 'immigrant-host' model. This model has been developed in various ways since Park's time, and it has served as the guiding framework for some interesting field studies. But it is probably more accurate to regard it as a loose collection of assumptions rather than a rigorously-detailed and systematic explanatory theory. The model contains a general image of the nature of society, a statement about the most important features and problems of migration processes, and some suggestions about the likely direction of change. The leading assumptions of the model can now be outlined:

(a) The 'immigrants' entering the host society are portrayed first and foremost as 'strangers' who bring with them a quite different, and usually inappropriate, cultural tradition. It is this 'strangeness', rather than their race or colour, which constitutes the major impediment to their social acceptability and economic success. They may, for example, lack the necessary 'urban' or 'industrial' skills, and their sheer unfamiliarity with the customs and cultural demands of the host society places them at a considerable disadvantage.

(b) The 'hosts', typically, are depicted as confused, hesitant and insecure (Glass, 1960). Lacking detailed information about the newcomers' ways and habits, they respond in ambiguous fashion to the presence of the migrants, reacting at certain times in a hostile manner and yet at other times displaying commendable hospitality and tolerance. Apprehension is far more common than straight-forward prejudice.

(c) The immigrant-host model embraces an 'order' or 'consensus' image of society, in which the host society is described as basically stable and orderly and characterised by an ultimate consensus of values. There are no fundamental conflicts of interests which divide the population, and the host culture is reasonably homogeneous.

(d) The 'cultural' or 'value' consensus of the host society is temporarily disturbed by the entry of the migrants which creates a problem of disorganisation or dis-equilibrium. In the resultant social interaction between hosts and migrants, the equilibrium is restored by a process of mutual 'adjustment'. The migrants gradually learn to 'adapt' to the values and expectations of the host culture, and for their part the hosts slowly 'accept' the migrants as permanent members of the society. As migrants – or their descendants – are socialised into the dominant values, and as misunderstandings are increasingly resolved, so the newcomers are incorporated into the over-arching consensus.

(e) The process of adjustment may be broken into a discernible sequence of 'stages' in which the spatial and social distance between hosts and newcomers is progressively shortened. Park, for example, described a 'race relations cycle', moving from the initial stage of 'contact' to 'competition' (over jobs, houses, political power), then 'accommodation' (peaceful co-existence) and finally 'assimilation'.

(f) The journey to full 'assimilation' does not necessarily proceed at a regular pace in every sphere of social life, and it may drag over several generations. Yinger (1981) described assimilation as a process of 'boundary reduction' between groups, and he suggests that it involves the following sub-processes: amalgamation (a biological matter, whereby differences in physical appearances are blurred through inter-marriage); identification (a psychological matter, in which feelings of allegiance and commitment to the host society are formed); acculturation (the process of change towards greater cultural similarity); and integration (a structural matter, whereby formerly separate sub-groups become inter-locked in a set of shared interactions).

Having outlined these broad defining features of the model, it is instructive to examine critically a particular example of a study informed by its assumptions.

Dark Strangers

Dark Strangers (Patterson, 1965) is the title of one of the first and most carefully researched studies of West Indians, those living in the

Brixton area of London in the 1950s. It provides a fascinating counter-part to the quite different account of racial conflict in Brixton provided by the Scarman Report on the Brixton Disorders of April, 1981.

Despite the modest disclaimer that her book offers only a rather 'impressionistic' picture, Patterson's assiduous fieldwork resulted in a wealth of observations, and she made a sustained effort to develop a more rigorous sociological understanding of migration and its attendant problems and processes. Patterson's argument is especially striking in its early abandonment of 'colour' as a central issue. Her research experience in South Africa and in the West Indies suggested that the notion of a 'colour bar' was a natural point of entry into the problems. Nevertheless, she argued that the immigrant-host frame-work offered a more serviceable and relevant orientation to the field:

> ... what we have in Britain at the present stage is not, or not yet, basically a colour or a race situation, however much it may appear so to many colour-conscious migrants – it is an immigrant situation. Although colour is a significant 'complicating factor', the essential point about West Indian migrants is precisely the fact that they are migrants, and their problems are little different from those facing any other group of migrants... The new West Indian migrants to Britain are, in fact, passing through the same kinds of dynamic processes, for example, as the East European Jews and the Irish in London in the last century, the Italians in Canada, the Puerto Ricans in New York, or even the southern rural Negroes in the urban north of the United States.

Patterson identified a cultural gap between the newcomers and hosts, in spite of superficial similarities of language and religion. In Brixton, the white population largely upheld 'respectable' norms which stress privacy, 'keeping themselves to themselves', cleanliness and tidiness, quietness and family propriety. But, she pointed out, 'No immigrant group has in the mass so signally failed to conform to these expectations and patterns as have the West Indians'. The newcomers tended to be more noisy and gregarious, less fastidious about house-keeping standards, and they had a higher proportion of common-law marriages. These departures from 'normal' expectations inevitably caused tensions between the two communities. Nevertheless, West Indians were described as having 'assimilationist' aspirations, and Patterson believed eventual assimilation was possible if both new-comers and hosts made appropriate efforts. The West Indians faced the task of 'adaptation', in which they were to undergo re-socialisation and acculturation into British ways. This involved, among other things, learning to queue at bus stops, formal marriage ceremonies, not building up exaggerated expectations, and the avoidance of 'chip-on-the-shoulder' attitudes. As for the hosts, they are presented with the more 'passive' role of 'acceptance' of the newcomers. The media should avoid lurid, sensational headlines on race issues; people needed to learn not to stare at West Indians in the street; everyone should be treated according to individual merits rather than group membership; and hosts must make an effort to learn more about the newcomers' cultural backgrounds. Patterson remained reasonably optimistic about the prospects for assimilation, because she believed there were no insuperable structural blocks which might stand in the way. Although Britain was an insular, conservative society, it was basically stable and peaceful, with social relationships 'harmonious and voluntarily ordered among the great majority of the society's members'. Also, although mild 'antipathy' to foreigners was a cultural norm, there was an absence of rigid, entrenched prejudice. She argued that emphasis on the 'prejudice-discrimination axis' overlooks the relatively favourable attitudes towards coloured people; and where discrimination did occur it was often for ostensibly 'good' reasons (e.g. 'other tenants would object'; 'children of a mixed marriage would suffer social stigma'; 'too many blacks would upset the white labour force', etc.) which made some sense, at least as far as the white respondents saw the situation. Patterson hoped these 'reasons' would eventually disappear, but she did not view them simply as insincere rationalisations for deep-rooted racism.

Patterson's study did not present a picture of a fixed or an inevitable pattern of absorption and change. On the contrary, a picture was presented that is fluid in the extreme. Yet the underlying assumption – the 'hope factor' informing the study – was that through various stages of varying difficulties a process of assimilation was possible and manageable.

Patterson cautioned that 'adaptation' and 'acceptance' need not always match up with each other, and absorption would not necessarily proceed in a smooth and unbroken fashion. Moreoever, the process would move at a different pace in different spheres of life. Based on her own field study in Brixton, Patterson reached the considered conclusion that the situation could be summarised as: 'A fair degree of migrant accommodation in work, somewhat less in housing, and the modest beginnings of migrant acclimatisation and local acquiescence in casual and formal social contacts.' Although most West Indians were semi-skilled or unskilled, and although they suffered from unofficial 'quota' systems by employers, most had managed to find work and had started to accommodate themselves to the disciplines and demands of British industrial life. And in housing, they had managed to overcome a long standing housing shortage and a more recent 'colour tax' whereby unscrupulous landlords asked higher rentals for old and dilapidated property. In the sphere of voluntary social relations, less progress had been made, and there was relatively little contact or mutual understanding between black and white groups. Still, Patterson hazarded the guess that the West Indian population would follow in the footsteps of the Irish towards more complete absorption, gradually raising their living standards and fanning out from the central areas of residential concentration. However, she did recognise that the situation was 'dynamic and uncrystallised', and she insisted that a laissez-faire policy was not sufficient; she made a plea for anti-discrimination legislation, and she advocated more positive state policies to ease the absorption of the newcomers.

Beyond the Immigrant-Host Model

Patterson's careful 1950s study is one of a number informed by the immigrant-host framework. Michael Banton was another who could see positive strength in the methods of enquiry it entailed, whilst doubting its underlying assumptions and the predictions to which it gave rise:

> The racial situation in Britain could develop in any of several different ways. Whether events will approximate more closely to an interpretation in terms of immigration and assimilation, or to one which envisages movement towards a pluralistic pattern of racial communities preserving their distinctiveness in respect of marriage and leisure-time associations, will be decided by the reception accorded to the present second generation of immigrant children when they leave school. This is not a long time to wait for an answer, for it has been estimated that by 1978 one in six of the school-leavers in Birmingham will be a young coloured person. When the second generation leaves the schools it will no longer be possible to represent race relations in Britain as a matter of immigration, or to see coloured people as strangers who could be sent back to their own countries. Thus the image of the coloured man will be modified. Will the pattern of social distance be modified? (Banton, 1967.)

Banton's questions are challenges to the *assumptions* in the immigrant-host framework. Indeed, a number of criticisms can be levelled at the model: (1) its inadequate description of 'stages' of adjustment; (2) its relatively unsophisticated advancement of 'assimilation' as a policy goal; (3) its under-estimation of the extent of 'prejudice' and 'discrimination'; and (4) its theoretically underdeveloped sense of 'social structure'.

(1) Stages of adjustment. Rather confusingly, Park referred to a race relations 'cycle' (presumably a pattern which repeats itself) and yet he also described the path to assimilation as a 'progressive' and 'irreversible' sequence. This initial uncertainty is a continuing feature of much immigrant-host literature: on the one hand, there is a basic optimism about a smooth, definite trend towards inter-racial harmony; on the other hand, there is a quite sensible appreciation of the possibility of stops and starts, long pauses, and even some regrettable reversals. It would be rather unfair, perhaps, to condemn the approach for this lack of precision – reality is, after all, highly complex – but the basic concepts ('acceptance', 'accommodation', etc.) are not clearly spelled out, and in practice it remains difficult to identify the exact stage of 'adjustment' which has been reached.

(2) Assimilation. The in-built assumption that assimilation is the 'natural' or 'desirable' goal has also been subjected to criticism. It seems that the anticipated adjustment is rather one-way, with the migrants being expected to take on the values and norms of the receiving society, and this overlooks the potential of their own cultural contributions. A clue to the possible benefits of 'cultural exchange' or 'cultural enlargement' (rather than one-way assimilation) is provided by the following comments on British society: 'While it has developed most admirable qualities of self-discipline, professionalism, self-containment, considerateness to others and respect for the law, it has failed fully to develop such other qualities as emotional warmth, psychic openness, capacity to uncoil and relax, ability to enjoy human diversity, generosity of spirit and the like.' (Parekh, 1978.) Moreover, the model normally underestimates the desire by migrants and their descendants to maintain their original cultures (see Chapter 4 on 'ethnicity'). If this is the case, then 'cultural pluralism' is more likely than 'cultural assimilation'. And even if the migrant groups do wish to achieve full (cultural and structural) integration, then they may be prevented from doing so by formidable forces such as widespread prejudice and the intractable structural features of British society.

(3) Prejudice and discrimination. The attempt to break away from 'colour' (or the black-white framework) and focus instead on migrant status was useful insofar as it enlarged understanding of relevant factors, but in the final reckoning it was unrealistic to relegate 'race' or 'colour' to minor significance. In the United States, for example, blacks have largely remained submerged in the 'underclass' for some centuries while successive waves of white migrants (Irish, Poles, Scandinavians) have leapfrogged to prosperity. And in Britain, research (Daniel, 1967) has revealed that white migrants (Cypriots, Hungarians) do not face problems of the same magnitude as those encountered by coloured groups. And so Allen (1971) has interpreted the re-definition of Britain's coloured population as 'immigrants' as little more than a rationalisation which seeks to avoid the brutal fact of racial prejudice. Racial prejudice in Britain has a long history, dating from the earlier settlements in the mid-sixteenth century. Since this period, Walvin (1973) argues, 'with the odd exception, white responses have been bounded on one side by open and legally approved cruelty and on the other by indifference and moral insensibility'. Writers working in the immigrant-host tradition certainly recognised the existence of prejudice and discrimination, but their under-estimation of these factors was starkly revealed by painstaking documentation of their massive and widespread presence in the 1960s and 1970s (see Chapter 3).

(4) **Social structure.** Conflict theorists argue that the immigrant-host model suffers from the limitations of a 'consensus' or 'order' view of society. In other words, it assumes a basic harmony of interests and values in the host society; it tends to view immigration as posing a problem of 'adjustment' because of the clash of values and consequent 'mutual misunderstandings'; and it frames the solution very much in terms of re-socialisation and cultural integration. Against this conception, the critics maintain that a conflict view of race (Horton, 1966) offers a more informative and analytically useful understanding of the relevant forces at work. For the conflict theorists, Britain is a sharply divided, class-stratified society in which different interest groups contest a struggle for power. The disadvantaged position of coloured migrants is explained by their historical role as cheap labour, and their continued exploitation is guaranteed by the racism which capitalism generates to serve its own intersts. The root of the problem, then, does not lie in restricted opportunities due to a clash of values, but in an exploitative economic order which can only be resolved by radical structural transformation (see Chapter 5).

But it is important not to discard the many insights and issues posed by the immigrant-host studies: after all, the New Commonwealth arrivals were, indeed, migrants, and Krausz (1971) illustrates the many parallels in the migration patterns and attendant problems of black and white migrants. The model effectively drew attention to the dislocation caused by migration, it bravely addressed the complexities of assimilation, and it demonstrated the dynamic processes of change, rather than settling for a misleadingly static view of black-white conflict. Also, it stood as a reminder that the migrants brought different sets of cultural values, and inevitably this raised important policy issues of how far cultural diversity could be accommodated within one nation state. So the model insisted that there were phenomena to be explained and problems to be solved. If it failed to supply satisfactory answers to all the issues, at least it stimulated further development of the debates.

In the next chapter we will shift focus from the migrants to the hosts and explore the latter's racial prejudices and discriminatory practices.

Chapter Three

Racism

Within the immigrant-host framework the expectation was that, after an initial phase of hostility, familiarity would promote mutual respect, and immigrants would merge – become *integrated* – into British society. A famous definition of 'integration' was provided by a Labour Party Home Secretary: 'not a flattening process of assimilation, but equal opportunity, accompanied by cultural diversity, in an atmosphere of mutual tolerance' (Jenkins, 1967). Nevertheless, in spite of these lofty intentions it became clear that relations between 'hosts' and 'immigrants' were marked by continuing hostility and intolerance. And that is why the concept of 'prejudice' became central to a great deal of research and theory in race relations. This tradition of 'prejudice' studies deserves special attention.

Prejudice

In the strict dictionary sense, it is possible to be prejudiced in favour of a group, but in social science the term is normally reserved for derogatory attitudes, as in the following frequently cited definition:

> An avertive or hostile attitude towards a person who belongs to a group, simply because he belongs to that group, and is therefore presumed to have the objectionable characteristics ascribed to the group. (Allport, 1954.)

This definition furnishes a basis for identifying some of the key features of prejudice:

(1) Prejudice consists of negative 'attitudes' or 'beliefs' which are directed at some 'out-group'. Of course, not every out-group is denounced or pitied, but anything which marks off a group as 'different' makes it a potential target for disapproval.

39

(2) As the term suggests, an element of pre-judgement is involved. Instead of treating people on their individual merits, they are portrayed in terms of misleading stereotypes which allow little room for fairmindedness or sensible negotiation.

(3) A certain amount of stereotyping is inevitable and even necessary in social relationships, but prejudice is additionally unfair because it involves a strong measure of mis-judgement as well. For instance, the objectionable 'differences' may be imagined or highly exaggerated, and the attractive features of the group may be totally ignored.

(4) Some people subscribe to racial prejudices because they have been misinformed or have fallen prey to common misconceptions in their culture. Nevertheless, the race debate is not a neutral, dispassionate affair which is easily resolved by patient regard for the available evidence. Prejudices involve emotions and feelings as well as simple information; indeed, some psychologists suggest that prejudiced people have underlying personality needs which lead them to denounce others.

Clearly, there are a large number of candidates for the unenviable role of 'victim': gypsies, foreigners, Jews, sexual minorities, left-wingers, right-wingers, dwarves, even sociologists. But the field of race relations provides particularly rich examples of the potent nature of prejudice. Here are some common prejudiced stereotypes: Asians are seen as 'shifty' and 'cunning', and stand condemned for alleged avarice and low standards of physical hygiene. Their 'alien' presence is signalled by their apparently incomprehensible languages, 'heathen' religions, impenetrable cultures, and their 'enslavement' of women. For West Indians, the stereotypes often draw a link to criminality with special emphasis on the phenomenon of 'mugging', or dwell on noisy music, drug taking and wild parties. Such stereotypes have a long history, and even as far back as the 18th century the British had formed discrediting or patronising views of the African: 'The Negro was held to be peculiarly sexual, musical, stupid, indolent, untrustworthy and violent.' (Walvin, 1973.)

Sometimes the selected features which are seized on are patently false (differences in intelligence, for instance), but the more subtle and sinister stereotype is that which starts from something real, but distorts it out of all recognition. So the Asian cultural emphasis on the extended family and on village ties undergoes a curious transformation: it is alleged that they actually prefer to live in overcrowded conditions!

Such a mischievous claim not only stigmatises the group as 'primitive' in their standards, but it conveniently overlooks the structural conditions which force many Asian families in Britain to live – reluctantly – in less than ideal conditions.

Another strange feature of racial prejudice is that the characteristics which are condemned in others are not always obviously discrediting. The alleged sexual prowess or musical talents of West Indians, for example, might be expected to elicit grudging admiration in some quarters. And the 'clannish' tendencies and mutual aid patterns found among Asian groups are not very distant from the qualities celebrated in 'traditional' working-class culture in Britain. Yet these qualities, when supposedly discovered in other 'races', are framed in a slanted way: the sexually prodigious blacks contribute to high rape and illegitimacy rates; their otherwise admirable spontaneity tends to lead to all-night parties which disturb their white neighbours; the clannish Asians are supposedly using their social networks to conspire against us. Moreover, the irrational element in racial prejudice is readily demonstrated by the inconsistency of popular attitudes. Thus, West Indians are criticised for (allegedly) being lazy and workshy, while Asians are blamed for the opposite reason that they are supposedly too hard-working ('they steal our jobs and grab all the overtime they can get'). Whatever they do – or are believed to do – they cannot win.

Studying Prejudice

There were a number of studies in the 1960s which tried to measure the extent of prejudice against coloured immigrants. Characteristically, the study of prejudice entails asking a sample of the population whether they agree or disagree with a list of positive and negative statements about groups of people. Then the responses are analysed by scoring the number which are prejudiced or unprejudiced and then distributing the population into groups with low or high scores.

One of the most ambitious surveys of this type was included in a massive study by the Institute of Race Relations in the late 1960s (Rose, 1969). After submitting a questionnaire to two thousand five hundred whites in five towns in England, the researchers concluded that thirty-five per cent of the sample displayed 'no hostility', a further fifty-five per cent shared 'doubts and uncertainties', while the remaining ten per cent were described as 'intensely prejudiced'. The latter group were more likely to be found among the lower middle-class and skilled working class, among Conservatives, the poorly educated, those with little personal contact with migrants, and among those with 'authoritarian' personalities. Overall, however, the findings did not present too bleak a picture, since they seemed to indicate that pronounced racial prejudice was not widespread. Indeed, it was suggested that 'what is needed (in short) is not an effort to make people unprejudiced, but rather to remind them that they are unprejudiced'. But more recently, in a 1984 report on British social attitudes, the apparently larger figure of thirty-five per cent of the sample identified themselves as 'racially prejudiced' (Jowell & Airey, 1984).

Plainly, there are recurrent methodological problems associated with this kind of survey, and so the results always need to be treated with caution. Apart from the obvious matter of the representativeness of the sample, sensitive and probing questions are required, otherwise the answers will be uninformative or positively misleading. Bald figures or head-counts – ten per cent belong to this group, twenty per cent to that group, etc. – are usually less revealing than a more detailed analysis of the underlying processes. If, for example, we investigate the 'doubts and uncertainties' group, some interesting tensions are disclosed. On the basis of her fieldwork in London in the 1950s, Ruth Glass (1960) aptly described this group as holding attitudes of 'benevolent prejudice'. Far from being severely hostile or unfailingly sympathetic towards ethnic minorities, they were typically muddled, confused and insecure. Their ambivalent outlook was a curious blend of competing values, of passive tolerance and latent prejudice, and different situations determined which element prevailed at any given time. For Glass, there was an urgent need to develop a 'philosophy of tolerance' to help overcome the 'sluggishness of good will' and prevent the mobilisation of intolerance.

Glass's sensitive exploration of the social climate of prejudice illustrates the value of moving beyond simple quantitative methods and mere head-counting. This is not, of course, to deny the role of attitude surveys in providing useful data on how people actually feel, and in acting as some sort of empirical check on otherwise unsupported claims about the extent of prejudice. But there is a danger that the 'snapshot' approach of these surveys freezes people and situations in too rigid a fashion. The temptation is to regard people as rather fixed in their attitudes ('some people are like this', 'some people are like that') and thereby overlook the extent to which their attitudes (and personalities) may be shaped by their cultural heritage and social circumstances. If these circumstances change, so we might expect some degree of movement in the profile of opinions and beliefs in the population.

Another criticism of these surveys is that the attitudes expressed do not always provide a reliable indication of how people are likely to behave in real-life situations. But the most important criticism of the 'prejudice' approach is the way in which it reduces the issues to the level of 'individuals'.

Sociologists accept that some individuals are more inclined than others towards prejudice, but they challenge the notion that racial hostility is basically a matter of the idiosyncratic attitudes and behaviour of a small number of disturbed personalities. In a country like Britain, for example, racial prejudice is far from being the exclusive property of a few scattered bigots. Just by growing up in this society, by incorporating its culture and history, and by being exposed to the mass media, many 'normal' people will become familiar with negative racial stereotypes. Prejudice, then, is enshrined within popular cultural traditions and dominant social institutions; it is not a matter of the free-floating attitudes of a few individuals. Furthermore, the causes of prejudice are not limited to the search for a 'prejudice-prone personality' or a few key 'psychological' factors. A major task of sociology is to demonstrate how the level and intensity of racial prejudice in a society responds to shifting social forces and power struggles. For example, where there is a social situation of economic or political conflict, the flames of prejudice are likely to be fanned. So we can see that sociologists shift the focus away from abstract 'attitudes' or 'personality dynamics' towards a wider social canvas. Prejudice is located within a social and historical context, and it is there that the major causes are identified. If racial 'prejudice' is the individualistic notion studied by psychologists, sociologists focus on *racism*. Three distinct uses of this term can be identified.

Racism

1. Racism as Ideology – Cultural Racism

Most commonly, 'racism' refers to a whole cluster of cultural ideas, beliefs and arguments which transmit mistaken notions about the attributes and capabilities of 'racial' groups. The term indicates a generally available cultural complex which falsely claims that certain 'races' (often fanciful) are condemned to a permanent position of moral, cultural and intellectual inferiority. The racist beliefs may be consciously incorporated within some pseudo-scientific doctrine, and indeed Banton (1977) has proposed that the term strictly applies only to those 'biological' explanations of racial inferiority – or theories of racial typology – which flourished in the nineteenth century. However, most sociologists prefer to adopt a broader and looser formulation of racism.

Rex (1970), for example, states that racism is present whenever any 'deterministic belief system' regards group characteristics as narrowly 'fixed' and therefore leading inevitably to rather rigid and exclusive barriers between one group and another. The belief system may well take the form of an explicitly 'scientific' theory (based on biology or psychometrics), but other grounds are possible. Thus, apartheid in South Africa is currently defended on the dubious grounds of alleged 'cultural' and 'historical' differences, without any obvious reference to biological arguments. Alternatively, corrupted theological doctrines may be employed to justify racial disadvantage (e.g. the argument that God purposely created different tribes, or that black suffering is the result of God's curse on the descendants of Ham). In addition to these systematic doctrines, however, racism may appear also at the less ordered and more inconsistent level of 'folk wisdom' or 'common-sense'. But even at this level the presence of racism can be related to structural and historical factors (e.g. history of British Empire).

2. Racism as Practice – Racialism

The term 'racism' is also used to refer to behaviour, policies or types of treatment which are informed by racial antipathies. This includes individual acts (a white employer refusing a job to a black applicant simply because he is black) and institutional policies (local authority refusing to make reasonable housing provisions for ethnic minorities). Prejudice does not just lurk inside the minds of people: it also finds expression in the ways they treat one another. Unfortunately, the use of the term 'racism' in this sense leads to complications since 'racism' then refers not only to ideas and beliefs rooted in culture, but also to 'behaviour' influenced by these beliefs.

It seems far less confusing to reserve the term 'racism' for the cultural attitude and observe the usual convention of adopting the term 'racial discrimination' or 'racialism' to describe the differential treatment of racial groups. We should note, however, that some schools of thought avoid such a distinction. So for Stuart Hall, writing in a neo-Marxist vein, racism is 'a set of economic, political and ideological practices' (Hall, 1980).

However, there is no direct link between racism (the attitude) and racialism (the behaviour). It is quite possible, for example, to imagine a white Afrikaaner reluctantly complying with apartheid because of possible sanctions against him (racialism without racism). However, racism and racialism are likely to feed each other in circular fashion. People who harbour prejudices are likely to find that it influences the way they act towards minority groups, no matter how much they try to conceal their feelings. And the behaviour also influences attitudes: if people are in the habit of treating minorities badly, then they will find that their negative attitudes are reinforced. If, for example, a minority racial group is habitually refused decent jobs, housing or education, then its resultant low standards of living will appear to justify the initial prejudice ('they must deserve it').

3. Racism as Social Structure – Institutional Racism

This version depicts racism as an enduring structural feature of a society, recognisable by social patterns of disadvantage and inequality which run along racial lines. Thus, Mason (1982) defines institutional racism as: 'any situation in which groups, socially defined as races, are systematically disadvantaged in respect of social rewards, capacities or opportunities'.

So alongside cultural racism (beliefs and attitudes) and racialism (differential treatment) we must place institutional racism, which draws attention to the ways in which racism penetrates the dominant organisations and power structure of society, resulting in distinctive patterns of social disadvantage. Racist assumptions are enshrined as the working basis for major institutions and official bodies; racialism becomes entrenched in routine procedures and rules.

Carmichael and Hamilton (1969) make a dramatic distinction between 'individual racism' and 'institutional racism':

> When white terrorists bomb a black church and kill five black children, that is an act of individual racism, widely deplored by most segments of the society. But when in that same city – Birmingham, Alabama – five hundred black babies die each year because of the lack of proper food, shelter and medical facilities, and thousands more are destroyed and maimed physically, emotionally and intellectually because of conditions of poverty and discrimination in the black community, that is a function of institutional racism. When a black family moves into a home in a white neighbourhood and is stoned, burned or routed out, they are victims of an overt act of individual racism which many people will condemn – at least in words. But it is institutional racism that keeps black people in dilapidated slum tenements, subject to the daily prey of exploitative slumlords, merchants, loan sharks and discriminatory real estate agents.

But certain difficulties arise if we stray from the purely descriptive level of using the term 'institutional racism' to indicate objective patterns of social disadvantage. For example, do the social institutions deliberately discriminate along racial lines ('conspiracy version')? Is institutional racism simply the accidental by-product of non-racist decisions ('unintended consequences version')? Mason draws attention to these and other rival versions and shows how these differing interpretations make it difficult to 'prove' the existence of institutional racism satisfactorily. Because of the ambiguities surrounding the term, there is a danger of it being employed as a political slogan rather than as an analytical tool.

The task now remains to decide whether modern Britain can be described as a 'racist' society.

Measuring Racism

Walvin (1984) notes that racial animosity and discrimination are not new in Britain. On the contrary, they are all too visible in the troubled history of black people in this country since the sixteenth century. Nevertheless, it is not an easy task to chart the ebb and flow of the tide of racism, nor to assess the depth and range of the problem at any given time. Invariably we are left with imprecise measures and rough estimates, and even then the 'factual' results are selectively interpreted according to the values and theoretical positions of those who enter the debate. Take, for example, the following two judgements:

> In talking about racist resentment, I did not at all wish to suggest that Britain is a racist society, nor that every Briton is a racist. Such a suggestion would be utterly false and grossly unfair. When all is said and done, Britain is one of the most decent and civilised societies in the world, and is characterised by a considerable sense of fairness and humanity (Parekh, 1978).

> Our record of tolerance is clearly not compatible with our image of ourselves as a liberal and tolerant nation... we must divest ourselves of the comforting myth of our national tolerance and painfully recognise that Britain is an endemically racist society (Husband, 1975).

These conclusions stem from ultimately contrasting images of society. Clearly, the 'radical' who adopts a conflict model is far more likely to regard entrenched racism as the inevitable outcome of a basically exploitative society; those who adopt 'liberal' or 'pluralist' models are attracted towards a more 'balanced' picture of the good and bad features of British race relations; and for extreme 'right-wingers' the problem is not racism at all but the presence of 'alien' people on British soil. These contrasting interpretations have to be remembered when examining the following empirical evidence.

(a) Cultural Racism

The association of dark skin with social inferiority is deep-rooted in our cultural heritage. Some writers relate this association to basic structures of thought and language which, for example, are expressed in the universal contrast between night and day, dirt and cleanliness, good and evil. This means that blackness stands as a symbolic representation of the things we fear or hold in contempt. Fryer (1984) illustrates these connections:

> The very words 'black' and 'white' were heavily charged with meaning long before the English met people whose skins were black. Blackness, in England, traditionally stood for death, mourning, baseness, evil, sin and danger. It was the colour of bad magic, melancholy, and the nethermost pit of hell. People spoke of black arts, blackmail, and the Black Death . . . White, on the other hand, was the colour of purity, virginity, innocence, good magic, flags of truce, harmless lies, and perfect human beauty.

Nevertheless, the expansion in geographical 'discoveries' and inter-racial contact from the sixteenth century on prompted the creation of further images and additional myths. For example, Walvin (1978) documents the influential role of returned travellers in popularising fanciful stereotypes and circulating lurid tales about foreign races. Patronising attitudes towards these 'primitive', 'innocent' and 'ignorant' people rested alongside more alarmist descriptions of their 'savage', 'heathen', and 'promiscuous' habits. And later, during the rapid expansion of the British Empire in the late nineteenth century, writers like Kipling fired the public imagination with vivid portraits of 'new-caught sullen peoples, half-devil and half-child', who apparently lagged well behind the British 'race' in civilised behaviour and nobility of mind. The remarkable accomplishments of the colonial powers certainly offered plausible support for spurious claims of white superiority. And the experience of colonial subjugation and enslave-ment imposed a lasting stigma on people with dark skins. History therefore provides a potent range of racial imagery, and this cultural legacy has been passed on to succeeding generations in varying forms (creative literature, school textbooks, pseudo-scientific theories, general folk-lore).

But it is misleading to regard cultural racism as merely some curiously influential survival from the colonial past. Culture is not normally handed down in an untampered form, but is constantly being re-created and transformed. Cultural racism, then, consists of a shifting network of interlocking ideas, images and assumptions, and each generation contributes to the re-shaping of this cultural complex. In modern Britain, for example, the imperial myths have hardly been swallowed wholesale; there are various counter-currents (intellectual and religious traditions, political ideologies, even the decent sentiments of the 'benevolently prejudiced') which represent a challenge to the dominance of racist assumptions. But we also have to recognise new sources and manifestations of cultural prejudices. Thus, a recent report by the Policy Studies Institute (1983) discovered that racial prejudice and racial talk are pervasive in the Metropolitan Police Force. The researchers found that a rhetoric of racial abuse ('nigger', 'coon', 'wog') was not only tolerated but actually cultivated in the occupational cultures of police, a group holding a powerful and publicly sensitive position. Likewise, the mass media have been identified as a particularly insidious source of racist sentiments (Hartmann and Husband, 1974). They have been accused of treating blacks in Britain as alien 'outsiders' and therefore as a 'problem' rather than an asset. Instead of vigorously condemning white racism, they have exaggerated immigration figures; instead of investigating the underprivileged conditions of blacks in this country, they have spot-lighted black crime rates. Admittedly, the media do not present a uniform picture, and no doubt counter-examples could be found. But the media are important shapers of public opinion, so any biases in their presentation are a serious cause for concern. Another source for cultural racism lies in the materials used by schools in socialising the young to a view of history and other cultures. A constant strand of complaint from parents of ethnic minority children relates to how the school curriculum ignores their presence and even reinforces racism. 'Little Black Sambo' remains alive and well in dozens of storybooks; the glories of imperial conquest are daily celebrated in classrooms; the superiority of the Christian over other religions is expressed in insensitive ways. By sketching how a school system can perpetuate, or at least not challenge, cultural stereotypes of a racist nature, we start to show how cultural racism becomes institutionalized.

(b) Racialism

Simply asking hypothetical questions in an opinion survey does not in itself establish how people actually behave towards one another.

Even the previously-mentioned report on the Metropolitan Police did not claim that they acted in a consistently discriminatory manner towards minority groups. So independent evidence has to be unearthed in order to assess the extent of racial discrimination in this country. Firm evidence for the widespread nature of racialism is provided by a painstaking series of studies conducted by Political and Economic Planning (PEP), a research organisation which later merged in the Policy Studies Institute (PSI). In an early PEP study (Daniel, 1968), a wide battery of research methods was employed. Apart from questionnaires and interviews with random samples of 'whites' and 'coloureds', the researchers investigated a selected group of 500 'potential discriminators' (e.g. recruitment personnel, building society managers, landlords). In addition, they developed the useful ruse of 'situation tests', where they sent professional actors (representing a white Englishman, a Hungarian or Cypriot migrant, and a coloured migrant) after the same job or flat. The disturbing conclusion was that racial discrimination ranged 'from the substantial to the massive' in many spheres: employment, housing, and services such as insurance, banking, shops and building societies. Coloured migrants were clearly less successful in applications for jobs, bank loans, mortgages and other valued resources. Also, far from being over-sensitive, they actually underestimated the amount of racial discrimination they suffered. And this discrimination could not be explained away by 'rational' criteria such as inferior qualifications (the better-educated were likely to experience an even greater degree of job discrimination!). A similar PEP study in the mid-1970s (Smith, 1977) concluded that racial discrimination had diminished to some extent. Nevertheless, there was still marked discrimination in the job market (especially for non-manual and unskilled workers), in privately-rented accommodation, and in the council house sector (where migrants were allocated inferior accommodation).

Both of these PEP reports strengthened the case for firmer antidiscrimination legislation. The second report indicated that earlier legislation (e.g. the 1965 Race Relations Act) had made some impact, but it also provided documented proof that discrimination still persisted. In recognition of this stubborn persistence, the 1976 Race Relations Act broadened the scope of legislation to restrict practices which, irrespective of intention, had the effect of discriminating against ethnic minorities (e.g. laying down rigorous but unnecessary language qualifications for manual jobs). Nevertheless, the history of government measures to outlaw discrimination and promote racial harmony is hardly an unqualified success. Dummett and Dummett (1982) argue that successive British governments must accept the major blame for continued racialism in this country. Instead of endorsing the notion of a truly multi-cultural, multi-racial society, governments have increasingly offered concessions to mounting racist demands. Instead of launching a concerted campaign against racism and against racially motivated attacks on blacks, they have passed a series of immigration laws which enshrine racist assumptions: blacks are seen as a 'problem' and their numbers must be limited; white 'patrials' are perfectly acceptable, but the 'alien' invasion threatens to 'swamp' the country. Quite apart from the distress caused to separated relatives, the harsh enforcement of immigration laws convinces the 'hesitant, ambivalent and confused' whites that they were right to feel apprehensive, and it encourages racists to make fresh demands. Governments have certainly maintained a 'respectable' face by passing relatively toothless and ill-designed anti-discrimination legislation, but many of their own practices simply reinforce racialism. Their positive measures have not radically altered the patterns of social disadvantage which the black population continue to suffer.

(c) Institutional Racism

The main preoccupation in the PEP/PSI studies gradually shifted from concern with 'prejudice' and 'discrimination' towards the documentation of the social patterns of disadvantage among Britain's black population. This shift was signalled in Smith's 1974 report which noted that disadvantage stems from various sources, not from discrimination alone. For example, the language problems of migrants might hamper their economic progress; and once migrants are recruited as a replacement population in the less prestigious jobs, the 'normal' structural features of British society (class differentials in power and opportunities) may result in the perpetuation of disadvantage. Obviously, then, it was important not to confuse discrimination and disadvantage, and the plotting of 'life chances' assumed a new priority. The 1974 report duly confirmed the underprivileged status of black migrants and their British-born descendants. Although there were interesting differences between the various 'ethnic' groups, the broad job picture was clear. Black males were over-represented in manual jobs, especially in the semi-skilled and unskilled sectors; they earned less than their white counterparts, and they were more likely to work shifts. In the housing sphere, blacks tended to be concentrated in less desirable areas of cities. Tenure patterns did not immediately suggest disadvantage – 'Asians', for example, were more likely than whites to be owner-occupiers – but the quality of housing was generally poorer, both in the private and the public sector. Overall, the gap between blacks and whites was clearly marked in most spheres of life.

A Home Office review (Field, 1981) of authoritative research findings criticised the PEP report for over-sampling inner-city areas, and hence exaggerating the gap between whites and blacks. Taking the period 1961–81, they recorded absolute improvements in the housing and job conditions of the minorities, and offered the following qualified conclusion: 'The trends described certainly do not support the notion of ethnic minorities as constituting a social group barred from all avenues of social progress, but nor do they show gains on all fronts'. But the latest PSI study, based on research in 1982 (Brown, 1984) did avoid over-sampling inner-city areas, and it also included a sample of women for the first time, so its conclusions merit attention. Like the Home Office study, they acknowledged 'considerable improvements' in housing conditions: the high level of owner-occupation has remained steady among Asian groups, while owner-occupation and council tenancy have risen for West Indian groups; there has been a marked decline in household size and overcrowding; there is less sharing of amenities with other households. Against this, there is little sign of any dispersal of the black population (the modest dispersal that has taken place is mainly into adjoining areas previously identifiable as clusters of 'immigrant settlement'). And they conclude that:

> the quality of the housing of black people is much worse than the quality of housing in general in this country. Blacks are more often at higher floor levels, and those with houses are less likely to have detached or semi-detached property; black families have smaller property on average, and, with larger household size, their density of occupation is much higher; black households more often share rooms or amenities with other households; the properties black families own or rent are older; and they are less likely to have a garden.

As for jobs, the only optimistic sign was that the status gap in the jobs secured by young blacks and whites was not so great as in the past. However, in the grim climate of economic recession, the unemployment rates of blacks was up to twice as high as that of whites (in 1974 it had been the same). Elsewhere, little had changed:

> The survey gives us a depressing picture of the economic lives of people of Asian and West Indian origin in Britain today. They are more likely than white people to be unemployed, and those who are in work tend to have jobs with lower pay and lower status than those of white

workers . . . there has been little convergence of the types of
job done by the majority and minority ethnic groups . . .

Overall, then, the 1982 PSI research found little change in the
structural situation of black citizens: the disadvantaged position of the
original migrant workers persisted in the second and subsequent
generations.

In this chapter we have defined some key concepts, and we have
looked at some empirical evidence concerning the problems of 'racism'
in Britain. In order to deepen our understanding of the nature and
meaning of these problems, we must now turn to the more theoretically
informed debates in the following chapters.

Chapter Four

Ethnicity

As we noted in the previous chapter, the immigrant-host model hinged on the belief that migrants from the Caribbean and the Asian sub-continent would eventually become 'acculturated', gradually shedding their distinctive identities and cultural norms, and slowly becoming socialised into the dominant values and folk-ways of the host society. The model, admittedly, conceded that only a modest degree of cultural assimilation was likely for 'primary' settlers, and it recognised that continued 'colour' discrimination might impede the process as far as the second generation was concerned, but nevertheless the envisaged trend was firmly in the direction of a cultural 'melting pot'. However, this framework of assumptions was disturbed in the 1960s and 1970s by the dawning realisation that migrant cultures were not simply short-lived phenomena destined to fade away rapidly under the dual impact of disruptive migration and the seductive attractions of the host culture. On the contrary, migrants and their descendants appeared to be stubbornly retaining many elements of their 'original' cultures, modifying them to only a limited extent, and sometimes emphasising them even more fervently with the passage of time. It became increasingly obvious, therefore, that cultural allegiances – 'ethnicity' – merited special attention.

This rediscovery of the importance of the 'ethnic factor' was not confined to Britain. Several commentators suggested that a process of 'massive retribalisation' was taking place in most Western societies, expressing itself in a renewed awareness of linguistic, religious, cultural and national identities. In the United States, for example, some writers identified a process of 'dissimilation', in which native-born Americans were re-asserting the ethnic traditions of their ancestors. Other cited examples included the persisting 'language divide' in countries like

Canada, Belgium and Wales; mounting religious conflict in Ulster and Holland; and the increased popularity of regional independence movements in nation states like Britain and Spain. These types of issues, it was argued, could not be explained fully by conventional 'political' or 'economic' analysis, since they involved an underlying 'ethnic' or 'cultural' dimension which gave them their special character.

Sociology in the 1950s and 1960s was taken somewhat unawares by these developments, and Burgess (1978) attributes this to the misleading influence of two strands of thought which he calls the 'liberal expectancy' and the 'radical expectancy'. The liberal expectancy had broadly assumed that the processes of modernisation and industrialisation would lead to the early dissolution of 'primitive' ethnic affiliations, as people adopted a more 'rational' and 'individualistic' approach to life. The radical expectancy shared the view that ethnic groups would become superfluous and irrelevant, but it assumed that people would abandon the 'false consciousness' of ethnic groups for the supposedly more 'realistic' arena of class struggle. In this radical scenario, ethnic groups would decline as members aligned themselves with their appropriate social class interests. However, the liberal and radical expectancies were apparently challenged by the train of events implied by 'massive retribalisation', and this prompted fresh academic interest in the whole question of ethnicity.

The Ethnic Dimension

An 'ethnic group' has been defined by Schermerhorn (1970) as 'a collectivity within a larger society, having real or putative ancestry, memories of a shared historical past, and a cultural focus on one or more symbolic elements defined as the epitome of their people-hood'. In a similar vein, Yinger (1981) suggests that the term refers to 'a segment of a larger society whose members are thought, by themselves and/or by others, to share a common origin and to share important segments of a common culture, and who, in addition, participate in shared activities in which the common origin and culture are significant ingredients'. From these definitions we can extract some key features of ethnic groups: shared culture, regular social interaction, and a sense of 'belonging' accompanied by an almost cult-like mystique which secures the bonds of unity between the members. The key term in ethnic studies is 'culture', which Khan (1982) defines as: 'the system of shared meanings developed in a social and economic context which has a particular historical and political background'. Culture is the distinctive 'design for living' that a group possesses, the sum total of its rules and guides for shaping behaviour and patterning its way of life. These cultural bonds can be so strong that when members move from one country to another – as in the case of New Commonwealth migrants to Britain – they frequently make determined efforts to sustain their ethnic identity by pursuing traditional religious and cultural customs, maintaining dietary habits, and keeping alive the languages and dialects of their homelands. It can be anticipated, also, that certain types of social experience and group formation are particularly conducive to the emergence of cleary-defined ethnic groups, and the most familiar examples of ethnic groups are usually based on nations, territorial units, religious codes, common language, and tribal or clan membership. Some writers have further suggested that 'race' is another likely source of 'ethnicity', so that we might expect the boundaries between races to coincide with the boundaries between ethnic groups. However, the connection is not quite that simple, and it needs to be spelled out in greater detail.

Various attempts have been made to establish the relevance of cultural factors in race relations situations. In the United States, especially, there has been a rather long-standing reluctance to acknowledge the cultural distinctiveness of the black population. Following the lead of respected researchers like Frazier and Myrdal, the American black was portrayed first and foremost as an American, thoroughly steeped in American culture. Anxious to combat racist notions, researchers tended to emphasise the cultural similarities of black and whites; alleged features of 'black culture' were explained away as stemming from lower-class culture in general, or from the general cultural milieu of the southern USA, and so it was denied that there was a distinctive 'black culture' at all. Blauner (1972), however, took issue with this dominant line of argument. Blauner insists that the historical experience of slavery, the forced entry into American society, remains a formidable shaping influence in black consciousness. He further argues that there is a recognisable black culture, forged from diverse sources: slavery, the African heritage, and the experience of racism and poverty. Themes like 'soul' and 'survival' are especially prominent, and cannot be regarded as a normal part of the general lower class culture. Moreover, Blauner points out that culture is not something fixed and static: it is constantly being created and re-created, and so black culture was able to incorporate notions like 'Black is Beautiful' and 'Black Power' in the 1960s. Finally, Blauner contends that the denial of a black culture is itself racist, or 'neo-racist', since it refuses to recognise the independent integrity of the black experience.

If it could be argued that blacks in the United States – after centuries of residence in that country – retained a distinctive culture, how much more pertinent the whole question of ethnicity seemed in a country like Britain, with its more recent upsurge in immigration from the New Commonwealth. Consequently, the new emphasis on ethnicity was eagerly borrowed by British race academics.

However, the connection between race and ethnicity is by no means straightforward. In our first chapter we showed the untenable nature of the argument that innate biological characteristics somehow 'determine' the cultural content of the racial group concerned. So, depending on circumstances, people of different 'races' may combine to create a common 'culture'; conversely, people of a given 'race' may create quite different 'cultures'. This means that there is no exact match between 'race' and 'ethnic' group; and so, strictly speaking, the terms should not be used interchangeably. Indeed, Lyon (1972) has attempted to distinguish race and ethnic group analytically. Firstly, an ethnic group is defined culturally, whereas a racial group is physically defined. Secondly, he maintains that an ethnic group voluntarily erects barriers between itself and other groups, whereas a racial group tends to be forcibly excluded and prevented from freely interacting with other groups. Thirdly, Lyon argues that ethnic groups enjoy a sense of solidarity and demonstrate a capacity for mobilisation of their collective interests, whereas racial groups tend to be little more than residual categories which have dim prospects for collective efforts. Lyon's conceptualisation certainly represents a brave attempt to sort out important terms and to avoid confusion, but ultimately it fails to establish a clear distinction. For instance, there is no convincing reason why a racial group cannot be 'self-defined', developing a positive sense of purpose and mutuality, and displaying considerable organisational talents (white racists and Black Power advocates are hardly likely to regard race as a mere residual category!). The experience of racism itself may help forge a unifying cultural identity, as we have already seen in the case of blacks in the United States. Moreover, members of a racial group tend to grow up together, to share common territory and social experiences, and so to that extent we might expect a common culture to emerge. So, in the end, the rigid separation of 'race' and 'ethnic group' cannot be sustained, and that is why the study of ethnicity is potentially so valuable for a deeper understanding of race relations. At its simplest, the underlying argument of this chapter is that race relations in Britain cannot be understood properly without taking due account of the ethnic affiliations of the groups concerned.

Studying Ethnicity

The reorientation in academic studies towards a greater emphasis on ethnicity was a welcome addition to the race relations literature. From the 1960s onwards there was a concerted effort to map out the field of 'ethnic studies', and this resulted in the launching of extremely valuable ethnographic studies of the communities concerned. Researchers carefully documented the distinguishing cultural features of selected groups of New Commonwealth migrants, charting the ways in which these groups differed in such things as language, religion, core values and social attitudes, kinship patterns, diet and routine life styles. Meanwhile, there was an increasing appreciation of the sheer complexity of cultural adaptation as migrants moved from one culture to another. This process could not be described as a simple matter of complete 'assimilation', but neither was it a matter of successfully preserving the 'original' culture intact. The process of adaptation was additionally complicated by the position of the second generation, who were frequently described as caught 'between two cultures' (Watson, 1977). In order to understand the transitions and upheavals entailed, Lea and Young (1984) suggest we must consider:

(1) The culture of the country (e.g. India, Jamaica) from which migration takes place.

(2) The particular sub-culture of those who migrate (e.g. Sikh Punjabis, Hindu Punjabis).

(3) The sub-cultures (e.g. second generation youth cultures) which spring up as part of the shifting process of adaptation to the country of immigration.

Lea and Young also take pains to warn against the dangers of assuming that the migrant culture is homogeneous (e.g. there will be generational, sexual and social class variations on cultural themes). Moreover, the view that ethnicity is somehow a desperate hanging-on to some archaic or 'primitive' or inappropriate form of 'life ways' is one that must be treated critically. Indeed, as we shall see, an important strength of some studies is how they describe and explain the *new* forms of communal life which emerge in multicultural Britain.

By considering some recent ethnographic studies we can explore these aspects further.

Sketches from Contemporary Ethnographic Studies

(1) Pakistanis

Pakistani communities, both in Britain and in Pakistan itself, have been subjected to close study by *Khan* (1977) and by *Dahya* (1973). By reaching beyond the normal confines of ethnographic research to include both 'home' and 'host' societies, this allows them to trace interesting continuities and discontinuities entailed in the process of migration. But the subtle process of change and adaptation is not merely a mechanical response to new circumstances or external constraints. Rather, the subjective attitudes, intentions and aspirations of the migrants themselves help shape the outcome in important ways. The favoured lifestyles and cultural affiliations of the ethnic groups concerned influence their experiences in Britain.

Most Pakistani migrants to Britain are drawn from the rural areas of the Punjab, Campbellpur and Mirpur. Khan describes the typical village life and cultural features of the Mirpuris, who inhabit the Kashmir region yet speak a Punjabi dialect. The typical household consists of three generations, with the eldest male having the greatest authority. The extended family has great importance, and frequently marriage takes place between cousins. Like most South Asian groups, arranged marriages are the norm. The Mirpuris belong to the Sunni sect of Islam, and women are expected to observe the regulations of purdah (involving wearing the veil, shunning the company of male strangers, etc.). Nevertheless, the general respect shown to traditional customs allows women to participate in the normal round of gregarious outdoor village life. Overall, there is a system of mutual inter-dependence (along village and kin lines) and individual subordination to group norms.

The possession of land is of extreme importance in providing status and livelihood, but the system of male inheritance of land (sub-division – property divided between the children – rather than primogeniture – property inherited by the first born) results in a large number of small land-holdings which afford only a modest living. The small landholders are certainly more prosperous than landless labourers, but largely they are restricted to subsistence farming rather than more profitable cash crop production. The economic spur to migration, then, is not so much to earn a living but to supplement and build on the resources the kin group already possess. Migration is seen as an economic investment intended to raise their social and economic status in Pakistan, rather than a serious bid for a gratifying 'new life' in Britain. Consequently, the Pakistani who travelled to Britain (at least in the earlier years of post-war migration) was typically a transient rather than a permanent settler. The intention was to return eventually to Pakistan, and this signified a particular scale of values.

The concept of the 'myth of return' draws attention to the continued importance of homeland and village kin ties to the migrant. In spite of raised standards of living in Britain, many will still claim they wish to return eventually. Nevertheless, although this wish may never be fully or consciously abandoned, the implementation of the desire becomes more difficult. However, the myth has a useful function in preserving homeland values against 'Western' ideas, and it is a useful protection against the stings of racial prejudice insofar as it portrays them as no more than 'temporary hardships'.

The orientation to Pakistan is perhaps most vividly represented in the resurrection of features of that way of life within Britain. Thus, it is possible to see the migrant community attempting to carve out a life style which approximates to an extension of village life, with some necessary modifications to adjust to the new context. Of course, in the early years of migration it was not possible simply to recreate village life in Britain. Early settlers, often discharged seamen, were drawn from different villages and kin groups, yet had to share accommodation with others. So Dahya describes a 'fusion' taking place between different Pakistani groupings. Nevertheless, with the pick up in numbers generally – and more particularly with the phenomenon of sponsored migration (where the village-kin group sponsors someone to join another member in Britain) there has been a gradual process of 'fission' or internal division, first along regional then along village-kin lines. There had always been certain divisions within the Pakistani population in Britain, but over time village-kin divisions became more distinct, as larger family units were established in Britain.

Khan also points out that there are two opposing trends within the Pakistani communities: internal differentiation and solidarity. The differentiation or cleavages occur along village-kin lines, and between the more 'Western-oriented' elites and the migrants from poorer rural origins. Consequently, she argues, leadership tends to be unstable, with self-appointed 'leaders' finding it difficult to establish a wide ranging authority or credibility. Moreover, these 'leaders' are in an ambivalent position, since they are aware that their activities on behalf of the ethnic community might hinder their own 'integration' into British society. Dahya, on the other hand, argues that the ethnic entrepreneurs and community 'brokers' have a vested interest in the retention of ethnic links, since it provides a steady supply of customers for their 'ethnic' shops and services. But alongside this internal differentiation there is movement towards an over-arching solidarity among Pakistani groups. There is considerable separation between these communities and the rest of the 'host' population, and the sheer scale of racial hostility helps unite the Pakistani groups. Thus, the structured exclusion from 'white' society helps maintain the internal solidarity of these groups.

Dahya, however, departs from the usual line of depicting Pakistanis as little more than the unwitting victims of white prejudice. He questions whether racial disadvantage can simply be read off as the direct and sole result of racial prejudice and discrimination. The concentration of ethnic minorities in inferior housing in inner city areas, for example, has frequently been attributed to discrimination by urban gatekeepers (building society managers, estate agents, council housing officials) which forces the groups concerned to settle for less desirable property (cf. Rex and Moore, 1967). But Dahya restores migrants to an active position, by suggesting that they actually choose to live together in the inner city. Areas of residence are deliberately chosen because of convenience (transport routes, proximity to jobs), entrepreneurial opportunities (shops, services), and cheap accommodation (which frees money which can be sent home to sustain the homeland economy). He describes Pakistani communities as an 'army on the march' who choose to live together to defend their ethnic identity, rather than being forced into it by outside pressures.

These studies of Pakistani communities point to certain continuities between life in Pakistan and life in Britain. The 'village institutions' are resurrected within Britain, and mutual aid, pooling of resources, and religious practices are successfully perpetuated. At the same time, important changes are in process, both in Britain and in Pakistan itself. In Britain, Pakistani households tend to be smaller, the system of arranged marriages pays more respect to the wishes of the young couple, and the second generation are more visibly affected by the influence of British cultures. And when people return to Pakistan for a visit, they are sometimes surprised at the changes which have occurred in the life-styles and living standards of the 'homeland'.

(2) West Indians

The early studies of minority groups in Britain assumed that West Indians would be most likely to achieve successful integration. Their language, religious affiliations and educational system indicated their strong ties with Britain, and the first wave of migrants arrived with a firm identification with the 'mother country'. Further, their immigration was more speedily accomplished than that of the Asian groups, and soon a second generation was entering British schools and growing up with no first-hand knowledge of the Caribbean. Unfortunately, the optimistic expectations were increasingly shattered as the West Indian population suffered continuing discrimination and outright violence (e.g. in 1959 there were 'race riots' in Notting Hill and in Nottingham, where white mobs attacked West Indians). Moreover, certain observers developed the notion of an 'internal colony' to describe the disadvantaged plight of West Indian migrants in Britain. Pryce (1979), for example, argues that colonisation not only made Jamaica politically and economically dependent on Britain, but it also created a class-divided and colour-conscious society. The oppressive features of that society continued under 'neo-colonialism', when Jamaica became politically independent but remained economically weak. Pryce underlines the irony that the poor and oppressed who escape to Britain find themselves similarly trapped within British ghettos, since a system of 'internal colonialism' is formed within 'metropolitan society'. So there are clear structural parallels between life in the West Indies and in Britain, and the same unremitting pressures and blocked opportunities confront the 'have-nots'.

Hall *et al* (1978) describes the 'colony society' in the following terms:

> In another sense, the foundation of *colony society* meant the growth of internal cultural cohesiveness and solidarity within the ranks of the black population inside the corporate boundaries of the ghetto: the winning away of cultural space in which an alternative black social life could flourish. The internal colonies thus provided the material base for this cultural revival: first, of a 'West Indian consciousness', no longer simply kept alive in the head or in memory, but visible on the street; second (in the wake of the black American rebellions), of a powerful and regenerated 'black consciousness'. Here began the 'colonization' of certain streets, neighbourhoods, cafes and pubs, the growth of the revivalist churches, hymn singing and mass baptisms in the local swimming baths, the spilling out of Caribbean fruit and vegetables from the Indian shops, the shebeen and the Saturday night blues party, the construction of the sound systems, the black record shops selling blues, ska and soul – the birth of the 'native quarter' at the heart of the English city.

Hall *et al* argue that the first-generation migrants adopted a 'strategy of acceptance', a life of struggling respectability against a background of discrimination and disadvantage. However, the second generation have been less tolerant of racial injustices, and they have gradually developed a strategy of 'resistance' or 'rebellion' which has helped the growth of the cultural cohesiveness described above. Pryce, on the other hand, detected little signs of social cohesion among the black groups in his earlier Bristol study and he gives much more attention to the diversity of life-styles within the ghetto. One of the more interesting examples of this diversity is Rastafarianism, which was not yet prominent in the late 1960s when Pryce began his fieldwork. However, this movement has been intensively studied by Cashmore (1979), and it is worth looking at his study in greater detail.

There was a marked upsurge in the popularity of Rastafarian ideas and lifestyles among young British blacks in the 1970s. They were easily identifiable by their rolled, uncut hair (dreadlocks) and the Ethiopian colours of red, gold and green. The reggae music of Bob Marley and others created a positive public awareness of their existence, but they also attracted a controversial reputation for drug-taking and criminal activities, a reputation which Cashmore shows is unwarranted. Cashmore's stated intention was to 'uncover the social foundations of a particular conception of reality', and this involved him in constructing the 'conceptual maps' of Rastafarians, highlighting their motivations, dispositions and cognitive states. This was, to say the least, a methodologically difficult task, and Cashmore frankly concedes that he relied heavily on 'intuition and inference'. At the same time, however, he researched the historical and material reality within which these subjective states were formed and sustained.

Cashmore claims that the 'movement' is an extension of a Jamaican historical tradition in which political objectives are couched in visions of redemption and supernatural transformations of the world. This tradition blurs the dividing lines between secular and religious objectives, and between the supernatural and the 'everyday' world. A particularly important period in this tradition came in the 1920s and 1930s with the writings of Marcus Garvey, in which he argued against 'integration' and depicted Africa as the spiritual homeland and eventual destination of blacks throughout the world. Although Garvey enjoyed a rather chequered political career, his prophecy (that the crowning of a black king in Africa would herald a new dawn) was seized upon and developed after the assumption to power of Haile Selassie as Emperor of Ethiopia in 1930. But what is surprising is how this somewhat distinct and esoteric cult came to be developed creatively by young Black Britons in the 1970s. Cashmore suggests six factors favourable to development of this kind of ethnicity.

(1) Concentration of a frustrated black population in urban areas.

(2) The unfulfilled aspirations and general disillusionment of this

population made them very receptive to new ideas which suggested some sort of solution to their disaffection.

(3) A cultural apparatus which percolated Rastafarian ideas through the popular and widely available medium of music.

(4) The survival of a gang structure from the 1960s – the remnants of the urban 'rude boy' culture common in downtown areas of Jamaica, and which had existed for a while alongside skinhead culture in Britain in the 1960s. This provided a vehicle for the transmission of ideas.

(5) Rising self-awareness and a sharpened political sense among blacks, who were less convinced by integrationist promises.

(6) Gradual state of 'drift' which loosened the ties to the dominant moral order, including the culture of their parents. This heightened the socialising influence of the street peer group.

Cashmore describes a 'kaleidoscopic array of beliefs and ideas', but the central concept which assists in forming 'boundaries' to the movement is that of Babylon. This concept refers to the whole structure and ideology of white oppression of blacks, originating with imperialism. Not only were blacks abused in physical ways (slavery and ill-treatment) but the whites spread an ideology which perpetuated black subordination and created a lingering sense of inferiority among blacks themselves. Christianity, for example, seemed to preach that blacks should remain meek and mild because they would thus reap their ultimate reward in heaven. So blacks have to purge 'internal' sources of oppression as well as external ones if they are to achieve freedom. This involves finding the 'true self' which can be explored through biblical guidance. The notion of 'brotherhood', however, emphasises that blacks are ultimately united in their common struggle, rather than seeking individual salvation. Indeed they are joined by the belief that God (Jah) resides within every one of them.

Cashmore presents a defence for some of the aspects of Rasta culture which have been most often criticised. Feminists, for example, have condemned the subordinate status of Rasta women ('queens'). Against this, Cashmore argues that one of the main tasks of the movement is to elevate and raise the status of black manhood, which has been severely undermined by the 'matrifocal' emphasis within black culture. Moreover, although Rastas do not marry (marriage is regarded as sinful), Rastafarians claim that their sexual relations are characterised by respect and honour, which they sharply contrast to the decadence and exploitation of 'Western' culture.

Another criticism levelled by radicals is that the Rasta culture is essentially escapist: the message seems to be to stand back and let Babylon crumble from its own corruption. Some radicals have interpreted it as a form of rebellion which has lost its way, taking a 'quietist' route. And certainly Cashmore points out that most of the 'members' are drawn from the lower ranks of the working class, those who presumably should be in the forefront of rebellion. But Cashmore insists that it is not simply an instrumental movement seeking material advantage. Rather, it pays serious attention to the need for identity and culture as well. There is a 'quantum leap' between a solely secular political movement and that of Rastafarianism, which blends secular and religious viewpoints within one world view. Thus, it does not fit neatly into radical accounts of 'protest' groups. Here is how Rex and Tomlinson (1979) sum up its contribution:

> Black youth are in need of a philosophy and a culture which gives them an identity and self-respect in contrast with the degraded self-image which white society imposes on them. This was what, first, Black Islam, and then the Black Power movement did for the ghettoized descendants of slaves in the USA. The blacks of contemporary Britain are also the descendants of slaves deprived of a culture, even if they have not experienced the degradation of the ghetto to the same extent as the American blacks. It looks as though Rastafari in its British growth and development will provide them at least with the beginnings of a culture of self respect . . . it is probably the most important single fact about West Indian society and culture in Britain.

Ethnicity: A Critique

The preceding ethnographies by no means exhaust the entire repertoire of available studies, but they do illustrate the general direction and familiar preoccupations of this approach. In turning to some of the critical debates surrounding ethnic studies, our discussion will be organised around two issues, their *descriptive accuracy* and their *explanatory value*.

(A) Ethnicity as Description

There are great methodological problems in 'reading' a culture accurately, and this leaves a wide latitude for descriptive errors and intruding value-judgements. So it is perhaps not surprising that students of ethnicity themselves disagree on most of the following issues:

(1) How 'different' are ethnic cultures? Plainly, these differences are sometimes clear-cut (as in the case of religious belief-systems), but more frequently they involve subtle variations in emphasis, and in many essentials the ethnic minorities subscribe to the same values as the majority culture. It is worth noting, for instance, that some recent research (Field, 1984) arrived at the conclusion that the attitudes of 'blacks' and 'Asians' living in Britain are not dramatically different from those of their white counterparts. Some commentators even suggest that such an apparently 'divergent' movement as Rastafarianism is more correctly viewed as a case of 'symbolic ethnicity' (Gans, 1979), a matter of cultural fashion and stylised identity which does not bite too deeply into the lives of its 'followers'. Rather than indicating an all-consuming commitment to 'alternative' values, the popularity of Rastafarianism, is sometimes based on the relatively casual matter of surface style. And this is only one of the problems of interpretation confronting ethnic researchers. It soon becomes obvious that these researchers face the difficult task of striking the correct balance, one which gives due weight to cultural variations without at the same time exaggerating the gap which exists between the various ethnic minority cultures, and between them and the rather under-researched 'host' culture (or, more appropriately, host *cultures*).

(2) How problem-ridden are ethnic cultures? Accusations of ethno-centrism are frequently hurled at writers on ethnicity, and one of the most heated debates concerns the position of the 'matrifocal' family structure in West Indian culture. Critics argue that not only has the frequency of single-parent, female-headed family units been grossly exaggerated, but researchers have been blinded by their own cultural values and have wrongly interpreted this type of family structure as 'weak', 'pathological', and 'inadequate'. This overlooks the need for cultural relativism (does it seem a problem to the people concerned?) and it underestimates the strengths of West Indian family life. In addition to charges of ethnocentrism, it is frequently alleged that sexist assumptions creep into the descriptions of Asian females. Thus, a distorted stereotype of 'passive' Asian females is circulated, in which they are portrayed as 'subjugated' and 'oppressed' by patriarchal Asian culture. Parmar (1982) argues that this patronising over-simplification ignores the brave and constructive role played by Asian women in resisting racism, capitalism, and patriarchy. These criticisms of ethnic studies certainly deserve attention, but it is also important to note that mainstream ethnicity writers do not always agree on these descriptions and evaluations. Moreover, not all the researchers are white (Pryce is Jamaican) or male (Parmar is just as scathing about white feminists). And it would be curious if ethnic cultures contained no 'internal' problems, tensions or weaknesses, especially given the damaging history of racism and the dislocating impact of migration.

(3) Is there a 'generation' gap in ethnic cultures? A recurrent topic of interest in ethnic research is the changing nature of cultural attachments over time, and so a great deal of attention has been paid to the second generation. Do they faithfully preserve the cultural heritage of the first generation or do they break loose from this tradition? It is commonly argued that first-generation West Indian migrants were typically 'compliant' and 'assimilationist' in orientation, whereas the second-generation are more truculent, alienated and militant. Indeed, the youngsters are portrayed as 're-discovering' elements of black history (Rastafarianism, Black Power) and creatively developing them in ways disapproved of by the first-generation. Likewise, Asian youth are sometimes depicted as bridling at customs like arranged marriages, and as flirting with 'Western' values and behaviour in a way which suggests a slow movement away from the culture of the first-generation. However, writers differ as to the extent of the culture gap between the first and second generations, and on whether this is indeed a 'culture gap' or simply an 'age' gap which becomes less marked as youth grow older.

Of course, these disagreements and criticisms do not constitute objections in principle to the ethnic approach. They simply point to the difficulties of cultural analysis and the margin for mis-interpretation. Nevertheless, there still remains the problem of determining the explanatory value of ethnic research: is the approach confined to the cataloguing of 'exotic' cultural differences, or does it have real theoretical significance?

(B) Ethnicity as Explanation

We will focus on two main questions in this section:

(1) Why do people cultivate allegiance to ethnic groups?

(2) What explanatory value has 'culture' for an understanding of race relations?

(1) The sources of ethnicity. Part of the theoretical problem consists in explaining why ethnic groups achieve prominence in the first place. McKay (1982) identifies two opposing schools of explanation for the importance of ethnic groups in modern industrialised societies: the

'*primordialist*' and the '*mobilisationist*' arguments. Primordialists contend that the strength of ethnicity derives from the way it meets the human need for deep-seated, sacred, non-contractual attachments. Ethnic allegiances answer our 'natural' need for belonging and community, and so ethnic groups emerge spontaneously from the innermost recesses of human nature. A more technical version of primordialism is afforded by 'sociobiology' (van den Berghe, 1978) which suggests that ethnic or racial attachments are coded in the genes. Ethnicity is explained in sociobiology as a particular example of 'kin selection', or the tendency to show favouritism to people of similar appearance or kin networks, in order that the common genes have a better chance of evolutionary survival.

The 'mobilisationist' school, on the other hand, suggests that ethnic loyalties are peripheral rather than primordial, and so groups only mobilise ethnic symbols when it offers them some strategic advantage in obtaining access to social, political or economic resources. In the British context, these mobilisationist arguments are usually translated into the concept of 'reactive ethnicity', which conveys the tendency for ethnic group members to construct ethnicity as a defence against racism and discrimination. Thus, Ballard and Ballard (1977) describe the ethnic ties of first-generation Sikhs as little more than a somewhat muted expression of their cultural traditions; the second-generation, however, attempted to strike compromises with British society, but were stung into 'reactive' pride in ethnicity because of the continuing experience of repeated rebuffs and racist humiliations. Moreover, this victimisation created a greater awareness of the similar problems faced by other ethnic groups, and so the second generation are increasingly reaching beyond the more parochial loyalties of their predecessors to embrace a more over-arching pan-Asian identity. As members of single ethnic groups or cross-alliances, the members manipulate ethnic symbols to build a positive identity and to engage in political and economic activity to promote their material interests.

These mobilisationist views helpfully avoid the rather mystical and circular arguments of the primordialist approach, and they appear more useful in understanding the ebb and flow of ethnic loyalties. However, it is not always clear what particular 'interests' are being promoted or defended. If the interests involved are not just material, but include identity, then this merely seems to take us back to primordial arguments. Also, just how strong are the tendencies to 'race' (or 'black' or 'Asian') alliances in comparison with specific 'ethnic' ties or even broad 'class' groupings? How much is the stress on ethnicity due to 'reaction', and how much to a more straightforward 'choice' to follow cultural traditions? Ethnicity obviously involves both 'emotional' and 'strategic' factors, and it would be premature to claim that these questions have been resolved.

(2) **Cultural explanations.** 'Radicals' of various persuasions have been extremely unhappy about the heavy reliance of ethnicity studies on 'culture' as a key to understanding race-related issues. They argue that the logical consequence of ethnicity studies is to attach ultimate 'blame' to the ethnic minorities themselves. Attention is almost exclusively focussed on the 'migrants' and their cultural peculiarities, and heavy emphasis is typically placed on 'pathological' or 'inappropriate' features of these cultures. It is only a short step, then, to 'blaming the victim': crime among West Indian groups is attributed to their 'weak' family structures or 'macho' cultures rather than to the economic deprivations created by capitalist processes; the disadvantaged economic position of Asian women is seen as resulting from their culturally-approved 'subordinate' role rather than from the exploitation of cheap labour in Britain. The predominant emphasis on cultural minorities conveniently deflects attention away from the cultural racism of the 'hosts' and the institutional racism of British society. 'Race' problems are subsequently framed in terms of 'mutual misunderstandings' and the solutions are posited along the tame lines of 'multi-cultural education' and 'cultural pluralism'. Bourne (1983) bitterly attacks ethnicity theorists as little more than 'cheerleaders' for cultural diversity who thereby absolve themselves from combatting the racism endemic in capitalist society. For the radicals, the underlying problems are structural ones of power and conflict, and these issues cannot be tackled by abstract debates about 'culture'. Racial disadvantage, they argue, is not the 'natural' outcome of a multi-cultural society in which some ethnic groups cling to inappropriate values: it is the structural outcome of an exploitative, oppressive society which can only be transformed through radical change.

In their eagerness to make political points, the radical critics have undoubtedly caricatured ethnic studies, and it is arguable that not all ethnographers are quite so naïve or politically insensitive as the critics make out. Few writers lay heavy stress on the 'pathology' of ethnic cultures, and if 'weakness' or 'inadequacy' are highlighted it is usually against a background of structural strain (cf. Pryce). Clearly, the issues of culture conflict and cultural misunderstandings cannot be ducked in a society in which the notion of an 'alien wedge' destroying 'British culture' is so politically entrenched, and so we should be grateful to ethnicity theorists for pursuing these matters. Moreover, the emphasis on ethnicity has had the welcome effect of restoring the ethnic minorities to the position of 'active subjects', fully human beings with their own aspirations, allegiances and consciousness. If nothing else, ethnicity studies have successfully challenged the notion of migrants as mere empty vessels or passive victims without a history and a consciousness of their own. Of course, this emphasis becomes dangerous if it is assumed that there is some permanent cultural 'essence' attached to ethnic groups, such that they will behave in the same manner regardless of circumstances. As Ballard and Ballard point out, we cannot assume that minority group behaviour is the direct expression of internal cultural preferences, but neither is it a direct reaction to external, objective constraints (material deprivation, prejudice, etc.):

> It should be recognized that the external constraints, such as the migrant's position in the labour and housing markets, or the discrimination he faces, are ultimately prior to the internal preferences of the group . . . It is the external constraints of discrimination which set the limits within which South Asians and West Indians in Britain may operate. *But the particular behaviour of different groups may only be finally explained in terms of the culturally determined choices made within these limits as well as the various ethnic strategies used to counteract, circumvent or overthrow those constraints.* (R. and C. Ballard, 1977)

So always we have to examine the interplay between 'cultural' and 'structural' factors. In the next chapter we introduce the 'structural' accounts of race relations.

Chapter Five

Structure and Conflict

The broad contours of racism in Britain were sketched out in an earlier chapter, where it was argued that 'coloured' people suffer from various forms of social disadvantage (institutional racism) and endure continuing problems of racial prejudice (cultural racism) and discrimination (racialism). These three inter-linked elements of racism form a complex and shifting reality, but nevertheless the available evidence consistently suggests the presence of significant racial tensions and structured racial inequalities in modern Britain. It is now time to move beyond the mere documentation of racism towards a search for its major causes. Why does 'race' acquire such a loaded social significance that it leads to the victimisation of black people and the sharp limitation of their life-chances? Why do exclusion boundaries tend to form around socially-defined racial groups? The main concern of this chapter is with 'structural' explanations of racism, and especially those versions which lay stress on deep social conflicts. The discussion is centred round two important topics: the relationship between 'race' and stratification systems, and the role of racist ideologies.

Race and Stratification

The sociological literature on race relations makes frequent reference to the location of racial minorities within stratification systems, and conflict models especially are inclined to regard the class structure as having a crucial influence on race issues. This is particularly true of the various Marxist accounts of racism in Britain, and indeed sometimes 'racial' groups disappear entirely from the analysis as they are submerged in a more general discussion of class conflict. Apart from the Marxist accounts, there are also studies which follow in the tradition of Weber, and Rex is the most prominent representative of this kind of approach. Although the Weberian approach is sometimes described as 'reformist', and although it rejects the Marxist notion of a historical class struggle fought to a revolutionary conclusion, it has more in common with the 'conflict' school than with functionalism. Some of the differences between these Marxist and Weberian approaches can be highlighted by looking at the work of Castles and Kosack on the one hand, and Rex and Moore on the other.

(1) **Castles and Kosack** (1973). These writers approach race relations from a Marxist standpoint, and emphasis is placed upon class conflict within capitalism. Capitalism is described as driven by a relentless search for profits, and in this search it has created a situation of under-development in ex-colonies (West Indian islands, India, Algeria, etc.). Moreover, the uneven development of capitalism has led to a split in Europe between the prosperous 'metropolis' countries like France, Germany and Britain, and the more backward areas like Turkey, Yugoslavia and Greece. These less developed nations – the ex-colonies and the poorer European countries – offer convenient reserves of cheap labour which can be drawn upon when the metropolis centres have labour shortages, and this is precisely what has happened in the post-war period of economic expansion. The prosperous capitalist countries of Western Europe enjoyed better living conditions and improved occupational mobility opportunities, and so the native population deserted the low-status, low-wage menial jobs, thereby creating a labour shortage which was solved by drawing migrants from the less developed countries. The migrants constitute a 'replacement population' filling the undesirable but essential jobs vacated by the indigenous population, and so they settle in the lower ranks of the working class.

It is their emphasis on the labour needs of capitalism which encourages Castles and Kosack to insist that there is no clear division between New Commonwealth migrants to Britain and the European or Arab 'guestworkers' in Germany and France. Admittedly, the legal and civil rights of the guestworkers are more precarious, and they are less likely to be accompanied by their families, but basically they fill the same economic role. Consequently, Castles and Kosack decide to break away from mainstream race relations approaches and they abandon ethnic and phenotypical considerations in favour of an emphasis upon class position. Furthermore, they break away from the cruder versions of the immigrant-host model which portray a rather homogeneous host society, and underline instead the class-divided nature of the receiving societies: 'Western European societies are class societies based on the ownership and control of the means of production by a small minority, and on the concomitant domination and exploitation of the masses. Social relationships are characterised not by harmony and free will, but by conflict and coercion'. The migrants, therefore, arrive into an hierarchical social order which is understood in terms of the Marxist distinction between two main classes, the bourgeoisie and the proletariat. Nevertheless, the migrants do not simply enter a class society: they also have an impact upon it. Castles and Kosack admit that the evidence on the long-term effects of migrant labour is sketchy, but they speculate on possible consequences. Most importantly, they believe the migrants create an internal split within the working class, even though the long-term interests of the native working class and the migrants coincide. The basic insecurity of the native working class makes them prey to racism, and they see the migrants as a threat rather than potential allies in a common struggle against capitalist exploiters. This split is both objective (in terms of the different kinds of jobs allocated to the two groups) and subjective (migrants have lower social status, and are the victims of prejudice), and it hinders the development of class consciousness.

Basically, then, Castles and Kosack explore the system needs of capitalism, the influence this has on migration patterns, and the consequences of this migration on the receiving societies (where capitalists benefit from cheap labour) and the sending societies (which are drained of talent). In swinging the debate away from familiar race relations preoccupations towards economic and class categories, they have been accused of explaining everything in terms of the economic base, and it is certainly true that they underestimate the importance of ethnicity. However, they do allow that political and cultural factors are important: for example, they argue that the increasingly restrictive immigration legislation in Britain was determined not by the economic interests of capitalists (who benefit from a large 'reserve army of labour'), but by wider political processes and cultural debates (e.g. in mass media).

The approach of Castles and Kosack has the virtue of setting British race issues against a historical backcloth and within a global context of political and economic relationships between nations. Of course, there are important differences between 'liberals' and 'Marxists' on the nature and consequences of these connections. Liberals usually admit that colonialism involved conflict and exploitation, but they also stress the beneficial consequences, especially the ways in which the more industrialised nations have assisted in the 'modernisation' of less developed countries. Modernisation theories (Hoogvelt, 1976) assume that 'development' is represented by the types of technology and social organisation which exist in Western countries. Overall, the influence of the Western countries has been to encourage the colonies and ex-colonies to overcome all those 'obstacles' (social, cultural and technological) which prevented their development, and in this respect they have set a useful example to the less favoured nations. Some branches of 'classical' Marxism also believe that the capitalist countries had a 'progressive' role to play in dragging peasant societies out of their stagnation and setting them on the road to capitalist development and the eventual socialist revolution. But some neo-Marxists (e.g. Frank, 1967) argue that, instead of generating capitalist development in these countries, the major powers have imposed 'dependency' or 'under-development'. This notion is captured by Harrison (1979):

> Colonial powers laid the foundation of the present division of the world into industrial nations on the one hand, and hewers of wood and drawers of water on the other. They wiped out indigenous industry and forced the colonies to buy their manufactures. They undermined the self-sufficiency of the Third World and transformed it into a source of raw materials for western industry ... In this way the colonial powers created the world economic order that still prevails today, of industrial centre and primary-producing periphery, prosperous metropolis and poverty-stricken satellites.

Whatever their particular disagreements, both 'modernisation' and 'dependency' theorists agree that a large gulf still separates the metropolis and satellite countries.

(2) Rex and Moore. In the course of their field study of Sparkbrook in Birmingham in the mid-1960s, Rex and Moore (1967) argued that much racial conflict can be understood by examining basic urban processes and problems, and the key urban process they highlight is that of competition for scarce yet desired housing. Whereas Marxists identify two main classes in terms of relationship to the means of production, Rex and Moore adopt a more flexible Weberian position which defines a variety of classes according to given 'market situations', and they point out that one such market is housing. This leads them to coin the notion of 'housing classes' to designate groups which occupy varying positions of strength in the housing market and system of housing allocation. These housing classes do not coincide with the Marxist classes (although there is some relationship between them), since one Marxist class would consist of several housing classes characterised by different interests and market situations. Another typical Weberian emphasis is their desire to develop analyses of the 'subjective' aspects of class situations, necessitating an exploration of popular world-views, including the ways in which people define their own class membership. Although there is no rigid consensus of values, Rex and Moore suspect that nearly everyone aspires to the 'suburban ideal' of 'relatively detached family life'. Nevertheless, the competitive class struggle for this kind of privately-owned, detached or semi-detached suburban housing creates winners and losers, and the less powerful classes have to settle for less desirable housing (flats, terraces), tenure systems (council or private tenancies) or areas of residence (slums, inner-city areas, problem estates).

Rex and Moore acknowledge both the depressed economic situation in the ex-colonies and the economic motives which inspire migration, and they are also sensitive to the continuing bonds between migrants and their countries of origin. But the main focus of the Sparkbrook study was an investigation of the disadvantaged position of New Commonwealth immigrants in the housing market. As far as the 'private' sector of house purchase is concerned, they faced various problems: usually their incomes were low and their savings modest, and in addition they experienced discrimination by vendors, estate agents and building society officials. In the 'council' sector they were confronted by unrealistic residence requirements and long waiting lists which overlooked the special circumstances of their recent arrival; and when they did qualify for council tenure, they were frequently given inferior accommodation on the basis of housing visitor reports which embodied public prejudices. The only solution for many immigrants, therefore, was to gravitate towards old, large and decaying property in inner-city twilight areas like Sparkbrook. These unattractive houses were purchased by communal pooling of resources or by high-interest, short term loans from banks and finance companies (since building societies were cautious about lending money for short-lease property). Generally this put serious financial strain on the migrants, and this accounts for the high proportion of multi-occupation and sub-letting: in order to maintain repayments, the purchaser was forced to take in lodgers, many of whom were fellow migrants unable to obtain alternative accommodation. Unfortunately, these areas of settlement usually suffer from various manifestations of urban deterioration, and it is against this background of decay that racial hostilities are intensified. White residents blame the immigrants for 'creating' the general housing problems, the migrants are resented for altering the 'character' of the area, and racist stereotypes enjoy wide circulation.

However, Rex and Moore argue that it is the discriminatory policies and inadequate housing provision which cause concentrated settlements of migrants, and they show that the migrants are little more than scapegoats for wider social ills.

The Sparkbrook study was enormously influential in directing attention to insitutional practices and policy inadequacies which magnify racial tensions, and it served as a useful catalyst for interesting debates on race issues. But a number of the particular details of urban patterns and processes were questioned, and Rex later admitted that Sparkbrook was an untypical area (e.g. in areas like Handsworth, also in Birmingham, single-family owner-occupation was more common among New Commonwealth migrants). Moreover, the notion of 'housing classes' was subjected to fairly rigorous analytical challenge from some quarters, and it was even suggested that the basic arguments could be accepted without the necessity of devising new 'classes'. Also some 'ethnicity' theorists claimed that migrants actively sought out inner-city areas (in order to retain ethnic ties and to exploit the greater entrepreneurial opportunities these areas afforded) rather than being forced into them because of discrimination or financial necessity. But perhaps the most pressing issue concerns the extent to which housing and environmental conflicts are responsible for racial tensions.

In a later work, Rex (1978) states that housing conflicts are only one source of racism, and he is not at all hopeful that mere urban improvement in itself will remedy matters. There are many reasons for racism – the colonial legacy, class conflict, widespread fear and insecurity – and the full citizenship of black people will require a concentrated effort to resolve the deep-seated problems of British society.

The Underclass

It is one thing to claim that racial conflict is largely a derivative of class conflict, but it still remains a perplexing task to specify precisely how racial groups fit into stratification systems. Various 'extreme' conceptualisations have been offered, including the notion of a 'plural society' (where racial or ethnic groups of more or less equal ranking lead separate existences, mixing only for limited economic purposes) and the 'colour-caste model' (where black and white groups are both stratified internally along class lines, but a rather rigid caste-like barrier between them symbolises and maintains the superior status of whites). In Britain, however, most of the analyses have related racial groups to conventional Marxist and Weberian categories. Nevertheless, even within these traditions there is plenty of disagreement. Miles (1982) helps structure the relevant debates by identifying some dominant stances:

(1) **Unitary Working Class.** Westergaard and Resler (1976) contend that too much attention has been paid to the special problems created by racial discrimination. Coloured people and the white working class share the same basic relation to the means of production, and it is this common class membership which oppresses them: 'Preoccupied with the disabilities that attach to colour, liberal reformers and research workers have been busy rediscovering what in fact are common disabilities of class: widespread and long-standing conditions inherent in the workings of capital, market and state in a divided society'.

(2) **Divided Working Class.** Castles and Kosack, as we have already seen, also work largely within a two-class model (bourgeoisie and proletariat), but unlike the previous authors they believe that black migration has created an objective and subjective split within the working class: 'In objective terms, immigrant workers belong to the working class. But within this class they form a bottom stratum, due to the subordinate status of their occupations'.

(3) **Underclass Thesis.** Rex and Tomlinson (1979) use the term underclass to signify a disadvantaged group which does not share the same experiences or privileges as the white working class. In their Handsworth study they found a 'structural break' between the white working class and the coloured underclass in a range of market situations (employment, housing and education), and of course racial discrimination is another distinguishing factor. They describe coloured people as leading a 'marginalised' existence since they have not yet been fully incorporated into traditional working class organisations (such as trade unions and the Labour Party).

(4) **'Racialised' Class Fraction.** Miles accepts the broad distinction between bourgeoisie and proletariat, but he emphasises the existence of different 'fractions' or sectional interest groups within each. So the working class is not 'unitary' and it is not simply 'divided' into two main camps. As for the 'underclass' thesis, Miles insists that this exaggerates the disadvantage suffered by black groups, and it places too much emphasis on racial discrimination rather than class dynamics. In Miles' conceptualisation, therefore, black people appear at different class levels (mainly within working class, but also in middle class groups) but always as a distinctive fraction which has been 'racialised' (endowed with overtones of racial inferiority).

It is exceedingly difficult to choose between these apparently rival views on the position of racial minorities within the British class system. Although there is agreement that coloured people are over-represented in the lower reaches of the stratification system, it is also clear that they are not exclusively confined to those zones, and this makes the articulation of precise lines of division a daunting task. In order to explore these problems further, it is instructive to take a closer look at the 'underclass' notion.

The notion of an underclass was first developed in the United States, where it was used to refer to that section of the population which seemed permanently trapped in a situation of poverty and unemployment. Although the term is not necessarily confined to black people, it had particular relevance to those people living in the black ghettoes like Watts, which erupted into violence and riots in the 1960s. Briefly, the sense of hopelessness and despair in these ghettoes was transformed into desperate action and protest, a dramatic expression of their feelings of marginality. Likewise, some British commentators (Young and Lea, 1982) have described the 'marginalisation' of black people as a major factor behind the British 'race riots' of the 1980s. Young and Lea suggest that the black population has been squeezed to the very margins of society, and this has denied them the normal channels for resolving their grievances. Unlike the white working class, they are distanced from traditional trade union and political party activity.

This theme of marginalisation is pursued also in Rex and Tomlinson's study of Handsworth. What Rex and Tomlinson argue is that there has not been any marked sense in which ethnic minorities have gained access to those key political, educational, economic and cultural institutions which would enable them to compete on equal terms with whites. Despite their characteristic working-class employment profile, it does not make sense to describe ethnic minorities as part of the working class; rather, they constitute an underclass. Rex and Tomlinson allow that the concept of 'underclass' does not imply that everyone within it is unemployed, but they do point out that ethnic minorities are subject to higher unemployment rates. Some evidence for this is supplied by the 1981 *Labour Force Survey* (see table overleaf).

However, the distinctiveness of the 'underclass' position persists even for those who are employed, and this distinctiveness is captured in the idea of a *'dual labour market'*. A dual labour market is one which shows clear divisions between two employment groups: the primary market (characterised by high pay, security of employment, and good training and promotion prospects) and the secondary market (characterised by low pay, insecurity of employment, and few opportunities for training or promotion). The expectation is that the

Ethnic Groups: Economic status of adults, percentages

Males	White	West Indian	Asian	Other	All
Self-employed	9	4	14	8	9
Employees	61	65	55	50	60
Out of employment	8	19	15	10	10
Economically inactive	22	12	17	32	22
Females					
Self-employed	2	1	3	3	2
Employed	40	56	30	38	40
Out of employment	4	11	7	7	5
Economically inactive	53	32	60	53	53

(Source: *Social Trends*, 1983)
[Reproduced with the permission of the Controller of Her Majesty's Stationery Office]

underclass are highly concentrated in the secondary market, and this creates a vicious circle: the stigmatised racial minority can only land jobs in the secondary market; and their over-representation in this market serves to reinforce their inferior social status. Again, the *Labour Force Survey* gives some indication of this pattern of under-representation in the more desirable jobs.

Ethnic Groups: People in employment by sex and socio-economic group, percentages.

Males	White	West Indian	Asian	Other	All
Professional, employers, managers	22	6	20	24	22
Intermediate and junior non manual	18	7	14	23	18
Skilled manual and non professional	38	49	35	27	38
Semi-skilled and unskilled	21	38	31	24	21
Females					
Professional, employers, managers	8	2	7	5	7
Intermediate and junior non manual	53	50	41	52	52
Skilled manual	7	4	13	8	7
Semi-unskilled	31	42	38	34	32

(Source: *Social Trends*, 1983)
[Reproduced with the permission of the Controller of Her Majesty's Stationery Office]

However, this table also indicates that ethnic minorities are not exclusively concentrated in the lower reaches of the occupational hierarchy and so this creates some difficulty in establishing whether they are truly an underclass. Rex and Tomlinson certainly recognise this spread over the occupational range, and they even allow that Asians in Britain may have a 'Jewish' future (where they prosper but remain separate from the rest of the population). But they insist on the notion of an underclass because of the *predominance* of ethnic groups in shift work, in low status occupations and in dirty industries. Nevertheless, the admitted spread of occupations poses problems for the underclass model. As Braham (1980) states, 'To say that skin colour involves a number of disadvantages is not to say that all black people occupy the same position in the labour market, and to establish that black workers are concentrated in less skilled jobs is not to establish the existence of a black "underclass".' And this lack of a clear 'structural break' between whites and blacks is one of the reasons why the 'unitary working class model' and the 'racialised class fraction' model depart from the underclass thesis. Some of the disagreements also stem from the basic ambiguity surrounding the meaning of the term 'underclass'. However, these disagreements also relate to the political strategies which black groups might adopt. Marxists tend to favour the 'unitary' and 'divided' conceptions, because they believe that whites and blacks should join forces in the class struggle. But the Weberian notion of underclass is less convinced of the unity of interests and revolutionary potential of the working class. Thus, Rex and Tomlinson believe that separate ethnic organisations and political activities are a fruitful means of furthering the special interests of the ethnic groups concerned, at least until they gain full entry into the dominant institutions of society. They also argue that the major political parties should call a truce over race issues and develop a high-profile strategy to overcome racial disadvantage. Multi-cultural education, housing and employment policies, and anti-discrimination measures are needed to rectify the plight of the underclass. As a Weberian, Rex places his trust in reform rather than revolution, but it must also be said that he remains rather pessimistic about the prospects for improvement. In spite of his belief that ethnic groups should engage in 'effective political organisation on their own behalf', he realises that the 'deterministic belief system' of racism severely limits their opportunities.

Racism as Capitalist Ideology

One of the chief preoccupations of the Marxist treatment of race issues concerns the nature, origins and functions of misleading racist ideologies. An ideology is a set of beliefs, ideas and values which has a recognisable shape and an organising cluster of recurrent themes. Sometimes the ideology is articulated in the form of systematic theoretical and philosophical statements, but it also appears at the more inconsistent level of 'commonsense' or 'folk wisdom'; so racist ideologies are represented in pseudo-scientific theories ('biological determinism') in media portrayals and in 'street-level' myths and rumours about disreputable habits of coloured people. Miles (1982) suggests that the defining feature of racist ideology – or 'racism', as he prefers – is that it ascribes negatively-evaluated characteristics in a deterministic manner to a group which is additionally identified as being in some way biologically distinct. Several examples of these racist beliefs and stereotypes have already been reviewed in earlier chapters, so the main focus in this section is on the origins and functions of racism.

Marxists take issue with those explanations of racism which stress universal moral failures (selfishness, cruelty) or narrow psychological causes (misperceptions, personality disorders), and argue instead that racism is rooted in historical and material situations of struggle and conflict. More specifically, the source of racist ideologies is traced to the emergence of capitalism and its process of world-wide expansion. Cox (1970) even speculates: 'It is possible that without capitalism, a chance occurrence among whites, the world might never have experienced race prejudice'. The exploitative processes of colonial expansion (the Iberian conquest of South America, British penetration of India, the European scramble for African territory) are therefore portrayed as the fertile seedbed of racism, both creating and transforming the nature of inter-racial relationships and concurrently spawning racist beliefs. Now, many liberals would agree that colonialism had a profound influence on race relations, but they tend to locate the conflicts in the past and view current race problems as resulting from the unfortunate cultural legacy which has been handed down from those years. But the distinctive thrust of Marxist theories is the claim that the production relations of capitalism harbour the conflicts and tensions which create the 'necessity' of racism. And, since capitalism still predominates in the West, its inherent (but shifting) contradictions continue to fuel racist sentiments in various ways. Consequently, a Marxist approach addresses not just the initial 'production' of racism by the capitalist system, but also the ways in which racist ideologies are 'reproduced' and progressively transformed as capitalism itself alters and encounters new problems. And the key to the lasting connection between 'capitalism' and 'racism' is located in the important functions which racism serves for the perpetuation of the capitalist system. These functions can be grouped around three headings: legitimisation, divide-and-rule, and scapegoating.

(1) Legitimisation. Colonial conquests were carried out by supposedly 'civilised', 'Christian' nations which were ultimately obliged to justify and legitimate their actions. The doctrine of racial superiority was a very convenient device for this purpose, allowing the subjugation and exploitation of the colonised to appear somehow natural, pre-ordained and even in the long-term interests of those who were subjugated. So it can be argued that racism serves as a powerful rationalisation for questionable practices, and it also protects privileged or ruling groups from damaging criticism by putting a gloss on exploitation or callous neglect. The social deprivations of blacks in present-day Britain, for example, may be attributed – via racist stereo-types – to their alleged innate inferiority rather than to any serious defects or injustices in the social order.

(2) Divide and Rule. The prevalence of racist beliefs drives a wedge between white and black workers, and this creates a divided working class which is thereby weakened in the struggle against employers. Indeed, this wedge may be deliberately encouraged by employers who can use it to manipulate the work-force to keep wages low. After the Emancipation of slaves in the southern USA, for example, some unscrupulous plantation owners employed agitators to stir up friction between blacks and whites, and this allowed them to play off one group against the other.

(3) Scapegoating. Racism encourages a scapegoating process in which the inherent frustrations and tensions of capitalism are allowed a 'safe' outlet by being directed at a visible and relatively vulnerable target group – blacks – rather than being directed back to the basic structure of capitalism. This scapegoating process allows a temporary release of pent-up strains and frustrations among the white population, and it deflects attention away from the serious crises of capitalism. Housing shortages are then blamed on an influx of alien immigrants rather than on the normal processes of an unjust housing market; unemployment is blamed on aliens taking all the jobs rather than on the crisis of profitability within capitalism.

These 'functions' help to underline the point that ideologies have real and important effects on the economic and political life of a country, and this is why Marxists sometimes represent racism as a set of 'practices' which exert a definite influence on the ideological, political and economic 'levels' of society. But always the emphasis is on the economic forces which generate and sustain these ideologies.

Policing the Crisis

One of the most illuminating accounts of these functions is the study by Hall *et al* (1978) who offer an interesting and immensely detailed version of the scapegoat argument. Their starting point is the debate about 'mugging' in Britain, a debate which became more and more prominent in the early 1970s after some heavily-publicised cases. Curiously, the mugging scare did not seem justified in terms of an unprecedented rise in the relevant crime figures, and so they used the notion of a 'moral panic' to draw attention to the exaggerated nature of the fears and rumours surrounding the issue. Moreover, a central feature of the debate was the close identification of mugging with blacks, an identification which seemed 'natural' and 'reasonable' in light of some familiarity with the crime debates in the United States. Hall *et al* skilfully demonstrate how certain groups created, sustained and transformed the moral panic about mugging. Thus, police groups seized the initiative, forming pre-emptive patrol groups even before the media bestowed a great deal of publicity. However, media coverage was certainly important in orchestrating public opinion and shaping public debate. But the main argument is that the association of mugging with the black presence in Britain was not simply accidental, a case of mistaken perceptions or unfortunate speculation. Rather, the moral panic was linked to the growing crisis of capitalism: '. . . the nature of the reaction to mugging can only be understood in terms of the way society – more especially the ruling-class alliances, the state apparatuses and the media – responded to a deepening economic, political and social crisis'. In particular, Hall *et al* focus on the crisis of 'hegemony'.

'Hegemony' (a term deriving from the Italian Marxist, Gramsci) draws attention to the ways in which ruling classes attempt to maintain their domination by ideological and cultural means. As well as exercising economic power and state coercion (police, military), the ruling class strive to win the hearts and minds of people and thereby gain 'consent' rather than mere obedience. However, this bid for hegemony is not always successful, and a crisis of hegemony occurs when there is a loss of faith in the social order, or when opposing groups challenge the legitimacy of the ruling groups. Hall *et al* chart the changing ways in which the state has struggled to secure hegemony in post-war Britain. In the early period of post-war growth and prosperity, hegemony was relatively successful, but the deepening problems of capitalism intensified, and in the 1960s hegemony was fractured by various social movements (student protests, youth culture, women's movement, industrial disorder, the rising waves of permissiveness, etc.). So a different 'control culture' emerged in order to re-establish authority, and the 'drift' of the state was arrested by a swing to 'law and order' (representing a move from 'consent' to 'legitimate coercion'). By focussing on such a potent symbol as 'law and order', the state was able to rally support for its campaign against not just muggers but also the wider forces of social unrest. The state was also able to capitalise on the symbolism of 'race', and that is why the identification of mugging with blacks was so important:

> ...the race theme was concrete and immediate... Their Saturday night parties were a constant reminder of the sacrifices demanded by the regime of work and the taboo on pleasure enshrined in the Protestant ethic. Their presence in the job queue recalled a century of unemployment and summary dismissal – evidence that a few years of 'full employment' cannot liquidate a whole class experience of economic insecurity. The black immigrant moved into the declining areas of the city, where Britain's 'forgotten Englishmen' lived on the very tightest of margins; he entered this 'tight little island' of white lower-middle and working class respectability – and, by his every trace, his looks, clothes, pigmentation, culture, mores and aspirations, announced his 'otherness'. His visible presence was a reminder of the unremitting squalor out of which that imperial noon had risen... The symbolism of the race-immigrant theme was resonant in its subliminal force, its capacity to set in motion the demons which haunt the collective subconscious of a 'superior race'; it triggered off images of sex, rape, primitivism, violence and excrement.

So the rich symbolism of the young black mugger was very powerful in its effects: in offending the latent 'sense of Englishness'; in connecting up with fears about 'youth today'; in offering a plausible explanation for the very real troubles people were experiencing; and in crystallising fears about 'inside conspiracies' by liberals who were imposing an alien presence and destroying valuable traditions and institutions. Race was certainly not the only symbol, but it brought together many of the preoccupations and fears of people living in a capitalist society experiencing deep crisis. Yet it enabled this crisis to be masked by a series of false resolutions (cries for law and order, desire for re-establishment of firm authority, stricter immigration legislation) which deflected attention away from the true source of the troubles. And in the process the moral panic inflamed racism and made life much harder for the scapegoated black communities in Britain.

Making Sense of Racism

The Marxist approach stresses features such as class conflict, labour exploitation and the history of capitalist expansion, and it attempts to uncover the economic forces which govern migration patterns and the emergence of racism. However, there are several variations on the basic Marxist themes, and different schools of thought debate the detailed factors and processes which underpin racism. A very crude Marxist account would run along the following lines: economic forces and conflicts are the main causes of racism; the origins of racism are directly attributable to the development of capitalism; racism performs vital functions for the capitalist system; an all-powerful state represents the economic interests of the dominant class by regulating the entry of coloured labour and by manipulating popular racism as the needs of capitalism dictate. However, the search for convincing evidence and for more sophisticated arguments tends to expose some of the weaknesses in the basic framework:

(1) There is a tendency to employ economic factors as a rigid formula to explain all aspects of race relations, and this under-estimates the role of other factors. Thus, Braham (1980) is probably correct in insisting that '. . . the dominant Marxist position appears to say little more than that racism is an ideology is a mechanical reflection of the mode of production of an economic base'. The independent force of ethnic, cultural and political factors is neglected by a Marxist approach which is obsessed with economic classes. The approach of Castles and Kosack, for example, not only loses sight of the ethnic affiliations of migrant labourers, but it also seems to dismiss 'racial' conflict as a matter of little interest. In recognition of these problems, some Marxists insist on the 'relative autonomy' of the economic, political and ideological spheres, but this tends to lead to rather untestable statements about the complex inter-relations of these three spheres.

(2) 'Conspiracy' versions usually describe a united ruling group which successfully manipulates racist feelings among the population. In reality, however, the dominant class is likely to be composed of competing interest groups or 'class fractions' whose short-term interests diverge. Thus, employers in low-growth industries may support immigration because it provides a cheap labour force; employers in prosperous industries may have no need for low-skill labour, and may oppose immigration because of fears of social unrest; and politicians have to balance the scales between economic pressures, political demands, and the desire to maintain good relations with New

Commonwealth countries. Similarly, it may be in the interests of the ruling groups to stir up racist feelings (in order to take advantage of blacks), but the same groups may support anti-discrimination legislation in order to prevent widespread social conflict. It can be seen, then, that a convincing conspiracy-type explanation needs to provide firm evidence on the dominant motives and actions of key groups: what, in fact, were their intentions? what interests were they promoting? how did they reconcile competing demands?

(3) More 'structuralist' versions of Marxism rely less on the intrigues of 'conspirators', and concentrate instead on the 'system needs' of capitalism. So it is argued that capitalism has certain broad system needs or requirements, and these needs mainly concern the establishment of conditions which assist the process of capital accumulation. Racism is seen as 'necessary', or at least useful, to capitalism, insofar as it performs the three previously-mentioned 'functions' (legitimisation, divide-and-rule, and scapegoating). Quite simply, racism arises because of its affinity with capitalist interests. However, there are certain problems with these structural explanations. Firstly, the identification of 'functions' does not demonstrate the initial 'causes' or 'origins' of racism, and so it is unwise to assume that racism was created precisely because of these intended functions. Secondly, it is not necessarily the case that the consequences of racism are indeed 'functional' for capitalists (e.g. the experience of racial prejudice can sharpen the political awareness of blacks and whites and lead to joint action against employers or politicians). Thirdly, the highly abstract level of the arguments lead to rather loose generalisations. For instance, the presumed 'connection' between capitalism and racism rests on a rather uncertain definition of 'capitalism' (which strangely includes the slave trade) and a special definition of 'racism' (which excludes the 'ethnocentrism' which existed before capitalism). Sweeping generalisations also overlook the diversity of views within and between racial groups, and they neglect the shift of racial attitudes over time. Finally, this structuralist approach is notoriously self-fulfilling and non-falsifiable (e.g. whether the state endorses racism or launches anti-discriminatory measures, arguments can be floated to show that this is in the interests of capitalism).

Many liberals would part company with the Marxist views that capitalism is inherently oppressive and exploitative, and that the class struggle is the major focus of attention. On the other hand, various elements of the Marxist approach to racism would be accepted by liberals and Weberians, and it is a caricature of liberalism to imagine that it pays no heed to economic issues or social conflicts. However, most liberals would shy clear of a unifying framework like Marxism, preferring to emphasise the multi-faceted nature of race issues. Some indication of this attitude is provided by Banton and Harwood (1975) who argue that:

> current notions of race are an integral part of the history of Western Europe, drawing upon many aspects of that story. These notions cannot be separated from the rest of that history and attributed to single factors like capitalism, colonialism, scientific error or personal prejudice. The sources of popular imagery concerning race are very diverse and the interrelations between their growth and contemporary political affairs are far too complex for the whole historical sequence to be explicable in simple terms.

The history of race relations is indeed a complex matter, but we hope that the models and theories covered in this section will help to shed some more light on this very important area.

Bibliography

Allen, S. *New Minorities, Old Conflicts* (Random House, New York, 1971).

Allport, G. *The Nature of Prejudice* (Addison-Wesley, Cambridge, Mass., 1954).

Ballard, R. 'Race and the Census' *New Society* 12 May 1983.

Ballard, R. and Ballard, C. 'The Sikhs: The Development of South Asian Settlements in Britain' in J. Watson, 1977.

Banton, M. *Race Relations* (Tavistock, London, 1967).

Banton, M. *The Idea of Race* (Tavistock, London, 1977).

Banton, M. 'Analytical and Folk Concepts of Race and Ethnicity' *Ethnic and Racial Studies* vol. 2 no. 2 April 1979.

Banton, M. and Harwood, J. *The Race Concept* (David and Charles, Newton Abbott, 1975).

Blauner, R. 'Black Culture: Myth or Reality?' in D. Bromley, 1972.

Bourne, J. 'Cheerleaders and Ombudsmen: The Sociology of Race Relations in Britain' *Race and Class* vol. 21 no. 4 1980.

Braham, P. *Class, Race and Immigration* (Open University Press, Milton Keynes, 1980).

Bromley, D. and Longino, C. (eds.) *White Racism and Black Americans* (Schenkman Pub. Co., Cambridge, Mass., 1970).

Brown, C. *Black and White in Britain: 3rd PSI Survey* (Heinemann, London, 1984).

Burgess, M. 'The resurgence of ethnicity' in *Ethnic and Racial Studies* vol. 1, 1978.

Carmichael, S. and Hamilton, C. *Black Power* (Penguin, Harmondsworth, 1969).

Cashmore, E. *Rastaman* (George Allen and Unwin, London, 1979).

Castles, S. and Kosack, G. *Immigrant Workers and Class Structure in Western Europe* (Oxford University Press, 1973).

Centre for Contemporary Cultural Studies. *The Empire Strikes Back* (Hutchinson, London, 1982).

Cohen, A. (ed.) *Urban Ethnicity* (Tavistock, London, 1974).

Community Relations Commission *Five Views of Multi-Racial Britain* (Commission for Racial Equality, London, 1978).

Cox. O. *Caste, Class and Race* (Monthly Review Press, New York, 1970).

Dahya, B. 'Pakistanis in Britain: Transients or Settlers?' *Race* vol. 14 no. 3 Jan. 1973.

Dahya, B. 'The Nature of Pakistani Ethnicity in Industrial Cities in Britain' in A. Cohen, 1974.

Daniel, W. W. *Racial Discrimination in England* (Penguin, Harmondsworth, 1968).

Dummett, M. and Dummett, A. 'The Role of Government in Britain's Racial Crisis' in C. Husband, 1982.

Eysenck, H. *Race, Intelligence and Education* (Maurice Temple Smith, London, 1971.

Field, S. *et al. Ethnic Minorities in Britain* (Home Office Research Study no. 68, London, 1981).

Field, S. *The Attitudes of Ethnic Minorities* (Home Office Research Study no. 80, London, 1984).

Fryer, P. *Staying Power* (Pluto Press, London, 1984).

Frank. A. G. *Capitalism and Underdevelopment in Latin America* (Monthly Review Press, New York, 1967).

Gans, H. 'Symbolic Ethnicity' *Ethnic and Racial Studies* vol. 2 no. 1 1979.

Glass, R. *Newcomers* (George Allen and Unwin, London, 1960).

Glazier, N. and Moynihan, D. (eds.) *Ethnicity: Theory and Experience* (Harvard University Press, 1975).

Goldthorpe, J. *The Sociology of the Third World* (Cambridge University Press, 1975).

Hall, S. *et al. Policing the Crisis* (Macmillan, London, 1978).

Hall, S. 'Racism and Reaction' in Community Relations Commission, 1978.

Hall, S. 'Race, Articulation and Societies Structured in Dominance' in UNESCO 1980.

Harrison, P. *Inside the Third World* (Penguin, Harmondsworth, 1979).

Hartmann, P. and Husband, C. *Racism and the Mass Media* (Davis-Poynter, London, 1974).

Hoogvelt, A. *The Sociology of Developing Societies* (Macmillan, London, 1976).

Horton, J. 'Order and Conflict Theories of Social Problems as Competing Ideologies'

American Journal of Sociology vol. LXXI no. 6 May 1966.

Husband, C. *White Media and Black Britain* (Arrow Books, London, 1975).

Husband, C. *'Race' in Britain* (Hutchinson, London, 1982).

Jenkins, R. Speech extract in *Race* vol. 8 no. 13 Jan. 1967.

Jensen, A. 'How Much Can We Boost I.Q. and Scholastic Achievement?' *Harvard Educational Review* 39, 1969.

Jowell, R. and Airey, C. *British Social Attitudes* (Social and Community Planning Research, 1984).

Kamin, L. *Intelligence: The Battle for the Mind* (Pan, London, 1981).

Khan, V. 'The Pakistanis: Mirpuri Villagers at Home and in Bradford' in J. Watson, 1977.

Krausz, E. *Ethnic Minorities in Britain* (Paladin, London, 1971).

Layton-Henry, Z. *The Politics of Race in Britain* (George Allen and Unwin, London, 1984).

Lea, J. and Young, J. *What is to be done about Law and Order?* (Penguin, Harmondsworth, 1984).

Lyon, M. 'Race and Ethnicity in Pluralistic Societies' *New Community* vol. 1 no. 4 Summer 1972.

Mason, D. 'After Scarman: A Note on the Concept of Institutional Racism' *New Community* vol. 10 no. 1 Summer 1982.

McKay, J. 'Primordial and Mobilisationist Approaches to Ethnic Phenomena' *Ethnic and Racial Studies* vol. 5 no. 4 1982.

Miles, R. *Racism and Migrant Labour* (Routledge & Kegan Paul, London, 1982).

Moore, R. *Racism and Black Resistance in Britain* (Pluto Press, London, 1975).

Parekh, B. 'Asians in Britain: Problem or Opportunity?' in Community Relations Commission, 1978.

Park, R. *Race and Culture* (Free Press, Glencoe, 1950).

Parmar, P. 'Gender, Race and Class: Asian Women in Resistance' in Centre For Contemporary Cultural Studies, 1982.

Patterson, S. *Dark Strangers* (Penguin, Harmondsworth, 1965).

Policy Studies Institute. *Police and People in London* (PSI, London, 1983).

Pryce, K. *Endless Pressure* (Penguin, Harmondsworth, 1979).

Rex, J. *Race Relations in Sociological Theory* (Weidenfeld and Nicholson, London, 1970).

Rex, J. *Race, Colonialism and the City* (Routledge & Kegan Paul, London, 1973).

Rex, J. 'Race in the Inner City' in Community Relations Commission, 1978.

Rex, J. and Moore, R. *Race, Community and Conflict* (Oxford University Press, 1967).

Rex, J. and Tomlinson, S. *Colonial Immigrants in a British City* (Routledge & Kegan Paul, London, 1979).

Rose, E. *et al. Colour and Citizenship* (Oxford University Press, 1969).

Scarman Report. *The Brixton Disorders 10–12 April 1981* (HMSO, 1981).

Schermerhorn, R. *Comparative Ethnic Relations* (Random House, New York, 1970).

Smith, D. *Racial Disadvantage in Britain: The P.E.P. Report* (Penguin, Harmondsworth, 1977).

Social Trends 1983 and 1984 (HMSO).

Taylor, S. 'Riots: Some Explanations' *New Community* vol. 9 no. 2 Autumn 1981.

UNESCO 'Moscow Declaration 1964' *Race* vol. 6 no. 3 Jan. 1965.

UNESCO *4th Statement on Race and Racial Prejudice* (UNESCO, Paris, 1967).

UNESCO *Sociological Theories: Race and Colonialism* (UNESCO, Paris, 1980).

Van Den Berghe, P. 'Race and Ethnicity' *Ethnic and Racial Studies* vol. 1 1978.

Watson, J. *Between Two Cultures* (Basil Blackwell, London, 1977).

Walvin, J. *Black and White* (Allen Lane, London, 1973).

Walvin, J. *Passage to Britain* (Penguin, Harmondsworth, 1984).

Westergaard, J. and Resler, H. *Class in a Capitalist Society* (Penguin, Harmondsworth, 1976).

Yinger, M. 'Toward a Theory of Assimilation and Dissimilation' *Ethnic and Racial Studies* vol. 4 no. 3 1981.

Young, J. and Lea, J. 'Urban Violence and Political Marginalisation' *Critical Social Policy* vol. 1 no. 3 Spring 1982.

Section 2

The Sociology of Development
Aidan Foster-Carter

Chapter One

Sociology and Development

Introduction

The sociology of development is an unusual kind of 'specialism' – and hard to cram into a short section. First, this 'specialism' is actually the study of most of the world! Conversely, the 'general' sociology you learn is in reality about that minority who live in 'Western' societies. So often, Western sociologists generalize about urbanism, industrialism, education, the family, etc; ignoring the fact that *most* people actually live in the Third World, in rather different *kinds* of cities (or not in cities), undergoing very different *forms* of industrialization (if any), with a wide variety of education systems, family structures, etc. So really it's the sociology of development which should include all the rest of sociology, rather than the other way round!

However, and secondly, the sociology of development includes more than sociology alone. It has to be *interdisciplinary*. You can't just leave out (say) politics or economics. Otherwise you end up with what's been called the 'underlabourer' notion of sociology – a sort of cringing hyena, waiting in the shadows while the fat cats of economics and politics take the meat, before sidling up to the carcass for whatever pickings are left: religion, the family, etc. I don't mean that these pickings are unimportant, obviously. But they really are not the whole body of the subject, and a diet confined to them would be seriously unbalanced.

Anyway, all social reality is in some sense a seamless robe, and disciplinary divisions are arbitrary. The founders of sociology, notably Karl Marx and Max Weber, certainly tackled economic and political issues in a sociological way. And one particular reason for doing this in our field is that in development we simply don't know (or people don't agree) what *is* the key dimension. Is it economic factors, or political, or social, or even psychological ones, which advance or hold back the development of societies? I hope you can see why it would be wrong to define the subject in such a way as to rule out any of these in advance.

Thirdly, there is an important but boring point which I shall stress only this once – though it applies to every sentence in this book. The Third World – the object of the sociology of development – is not homogeneous. On the contrary, it is highly *diverse*. It consists of three or four continents, each containing dozens of different countries and hundreds of once separate cultures. How on earth can we dare to generalize about all that? 'With great care' is the only possible answer. So, although this short book inevitably contains many generalizations, there will always be somewhere to which a particular point doesn't apply. (And besides, somebody else might read the balance of the evidence differently.)

Nonetheless – and this is my fourth introductory point – there have been two main perspectives in the sociology of development which *have* tried to generalize about the Third World. Usually known as *modernization theory* and *dependency theory*, they are dealt with in subsequent chapters. As adversaries, giving very different accounts of why the Third World is underdeveloped, these two schools have often clashed in heated debate. In this section, however, besides assessing them as theory, I make a conscious attempt to pull these two old war-horses off the jousting field, put saddle and harness on them, and see if they can still carry a load. To be precise, the substantive chapters – on industrialization, urbanism, education, health, etc. – try to concretize the arguments of the theory chapter, and assess which (if either) of the two perspectives best helps us understand what's actually going on in the Third World in these particular areas.

Terms and Definitions

Development/Underdevelopment. This section's title is *The Sociology of Development*. But what does 'development' *mean*? Some of the overtones are obvious: a sense of *process*, and more than that of *progress*. But *what* process? and what *is* progress? On such matters there is no agreement.

We may make progress, however, by looking at two or three arguably related themes. Not the least of the problems of the sociology of development is how, if at all, it relates to other areas of sociology. One obvious candidate for a predecessor is *social evolutionism*: pioneered by Comte and Spencer, and still persisting (or revived) in parts of the later work of Talcott Parsons. What is interesting here is the idea of societies as developing through a *fixed series of stages*, in a definite order.

But should we think of *societies* in such terms? Probably the simplest way I can introduce to you the first major school in the sociology of development, *modernization theory*, is to say that on the whole this *is* how they think about social development: as proceeding through certain stages, in a fixed order. On this basis, we can think of the world as a kind of continuum, with different 'societies' (which by now probably means nation-states, although it didn't always) ranged at various points along what is claimed to be the same route. Latecomers follow in the footsteps of pioneers. As Marx said, the more developed society thus shows to the less developed the image of its own future. One contemporary modernization theorist who explicitly thinks along these lines is *Walt Rostow*, whose 'stages of economic growth' we shall consider in the next chapter.

Such a view gives us a vocabulary, and a particular way of using it. Countries which have made it, or are far along, are *developed* (which doesn't imply that they've stopped, but rather that they're over the hump – or, in Rostow's famous metaphor, the 'take-off'). Conversely, there are other as yet *less developed countries* (often abbreviated to LDCs). These may also be called – optimistically, and in a sense begging the question – *developing countries*. Yet a third term for the same thing, seemingly more neutral, is *underdeveloped* – first used in this sense in the 1940s.

However, according to *dependency theory*, the second major school in the sociology of development, this whole terminology is by no means neutral. From their very different standpoint, and as one of them (André Gunder Frank) put it, *under*development is not at all the same as *un*development. If by the latter we mean a relative lack of development (such as we may presume to have been the lot of Europe too in pre-capitalist or pre-industrial times), this is *not* the same as what prevails in the Third World (see below!) today. For, according to dependency theory, evolutionist assumptions are quite inappropriate. Underdevelopment, far from being a stage on the way to development, is a totally different situation – on a road that leads nowhere. And this in turn is because it is not (or not only) a process, but a *relation*: it is something (something not very nice, either) which someone has done to somebody else.

Hence Gunder Frank, like a guerilla capturing an enemy's gun, takes the word 'underdevelop' and turns it around – as seen in the title of another classic dependency work, Walter Rodney's *How Europe*

Underdeveloped Africa (1972). Underdevelopment, on this view, involves imperialism and exploitation. Third World societies have been prevented from developing because this serves the interest of the West.

As yet, I make no comments on the relative merits of modernization and dependency theories: that task comes later. For now, you should just be aware of their overlapping vocabularies which nonetheless mean very different things.

First/Second/Third World. 'Third World' (we shall come back to First and Second) is widely used in practice as a synonym for developing coutries or less developed countries (LDCs). However, its implications are somewhat different, in two ways. First, it was an attempt to get away from 'Cold War' assumptions that the entire world was divided into only two power blocs, West and East, headed by the USA and USSR. Second, 'Third World' was a *self-conscious* grouping, one possessing awareness of its own identity. (To adapt what Marx says about class: a group *for* itself, rather than a mere category or group *in* itself.)

But if we know what the Third World is (or think we know), what about the first and second worlds? Both usages are in fact rare, and the latter almost nonexistent. Implicitly, the First World is the 'West', the Second World the 'East' – using West and East in a *political* sense, for capitalist and communist respectively.

However, as Worsley (1979) has pointed out, this poses a problem, since we now have both political (capitalist/communist) *and* economic (developed/underdeveloped) criteria at work. This should logically give us four categories, not three, because the Third World would then have to be divided into capitalist and communist Third World countries as well.

North/South. This is the most recent addition to the vocabulary of development, having been largely popularized by the Brandt Report (1980), in whose title it appears. Basically, 'North' = East plus West, and 'South' is the Third World. (It works quite well on a map, if you think about it; only Australia and New Zealand are awkward.)

But what is Development?

For the rest of this section I shall use all the above terms, blithely and more or less interchangeably. You should nonetheless now be aware of their somewhat differing resonances. However, there is a more substantial issue to be addressed concerning 'development': namely what is it? Most of the literature tends to assume that the content of development is *economic*; i.e., usually, to increase national output and wealth, often by industrialization. But is this wholly valid? In principle, at least three other types of development goal can be distinguished.

(a) **Social.** When development studies got started as a field of study, after World War Two, it was taken for granted that the main problem was simply how to provide economic growth. Once this was done, it was assumed, the wealth thereby created would sooner or later 'trickle down' to the grass roots and make people better off – although this might not happen right away, Or, to put it another way, questions of *production* seemed much more important than arguments about *distribution.* As the late Kenyan politician Tom Mboya memorably put it, what is the use of arguing about how to cut the cake before you have even baked it?

This view was never universally accepted, however, and in recent years it has been widely criticized. An alternative view is to argue that, especially in the poorest countries, the prime task of development must be the immediate fulfilment of *basic needs*. These can be defined either broadly or narrowly. Minimally, they encompass food, shelter, and clothing; essential services, like drinking water, sanitation, health, education, transport; and job opportunities. Some would extend the concept to more qualitative factors: the environment, decision-making, and the rights of women and minorities.

For advocates of 'basic needs', merely maximizing growth of gross national product (GNP) is not development. More precisely, it neither *constitutes* development, nor will it necessarily *cause* development. At the same time, it would be misleading to suppose that you necessarily have to choose between *either* economic *or* social priorities in development. On the contrary, basic needs advocates would claim that theirs is a better *economic* strategy too: because a healthy, literate, and employed population is a better investment and an essential starting point for any development programme.

Still, it is interesting to note that attempts to create a social *indicator* (one that would measure social development, just as GNP per capita – arguably – measures economic development) reveal that countries may score very differently in each respect. A well-known social indicator is the Physical Quality of Life Index (PQLI): a weighted average of life expectancy, infant mortality, and adult literacy. Some countries with low per capita GNP, like Sri Lanka and Vietnam, score high on PQLI. (Thomas, 1983, p. 25ff.)

(b) **Political.** 'Political development' can often be a rather empty phrase, which ideologists of different persuasions then proceed to fill according to their own preconceptions. Thus American political scientists in the 1960s tended to use Western-style democracy as an index of political development; whereas by the 1970s some of them, ominously, had decided that maintaining 'order' even without democracy was more important. Others have claimed that the one-party systems found in many Third World as well as communist countries are either more appropriate or (even) more democratic.

A provocative attempt to redefine political, economic and social development was made in 1971 in a Tanzanian policy document called 'Mwongozo' (guidelines). This baldly stated:

> For people who have been slaves or have been oppressed, exploited, and disregarded by colonialism or capitalism, 'development' means 'liberation'. Any action that gives them more control of their own affairs is an action for development, even if it does not offer them better health or more bread. Any action that reduces their say in determining their own affairs or running their own lives is not development and retards them even if the action brings them a little better health and a little more bread. (cited in Rweyemamu *et al*, 1974, p. 24)

You can see the influence of dependency thinking here, in stressing autonomy and control over one's own destiny as political values, even at the expense of material development goals.

(c) **Cultural**. Almost inevitably, development involves cultural changes, often profound ones. The question is: what kind of changes? who says? and at what price? Probably the most striking example is in Iran; where the former Shah's modernisation strategy was evidently felt by many people to be profoundly un-Iranian, thus producing a specifically Islamic cultural reaction (rather than, as many had predicted, a Marxist political revolution) in the form of Ayatollah Khomeini. Iran today looks like a clear case in which the economic goals of development have been consciously subordinated to the cultural priority of creating a strictly Islamic society.

Nevertheless, as with political and social dimensions, I would argue that it is not usually a case of *either* cultural *or* economic development. Rather, if we look at examples of clear-cut economic development such as Japan, we find that tradition has not wholly been abandoned. Indeed, we can say that rapid and drastic modernization in some spheres may be accompanied and even *legitimated* by appeals to traditional values or practices in other spheres. The almost universal use of nationalism, by regimes of every kind, to mobilize their people for development is the most obvious case.

The Third World: a Descriptive Taxonomy

Generalizing about the Third World has its limitations. The societies which compose it are exceedingly diverse in all kinds of ways. Even in so short a section as this, it may be desirable to illustrate at least some of that diversity. This section will therefore give brief information about the major regions which make up the Third World.

1. Sub-Saharan Africa

Africa south of the Sahara has mostly tropical or subtropical climates. Physical environments range from rain forest to desert, with much savannah and bush land. Parts of Africa (e.g. South Africa, Zaire) are extremely rich in mineral resources. With localized exceptions, population density is low. Africa's major religions (as well as traditional animist beliefs) are Christianity and Islam; the latter has been established in West Africa for a thousand years and more, and continues to make gains.

Many pre-colonial African societies were relatively small-scale (sometimes called 'tribes', although controversy surrounds this word), and state formation had not proceeded far. There were major exceptions, though, e.g. the empires of Ghana and Mali in West Africa – names which were later taken by newly independent states.

Africa had a very specific experience of the world system and colonialism. First, it was uniquely subject to the massive depredations of the slave trade over some three centuries. Millions of people were forcibly taken to the Americas, with drastic effects on their societies. Secondly, formal colonialism in Africa was both late and comprehensive. It didn't really get going in earnest until after the Congress of Berlin in 1884–5, at which European powers carved up the map of Africa. But once it did get going it was almost universal: only Liberia and Ethiopia escaped.

The direct colonial phase lasted much less than a century. Most of Africa resumed its independence in the 1950s or 1960s. But the 50-odd states that have now come into existence are often small (in population), weak and fragmented; the ideology of 'Pan-Africanism' (calling for a united Africa) has had little concrete impact. Notoriously, the lack of fit between the new nations' boundaries and those of pre-colonial societies can lead to ethnic conflict being a major factor in political life.

Despite recent explosive urban growth, Africa remains overwhelmingly an agricultural continent. Much agricultural labour is done by women. The technological level is often low: the hoe (rather than bullock, let alone tractor) plus human muscle power remain the major instruments of production. All in all, in a Third World whose diversity is increasing, much of Africa looks to be the least developed and have the worst problems. For example, despite the predominance of agriculture many African states cannot feed themselves.

2. North Africa and West Asia (the 'Middle East')

This region stretches from Morocco to the Gulf, or perhaps beyond. It has a number of common characteristics. Much of it is desert, with long established agriculture along such major rivers as the Nile and Euphrates. 'Desertification' is quite a recent (and continuing) process in historical time; in Roman days, North Africa was the granary of the empire. The region is not rich in natural resources, with one crucial exception: oil.

This area was the cradle of the earliest known human civilizations, including of course Egypt. Much later, it was unified by the conquests of early Islam (which originated in what is now Saudi Arabia), and much of it thus acquired a common identity: a single written language, Arabic (although spoken variants can be mutually unintelligible); and a common faith, Islam (albeit with important sectarian differences, notably between Shias and Sunnis). Islamic seats of learning preserved the Graeco-Roman classics during Europe's 'dark ages', and also made important contributions to science.

Some places, Iran and Turkey, are Islamic but not Arab. Yet Turkey made its own contribution to the unity of the region in the form of the Ottoman Empire, which ended only with the First World War. Different coutries were also colonized or semi-colonized by France, Britain and Italy. In recent years, possession of the world's major oil resources has dramatically transformed both the wealth and importance of several states in this region.

3. South Asia

I use this term to designate what is sometimes called the 'Indian subcontinent'. It contains almost a billion people, most of whom live in one country, India. Historically it was the seat of a number of civilizations, the last before the British Raj being the Moghuls. The Moghuls were Muslim, and Islam is the major religion of (and was indeed the basis for the creation of) Pakistan and Bangladesh. Hinduism is the main religion in India; its caste system has made it of special interest to sociologists. India is also the birth place of Buddhism, which is strong in Sri Lanka.

The area contains a relatively small number of rather large language-groups, and both India and Pakistan have experienced regional conflicts. Much of it, especially Bangladesh, is densely populated. Monsoon agriculture predominates. In some parts of India, notably the Punjab, the 'Green Revolution' has recently led to dramatic increases in yields, but in most of the region agrarian poverty remains widespread.

The unevenness of development within nations (and sectors), as well as between them, is illustrated by the little known fact that India is *also* the world's tenth ranking industrial power, and Indian transnational corporations (TNCs) are active elsewhere in the Third World.

4. East and South-East Asia

This region too is in a sense dominated by one country, China: with the world's largest population (around a billion), it is also the world's oldest continuously existing civilization, and its culture has long influenced the rest of the region. More recently, since the communist victory in 1949 it has been widely seen as a symbol (of hope or fear, depending on one's perspective) of an alternative socialist type of development; although trends since 1976 suggest that this may be changing.

Otherwise the area is rather diverse. The three other Chinese states – Taiwan, Hong Kong and Singapore – plus South Korea, form one category of small but dynamic capitalist industrializing countries. There are also six other Asian communist states around China, all but one hostile to it. Vietnam, Laos and Cambodia have not long emerged from decades of bloody war (or, in Cambodia, even bloodier aftermath under the genocidal Pol Pot regime); but North Korea and Mongolia have seen some industrialization. Meanwhile, Afghanistan seems likely to become the USSR's 'Vietnam'.

That leaves a number of diverse and sizeable countries. Their colonial experiences were varied: Thailand avoided it, Burma and Malaysia had the British, Indonesia (the world's fifth largest country by population, and immensely rich in natural resources) the Dutch, and the Philippines had Spain followed by the USA. (Indo-China was French). Religion is also very diverse: Buddhism is strong in several countries, Indonesia has Muslim and some Hindu influences, while Christianity has adherents in most places (including some 25% of the population of South Korea).

5. (a) Latin America

In some senses Latin America is the original Third World. It was colonized early, from the late fifteenth century, mostly by Spain and Portugal. It was also independent early, from as long ago as the 1820s (before most of Africa had even been colonized in the first place). The original inhabitants – still called Indians, for no better reason than that Columbus didn't know where he was – lived in societies which ranged from very small scale hunting and gathering bands to the major theocratic empires of the Inca, Aztec, and Maya. Their numbers today vary: almost non-existent in Argentina and Uruguay, a majority in Peru and Guatemala, but in no case possessing much power. Most were converted (often forcibly) to Christianity; but the traditional role of the Roman Catholic church in supporting an often oppressive status quo has in recent years been challenged from within, with the emergence of 'liberation theology'.

The continent's other inhabitants are descendants of voluntary settlers from Europe (and parts of Asia), and involuntary settlers from Africa. Population densities are mostly low. Many countries (especially Brazil) are rich in resources, which have been the basis for successive supplies to the West: gold and silver initially, then sugar, rubber, coffee, tin, copper, and much more.

In this century some larger countries – Brazil, Mexico, Argentina – have undergone a certain degree of industrialization, which continues. Whether this has or will transform the basic structures of under-development is hotly debated, and it is no surprise that it was Latin America that gave birth to dependency theory.

Politically, in the wake of Castro's triumph in Cuba most countries experienced guerilla movements, nearly all of which were crushed (including the death of Che Guevara in Bolivia in 1967). Political democracy has been precarious in most countries, with alternations of civilian and military regimes (the latter mostly, but not invariably, of the right). Today the smaller countries of Central America seem the focus of interest, with a recently victorious revolution in Nicaragua, and civil war in El Salvador.

(b) The Caribbean

This sub-region of the Americas perhaps deserves brief mention in its own right, having a number of sociologically distinctive features. Populated largely by the descendants of African slaves (and, in some cases, the Indian indentured labourers who followed them), it consists of a multiplicity of small, mostly island states. Historically dominated by plantation agriculture, Caribbean states find it hard for reasons of scale to diversify.

The region's languages are Spanish and French (Haiti) as well as English, reflecting a variety of colonizers who stayed a very long time (up to four centuries). The English-speaking territories, it is perhaps worth pointing out, are the one part of the Third World in which governments regularly lose office through the ballot box.

6. Conclusion

In the face of all the diversity, to dare to speak of a 'Third World' at all embodies a claim: that despite the endless variety of geography, history and culture, there is also at some level an element of commonality – in economy, politics, or society – in experience or structure. More precisely, there are at least two variants of this claim, corresponding to the two major perspectives in the field. To put this roughly, the two claims are:

a) **Recapitulation/Diffusion**. What the Third World shares is being 'behind' the advanced countries in various ways; it also shares the opportunity to ameliorate this by receiving benefits diffused from the West; and it will share a common future in following gradually in the West's footsteps.

b) **Unevenness/Dependence**. What the Third World shares is a similarity of experience; namely, being historically subjugated and reduced to a subordinate position in the world economy; which is not like anything the West went through; and which must be escaped from, not built upon, if real development is to take place.

Chapter Two

Theoretical Perspectives

Modernization versus Dependency Theory

I have already said that I shall use the above framework as a framework for this section – and this chapter in particular. The structure of this 'theory' chapter is as follows. I begin by comparing and contrasting one of the most famous examples of each school, W. W. Rostow and A. G. Frank. I go on to look at further varieties of modernization theory, and suggest tentatively that part of its agenda may still be valid. I also examine recent Marxist criticisms of dependency theory, especially by Warren. Finally, I mention Barrington Moore as an example of an important theorist who cannot be slotted readily into either of the two main camps.

Two Exemplars: Rostow and Frank

In order to illustrate the modernization and dependency perspectives, and the differences between them, we shall first look at the work of a major writer from each school. There are dangers in this procedure. Both these perspectives are in fact extremely diverse. Each contains within its boundaries different schools of thought, stressing different factors in development.

Also, by focussing on just two writers each of whom helped 'set up' the perspective in question, we run the risk of having a rather stale and dated analysis. Both Rostow and Frank produced their best-known work in the 1960s. But the world moves on, as does social science; new issues and debates have arisen, not least in response to these writers themselves.

Nonetheless, there is no denying that Rostow and Frank are both the best known and probably (for better or worse) the most widely influential representatives of the modernization and dependency paradigms, respectively. It is therefore appropriate to look at some of their major themes. In doing this, we shall also examine some of the criticisms and debate which their work has inspired and provoked.

Rostow

Walt Whitman Rostow is an American economic historian. Originally a specialist on British economic history, he became more widely famous (or even notorious) in two different spheres. As an academic, which most concerns us here, he coined and popularized the idea of a 'take-off' into self-sustaining economic growth as being the key stage of the development process; above all, in his book *The Stages of Economic Growth: a non-communist manifesto* (1960).

In addition, as that sub-title indicates, Rostow's work had political purpose. He explicitly (and rather immodestly) saw his theory of stages of economic growth as an alternative to Marx's. At the time of the Vietnam War he was an adviser to President Lyndon Johnson and acquired a reputation as a 'hawk': a role which helps to explain the sometimes bitter controversy which his work has evoked, especially from Marxists.

Rostow propounded a schema of five stages through which all developing societies must pass. The first of these he terms *traditional.* Although well aware that this lumps together a huge variety of actual societies, ranging from Stone Age cultures to (say) France on the eve of the Revolution, Rostow believes that for purposes of his model their common features matter more than the differences. These features include: 'pre-Newtonian' science and technology; a basically agricultural economy; and a rigidly ascriptive social structure, usually based in kinship.

In this sense, presumably, the vast majority of human societies – indeed, all of them until barely two hundred years ago – have been 'traditional'. In some, however, there began to be stirrings of new social forms and forces. This is Rostow's second stage, the *preconditions for take-off.* Often triggered off by some impulse from outside (although this is a point Rostow never systematically develops), changes begin across a whole range of institutions. In the economy, agriculture is augmented by an increase in trade, services, and the beginnings of industry (especially extractive industry, such as mining). The economy as a whole becomes less self-sufficient and localized, as trade and improved communications facilitate the growth of both national and international economies. Socially, these processes are related to the emergence of an elite group, able and willing to reinvest their wealth rather than squander it. Rational scientific ideas also play a key role: the natural world is no longer taken as given. At least one of the preconditions for social and economic progress is thus the *idea* that progress is possible at all, as opposed to fatalistic acceptance of the natural and social *status quo*.

This brings us to the key third stage, the *take-off* itself. Rostow characterises this in both quantitative and qualitative terms. Investment as a proportion of national income rises to at least 10%, thus ensuring that increases in per capita output outstrip population growth. One or more manufacturing sectors (but not, as yet, the whole range) come to assume a leading role. Political and social institutions more generally are reshaped in order to permit the pursuit of growth to take root. All this typically takes about twenty years, and Rostow attempts to date the actual take-off of those countries which have experienced them: 1783–1803 for Britain, which was the first; followed amongst others by the USA (1843–1860), Japan (1878–1900), Russia (1890–1914), and India and China (1950 onwards).

Rostow's last two stages can be dealt with briefly; in a sense, they are not part of the sociology of the Third World, inasmuch as any society that has got this far is by definition no longer underdeveloped. The *drive to maturity* is a period of consolidation. Modern science and technology are extended to most if not all branches of the economy, which thus acquires a wider range of leading sectors. The rate of investment remains high, at 10–20% of national income. Political reform continues, and the economy 'finds its feet' internationally.

Finally, there is the *age of high mass consumption*. This involves yet further consolidation and advance, and as such is not clearly distinct from the drive to maturity. Such is the productive power of the society by this stage that three broad strategic choices of orientation are available. Wealth can be concentrated in individual consumption, as in the USA; or channelled into a welfare state as in Western Europe; or used to build up global power and influence – which is how Rostow characterizes the USSR.

Such, in bare outline, is Rostow's theory. It has been extremely influential, perhaps especially at a common-sense level: the word 'take-off' has passed into ordinary use. It has also been hotly debated and fiercely criticized, from a variety of viewpoints. Before looking at some of the critique in detail, however, let us note some key characteristics of the *kind* of theoretical model that Rostow is using. Four linked aspects can be singled out: theoretical traits which Rostow arguably shares with others of the modernization school, even if his particular version is perhaps more extreme.

1. Rostow's theory is *evolutionist*. It sees socio-economic change as unfolding through a fixed set of stages.

2. It is also *unilinear*. All countries must pass by the same route, in the same order. There are no 'leaps', short cuts, choices, or alternative routes.

3. Further, it is *internalist*. Despite occasional tantalizing hints (as mentioned above) that outside influences do play a role, Rostow firmly takes the given society as his unit of analysis and assumes that all the crucial dimensions of change are internally generated within each society.

4. Finally, and in a sense summarising the above, it is *recapitulationist*. The presently underdeveloped countries today have to follow precisely the same basic path as did the now developed countries in their day. In this sense Rostow might even agree with Marx, who also said that the more developed society shows to the less developed the image of its own future.

How might such an account be criticized? A. G. Frank, in addition to putting forward a very different model of his own (see below), is the author of a major critique of the modernization approach in general and Rostow in particular. Frank (1969b) suggests three criteria for assessing any theory in the social sciences: empirical validity, theoretical adequacy, and policy effectiveness. (Crudely, we could thus ask: does it fit the facts? Does it make sense? and is it any use?)

Rostow has been found wanting on all three counts, and by no means solely by Marxists like Frank. Even to apply the model presents a host of difficulties, only some of which can be mentioned here. Thus other economic historians challenge on empirical grounds Rostow's central claim that an investment spurt characterizes the actual take-off. From a different tack, Frank himself points out that a number of countries in Latin America and elsewhere never had a 'traditional' stage at all, yet still seem to be locked into underdevelopment. He calls these *tabula rasa* (literally, 'clean state') countries; where there were either no pre-existing societies at all (e.g. Uruguay) or these were wiped out or marginalized by European conquest – which for Frank is where *both* the modern history of these countries *and* their underdevelopment begins.

The empirical problems in Rostow's work are linked to theoretical difficulties. There is wide agreement among critics that his major conceptual weakness consists in failing to emphasize *inter* – as well as *intra* – societal connections, i.e. relationships *between* as well as within societies. Thus for the Nobel prize winning Swedish economist, Gunnar Myrdal (1963) there are crucial differences in initial conditions faced by today's developing countries; not least, that they have to try to develop in a world context which *already* contains their precursors, i.e. a powerful block of already developed countries, whose interests may well clash with theirs (e.g. if they want to industrialize).

For other writers, the changed situation is in some ways actually beneficial. Thus the economic historian Alexander Gerschenkron (1962) has stressed what he calls the advantages of backwardness. On this view, late developing countries do *not* have to repeat the same stages as early developers; for example, they can use, where appropriate, technologies already developed elsewhere. But in either case the methodological point, and the critique of Rostow, are the same. Relations *between* countries, in space and time, are at least as important as what goes on within a society. In this sense, the evolving international context makes it likely – some would say certain – that stages or patterns of development are *not* everywhere the same. Reinhard Bendix has put this graphically: 'Industrialization cannot occur in the same way twice . . . Once [it] has occurred anywhere, this fact alone alters the international environment of all other countries' (quoted in Goldthorpe 1984, p. 137). Finally, over and above any empirical and theoretical weaknesses, Rostow's model is arguably not much help for policy purposes. For one thing, it seems as if the take-off can only be identified *ex post facto*, after the event (perhaps even decades after), which is not a lot of use to development planners in the here and now! Secondly, as Myrdal has acutely observed, there is in Rostow both a *teleology* and a problem of *agency*. That is to say, the process of take-off and growth is basically portrayed by Rostow as unfolding, in a rather automatic way, towards a given end-state; which makes it very difficult even to raise crucial questions of policy choice or planning development. Myrdal attributes this to Rostow's implicit bias in favour of laissez-faire capitalist development; which leads him to ignore the fact that virtually every single actual take-off (except perhaps those of the UK and the USA) has been an actively pursued project, in which the *state* has played a crucial economic role. This is as true of such capitalist take-offs as Bismarck's Germany or Meiji Japan as it obviously is of the USSR.

Frank

Andre Gunder Frank is an American economist – for all practical purposes; although he actually holds German citizenship – who received a conventional training in economics at Chicago. He went to

Latin America in the early 1960s, and drastically changed his views under the impact of both the Cuban Revolution and the then emerging 'dependency' school of thought. With the publication of his book *Capitalism and Underdevelopment in Latin America* (1969), followed by other works, Frank rapidly came to be taken in the English-speaking world as the leading representative of what has been variously called 'dependency', 'neo-Marxism', or 'underdevelopment theory'. In particular, his key term 'the development of underdevelopment' can be seen as the radical counterpart of Rostow's 'take-off'.

Whether methodologically or politically, Frank's starting point could scarcely be more different from Rostow's. Rather than taking a society as the unit of analysis, Frank sees national economies as structural elements in a global capitalist system. It is this system, not individual societies, which is the necessary unit of analysis.

Furthermore, this system is structured, and unevenly so. In a famous metaphor, Frank characterises it as a whole chain of 'metropolis-satellite' relations. This chain links the entire system: from the ultimate global metropolis which is no one's satellite (i.e. the USA); via a whole series of intermediate units which are simultaneously both metropolis and satellite (e.g. Latin American capital cities, which Frank sees as both exploited by the USA and themselves exploiting their own hinterlands); right down to the ultimate satellite – e.g. a landless rural labourer, who has nothing and no one to exploit (and, one should add these days, is probably female).

The nature of the whole chain is, to put it crudely, a gigantic and systematic rip-off. In Frank's terms, 'surplus' is continuously appropriated and expropriated upwards and outwards, at all levels, from bottom to top. This occurs because each metropolis has monopoly economic power in its bit of the system, rather than a free market. The system has been like this since it began (i.e. the 16th century, in Latin America), and remains so. Given this, any real development will require a revolutionary break from the system.

On the basis of this overall model, Frank formulates a number of more specific (although still pretty general) hypotheses. First, the development of satellites is limited simply because they are satellites. Development along metropolitan lines is precisely *not* possible for satellites, given their subordinate position in the system. What satellites experience is *under*development; which crucially Frank redefines as an active process of distortion, characteristic of the relatively modern fate of the Third World, and hence in no way to be equated with 'tradition' or any sort of original state. Conversely, the now developed countries never experienced *under*development, in this sense; they were only *undeveloped at the outset*, which for Frank is very different.

In fact, Frank does not deny that some development has taken place in Latin America. But his second hypothesis, consistent with his overall approach, is that satellites can only develop when their ties with the metropolis are relatively weakened. Frank offers two different sorts of example of this. Isolation, whether geographical or economic – Frank cites Paraguay at one time, and above all Japan – is not a bad but a good thing, as it avoids satellization and permits 'self-generating' development. Alternatively, once a country has become a satellite its only chance is to seize brief opportunities when the grip of the metropolis temporarily weakens – whether because of war or recession. For example, for Frank such industrialization as a few Latin American countries have achieved in this century was principally made possible by the two World Wars and the 1930s depression.

This cannot last, however. Sooner or later the metropolis reasserts its control, the errant satellite is reincorporated, and its briefly promising development is 'choked off'. Exactly what processes this refers to is not always clear, but Frank evidently has in mind the penetration of even the more advanced Latin American economies in the 1960s by trans-national corporations.

Frank's third hypothesis is perhaps the boldest of all. The regions most 'ultra-underdeveloped' today, he asserts, are precisely those which had the closest ties to the metropolis in the past. The Brazilian *nordeste* (north-east) is probably his strongest case. Its appalling poverty and apparent backwardness today are not in the least 'traditional', but on the contrary in the days of 'King Sugar' this was originally the most flourishing part of Brazil. It was, in a sense, used and then thrown on the scrap-heap as economic interests 'moved on' both historically and geographically.

As with Rostow, so with Frank. Utterly opposed as their perspectives are, we shall follow the same procedure of first drawing out some characteristics of Frank's theoretical model as such, before passing on to some specific criticisms.

1. Frank's model is *externalist*. At least for the Third World, all decisive and determining change is seen as coming from, and imposed by, outside forces.

2. It is also *bilinear*. Metropolis and satellites pursue totally different paths from the beginning, determined by their different structural roles in the system.

3. Further, it is *stagnationist*. For the satellite, and in some sense for the system as a whole, nothing ever changes: the structure remains the same. (This may sound rather absurd: evidently Frank is not claiming

that the world or any part of it is exactly the same today as it was four centuries ago. Nonetheless, his concept of 'continuity-in-change' definitely emphasises the continuity rather than the change.)

4. Finally, it is *discontinuist*. So far from following in the footsteps of metropolitan development, the satellite not only starts out on a different road (albeit a road not of its own choice, and one which turns out to be a cul-de-sac), but will have to make a radical break with the entire system if it ever wants to really develop. In no sense does development emerge by evolution within the system. Frank never specifies what this involves, but at least initially he seems to have taken Cuba as an example.

Passing now to more specific criticisms, one could say that Frank's own aforementioned three criteria for assessing theories have boom-eranged back on him. Certainly critics have identified empirical, theo-retical, and policy weaknesses in his work as they have with Rostow. Empirically, indeed, the criticisms are very similar. It turns out to be often difficult to apply Frank's model – in particular, his view that no real development at all is possible under capitalism. It is far from clear what this means; but if it means what it appears to mean then it appears not to be true. For, while some aspects of North-South relations past and present seem to fit Frank's model, others equally clearly do not, e.g. the growth of 'newly industrialising countries'.

Secondly, with Frank as with Rostow, critics have attributed empirical problems to theoretical deficiencies. It is difficult to identify his 'metropolis' and 'satellite' with any actual sociological entity: they are a curious mix of geographical and social, being apparently consti-tuted at different levels by countries, classes, or even individuals.

Finally, there are policy problems. Even supposing Frank's analysis to be correct, what is to be done? Presumably, one must 'delink' from the world system in some way. Yet it is not clear in what sense this is possible. Frank himself, like Wallerstein, now seems to regard even communist countries which have tried to go it alone (like Cuba) as being still bound up in the world system. Here too, perhaps, less sweeping and polarized alternatives would seem more apt, looking in detail at practical and feasible ways of trying to reduce dependence without hoping to abolish it entirely.

Critics of Dependency Theory

Naturally, dependency theory had always been liable to counter-attack and critique from the 'right', by modernization approaches. More unexpected, perhaps, was an increasingly vigorous assault from the 'left' which gathered momentum in the late 1970s and early 1980s, by critics for whom dependency theory in various ways was not Marxist *enough*. The best known of the these critics is Bill Warren.

Warren

Despite the recent dominance of dependency theory, being an avowed Marxist is not inconsistent with enthusiastic support for capitalism as a means of promoting development. Thus the late Bill Warren, in his book *Imperialism: Pioneer of Capitalism* (1980), argued vigorously and heretically that:

(a) The prospects for capitalist development in much of the Third World are good;

(b) Such development has in fact already been taking place – i.e. in the spread of both capitalist relations and the development of the productive forces, in both industry and agriculture – especially in the period since 1945;

(c) Even before that, 'colonialism itself acted as a powerful engine of progressive social change': not only in destroying pre-existing social systems, but also in implanting a capitalism which has now taken firm root;

(d) *Internal* aspects of the Third World (e.g. traditional institutions and ideas) are more of an obstacle to development than is 'imperialism';

(e) The net effect of the relationship between 'imperialist' and Third World countries is beneficial to the latter's economic development and even industrialisation;

(f) The rise of 'indigenous' capitalisms' in various places means that we are now living in 'an era of declining imperialism and advancing capitalism';

(g) Although this theme is very 'underdeveloped' in Warren's work, he believes, as a Marxist, that the above trends will lead to the creation of an industrial proletariat and ultimately to socialism;

(h) The *nationalism* prevalent in much of the Third World is for Warren wholly negative: it puts a brake on capitalist development and it diverts the proletariat away from pure socialism.

In making such claims, Warren was self-consciously breaking with not only dependency theory, but *also* the whole Marxist traditional view of imperialism as harmful to the Third World – although Warren claimed his own view was closer to Marx's own.

Not surprisingly, Warren's views have provoked a storm of criticism.

(i) Although some countries may be developing or even industrializing, this does not prove that all others can or will follow. The argument here is similar to one in social mobility studies: the fact that some individuals rise out of one class into another does not mean that classes themselves thereby cease to exist. On the contrary, by relieving potential tension such mobility may actually strengthen the class system, not weaken it.

(ii) Warren's rosy view of colonialism (he never mentions the slave trade!) and stress on internal Third World obstacles are viewed by some as both inaccurate and insulting: a form of 'blaming the victim', and theoretically a step backwards into what is in effect a version of the crude tradition/modernity division associated with modernization theory.

(iii) More subtly, his obsessional hatred of nationalism seems unrealistic as well as inconsistent, since by his own account it is national independence which has led to today's greater freedom of manoeuvre for the Third World to develop.

Although Warren's is an unusually extreme view, aspects of his critique of dependency theory are shared by others, both Marxist and non-Marxist. In a sense, the extreme formulations of some versions of dependency theory (e.g. A. G. Frank) have produced an equally extreme counterblast. In the mid 1980s, a somewhat more moderate dependency position might well concede some points, while standing firm on others. Thus:

1. Historically, the 'creation of the world' *was* a drastic, contradictory, often brutal process, creating global inequalities which persist to this day.

2. Some countries may still industrialise, but the overall system remains structurally unequal.

3. Capitalist development is a dynamic but profoundly uneven process, benefitting some and disadvantaging others at many levels: ·
individual, class, nation, and gender.

4. Rather than falsely polarizing 'external' versus 'internal' obstacles to development we must focus on how they are *linked* (e.g. alliances between TNCs and local Third World bourgeoisies).

5. To speak of a Third World is simply to recognize that for some groups in particular contexts – most of the world's population, in fact – the economic and social structures they face differ strikingly in degree, and probably in kind as well, from those in the already industrialised capitalist countries.

6. But generalization is unwise. If it was wrong to deny with Frank that capitalism could any longer develop the Third World, it would be equally misguided to assume with Warren that a *general* process of

capitalist development is now unfolding. Each concrete case must be examined on its merits.

Varieties of Modernization Theory

There's obviously much more to modernization theory than Rostow alone. The feature he most clearly illustrates is a *stages* approach. What other theoretical 'moves' are typical of modernization theory?

One very common tendency, going back to the sociological classics, is to picture development not so much as a series of stages but as a basic *dichotomy*, or pair of opposites. You're probably familiar already with Tonnies 'gemeinschaft/gesellschaft' (community/association), or Durkheim's 'mechanical vs organic solidarity'. In modern times, Talcott Parsons' 'pattern variables' have been used by Hoselitz (1960) in a similar way. All you do, basically, is set up two opposite pairs of characteristics, and then claim that one lot are 'traditional' and apply to the Third World, while the other lot are 'modern' and apply to the West. So, for example, the West is described as achievement-orientated and having a highly specialized division of labour, while the Third World is the opposite: ascriptive oriented (it's not what you achieve, but who you're born, that counts), and with very little role specialization.

One problem with this kind of 'study of paired contrasts' is that there's no movement in it, no process. This can be remedied by a second approach, *diffusionism*. On this view, development consists of those who've got it giving it (or some of it) to those who haven't. Depending on the author, the 'it' can be anything from capital or technology to political institutions or cultural values. This is the theoretical basis for the idea of *aid*. On this view, too, even *within* a Third World country the same process takes place. There is a 'traditional' sector and a 'modern' sector, and development means that the modern will gradually spread its influence and absorb the traditional. Such theories (of which there are several kinds, economic and sociological) are known – for obvious reasons – as *dualist*.

A third approach in modernization theory might be called *psychologism*. It's tempting to call this one 'When All Else Fails', since so often that seems to have been the mood in which it has been taken up. Despairing of finding economic or social or political explanations for underdevelopment, this approach locates the problem firmly in the *cultures* (or even the psyches) of Third World peoples – who are thus said to be passive, conservative, fatalistic, or superstitious, when what they need is to be creative, innovative, entrepreneurial, get-up-and-go types.

What can we say about these different 'modernization' approaches (which I've only sketched here)? For one thing, they're rather too close for comfort to Western 'commonsense' ideas about development. You should remind yourself what the alternatives are. A dependency theorist like Frank would reject dichotomies, firstly, saying we have long lived in a single, capitalist world: *nothing* is 'traditional' any more, even if it looks that way. Likewise, Frank would reject *diffusionism*, or at least re-evaluate it. In his (perhaps extreme) view, the West has 'diffused' nothing but trouble to the Third World: political oppression, economic exploitation, and the very structures of under-development itself. As for *psychologism*, Frank would see this as 'blaming the victim', and as such implicitly racist.

Others (including other Marxists) may take a more balanced view. Perhaps some traditional sectors do survive, even if linked to capitalism. Probably the balance sheet of 'diffusion' isn't either wholly positive or wholly negative: there has been good and bad. As for 'psychologism', while avoiding extremes we can surely recognize – in the spirit of Weber's famous 'Protestant Ethic' – that there do exist real sociological questions about socio-cultural innovation: who does it, when, where, and why? Yet, like Weber (but unlike psychological approaches to development) we should avoid monocausal deter-minism, i.e. singling out one factor alone as *the* key to the whole process. Instead, we need to look at the interplay of economic *and* cultural and other factors, in concrete cases. There is, I would argue, too little work on cultural aspects in the sociology of development. Dependency theory has become *over*-economistic. Maybe to pay *some* attention to culture could be a lesson which modernization theory still has to teach us.

Barrington Moore's 'Routes'

By no means all contributions to the sociology of development can be easily pigeon-holed as 'modernization' or 'dependency'. An out-standing example is the influential work of Barrington Moore (1966), which might be described as modernization in form and Marxist (but not dependency, as we shall see) in content.

Moore looks at what he calls the 'routes to the modern world' followed in six countries: Britain, France, the USA, Japan, China, and India. He is particularly concerned to explore connections between the types of political regime which resulted from modernization, and the varying patterns of class alliances which preceded and precipitated it.

Importantly for Moore, these classes include losers as well as winners; and his overall focus is less on the characteristic inheritors and protagonists of industrial society, the bourgeoisie and proletariat, than on their agrarian counterparts – the 'lord and peasant' of his book's subtitle. Particularly crucial is how these classes respond to the challenge of commercial agriculture.

On the basis of his six case studies (and making reference also to Germany and Russia), Moore delineates three 'routes to the modern world'. The first – as in Britain, France, and the USA – is *bourgeois revolution* leading to *capitalist democracy*. Here a social group develops with an independent economic base, namely an urban trading and/or manufacturing class, and attacks obstacles to its economic and political success. Its allies in this process vary markedly. The old landed upper class either form part of the tide, as in England; or if hostile are swept away by revolution (as in France) or civil war (as in the USA, where the Southern plantocracy rather awkwardly fill this slot). As for peasants, they either pushed the same way (France), or were overwhelmed by the capitalist advance (England, e.g. the enclosures), or they never existed in the first place (USA).

Route two is variously characterized as *revolution from above*, 'capitalist and reactionary', or 'abortive revolution'. Its eventual outcome, at least temporarily, is *fascism*. In Germany and Japan (and presumably Italy), the bourgeois impulse is much feebler, and any attempted bourgeois revolution crushed. Instead, a relatively weak commercial-industrial class relies on dissident elements (junkers, samurai) from the older and still dominant ruling class to force through a programme of economic modernization from above. This can lead to rapid industrialization, but within strict political limits.

In route three, finally, the dead weight of the great agrarian bureaucracies of Russia and China stifled even more effectively any impulses to commercial or industrial (let alone political) modernization, whether from below or above. Since the new urban classes were too weak – and the old classes, in a sense, too stupid – there remained in the absence of modernization a huge peasantry, which would ultimately overthrow the old order. So route three is *peasant revolution* and its outcome *communism* – which then proceeds, as Moore lugubriously notes, to make those same peasants its victims.

And India? A check on generalization, it seems, since it cannot (at least as yet) be readily slotted into any category. Its particular history means that no class has been constituted in such a way as to have an interest in rechannelling agricultural surplus so as to get growth started. Aspects of democracy coexist alongside much rural misery, yet there is little sign of revolution. India, one senses, represents unfinished business.

Moore's work has been massively influential, or at least inspirational. His development of Marxist class categories in a comparative framework firmly grounded in empirical evidence has proved something of a model for more recent large-scale comparative grand theorizing, such as the work of Perry Anderson, Theda Skocpol, and Immanuel Wallerstein. He graphically showed that development was not a smooth process, but one full of conflicts and revolutions. (Even his chapter on England is titled 'England and the contribution of violence to gradualism'.) And Moore showed both the importance and the specificity of history. In all this, his work represented an implicit blow against culturalist, unilinear, or evolutionist strands in modernization theory.

On the other hand, it has proved persistently difficult to apply Moore's perspectives more widely. Moore himself cautioned against this, insisting that what he said only applies to the countries he said it about. In particular, he chose not to study 'small' countries on the grounds that 'the decisive causes of their politics lie outside their own boundaries' (1966, p. xiii). This indicates the major respect in which Moore remains closer to modernization than to dependency theory. In his study just about everything – even for India, which was after all a colony – is explained by events or trends inside the society concerned.

This leads Moore to ignore the crucial question which a dependency theorist might ask, namely: how far is the 'availability' of a particular route to any country at a given time determined by the routes which other countries have already followed. It hardly seems coincidental that Moore's three routes and six cases also form a *chronological* sequence. In a nutshell, might not the earlier success of the UK *et al.* have made it harder for 'latecomers' to follow the same road, and hence made more statist and/or revolutionary approaches more likely?

Chapter Three

Industrialization

Introduction

Industrialization is at once a central and an elusive topic in the sociology of development, as indeed in sociology more generally. Its centrality lies in the fact that it is the advent of modern industry, above all else, which is widely held to clearly distinguish contemporary Western society as a whole from all previous social forms. In this sense, the Industrial Revolution is cited by Nisbet (1967) as one of the 'two revolutions' – the other being political, namely, the French Revolution – whose transforming impact gave rise amongst other things to the new discipline of sociology itself. In similar vein, Lee and Newby (1983) have recently used various aspects of industry and industrialization as a peg on which to hang an entire introductory textbook in sociology.

These examples also illustrate the topic's elusiveness, in the sense that in such approaches there is little to prevent 'industrialization' from becoming equated with the entire subject matter of sociology. Similarly, there has been much debate as to whether we should still characterize Western societies as 'industrial', or prefer some other term such as 'post-industrial' (see for instance Kumar, 1978). Likewise, those interested in East/West comparisons have argued over whether there is a 'logic of industrialism', such that the political differences between the USA and USSR will gradually be eroded in a process of 'convergence' (Kerr, 1962).

These are interesting and important issues, but I shall not deal with them here. My focus will be narrower, in two senses. First, although not denying that the growth of industry links in to broader processes of social change (e.g. urbanization), I have tried to cover at least some of those processes in other chapters and will not repeat them here.

Secondly, this chapter will specifically address what might be called the 'North-South' issue in industrialization, namely: can the same or similar processes of industrialization as characterized the West's own development be expected to recur in the Third World? Are they indeed already taking place? Can we look forward eventually to a wholly industrialized world? Or are there reasons why this is impossible, unlikely, or even undesirable?

Definitions

A particularly clear and helpful account of many of the issues covered in this chapter has recently been provided by Wield (1983). In terms of definitions of industry, Wield suggests three. One is *residual*: 'industry' means everything that isn't agriculture. Another is *sectoral*: energy, mining and manufacturing. More useful than either of these, however, is the third: 'a particular way of organizing production using machinery and a complex division of labour'.

This last definition is better because it is more discriminating than the other two. No. 1, for instance, wouldn't allow us to speak of industrialized agriculture; while no. 2 fails to distinguish *scale* of production – often very varied in the Third World. Plumping for no. 3, then, Wield suggests this can be unpacked in either of two ways, which we might call 'micro' and 'macro' respectively: the industrial production as such, and the broader social process of industrialization. Although as already stated our main concern is with the latter, it is important to have a fairly precise idea of the former too, and I cannot do better than quote Wield's definition (adding my own emphases):

'Industrial production processes are characterized by:
(a) the possibility of utilizing *technologies* with complex *machinery* associated with a large *scale* of production;
(b) the utilization of a wide range of *raw materials* often already processed through the use of complex technologies;
(c) a relatively complex *technical division of labour* within units of production;
(d) complex *co-operation and co-ordination* of specialized tasks inside the unit of production;
(e) a diverse range of *skills* within the work force.' (Wield, 1983, p. 8.)

As Wield observes, the distinctiveness of all this becomes clearer if we contrast all the above with small-scale *artisan* or intermediate *handicrafts* production. It is characteristic of the Third World that all these co-exist side by side. This leads into the second, broader or 'macro' notion of industrialization. Briefly put, this implies that the 'micro' model outlined above will spread, and carry all before it sooner or later, with consequent broad social changes. Whether this is indeed on the cards in the Third World is precisely the issue of this chapter. That it cannot be taken for granted is already clear from the case of *extractive* industry (mining), long prevalent since colonial times in parts of the Third World without necessarily having any 'spill-over' transformative effects on the wider society as a whole.

In order to capture these broader aspects, a single measure is not enough. Sutcliffe (1971), the author of a major study on industry and underdevelopment, proposed a threefold definition of an industrialized country as one where the industrial sector: (i) contributes at least 25% of GDP (gross domestic product); (ii) consists 60% or more of manufacturing; and (iii) employs more than 10% of the population. We shall see how Sutcliffe applies this below.

Strategies for Industrialization

Looking at the specifically economic choices faced and paths pursued by Third World governments today and in the recent past, we can distinguish two broad types of development strategy; corresponding at least roughly to the modernization/dependency dichotomy. First, however, we should recall that the traditional economic role for the Third World was not industrial at all, but rather to specialize in producing minerals or cash crops to 'feed' the industrialization of the West. Despite the changes discussed below, this model still characterizes the economic structures of many Third World countries (above all, in Africa). It is also still legitimized by a powerful strand of conventional neo-classical economic wisdom. The doctrine of *comparative advantage* (from Ricardo onwards) advocates that countries should specialize in those branches of production in which they have 'natural' advantages. On this argument, raw material production is what Third World countries are good at and suited for, at present. By specializing in this area, and exchanging their raw materials for industrial goods produced elsewhere, they will eventually earn enough revenue to permit local capital accumulation and hence a gradual diversification of their economic structures.

This model has been much criticized. Empirically, there is a persisting (and probably insoluble) debate about the *terms of trade* between raw materials and industrial goods. Some economists, like Gunnar Myrdal (1963), believe that the long-run trend is against raw material producers; that is (over-simplifying somewhat), the more you produce, the less (relatively) you earn. On this view, then, putting all your eggs in the basket of primary production is a dead end, because you will never in fact earn enough to make the switch to industrialization. Instead, like Lewis Carroll's Red Queen, it takes all the running you can do even to stay in the same place; because year by year the price you must pay to import industrial goods consumes an ever greater proportion of your own earnings from primary products. Whether or not this is universal or inevitable, it certainly corresponds to the actual experience of a number of Third World countries.

1. Import-substituting Industrialization (ISI). The critique summarized above was first formulated by an important group of Latin American economists from the 1940s onwards. Including the Argentinian Raul Prebisch and the Brazilian Celso Furtado, this group is known as ECLA (after the UN Economic Commission for Latin America, where many of them worked). Sometimes their approach is also called 'structuralist', which in a sociological context can be rather confusing.

Rather than *development towards the outside* (as above), the ECLA group advocated *development towards the inside*. In practice – and, since several of them went on to hold government office, this *was* a practice and not just a theory – this took the form of *import-substituting industrialization* (ISI). The idea here was that, rather than specializing in primary production for export, you should try to cut down on imports of industrial goods by manufacturing at least some of them locally. This did not mean basic or heavy industrialization (steelworks, etc.), at least not at first; but more likely light industries producing consumer goods (textiles, household products, soft drinks, etc.) for the home market. Because value-added is greater in industry than agriculture or mining, this would be a surer way of accumulating capital and later diversifying the economy.

As is often the case, this was not a purely economic doctrine. The ECLA group had a political and social project too. Representing in a sense the outlook of a new but weak industrial middle class, they wanted to modernize and overhaul what they regarded as the backward and even feudal social structures of their countries. In particular, they hoped to erode the power of the coalition of traditional rural landlords and import-export merchants who effectively ruled in much of Latin America. Further, they wished to enfranchize (often literally) the working classes and peasants, thus creating a modern democratic political community and an integrated national society. All in all, this was a programme with strong echoes of the French Revolution and the world-view of a rising bourgeoisie.

As a practical strategy, however, it ran into difficulties. One area of controversy focusses on the role of the state. Although not socialist, the ECLA approach was not content to leave everything to market forces; regarding them not as natural, but as the outcome of an unequal specialization which had been imposed upon Latin America historically by the Spanish and Portuguese colonialists. So they saw an economic role for the state, in particular to create tariff barriers to shelter the new infant industries during their early years.

Neo-classical critics, however, said this was inefficient. In the absence of competition, there was no way of choosing rationally what branches of production you should specialize in. Also, protected markets have a habit of remaining so well beyond infancy, leading to a maze of tariff barriers which serve no function except to inhibit trade and growth. Although there is a strong dose of ideology in these arguments, it is probably true that in many cases tariffs were applied with insufficient finesse.

A second problem with ISI was that it produced a peculiar kind of vicious circle. To set up industries, you obviously need capital goods. In the first instance, these must be imported; which means they must be paid for, with foreign exchange. How to earn the foreign exchange? In the short run, what option was there but to concentrate even more intensively on the traditional primary production for export; which of course is what you're trying to get away from, but right now it's all you've got!

There was an alternative source of funds, but that had its problems also. The ECLA approach originally had nothing against foreign capital as such, so in many cases the answer was to invite foreign companies in to do the industrializing. But this too often backfired. In theory, foreign capital was supposed to help set up branches of industry and thereby stimulate local business to follow suit. In practice, TNCs (transnational corporations) increasingly came to monopolize these new markets into which they had been invited. Not only did they not encourage local firms, but often they actually displaced or swallowed them up. After all, it is not easy for a small new indigenous enterprise to compete against the resources, know-how, assets, and sheer power of a TNC. So, paradoxically, the ISI strategy which had been intended to create less dependent and more autonomous economies all too often ended up trapped in new forms of dependence.

Even if these problems could have been overcome, there was a third source of difficulty with ISI. It assumed the existing pattern of demand.

If your industrialization consists of making at home what you currently import, then what are these goods? In practice, given the highly unequal income distribution in countries where most people lack effective purchasing power, this means concentrating on the luxury goods consumed by a small elite: televisions, consumer durables, cars, etc. An industrial strategy based on those sorts of goods simply reproduced the existing inequalities: it had no relevance to basic needs, and it did nothing to put purchasing power in the hands of the mass of the people and unleash the kind of Keynesian dynamic of large-scale demand which the ECLA group had intended. It was a skewed, wrong-way-round sort of industrialization: starting with what in Europe's industrialization had come later, and only then (if ever) going on to the sort of basic industrialization and mass consumption goods which Europe had begun with.

2. **Export-oriented Industrialization (EOI).** The crisis and blockage of ISI lent weight to a very different approach which increasingly emerged in the late 1960s and 1970s, especially in parts of Latin America and East Asia. (The contrast between Brazil before and after the 1964 military coup is probably the most striking example.) In one sense the strategy of *export-led* growth was not novel; in that it advocated production for the world market rather than for home demand as an engine of growth, and it justified this in terms of the doctrine of comparative advantage.

Two things were new, however. The obvious one is the *content* of the exports: no longer the traditional agriculutral and mineral primary products, these now comprised manufactured goods. In the first instance, these were and to a large extent still are light industrial products, especially textiles. (Check where your own clothes and shoes were made, and you'll see what I mean!) Increasingly, however, several *newly industrializing countries* (NICs) have diversified into such areas as electronics, steel, ship-building, and even computers.

The second novelty is more contentious. Although the NICs profess an often brashly capitalist ideology, closer inspection reveals that their growth has by no means been the work of market forces unaided. On the contrary, their economies are characterized by often massive *state intervention* – not infrequently on as large a scale as was ever the case with ISI! From Brazil to Taiwan, Mexico to South Korea, these are highly statist economies (Wade and White, 1984).

Needless to say, the NICs have not been without their critics. Dependency theory in particular obviously finds them a great challenge (it shouldn't be happening!), and has tried to develop a critique; some parts of which are more convincing than others. For example, it stretches credulity to argue that the NICs represent 'development of underdevelopment', in A. G. Frank's sense. On whatever index you choose – quantitative growth rates, structural change (e.g. from agriculture to industry, or from light to heavy industry), and in many cases actual incomes and living standards – there has been undeniable progress. Indeed, I think one has to admit that what has been called the 'stagnationist' thesis of dependency theory – i.e. Frank's extreme view, that no further progress under capitalism is possible anywhere in the Third World – has been definitely disproved by the experience of the NICs.

However, to concede this does not exhaust the dependency critique. There are at least three more strings to the dependency bow, and these may be more on target. One is to suggest that all this has been accomplished under the dominance of foreign capital, hence it does not constitute genuine or autonomous development. I'll return to this.

A different tack is to point to the *political preconditions* of this economic model. The NICs' comparative advantage is based on low wages, kept low by political suppression of trades unions and democracy. It is true that virtually all NIC governments are more or less politically authoritarian. It is not clear, however, at least to me, that they are more authoritarian than most other Third World governments, of left or right; the great majority of which have not 'delivered the goods' economically speaking, as the NICs have. (This is not to condone authoritarian government anywhere, but merely to make a comparative sociological observation.)

To further confuse the picture, the conventional economists' measure of inequality – the Gini coefficient – appears to suggest that at any rate the East Asian NICs (notably Taiwan and South Korea) have rather *less* inequality than most other Third World countries. Likewise on low wages, it would seem that most NICs have now moved on from what was undoubtedly their original selling point of cheap labour, into industries which are more skill and capital-intensive. This can be seen most clearly in textiles, which are increasingly shifting to countries like Indonesia, Morocco, or even China – where wages are appreciably lower than in NICs like South Korea.

This last consideration leads conveniently into dependency theory's strongest argument against the NICs. Rather than a rearguard action which says it isn't happening, or that anyway it isn't development, this focusses wisely on the *generalizability* of the NICs' experience as a *model*. If they can do it, does that mean everybody can and should do it? Certainly, in the ideological struggles which are rarely far below the surface in scholarly economic debates, this is what is usually claimed. The NICs are frequently touted as sensible, practical regimes, which have followed the natural laws of economics instead of trying to impose alien or unworkable ideologies, and hence have reaped a rich reward.

And this message is widely believed. Thus many other Third World countries have been busily setting up *export processing zones* (EPZs): enclaves into which foreign investors are invited, on very generous terms (infrastructure provided, import duties waived, tax holidays, full remission of profits, etc.), to employ cheap local labour (often female) producing light industrial goods for export. They hope thereby to repeat the experience and success of the NICs. But will they? It is perhaps too early to tell, but even so there are strong reasons for doubt.

Clearly the argument hinges on what you think have been the conditions for and causes of the NICs' success, and whether these conditions exist or could be replicated in other parts of the Third World. One problem is that there is no general agreement on what the key factors are, so the discussion that follows can only be suggestive, at best. One *internal/cultural* consideration would be to note that the East Asian NICs, the so-called 'four little tigers' or 'gang of four' – Taiwan, Singapore, Hong Kong and South Korea – have a common link: three are wholly or overwhelmingly Chinese, and the fourth shares with them a strongly Confucian cultural heritage. On this basis, by a kind of analogy with Weber's 'Protestant Ethic', there has been suggested a 'Confucian ethic' for these countries, emphasizing such values as respect for authority, social cohesion, and education as a basis for their economic success.

I doubt that this is the whole story, and obviously it doesn't explain Brazil; but equally, I doubt that such factors can be wholly ruled out. In which case, other countries which lack Confucianism or a similarly strong fundamental ethic presumably will not be able to follow suit on this basis. (As a caution against single-factor explanations, however, you should notice that another thing which the 'gang of four' (partially excepting Singapore) have in common is that they are almost wholly *mono-ethnic*, a very unusual situation in the Third World; hence the ethnic and national problems which stymie so many other countries' progress simply don't arise, which is an obvious bonus.)

Most dependency critiques, however, emphasize *external/economic* factors. They point out that the NICs 'took off' in the 1960s, at a time when the world (and in particular the Western) economy was still growing, and did so by specializing in labour-intensive areas such as textiles which the increasingly capital-intensive and high-wage Western economies either could afford to shed and lose or simply could not compete in. Several things, arguably, have changed since then. One is that the existing NICs have (so to speak) taken up all the space there is, often literally, as Western countries turn increasingly protectionist and put up tariff barriers and quotas against textiles and electronic goods produced in Third World countries, in order to protect their own troubled industries in these fields. This growing protectionism in turn is a product of the deep recession which has gripped the world economy for over a decade, and which shows no clear sign of easing yet. So who are all the new would-be NICs going to sell the products of their EPZs to?

Some might say this is an unduly static or short-sighted view. It is true that dependency theorists have often held to a *zero-sum* view of world capitalism, assuming that a gain in one part of the system automatically entails a loss somewhere else. As such, they tend to overstress how much capitalist development has been achieved *externally* (some places exploiting other places), and underestimate how much is due to *internal* factors (increases in productivity brought about by technical progress). More generally, Marxists of all kinds are all too prone to wishful thinking, pronouncing capitalism to be dead or moribund – when time and again it proceeds to confound them by making a miraculous recovery.

Yet even allowing for all that, I would still stick my neck out and suggest that for many countries EPZs and export-led growth will turn out to be a cruel con-trick, and no less a dead-end than was the traditional export of primary products. The world (read 'Western') market is limited, and currently stagnant and saturated. Most countries setting up EPZs have little to offer except cheap labour (indeed, they must compete with each other to see who can be the cheapest – a contest in which the all-time winner now seems likely to be China, of all places!). This may enable them to get a slice of labour-intensive industries like textiles, but it is hard to see how they will make the crucial shift which the NICs have made into either traditional heavy or more technically advanced industries.

Above all, and quite unlike the NICs of East Asia or Latin America, most EPZ-mongers seem content to pin all their hopes on foreign businesses. Rather than encouraging either state enterprise or indigenous firms, they are left at the mercy of TNCs who as a result have a field day. Thanks to recent advances in technology and communications, TNCs are thus enabled to do two very convenient things.

1) They can *break down* their production processes into discrete components and physically locate each one where it can be done most

cheaply. This means that Third World countries do not acquire entire industries, but only those stages which are labour intensive – and hence most technologically backward. This *decomposition* of production processes has gone further than many people realize. In the semiconductor industry which underpins the current revolution in electronics and computers, it is quite usual for the components to be manufactured in an advanced country, assembled in a Third World country (this is the labour-intensive stage: e.g. 'sewing' silicon chips together, a task largely performed by young women workers in South East Asia, often recruited explicitly under racist and sexist slogans about 'the traditional nimble fingers of the oriental female'); and then returned to the advanced country for final processing and packaging. Another example is of trousers, cut out in West Germany, airfreighted across the Mediterranean to Tunisia to be made up, then flown back to Germany for finishing and sale. Quite likely, your own jeans or calculator or stereo have been produced on this roundabout basis.

2) Even without this decomposition, the *competition* between different Third World countries to attract customers to their own EPZs is a virtual incitement to TNCs to play off one against another. You set up in one place, take advantage of all the grants and tax concessions, and then when these are finished you just pull out, set up somewhere else, and take another set of hand-outs. Nor is this process confined to Third World countries. If you live anywhere north of Watford, you may well be aware of examples in your own region. With both national and local governments, in the West as well as in the Third World, increasingly desperate to attract new jobs to their own communities, it is hard to see how this situation will quickly change. Needless to say, the ever-present threat of potential relocation also acts as a powerful curb on trade union campaigns for better wages or conditions.

I have deliberately spent some time on this discussion of NICs, EPZs, TNCs and so forth, because these are the key development issues of the 1980s and 1990s. In many ways they strain and take us beyond the 'modernization vs dependency' framework, which I have largely used to structure this book and which served us well enough in the 1960s and 1970s. Even so, I shall conclude this section by suggesting that at least one version of dependency theory can cope with the NICs. This is Wallerstein's *world-system theory*.

Whereas A. G. Frank uses a dichotomous model of *metropolis* and *satellite* to characterize the world system, Wallerstein makes a triple distinction: *core, periphery* and *semi-periphery*. This addition of a third term makes the model much more plausible and flexible. Instead of being committed to maintaining the 'development of underdevelopment', Wallerstein can thus predict that *sometimes* (not always) *some* countries (not all) can move up or down. More precisely, at times of economic recession in the existing core he predicts that there is limited scope for a few countries to rise in the system, either by 'seizing the chance' (a bit like ISI) or through 'development by invitation' (having the TNCs do it for you).

It is, if you like, a kind of international social mobility theory, in which the 'actors' are national economies. And crucially, as with any social mobility model, the existence of some opportunities for mobility does *not* imply that the entire system is an open one. On the contrary, in both cases, certain kinds of mobility are compatible with and even reinforce an overall *structure* which is hierarchical and unequal.

Other Marxists of course, like Warren, take an opposite view and see capitalist growth and development proceeding virtually all over the Third World. Time will tell who is right. A crucial test case will be whether the next 'rung' of Third World countries below the NICs – Malaysia or Indonesia, Peru or Colombia, say – will be able to follow the Brazils or Taiwans, and move on from low-wage textiles and assembly into diversified but increasingly balanced national economies.

So, for some on the right, the experience of the NICs simply goes to show that the market knows best. But that conveniently ignores the considerable role of the state in almost all NICs: providing grants and incentives, setting up actual enterprises, allocating credit and investment funds, controlling (or suppressing) wage negotiations, developing technology, carefully selecting foreign investment, seeking out markets – all this in addition to the usual fiscal and monetary policies.

Meanwhile, on the left, some try to salvage a modified dependency position with concepts like the *new international division of labour*. As discussed above, this implies that basically TNCs and developed countries still rule the roost; and if today some industrialization is taking place in the Third World, it's only because that suits them. The essential nature of the world system has not changed. Or has it?

The NICs, however, do seem to be doing something about it. Moreover, and crucially, on closer inspection at least part of what they are doing cannot simply be attributed to the interests of the already developed countries. On the contrary, there are often contradictions and clashes of interest. For example, South Korea's steel, construction and ship-building industries are a real threat to established producers.

Part of the response to this would be to say that this is because TNCs have no national interest. They go where the profits are, even if that means relocating part or even whole industries overseas, and hence harming their own original national economy (as has arguably been the practice of many British TNCs in recent years). However, this is not the whole picture. Third World 'actors' include not only national governments but also, increasingly, *their own TNCs* – which are a growing force on the world scene, and major investors in their own right (albeit often with support from their governments) in other countries' EPZs.

Perhaps it is helpful then to consider dependency theory as indicating not a total system and straitjacket, so much as a linked series of obstacles which are very difficult to overcome – but which nonetheless certain actors may be able to deal with. At all events, it becomes increasingly difficult to categorize Third World strategies of the 1980s into neat boxes: capitalism vs socialism, or even export-orientation vs import-substituting industrialization.

Sutcliffe Reconsiders

Bob Sutcliffe, whose 1971 study was cited earlier (p.118), has recently reviewed the position as he sees it almost fifteen years on (in Kaplinsky, 1984). To recap, he defined an industrialized country as one where the industrial sector: (i) contributes at least 25% of GDP (gross domestic product); (ii) consists 60% or more of manufacturing; and (iii) employs more than 10% of the population. Not many new countries, he notes, have passed his threefold 'test' of industrialization since then. Uruguay, Israel, Yugoslavia and Portugal have crossed the borderline to join those that were already there (Western and Eastern Europe, North America, Japan, Australasia, Argentina, Hong Kong, Malta and Singapore). But the only wholly new arrivals are South Korea and probably Taiwan. Others, NICs and near NICs, which might pass on the first two (sectoral) criteria fail on the third, industrial *employment*.

This leads Sutcliffe to question over-optimistic views, such as Warren's, of industrialization as a *general* process in the Third World. For one thing, the North-South 'gap' in manufacturing output per head remains wide. A NIC like South Korea has certainly undergone structural change: in terms of percent of labour force in and the sectoral share of industry, it appears as industrialized as the UK. Yet its manufacturing output per head in 1978 was $621, compared with the UK's $2,667. From such data Sutcliffe concludes that real structural industrialization can take place at much lower rates of labour productivity than happened in the West.

However, secondly, some alleged structural shifts from agriculture to industry are misleading, since they may simply indicate bad *agricultural* performance. As Sutcliffe caustically notes, ' "industrialization" here is a sign not of economic advance but of economic decline' (1984, p. 127). Thirdly, Sutcliffe detects a complicated set of trends at work which are best quoted in his own words:

> A form of industrialization has been taking place in quite a widespread manner. But in many countries it is composed of different elements which are not homogeneous and do not unambiguously represent economic modernisation... What seems to be happening is that modern industry is growing at high and rising productivity levels and at the same time small-scale, more primitive industry survives at low, possibly declining productivity levels, but provides a meagre living for a growing share of the people. What may be occurring therefore is a process of internal polarisation, one which is more complex and extreme... and one which is very different from what took place in the successful industrializations of the past. (1984, pp. 128–129)

More broadly and reflectively, Sutcliffe also considers something to which we should now turn our attention: namely, the costs of industrialization.

The Costs of Industrialization

As Barrington Moore (1966) has gloomily noted, there is no evidence that the majority of people anywhere have ever actively wanted an industrial society, and plenty that they have not. Whatever its long-run material and other benefits, industrialization *at the time* is a costly process: economically, politically and culturally.

As an *economic* process, first of all, industrialization by definition involves shifting the balance from consumption to investment, often at a high rate and for a long period. It is, literally, a case of jam today versus jam tomorrow; and, if the latter is chosen, people must tighten their belts as they invest in the future. This iron necessity applies equally to capitalist and socialist regimes. Doubtless as a result, industrialization so far has everywhere been associated with *political* authoritarianism. We should think of it, not so much as an abstract social *process*, but a definite *project*: as something which some people do at the expense of others.

The choices and conflicts which arise here can be viewed in two linked ways. In part, they are *generational*: one generation (or part of it) foregoes consumption (i.e. gives up goodies), in order that the investment thus created may enable their children (or grandchildren) to consume more and better than they ever could have, without that sacrifice. But industrialization is also very much a *class* question. By definition, in societies which are initially agrarian it is peasants who get squeezed, sometimes mercilessly: by enclosures in England, by collectivization and requisitions in the USSR. As these examples may suggest, who does the squeezing can vary. Moore's account, as we saw, found several possible combinations and alliances of rising bourgeoisie, modernizing sections of old rural oligarchies, and so on. As for the link between generation and class, this consists in *social mobility*. Not least among the tragic ironies of Soviet industrialization in the 1930s was that the 'workers' on whose behalf the 'peasants' were smashed were in most cases the sons and daughters, brothers and sisters of those same peasants.

Industrialization also has its *cultural* costs. Old ways are shattered, or eroded. Small-scale activities become uneconomic and disappear. A brash new smoky squalid urban industrial society thrusts its way onto centre stage, while the old rural world is pushed to the margins. The impersonal replaces the personal, community is superseded by organization. There are echoes here of the famous themes of Nisbet's *The Sociological Tradition* (1967), which identified precisely these such unprecedented changes as provoking the reflections out of which sociology itself was born.

There is of course another side to all this. Modernization theorists, and not only they, would retort that whatever the rigours of the 'steep ascent' the eventual plateau of industrial society is well worth it. At least since 1945, Western societies have enjoyed a combination of economic well-being, political democracy, and cultural breadth which is historically quite without precedent. None of this would have been possible without industrialization. Sacrifice there certainly was, but it wasn't in vain. And the rest of the world both can have and is entitled to share the same benefits.

Still, as we have seen this process is far from being problem-free. Perhaps it is not too utopian to suppose that by now, after some 200 years of global industrialization, we could learn some lessons and apply them to the process in the future. It is already clear that there is no single royal road to industrialization. Different countries vary widely in their size, climate, and resource endowments, as well as their history, social structure and type of political regime. The balance of market and planning may vary considerably; althouth any industrialization process nowadays (whatever the monetarists say) is likely to involve a good deal of state intervention.

Nor is it always necessary – or even possible, in some countries – any more to 'sacrifice' agriculture to industry. A steelworks in every country may not be a feasible goal. Some smaller agrarian countries might do better to concentrate on feeding themselves and developing agro-industries. In technology, too, there are choices. Thanks to the work of E. F. Schumacher (1974), it is increasingly recognized that 'small is beautiful'. Or can be, since it would be wrong to generalize. But relatively small-scale production and organization may be appropriate in specific cases. In particular, Third World countries where labour is abundant may well at first choose relatively labour-intensive, 'older' or intermediate technology, rather than the very latest expensive machinery which creates hardly any jobs.

Finally, we should note the paradox of being a 'late developer'. On the one hand, the firstcomers have so carved up the world and ensconced themselves within it that it sometimes seems as if newcomers can hardly get a look in. On the other hand, just as technologically nobody has to re-invent the wheel, socially too it should be possible (at least in principle) for today's would-be developers to take a long, hard look at the harsher sides of earlier industrialization experiences: to learn something from their mistakes, and to make choices at once more purposive and less brutal.

But is it Possible? – The Ecological Dimension

With this stark question, Goldthorpe (1984) opens his own chapter on a set of considerations which can scarcely be ignored (though they all too often have been) in any discussion of industrialization. Irrespective of dependency arguments about socio-political blockages to industrialization, and criticisms of the human costs of the process, are there *ecological* constraints which in any case rule out any prospect of a world-wide industrial society?

Some have certainly argued so, in no uncertain terms. Thus the Ehrlichs state baldly that 'our environment cannot stand "world industrialization" '. And they do not hesitate to grasp the nettle: 'Most of these countries [LDCs] will never, under any conceivable circumstances, be "developed" in the sense in which the United States is today. They could quite accurately be called the "never-to-be-developed" countries' (quoted in Goldthorpe, 1984, p. 106). On the other hand, no less robust opinions can be found which dismiss such views, and stress the possibilities for global abundance. Although there is no space for a detailed rehearsal of all the arguments here, we shall follow Goldthorpe in breaking the issue down into four distinct areas: pollution, food, non-renewable resources, and energy.

That *pollution* is frequently a local problem is undeniable, especially in the early stages of any country's industrialization where there are often all too few controls on such 'externalities' as the dumping of wastes. For it to be a *global* problem involves further claims; e.g. that vast increases in energy consumption would alter the heat balance and the climate, or that cumulative discharge of wastes may irreversibly affect ecological cycles. There is no clear evidence yet, thankfully, for such global changes. Local problems, however, are unfortunately only too familiar, and require constant vigilance on the part of governments and pressure groups to prevent a given industry's 'external' costs being dumped on outsiders and future generations. Alas, in this business of 'fouling one's own nest' it is not infrequently governments themselves who are among the worst offenders.

Food is not strictly a matter of industrialization, but there are at least two important links. First, an increasingly industrialized globe needs to be fed. In the past there has been much alarm about this, as expressed in books with titles like *Famine 1975!* The fact this date has after all come and gone suggests, as Goldthorpe puts it, that the Malthusian spectre has receded. As discussed elsewhere in this book, the Green Revolution (whatever its economic and social implications) has *technically* solved the *global* food problem. Shortages that remain, however appalling (e.g. the 1984/5 famine in Ethiopia), are largely localized to one continent, Africa. Or is this too complacent? For the second issue here concern the *nature* of this agricultural success, itself highly 'industrialized' and based on resource-expensive fertilizers, which some critics maintain is exhausting the soil.

This leads into the question of non-renewable *resources*. (Even *renewable* resources, it should be noted, can be at risk: forests are being torn down as far apart as Indonesia and the Brazilian Amazon, and it is reckoned that each *minute* some 14 hectares of tropical rainforest are being lost to the world (Redclift, 1984, p. 26)). Mineral endowments, in contrast to agricultural, are literally finite. The issue is therefore threefold. First, at the moment new resources are still being discovered, but this process will obviously reach its limit eventually. Secondly, even used mineral resources are not lost. As Goldthorpe has said, all the iron that there ever was in the earth is still there; in other words, the process of recycling 'scrap' is likely to become relatively more economical. Thirdly, in this as in other aspects it is obviously prudent to seek where possible to develop new technologies, which minimize dependence on non-renewable resources.

Much the same applies to *energy*. In the most notorious case, oil, reaction to the OPEC price increases since 1973 has already led to many industrial processes becoming somewhat less oil-dependent. Other fossil fuels remain much more abundant: thus only 1–2% of available coal has yet been extracted. Nuclear energy is as yet expensive, and carries political and social risks. But the future for the Third World may well lie in developing wind, tidal and solar power, which are inexhaustible as long as the sun continues to be – although effective technologies for harnessing these scarcely exist as yet.

This brief review of ecological factors affecting industrialization should encourage neither alarmism nor complacency. Ecological issues were neglected for a long time, but the very publicity and awareness they now raise gives some hope of solutions being found.

Finally, in a sociological text it would be wrong not to make a brief comment on ecology as *social* theory. Ecological debates on both sides have been bedevilled by heavy doses of ideology. The fact that some of us in the West are feeling a certain disenchantment and boredom with our industrial civilization, from which we have gained so much, is hardly a good reason to deny its benefits to a Third World which has yet to experience this and may badly want to. Those in the West who want to go 'back to nature' are liable to forget, not only that this 'Nature' is not so much a reality as a cultural concept like any other, but also that many in the Third World would like nothing more than to get *away* from nature – or at least from being at its mercy in terms of food, shelter, and life-chances generally.

Conversely, ecological optimists often seem guilty of an arrogant complacency, as well as projecting from past 'success' to assume that nothing can ever run out or go radically wrong. Like everything else, these ecological issues turn out to be empirical questions, with no uniform or fixed answers. It is something that has to be watched.

Chapter Four

Urbanization

Definitions

Probably we all think we know what a town is, even more so a city. Nevertheless, as Hardiman and Midgley (1982) observe, there are a lot of problems of definition and comparison in this field. There is no single agreed usage for such terms as 'town', 'city', 'metropolis', etc. let alone for more theory-laden words like 'urbanism' and 'urbanization'. Four particular problems may be mentioned.

In the first place, different countries may use different and arbitrary measures of what's urban and what isn't, thus making cross-national comparisons of urbanization very hazardous. Secondly, even where a minimum figure is agreed for a settlement to count as urban, it is often too low, as the average size of *all* settlements continues to increase. Once, a population of 2000 might have served to distinguish an urban place. Today, it is more likely to mean a biggish village – yet this figure is still sometimes used as a threshold of urbanism. Thirdly, for obvious reasons, definitions of cities tend to be related to administrative boundaries. Yet this too can be sociologically misleading. With continued growth, cities tend to overspill their boundaries. Should we regard the eastern seaboards of the USA and Japan as a series of cities, or as each a gigantic sprawling megalopolis? Finally, whatever threshold you use there will be bumps and lumps in the figures, as rising populations continually entail the redefinition overnight of a 'village' of 19,999 into a town of 20,001.

Kingsley Davis (cited in Hardiman and Midgley, 1982, p. 126ff) has done more than most to try to bring statistical and conceptual order to this chaos. His suggested threshold definitions of 20,000 for an 'urban place' and 100,000 for a city are now widely used, e.g. by UN agencies.

133

Davis defines 'urbanization' as a growth in the proportion of the country's population living in cities. Thus cities can grow in size without urbanization occurring if the rural population increases at an even greater rate. This is an important point. In Europe urbanization developed rapidly due to massive rural-urban migration. In the Third World urbanization is much slower because rural populations continue to rise rapidly despite migration to the cities.

Urbanization Historically

There have been cities for at least 5000 years, in both what are now the developed and underdeveloped worlds. Some were very large. According to Goldthorpe (1984), Rome at the height of its power around 150 AD had about a million inhabitants, and presided over an empire some 10% of whose 100 million population were urbanized. Yet, by the 9th century, Rome itself had shrunk to a mere 20,000, and would not reach a million again until this century. This shows one difference between the pre-industrial and the modern city. The former quite often fluctuated in size, due to war or natural disaster. In the latter, by contrast, with rare exceptions (and apart from the process of suburbanization in the First World, itself arguably a form of further urbanization rather than a counter-trend) the movement is strictly one way: in and up, often at rapid rates.

Historically, like today, the biggest cities of all have often been in the Third World. China in the thirteenth century had several urban centres each with over a million inhabitants. Nonetheless, such pre-industrial cities typically still contained only a small percentage of their countries' total population. And, almost by definition, their function in the societies tended to be as commerical, administrative or military centres rather than any 'industrial' role.

England, the first industrial nation, was also the first to urbanize. An urban majority was reached as early as 1851, and fifty years later the UK was still the world's only predominantly urbanized society. The British figure peaked at over 80% in 1951, but according to Goldthorpe has fallen slightly since because of the rise of commuting. Hardiman and Midgley (1982) by contrast, quote a still higher figure of 91% urbanized for the UK in 1980: a discrepancy doubtless due to differences of definition as outlined in the previous section.

Facts and Figures

Urbanization as a global process is a product of the twentieth century, and indeed largely of the latter half of that century. As recently as 1960, only 20% of a world population of 3 billion lived in cities. Even this, however, reflected a massive increase (both absolutely, and in percentage terms) during the epoch of the Industrial Revolution. In 1800, only 1.7% of the world's 900 million people lived in cities; so a century and a half later, while the total population had increased three-fold, city-dwellers were almost *forty* times more numerous (up from 15 to 590 million approximately). Such is urbanization, in Davis' sense.

And urban growth continues apace. By 1980, 41% of the world's population was urban, meaning some 1,560 million people. During the 1970s, too, the numerical balance shifted to the Third World: so the 'typical' urbanite in our world lives not in the West but in the South. These processes will continue, such that a majority of *all* the world's people will be urban by the year 2000. Overall, between 1900 and 1975, while world population rose two and a half times (1,600 to 4,000 million), urban numbers multiplied no less than tenfold (150 to 1,500 million).

Distribution by continent remains uneven, however. As of 1980, both Asia and Africa had urban populations still under 30%. The African figure was slightly ahead of Asia's, and it is indeed in Africa that the world's fastest urban growth is currently taking place. However, because it starts from the lowest base-lines, this does not yet show up very much in overall size or percentages. Within Asia, there is much variation. Urbanization is highest in West and East Asia (the latter of course including two city-states, Hong Kong and Singapore), and lowest in South Asia. Latin America, by contrast was already 50% urbanized by 1960. The 1980 figure approaches 65%, and the projection for 2000 is 75% – virtually on a par with that in the North.

This higher Latin American urbanization reflects the cumulative effect of a high rate of natural increase within cities plus a good deal of continuing rural-urban migration. And it is worth mentioning that this continent contains the monster of them all: Mexico City, already esti-mated to have some 16 million people, and scheduled to rise by the end of the century to a staggering 25 million – i.e. more than most entire countries!

Third World Urbanization

As always, however, facts do not speak for themselves. It is time to begin to try to link all these figures to major analytical debates. And here, as ever, one of the main bones of contention between modern-ization and dependency approaches concerns 'recapitulation'. Is the Third World's urbanization following the pattern of the West's, such that we may accurately speak of a single global process?

There are a number of complex issues and factors here, and they are admirably summarized by Hardiman and Midgley (1982, p. 132ff). We might say that the South's urbanization, paradoxically, is both more and less than – but, in either case, significantly divergent from – the North's. On the one hand, the pace of urban growth in the Third World today is historically unprecedented, with rates of growth typically twice as fast as they were in late 19th century Europe. On the other hand, this rapid urban *growth* goes along with relatively *low* rates of urbanization (remember Davis' definition). The clue is that, because Third World *rural* populations are also increasing rapidly, the overall proportion of the population living in cities increases slowly compared to 19th century Europe.

Putting it another way, much (probably most) Third World urban growth is due more to natural increase than to migration. Davis notes that today's cities in LDCs have high fertility and low mortality, whereas in 19th century Europe both were high (hence rates of natural increase, as distinct from immigration, were relatively lower – at least at first). Muddying the waters, Todaro points out an 'interference' factor: high urban natural increase may itself be attributable to the age-structure of migrant populations, many of whom are young adults at the peak of their fertility. Besides, as mentioned above, some Third World urban 'growth' is simply statistical reclassification. The pitfalls are many.

Two major differences remain to be mentioned: one quantitative, the other qualitative. Third World cities tend to be fewer and bigger rather than many and smaller. A rather common extreme, arguably specific to the ex-colonial Third World, is what Linsky called the 'primate city': a single city (normally the capital), many times larger than the next biggest, and not infrequently containing a substantial percentage of an overall national population which may not itself be all that large.

Finally, and most notoriously, what makes Third World urbanization different is that (unlike in the West) it has often *not* been accompanied by industrialization. Rather than an expansion of classic industrial factory work, the cities of the South have instead come to feature massively swollen 'tertiary' or 'service' sectors, in which millions of people earn a precarious living in an astonishing variety of ways – relatively few of which, however, involve production, at least in any large scale context.

As we have seen there are contentious general issues here. Not a single Third World country is totally devoid of factories, and some have substantial urban industrial sectors. But in many countries this 'formal sector' seems relatively small by comparison: whether looking back to how it happened in Europe, or looking sideways to the much larger 'informal sector' which seems so distinctively to characterize the contemporary urban explosion in the Third World. Let us now examine this more closely.

The Informal Sector: What's in a Name?

The terms use to refer to some Third World urban dwellers have changed significantly. Two decades ago, when the sociological distinctiveness of these new Third World urbanites was first becoming clear, some referred to them as a 'lumpen-proletariat'. This Marxist term implies socially and politically unstable sections – beggars, hustlers, prostitutes, and so forth – marginal to mainstream economic life and without revolutionary potential. Others, like Fanon, reversed the politics of this view. It was the very marginality and indeed poverty of these, the 'wretched of the earth', which made them a 'revolutionary force', along with peasants, but *unlike* (contradicting Marx) the tiny proletariat proper, so small and privileged in the Third World as to constitute a 'labour aristocracy'.

Such sweeping visions tended to precede rather than follow empirical investigation. Admittedly, it was (and perhaps still is) understandable if observers have nightmares about just how Third World cities are going to cope with so many people, in the absence of widespread industrialization. But the evidence suggests both more stable social structures, a wider range of economic activities, and less radical politics than in the Fanonist vision. As a result, from the early 1970s a rather different and at first sight more neutral term, the 'informal sector', became prevalent – although this too has had its critics.

Bromley (1978) provides a useful ideal-type of this model of the urban economy, in terms of seven criteria. The *informal sector* is characterized by: ease of entry, indigenous resources, family ownership, small scale, labour-intensive or adapted technology, skills acquired outside the formal school system, and unregulated and often highly competitive markets. The *formal sector*, by contrast, is in each respect the opposite: difficult to get into, often using overseas resources, corporately owned, large scale, with capital-intensive and often imported technology, formally obtained (often expatriate) skills, and operating in highly protected quasi-monopolistic markets.

Such an approach has had the merit of encouraging both more research on the informal sector by academics, and a less negative attitude towards it by governments. For obvious reasons the informal sector tends not to show up in official statistics, and sometimes operates at or beyond the margins of legality. Hence the official mind tends to classify it as a problem, and sometimes to act accordingly – in rounding up or harassing street-vendors, in demolishing squatter settlements, expelling 'vagrants' back to the countryside, and so on. Against this, the International Labour Office in particular in a series of reports during the 1970s urged the merits of the informal sector, seeing it as more of a solution than a problem, providing goods and services to fill the gaps in the less flexible formal sector, and generally keeping people out of mischief.

Nevertheless, the term 'informal sector' itself has attracted increasing criticism. Once again Bromley (1978) provides a convenient summary. The model is too dualistic: we need more than just the two categories 'formal' and 'informal', probably a continuum. It also falsely implies separateness of the two sectors: it downplays their inter-action, and indeed the possible domination of one sector by another. This is important, because much field research suggests that in various ways the informal sector (directly or indirectly, and consciously or otherwise) is bound in with and serves the formal sector. For example, research carried out on a rubbish dump (literally!) in the Colombian city of Cali showed how waste paper collected by scavengers eventually found its way, through a series of middlemen, to one of the biggest paper mills in the country for recycling (Birkbeck in Bromley and Gerry, 1979).

Bromley is also worried about what the term 'informal sector' lumps together, and equally what it splits up or leaves out. In policy terms, the use of a single term might imply that a single government approach will do for diverse areas of the informal sector such as furniture, fireworks, foodstuffs, and prostitutes – which is unlikely. Related to this is a simplistic assumption that, if only policy makers will take heed, the informal sector will thrive and hence disappear as such (by becoming formal!). Analytically, meanwhile, the phrase confuses different sorts of units: neighbourhoods, households, individuals, activities, and enterprises. Only the last, says Bromley, are at all likely to be 'either/or' (formal or informal). All the rest are liable to be 'both . . . and', with much overlapping. And this goes along with the false equation of the informal sector as identical to the urban poor. In reality, not all the poor are in the informal sector, and by no means is everybody in the informal sector necessarily poor.

Finally, in this critique, there is what the term 'informal sector' leaves out. Two important things, according to Bromley. One is the countryside; where there are similar and indeed often linked activities (artisans, petty traders, etc.) – yet who in the rural context are often perversely regarded as 'traditional'. The other is the State: here, as so often in development studies, an implicit but unstated subject and key actor, which really ought to be painted in to complete the picture – even if it is also the painter.

If not 'informal sector', what else should we call it? Those concerned to apply Marxist economic categories (often going beyond, or even against, dependency theory in order to work out the empirical micro-implications) have lately used terms such as *petty commodity producer* in both urban and rural contexts – in the latter case preferring this term to the analytically vague word 'peasants'. A broader-based term is offered by Bromley and Gerry, namely *'casual work'*. They define this as 'any way of making a living which lacks a moderate degree of security of income and employment', whether productive or not, working for oneself or others, legally or otherwise.

One advantage of this term is that it can cope with the range of *forms* of employment found in Third World cities, to which the contrast of wage labour 'versus' self-employment does scant justice. Such inter-mediate forms include: short-term or 'casual' waged work (by the day, week, month, or season); 'disguised' wage-work (e.g. out-work, or commission sellers); and 'dependent' work (dependent, that is, on larger, 'formal' enterprises for anything from credit and materials to premises and sales outlets).

Even so, I dare say that despite its theoretical shortcomings the term 'informal sector' (rather like the equally criticized term 'underdevelopment' itself) will survive. The real point, as always, is to be aware of the different analytical issues that arise from this empirically and concep-tually complex yet fascinating area.

Housing and Settlements: Slums of Hope?

The previous section focussed on aspects of *work*; and we noted that it was wrong to equate this sector with others, such as housing, in the rather blurry way that a term like 'informal sector' might imply. So having looked at work in its own right, we must now do the same for housing and settlement.

Everyone has seen pictures of shanty-towns: barrios, favelas, bidon-villes, bustees – the names are as numerous as the countries where they exist, which in effect means virtually the entire Third World. And there is, of course, substantial overlap with the informal sector. Many millions who have no regular job, equally have no 'regular' housing; for both work and shelter they fend for themselves. Yet in both spheres of life, the result is social structures both more organized and systematic than the chaotic randomness which may be the observer's first impression.

One problem, however, is that in few areas of the sociology of development are approaches quite so coloured by the observer's biasses. As Hardiman and Midgley (1982) note, sociology as a discipline tends to have anti-urban prejudices in any case, at least in its implicit nostalgia for alleged lost 'community'. So it was predictable that many, whether from a modernization or dependency perspective, should hasten to categorize Third World slums under the heading of social pathology. Phrases like Oscar Lewis' famous 'culture of poverty' may have different explanatory force from the preferred dependency term 'marginality', in that (to oversimplify) the former blames the victim while the latter blames the system. Yet both share an implicitly negative attitude: this is a social problem.

Against this view, John Turner maintains that 'the slum is not a problem . . . but a viable solution to the problems of rapid urbanization' (Hardiman and Midgley, 1982, p. 143). Philosophically Turner is an anarchist, which at least lets in a bit of ideological fresh air. 'Spontaneous settlements' – a more neutral term than 'slums' – do a job: they offer cheap accommodation, provide access to employment, and generally give the new migrant a foothold in the city. What's more, by definition these are settlements in which people do their own thing rather than have things done to them (whether for or against them). Turner is all for self-help, both as individual and collective action. Thus, to take an actual example from Ecuador, squatters might set up house right on a city garbage dump where they work, and then petition the municipal authorities to provide such services as standpipes and electricity.

Turner's views are controversial, and all the issues are complex. It's hard not to sympathize with Lloyd's (1979) view that the notion of 'marginality' is vague to the point of uselessness, if (say) up to 75% of the urban population are to be classed as 'marginal'! As for the 'culture of poverty', one can make two points. Empirical variation is likely: some slums may be as Oscar Lewis described in Puerto Rico, while others seem preoccupied with self-improvement. Besides, it isn't a point of culture 'versus' structure: they may well be interdependent.

There is also empirical evidence that many slum dwellers are neither disorganized, apathetic, or even especially radical. Voluntary associations (often ethnic-based) to help new migrants on arrival in the city have a long history all over the Third World. And the desire to 'get on', even in appalling material circumstances, seems often as powerful as that for radical change. But generalizations are hazardous. In a sense the Third World slum, like the informal sector, is *both* a problem *and* a solution. Stressing the often amazing resourcefulness of the people and communities involved is helpful, insofar as it checks governments from having a jaundiced and hostile attitude – especially if, as so often, the State has nothing positive to offer once it has bulldozed the shanties or driven the hawkers off the streets (probably they'll both be back in the morning). And yet to praise people's resourcefulness must not entail complacency about their adversity, such that the government feels let off the hook. Ultimately, and despite the formidable difficulties, the resources and planning necessary to provide even a halfway decent urban environment – be it for housing, work, travel, or whatever – can only come from the state.

Internal Migration and Social Classes

Movement by individuals or households between countries – *inter-national* migration – is a major factor of modern society, as the ethnic profile of the postwar UK illustrates. Still more widespread, and arguably more fundamental, is *internal* migration: movement within national boundaries, almost always meaning from country to town. Although in industrialized countries this has virtually ceased as a systematic social process, it was of great historical importance in its time. In the Third World today, notwithstanding that much urban growth arises from natural increase rather than migration, the latter is a major social movement – literally! – and has been extensively studied. We want to know who migrates, how, and why, and with what consequences (for themselves, and for society as a whole).

Inevitably over-generalizing; migrants tend to be young unmarried adults. Mostly, they are male; and even if they are not (as in Latin America), men tend to migrate before women. Some studies have found that migrants have above-average education levels, or that they come from middle-income groups, rather than the very poorest or richest. Reasons for migration can involve all sorts of combinations of 'push' and 'pull'. We in the West tend to romanticize the countryside, but many in the Third World have good reason to try to get away from land scarcity, poverty, underemployment, a general lack of opportunities, or in extreme cases famine or violence. On the other side of the coin, despite the risks of urban life, people are lured by the possibilities which it offers, at least in principle and for some: better education, health, social services, living standards; perhaps a job, at all events some way of making ends meet. And, vaguer but just as real: the lure of the bright lights, the excitement (however enervating) of modernity, its open-endedness compared with what Marx witheringly called 'the idiocy of rural life'.

So they come. *How* they come is interesting, and seems to indicate differences from as well as similarities to the 'same' processes in the West. The main difference can best be summarized in Marxist terms. Unlike in the West, proletarianization in the Third World is far from complete, and shows every sign of remaining that way. People do not lose their links with the land entirely, or only very slowly. Individuals and especially households pursue complex strategies and create intricate patterns, to the despair of those who would like to find classes in neat clear-cut boxes. Sometimes there is *step* migration: first to a local small town, then on to a larger city. Sometimes there is *seasonal* migration, by the year or shorter and longer periods. Importantly, not all migration is rural-urban (or the return flows). Intra-rural migration is becoming more common. People have long gone to work for plantations; now they go to work for agri-businesses, and a country like Mexico has been described as having vast seasonal armies of millions of migrant labourers, roaming the countryside in search of employment.

The links to theory are interesting here, and may be worth spelling out. To describe what is going on at a macro-level, the appropriate broad categories seem to me to be Marxist ones like proletarianization (or lack of it) and accumulation. Nevertheless, the sheer complexity (empirical and analytical) of the *actual* social relations involved poses great challenges for a Marxist approach. To find definite classes, or even classes definitely in formation, let alone to impute particular forms of political consciousness and predict particular kinds of political action – all this is hazardous, and certainly can't be done from first principles. Rather, one must first go out and look.

Chapter Five

Rural Development

Facts and Figures

Despite growing urbanization, the great majority of the Third World's population – over 2 billion people – still lives in the countryside. Moreover, despite rural-urban migration, this figure is increasing in *absolute* terms by an average of some 2% p.a., even while the relative proportion of rural inhabitants in total population declines. By continent, only in Latin America are rural dwellers a minority, outnumbered in 1985 by an estimated 2:1. Yet even here their *numbers* are increasing in almost all countries. In Africa and Asia, by contrast, the proportions are more or less reversed, with some 70% of the population still rural. (Needless to say, these are averages; figures for individual countries may differ widely.)

While we in the West tend to sentimentalize the countryside, in the Third World rural life often means poverty. Almost three quarters of the global poor (550 mn out of 750 mn) live in rural areas (Hardiman and Midgley, 1982). Another striking statistic of global difference concerns *agricultural productivity*, especially in relation to food. A single farmer in the USA feeds, on average, 65 people. In some parts of the Third World (especially Africa) by contrast, even countries which are overwhelmingly agrarian (i.e. agriculture is almost all there is, or all that anybody does) cannot feed themselves. In fact, according to Adamson (1984) the nature of the global food problem is often misunderstood. For one thing, there isn't a *global* food problem. World grain production reached record levels in 1984; it grew by 7% as against 1983, while population grew 2%. Each of us needs the equivalent of some 250 kg of grain per year; the 1984 harvest yielded 50% *more* than this, for every person in the world.

143

The catch, of course, lies in the *distribution* and *use* of the grains grown. Europe and North America between them produced enough to feed the entire world. Asia and Latin America produced enough to feed themselves; Africa, however, only produced 50% of its grain needs. And where did the North's surplus in fact go? A breakdown of the US figure reveals that 13% was eaten directly, 27% was sold commercially overseas, while 20% went to replanting and storing (the latter contributing to pile yet higher the infamous 'mountains' of food surplus possessed by both the USA and the EEC). I have left till last the largest and smallest figures. 40% of US grain went for cattle feed. And just 0.5% went as aid to the hungry.

Even so, Adamson argues against the popular myth that half the world's population is starving. On the contrary, the proportion of those who are *overfed* (2%) is greater than those visibly under-nourished (less than 1% – although this still represents tens of millions of hungry human beings). Some 90% of the world's population are at least tolerably well fed. But that still leaves 10%, or over 450 million, who are not.

Variations by Region

As Hardiman and Midgley note (1982, p.102 ff), patterns of access to and control over land vary widely from place to place. *Latin America* exhibits an extraordinary range of scales and types of land ownership and tenure. Very large and often inefficient *latifundia*, large estates where social relations may be seemingly feudal (although the aptness of this term is hotly controversial), exist alongside and dominate tiny *minifundia* (very small family farms). Land and labour productivity is low, technology is poor, and large numbers of small producers are in practice dependent on their landlord – whether providing unpaid labour, or as sharecroppers (handing over a portion of the crop), but in either case lacking basic security of tenure. Alongside this there also exist more modern and better capitalized farms, both family-sized and larger.

The *Asian* picture is significantly different. Although land concentration is high (i.e. smallholdings being grouped together in larger units), what counts as a 'large' unit is much smaller than in Latin America. Population density is much greater, making land scarcity the critical problem (unlike in Latin America or Africa, where 'colonization' in the geographers' sense – i.e. bringing new land under cultivation – is still a widely available option). Absentee landlords are numerous, and resulting tenancy and sharecropping arrangements are at once onerous but also more 'decentralized' than in Latin America. Technology and hence land and labour productivity is poor, while production is labour-intensive and more for subsistence than export. Rural poverty is a major problem, especially in South Asia, as illustrated in the rise of moneylenders and the often permanent indebtedness of very many people.

One reason for the severity of Asia's problems is the breakdown of traditional agrarian relations under the impact of the colonial introduction of private property in land. In *Africa*, by contrast, precapitalist forms of customary tenure are still found to some extent. This (plus low population density) has helped prevent land concentration and inequality on the scale experienced elsewhere in the Third World. On the other hand, productivity and technology alike are very low. Much, probably most African agriculture still revolves around humans wielding hoes, rather than oxen drawing ploughs – let alone tractors. There is still much shifting cultivation (so-called 'slash and burn'). And ironically, although subsistence agriculture still predominates, it is Africa alone of the Third World's continents which for the most part is chronically (and increasingly) unable to feed itself; as witness the famines of the Sahel and, more recently, Ethiopia.

Rural Communities: an Ideal-type?

Modernization and dependency theorists are apt to disagree dramatically about how we should conceptualize rural communities in the Third World today. For the former, tradition still largely holds sway, obstacles to progress are internal, and cultural characteristics are particularly problematical. For the latter, by contrast, the main problem is the 'modern' (but non-beneficial) externally imposed economic constraints of capitalism.

Hardiman and Midgley (1982) to some extent try to have it both ways. They begin by constructing a sort of Weberian 'ideal-type'. Rural communities are *small-scale* societies, often not very densely populated, in which face-to-face interaction looms large, yet the scope of individuality is limited. Family and *kinship* are omnipresent and multifunctional: rather than being just one sphere of life among others (and a declining one at that), kinship permeates and links all aspects of society – economic, political, juridical, religious, and social welfare. *Territory* is important both instrumentally and symbolically. *Means of production* are technically simple; and the *division of labour* is based principally on age and sex. Methods of cultivation are traditional, hence *labour-intensive*, depending mainly on inputs of human energy.

The primary goal of production is *subsistence*; any cash crops are secondary, and self-sufficiency is the goal. Culturally, *ritual* is important: a harsh environment breeds a sense of being at the mercy of nature, fatalism, superstition, and supernaturalism – albeit not necessarily excluding scientific beliefs and practices. Finally, economic self-sufficiency has its political and 'jural' counterparts, inasmuch as traditional communities have little *separation of spheres* between (e.g.) executive, legislative and judicial realms.

Hardiman and Midgley go on to add qualifications to this picture. They stress that such 'communities' were not and are not homogeneous, consensual and static, but rather experience differentiation and conflicts – even before the impact of 'social change'. Nonetheless, I think there are real pitfalls in setting up the problem in this way. The most obvious risk is *over-generalization*. Some of these characteristics, especially the first and last, might fit pre-colonial Africa – but would scarcely do for the civilizations of East and South Asia, densely populated and long since linked to a wider state. Secondly, the content of this ideal-type is heavily *Durkheimian*: tradition is implicitly equated with simplicity, diffuseness, and lack of differentiation. Yet much anthropological evidence has brought out the intricacy and complexity of social relations, even in small-scale societies with low levels of technology.

Above all, as with any attempts to construct the 'traditional', what is in question is its precise resemblance to the Third World *today*. Rather like those anthropologists who began with the notion of 'tribe', and then found that with urban migration they had a self-inflicted conceptual problem of 'detribalization', it is perhaps an unwise procedure to begin with a supposed pre-existent reality and only later introduce 'change' from the outside. Granted, that may be the way it actually happened. But surely what we need to do today is to analyse the actual complex and mixed social forms we find in the rural Third World, in terms of their own dynamics and reproduction. True, Hardiman and Midgley go on to look at how this earlier ideal-type is eroded by such trends as the effects of labour migration, the penetration of a cash economy, the spread of urban values, and a general increase in the number, intensity and variety of the links which tie the small community to wider national and indeed international contexts. But the very determining power of those ties inspires the methodological thought that perhaps then this would have been the place to start an analysis of present-day rural realities, rather than bring it in later.

Rural Change, Colonial and Since

By way of contrast, Johnson (1983) adopts an approach which emphasises the drastic degrees of transformation which Third World rural social structures have long since undergone, both under the impact of colonialism and subsequently. In general, colonialism profoundly affected what was grown, who was to grow it, and how. The introduction of the Western concept of *private property* in land often had a revolutionary effect (as Marx noted for India), transforming old social relations and creating new ones. Money *taxation* (by head or hut) had scarcely less drastic effects; including *labour migration* to various sources of employment (rural plantations, mines, or towns). Alternatively, the spread of commercialized *markets* sometimes presented itself to more fortunate peasants as opportunity rather than compulsion, such that they began producing *food* for these other sectors (plantations, mines, towns). More than this, some peasants began growing *cash crops*; which often brought them into competition with the large-scale *plantations* created for this purpose by colonialism.

Most of these trends continue today. The commercialization of small-scale agriculture, in particular, has a number of effects. Staple foods are increasingly being displaced by *commercial crops*; including 'luxury' grains, like wheat and (in some cases) rice, which may not meet the foods needs of those who grow them. *Land concentration* in fewer holdings means that large numbers are being *displaced* from the land, hence peasant producers are becoming more differentiated, i.e. some are becoming wealthy farmers, others poor farm labourers. The effects on *labour* are contradictory: an increasingly large agricultural *proletariat* may be simultaneously being augmented by peasants made landless and displaced by mechanization.

Johnson notes elements of persistence as well as the changes mentioned above. Many peasants still use very basic technologies and stick to well-tried practices. (So-called peasant 'conservatism' reflects the fact that, for poor small-scale producers, any innovation carries enormous risks.) Much agricultural production is still carried on by households using family labour. Most of them still produce their own food, over and above any cash crops. And there still survive, often on a large scale, such seemingly 'pre-capitalist' forms of land ownership and labour use as share-cropping and debt bondage.

This account by Johnson could be criticized as overly *economistic* (although, to be fair, her brief was to write a text unit on production). Nonetheless, I think this approach has two sociological merits. First, the sorts of things she focusses on, whether or not they 'determine' other aspects of existence, certainly form the essential framework or context within which rural Third World people must live – and over much of which they have little control. As such, this seems a sensible place to start from. Secondly, you may have noticed that almost all the factors Johnson mentions are *processes*, rather than *states*. Instead of the unavoidably static construction of ideal-types, which then (so to speak) have to be jump-started into life from some outside force, this places movement and change at the centre of the analysis – which is as it should be.

Peasants

There is no general agreement about what constitutes a peasant. It has been said that 'peasants are the majority of mankind' (Shanin, 1971, p. 238). This implies that over vast reaches of place and time, through an immense variety of cultures and social structures, hundreds of millions of people have enough in common to justify the use of a singular term to describe them. For one thing, as the root of the word implies, peasants live in the countryside. Yet it is not as simple as that, in several ways. Not all peasants live in the countryside; Bryan Roberts (1978) entitled his book on Third World urbanization: *Cities of Peasants*. (The *migration* which this refers to is discussed in a separate section.) And not all rural dwellers are peasants. Some may be agricultural labourers. Some may be 'communal cultivators', and not yet peasants (we shall return to this below). And yet others, importantly, may be landlords.

So peasants don't usually (perhaps ever) occupy the countryside alone. In fact we might say that peasants are rural dwellers with two crucial linked qualifications: (1) they are in some form of subordinate class/status relation to others; (2) they form part of some wider social/political/economic structure. We could call these *vertical* and *horizontal* linkages, respectively.

In terms of the vertical linkage, we might treat the landlord-peasant relationship as an earlier rural version of bourgeoisie and proletariat, rather as we saw Barrington Moore (1966) did. Like bourgeoisie/proletariat, landlord/peasant is of course an oversimplification of real situations which are both more complex and in motion. Complexity consists in (1) *sub-divisions* (e.g. rich/middle/poor peasant, discussed below); (2) *intermediate groups* (e.g. rich peasants or 'Kulaks', on the ascent to becoming capitalist farmers: an example which also illustrates *motion*) and (3) *mixed forms*, often much more confusing in rural than in urban areas due to the incomplete nature of proletarianization. Gunder Frank (1969a, pp. 271–2) has put this well, referring to the likelihood of: 'a single worker who is simultaneously (i) *owner* of his own land and house, (ii) *sharecropper* on another's land . . . , (iii) *tenant* on a third's land, (iv) *wage worker* during harvest time on one of these lands, and (v) independent *trader* of his own home produced commodities.' (emphases added.) To 'his', one should add 'hers': for women are fully involved here too, and once you start considering *household* strategies the picture becomes yet more tangled – with wives and husbands, daughters and sons all often doing different things, not infrequently in different places.

However, unlike the bourgeois/proletarian relation (at least in its Marxist form), to speak of a landlord/peasant relation does not necessarily imply any particular theory of exploitation. There can be several types of linkages. We can consider them (like many social phenomena) under three headings, separable conceptually but empirically linked: economic, political and cultural.

There is bound to be an *economic* relation of some kind. In Marxist terms, surplus can be transferred in a variety of ways, typically *not* full wage labour (else we should speak not of peasants, but of farm labourers). These include *sharecropping*, giving up a share of the crop to the landlord (on whose land it has probably been grown); and/or various forms of unpaid *labour service* of a 'feudal' nature. Marx of course speaks of a 'feudal' mode of production, but not a peasant one; hence some Marxists criticize the term 'peasant' as being loose, unscientific, and merely descriptive.

At all events, the lord/peasant relation is typically not economic alone. *Politically*, Marxists stress the non-economic coercion inherent in feudalism. *Culturally*, this is often viewed (by all concerned) as a system of mutual dependence, with rights and responsibilities on both sides; even if to the outsider it looks profoundly unequal. More generally, those who claim that there *is* an entity called peasants who do have something in common often locate that something in the cultural realm. Peasant culture is characterized as wary, fatalistic, deferential, and having a particular view of the 'order of things'.

Yet the 'vertical' links discussed hitherto may not exhaust the topic. In large parts of contemporary Africa, for instance, one might want to use the term 'peasants' even in contexts where no 'feudal' or other landlord class – least of all a traditional one – is necessarily in evidence. A century ago, however, 'peasant' might not have been the right word to use. In order to see why, let us now examine what I have called the 'horizontal' dimension of peasantry. This aspect has been summarized by Kroeber and Redfield, who define peasants as 'a part society with part culture' (quoted in Shanin, 1971, p. 245). And Redfield adds: 'there is no peasantry before the first city' (*ibid* p. 255).

Like the 'vertical', such horizontal linkages to a wider world can be seen as having economic, political and cultural dimensions. *Economically*, peasants are likely to be involved at least to some degree in *markets*, and producing for markets, whether they sell directly or deal through merchants or middlemen. In *politics*, too, there may be middlemen; indeed, it is a classic theme of the political sociology of the Third World how often politics takes a 'clientelist' or 'brokerage' form – a fact usually attributed to peasants' political tendencies. More broadly, peasants are at least in some sense members of (albeit often substantially excluded from participating in) a wider political order, i.e. an empire or nation-state. If nothing else, they are liable to be drafted into the military: most Third World armies are largely composed of peasant conscripts. *Culturally*, according to Redfield (cited in Shanin, 1971, p. 337 ff), peasants have a folk culture or 'Little Tradition' which stands in contrast to (although historically in some instances it is transformed into) the kind of 'Great Tradition' typical of city civilization.

Peasantization

After this necessary detour, you can probably see why the term 'peasant' might *not* have been applicable a century ago to large swathes of Africa, where not only vertical but also these kinds of horizontal linkages scarcely yet existed. Ken Post (1977) has usefully formalized the distinctions between traditional or tribal 'communal cultivators', and the peasants whom they gradually become. *Land ownership* is originally communal (although its *use* may be individual), but becomes individual; indeed, the notion of *ownership* may appear for the first time. Both the social *division of labour*, and *political* hierarchy and obligations, are inseparable from kinship; but with 'peasantization' they each become increasingly autonomous spheres. *Markets* were absent or peripheral, but become increasingly central. And *culture*, once largely homogenous, becomes separated into Redfield's 'great' and 'little traditions'.

Note that Post's contrasting ideal-types represent an actual historical process, which he calls '*peasantization*'. The word is both ugly and surprising yet the idea is essential. We perhaps tend to think of peasants as the ones who were always there in the first place, and whom history tends to bundle more or less unceremoniously off the historical stage as modernization and industrialization take hold. Such an approach may do for Europe, but for much of the Third World (especially Africa) the *creation* of peasantries is a relatively recent and even continuing process. Moreover, in a contradictory compression of what in Europe were separate and successive process, peasantization and proletarianization may be taking place side by side. Palmer and Parsons (1977, p. 2) put this point well, in summarizing the pioneering contribution of Giovanni Arrighi's (1967) work on Rhodesia (now Zimbabwe): 'Arrighi brought out the historical contradictions inherent in capitalist development, first stimulating the growth of a peasantry to supply its food-stuffs, and then proceeding to break up that peasantry in order to obtain its labour'.

Proper Peasants?

Drawing some of the threads together, Shanin (1971, pp. 14–15) suggests a four-part 'ideal type' of peasants. The *family farm* is the basic unit of socialization, involving just about everything: labour, consumption, property, socialization, sociability, and welfare. Secondly, *land husbandry* is the major means of livelihood, directly providing for most consumption needs, at a low level of specialization and technology. Then there is the specific *culture* of small rural communities, stressing tradition and conformism. Finally, there is the peasantry as *underdog*, dominated by outsiders: yet whose linked economic, political and cultural subordination does not prevent them sometimes turning into 'the revolutionary proletariat of our times' (p. 15).

Not everyone would agree with this characterization. In general, Weber's 'ideal type' approach (of which the above is a good example) does not command universal assent. More specifically, Marxists who emphasize relations of production as basic would find more differences than commonality in all of the above. In particular, they would direct attention to the specific relations of particular groups of producers with emerging capitalism; and would probably predict growing class differentiation and polarization among 'peasants', thus eroding whatever homogeneity may once have existed.

Shanin himself insists that 'like every social entity, peasantry exists only as a process, i.e. in its change' (1971, p. 17). What is at issue, though, is what the processes are. The major controversy surrounds the first of Shanin's four points, namely the nature of the *family farm* and its dynamics. Shanin, following the Russian 'populist' agronomist Chayanov (cf. Shanin, 1971, pp. 150–9), regards peasant economy as a distinct type with its own logic, which for complicated reasons has no necessary inbuilt tendency to polarize into separate capitalist classes. This view was opposed in theory by Lenin and in practice by Stalin, with his brutally enforced collectivization of the Soviet peasantry.

While there is probably no single general answer to this question, my own sympathies are more with Shanin. An over-economistic Marxism tends to neglect cultural variables (e.g. the persistence of kinship ties) in its analysis; while in practice it is too hasty in finding 'classes', presuming their interests to be mortally opposed (e.g. rich 'versus' poor peasants), and taking action accordingly. As a result, communist regimes – even those whose revolutions were largely won with peasant support, ironically and tragically – have often pursued wrongheaded or harsh policies with a detrimental effect on both peasant economic output and political support.

Nonetheless, capitalist development in the long run is likely to erode the peasantry. Just how long that run can be, however, is illustrated by France, whose peasantry remains numerous and politically vocal – although it may be a moot point whether family farms possessing tractors, combines, and colour TV are still strictly 'peasant'.

Peasants and Politics

One major controversy over peasants concerns their politics, about which there exist diametrically opposed views. Some (including Marx) saw them as inherently conservative because of their conditions of life, which put caution at a premium and discouraged collective action. Yet, as Eric Wolf (in Shanin, 1971, p. 264) points out, 'six major social and political upheavals, fought with peasant support, have shaken the world of the twentieth century' – in Mexico, Russia, China, Vietnam, Algeria, and Cuba. Indeed, it looks at first sight as if peasants have been doing what Marx thought was the proletariat's job.

Although the issues are complex and each case is different, Wolf suggests that normal peasant passivity has in this century been challenged by three crises: demographic, ecological, and 'power and authority'. Importantly, peasants often see themselves as acting in self-defence, standing up for an old order against the encroachments of (e.g.) large-scale commercial agriculture. John Womack (1972), in his book on Zapata and Mexico, captures this aspect brilliantly. His book begins (p. 14): 'This is a book about country people who did not want to move and therefore got into a revolution. They did not figure on so odd a fate'.

Wolf makes the further point that the key force in such processes is neither the richer peasants who usually have a stake in the status quo, nor the poorest who lack land and hence tactical power, but the 'middle' peasants. It is they who may have both the reasons and resources to resist, and hence find themselves (albeit usually with outside support) making a revolution.

The 'Green Revolution'

In a number of Third World countries, especially in Asia and Latin America, increased crop yields made possible by scientific break-throughs have brought about dramatic changes in agriculture. There are in fact two good reasons for scrutinizing this 'Green Revolution' (as it has come to be known) in a sociological text: not only for its empirical importance, but also because it provides an object lesson in the inter-relation between technical and social factors.

Byres and Crow (1983) have studied the Green Revolution in India, and I largely draw on their account in what follows. As they say (p. 6), ' "Green Revolution" is a slogan which adhered retrospectively to a particular technocratic approach to agrarian change'. What does this imply? In principle, there are a number of ways of boosting agricultural production: increasing crop yields, extending acreage, or having more crops per year. And any of these could in principle be approached in different ways. One could alter the *technical* conditions of production: either *biochemically* (improved strains of seed, fertilizer, pesticide, etc.), or *mechanically* (more machinery, e.g. tractors and combines). Alternatively, and perhaps less obviously, changing the *social* conditions of production may also bring about increased production: paying farmers more for their crop, giving security of tenure, or re-distributing land to the landless.

So it is a complex picture, in which there are both interrelations and choices. To dramatize the choice somewhat, the Green Revolution may be seen by governments as the only alternative to a red one. In situations where land shortages and rural inequalities not only caused discontent but placed limits on increasing food production for city and country alike, technical breakthroughs in developing high yielding varieties of grains such as wheat and rice came as something of a godsend, potentially staving off food crises and social unrest – and avoiding the need for any serious and systematic land reform.

However, this 'technical' solution has not in practice proved to be socially neutral. Abundant research evidence shows that the full benefit of high yielding varieties (HYVs) only goes to those well placed to take advantage of them. Without going into all the details, the key link here is in a broad sense 'mechanical'. HYVs need irrigation, which means tubewells, which cost money. The time constraints of multiple cropping favour those who can afford to mechanize harvesting. And, at least in India, the whole new technological 'package' was heavily commercialized: seed (formerly saved from last year's crop) must now be purchased, along with the fertilizers and pesticides without which HYVs would hardly thrive.

So who benefits? At one level, the Indian state and nation as a whole. For the Green Revolution has solved or at least staved off India's chronic food crisis: an achievement which, compared with the position twenty years ago, should not be under-estimated. Yet a more detailed scrutiny shows that the gains are in many ways uneven: accruing principally to particular crops, in specific favoured areas, and to some social classes more than others. The Green Revolution is a *wheat* revolution (or, in other countries, a rice revolution). It has boosted production of the cash crop sold to cities, but not of the millet and maize which the rural poor themselves eat; and it has elbowed out the lentils and pulses which helped balance rural diets. By region, it is over-whelmingly the well-watered plains of the Punjab which have become the granary for the rest of India. This has two consequences. Not only is rural life not improved for most Indians; but the Punjab's increasing sense of its own advance and importance is undoubtedly one factor in fuelling separatist political demands, the suppression of which led to Mrs. Gandhi's assassination in 1984.

Specific crops and regions aside, the *class* effects of the Green Revolution are particularly interesting. For, although it is a strategy which involved 'betting on the strong', it has not exactly strengthened the status quo. On the contrary, whereas until the 1950s the landlord class was dominant, it is the *rich peasants* who have gained most from the Green Revolution and 'emerged as masters of the Indian country-side' (Byres and Crow, 1983, p. 47). It was they who had both the incentive and the resources – including, importantly, *access* to institutional credit as much as actual pre-existing wealth – to benefit most.

What of the others? The effects are complex, but those less well placed lose out in various ways. Poorer peasants increasingly lease their land to those richer (who can take advantage of economies of scale). Sharecroppers become in fact or in effect wage labourers, as mechanizing landlords now need their labour less than they want back the land that the sharecroppers occupy. There is growing landlessness (albeit slowly, so far); growing proletarianization (albeit incomplete: labour is still often 'attached' via loan-debts and other forms of personal dependence); and, in particular, a big increase in migrant labour (as Hindu migrants from Bihar, say, travel across India to work on Sikh farms in the Punjab; again, a factor not unrelated to recent communal tensions).

In this account I have focussed on the Indian case, following Byres and Crow (1983). Elsewhere, the details might be different. Other interpretations are possible too. In fact, the Green Revolution literature is often rather polarized in predictable ways. Modernization theorists portray it as a more or less unproblematic success story, in which 'science rules OK'; whereas some dependency approaches leave you with the impression that nothing has changed at all, or only for the worse. I hope the above section has shown how and why both these views are inadequate. Change there has certainly been, both economic and social. But, not unusually, it has benefitted different interests unequally. And if, as seems plausible, the long-term effect is increasing inequality in the countryside, one may wonder whether the technical solution afforded by the Green Revolution will for all time stave off demands for revolution of a different hue – or, at least, for some alterations in the social conditions of production as well.

Peasants in Hyden

The Swedish political scientist Goran Hyden (1980) has written a fascinating book to try to explain why Tanzania has had such uneven success in implementing *ujamaa* socialism, increasing agricultural output, or indeed effecting any kind of rural change. In Tanzania, as in much of Africa, the subsistence-oriented 'peasant mode of production' is particularly resilient. The 'economy of affection' (familial and communal ties) still looms large. Moreover, rainfed agriculture and low population density meant there was no pressure for either cooperation or state-sponsored irrigation to develop, as happened in parts of Asia. The result is that output and productivity levels are very low.

Enter the State. According to Hyden (1980, p. 9) 'economic history is largely the story of how to capture the peasants'. Only in Africa has this still not widely happened yet, as peasantries with their own means of production cling to their independence and tenaciously resist the state's efforts to get a handle on them; even, ironically, in an at least arguably well-meaning socialist state like Tanzania, stressing the African cooperative traditions of *ujamaa*.

What ensues is a game of cat and mouse, delightfully illustrated in the successive chapter titles of Hyden's book. Small is powerful; small rebuffs modern and big; big slips on small; small goes into hiding; small the deceitful; small as infiltrator; the pervasiveness of small; is small really beautiful?; why small remains unexplored. The sly strength of peasantries in evading, resisting and when all else fails infiltrating and subverting state institutions and policies is made very clear. (In fact, Hyden remarks, it is easier for the State to control foreign capital, even, than the peasants!)

Theoretically, Hyden draws on both mainstream and Marxist approaches. He portrays capitalist and precapitalist modes of production in an uneasy kind of symbiosis, with the former in some circumstances strengthening the latter rather than undermining it. He sees the principal barriers to increased production as internal; if anything, capitalism has not exploited the Third World enough. And, like modernization theorists, he insists that peasant institutions and values will have to change.

This last point is crucial. For Hyden does *not* say that small is beautiful; in fact he explicitly queries it. Wherever his sympathies lie, the logic of history and development alike dictate that one way or another, sooner or later, states must take their agriculture in hand and turn it into a modern, efficient, productive sector, guaranteeing a surplus to both feed and invest in urban and industrial development – which in turn will benefit agriculture. One may hope that this will be done *with* the peasants, rather than against them; not only on humanitarian grounds, but also realistically because of their considerable ability to sabotage any programmes and policies which they disapprove of. But, one way or another, it must be done.

Transformation or Improvement?

There is widespread agreement that over much of the Third World existing agrarian relations are unsatisfactory, whether from the view-point of economic efficiency ('delivering the goods', in the form of cash crops or food self-reliance) or social justice. There is much less consensus, however, about what can or should be done about this – and by whom.

It is conventional and convenient to distinguish, as Long (1977, p. 144) does, two basic approaches to changing agriculture. The *improvement* approach seeks to work with and within existing systems of peasant production, in order to make them work better. The *transformation* system, by contrast, aims to make a complete break and establish new organizational forms for agriculture. The former can include the provision of various types of inputs and assistance to existing communities, either singly or in 'packages' such as community development programmes. The latter includes a wide range of different kinds of initiative: plantations, state farms, settlement schemes, land redistribution and reform, or revolutionary measures such as the Chinese commune.

As may be readily seen, 'transformation' in this sense is not only varied but has been going on in the Third World for quite some time already. Long (1977, p. 144) describes it as involving 'a radical break with existing peasant systems in terms of scale of operation, production techniques, and socio-legal structure'. Each of those three points would apply to a capitalist plantation producing sisal in colonial Tanganyika, for instance, as much as to a collective farm in the USSR. So we should be careful to distinguish these three dimensions of *scale, technology,* and *ownership* when trying to assess the arguments for and against the two approaches.

Critics of peasant agriculture suggest that it is inherently unsuited for adaptation to the needs of a modern state. Being principally concerned with subsistence and self-sufficiency, peasants lack the incentive or initiative either to adopt modern technology, or to expand their operations up to a level where they can begin to reap economies of scale. One reason for this is that they tend to see land as more than just a commodity to be bought and sold, and indeed their whole way of life as more than just a question of production inputs and outputs. This sentimental peasant attachment to old ways puzzles and exasperates their critics, who are, however, themselves ideologically divided from this point on. Advocates of large-scale *capitalist* farming are content to create a market in land and wait for the normal market processes to take hold. Socialists, however, have often had an additional and to some extent different set of self-imposed worries.

In a sense trusting peasants both more and less than their capitalist critics, socialists like Lenin envisaged capitalism as evolving in agriculture along two routes simultaneously: not only by the formation of big estates (or, in the European case, their *transformation* from semi-feudalism into large-scale modern farming), but also through a process of differentiation within the peasantry itself. For socialists, then, considerations of politics as well as economics enter in; and their fear of peasants is less that economically they will deliver too little than that politically they will be trouble.

Chapter Six

Population

Demography and development form a paradoxical pair. They are obviously connected, yet the nature of the connexions is both unclear and controversial. Sometimes mistakenly regarded as dry-as-dust number-crunching, and certainly demanding statistical and analytical skills, population dynamics are in fact a profoundly sociological topic: impacting as they do upon such areas as health, gender, the state, industrialization, cultural change, and indeed just about everything.

Population is also a highly political and often polarized topic. Extreme positions abound. For the prophets of imminent eco-doom, population is *the* problem: a time-bomb which if not defused and checked will destroy global civilization in a cataclysm of famine, war and general Malthusian catastrophe. Equally robust views are found at the other extreme, where a distinctly odd coalition of forces – Marxists alongside right wing nationalists, the Roman Catholic church along with optimistic scientific rationalists – denies that there is a problem at all. The world can feed far more people than its present population, and we have neither the right nor the need to limit births. Any move to do so is a (depending on your viewpoint) capitalist, racist, atheist or anti-scientific conspiracy.

Not surprisingly, the clash of positions like these tends to generate more heat than light. Yet within both of these two extremes, as well as between them, can be found defensible views concerning population analysis and policy. A case can be made that population growth is now outstripping and hence cancelling out economic advance in the Third World, such that birth control is the crucial precondition for any other effective steps towards development. The most spectacular convert to such a view is undoubtedly China, which since the early 1970s has dramatically switched sides. We shall discuss the Chinese case later.

158

Equally, however, one can construct a respectable case for the opposite view. Not necessarily that population is no problem; but that, if the West's experience is anything to go by, economic development and a consequent spread of at least the beginnings of affluence must come first, precisely in order to give people an incentive to start limiting their family size. According to this argument, if governments ignore this fact and try to provide family planning in isolation, they are unlikely to succeed – indeed, such measures may well blow up in their faces.

As we shall see, advocates of this view are on surer ground in worrying about the policy and implementation problems than in their reading of the European historical record. But already this discussion has implicitly raised two pairs of analytical distinctions which we should now make explicit, to be borne in mind in the rest of the chapter. One, which should be familiar in general terms, is the relation between *economic* and *cultural* factors, and their respective role in population change. Is it true that, as a former Indian minister put it, 'development is the best contraceptive'? – implying that economic development is a necessary precondition for the birthrate to decline, rather than vice versa? Alternatively, can people's *attitudes* and hence behaviour regarding procreation change even without or before such development?

This has already raised the other pair of distinctions, which concerns the relationship in all this between *individual* (or family) and *state* policies – or, if you like, micro and macro. Can government policy of whatever kind – stick, carrot, or a combination of the two – be effective in changing people's ideas and practices in this field? and if so, how?

Population Facts and Figures

At the time of writing, the total human population of the world is around 4.5 billion. Within a few years of publication, it will pass the 5 billion mark. 6 billion will be reached before the century is out. Nor is it going to stop there. Any stabilization measures will take time to have effect. (If you think about it, population policies only 'bite', not when and because people have fewer children, but when that smaller generation is *itself* grown up and producing fewer children.)

This situation of rapid population growth is both historically new and unevenly distributed. Taking the very long view, for thousands of years before the Neolithic revolution introduced settled agriculture (and hence the increased productivity which could feed more mouths), world population probably remained stable at a tiny fraction of its present level: perhaps 5–10 million. (Hunters and gatherers need a lot of space.) The great agrarian civilizations were more productive, and by the time BC became AD the figure was probably 200–300 million.

It says much for the demographic stability of pre-industrial societies that this figure was still much the same a thousand years later; thanks to the characteristic combination of high birth *and* death rates, plus periodic crises – famines, plagues, etc. – which meant that in those days populations could fall as well as rise. Things began to pick up again in the early modern period: 400–500 million in 1500, and 550 million by 1650 (though still giving a global rate of increase of no more than a million a year).

Only in the last 200 years has the picture changed out of all recognition, such that growth (and increasingly rapid growth) has become the norm. This timing suggests that, just as the first big spurt coincided with the agrarian revolution, so today's 'population explosion' is connected with industrialization. As we shall see, however, the exact causal relations are not so straightforward as might be supposed. Be that as it may, the numbers are not in doubt (and in modern times, of course, our ability to measure them exactly has been greatly enhanced thanks to national censuses). The billion mark was reached around 1830. It took a century to double to 2 billion (1930), but only thirty years to add the next billion (1960) and sixteen years the one after that (1976). Put another way, 'doubling time' from 2 to 4 billion took 46 years, less than half the previous doubling time.

Population Distribution

The world's population is not evenly distributed, either by absolute number or in terms of *density* (relative to land area). About two-thirds of humankind live in the Third World. Of these, some three quarters (close to 2.5 billion) are in Asia, which thus contains over half the world's population. Even this figure is overwhelmingly accounted for by the world's two mega-nations, China and India, with populations currently of the order of 1000 and 700 million respectively. (These two countries' particular population problems and policies form the subject of a separate section.)

Overall, Asia has a density of some 95 persons per square kilometre (ppkm²). Coincidentally, Europe's density figure for its half a billion people is almost exactly the same. But the other two major Third World continents, Africa and Latin America, present a very different profile. With populations around 500 and 400 million respectively, their *densities* are in both cases less than 20 ppkm² – i.e. only a fifth of the figure for Asia or Europe. This figure should serve as a caution against any naïve view that the *entire* Third World - and *only* the Third World - is densely populated.

Admittedly, population density figures must (like all figures) be interpreted carefully. Like any average, figures for continents conceal a wide range of national and regional variation. Qualitatively too, density per land area alone tells us nothing about the *nature* of the land: whether it is mountains, desert, or fertile soil; whether it has mineral resources; and whether in either case it has a society and level of technology well able to use these resources to sustain a large population.

Also, of course, 'snapshot' density figures in themselves do not reveal the crucial factor, *rate* of growth. Looking at this, we find that it is in fact Africa and Latin America which have the highest rates of natural increase. In 1975-77 these were 2.8% and 2.6% per year respectively, and the African figure was still rising. The figure in Asia was 2.3%; while Europe's was a mere 0.7%. Yet, just twenty years earlier during 1950-55 the European rate had been almost twice as high, at 1.3%. What factors then account for changes in rates of natural increase? And what kinds of policy intervention are appropriate or feasible?

Demographic Transition and the European Experience

Demographic change is a function of three variables: births, deaths, and migration. (You could say: movement into and out of the planet, and movement into or out of particular countries.) In practice, although migration in particular places and times can be very important, it is births and deaths - and particularly the former - which have received most attention.

Reviewing the experience of Europe, a number of writers (including Blacker, Davis, Notestein and Thompson) have detected a particular pattern of 'demographic transition'. Some describe it as having three stages, others four. In either case, the starting and end points are agreed: these are situations of relative population stability, but with very different causes. At the outset, traditional societies are characterized by high fertility *and* high mortality. Blacker calls this the 'high stationary' stage. From society's point of view, the high birth rate cancels out the high death rate. From the individual's point of view, it is necessary to produce a large number of children in order to ensure that at least some survive into adulthood.

In contrast, the final or at least modern stability (for Blacker, 'low stationary') is a result of *low* rates of both birth and death. Now improved living standards and medical advances have dramatically reduced death rates in industrial societies. Since virtually all children born can now be expected to live into adulthood, people no longer need to have so many of them. Affluence too, it is argued, provides a further incentive for having fewer children. People want material possessions and children are a very costly investment. And, of course, a range of effective contraceptive technologies are now available and widely distributed. In some industrial societies (particularly in Eastern Europe, which is interesting), birth rates have now fallen to or even below the point where existing numbers are maintained; in other words, zero or even negative population increase.

What about the intervening stage or stages? The point is that death rates begin to fall before birth rates start to follow suit, and it is a moot point really whether you call this two stages or one. (Blacker distinguishes 'early' and 'late' expanding stages: the former with sharply declining deaths while births remain on a plateau, the latter once births have begun to come down whilst the fall in deaths has also levelled off.) Either way, the obvious result of lower death rates while births remain high is a population explosion: that is what happened in much of 19th century Europe, and that is what is happening in the Third World today. It is obviously of more than antiquarian historical interest to know just how and why Europe shifted out of exploding transition into its modern steady state, since any lessons learned may be applicable to the Third World.

One of the most comprehensive and interesting studies of Europe's experience has been carried out by van de Walle and Knodel (cited in Goldthorpe, 1984, p. 33ff). They were particularly concerned to try to isolate the onset of widespread use of contraceptives, as distinct from the pre-existing differences in 'natural fertility' of various communities. What Goldthorpe pithily calls 'stopping behaviour' (indicated by a noticeable decline in married fertility) was found to occur all over Europe around 1900: rarely earlier than 1880 (except in France), or later than 1920.

This discovery is on the face of it bad news for purely socio-economic explanations, since Europe itself at this time exhibited wide diversity. England was highly industrialized and literate, Hungary mainly illiterate and overwhelmingly agrarian – yet fertility decline began in both at around the same time. So it looks as if the cultural diffusion of ideas is more important. But perhaps we should not polarize economic and cultural factors too sharply here. Just as urbanism affects even those who do not themselves live in cities, so one might suggest that the onset of industrialism in Europe set in train complex changes in attitudes, expectations, and behaviour, which sometimes worked themselves out in advance of actual industrialization in any particular place. Cultural change can follow economic change without being its consequence, and may precede it without necessarily being its cause.

Third World Issues: Culture and Economics

That which in Europe is of historical interest assumes great practical urgency in the Third World. Clearly, developing countries are well into the second stage of demographic transition; but how are they going to get home and dry into the final steady state? Already in the Third World, as occurred earlier in Europe, social improvements and medical advances have begun to reduce death rates. Birth rates, however, have not yet (with some exceptions) followed suit.

What then are the factors which affect fertility in the Third World? As you might expect, there is a range of different theories. Moreover, any explanation has to be adequate to explain both overall trends and individual motivations. Hardiman and Midgley (1982) note that here too there are 'cultural' and 'economic' camps. The former may well imply that high fertility is irrational, but persists as a kind of cultural lag (often contained in religious or similar norms) from the time when traditional societies really did need as many births as possible.

But there are difficulties here. Perhaps surprisingly, not many of the world's major religions do in fact frown on birth control; the Roman Catholic church is almost the only one which does. On a different tack, it is interesting that Hardiman and Midgley use the same historical evidence from Eastern Europe as Goldthorpe does to reach an opposite conclusion. For them, the fact that birth rates fell in Bulgaria *before* industrialization shows that cultural factors (in the form of alleged rural traditionalism) are *not* paramount; while for Goldthorpe this proves that socio-economic conditions are no match for the power of ideas (i.e. knowledge of, and preference for, modern contraceptive methods). Perhaps the moral is that we must be very careful, both to distinguish conceptually what we mean by terms like 'cultural' and 'economic', and to analyze empirically how they interact in practice.

The main objection to culturalist explanations of high fertility, however, challenges head-on the basic premise that having many children *is* irrational. According to this view, the logic of *states* (taking the longer, macro view) and of *households* (who must ensure their own survival in the here and now, and who may have no cause to believe that tomorrow will be much different from yesterday) are liable to diverge, perhaps sharply. For peasants in particular, over and above the felt need for many births in order that at least some children will survive (a view in itself still not wholly irrational, despite falling death rates), more children represent both an extra labour input and insurance for old age – factors which may well counter-balance the (relatively brief) period when they are nothing but an additional mouth to feed.

Admittedly this view is sometimes taken to extremes. Perhaps out of a laudable desire to avoid that ethnocentrisism which would dub any puzzling behaviour as 'irrational', some of the more mathematically-minded economists have not only declared that 'children yield utility' but have actually proceeded to try to calculate it, in terms of 'inter-generational wealth flows' and the like. As with parallel attempts to reduce rural-urban migration to mathematical cost-benefit calcula-tions, one suspects this is overdone. As Hardiman and Midgley drily observe, conception is more a matter of emotion than of economics. (To put it another way, it is not usual to make love while holding a pocket calculator.) Nevertheless, a modern classic study like Mamdani's (1972) in the Punjab supports the broad view that poor peasants see children as an economic asset – perhaps their only one. In this instance the villagers were polite enough to accept the contraceptives offered by a high-powered US family planning project, whose experts then puzzled over why the project was having no visible effect: but they simply didn't actually take the tablets!

Finally, Hardiman and Midgley note how some have tried to argue that economic development alone will not cause fertility to fall unless linked with social development, 'basic needs', and similar distributional issues. This hypothesis helps explain some kinks in the statistics, but (like most attempts at a general theory, in this field) fails to iron out others. As ever, there are still counter-instances in both directions; and, as ever, it is not easy to spell out precisely the alleged links in the model's chain.

Population Policies: India and China

It is hardly surprising that the two biggest countries in the Third World and indeed the whole world (both have populations well over twice as large as anywhere else) should be in the forefront of policy measures to control their rates of increase. Although China and India are untypical by the very scale of their problem, and their approaches have been rather different, nonetheless their experiences are interesting and instructive.

India, according to Goldthorpe (1984, p. 37) was the first country in the world whose government actively favoured family planning – from soon after independence in 1947. As successive degrees of encouragement failed to have a noticeable impact, however, with the birthrate remaining over 40 per 1000 in the late 1960s, the stakes got higher. Ironically, Dr. Karan Singh, the very same minister who had coined the slogan 'the best contraceptive is development', now did a U-turn and called for a 'direct assault' on the 'vicious circle' of population growth. His wish was granted, but it got seriously out of hand. There were widespread reports of excessive pressure and even compulsory vasectomies and sterilizations, which played a major part in the late Indira Gandhi's losing the general elections of 1977. She got back in later, of course, and with or without her the family planning programme went on, albeit in a lower key. Yet any progress is slow, not least because even if birth rates do come down death rates are still doing likewise. Thus according to figures quoted by Hardiman and Midgley (1982, p. 70), although India's crude birth rate declined from 43 to 35 per 1000 between 1960 and 1978, a parallel fall in the death rate (from 21 to 14 per 1000) meant that the overall rate of natural increase in 1978 was only fractionally less than it had been almost twenty years earlier: 2.1% as against 2.2%.

By contrast, the equivalent figures for China for the same years are in every respect more dramatic: birth rate halved from 36 to 18, death rate slashed from an already low 15 to an extraordinary 6 (in part a statistical freak, this; though seemingly lower even than in most developed countries, this reflects an age-structure in process of change, in which – so to speak – the first generation that is living longer has not yet begun to die off); and the overall rate of natural increase sharply cut from 2.1% to 1.2%. All this is the more remarkable considering that China was a late starter in these matters, the communist government having been strongly against population control for some twenty years after it took power in 1949.

Then again, China arguably has both organizational and cultural resources (in the form of the Communist Party and the Confucian heritage, respectively) for implementing the edicts of central authority. Nonetheless, China has had its problems too, notably since the introduction of a 'one-child' policy in the late 1970s, backed by a whole range of sticks and carrots: financial inducements for couples who adhere to the policy, withdrawal of certain welfare benefits from those who do not. While it is as yet too early to judge the success or overall results of this policy, certain illuminating and disturbing effects are already becoming apparent.

In general, the form of the policy seems to run counter to the Chinese government's overall attempts to loosen state control, while its content goes against many deeply ingrained cultural assumptions. For one thing, traditional preference for male children has led to statistics in some Chinese provinces showing up an extraordinary preponderance of male births which can only be attributed to a revival of female infanticide. In other words, if you're only allowed one child then it had better be a boy. (However, according to recent reports, rural couples whose firstborn is a girl are allowed another try.) Also, in a society where aged parents are still provided for by their children, it has been calculated that if successful the new policy – coupled with an already changing age structure, as people live longer – would lead to an impossible burden, whereby each working adult of the next generation might eventually be responsible for up to 6 elderly relatives.

Or again, even if the new policy is taking effect in towns (either because social control is easier there, or because urban couples are inclined in any case to have fewer children), it faces an uphill struggle in the countryside. Chinese peasants, like those elsewhere, have both economic and cultural reasons to prefer several children. At all events one seems an impossibly low figure. There is evidence that at any rate the increasing numbers of wealthier peasants are ignoring the new policy and cheerfully paying the economic penalties, secure in the knowledge (or belief) that they can afford to – not least, because an additional child is seen not so much as a mouth to feed but as an extra pair of hands (and, of course, a provider for one's old age: peasants don't get pensions, even in China).

The World Fertility Survey (WFS)

As it happens, possibly the biggest social survey ever is about population in the Third World. Started in 1972 and still being written up, the WFS has involved sampling 42 developing and 20 developed countries, whose population adds up to around 40% of the world's total. In each country several thousand women have been interviewed (nearly all the interviewers are women too), so the total global sample numbers some 340,000. Most of the research was done in the late 1970s, and by the mid 1980s most of the country studies have been published. What do they show?

In the first place, it looks as if in every continent of the Third World bar one fertility has begun to decline, albeit slowly. Women used to have 4–5 children each, twice as many as their First World sisters and twice what is needed simply to replace (i.e. maintain) existing population levels. That figure has now fallen by an average of one child per woman. The exception is Africa, where birth rates continue high; and where one country, Kenya, for no very clear reason has the world's highest rate of increase at around 4% a year.

Awareness of contraceptive devices is also well-nigh universal. Access to and use of them is another question, however. Goldthorpe (1984) reads the evidence as suggesting 'spacing' rather than 'stopping' behaviour. That is, Third World women so far are using contraception to save their health from the risk of too frequent pregnancies, rather than (as in Europe) to ensure that after a given point they have no more children at all.

The WFS has found too a correlation between fertility and certain socio-economic indicators. On the whole, fewer children are born to women with more education, or who live in towns, or who are employed outside the household.

The WFS figures tend to confirm other general surmises. Thus Bogue and Tsui (cited in Goldthorpe, 1984, p. 34) already in 1978 identified five socio-economic factors as correlating with fertility decline. Working from aggregate national rather than individual data, they found the highest rates of decline among those Third World countries which were: richest, most urbanized, most industrialized, best educated; and which had the lowest infant mortality rates. Over and above all these, however, government family planning programmes were found to have an important effect in their own right. On this basis, Bogue and Tsui concluded that by the late 1970s an overall global downturn in fertility had at last begun.

Chapter Seven

Health

Introduction

Commonsense might query what health has to do with sociology anyway; isn't it a matter for expert medical professionals? However, as sociologists are so fond of pointing out, commonsense can be misleading. Not only is the sociology of health and medicine an important and fascinating field in its own right, but in the Third World context the issues which it raises are of great practical urgency and theoretical importance. This chapter will try to show how many health problems in the Third World need to be analyzed as *social* phenomena.

Colonialism and Health

Colonialism affected people's health, directly and indirectly, in a number of ways. A 'modernisation' account would see this as wholly or largely positive: bringing the benefits of modern Western medical techniques to populations previously at the mercy of all kinds of dread tropical diseases which they were unable to cure or prevent.

Although as we shall see there has indeed been progress in such areas as life expectancy and infant mortality, the above view is much too simple. To be brutal, colonialism in its early stages killed millions of people: not only in various acts of genocide, or the massive depredations of the slave trade, but also by introducing hitherto unknown European diseases to Third World populations unable to resist them. However unintentional, the effects were devastating. Far more Indians died of disease resulting from Western conquests and settlement in the Americas and the Caribbean that were killed outright.

Even at a later stage, when rudimentary health services began to be introduced into colonies by now 'pacified', they had serious limitations. The fact that most such services were initially designed to serve only European colonial officials (plus, later, indigenous employees of the administration) had two harmful effects. One was that these services' scale (small) and location (urban) meant that they simply did not reach the vast rural majority. The other, less obvious, was that the Third World thus inherited a *type* of medical care – European-style, curative in intent, patient-centred, and hospital-based – of doubtful relevance to its actual problems and needs. Both these factors remain today as major question marks over the quantity and quality of Third World health provision.

Less directly, but of stark contemporary relevance today, the fact that colonialism often entailed the replacement of growing food for one's own subsistence by cash crop production for foreign markets has been one factor in precipitating a chronic food crisis in many Third World countries. In extreme cases, the result is famine and mass starvation. Less visibly, there is evidence that 'mono-cultivation' (growing a single cash crop) has led to many people's diets becoming less balanced over time. An example which haunts me is from 'socialist' Tanzania, even, in the early 1970s. In an area of protein-deficient diets, people were forbidden to pick cashew nuts from the trees – because they were earmarked for export, to earn foreign exchange.

Traditional Medicine and Healers

All societies, by definition, have had some procedures for dealing with the sick. Many had specialized practitioners in this field, such as herbalists or midwives. In the Third World, however, the colonial impact often led to such knowledge being dismissed wholesale as unscientific 'mumbo-jumbo', and its practitioners being labelled as 'witch-doctors'. 'Scientific' medicine was equated with modern Western techniques – even while, ironically, these were scarcely available to most people, who largely continued (and still do) to have recourse to traditional remedies, nowadays often in conjunction with Western ones.

It is true that some indigenous practices were unhygienic or even dangerous, and many practitioners probably could not give a 'scientific' account of what they did or why. Nevertheless, the balance of opinion and practice is now changing, in several ways. First, many traditional herbal remedies have been found to work, and chemical analysis can show how and why they work. Second, there are techniques which appear to succeed even though their theoretical basis is not well understood – the best known being Chinese acupuncture. Related to this, even in the West itself there is a decline of exclusive faith in 'established' medicine, coupled with an open-mindedness to alternative traditions (e.g. homeopathy or osteopathy) which the dominant medical profession has tried to marginalize or suppress.

Above all, and good news for sociologists, there is increasing recognition that medical relations are also social relations. Traditional healers undoubtedly had and have important social roles – in their communities generally, and in their relations with individual patients – which contribute to their success and the continuing respect in which they are often held. The coming years may well see greater tolerance and even interaction between traditional and modern medicine, to their mutual benefit – which in turn should enhance the health and well-being of Third World peoples.

Health Data

Data in this field suffer from all the usual pitfalls. Many figures do not exist; some which do exist may not be accurate; and as always there is the question of what figures mean. There can also be statistical freaks: a country with apparently high infant mortality may simply have a better death reporting service. Demographic change also interferes: some Third World countries have lower death-rates than some in the West, simply because the age-structure of their populations is changing.

Nonetheless, certain demographic indicators are widely agreed to provide useful evidence of changing patterns of health. Crude death rates have shown a steady decrease over the last thirty years. More specifically, *infant mortality* is declining, but in a pattern illustrating regional diversity: falling fastest in East Asia, and most slowly elsewhere in Asia and in Africa. Yet overall Third World infant mortality is often still five or six times greater than in the West, and many countries still have rates as high at 100–150 per 1000 (Hardiman and Midgley, 1982).

Life expectancy is another useful indicator. Again there has been steady global progress: in the Third World, the average rose from 32 in 1939 to 49 in 1970 (while in the West it has gone up from 56 to 70). However, like many averages these figures are misleading, and in two ways. First, they do not mean in the Third World – although they may do in the West – that these are the ages at which most people actually die. In many Third World countries 40% of *all* deaths are of children under 5 – compared with under 3% in the North.

Secondly, once again global progress conceals variation by country and region. While several Latin American countries have life expectancies of around 70, comparable to the North, Asian averages are closer to 60 and African figures are around 50 or even lower. All in all, 'life-chances' in the most literal sense still differ greatly on our planet, both as between North and South and within different regions of the South.

Incidence of Disease

Similar differences are evident in patterns of incidence of disease, which are clearly related (amongst other things) to two factors: *diet*, and *age*. Thus the two major causes of death in the North are neo-plasms and cardiovascular disorders – in plain English, mostly cancers and heart disease – which are associated not only with older populations but also (it is increasingly argued) with over-rich and fatty diets.

The South's problem is the opposite in both respects. Far and away the biggest killers are communicable diseases: most of them not exotically tropical, but including many infections which were common in the North too within living memory – like tuberculosis or diphtheria – or which are still widespread but regarded as minor, e.g. measles or diarrhoea. It comes as a shock to think of measles or diarrhoea as major killers. Yet children in the Third World are especially vulnerable here; all the more so when (as often) they are already weakened by malnutrition and inadequate diets. In fact the largest single disease-affected group in the Third World is children.

Disease, like most things, is also *gender*-specific in ways which are clearly social. Although under equal conditions women's life expectancy is a few years higher than men's, over much of the Third World this gap is narrowed, and in some cases (notably the Indian sub-continent) it is actually reversed. Factors here include nutrition: in some societies men and male children eat first and get the lion's share, while women and girls (who have probably prepared everyone's food) must make do with what is left. Childbirth is also hazardous: too many pregnancies, too little space between them, insufficient care at all stages (from ante-natal to the delivery itself to post-natal) and poor nutrition all take their toll, separately and in conjunction.

Two other factors of disease incidence are worth mentioning. One is obvious: in the South as in the North, only more starkly so, the *poor* suffer ill-health much more than the rich. The other may be less obvious. Despite the obvious health hazards of Third World urban slums, *rural* populations are even worse off: they have far fewer doctors, they are much further from hospitals and health centres, and are even less likely to have access to clean water or effective sanitation. I mention this, because of a tendency in the North to romanticize especially the alleged virtues of rural poverty in the South, as some sort of natural 'world we have lost'.

Needless to say, all of the above factors also interact, and their cumulative weight can be appalling. Thus the health prospects for female children of the undernourished rural poor may be very grim indeed.

Patterns of Disease

It may be useful to go into some detail on the types of diseases prevalent in the Third World, for three reasons. The first is related to the general issue of *recapitulation*. How far is the South's experience of health and disease repeating the North's history in this field? Secondly, there is the claim of *sociology*. If you're ill, you need a doctor, not a sociologist. Such is the commonsense view. And yet we are entitled to ask how far in the South today, as in the North yesterday, medical problems may have social causes and require political solutions (e.g. environmental and sanitation improvements). Finally, facts are important in themselves – and these facts are particularly striking, even shocking. For the fact is that millions in the Third World still die of communicable diseases which are preventable, yet which are endemic in many areas (especially rural areas), and whose incidence is in some cases actually on the increase. Or, even where not fatal, such diseases can be chronic and debilitating, thus affecting individuals' and indeed whole communities' chances of living and working effectively.

Communicable diseases are grouped according to their *vector*, i.e. what carries them. In most cases, not to mince words, this is shit. Infections transmitted through *human faeces* (often via flies) include:

– *diarrhoeas*: a major killer, especially of young children.
– *bacterial or viral diseases*: including polio (on the increase in some countries), cholera (of which new strains have developed since the 1960s), hepatitis and typhoid.
– *parasitic infections*: including two, ascariasis and hookworm, which infest an estimated 650 and 450 million people respectively.

Partially, excepting this last category, much of the above would have been familiar in nineteenth-century Europe.

A second major category is *air-borne* diseases, which account for up to a third of all deaths in the Third World. These include such familiar names as: tuberculosis, pneumonia, bronchitis, whooping cough, diphtheria, meningitis, and influenza. Their familiarity (as names) is instructive. All these are found in the West, but are treatable hence rarely fatal – although it is not so long since many were killers here too. This category also includes the single total success story to date: smallpox, now eradicated worldwide and existing only in laboratories.

A third category, more specifically tropical, involves *insect* or other animal vectors. The best known is the chronic fever *malaria* (which was once found in England), transmitted by mosquitoes. Half a billion people are still at risk from this disease, although campaigns (of drainage, etc.) have had some effect: three-quarters of malarial areas in 1950 were malaria-free by 1970. But resistance, both to insecticides (e.g. DDT) and medications, is a growing problem. Other diseases in this category include schistosomiasis (bilharzia), carried by a water snail, which debilitates some 200 million people; trypanosomiasis (sleeping sickness), which affects 30 to 40 million people and is usually fatal; filarial parasites, including elephantiasis, with 250 million sufferers; and onchocerciasis (river blindness).

Still a fourth group of diseases travel by *contact*, including leprosy, yaws, and VD. They affect relatively fewer but still very many people; perhaps 10–15 million for leprosy, and 40 million for yaws. As for VD, global incidence of syphilis and gonorrhea in the late 1960s was over 50 million and 160 million respectively. Now there is AIDS too, which at least in its Third World manifestations (in Central Africa, so far) has no particular connection with homosexuality. And this category or the previous (scientists are not sure) will include *trachoma*, which affects no fewer than 600 million people and is the major cause of blindness in the world (Hardiman and Midgley, 1982).

I have deliberately given a lot of detail above, because I trust you find these facts as appalling as I do. In most cases (not all, admittedly), millions of people – especially small children – are still dying of perfectly preventable diseases. We know, from the West's experience, how to prevent or at least severely check the worst effects of many of the major communicable diseases. Moreover, we know that the necessary measures are not usually on the frontiers of medical technology (expensive 'wonder-drugs' and the like), but would involve relatively cheap and simple actions such as immunization. In some countries, hearteningly, action on immunization is beginning to be taken. Brazil in 1984 had a massively promoted national campaign aiming to reach every child. And even in strife-torn El Salvador, in early 1985, a day's truce was declared in the civil war so that a mass vaccination programme for children could be carried out.

Yet although such medical programmes are vital, our own history teaches us that the crucial first steps are not medical at all, but social.

Health and Social Factors

Not only were many of the diseases outlined above familiar in the West in the 19th century; but the crucial fact is that in most cases their incidence had fallen dramatically by the early 20th century, *before* their defeat was consolidated by the discovery of antibiotics and vaccines. One way or another, therefore, the fall in disease was connected with improvements in living standards: improved diets, less crowded housing, more education, cleaner water, better sanitation, disposal of wastes, and the like. Although all the precise connections are not fully understood or agreed, the general correlation is pretty clear.

An awful lot of it boils down (as you might say) to *water*. Indeed, some estimates suggest that as much as 80% of all Third World disease is water-related. The connections are clear from the account given above. Yet few people in the Third World, urban or rural, have access to an adequate quantity or quality (and both aspects are crucial) of water. Piped water supplies are still far from the norm, especially in rural areas. Even where they do exist, they may be polluted. Where there is no piped supply, as in most rural areas, water must be fetched. Water is heavy to carry: yet carried it is, almost invariably by women and children, often on their heads over long distances. Not surprisingly, water so obtained is little and precious, such that to use it for washing may well seem a luxury.

Water is also a major factor in *sanitation*. Most of the Third World, urban or rural, still lacks adequate and effective sewage disposal systems. Yet, for as long as this lack continues, faecally-transmitted diseases will continue to infest and kill millions of people – just as they did in the dank cities of early-industrializing Europe, a century and more ago. *Overcrowding* is another social factor contributing to ill-health: not only through high-density urban slums and consequent infection, but equally in 'under-populated' rural areas where many may share one room and eat from a single pot.

Health Policies

Conditions like those described above cry out for action. Yet effective health policies in the Third World are hampered by tradition. Not, for once, 'tradition' in the modernization theorists' sense, meaning backward cultural practices (although to be sure these do play a part), but in this case the tradition is the Third World's colonial inheritance. Colonialism fostered a lop-sided health care system. I described it above as 'curative . . . patient-centred, and hospital-based', and it is now time to go into this in more detail.

Preventive/curative is one of the most basic distinctions in the sociology of health. They are not, of course, in principle opposed: a good health system will include both prevention and cure. Nor is it universally the case that prevention is cheap while cures are costly. Yet overall it is increasingly now agreed that Third World health care has put the cart before the horse. Far too many resources have gone into building, maintaining and staffing costly Western-style hospitals at the expense of all other health priorities. Despite their vast cost, these hospitals still mostly reach only the privileged and city-dwellers. Even more seriously, this system only intervenes once patients are already ill. It does little or nothing to prevent them *becoming* ill, a task which would entail very different priorities: public health campaigns, mass immunization, adult education (e.g. about balanced diets or personal hygiene); draining swamps, building latrines, providing clean piped water, and generally mobilizing people to participate in improving their own health, not only as individual 'patients' but also as whole communities.

In the West, on the whole, the development of preventive and curative medicine went hand in hand. If anything, 'social' public health measures often *preceded* strictly 'scientific' improvements in medicine itself, e.g. antibiotics. Moreover, many public health measures are relatively cheap. It would only cost $1 million – chickenfeed, for a government – to provide basic immunization for every single child in Peru. Even those measures involving public works can be inexpensive if communities are mobilized, e.g. to build their own latrines. Indeed, some economists would argue that this kind of expenditure isn't even a cost or a drain on resources at all, but an investment. After all, a healthy population constitutes 'human capital' for development; conversely, people who are disease-ridden and under-nourished cannot work very productively in industry or agriculture.

Why then is more not being done? And why does so much that is wrong continue to be done? Part of the answer is sheer 'systems inertia'. A given structure has been inherited, and will continue until and unless enough people are motivated to seek to change it. But there are also vested interests involved in at least three ways. One is the clientele. Existing curative hospital-based medical systems serve and suit the wealthier urban classes pretty well. After all, *their* living conditions (unlike those of the majority of their compatriots) are already such as to ensure few problems on the preventative/public health side.

A second group with an interest in the status quo are Western TNCs, who supply almost all the equipment and above all the drugs to Third World hospitals. These are dealt with in a separate section. The third and perhaps the most important group also deserves a section to itself: the medical profession.

TNCs and Health

The role of TNCs in relation to health has been particularly controversial in recent years. By their own lights, they would probably see themselves as providing to the Third World the advantages of up-to-date drugs, or such modern conveniences as powdered milk for infants. Argument rages, however, on the way TNCs set about this.

The fact that (as we have seen) the Third World's major priority ought to be prevention rather than cure is not in itself the TNCs' fault. They can hardly be blamed for seeking to supply a market whose value has been estimated at $20 billion annually. The question is how they go about it. Several studies have lent weight to numerous Third World complaints, which include the following:

1) The drug companies – which are very few, very big, and of course all based in the First World – use their monopoly power to maintain high prices for an artificially wide range of 'brand name' drugs, in cases where the basic 'generic' drug could in fact be supplied much more cheaply. Since even the Conservative government in Britain is currently in conflict with the drug companies on this issue, one can imagine how weaker Third World governments fare.

2) Particular drugs which may be dangerous are nonetheless sold in the Third World. This may include pre-testing, before a product is deemed safe for the West; or dumping of drugs now banned in the West, e.g. because of harmful side-effects. Most often, it involves drugs which in the West would be prescription-only being sold freely over the counter, often with inadequate instructions and warnings.

3) Very little drug research and development is done in the Third World, or for that matter on Third World diseases.

Of course, in principle it is up to Third World governments to act to prevent abuses like these: e.g. by legislation; by setting up their own basic pharmaceutical industries; or by sticking to the World Health Organisation's list of 200 basic generic drugs. But the drug TNCs still exercise considerable power – not least, as a crucial part of the entire inappropriate individual and curative-based system, whose few actual

Third World beneficiaries are precisely the urban elites who sustain and indeed mostly constitute the governments in question. (This is a good illustration of how wrong it is to counterpose 'external' *versus* 'internal' causes of underdevelopment; for a case like the above precisely shows how 'external' dependency becomes internalized and takes root within the actual structures of Third World societies.)

The issue of powdered baby milk illustrates a similar point, in a slightly different way. Here, although in principle it is surely progress for women to have the option of bottle-feeding if they so choose, the concrete issue concerns the way in which TNCs set out through powerful advertising campaigns to create the impression that bottle-feeding was the only 'modern' method. Since Western cultural aspirations are more widely internalized than the means to fulfil them, the consequence was that (especially in Africa) women went in for bottle-feeding who could not afford it. As a result, either through over-dilution or unsterilized bottles or both, very many babies have suffered malnutrition and death who could have fed much more healthily from their mothers' breasts. Worst of all, even though this issue has generated considerable publicity, it is not clear that all the TNCs concerned have yet stopped pushing their product in the Third World.

The Medical Profession in the Third World

Just as there is no reason why health care provision should take any particular organizational form, the same applies to health personnel. In particular, one may well feel that there is no obvious logical rationale why workers in this field should be so starkly divided between a small highly trained and generously paid elite (mostly male) on the one hand, and a much larger group (mostly female) whose skills receive less formal accreditation and who therefore receive much lower pay and status.

Like the West, the Third World has doctors and nurses too (although the latter are not always so predominantly female). It may seem a harsh judgement, but in many ways doctors seem as much part of the problem as of any solution. Their whole training fits them for curative medicine, and to defend a curative-based system – or indeed to extend it, as general hospitals acquire even more expensive specialist units, and medical schools expand into ever-costlier areas of post-graduate expertise in order to train a handful of students. (In Peru, to train a single doctor costs six thousand times more than to educate a peasant child.) In most countries, doctors have lucrative private practices, as well as or instead of – but in either case at the expense of – any state or public post. (As a general aside, it is not widely realized in the West that most people in the Third World *pay* directly, in one way or another, for any medical care they receive: doctors' bills, medications, etc. Ironically, it is only in some rich Northern countries that medical care is free, not in the poor South.)

Nor is this all. As Hardiman and Midgley put it (1982, p. 170), these doctors 'are trained to treat the diseases of the urban rich rather than . . . of the rural poor'. Figures for number of doctors per patient, already predictably low for much of the Third World in any case, are positively appalling when broken down by urban and rural areas. In Kenya, in 1975, the rural ratio was an astonishing *62 times* higher than the urban one (*ibid*. p. 171).

And not only do Third World doctors not like working in rural areas; many choose not to use their skills in and for the Third World at all. The so-called 'brain-drain' of professionals from South to North especially affects doctors. Of some 60,000 foreign doctors in the USA, the majority are of Third World origin. And the British National Health Service relies heavily on doctors from the Indian sub-continent, who are therefore no longer available to work in their countries of origin.

The point here is not to be judgmental about individuals or even social groups, but rather to note that as a *system* none of this does much to promote better health in the Third World. What then can be done instead?

Healthy Socialism

Fortunately, there is evidence that there are alternatives and that they do work. Such evidence comes mainly from two rather different sources. One, as already mentioned, is the experience of the now developed Northern countries (West and East) in public health and preventative medicine. The other is that minority of Third World countries which (in some cases while remaining quite poor) have pursued a socialist development strategy. This does not necessarily entail revolution. Examples include China, Cuba, Vietnam and now Nicaragua, but also cases of social democracy like Costa Rica and Sri Lanka.

What all these, and some others, have in common is simply that their governments have in various ways given priority to preventive medicine and primary health care. As we have seen above, what needs to be done is not really very technically controversial, complicated, or even expensive. But most Third World governments lack the organizational means or the political will to implement change.

Probably the best known area of innovation involves so-called 'barefoot doctors'; or, more exactly, medical auxiliaries. Such terms in fact can cover a considerable range of ideas, roles, and practices in different countries, all of which share the aim of bridging the gaps between doctor/nurse and doctor/patient by creating intermediate personnel. Often, such a role will be at least in part preventative: working out of a local community and promoting immunization and public health measures, as well as dealing with minor ailments in local health centres while referring more serious cases onward to a doctor and perhaps ultimately thence to hospital (for both of these, despite all that has been said above, obviously still have a crucial place in a balanced system of health care provision).

Conclusion

Historically, indigenous Third World health practices were largely suppressed, superseded or marginalized by colonial health systems, which in turn have shaped health provision today. *Culturally*, indigenous beliefs and practices (which in some cases no doubt were and are indeed unhealthy, unscientific, or both) have been widely blamed or denigrated. Yet, ironically, a no less irrational acquired cultural attachment to the idea of 'West is Best' has if anything done even more damage, or at least failed to fulfil its promise of betterment.

Socially, systems of health provision often grossly unequal (in their impact on town and country, rich and poor, men and women) are tenaciously defended by the few who benefit from them and the even fewer professionals who staff them. *Politically*, this pressure is hardly if at all resisted by governments who either share these priorities, or lack the political will or means to confront and change them – especially if this entails the difficult and dangerous task of in some degree actively mobilizing dispossessed groups and communities. *Economically*, it is almost the worst of all possible worlds. Governments grudgingly devote relatively small proportions of their budgets to financing costly, inappropriate and expensive systems of health care which reach hardly anybody – and the no less costly medical schools which preserve them. Conversely, cheap preventative public health measures are neglected; and health expenditure as investment in 'human capital' is scarcely considered.

What then of modernisation *versus* dependency theory? As always, there is no single or uniform answer; and nor do these two approaches necessarily cover or exhaust all the important or interesting issues in any particular field. My own view is probably clear enough from the foregoing discussion: the Third World's lop-sided, 'cart before horse' acquisition of Western-style curative medicine without its preventative complement is a rather good example of the sort of thing dependency theory is on about.

There is no need or call for exaggeration here. It is unnecessary, and in my judgment false, to claim that over most of the world health conditions were *better* before the coming of Western medicine. The onward march of such statistics as rising life expectancy and falling infant mortality testifies to global progress, albeit still too slowly and unevenly. From this, the broad picture, modernization theory might draw some comfort; as also from the point about *recapitulation* stressed earlier, that many of the public health problems and diseases that the Third World faces today were much the same in 19th century Europe.

But such similarity of *problem* is surely outweighed by the acute differences in the *solutions* adopted, and their effectiveness (or lack of it). As so often, the way in which the Third World acquired the potential benefits of Western 'progress' – partial, uneven, and perverse – has largely worked so far to limit its impact and prevent its promise from being fully realized. How long those affected will tolerate this is another question.

Chapter Eight

Education

Introduction

Every human society has always had some form of education; if by this we mean the passing on from generation to generation of such knowledge, skills and values as the group in question possesses and prizes. It has been the distinctive contribution of modern industrial societies to *formalize* this process: that is, to have it done in specific places (schools), by specific personnel (teachers), to age-specific groups (children and young adults), and in a specific way (book-learning).

For modernization theory, as you might expect, modern education is a good thing. If anything that is an understatement. Education is seen as *the* major means of accomplishing modernization, at both societal and individual levels. From the viewpoint of governments, education has a threefold value. *Economically*, it provides the trained 'human capital' (at a price, to be sure; but this is an investment) which will 'staff' development and hence enhance it at every level: efficient administrators, knowledgeable entrepreneurs, literate clerks, skilled workers, scientifically aware peasants. *Politically*, it helps the vital task of nation-building by welding a nation out of what may well be diverse ethnic groups and tribes: an important task of political socialization, as indeed of social control. *Culturally*, likewise, it frees people from ignorance, superstition and backwardness, creating a modern consciousness and community.

Such goals and aspirations are mirrored at the level of the individual too. For an early modernization theorist like Lerner, education (especially literacy, and alongside other factors like urbanization and exposure to mass media) plays a crucial role in producing modern 'mobile personalities', characterized by rationality and 'empathy' (the ability to put yourself in other people's shoes). Similarly, Inkeles and Smith's large-scale survey of some 6000 men in six Third World countries in the mid 1960s found education to be the most important single factor in producing 'individual modernity', which they summarized as involving informed participation, personal efficiency, individual autonomy, and open-mindedness (quoted in Goldthorpe, 1984, p. 241). And certainly education is almost universally seen in the Third World as the only way to get on: to escape from agriculture, get a white-collar job, make something of yourself.

Dependency theory, not unexpectedly, casts a distinctly critical eye over most of this. Some of its criticisms overlap with the more general radical critique of education within the Western sociological debate, while others are specific to the Third World context. While there is no general hostility to modern education systems as such (except for the rather different argument of Illich, which we discuss below), there is much querying of the particular form it has taken, its priorities, implications and effects.

Using the same three headings as above: *economically*, existing education systems are criticized as top-heavy, spending too much on secondary and tertiary provision for a small elite at the expense of primary education for the masses. But this is not surprising, since *politically* the colonial origins of Third World education systems were designed precisely to foster and bolster an indigenous elite, first as auxiliaries to the colonial power and now (since independence) as a ruling class still subordinate to neo-colonial metropolitan power and influence.

No small part of that influence is *cultural*. For a distinctive and tragic result of modern education in the Third World, on this view, is a specifically *cultural dependence*; what Frantz Fanon, the revolutionary French-Caribbean psychiatrist who fought with the Algerian independence movement, called a 'colonized personality'. In total contrast to the almost lyrical view of someone like Lerner, in which the modern personality is seen as some sort of liberated free spirit, the cultural dependency approach paints a sad picture of an isolated and rootless elite infected by individualism, over-identifying with the West, hence ignorant and scornful of (or in any case cut off from) their own societies. In some cases, they may not even speak 'their own' language, but only (or primarily) English or French.

In sum, where modernization theory sees beneficial *diffusion* of Western institutions or cultural values, critics see the creation of harmful *dependence*.

Indigenous Education and Colonialism

Prior to the introduction of modern education, different societies in what is now the Third World had a great variety of education and socialization systems. On the one hand, China had had centuries of entry to the governing bureaucracy by a stiff formal examination. At the other extreme, small-scale preliterate societies (e.g. in Africa) might have had nothing we could recognize as schools at all. Nonetheless, various socialization processes took place, such as initiations and the learning of practical skills, often under the direction of many adults, sometimes in specific places, at particular ages, in groups usually segregated by sex. (You may recall Kunta Kinte in such a scene, in the first episode of *Roots.*)

Elsewhere, there were surplus-producing societies (producing a surplus over and above subsistence) which had a state machinery and written languages. These usually had some form of schooling, often under religious control (e.g. Islamic societies). The coming of colonialism continued the link between education and religion in a new way, inasmuch as it was often Christian missionaries rather than the colonial state as such which first set up Western-style schools. In colonies of mixed religious affiliation, such as Nigeria, this produced an ironic result. The relatively more developed Muslim northern societies did not want Christian missions, which as a result were largely confined to the then less developed smaller-scale animist societies of the south. As a result, the South educationally 'overtook' the North, and there was created a preponderance of better-educated southerners in late-colonial and post-independence Nigeria: a fact which contributed to the rivalries and mutual suspicion which in the mid-60s produced the Biafra war.

Educational Data and Trends

Hardiman and Midgley (1982) provide a useful global progress report. As ever, the data (where available) may be suspect. School enrolment ratios and claimed literacy percentages are especially likely to be inflated, e.g. by ignoring absenteeism and drop-out rates – the latter often very high in the Third World.

Nonetheless, taking a broad sweep over the last thirty years, the picture that emerges is one of broad advance – but unevenly so, and lately with worrying signs of deceleration. In the period 1950–1965, *primary* school enrolments worldwide increased by 95 million. Yet a UNESCO projection for 1970–1985 suggests that, although *percentage* enrolments are still going up, this has now slowed to a rate such that absolute *numbers* of children *not* in school are also on the increase. If correct, this means that over 100 million *more* children in the 5–14 age group are now not in school than in 1970 – even while the percentage enrolled has gone up from 44 to 48%.

A further implication of these figures is that at any given time over half the Third World's children are still not at school. This may be too pessimistic: other sources suggest that a clear majority do now get at least some schooling (over 60% in 1975, according to World Bank data.) Whatever the figure, it seems that the much touted goal of universal primary education is still a long way off. Also clear is the high *unevenness* of educational provision within the Third World, in terms of just about any dimension of stratification you care to name: regional, class, ethnic, gender, or urban-rural. This will be further examined in a separate section.

Not only is primary education coverage incomplete, but thereafter Third World schooling is sharply pyramid-shaped. Only a very small proportion go on from each stage to the next, so once again there is a striking gap between percentage and absolute numbers. Undoubtedly there has been advance. *Secondary* school enrolments rose by no less than 920% between 1950–1975, which means they grew twice as fast as primary enrolments. (In many cases, this reflected a rapid post-independence expansion of secondary education, in countries like Zambia, to fill the huge gaps left by the colonial education system.)

Yet even the most developed Third World countries rarely have even half of the relevant age group in secondary school. Usually the figure is much lower than this. It is ironic, then, that *budgets* catering for this minority are often higher than those for the entire primary school system (which is all the education the majority will ever get). Secondary schools are typically much better equipped and staffed.

Similar considerations apply even more forcefully to tertiary or *higher* education. Universities are often the most expensive sector of the lot (in part inevitably so, since they need laboratories, etc.), even though they serve only a tiny minority. Here too there have been dramatic percentage increases, as newly independent countries set up new universities in order to turn out indigenous replacements for colonial expatriates. Yet, to put things in proportion, even despite a tenfold increase in numbers of Third World students between 1950 and 1975, the South still lags far behind the North. In all LDCs, in 1970, there were less than 6 million students; while the developed countries, despite their smaller overall population, had over 20 million.

Besides the school and college system, what other developments have there been? Perhaps understandably, provision of special schools or pre-school education is deemed a luxury in most of the Third World, except for some communist countries. (North Korea claims to be the first country in the world with 100% creche and kindergarten provision.) So the only major area of non-school educational activity has been *adult education*, especially in relation to *literacy*. Global literacy rates do indicate progress: illiteracy went down from 44% in 1950 to 34% in 1970, and the trend continues. On the other hand, most of this is probably due more to expanding primary education than working with existing adults. There are estimated to be still some 800 million people (of whom at least 60% are women) who cannot read and write. And, as we saw with other statistics, here too the absolute numbers may be growing even while the percentage declines. Only in socialist countries like Cuba or Tanzania have mass literacy campaigns, aimed at adults, noticeably dented the existing illiteracy statistics.

Education and Inequality

The inadequacies of educational provision in the Third World become even starker if we break down national or global data into particular real groups, and consider their *access* (or lack of it) to education.

By *region*, first of all, educational coverage is much better (especially at primary level) in most of Asia and Latin America than in much of Africa. The most developed Third World countries, especially in East Asia, have enrolment figures little worse than those in the West – i.e. almost universal education.

Within particular countries, however, there arise several different dimensions of unequal access. A major one is *urban/rural*. Almost without exception, there is more and better educational provision in city than in countryside – even though most of the population are rural. Sometimes the differences are stark: Buchanan (1975, p. 29) claims that in the West African state of Mali only 3% of rural children got any education at all – compared with 75% in the capital, Bamako.

Gender is also an important aspect of inequality in this as in most other spheres of existence. Almost all enrolment rates everywhere, except in the richest LDCs, show a lower proportion of girls than of boys in school. Although there has been progress, the drop-out rate for girls still tends to be higher; and the sex gap increases at secondary and higher levels.

A particularly difficult and often divisive problem is that of *ethnicity*. Most Third World nation-states incorporate within their boundaries a number (in some cases, a large number) of different ethnic groups. This raises a number of educational problems. The most difficult of these concerns *language*, and a separate section is devoted to this. But even apart from language, different peoples may for historical reasons have (or believe they have) unequal access to education: minorities (especially remote ones) claim they are excluded by the majority, and so on. (Of course, such problems are not confined to the Third World. In Western Europe, too, old national minorities and new immigrant communities alike often feel they get a raw deal from the education system.)

Last but by no means least, there is *class*. Controversy rages as to how or how far you can apply class analysis (Marxist or otherwise) in the often very different context of non-Western societies. Suffice it to say that, in the Third World just like everywhere else, those individuals or groups who have wealth and status and power (on whatever basis) seem well placed to ensure that their children get in and get on better than other people's in the education system. In other words, *social mobility* is as constrained in the Third World as anywhere else – probably more so, in many cases, since inequalities of all sorts are often harsher in the South than in the North (another reason, incidentally, why 'averages' of e.g. GNP per head can be very misleading).

Any exceptions are likely to be few and temporary: for example, Szentes' (in Cliffe and Saul, 1973, p. 341ff) interesting argument that, in Tanzania and similar then newly independent countries, a rapidly expanding bureaucracy and education system entailed large-scale elite recruitment from the sons and daughters of peasants, simply because there wasn't anybody else; and that this prevented crystallization of a closed ruling class. However, any such expansion has now ceased, and it would take a brave optimist to maintain that recruitment of subsequent generations of the elite would remain so broad-based.

Two last brief comments on all these inequalities: they reinforce one another and they get worse the higher you go in the education system. The boy child of a wealthy urban elite family, belonging to a dominant ethnic group, has educational opportunities almost infinitely better than a girl from a poor rural minority tribe. And even if that girl makes it to and through primary school, what chance has she got at secondary level? – which may well mean leaving home and moving to the city, to be taught in a language not her own; even while rich boy stays on his home ground, and learns in the language he speaks at home anyway. Small wonder if poor girl's parents put pressure on her to stay home, help in the house and on the farm, and then get married . . . In such ways do Third World education systems, like those elsewhere, serve – wittingly or not – to reproduce and reinforce existing social inequalities.

A Relevant Education?

So far we've mostly considered educational provision in *quantitative* terms: numbers enrolled, and so forth. However, the *qualitative* dimension is also very important, i.e. how good is the education? Some aspects of this are fairly straightforward. Most Third World educational facilities are much less well equipped than in the West, and their teachers may well be less qualified too. As ever, the problems are most acute at primary schools; many of which suffer from excessive pupil-teacher ratios, severe shortages of equipment, ageing or inadequate facilities, and poorly trained teachers.

Over and above such matters, however, there remains the crucial question: what *kind* of education do people get in the Third World? and is it the kind they *should* be getting? These are difficult and controversial issues. Partly, it is a debate about priorities. We have already noted that often more money gets spent on the few enjoying secondary and higher education, than on the many who will know only primary school. But some critics go further, arguing that the *content* of education is also inappropriate – too 'academic', geared to the few who will go on to secondary school, and hence having nothing to say to the great majority whose lot will be to return to the slum or the farm.

It gets worse. Not only does schooling not help the majority but it actually does them a disservice – by encouraging aspirations to urban lifestyles and white-collar careers which the system can't in fact deliver. Education is thus blamed, not only for not being relevant to agriculture, but for putting people off farming in any case and filling their heads with all kinds of fancy ideas.

Even the education received by the privileged few who do leap the hurdle into secondary school and beyond can be criticized. Still too much book-learning, not enough practicality; too much arts, too little science and engineering; too much oriented around the old colonial power, too little devoted to one's own country. There is surely much truth in this, even though it is hard to generalize and things do change. Many West Indians did indeed suffer geography lessons that taught them more about Britain than the Caribbean. And even in Tanzania, the one and only university started life in the early 1960s with a Faculty of Law, of all things; and didn't acquire a Faculty of Engineering until a decade later.

Going back to the debate about primary education, however, there is a real dilemma. Even if the critics are right, what is to be done? Already in colonial times in East Africa there were some attempts to suggest a more agriculturally-based primary school curriculum – but these were roundly condemned by the rising nationalist movements as an insidious plot to confine Africans forever to the role of hewers of wood and drawers of water. Yet now the nationalists are in power, they too face the same problem. Any move towards a more practical primary education, such as President Nyerere of Tanzania has advocated, runs the risk of still being interpreted as an attempt to 'freeze' and preserve existing inequalities of access and life-chances.

Yet if nothing is done and things go on as they are, the more visible become the perverse effects described by Ronald Dore (1976) as *The Diploma Disease*. (Other terms for the same sort of things include 'qualificationism', 'certification', and 'credentialism'.) Where the demand for jobs greatly exceeds the supply, educational qualifications – say, a primary school leaving certificate – seem like a simpler way of selecting candidates than actually trying to test whether they have relevant abilities or skills. Those who lose out in this process are likely to respond by staying in the education system, re-sitting until they pass; while others stay on to move up a stage and acquire O-levels, and so be better placed. This of course ups the ante for everybody; now, you need O-levels to get a job. And so on . . .

In the end, even a country like Sri Lanka (poor, but with an extensive education system) winds up producing excess numbers of unemployed university graduates! – who still can't get jobs, because there are scarcely more jobs around than there were in the first place; and whose paper 'credentials' (which haven't delivered the goods for them in any case) bear no necessary relation to the possession of any useable or useful skills. It's an ironic and gloomy picture. Despite surface similarities, Dore is careful to distance his critique from 'trendy de-schoolers' like Ivan Illich. Far from wanting to abolish schools, his concern is that they should do their job better – if they can only get away from the 'formalism' and 'ritualism' which the wild goose chase after exam success and the attendant piece of paper imposes upon them.

Education, Economics and Development

The foregoing discussion has highlighted the relationship (or lack of it) between education and the economy, in terms of employment structures and prospects (or, again, the lack of them). This can be looked at from either a micro- or a macro-perspective: as individuals see it, or as governments.

As to the former, individuals are not wrong in this perception of differential rewards for the educated few. Silvey (in MacPherson, 1982, p. 78) cites a study which estimated a graduate's earnings to be more than six times those of a primary school leaver. But so narrow is the apex of the pyramid that the vast majority are doomed never to make it, and hence to disappointment.

Governments have often experienced a not dissimilar frustration, as their macro-calculations go awry. In retrospect, during the 1960s, too much faith was placed in education as *automatically* producing the 'human capital' that would promote development; just as earlier, in the 1950s, it was thought that *real* capital alone – 'aid' – would do the trick. Today, it is recognized that creating formal employment is a problem in its own right.

Yet it seems reasonable that there should be *some* connection between education, employment and development. The problem is that it is not easy to establish the precise linkages. Bairoch (1975) noted that the now developed countries had their own industrial revolutions in the nineteenth century with mostly very low literacy rates (technologies were simpler then, admittedly). The same author cites studies from the early USSR as suggesting, nonetheless, that increased literacy does more for industrial productivity than formal apprenticeships. (This may add an economic reason to the political and social motives for socialist regimes, e.g. in Cuba, Nicaragua and Somalia, to conduct massive literacy campaigns as one of the first steps in their development strategy.)

Inevitably, however, there is a timelag before the benefits of better education show up in the economy. And still the exact relations can be hard to specify. Anderson and Bowman (cited in Hardiman and Midgley, 1982, p. 201) find certain correlations. 40% literacy seems to be a kind of threshold, in that the very poorest countries are mostly below this. At the other end of the scale, the richest Third World countries tend to have literacy rates of 80% and above. But in between there is no very clear correlation. As they suggest, GNP alone is too crude a figure; one must also look at income distribution, demographic factors, and above all the structure of employment.

Over most of the Third World demand for education remains high, despite the fact that in many cases (especially for secondary and higher education) people have to pay for it – as is also the case with health services. Yet educated unemployment (e.g. jobless school leavers) is also well-nigh universal in the South, sometimes alongside a lack of skilled human power in particular sectors. In conclusion, education may well be a necessary but is certainly not a sufficient condition for development, both economically and socially. In particular, expanding education and hoping for the best is no substitute for direct measures to create jobs.

Language and Education

When I taught at the University of Dar es Salaam in the early 1970s, I had the convenience of teaching in my own language: English is the official medium of instruction in higher and secondary education in Tanzania. For the students, however, English (which they wrote at least as well as British students) was not even their second but their *third* language. They will have grown up speaking one of Tanzania's several dozen vernaculars (local languages), such as Chagga or Ha, and then learned in Swahili, the national African language, at primary school before switching to English at secondary level.

Similar situations are by no means rare in the Third World. Although Swahili has few equivalents, the choice between vernacular and national languages as a medium of educational instruction has many aspects and is not easy. Suppose you have vernacular primary education; after all, children learn best in the language they're used to. What about secondary school? Quite possibly, by that stage children from different language groups may be studying alongside each other (they certainly will at university). Obviously they can't all be taught in different languages. What then?

Almost certainly, some language groups (peoples, 'tribes') will be bigger than others. Should minorities then learn the majority's language? and learn everything else *in* it? Where there is one dominant group and relatively few or small minorities, that is indeed what tends to happen. (And not only in the Third World: earlier in this century, you could be beaten in Wales or Scotland if heard to speak Welsh or Gaelic in schools.) But if there are a number of groups, this would be both impracticable and politically controversial: each group will be fearful of others gaining too much power, so to elevate any one such language to be *the* language of education would be to stir up a hornet's nest.

And that is why over large parts of the ex-colonial world, especially Africa, the official language (of education, and otherwise) remains that of the former colonial power: English, French or Portuguese. That way, no one indigenous language gets privileged: all are equal. It has other advantages too. Much of the world's scientific and academic literature is written in English or French, so to choose one of these as an educational medium saves an awful lot of translating. (In Tanzania lip-service is paid to the goal of ultimately 'Swahilianizing' the whole education system, and the Institute of Kiswahili Research is busy inventing technical terms – 'sociology' is 'elimu ya ujami'. But somehow one wonders whether, or when, it will actually happen.)

Adopting a European language has its negative side, however. For one thing, it disadvantages those unfamiliar with it – which is another way of saying that it gives yet another boost to those from privileged homes, where English or French may already be familiar. Similarly, for those alarmed about cultural dependency, it drives yet another wedge between the elites and their fellow-citizens, while simultaneously cementing further their ties with the former colonial power.

In some former colonies, 'pidgins' or 'creoles' have developed as a spontaneous mix of elements of European and indigenous languages. Yet even in such cases, such as Guinea-Bissau (the former Portuguese Guinea), governments have usually preferred to adopt the 'pure' European language for official and educational use. A partial exception is Papua New Guinea, that extraordinary country with its hundreds of language groups, where 'Tok Pisin' (talk pidgin) has official status alongside English.

It is tempting to multiply illustrations. Complicated political games can be played out in the realm of language. In Malaysia, for instance, Malays worried about Chinese predominance in the education system brought in proficiency in the Malay language as a qualification for university entrance – which is one reason why many Malaysian Chinese come to study in the UK. In Hong Kong, a longstanding debate as to which of English or Chinese should be the medium of instruction (there are universities which use each) will doubtless receive fresh momentum as the territory's reversion to China in 1997 draws nearer. And so on . . . There are endless examples, but no easy answers.

Polemics and Practitioners: Illich and Freire

It would be wrong to close this chapter without at least mentioning two major and much discussed figures who have helped shape thinking about educational problems in the Third World. Of the two, Ivan Illich is the better known. An Austrian who lives in Mexico, his radical diagnosis of and prescriptions for schools (and indeed many other conventional institutions) are famous beyond the Third World. Arguing that most people learn most of what they know (and what it is actually useful to know) outside school rather than within it, Illich goes so far as to recommend – in the title of his most famous book – 'deschooling society'. Learning and teaching should be a co-operative endeavour, and a lifetime process, occupying (say) two months a year over a 20–30 year period rather than all being squashed up front during the few years of childhood.

By contrast, the ideas of the Brazilian Paulo Freire embody a perhaps more workable radicalism. They were certainly developed in practice: Freire was formerly in charge of his country's National Literacy Programme, and insisted that literacy could only be effectively promoted among the poorest if it was linked explicitly to thinking critically about their own situation and what they might do about it. In a word (and a word unpronounceable in any language), this entails a process of *consciencization*: not just consciousness–raising, but people learning to think and act as subjects in their own right.

Needless to say, none of this went down a bomb with the right wing military dictatorship which seized power in Brazil in 1964; they closed down Freire's programme, and exiled him.

Cultural Dependency?

Let us now return to the idea of 'education as cultural imperalism' – itself the title of a book by Martin Carnoy. The basic point is tellingly put by a Senegalese writer, Sheikh Hamidou Kane (quoted in Buchanan, 1975, p. 31): 'More effectively than the gun, it makes conquest permanent. The gun coerces the body, but the school bewitches the mind'.

There is undoubtedly much in the Third World's historical experience which chimes in with this view. In colonial times, Western (often missionary) education could be profoundly culturally divisive, splitting communities and even families. In a classic study, Mayer (1963) reported how in a South African city urban Xhosa saw themselves as belonging to one or two opposed groups. *Red* were those who still wore the traditional ochre of their nation, and in general kept up their old beliefs and customs. The others, more westernized in their lifestyles, religion, and so forth were significantly called *School*. Similar episodes, differing in degree and detail, could be quoted from the length and breadth of the Third World.

And indeed beyond: for wherever 'modernity' came from the outside (whether or not at the barrel of a gun), it has always involved profound cultural conflict and agonising choices. Thus Rusisian intellectuals over a century ago found themselves divided into 'Westernizers' and 'Panslavists': the former arguing that only wholesale and immediate adoption of Western science, education and institutions could save Russia, the latter insisting that on the contrary it was essential to reaffirm whatever traditions made Russia unique and different. In the coming decades, Arab, Chinese and many other intelligentsias would each independently repeat the terms of this debate.

In retrospect, then, it showed astonishing optimism or ignorance or both for modernization theorists to assume that such cultural change was relatively unproblematical. Although it was admitted there would be 'strains', Lerner's claims in the mid 1950s that 'what America is, the modernizing Middle East now seeks to become', and his view of Islam as defenceless against the 'rationalist and positivist spirit' look bizarre in the mid 1980s, with a virulently anti-American Islamic neo-fundamentalism riding high in Iran and elsewhere.

Even so, I'm not convinced that the 'cultural dependence' school have got it quite right either. That there has been a continuing process of cultural Westernization of the Third World seems to me an undeniable fact. To some extent, how we evaluate it ethically seems to me beside the point, since at least some aspects are irreversible. For example, despite Illich schools are not actually going to be abolished in the Third World. So whether or not it was a good thing for Western-style education to come to dominate the Third World is really beside the point; it's there, and that's that. The point is that much that *was* foreign in the Third World has now taken root, to the extent that it is no longer useful or proper to regard it as other than indigenous. Religion is the obvious case: both Christianity and Islam are in a sense 'foreign' to everywhere outside Palestine and Saudi Arabia respectively, yet it would be sociologically ludicrous today to think in such terms. Similarly, no one is actually going to unpick the patterns that imperialism has woven upon our world. Dye them a different colour, perhaps. But things are not going to go back.

Yet people do muse upon these things, like the Russians I mentioned. And in this, I think, lies the Third World's salvation. It can, and in some sense always does, *react*: select, redefine, recombine cultural elements from many sources – its own traditions (themselves no single seamless web) and various newer influences (equally diverse). There is of course nothing automatic or evolutionary about this. It involves debate and cultural contestation – like Chileans under the Allende government rediscovering and reasserting their Indian musical inheritance, against the tide of Tin Pan Alley. That sort of thing is happening all the time, producing new syntheses (like the music of Inti Illimani) which surely enhance the whole world's cultural heritage.

In sum, if modernization theory couldn't see the problem, dependency couldn't see the solution. Modernization is never pure and naked: it always wears particular cultural clothes. But these garments are not necessarily straitjackets. Some put them on others; but the wearers usually adopt and transform them, and may well make them fit.

Chapter Nine

Women and Development

Introduction

Until quite recently gender issues were conspicuous by their absence from the sociology of development as with most of the rest of sociology. And, as in other areas, the gradual process of making amends for this astonishing oversight is proving very fruitful for the sociology of development, in two ways. Not only is it a matter of filling a gap, painting in a blank, putting in something which was left out. But perhaps even more importantly, awareness of a gender dimension often sheds new light on other already 'known' areas of sociology too. Where appropriate, in the various substantive chapters in this book I try to draw attention to gender-related aspects. But there is need also for a chapter in its own right on women, although inevitably this will only scratch the surface of what is if anything an even wider range of issues than usual.

Let us begin with some facts and figures. Women form 50% of the world's population; perhaps fractionally more, since on average they live longer than men. It is estimated that this half of us work two-thirds of all work hours in the world, and are responsible for 50% of world food production. Yet they receive only 10% of world income, and own a derisory 1% of world property. They have other obligations, too: one-third of all families are headed by women.

In Africa in particular, for example, women do 60–80% of all agricultural work, 50% of animal husbandry, and close on 100% of food processing. Or again, to break down an often quoted 'global' figure, of the world's 800 million illiterates, 3 out of 5 (480 million) are women. Illiteracy is in fact increasing, and once again the process is unequal by gender. During the 1970s male illiteracy grew by about 2 million p.a.; for females, the figure was 5 million p.a.

I mentioned in Chapter 7 (p.171) that women tend to live longer than men. In the First World where at least physical conditions (if not social conditions) for the sexes are relatively equal, the lifespan gap can be up to eight years. In the Third World, reflecting the enormous physical burdens which fall disproportionately upon women, this gap falls to two years. In India and Bangladesh it is actually reversed, and men survive longer than women.

Women in Development

Like other themes in this section, women's subordination has both economic, political, and cultural aspects. Also, given that Third World societies today are a mix of traditional and modern, internal and external influences, it is important to stress that *all* these can be sources of inequality. It would be equally wrong, in my view, to portray Third World women as uniformly sunk in bondage until rescued by the progressive West, as it would be to reverse the picture and conceive of the South as a utopia of sexual egalitarianism until evil capitalism came and brought in oppression. The real picture is much more complicated.

Some of the complexities and ambiguities are summarized by Paul Harrison (1981, p. 438ff). In general, women work a 'double day': not only eight hours or more in formal labour outside the home, but often the same amount of domestic labour within it. Lest any man still associates women's work with 'light' work, Harrison points out that three well-nigh universal and back-breaking tasks – fetching water, gathering fire wood, and grinding corn – are almost invariably performed by women. That much may be traditional, but the same is not true of other factors working to render women 'the poorest of the poor' (the title of Harrison's chapter).

Thus it is modern factory-produced consumer goods (whether made in the Third World, or imported from the West) which have dealt a body blow to indigenous handicraft production – often a traditional livelihood for women. Or again, it is modern systems of male labour migration which have redoubled the burdens upon women, who are left holding the fort in every sense – running the farm single-handed, bringing up children, etc. – while their menfolk migrate to cities or even overseas for long periods in search of wage employment. And it is well meant but ill conceived modern rural development projects which, as Barbara Rogers (1980) has illustrated, time and again benefit men whilst excluding or even harming women. Mechanization of ploughing, for instance, lightens men's load as this is usually a male task – while simultaneously putting far more pressure on other jobs, e.g. weeding and processing, which are done by women but which do not receive the benefit of mechanization.

Women and Life-chances

What sorts of factors should we look at, in order to assess and indeed compare the positions of women in different societies? Blumberg (quoted in Giele, 1977) lists seven 'life options': whether and whom to marry; termination of such unions; sexual freedom, before and outside marriage; freedom of movement; access to educational opportunities; power within the household; and control over reproduction and family size. On each of these, one can compare the position of men and women both within and across societies. Thus, on sexual freedom hypocrisy and double standards are well-nigh universal. A man (married or not) who 'sleeps around' rarely incurs any penalty, and may even earn unofficial kudos ('he's a bit of a lad'); whereas a woman who does exactly the same risks at best insults ('slag', and worse), or at worst in some societies severe punishment or even death.

Blumberg's seven criteria, however, mostly focus on household and family. Yet this is only part of the picture, and Giele provides a more comprehensive sixfold list of different spheres. First is *political expression*. What rights do women possess, formally and otherwise? Can they vote, in theory and practice? Can they own property in their own right? Can they express any dissatisfactions in their own movements? Second is *work and mobility*. How do women fare in the formal labour force? How mobile are they; how well are they paid, how are their jobs ranked, and what leisure do they get?

Third comes *family: formation, duration, and size*. Do women choose their own partners? Can they divorce them? What is the status of single women and widows? Do women have freedom of movement? Fourth is *education*; what access do women have, how much can they attain, and is the curriculum the same? Fifth is *health and sexual control*: what is women's mortality, to what particular illnesses and stresses (physical and mental) are they exposed, and what control do they have over their own fertility? Last, elusive but important, there is what Giele calls *cultural expression*. What images of women and their 'place' are prevalent, and how far do these reflect or determine the reality? And what can women do in the cultural field? In the next section, we shall briefly examine some of these issues in particular regions of the Third World.

Variations by Region

Although as Rosaldo and Lamphere have said 'sexual asymmetry is presently a universal fact of human social life' (quoted in Giele, 1977), nonetheless, both the forms and degrees of women's subordination vary greatly, from place to place and over time. In both respects the Third World is no exception, as the following (inevitably highly selective and compressed) thumb-nail sketch may indicate.

In many parts of *Africa*, women traditionally had more power and status than was the case in much of South and East Asia, or even in Europe. They had major socio-economic roles, as farmers, producers of craft goods, and traders – this last remaining important today, as with the market women in several West African societies. Also, women often participated in political decision-making through their own organizations. Some societies had female chiefs.

By contrast, in many *Islamic societies* (in West and South Asia, and North Africa) the role segregation and subordination of women was and is considerable. In extreme cases, the practice of *purdah* delineates largely separate spheres for men and women, corresponding to the 'public' and 'private' realms respectively. Women's participation in public life ranges from limited to non-existent. Often, even to enter the public domain (e.g. walk in the street) requires varying degrees of veiling. Although there is much variation, it may be salutary for anyone who thinks of development as automatically unilinear and progressive to note that, with the current wave of fundamentalist revival within Islam, even in hitherto more relaxed societies like Malaysia women are coming under increasing pressure to don the veil.

In *East Asian* societies the cultural heritage of Confucianism emphasized the subordination of women as one of the several parallel 'natural' hierarchies: young to old, children to parents, ruled to rulers. Although to a degree transformed by socialist revolution in some countries and capitalist industrialization in others, such norms are persistent. In South Korea, for instance, although women's education is far better provided for than in most of the Third World, it is hard for graduate women to find jobs, let alone make careers, and the pressure to marry is acute. And the divorce position is Victorian: although legal, it is rare because considered shameful – and the *father*, as head of household, is almost certain to win custody of children if he wishes. Working-class women face different problems. Far from being excluded from the formal labour force, millions work as factory workers – yet their pay averages less than half what men get, which is itself not high. And, on top of long hours of factory work, women as everywhere have primary responsibility for child care and running the home as well.

Women's position in *Latin America* is ambivalent. Saffiotti (in Rohrlich-Leavitt, 1975) suggests that the ideology of 'machismo' has effects in the sphere of women and work. Women are regarded as and socialized into being wives and mothers, dedicated to self-sacrifice. Wage labour is viewed as secondary, and not relieving them from these primary domestic obligations. Both from the viewpoint of society and their own husbands, therefore, women are seen as available to be pushed either into or out of the formal labour market as and when necessary. Such jobs as they do get, like elsewhere in the world, tend to be the worst paid and defined as the least skilled: in factories, as vendors, or domestic service. The last involves a particular irony. One plus for Latin America is that it has a rather larger proportion of middle-class women pursuing professional careers than is normal elsewhere in the Third World. Yet this is only possible because of the availability of other women to perform low-paid domestic service and child care.

Women in Historical Development

The recent growth of interest in gender issues in sociology has led to much research and speculation on the position of women in long-run processes of historical change. Some radical feminists have pictured an original human condition of matriarchy, but evidence for this is scarce.

What does seem plausible, however, is a relationship between different types of society (especially in agriculture) and the position of women changing – not always for the better. Ester Boserup (1970) put forward a theory relating to different ecological contexts. Hunting and gathering societies, first, have a relatively low sexual division of labour. Once settled agriculture begins, the pattern varies. Hoe-based agriculture and shifting cultivation, especially in Africa, seem to be related to an increase not only in women's role in farming but also in their political autonomy. Conversely, the introduction of dry plough agriculture is almost always associated with men's labour, as this is 'heavy' work; and women come to experience restrictions also on their mobility and commercial activities. However, the pattern is different in wet, paddy farming (notably rice). There, tasks necessary for intensive cultivation (irrigation, weeding, transplanting, etc.) ensure an important role for women in production, and concomitant status.

Although generalizing of this kind is always hazardous, it is a merit of Boserup's approach that it is not so much a 'stage' theory as one related to different environmental contexts. We could say: progress is neither unilinear (one way) nor is it indeed necessarily progressive (for the better). By contrast, it seems in many ways too simple to reduce this as Giele (1977) does to a three-stage general model of women's social position: from early high status (often very long ago indeed), via a lengthy period of constriction – most of recorded human history, in fact – to a prospect of some improvements in the present era.

It should be said, however, that this alleged 'curvilinear relationship between societal complexity and sex equality' (up, down, then up again) appears to be paralleled in the obviously related area of changing family structures. The standard view which associated the nuclear family with modern industrialism and the extended family with pre-industrial societies has been subject to a number of criticisms and qualifications. The one which concerns us here suggests that the very earliest hunter and gatherer societies also had something like a simple nuclear family structure; and that only with plough-based agriculture did the extended family, under a male patriarchal 'head of household', arise.

Women, Colonialism and Economic Change

The effects of colonialism on the position of women were not clear-cut. There were those who saw themselves as striving to rescue women from traditional forms of oppression. Missionaries in Kenya, for instance, caused controversy by forbidding the practice of female circumcision among their converts. In Korea, education for women was virtually founded by Christian missionaries. On the other hand, almost by definition missionaries brought with them their own Western ideas about 'women's place', thus introducing new forms of inequality (e.g. seeing women's roles as primarily domestic).

Other aspects of the impact on women of broader economic changes have already been mentioned, such as pressure on handicraft production and the rise of migrant labour. The latter should not be underestimated, especially in Africa, and its effects continue to loom large today. Millions of women do not see their husbands, or only very briefly, for months or years at a stretch. By no means all of them receive much in the way of cash remittances from male earnings. Meanwhile, they must look after farms and bring up their children alone – or with only the help of the elderly. In South Africa, notoriously, such arrangements are legally formalized in 'pass laws' and so-called 'homelands'. Elsewhere – including neighbouring independent countries which still supply labour to South Africa – economic pressures produce a not dissimilar result.

Even so, modernization theorists would doubtless stress the way in which development has transformed women's position and options out of all recognition. The rise of urban life, the increase in educational access, the opportunities for factory and other formal labour, all constitute major changes. Yet a rounded view must surely emphasize the unevenness and contradictions attendant upon such processes. To gain such advantages, women must not only often fight against concepts of their traditional role, but usually even if 'successful' they must continue to perform the lion's share of domestic labour as well. Factory work is a particularly ambiguous area, in which the price of gaining some measure of autonomy and income of one's own is often submission to new forms of exploitation: long hours, low wages, and the advances of chauvinist male bosses.

In India, poor peasant women work in the fields alongside men. One of the first social consequences of agrarian prosperity, for instance in the Punjab under the influence of the Green Revolution, is for wealthier farmers to show their new status by withdrawing 'their' women from agricultural labour – and keeping them in the home. Is this progress, for the women concerned?

Women in Export Manufacturing

As already implied, gender issues in the Third World are not just one 'area' among others. Rather, they raise questions that run the gamut of the entire development process: old and new, traditional and modern, internal and external, economic, political and cultural.

A striking modern example concerns the increasing numbers of young women, notably in South and East Asia and Latin America, who now work in factories producing goods (mainly textiles and electronics) for export to world markets. This is a trend of the 1970s and 1980s involving both 'footloose' Western TNCS and indigenous Third World firms. What is noteworthy in many cases is their positive preference for labour which is young (aged 14–25), female, and often newly recruited to the formal labour-force. How can we explain this new trend, and how is it liable to affect women's positions?

Diane Elson and Ruth Pearson (in Young et al, 1981) have made a particular study of these issues. At one level, capital seeks labour that is cheaper, pliable, and docile. Third World labour in general may well fulfil these criteria; especially in countries which offer to TNCs the 'carrot' of EPZs (export processing zones) with all their incentives, plus the 'stick' to the workforce of suppressing trades unionism. Young female labour may be especially suitable. But, importantly, the categories and labels used should not be taken at face value; they require historical explanation. Thus, if women are 'docile' (and they aren't always: world market factories in several countries have seen some explosive strikes, sit-ins, lock-outs, etc.), this may be partly a mask they put on in order to survive – like black slaves who pretended to be cheerful 'Uncle Toms'. Or it may represent a deference to authority already inculcated by traditional patriarchal structures, which capital can then adapt to its own uses and circumstances – e.g. by employing male bosses and supervisors, as is normally the case. Similarly, it is because of what Elson and Pearson refer to as women's 'material subordination as a gender' that women may also put up with lower wages, or accept a high rate of labour turnover – because they know they are going to leave and get married in any case.

The question of *skill* is of especial sociological interest. In this field as elsewhere, work that women do is typically classified as 'unskilled', and paid accordingly. Insofar as any element of skill *is* admitted, it is attributed to women's nature. Thus Elson and Pearson quote an official Malaysian brochure soliciting foreign investment, which manages to be both racist and sexist in claiming that 'the manual dexterity of the Oriental female is famous the world over'. The truth is that many women do indeed have these skills, not by nature but learned from other women in the household – and hence not recognized as skills to the patriarchal powers that be.

What are the consequences? Elson and Pearson suggest that there are three possible outcomes, and that factory work may either *intensify, decompose,* or *recompose* pre-existing forms of gender subordination. It is an empirical question, and examples of all three (as well as mixed forms) have been found. Intensification of subordination could be where wages are not even paid to the women themselves, but to their fathers. Alternatively, in the second case, decomposition of subordination, some women may use the money they make from factory work to increase their own autonomy, e.g. by getting out of the need for an arranged marriage. Or, in the third case, recomposition of subordination, it's old wine in new bottles. Nothing really changes; male dominance appears in a new form (e.g. women workers, male bosses).

But change it is, nevertheless. Elson and Pearson stress the negative aspects. Long bouts of shiftwork take their toll; stitching copper wires onto silicon chips can induce severe eyestrain. Moreover, dependence on the world market may be unstable anyway. Women who have reshaped their lives around wage income and then lose their job may face a bleak future, with little choice but to seek to survive in the service sector – which may in practice entail prostitution or related activities.

After the Revolution? Women in Socialist Countries

One obvious question is to ask how far and with what success the many and varied problems outlined above have been tackled in countries which claim adherence to socialism. Maxine Molyneux (in Young *et al* eds, 1981) has surveyed the position in a number of the countries we conventionally call 'communist'. She found a mixed picture, in which at least four things were generally positive.

In the first place, and not to be discounted, there is official ideological commitment to equality of the sexes. What this means in practice is admittedly varied. Among Islamic societies, whereas supposedly socialist regimes like those in Algeria, Libya or Somalia offered little more than lip-service, it was the avowedly Marxist-Leninist regimes like those in Afghanistan, South Yemen (formerly Aden), and Soviet Central Asia which had actually dared to tackle such traditions as polygyny (two or more wives), child marriage, the veil, and seclusion of women in general.

Secondly, entrance into the formal labour market is seen at least in principle as a normal expectation, even a duty, for women as well as men. Thirdly, there is commitment to full employment and mobilizing women; while in general, fourthly, such governments accept greater responsibility than those elsewhere in the Third World, both for the reproduction of a labour force and for social welfare.

On the other hand, state socialist regimes make little attempt to change relations *within* the home. If women are drafted into the formal labour force while still bearing the brunt of household tasks, this of course continues the 'double day'. Moreover, a particular form of family tends not only to be assumed but even idealized: gender-typing abounds, especially in images and ideologies of motherhood (or conversely, male leaders as 'fathers of the nation'). Finally, women still play less part in political life, and are heavily under-represented in the topmost echelons of power.

Interesting confirmation of some of Molyneux's analysis comes from the case of Vietnam, studied by Christine White (1982). In the period 1945–1975, during three decades of almost continuous war against first France and then the USA, the role of women in North Vietnam was crucial – to the point where by the end they were responsible for nearly all agriculture and the greater part of industrial production as well, and large numbers had acquired Party membership. After victory in 1975, however, not only did many women in leadership positions lose their jobs to newly demobilized men (which also happened in the West, after 1945), but party cards were called in and re-issued. The new issue gave preference to army veterans who are of course overwhelmingly male. (As an aside, but a very important one: the ways in which *military* regimes and the militarization of societies – common in the Third World – *generally* entrench and enhance specifically male power are only just beginning to be recognized.)

The case of Vietnam, though, is by no means wholly negative. Changes in agriculture mean that women are no longer unpaid family labour, and an effective marriage law reform has been implemented. Under socialism as under capitalism, there are particular gains and losses for women.

Women and Development Paradigms

Where does all this leave our twin rival perspectives, modernization and dependency? June Nash suggests (Nash and Safa, 1976) that both have tended to ignore gender issues. Modernization approaches not only simply overlook a good deal that women do (e.g. production within the home), but also duck the question of the ambiguous impact of much that passes for 'development' upon women. Dependency, meanwhile, fails to relate the external relations of structural dependence which it so much emphasizes to what is perhaps the most basic dependent relationship of all, the one which in a sense underpins all the rest – namely, that within the home. On reflection, the 'satellite that is no one's metropolis' at the bottom of Gunder Frank's metropolis-satellite chain should not be a landless labourer – but his wife. For that matter, Harrison (1981) has characterized women in general as 'the world's largest group of landless labourers'.

Women and Change

Most of the inequalities outlined above are well known to those who suffer them. Such knowledge is increasingly being articulated into action. Many countries in the Third World now contain women's movements of various kinds, which can differ in interesting ways from feminist movements in the West. A classic illustration is provided by Domitila Barrios de Chungara (in Johnson and Bernstein, 1982), a Bolivian Indian women's organizer and wife of a tin-miner, who describes how she went to an international women's conference in Mexico City and felt very alienated from the women on the platform –

as much for their elegant designer clothes, as for their insistence that men were the main problem and enemy.

By contrast, as Nash (in Nash and Safa, 1976) has put it, Third World women's movements are more likely to stress the need to transform the total process of uneven development of which women's subordination forms part. Class and sex exploitation are deeply interwoven; 'development' processes have profoundly affected women's roles; hence it seems both analytically problematical and politically inappropriate to isolate women's issues from their broader context. Not that this is a recipe for doing nothing. Such movements are no longer content to be left on the back burner, or told by men to wait until 'after the revolution'. But most would agree that, in their particular circumstances, the task is to fight with men against oppression rather than fight against men as such.

Struggle and change can take many forms, some less obvious and visible than others. An interesting argument which illustrates the pervasiveness of gender issues is provided by Adamson (1984). One of the great advances of the twentieth century, according to Adamson, is a very recent revolution in the education of girls. Only twenty years ago as few as 15% of girls received any education; whereas in 1984 three quarters of all six year old girls started school, a proportion barely lower than the figure for both sexes combined (80%). This constitutes more progress in the last twenty years than the previous 2000. For Adamson, its most radical effects have yet to be felt. As for the first time a generation of Third World women grows up where education is the norm and not the exception, they will demand more say in decision-making, at every level from the household to the state. As mothers, these educated women will have fewer children, whom they will be better able to look after – and educate in their turn. Thus improvements for women spread out and result in improvements for all in health, education, and population.

Possibly Adamson is too optimistic. Many (and disproportionately many) of those girls will drop out of school; and doubtless women's attempts to improve their lot will continue to meet resistance. In some countries, where Islamic fundamentalism is growing, the position of women may well deteriorate. Even so, I am tempted to share Adamson's sense that a mightly global social movement is now at last under way – perhaps, indeed, the mightiest of all.

Once, Marxists thought of the working-class as somehow encapsulating all exploitation, such that their liberation and overthrow of the existing order would constitute liberation for all. More recently, some.'Third Worldist' Marxists have suggested that at a global level it was the peasantry and not the proletariat who now fulfilled this vanguard role. Personally, I am sceptical (with some regret) of such dramatic visions – indeed, I think that to be able to transcend them in favour of a more complex if less dramatic world view is a sign of the maturing of sociology. Still, if I were ever tempted to see a single social group and their particular afflictions and struggles as the key to transforming our world, then for me it would be neither workers nor peasants as such, but rather those who were for so long astonishingly invisible to sociologists and socialists alike, the 'minority' who are in fact the majority: the subject of this chapter, gradually but irreversibly becoming the subject of history too.

Chapter Ten

Religion

The sociology of development has tended to neglect the rich field of Third World religion. This reflects its general over-emphasis on economic and political phenomena. Such a gap is unfortunate, since the material is both fascinating and important.

The above criticism cannot, however, be applied to social anthropology, whose opposite bias – towards the study of cultural aspects of social life – has here stood it in good stead. Of the works I shall mention, some are by anthropologists, some by sociologists, and some by historians. As always, it is far from certain that these disciplines are ultimately distinct.

The history of Third World religions can be seen in terms of hundreds or even thousands of separate cultural traditions (none of them static) coming into increasing contact with one another. This has not been an equal contact. The large-scale world religions of Christianity, Islam and Buddhism have over varying periods of time (centuries, in some cases) made substantial if uneven headway all over the globe; and this process continues.

Yet, although unequal, it is not a one-way process. Rarely are all traces of pre-Christian or pre-Islamic belief and practice submerged when a society or community converts. On the contrary, it is precisely in the 'syncretisms' or mixed forms which the Third World has produced that much of its interest lies.

Out of this potentially huge and fascinating field, I shall focus on three aspects which seem of especial interest to the wider concerns of the sociology of development. Two of them have been neatly summarized by John Goldthorpe: they concern religion as *cause* or *consequence* of economic development.

The first of these might be called, a bit irreverently, 'son of Protestant Ethic', referring to Max Weber's classic argument that capitalist development in the West was not originated by economic factors alone (although he maintained nothing so simple as that Protestantism *caused* capitalism).

Might Protestantism, or some other religious tradition, have the same dynamizing impact in the Third World as it arguably did in the West? There have been a number of studies of 'enterprising' groups along these lines. One particularly interesting current argument suggests a 'Confucian ethic'. Noting that the NICs (Newly Industrializing Countries) of East Asia, the so-called 'gang of four' or 'four little tigers' (South Korea, Taiwan, Hong Kong, Singapore) are all overwhelmingly ethnic Chinese or Confucian by tradition, this view suggests that there may be something in Confucianism conducive to rapid development. This 'something' might include: a respect for authority and the state; concern for education and learning; seeing oneself as part of a wider social whole; working together in harmony.

This may sound plausible, and certainly there is a correlation which needs explaining. However, there are problems. For one thing, Confucianism is not exactly a religion but more a social philosophy or ethic; still, for present purposes this may not matter. More damagingly, it was these very aspects that are now cited as virtues – deference, lack of individualism, etc. – which Weber in his original argument claimed could only maintain social conservatism! – inasmuch as they made innovation or rebellion impossible.

Perhaps the moral is to always be wary of single-factor explanations. Even if a Confucian ethic does act as a kind of social cement once growth is under way (and there's no doubt that the political cultures of all the East Asian NICs differ utterly from those of Brazil or Mexico, for instance), I suspect we must also look elsewhere for material, political, and other highly specific factors in explaining the total process of growth and development. Besides, Confucianism has been around for centuries, millennia even; whereas these growth processes are barely twenty years old. To explain the latter solely in terms of the former would therefore be a gross error of method. Even so, it would probably be wrong to rule such cultural factors out of the picture altogether. The challenge is how to 'operationalize' them, as part of a total explanation which can also account for why they come into play at some times but not at others.

Whether or not religion can be a cause of economic development, it has often been the subject of strikingly dramatic effects. This brings us to Goldthorpe's second category. It is by no means one confined to the Third World. On the contrary, whenever people have been faced by massive and seemingly inexplicable sudden changes in their lives, they naturally struggle to try to make sense of what is happening to them. And not infrequently, in pre-modern Europe as much as the Third World, the 'explanations' they come up with have a strongly religious cast.

For this purpose, the change could be a flood, plague, or natural disaster. Or it could be the startling and terrifying arrival of people of a colour never seen before, with seemingly magical powers over objects equally inexplicable and potent (aeroplanes, guns), who proceed to take you over and order you around. In a word, *colonialism* has been a powerful cause of specifically religious response, as have the slower but no less corrosive processes which it sets in train: changes in authority structures, in patterns of land holding, in communications, etc.

We are here in the territory of what is often called *messianic* or *millenarian* religion. The technical difference is that the former looks to a particular individual saviour, now or in the future, to deliver his or her people from their travails; while the latter anticipates a second coming or new kingdom. As this vocabulary would imply, millenarianism (I shall now use this as the general term) is very much a product of the impact of Christianity, usually in the context of European colonialism.

Sometimes colonialism alone provides the spur. Perhaps the most striking example is the 'cargo cults' or Melanesia in the Pacific, described by Peter Worsley in his book *The Trumpet Shall Sound*. In brief, noticing how the European colonialists were endlessly supplied with all their needs by air, members of these cults went through the motions of clearing their own airstrips and performing what they regarded as appropriate rituals, in order that they too might receive supplies of 'cargo'.

The forms of millenarianism can be extremely diverse. One highly visible expression is the growth, in colonies or ex-colonies, after a number of years of proselytizing by missionaries, of 'breakaway' indigenous churches and sects. (In South Africa alone, significantly, there are several hundred of these.) Sometimes these regard themselves as the true church, from which the 'white man's church' has strayed. Or again, they may be more or less *syncretist*: i.e. merging elements of Christianity with aspects of indigenous religion or culture which the missionaries' Christianity would want them to reject.

Often these syncretisms are associated with active social movements, leading in some cases to open political rebellion: e.g. the Taiping in 19th century China, the Tonghak in Korea at the turn of the century, or Kimbanguism and many other cases in Africa this century. Rebellion, naturally, invites the full force of government suppression (colonial or otherwise). Because of this aspect, some commentators have stressed the political aspect and significance of millenarianism, as often an early stage in what will later become secular nationalism. Vittorio Lanternari has thus dubbed them as 'religions of the oppressed'. Other explanations are closer to modernization theory. J. Milton Yinger sees millenarian cults as a kind of 'bridge' between traditional world views and the impact of the modern world, hence helping people to cope and assisting the passage from one to another.

The final aspect on which I want to focus is related to this second one. In a nutshell: how do we explain the Ayatollah? For a very striking feature of parts of the contemporary Third World is the resurgence of militant fundamentalist Islam, of which the Iranian revolution is only the most obvious example. To a large extent this caught sociologists on the hop. Those who had predicted the Shah's downfall tended to assume that the impetus would be secular, progressive, possibly socialist. As it turned out, however, all those forces in Iranian society have received even shorter shrift than they did under the Shah from what is turning out to be a militant and deeply reactionary theocracy.

Evidently, millions of Iranians see the world in profoundly religious terms. They thus reacted to the Shah's 'modernization from above' not only as being politically dictatorial (which it was) and economically unsettling (which it also was), but above all as culturally alienating. The worst, it seems, that could be said – the symbol that had real power – was neither poverty nor tyranny as such, but *foreignness*. What is needed instead is a return to fundamentals; neither capitalism nor communism, but a truly Islamic development policy.

The fact that many Westerners find all this both puzzling and distasteful is no reason for not trying to understand it. Apart from showing up the tendency of secular-minded Western sociologists to downplay what they all too often regard as irrational religion, it is important to put Islamic fundamentalism in a broader context in two ways. Islam is not the only kind of fundamentalism around; and fundamentalism is not the only kind of Islam.

The fact that fundamentalist *Christianity* is also registering substantial gains (e.g. in East Asia, and parts of Latin America) suggests that a more general process is at work, in which people cling to unquestioned truths (albeit in revitalized forms) as a guiding thread in times of uncertainty and upheaval. Nor should one neglect the way religion can function as ideology. There is something in Marx's 'opium of the people' jibe, insofar as some forms of fundamentalism do deflect people's attention away from changing gross inequalities of power in this world.

Nonetheless, the note on which I want to end is to stress that in neither Islam nor Christianity do the fundamentalists go unchallenged. On the contrary, throughout their history the major world religions have functioned as 'terrains of meaning', subject to radically different interpretations and conflicts which may have profound social implications. Islam and Christianity alike have always had their reformers, their populists, their 'protestants'. Nor has this process ceased. In Iran today, the most active and persecuted oppositionists are a group called the Mojahedin; also devoutly Muslim, but with a reforming bent which stresses science and social progress (e.g. in the position of women, and the rights of minorities), and which regards Khomeini's brand of Islam as reactionary and indeed un-Islamic.

Similarly, within Christianity the Third World has found a distinctive voice in recent years in the form of 'liberation theology'. Originating in Latin America, where the Catholic Church had for long been regarded as a bastion of the *status quo*, liberation theology gives a very different slant: reading the Old Testament as a people's struggle against oppression, and the New Testament as the gospel of and for the poor and disinherited. As a result, radical Christians have become a politically important force in several countries, notably Nicaragua (where several priests serve in the Sandinista government, despite Vatican disapproval) and El Salvador (whose progressive Archbishop, Oscar Romero, was gunned down in his cathedral by right wingers).

In conclusion, it is perhaps ironic that while in the West (or North) sociologists debate the hypothesis of secularization, in the 'South' religious categories and identities seem to be as imbued with meaning as ever. This alone should be sufficient reason not to neglect this area. Naturally, it is never the province of sociologists to pronounce on the truth or falsity of religious claims. But in surveying religion in the Third World today, sociologists of development should not forget W. I. Thomas' famous axiom: if people think something is real, it *is* real in its consequences. In all its diverse forms – possible catalyst for development; categories for coping with upheavals caused by development; or terrains of meaning *within* which struggles take place – religion in the Third World is sociologically very real indeed.

Bibliography

Adamson, P. 'Global Report' (BBC2 TV, 31.12.1984)

Alavi, H. and Shanin, T. eds. *Introduction to the Sociology of the 'Developing Societies'* (Macmillan, London, 1982)

Amin, S. *Unequal Development* (Harvester, Hassocks, 1976)

Anderson, P. *Lineages of the Absolutist State* (New Left Books, London, 1974)

Arrighi, G. *The Political Economy of Rhodesia* (Mouton, The Hague, 1967)

Bairoch, P. *The Economic Development of the Third World since 1900* (Methuen, London, 1975)

Bernstein, H. ed. *Underdevelopment and Development* (Penguin, Harmondsworth, 1973)

Boserup, E. *Women's Role in Economic Development* (Allen & Unwin, London, 1970)

Brandt, W. *et al. North-South: a programme for Survival* (Pan, London, 1980)

Brenner, R. 'The origins of capitalist development: a critique of neo-Smithian Marxism' *New Left Review* 104, Jul–Aug. 1977

Bromley, R. ed. *The Urban Informal Sector: critical perspectives* (Pergamon, Oxford, 1978)

Bromley, R. and Gerry, C. eds. *Casual Work and Poverty in Third World Cities* (Wiley, Chichester, 1979)

Buchanan, K. *Reflections on Education in the Third World* (Spokesman, Nottingham, 1975)

Byres, T. J. and Crow, B. *The Green Revolution in India.* U204, case study 5. (Open University Press, Milton Keynes, 1983)

Cardoso, F. H. and Faletto, E. *Dependency and Development in Latin America* (University of California Press, Berkeley, 1979 (1971))

Carnoy, M. *Education as Cultural Imperialism* (Longman, London, 1974)

Chambers, R. *Rural Development: putting the last first* (Longman, London, 1983)

Cliffe, L. and Saul, J. eds. *Socialism in Tanzania: an interdisciplinary reader* 2 Vols (East African Publishing House, Nairobi, 1974)

Crow, B. and Thomas, A. *et al. Third World*

Atlas (Open University Press, Milton Keynes, 1983)

Dore, R. P. *The Diploma Disease: education, qualification, and development* (Allen & Unwin, London, 1976)

Dore, R. P. 'Making Sense of History' (Review of B. Moore) *European Journal of Sociology* Vol. X, No. 2, 1969

Elson, D. and Pearson, R. 'The Subordination of Women and the Internationalisation of Factory Production'. In K. Young *et al*, eds. *op. cit.*

Fanon, F. *The Wretched of the Earth* (Penguin, Harmondsworth, 1967)

Frank, A. G. *Capitalism and Underdevelopment in Latin America: historical studies of Chile and Brazil* (Monthly Review, New York, 1969a)

Frank, A. G. *Latin America: Underdevelopment or Revolution* (Monthly Review, New York, 1969b)

Freire, P. *Pedagogy of the Oppressed* (Penguin, Harmondsworth, 1975)

Furtado, C. *Development and Underdevelopment* (University of California Press, Berkeley, 1964)

Gerschenkron, A. *Economic Backwardness in Historical Perspective* (Harvard University Press, Cambridge, Mass, 1962)

Giele, J. Z. and Smock, A. C. eds. *Women: roles and status in eight countries* (Wiley, London, 1977)

Gilbert, A. and Gugler, J. *Cities, Poverty and Development: urbanization in the Third World* (Oxford University Press, Oxford, 1982)

Goldthorpe, J. E. *The Sociology of the Third World: disparity and development*, 2nd ed. (Cambridge University Press, Cambridge, 1984)

Hardiman, M. and Midgley, J. *The Social Dimensions of Development: social policy and planning in the Third World* (Wiley, Chichester, 1982)

Harrison, P. *Inside the Third World*, 2nd ed. (Penguin, Harmondsworth, 1981)

Haupt, A. and Kane, T. T. *Population Handbook: international edition* (Population Reference Bureau Inc, Washington DC, 1980)

Hilal, J. 'Sociology of Development' (Dept.

of Sociology, University of Durham, mimeo, 1970)

Hoogvelt, A. *The Sociology of Developing Societies* (Macmillan, London, 1976)

Hoogvelt, A. *The Third World in Global Development* (Macmillan, London, 1982)

Hoselitz, B. *Sociological Aspects of Economic Growth* (Free Press, Glencoe Ill., 1960)

Hyden, G. *Beyond Ujamaa in Tanzania: underdevelopment and an uncaptured peasantry* (Heinemann, London, 1980)

Illich, I. D. *Deschooling Society* (Penguin, Harmondsworth, 1975)

Johnson, H. 'Production on the Land'. Block 3, Part A of *Making a Living: production and producers on the land*. U204, Third World Studies (Open University Press, Milton Keynes, 1983)

Johnson, H. and Bernstein, H. eds. *Third World Lives of Struggle* (Heinemann, London, 1982)

Kahn, J. and Llobera, J. eds. *The Anthropology of Pre-Capitalist Societies* (Macmillan, London, 1981)

Kaplinsky, R. ed. *Third World Industrialization in the 1980s: open economies in a closing world* (Cass, London, 1984) Also available as *Journal of Development Studies*, Vol. 21, No. 1, Oct. 1984

Kemp, T. *Industrialization in the Non-Western World* (Longman, London, 1983)

Kirkpatrick, C. H. and Nixson, F. I. eds. *The Industrialization of Less Developed Countries* (Manchester University Press, Manchester, 1983)

Kitching, G. *Development and Underdevelopment in Historical Perspective: populism, nationalism and industrialization* (Methuen, London, 1982)

Kerr, C. et al. *Industrialism and Industrial Man* (Heinemann, London, 1962)

Kumar, K. *Prophecy and Progress* (Penguin, Harmondsworth, 1978)

Laclau, E. 'Feudalism and Capitalism in Latin America' *New Left Review*, 67, May–June, 1971

Lea, D. A. M. and Chaudhri, D. P. eds. *Rural Development and the State: contradictions and dilemmas in developing countries* (Methuen, London, 1983)

Lee, D. and Newby, H. *The Problem of Sociology* (Hutchinson, London, 1983)

Lewis, O. *La Vida: a Puerto Rican family in the culture of poverty* (Panther, London, 1969)

Lipton, M. *Why Poor People Stay Poor: urban bias in world development* (Temple Smith, London, 1977)

Lloyd, P. *Slums of Hope?* (Penguin, Harmondsworth, 1979)

Long, N. *An Introduction to the Sociology of Rural Development* (Tavistock, London, 1977)

Love, J. L. 'Third World: a response to Professor Worsley' *Third World Quarterly* Vol. II, No. 2, Apr. 1980

MacPherson, S. *Social Policy in the Third World: the social dilemmas of underdevelopment* (Wheatsheaf, Brighton, 1982)

Mamdani, M. *The Myth of Population Control: family, caste and class in an Indian village* (Monthly Review, New York, 1972)

Michaelson, K. L. *And the Poor Get Children: radical perspectives on population dynamics* (Monthly Review, New York, 1981)

Molyneux, M. 'Women in Socialist Societies: problems of theory and practice'. In K. Young, *et al.* eds. *op. cit.*

Moore, B. Jr. *Social Origins of Dictatorship and Democracy: lord and peasant in the making of the modern world* (Penguin, Harmondsworth, 1966)

Myrdal, G. *Economic Theory and Underdeveloped Regions* (Methuen, London, 1963)

Nash, J. and Safa H. E. eds. *Sex and Class in Latin America* (Praeger, London, 1976)

Nisbet, R. *The Sociological Tradition* (Heinemann, London, 1967)

Open University *U204: Third World Studies*, 5 blocks in 8 volumes, 10 'case studies' atlas, and other materials; various authors (Open University Press, Milton Keynes, 1983)

Oxaal, I., Barnett, A. and Booth, D. eds. *Beyond the Sociology of Development* (Routledge & Kegan Paul, London, 1975)

Palmer, R. and Parsons, N. eds. *The Roots of Rural Poverty in Central and Southern Africa* (Heinemann, London, 1977)

Redclift, M. *Development and the Environmental Crisis: red and green alternatives* (Methuen, London, 1984)

Roberts, B. *Cities of Peasants* (Arnold, London, 1978)

Rodney, W. *How Europe Underdeveloped Africa* (Bogle-L'Ouverture, London, 1972)

Rogers, B. *The Domestication of Women: discrimination in developing societies* (Kogan Page, London, 1980)

Rohrlich-Leavitt, R. ed. *Women Cross-Culturally: change and challenge* (Mouton, The Hague, 1975)

Rostow, W.W. *The Stages of Economic Growth: a non-communist manifesto*, 2nd ed. (Cambridge University Press, Cambridge, 1971) (1960)

Roxborough, I. *Theories of Underdevelopment* (Macmillan, London, 1979)

Rweyemamu, J.F. *et al. Towards Socialist Planning* (Tanzania Publishing House, Dar es Salaam, 1974)

Saffiotti, H.I.B. *Women in Class Society* (Monthly Review, New York, 1978)

Sandbrook, R. *The Politics of Basic Needs: urban aspects of assaulting poverty in Africa* (Heinemann, London, 1982)

Schumacher, E.F. *Small is Beautiful* (Sphere, London, 1974)

Seers, D. 'The limitations of the special case' In *The Teaching of Development Economics*, edited by K. Martin and J. Knapp (Cass, London, 1967)

Shanin, T. ed. *Peasants and Peasant Societies* (Penguin, Harmondsworth, 1971)

Skocpol, T. *States and Social Revolutions* (Cambridge University Press, Cambridge, 1979)

Sutcliffe, R.B. *Industry and Underdevelopment* (Addison-Wesley, London, 1971)

Szentes, T. ' "Status Quo" and Socialism', Ch. 71 in Cliffe and Saul eds. *op. cit.*

Taylor, J. *From Modernization to Modes of Production: a critique of the sociologies of development and underdevelopment* (Macmillan, London, 1979)

Thomas, A. 'Third World: images, defin-itions, connotations'. In *The 'Third World' and 'Development'* U204, Third World Studies, Block 1 (Open University Press, Milton Keynes, 1983)

Thomas, C.Y. *Dependence and Transformation* (Monthly Review, New York, 1974)

Turner, J.F.C. *Housing By People* (Marion Boyars, London, 1976)

Vogeler, I. and De Souza, A. *Dialectics of Third World Development* (Allanheld, Osmun & Co. Totowa, N.J., 1980)

Wade, R. and White G. eds. 'Developmental States in East Asia: capitalist and socialist' *IDS Bulletin*, Vol. 15, No. 2, Apr. 1984

Wallerstein, I. *The Capitalist World Economy* (Cambridge University Press, Cambridge, 1979)

Warren, B. *Imperialism: Pioneer of Capitalism* (New Left Books/Verso, London, 1980)

Webster, A. *Introduction to the Sociology of Development* (Macmillan, London, 1984)

White, C.P. 'Socialist transformation of agriculture and gender relations: the Vietnamese Case' *IDS Bulletin*, Vol. 13, No. 4, Sep. 1982

Wield, D. 'Industrial Production: Factories and Workers' In *Making a Living: production and producers in the Third World*, Block 3, Parts B–C. U204, Third World Studies (Open University Press, Milton Keynes, 1983)

Williamson, B. *Education, Social Structure and Development: a comparative analysis* (Macmillan, London, 1979)

(World Bank) *World Development Report* Various years (World Bank, Washington, DC)

Worsley, P. 'How Many Worlds?' *Third World Quarterly*, Vol. I, No. 2, April, 1979

Young, K. *et al.* eds. *Of Marriage and the Market: women's subordination in international perspective* (CSE Books, London, 1981)

Section 3
Urban Sociology
Martin Slattery

The city and civilisation are inseparable: with the city's rise and spread, man at last emerged from the primitive state . . .
Some scholars regard the city as second only to agriculture among the significant inventions in human history. (Gideon Sjoberg, 1960, p. 1)

The reason why cities are ugly and sad,
Is not that the people who live in them are bad,
It's just that the people who really decide
What goes on in the city live somewhere outside.
(quoted in R. Friedland, 1982)

Urbanman

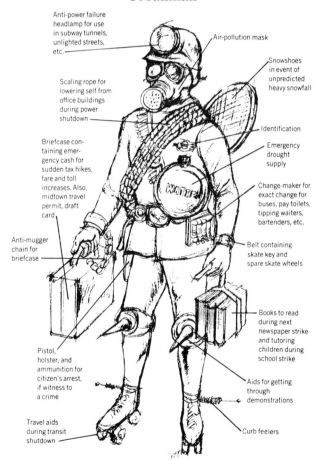

Anti-power failure
headlamp for use
in subway tunnels,
unlighted streets,
etc.

Air-pollution mask

Snowshoes
in event of
unpredicted
heavy snowfall

Scaling rope for
lowering self from
office buildings
during power
shutdown

Identification

Briefcase con-
taining emer-
gency cash for
sudden tax hikes,
fare and toll
increases. Also,
midtown travel
permit, draft
card

Emergency
drought
supply

Change-maker for
exact change for
buses, pay toilets,
tipping waiters,
bartenders, etc.

Anti-mugger
chain for
briefcase

Belt containing
skate key and
spare skate wheels

Books to read
during next
newspaper strike
and tutoring
children during
school strike

Pistol,
holster, and
ammunition for
citizen's arrest,
if witness to
a crime

Aids for getting
through
demonstrations

Travel aids
during transit
shutdown

Curb feelers

Introduction

The Urban Revolution of the past 150 years has transformed societies throughout the world by fundamentally altering not only where people live but how they live. This massive shift of population from the countryside to towns and cities has fundamentally altered not only the character and structure of society but the very environment we live in; not only our relationships with other people, but our whole 'way of life'. Many writers now argue that not only are advanced industrial societies like Britain essentially urban societies but that the world is increasingly becoming an urban world:

> Before 1850 no society could be described as predominantly urbanized, and by 1900 only one – Great Britain – could be so regarded. Today, only 65 years later, all industrial nations are highly urbanized, and in the world as a whole the process of urbanization is accelerating rapidly.
>
> (Kingsley Davies, 1973, p. 4)

Some therefore see the City as the centrepiece, the jewel in the crown of modern civilisation. Most of us live in or near to a major town or city. All of us have strong images of city life – we either love it or hate it. It is a place that hustles and bustles with life. Its bright lights attract us like moths and we feel enveloped in its atmosphere of rush, expectation and excitement. Cities are the focal point of modern economies, the homes of the major corporations and financial institutions. They are the powerhouses of modern politics, the centres of government, of law and order. They are the cultural centres of the modern world. They house the cinemas and theatres, music halls and playhouses, libraries and museums. Through television, radio and mass communications they beam messages and images round the globe. The city is the centre of modern progress.

Yet they are also places of danger, fear, isolation and ugliness – the 'dark side' of industrial progress, the centre of a whole spectrum of social problems from pollution to poverty, crime to congestion. Thomas L. Blair (1974) for example believes that we face an 'international urban crisis'.

Many now fear living in a 'human jungle' where crime, murder, suicide and riots seem almost commonplace, where people treat each other like animals, pushing past them, ignoring them and abusing them as they rush for the bus or push to get served in the shops and restaurants. Care and consideration for others no longer seems to exist. Thus whilst many love the city, others hate it and hark back to the 'Good Olde Days' of life in the country, living in small isolated villages amongst people you know intimately and grew up with, where you have a sense of place, a sense of community, an environment in which peace and quiet walk arm in arm with harmony and stability – a far cry from the noise and traffic, hustle and bustle of the city centre.

But what is it that makes the City tick, what is it about such huge concentrations of people and buildings that creates such excitement and such strife? Is it simply the place – its size and chaos? Do Inner City areas really 'breed' crime and poverty, do the suburbs 'breed' affluence and conservation, can town planners by redesigning cities, redesign people and recreate a sense of community? Do cities have a life of their own or are they the result of human action? Has the modern city simply got out of control?

Urban sociology is an attempt to answer such questions, an attempt to identify the key urban forces. This field of study has grown not only because the city has, but because many now fear that if the city dies so will modern civilisation. As the American National Resources Committee put it in 1973: 'If the city fails, America fails. The Nation cannot flourish without its urban-industrial centers.' Two years later New York went bankrupt!

Urban sociology however is not without its own problems, in particular:

(a) Problems of Definition. As a variety of writers have noted urban sociology has never clearly established itself, defined its boundaries in the way other sociologies have. Whilst the sociologies of crime, education and religion seem to have fairly clear cut areas of study, urban sociology has fluctuated between two opposing views:
(i) That urban sociology is the study of the City as a unique social institution with a life of its own separate from society at large and with its own internal laws of 'cause and effect'. Such a perspective tends to see different physical environments and geographical locations as generating different lifestyles and relationships. Compare for example life in a village and life in the city.
(ii) That the City is not separate from society at large but a reflection of it. From such a perspective the City is merely the arena in which

broader social, economic and political conflicts take place. Urban sociologists of this persuasion, study not only what goes on 'inside' the City but the forces outside that have shaped and changed our urban areas. Whilst the Founding Fathers of Urban Sociology and Community Studies took the first view in the early 20th century, the Radical Theorists of the 1970s and 1980s have taken the second. Urban sociology has thus undergone an 'Identity Crisis'.

(b) Ideological Bias – as will become evident, underlying much that is written about the town, village or city is a pro- or anti-urban bias, a disposition to praise and save the city or a romantic nostalgia for the community life in the past, in the village.

(c) Problems of Breadth and Scope – urban sociology is only one of the many disciplines that make up urban studies, a field that stretches from the geographer and town planner through to the economist and anthropologist. The problem is deciding where their individual boundaries start and finish, what the particular contribution of each is. As O.P. Williams (1971) pointed out: 'Urban is a catch-all adjective loosely used to classify a bloc of heterogenous studies that have little or no theoretical affinity.'

This section attempts to show not only how a variety of perspectives have developed within urban sociology but what its contribution to urban studies has been, what the advantages of a multi-disciplinary approach might be, what the advantages of a world perspective might be. However whilst the core of this section is an outline of urban theory, such theories are often highly abstract, even rather lifeless and so to help understanding and provide some background, chapter 1 briefly outlines the main trends in urban growth and development throughout the world. But cities are not only the laboratories of social scientists. Governments too experiment with them and the Inner City in particular has been the focus of considerable diagnosis and policy-making as politicians have desperately sought to cure this inner 'sickness', this stain on modern progress, this crucible of deviance, discontent and revolution. Chapter 4 outlines British attempts to save the urban soul because this topic is of considerable interest and highly relevant to the future of modern society and because it offers a 'testbed' for many of the theories and predictions of sociologists in the 1960s and 1970s.

As will become evident urban sociology is a fascinating and kaleido-scopic, as congested and sprawling as its subject matter. Like the city it has no beginning and no end. 'In an urbanised society, "urban" is everywhere and nowhere; the city cannot be defined and so neither can urban sociology.' (Pahl, 1970, p. 270).

Chapter One

Urbanisation

The aim of this chapter is not to provide a comprehensive overview of the process of urbanisation – that debate would take a book in itself – but simply to outline the main trends throughout the world today as background material for the sociological theories that follow. The chapter is divided up into three main sections describing urbanisation in the First, Second and Third Worlds, partly for ease of explanation; partly to emphasise the points that there is tremendous variation in the way cities grow and develop and that urbanisation itself does not necessarily follow or depend upon industrialisation. The final section links them back together again to show that though each city may seem unique with its own character and structure, it in fact forms part of an international urban and economic system.

The city is not a new phenomenon. What is new is its size. Cities existed over 5000 years ago usually at crossroads, as trading or market centres, or as the kingpins of great Empires or Civilisations such as those of Ancient China or Egypt. Rome may well have been the first 'million' city and the Roman Empire spread a vast network of towns and fortifications across Europe linked by road and sea; the remains of which still exist today. With the fall of the Roman Empire these urban areas disappeared too, until the rise of the great Nation States in the 14th and 15th centuries. Cities re-emerged as the courts of the new monarchs and so attracted power, privilege and luxury. However even as late as 1700 there were only six or seven cities in Europe of over 100,000 people. Gideon Sjoberg's study of the pre-industrial city is a classic analysis of such walled fortresses.

Elsewhere in the world though cities continued to grow and prosper. In East Asia, for example Sian in Ancient China and Kyoto in Japan were 'million' cities and the Aztec and Inca cities of South America became world famous. However with the invasion and colonisation of

221

such areas by Europeans from the sixteenth century onwards, such development stopped.

Urbanisation in the First (Capitalist) World

The **industrial** city however sprang from the economic and social revolutions of the 17th and 18th centuries. The following factors influenced its development:

(a) The Agricultural Revolution with its new machinery, new techniques of crop rotation and breeding and the large scale farming created by the Enclosure Movement **pushed** the peasants and small farmers off the land and created the surplus of food necessary to feed the new towns.

(b) The Industrial Revolution with its factories, mines and mills **pulled** such landless labour into the new towns with the promise of jobs, better wages and new freedoms.

(c) The Transport Revolution that followed – the canals, roads, and ultimately the railways – provided the means for men and goods to move quickly round the country.

(d) The Population Explosion of the 19th century provided the 'mass markets' for the new goods and services being produced. Between 1801 and 1901 Britain's population soared from 10.5 million to 37 million as the death rate fell dramatically in the face of improvements in food, health, hygiene and housing.

Britain experienced the first Industrial Revolution and it is usually described as a free market or capitalist one, one that appeared to 'take off' by its own momentum, one that was guided more by the 'invisible' hand of the market than by the State. In the late 18th century Britain not only had all the 'factors of production' necessary for an Industrial Revolution – in particular the vast resources and new markets of its great Empire and the financial and administrative system derived from its commercial activities – but it also had what Max Weber has called the 'Spirit of Capitalism': a culture of free enterprise as the merchants and bankers of the day searched for new investment and fresh profits.

At the centre of this Industrial Revolution was the city 'the central place par excellence, where men, machines and capital were co-ordinated to produce goods for world markets' (Blair, 1974, p. 29). Britain thus also experienced the first Urban Revolution. Between 1811 and 1891 the total population of England's large cities (100,000 inhabitants or more) increased from 1.2 million to nearly 9.5 million. London grew from 800,000 to over 4 million and by 1901 77% of the population were living in towns and cities. The transition from an agrarian to an industrial economy was complete with only 10% of the population employed in agriculture. England was now the commercial and financial centre of the world.

With industrialisation comes specialisation and such a division of labour affects not only workers but towns and cities. From being all-purpose centres of local activity and trade, there arose the new specialist industrial town based on one particular industry beit coal, iron-ore or textiles. Towns like Manchester and Newcastle became part of an economic network that stretched not only across Britain but across the globe as Britain became the 'workshop of the world'.

If the first stage of Britain's Urban Revolution was urbanisation – the movement of people and jobs into towns and cities, the second stage has been the movement out – not back to the country but out to the suburbs, to the new, satellite towns and commuter villages, to the growing tourist and retirement centres. Brian Berry has referred to this social revolution as a process of **counter-urbanisation** and it is obviously reflected in the 'flight from the Inner City' in the decline of population in the major conurbations. Between 1951 and 1971 for example Manchester's population fell by 22.8% and Liverpool's by 24.3%. The main factors involved in such urban decentralisation can be listed as:

(a) The Transport Revolution, the rapid development in the late 19th century of cheap public transport (trams, omnibuses and the railways) enabling even the working-classes to move out of the Inner City to the fresh air of the suburbs. The car and the motorway have produced a commuter revolution enabling people, especially in London to live out in the countryside and along the coast and yet work in the city.

(b) The Changing Location of Industry. Whilst the early Industrial Revolution produced a concentration of factories and warehouses in the city centre the twentieth century has seen their movement out – to the New Towns and the new Industrial Estates. Few industries now need to be based in one specific area and with the advent of the motorway they can pick and choose their location. As factories moved out, offices moved in.

(c) The Growth of Local Government. This dates from the 1880s and involved not only the provision of such basic services as gas and water but increasingly town planning and slum clearance. During the 1930s and 1950s masses of people were cleared from the inner city slums and rehoused on new estates and in New Towns on the outskirts of the major cities.

(d) The Housing Revolution. With the post-war growth in affluence, the greater availability of mortgages and the mobility of modern transport systems, more and more people have been able to afford a house in the suburbs or even the country. The very high cost of Inner City land has further encouraged both industry and people out to the outskirts. Accompanying such trends is an overall shift of population from the old industrial North to the new industries and services of the South and though there is some evidence of a slight shift back into the Inner City as young middle-class couples buy up cheap terraced housing and do it up, such a process of **gentrification** is only really pronounced in London.

The same general trends are evident in the rest of Northern and Western Europe – though not always exactly in the same direction and at the same pace. As Hall and Hay (1980) explain:

> Europe is a highly urbanised nation and furthermore it is increasingly becoming so. Some 86% of its population lived in metropolitan areas in 1950, with a further 2.3% added by 1970... Britain seems to be most advanced down the centralisation to decentralisation urbanisation path. Nations in Northern and Central Europe and the Benelux countries seem to be not too far behind, with their populations beginning to decentralise, although in some cases not yet their jobs. (Summarised in Spence *et al*, 1982, pp. 5–7)

America too has experienced mass urbanisation but not so much from the countryside as from Northern and later South East Europe, as immigrants poured into this 'land of opportunity' before and after World War I. According to James Richardson (1982) by 1900 virtually every major American city had been founded and increasingly a hierarchy of urban centres developed with key cities like New York becoming the financial and political centres of both the Federal Government and the new Multinational Corporations. The move to the suburbs began in the 1920s but according to Sternlieb and Hughes (1975) the American 'flight' from the Inner City was not only because of factors like those listed above but also because of fear – fear of the decay, crime, pollution and riots that have beset such areas. Between 1970 and 1977 the cities of America lost 4.6% of their population whilst the nation as a whole gained 6.4%. This decline especially hit such manufacturing cities as New York which went bankrupt in 1975 with a financial deficit of $5.1 billion. The suburbs have grown by 12%, twice that of the country as a whole and there has been a flight west and south – to the 'sunbelt' of California, to Texas and to the new 'post-industrial cities' of Dallas and San Diego. The 1980s however have seen some shift back due to the processes of gentrification and of **conversion**. Big business is now trying to convert the city centres of New York, San Francisco and the like into offices, hotels, government headquarters and residences for the rich. The poor (and their problems) are being shifted out to the fringes as the cities of America try to come alive again.

Urbanisation in the Second (Socialist) World

Trends here have been similar to those in the West but with the key difference that urban development in Communist countries is centrally planned rather than the result of market forces. Public need is the guiding light rather than the pursuit of profit. In this way socialist societies hope to eliminate the inequalities and major social problems that are a feature of capitalist cities. They aim to establish the 'classless' city and a proper harmony between town and country.

However within the Communist Bloc, attitudes towards urbanisation vary sharply. Whilst those countries in the Eastern Bloc under Soviet rule generally welcome it as a sign of economic and social progress, others like China have a deep distrust of cities since in the past they were seen as centres of luxury and debauchery, exploitation and oppression.

As in the West, urbanisation here has generally accompanied industrialisation with a surge of urban growth following the establishment of communist governments before and after World War II. As part of the overall programme for reconstructing the economies of East European countries devastated by the War, investment was channelled into industrial sectors in certain key areas. In the absence of capital the abundant and cheap labour of the countryside was directed into these new industrial centres which thus inevitably mushroomed. But the massive urban growth of the post-war period was not only due to migration but also to the very high birth rate in these cities – the post-war Baby Boom. Housing however was in very short supply so many workers had to commute daily from their villages. By the 1960s however the birth rate had slackened and migration was under control. Though all the countries of Eastern Europe have experienced massive industrialisation, the level of urbanisation varies enormously. In 1980 for example East Germany had 76% of its population living in cities but Yugoslavia had only 42%.

The Soviet Union, the centre of this Eastern Bloc, exemplified many of these trends. Whilst in '1971 barely one sixth of all Soviet inhabitants lived in cities, soon two-thirds will' (James Bater, 1980, pp. 1–2). In 1914 only 28 million people lived in Soviet cities; by 1979, 162 million out of a total population of 262 million will. In 1959 there were only three Soviet cities of over one million people, today there are twenty three with Moscow as the great Russian giant having over 8 million inhabitants. Such urban expansion however is despite rather than because of Soviet planning. Millions of peasants have found ways to get round the very strict controls on movement from the country into the city – controls that include residency permits and domestic passports. Nevertheless urban development in the Soviet Union is far more controlled and organised than that in either the West or Third World.

According to Soviet ideals, urban living is the highest form of socialist life, the perfect environment for developing socialist consciousness and a vital step in industrial progress away from what Marx and Engels called 'the idiocy of rural life'. The aim of Soviet plans is to create a balance both within urban areas and between the towns and country. They try to separate industrial and residential areas by 'green belts' but keep them close enough to prevent long distance commuting. Each neighbourhood in a Soviet city is meant to have local facilities to provide residents with their daily needs and a district service centre providing for 4 to 10 neighbourhoods. More specialised goods and services are to be found in the city centre. As French and Hamilton (1979) explain, neighbourhood organisation

> is based on the premise that for comfortable living in a socialist society, all citizens should have equal access with minimal outlays of journey time and effort, whether on foot or by public transport, to all the material, cultural, and welfare goods and services that they require. (p. 9)

The basis of such communal living is the **mikrorayan** or micro-district a self-contained unit comprising residential quarters, dormitories, communal eating and recreation facilities, creches, schools and local medical services. Each micro-district is linked to a major factory or industrial plant and such neighbourhoods have become the basic unit of Soviet house building. Other differences between Western and Soviet cities include:

(a) Layout. Instead of the outward sprawl of capitalist cities, Soviet ones have a fairly even distribution of population. They too have an Inner City but its not an area of blight and decay but one of life and energy. They have no Central Business District as in the West where shops, offices, restaurants and entertainment are huddled together but rather each of these facilities is in a separate part of the city. The only central feature of a Soviet city is the central square and the inevitable statue of Lenin for May Day parades and the like.

(b) Social Segregation. According to French and Hamilton (1979) there is little social segregation in terms of distinctly different residential areas as in the West. There are no slums in our sense of the word, only 'some tendency for social segregation by apartment building'. Other writers are less sympathetic, Mervyn Matthews (1979) for example has identified four main classes of Soviet housing – the Dachas and hilltop mansions of the Communist Party Leaders, the blocks of prestige flats for top Party officials, the flats and houses of State managers and highly skilled technical workers and the Soviet 'slums' (a word banned in the USSR). In his studies of socialist housing in Hungary (1972 and 1983) Ivan Szelenyi has identified similar social divisions with the intellectuals, bureaucrats and technicians living in the superior zones of the city centre and new multi-storey estates and the blue collar and unskilled workers living in the inferior zones of the outer suburbs and industrial areas.

(c) Transport. Whilst we in the West rely mainly on the car for urban transport, the vast majority of Soviet citizens get about via a very efficient and cheap system of public transport. Inevitably the problems of congestion and pollution are less.

(d) Social Problems. Though Soviet cities have their fair share of such urban problems as crime, alcoholism, prostitution and black marketeering, few of them are on the scale found in Western especially American cities.

Thus in French and Hamilton's view the apparent similarities between Western and Soviet cities are superficial. The two economic and political systems are fundamentally different. No western government can control the urban environment in the way a Soviet planner can. As Ivan Szelenyi (1983) also concludes:

> But, even if Western Europe is beginning a transition to something more like the North American model, our theme here is that Eastern Europe is not. It is developing a third model, all its own. Compared with most North American cities, the segregation of the East European cities is more moderate – as also are most of their urban and social inequalities. (p. 148)

Soviet cities however are still a long way from true socialism. Inequalities still exist and the planners do not have total control of urban growth. Therefore French and Hamilton suggest that it would be more appropriate to call them 'socialised' than socialist cities.

Other non-Soviet Socialist societies have developed alternative paths to Socialism. The Chinese revolutionaries of 1949 for example saw cities as centres of oppression and debauchery and they planned to turn them from consumer centres into centres of production. They aimed to eliminate the three key 'wasteful differences' – those between agriculture and industry, mental and manual work, country and city (Stretton, 1978). The central aim of Chinese planning especially since the Great Leap Forward has been what Larry Sawers (1978) called **engagement**, the integration of all the various elements of society into a single community. The aim has been to merge the city into the country-side and within cities to create a sense of involvement in the neighbourhood based not on planning from above but involvement at the grass roots. Thus in contrast to Western and even Soviet cities, Chinese ones do not focus on city centres. Though such centres exist they were generally built or influenced by westerners. Rather the overall impression of a Chinese city is of 'a continuous series of small towns. Each area had its own streets of shops, noodle stands, and play-grounds, with no apparent "center" of the city,' (C.C.A.S., pp. 107–8). The focal point of the Chinese city is the 'neighbourhood' which is usually planned around places of employment creating a commune-like structure similar to that in the countryside. Moreover, the revolutionary committee that runs the factory also oversees the surrounding neighbourhood to ensure this integration of production and residency, this sense of communality and political participation in local decision-making. The overwhelming impression of visitors to Chinese cities seems to be one of involvement, warmth and community. The Chinese take a deep personal interest in their neighbours' affairs and one result of this is an astonishing lack of crime and drug addiction. 'The organization of life in China's neighbour-hoods can perhaps be best viewed as a total community support system, one fostered and maintained by the residents of the neighbourhood themselves.' (R. Sidel, p. 147). The segregation of classes, of work and home, of citizen and government, the sense of violence and soulness-ness evident in many western and even Soviet cities does not seem to exist in China. Though Chinese cities have grown enormously since 1953 – there were only 9 'Million' class cities then, by 1979 there were 24 – they have not been uncontrolled and the Chinese emphasis on rural development has greatly helped stem mass migration to the cities.

Socialist governments like that in Cuba seem to have had similar success. As the distinguished urban specialist Jorge Hardoy described the former 'Pleasure City' of Havana (quoted in D. M. Smith. 1979, pp. 244–5):

'Touristic' Havana of pre-revolutionary decades has disappeared. In its place stands a society without un-employment or slums, with antiquated and crowded buses, but with beaches open to the people; with un-painted houses, but with an urban growth which has been ordered and controlled, once land speculation was eliminated.

Social classes have disappeared; schools, hospitals, and sports events are free; transportation will be free. Cuba is equalising itself from the bottom up, and nowhere is this transformation more evident than in Havana for one who has visited the country before and after the Revolution.

Urbanisation in the Third* (Developing) World

Whilst urbanisation in the first and second worlds is closely related to – if not caused by – industrialisation, that in the Third World is not. Whilst urbanisation in the first and second worlds is a sign of economic and social progress, of an increasing standard of living, this is less true in the 'Third World'. Whilst the Inner Cities of the western world are seen by many as the powder keg of the first world, the shanty towns of Latin America and Asia are even more explosive.

Urban settlements were first established more than 5000 years ago but as recently as 1900 only 1 in 8 people lived in urban areas. Before this century is out, half of mankind, 3 billion people, will live in urban settlements and two-thirds of that number will live in the 'Third World' (Gilbert and Gugler, 1982 preface). As Peter Hall comments some of this growth is 'mind boggling'. Mexico City for example has grown from 1.8 million people in 1940 to 9 million in 1970. By the year 2000 it is expected to be 31 million – making Mexico City 'the biggest urban area the world has ever seen. Sao Paulo in Brazil, in the half-century from 1950 to 2000, is expected to grow from 2.5 to 25.8 million; Shanghai from 5.8 to 22.7 million; Peking from 2.2 million to 19.9 million; Rio de Janeiro from 2.9 million to 19.0 million.' (Hall, 1984). The World Urban Explosion is therefore very much a Third World phenomenon as the following chart indicates. Urban life in the Third

---

* The term 'Third World' is a catch-all phrase referring to all countries not in the Western or Soviet Bloc. It implies that they are all poor and/or developing nations. This is correct but the gap between them is enormous and their lifestyles and social structures are very different. Some of the poorer ones are really a Fourth or Fifth world.

World for the majority of people centres on the **shanty towns** that surround the major cities. Housing here consists mainly of 'Used industrial and commerical crates, corrugated cardboard, drums and cans. People also live in caves, burrows, ditches, old iron tanks and concrete pipes. Millions of street sleepers live without any regular private shelter at all.' (Stretton, 1978, pp. 96–7). Such slums contrast starkly with the office blocks, skyscrapers, department stores and lavish hotels of the city centres and they clearly reflect the huge gap in developing countries between the minority of rich and the mass of poor.

World Urban Population, by region, 1950, 1980 and 2000

World Region	1950 Urban Population (Millions)	(%)	1980 (est.) Urban Population (Millions)	(%)	2000 (est.) Urban Population (Millions)	(%)
North America	105	64	196	79	256	86
Western Europe	177	60	260	74	321	83
Oceania	8	64	17	73	26	78
Latin America	67	41	237	64	464	75
Eastern Europe/Soviet Union	108	39	243	62	344	74
North Africa/Middle East	26	26	112	48	243	50
East Asia	112	17	358	33	591	43
Southeast Asia	23	13	90	24	207	34
South Asia	69	15	199	22	441	31
Subsaharan Africa	17	10	80	22	210	37
World	715	29	1792	41	3103	50
More Developed Countries	457	53	842	72	1107	77
Less Developed Countries	257	16	950	30	1996	35

(adapted from Brunn and Williams, 1983, pp. 10 and 454)

Such 'towns' however are neither as disorganised nor as desperate as they might appear, as this extract from J. E. Perlman (1976, p. 13) illustrates:

> From outside, the typical favela (shanty) seems a filthy, congested human antheap. Women walk back and forth with huge metal cans of water on their heads or cluster at the communal water supply washing clothes. Men hang around the local bars chatting or playing cards, seemingly with nothing better to do. Naked children play in the dirt and mud. The houses look precarious at best, thrown together out of discarded scraps. Open sewers create a terrible stench, especially on hot, still days. Dust and dirt fly everywhere on windy days, and mud cascades down past the huts on rainy ones.

Things look very different from inside, however. Houses are built with a keen eye to comfort and efficiency, given the climate and available materials. Much care is evident in the arrangement of furniture and the neat cleanliness of each room. Most men and women rise early and work hard all day. Often these women seen doing laundry are earning their living that way, and many of the men in bars are waiting for the work-shift to begin. Children, although often not in school, appear on the whole to be bright, alert, and generally healthy. Their parents . . . place high value on giving them as much education as possible. Also unapparent to the casual observer, there is a remarkable degree of social cohesion and mutual trust and a complex internal social organization, involving numerous clubs and voluntary associations.

Nor is the shift from the rural villages to the cities as great a cultural shock as it might appear. The peasants are often aware of urban life-styles from visits, friends and kin and such relatives often provide initial accommodation and help. They often see work in the city as only a temporary phase and maintain regular contact with their village. They adapt quickly to their new lifestyle and form their own small communities often with others from the same village or of a similar religion. Such community spirit not only makes life in the Shanty Town more bearable but gives the poor some measure of power through collective action. However the city also offers the opportunity, for those who wish, to escape such traditional bonds and to seek out alternative lifestyles.

The population explosion in the cities of the Third World however is not something to romanticise about. It is creating enormous social problems that such countries are largely unable to cope with. Unlike urbanisation in the first two worlds, here there is a massive imbalance between jobs and people. The manufacturing and industrial sectors are still very small so most people in the shanty towns are unemployed or part of the informal economy, scavenging, begging, providing such services as shoe-shining, rickshaws and running errands. Estimates by Souza and Tokman (1976) and Mazumdar (1976) for cities in 6 Latin American countries and two Asian ones suggest that between 39% and 69% of the urban labour force is in the 'informal sector'. Secondly, as the very existence of the Shanty Towns shows, there is a drastic shortage of housing, which Third World governments can do little to alleviate – even if they wanted to. Thirdly despite the desperate poverty in Third World cities, the people there are better off than their rural counterparts (Gilbert and Gugler, 1982). Not only are incomes often higher but the facilities much better than in the villages – education, clean water, medical aid, electricity and some subsidised housing are all generally available. Health and mortality rates bad though they are by western standards, are a significant improvement on those in rural areas.

This has led some Third World leaders to argue that the real source of their countries' poverty and problems is the City itself. It ruins any attempt at national planning and drastically distorts the distribution of wealth. As Julius Nyrere, President of Tanzania argued (1968) 'if we are not careful we might get into the position where the real exploitation . . . is that of the town dweller exploiting the peasants' (p. 28). Michael Lipton (1977) has gone as far as to argue that the key issue in Third World Development today is that of urban bias, the exploitation of rural areas by the towns and cities:

> The most important conflict in the poor countries of the world today is not between capital and labour. It is between the rural classes and the urban classes. The rural sector contains most of the poverty, and most of the low cost sources of potential advance, but the urban sector contains most of the articulateness, organization and power. So the urban classes have been able to 'win' most of the rounds of the struggle with the countryside; but in doing they have made the development process slow and unfair.

Third World governments have developed a variety of policies to deal with such imbalances. At one extreme there are those who are distinctly anti-urban and the most extreme example here is that of the Khmer Rouge who after seizing power in Cambodia, literally emptied the cities and forced people back onto the land. In the process over two million people were killed. Though far less brutal, the Chinese experiments during the 'Great Leap Forward' involved sending millions of the young and unemployed out into the countryside to work alongside the peasantry.

The alternative, pro-urban approach has involved building brand new cities like Brasilia, Islamabad and Ankara as national symbols of future progress. However, the cost of such cities is enormous, a huge drain on already meagre resources, and highly dependent on the government creating an 'Economic miracle'. Such miracles usually involve massive foreign aid so locking such countries into a world economic and financial system that is largely controlled by the West and the multinationals. Soon the interest on such debts outruns the initial loans, such countries default, face bankruptcy and the whole world banking system goes into crisis. Mexico and Brazil are two recent examples of a debt crisis that is threatening the world economy.

It is here that many socialist writers see the root cause of Third World poverty, underdevelopment and urban chaos. They see the world economic system as essentially a capitalist one by which the First World exploits the Third by a chain of **dependency** that deliberately keeps the poor countries underdeveloped and in debt. The cities of the poor South are chained to those of the rich North and as they are drained of their surplus wealth so they in turn syphon off the produce of their own countryside. From such a perspective, the glittering wealth of London, New York or Paris is a direct reflection of the poverty and deprivation of Delhi or Lima. Such theories of 'dependency' are briefly outlined in chapter 2 pp. 39–42, but as Peter Lloyd (1979) so clearly puts it:

> Primitive man is haunted by fears of natural disasters – of floods, droughts and earthquakes, whose incidence he cannot predict and against whose terrors he can but propitiate his gods. Modern man is haunted by the misery and squalor in which millions of his fellows live, the causes of which may be obscure to him though they are undeniably the product of his own activities.

The Economic Structure of the City

As theories like those above and as geographers and economists have long recognised, no city and few villages today live in total isolation. They are part of both national and international economic systems and a wide variety of urban relationships. The most basic of these is that of a town or city with its **hinterland**, the area that surrounds it and provides it with food, raw materials and workers. In return it provides shops, banks, employment, entertainment and a wide range of other facilities. A broader relationship is that between cities, such that they form an urban hierarchy or league table with London and the conurbations as the 'premier division' and the smaller regional towns as their satellites. Some writers see such relationships as reciprocal and mutually beneficial, others see the towns exploiting the countryside, the big cities as dominating the smaller ones, the South-East of England as draining the North and West.

The city today though is part of a world economic system such that changes in one part of the world, be they new EEC regulations or a Third World Revolution, have a direct impact elsewhere. The dominant influence on this urban system is the **multinational**. In 1971 for example Levinson calculated that between one and two thousand firms controlled 75% of world output and Stuart Holland has argued (1976) that in the UK alone over 50% of our national output is produced by the 100 largest companies. But such companies do not operate on a national basis. They have branches and plants throughout the world. Dunning (1975) has estimated that between 20% and 25% of British industry is American owned. Our cities are often the links in this economic chain of command. London as the headquarters of most of the major multinationals and companies in this country therefore acts as the focal point of an urban hierarchy, a spider's web of power and control that stretches out to the regions. Such areas are often dominated by a few very large firms. Merseyside for example is heavily dependent on Ford, Unilever, Plessey and Pilkington; Teesside on British Steel and I.C.I. The fate of such areas depends on such companies' investment strategies. If they pull out, as many have done recently, such areas die. Thus as Holland (1976) argues the life and death of today's cities rests primarily in the hands of big business, the world banks and central government and increasingly such organisations are adopting a world perspective in which the fate of a particular area or even country is of secondary significance to the pursuit of profit. Thus the prosperity of London and South East England can be seen as a direct reflection of such strategies – of the growing concentration of capital and the shift from manufacturing to tertiary industries. The decline of the Northern cities can similarly be seen as the reverse side of this trend and of the rise of such newly developing nations as Korea and Taiwan whose cheap labour and lack of unions serves the multinationals better than the men and women of Tyneside or South Wales.

The modern city is therefore a very different creature from that of the 19th century. It is no longer a centre of production but one of finance, communications and administration. It provides services rather than produces goods, it houses offices and shops rather than factories and warehouses. It is the centre of national and international systems of government, finance, commerce, media and transport. As cities have grown in importance so they have grown in size to **conurbations** – huge urban sprawls of interlinked cities and satellite towns like Greater Manchester and Strathclyde and to **megapolises**, the term used by Jean Gottman to describe the North Eastern seaboard of America, the almost continuous stretch of cities and suburbs from Boston to Washington. Over 40 million people live in what is possibly the largest, wealthiest and most productive urban area on the face of the earth, the financial, industrial and political heartland of America. Another such urban conglomeration is the 'Golden Triangle' in Northern Europe which includes London, Birmingham, Paris, Brussels, Antwerp, Bonn, Frankfurt, the Randstadt and the Rhine-Rhur.

We are, therefore moving towards the idea of the world as a 'global village'. As more and more people throughout the world move into cities and as cities are increasingly interlinked and interdependent so in a sense the world is shrinking. Through mass communications and modern transport systems the world is a smaller place and the key links in this urban chain are the **world cities** identified by Peter Hall (1984), cities of such size, wealth and power that they are not only national capitals but international centres of decision making, commerce, culture, transport and knowledge. Cities like London, Paris, Moscow, New York and Tokyo are now 'world capitals' in a world that is urbanising at a fantastic rate.

The Social Structure of the City

Just as geographers and economists have revealed the physical and economic layout of the city so historians and social scientists have unveiled its social make-up, its divisions of class, wealth and power, its varying images and character. Whilst some see the city as a land of opportunity and a cradle of civilisation, others see it as a breeding ground of crime and decay, as the unacceptable face of industrialisation. However no two cities are alike – compare for example Liverpool and Bath, Edinburgh and York – and even urban districts vary and gain reputations – compare for example the Gorbals in Glasgow and the Left Bank in Paris. We all know the 'good' areas in our city – and those to be avoided. We all recognise – albeit often unconsciously – that such reputations are based on the character not only of the area but of the people living there, that such physical and residential divisions and images are part of a labyrinth of social segregation such that even individual streets become part of a finely tuned system of social stratification both between and within social classes. Thus there are not only middle-class and working-class areas or neighbourhoods but respectable and rough working-class council estates and streets that separate the professional middle-class from the 'up and coming', blacks from whites. Such a network of homogeneous 'little worlds' not only helps create a sense of security and belonging but helps prevent class conflict. Keeping up with the 'local Joneses' becomes more important than attacking the lifestyles of the wealthy. Equally though they are part of a system of social control and inequality by which the well-to-do exclude 'undesirables' from their neighbourhoods, from the 'good' schools, usually by the high house prices of such areas, occasionally by applying political pressure on the local council. Thus the physical layout of a city – its mosaic of slums, terraces, high rise blocks, council estates, semi and detached housing – reflects its social make-up, its structure of wealth and power. Though Friedrich Engels' vivid description of Manchester in 1844 is of a time when social segregation was more blatant and harsh, it is still relevant today:

> All Manchester proper, all Salford and Hume are all unmixed working people's quarters stretching like a girdle, averaging a mile and a half in breadth, around the commercial district. Outside, beyond this girdle, lives the upper and middle bourgeoisie, the middle bourgeoisie in regularly laid out streets in the vicinity of working quarters . . . the upper bourgeoisie in remoter villas with gardens . . . in free, wholesome country air, in fine, comfortable homes, passed every half or quarter hour by omnibuses going into the city. And the finest part of the arrangement is this, that the members of the money aristocracy can take the shortest road through the middle of all the labouring districts without ever seeing that they are in the midst of the grimy misery that lurks to the right and left.

This chapter has attempted to outline the main features of urbanisation so far, to show that amid certain general trends there are individual differences, alternative ways to urbanise and to show that though cities seem to be like plants with their own natural and evolutionary pattern of growth and expansion, they are also shaped by powerful economic and political forces. The next chapter outlines the main theories advanced by sociologists to explain such patterns, such character, such power.

Chapter Two

Urban Sociology: Themes and Perspectives

The aim of urban sociology has been to discover and explain the key forces – economic, social and political – that caused the urban revolution and to understand the effect of an urban environment, an urban way of life on human behaviour and relationships. As pointed out in the Introduction such theories of urban change tend to fall into two main traditions.

(i) Those that see the city as a separate entity with a life of its own
(ii) Those that see the city simply as a reflection of society at large.

The development of urban sociology can be further divided into certain historical periods and as Janet Abu-Lughod and Richard Hay (1977) have argued the rise and fall of urban sociology has largely followed periods of urban crisis.

(a) The Founding Fathers of Urban Sociology and the Agrarian, Industrial and Political Revolutions of the 18th and 19th centuries.

(b) The Chicago School and the mass immigration into America after World War I.

(c) The Radical Conflict Theories of the 1960s and 1970s following the Black Riots in America.

(d) The Marxist and Dependency Theories of the late 1970s and 1980s and the urban crises of the Third World.

Thus like the city itself, urban theory has spread ever outward into new perspectives and neighbouring fields of study. This chapter attempts to outline this transformation in ideas from the Founding Fathers of Sociology through to today, as urban sociologists continue their search for a subject.

Traditional Perspectives in Urban Sociology

(1) The Founding Fathers and Urban Sociology

Even today the 'Holy Trinity' of Durkheim, Marx and Weber continue to exert an all pervasive influence on sociology and urban sociology is no exception. The present resurrection of urban sociology is largely due to writers in this field turning once again to them for inspiration. The Founding Fathers of Sociology were in many ways closer to revolution than their modern followers. They lived through the Revolutions of the 19th century – The Agrarian and Industrial, The Political and Intellectual. They sought to explain such massive social changes – Durkheim through the Division of Labour, Marx through Class Conflict, Weber through the rise of Rational Thought. All three saw urbanisation as a key feature of industrialisation but none of them considered the City as worthy of separate analysis. All three simply saw the growth of urban institutions and way of life as an expression of deeper, more widespread social and economic changes. To all three the modern world was an urban world.

(a) **Emile Durkheim** (1858–1917) viewed society not simply as a collection of individuals but as a living entity with the power to determine both its own destiny and the behaviour of its inhabitants. His functionalist model analysed society as a system of interrelated parts – the economy, family, government, etc. – held together by a central value system, a general consensus and set of norms and values into which members of society were socialised. Such a 'collective consciousness' provides the moral foundation by which society controls the aspirations and desires of individuals and so prevents intermidable conflict over the distribution of wealth. Durkheim further distinguished between the mechanical solidarity of small pre-industrial societies and the organic solidarity of modern mass industrial ones. In mechanical societies relationships are face-to-face, highly personal ones and the division of labour is limited. Everyone knows everyone else, most do a range of tasks rather than one specialised one and in such societies right and wrong, the rights and privileges of each individual are well known. The family and the Church act as the main agents of social control. However in large-scale industrial societies life is not so clear cut. There is an extensive division of labour, relationships are far more impersonal, there is a great variety of ethnic groups, sub-cultures and ways of life. There is a greater demand for individual rights and a variety of norms and codes of behaviour rather than a general consensus. Whilst Durkheim hoped that an organic form of solidarity would arise, he feared that in the transition from agrarian to industrial society, traditional controls would break down and the individual would be left rootless, isolated and over-ambitious so creating an enormous potential for social disorder, for normlessness, for **anomie**. The great fear of the 18th and 19th century Ruling Classes was the 'Mob', the mass of peasants recently arrived in the new cities and who were heavily involved in the French Revolution of 1789 and those in Europe in 1820 and 1848. Thus Durkheim's view of the city was ambiguous. He hoped it would stimulate economic progress, individual creativity and a new moral order. He feared it would lead to a breakdown of community and the growth of anomie.

(b) **Karl Marx** (1818–1883) and **Friedrich Engels** (1820–1895) were similarly ambivalent. Their theory of Historical Materialism led them to see the rise of the industrial city as a sign of progress, as a key step towards economic abundance and socialism, as a step away from the backwardness and 'idiocy of rural life' and as a major step towards class consciousness, unity and social revolution. By creating such huge urban centres capitalists were contributing to their own downfall because they brought the masses together and created a new 'working class'; a class that would now not only be face to face with its exploiters but increasingly aware of its oppression, increasingly organised and militant, increasingly moving from being a 'class in itself to a class for itself'. In Engels' words:

> The great cities are the birthplaces of the labour movements; in them the workers first began to reflect upon their own condition and struggle against it; in them the opposition between proletariat and bourgeoisie first made itself manifest; from them proceeded the Trades Unions, Chartism and Socialism. (Engels, 1969, p. 152)

Whilst welcoming these developments, Marx and especially Engels were also appalled by the conditions the working-class had to live in, by the immorality and exploitation of class relationships:

> The very turmoil of the streets has something repulsive, something against which human nature rebels. . . . The brutal indifference, the unfeeling isolation of each in his private interest becomes the more repellant and offensive, the more these individuals are crowded together within a limited space. (Engels, 1969, pp. 57–8)

Thus for Marx and Engels the new industrial city reflected the essential features of the Capitalist Mode of Production. The City acted as the centre for the new divisions of labour, new technology and structures of production; it represented the separation of society into two new classes the Bourgeoisie and Proletariat; it became the arena for the intensification of such class conflict and for the growth of 'Monopoly Capital' as the larger firms crushed the smaller in the perennial search for profit. In their view the City was the effect not the cause of capitalism.

(c) **Max Weber** (1864–1920) was the only one of the three to write specifically about the City. But not the modern industrial one rather the Medieval City of the Middle Ages, which he saw as the cradle of many of the key features of modern society – the rise of bureaucracy, of modern government and democracy, of the new Merchant Classes and early capitalist enterprises. Such cities helped the transition from feudalism to capitalism, they fostered the new spirit of Rationality – of order and efficiency, of reason rather than tradition. They stimulated the new ideas, culture and administrative structures that were to prove so vital to the rise of western capitalism. They encouraged individual enterprise and for a short time at least were independent, autonomous and the key centres of civilisation. However with the rise of the great monarchs, of the Nation State and development of capitalism, such cities lost their independence and in Weber's view degenerated merely into expressions of society at large. Weber deplored the new industrial cities and according to his biographer Don Martindale (1958) believed that: 'The age of the City seems to be at an end' (p. 62).

(2) The Founding Fathers of Urban Sociology

Though the Founding Fathers of Sociology did not believe in a sociology of the City, many other early sociologists did. Such writers were deeply concerned with what they saw as the loss of Community caused by industrialisation and like Durkheim feared the collapse of social order and morality. Such writers tended to concentrate on particular features of urban change.

(a) Ferdinand Tonnies and Urban-Rural Relationships

Tonnies is generally considered the founding father of Community Studies because of the distinction he made in his major work 'Community and Society' between the **gemeinschaft** relationships of traditional society and the **gesellschaft** ones of industrial society. By Gemeinschaft, Tonnies was referring to the sense of community, the intimacy of face-to-face relationships, the sense of place (social and geographical) and belonging that comes from being brought up in a particular locality amongst family and friends, according to time honoured traditions and under the control of the family and Church. Tonnies portrayed Gesellschaft relationships as much more superficial, impersonal and calculating. They derive from the competitive and highly mobile nature of industrial society where relationships are not an end in themselves but a means to profit and self-interest. Similarly role relationships in urban societies tend to be fairly specific, those in the village more diffuse. Thus for example whilst everyone knows the village bobby, few know their city cops. Whilst the Church and family are the cornerstones of traditional society and morality, business ethics provide the dynamism and values of society today. Whilst in the past social status was ascribed, determined by birth, today it is achieved through the 'Rat Race'. Thus Tonnies, unlike Durkheim, was deeply pessimistic about the effect of industrialisation and urbanisation on society. He saw it as the death of community, of civilisation and though he never said that specific locations – the village or the city – created different types of social relationship, later writers did.

(b) Georg Simmel and the Urban Personality

Simmel applied Tonnies' ideas specifically to the urban environment and argued in his most famous essay (*The Metropolis and Mental Life*, 1903) that city life creates a unique type of personality, a particular sort of mentality geared to the rush, complexity and calculation of urban life. In the market economy of the city, money, self-interest and rational calculation form the basis of relationships. There is no time for sentiment, the pace of life is too fast for habits to form and so to cope the individual becomes blasé – reserved and withdrawn. He treats other people as objects rather than individuals, as a means to an end. In this 'urban jungle', some thrive (the urban 'cowboy', the city 'slicker') some die or drop out (the suicide, the tramp, the homeless). However Simmel also saw the urban environment as potentially liberating, allowing the individual to escape traditional controls and the pettiness of small town life, to express his own individuality and creativity, whilst recognising its dangers – of the individual feeling lost, merely a cog in an enormous organisation of things with no-one to turn to.

(3) The Chicago School and the Urban Environment

The themes of European writers like Tonnies and Simmel were blended into a theory of urban sociology not in Europe but at the University of Chicago between 1916 and 1940. Faced by a massive influx of immigrants from S E Europe and the southern states of the USA, Chicago seemed about to be overwhelmed. There appeared to be no basis for social order or control and yet such cities survived and adapted. The geographers and social scientists of Chicago set out to explain how. Three of the most famous of these scholars were Robert E. Park, Ernest Burgess and Louis Wirth.

(a) **Robert E. Park**. As a student of Simmel, Park was fascinated by the ebb and flow of city life, by the variety of lifestyles it created, by the mosaic of 'urban worlds' from the suburbs of the middle-class to the twilight zones of the prostitute and ethnic minorities. To try and explain the underlying laws of urban life, how order arose out of apparent chaos, he and Ernest Burgess developed the theory of **human ecology**, a theory that combined Darwin's notion of a struggle for survival and Durkheim's of a moral consensus. From Darwin they drew the idea of the city being like a social organism with a life of its own, continually adapting to its environment. From Durkheim, Park drew the idea of an inbuilt tension between the individual's need for freedom and society's need for social control. Thus they argued cities change through a complex interaction of physical and moral forces. Park went on to explain the kaleidoscope of 'urban worlds' in terms of concepts used by biologists to explain the patterns of life and processes of change found in plant life. He argued that there was a 'struggle for existence' over territory, with the strongest and richest seizing the most favourable urban locations. As each area settled, it developed its own way of life, its own natural history. However in time change takes place. As the relative attractiveness of particular locations change, new groups invade someone else's territory. Existing inhabitants are pushed out and so in turn invade their neighbours until a new equilibrium emerges, a new pattern of urban settlement.

(b) **Ernest Burgess** made this idea of invasion, succession and equilibrium the basis of his famous theory of **concentric urban zones** (1925). He noted the tendency for most cities to spread outwards like ripples on a pond with each zone inhabited by a particular 'class' of people. In the city centre there tends to be a Central Business District (CBD) surrounded by a Zone of transition, then a belt of working-men's housing, a residential area of high class apartment buildings and finally a commuter zone of suburban areas in satellite towns.

Whilst the well-to-do could afford to choose where they lived and so tended to live well away from the grime and soot of industry, the poor and ethnic groups had no choice but to live in the Inner City. As the population of a city grows, as industry expands so by a process of invasion and succession, new patterns of social segregation emerge

Burgess's spatial model

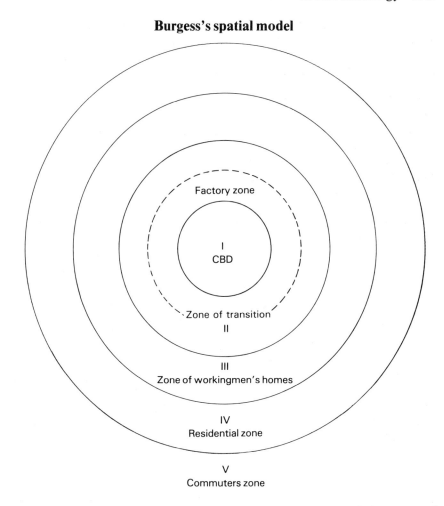

Factory zone

I
CBD

Zone of transition
II

III
Zone of workingmen's homes

IV
Residential zone

V
Commuters zone

from the suburbs of the middle-class to the ghettoes of the zone of transition.

The ecological theories of the Chicago School spawned a wealth of mapping exercises tracing such zones and a multitude of natural histories of both slum and affluent neighbourhoods as in Zorbaugh's *The Gold Coast and the Slum* (1929). Much of this analysis focused on the zone of transition and its apparent 'disorganisation', its lack of social and moral order, its constant state of flux. It was seen as the area with the least opportunity to stabilise, the area of greatest human demoralisation and the most likely to 'breed' crime and deviance.

Hence the mass of studies of juvenile gangs, prostitutes, drug addicts and ethnic groups, in this period. The essence of Human Ecology was its attempt to explain city life by the city as 'an externally organised unit in space produced by laws of its own' (Park, 1915) separate from society at large. This theoretical framework not only 'bred' a whole generation of 'urbanologists' but left a legacy of concepts that are still popular today – the idea of immigrants 'invading' a neighbourhood, of inner city areas 'breeding' crime. However such research increasingly became the basis for rejecting the theory of Human Ecology. Many cities did not display the concentric zones, identified by Burgess, the rich did not always move out to the suburbs (W. Firey, 1945) and it failed to identify the power of certain groups to determine the shape of the city and the lives of the inhabitants. It explained all as natural and beyond human control, it ignored the power of social forces outside the city.

(c) **Louis Wirth and the Urban Way of Life.** Though a member of the Chicago School in this period, Louis Wirth's analysis of city life was more a cultural than an ecological one. In his classic essay 'Urbanism as a Way of Life' (1983) Wirth proposed a minimum sociological definition of the City as a 'relatively large, dense and permanent settlement of sociologically heterogeneous individuals'. It was these characteristics that distinguished city life from that in the country. The very size, density and heterogenity of the city creates social segregation, impersonality and both social and geographical mobility. The individual no longer has a set place, his relationships with others (at work, in shops, on the street) are highly rational, superficial and transitory. Amid the city crowds it is easy to feel lost, amid the urban 'Rat Race' only the fittest thrive, amid the multitude of such daily physical encounters there is little social meaning. City dwellers tend to be nervous, irritable, even a little schizoid, can all too easily feel lost, alienated and powerless. To find some sort of security, some sense of belonging, city dwellers join a wide variety of associations or move into areas of likeminded people. But Wirth was not totally pessimistic. He saw the possibility of cities settling down and establishing some sense of permanence and character. Moreover he regarded urbanism not only as the way of life of the city but of modern society.

Wirth's essay encapsulated the insights of previous writers and inspired a wave of studies over the next twenty years into urban and rural ways of life. However like Human Ecology it too came under growing criticism:

(i) Wirth used Chicago as the 'laboratory' for his analysis but as

Herbert Gans (1968) has argued, Chicago in the 1920s was hardly a typical city. It experienced an unusually high influx of immigrants and so appeared especially 'disorderly'.

(ii) Wirth's argument that factors like population size and density create psychological stress is challenged by examples like Hong Kong where overcrowding is intense but rates of death, disease and social disorganisation are low.

(iii) The main criticism against Wirth though is his claim that this urban culture is the major influence on people's behaviour. Writers like Gans (1968), Williams (1973) and Castells (1972) have argued however, that the culture of urbanism is not a cause of city life but an effect, that what Wirth saw as an 'urban way of life' was in fact an industrial or capitalist one.

Despite such relatively recent criticisms, the Chicago School laid down the main framework for urban sociology right up until the 1960s. Attempts were made to refine its theories by writers like Hawley (1950) and Schnore (1959) in America, Peter Mann (1965) in Britain. Geographers mapped out the city in Social Area Analyses and sociologists and anthropologists mapped out its 'underworld' in a mass of highly detailed ethnographies but the major sociological tradition it spawned was that of community studies.

(4) Community Studies

As the title suggests, this tradition centred on analysing a wide variety of communities, often using them as social laboratories to test the theory that *where* you live profoundly influences *how* you live. The framework for this form of study was the idea of a **rural-urban continuum**. As Louis Wirth put it 'the city and the country may be regarded as two poles in reference to which, one or other of all human settlements tend to arrange themselves.' Whilst Wirth outlined the main features of the 'urban way of life' Robert Redfield (1947) described the typical folk or rural society

> Such a society is small, isolated, non-literate and homogeneous, with a strong sense of group solidarity. The ways of living are conventionalized into the coherent system which we call 'a culture'. Behaviour is traditional, spontaneous, uncritical and personal, there is no legislation or habit of experiment and reflection for intellectual ends. Kinship, its relations and institutions are the type categories of experience and the familial group is the unit of action. (p. 293)

In 1929 Sorokin and Zimmerman produced the definitive outline of the main differences between an urban and rural lifestyle. They compared the naturalness, health and sense of community of the country with the ugliness and social and mental disorders of the City, an environment which offers

> Neither the impulses for creative activity; nor for orientation, curiosity, and novelty; nor the lust for variety and adventure; nor the physiological necessity for being in touch with nature; not to enjoy with eyes the greenishness of the meadow, the beauties of the forest, the clear rivers, the waves of golden wheat in the fields; nor to hear the birds singing, the thunderstorms, or the mysterious calm of an evening amidst nature, these and thousands of similar phenomena have been taken from the urban man.

Underlying this tradition therefore was the belief that the shift to the City had destroyed men's traditional sense of community and that such social harmony could only be found in the past or in the village. The problem is that this term has never been satisfactorily defined beyond a rather romantic nostalgia for the 'Good Olde Days'. As George Hillery's review in 1955 showed the term 'community' had been used in 94 different ways; others have come to see the term as a 'catch-all phrase' capable of all and any interpretation. Worse it has an ideological, anti-urban bias. It implies that city life is essentially bad, inevitably unnatural and Margaret Stacey (1969) has advocated that it be withdrawn from the sociological dictionary and replaced by the more neutral term 'social system'. Nevertheless this 'quest for community' produced a flood of local studies in the 1930s, 1940s and 1950s. Probably the most famous were:

(a) Robert and Helen Lynd's study of the mid-American town of Muncie, Indiana (1929) as a typical 'Middletown'. They lived there for 18 months and studied six main areas of life there (work, family life, child rearing, religion, community and political activity and leisure).

(b) Frank Lloyd Warner's ambitious survey of Yankee City (1963), which produced a mass of sociological data in the days before advanced computer analysis.

Such studies inspired a host of imitators in America, Europe and even the Third World. British Community Studies included Arensberg and Kimball's (1940) of the isolated village of Luogh, County Clare, Ireland, Alwyn Rees's (1950) studies of rural Welsh villages and Roland Frankenberg's *Village on the Border* (1957). The full flavour of such studies is provided by Frankenberg's book *Communities in Britain*

(1966) in which he attempts to outline his own more refined version of the Rural-Urban Continuum.

However, by the mid-1960s this tradition added up to little more than a vast collection of 'one-off case studies', incapable of sustaining broad generalisations. It had been superseded by more advanced survey and computer techniques for collecting and analysing data. More importantly however the whole idea of the Rural-Urban Continuum, of certain physical environments 'creating' a sense of community was under attack.

Firstly, the 'Discovery of Community in the City.' Studies like Herbert Gans in Boston (1962), Oscar Lewis in Mexico and in particular Young and Wilmott's in East London (1962) showed, in direct contradiction to the Rural-Urban Continuum, the existence of tight-knit urban communities. As Young and Wilmott described Bethnal Green:

> Bethnal Green, or at any rate the precinct, is, it appears, a community which has some sense of being one. There is a sense of community, that is a feeling of solidarity between people who occupy the common territory which springs from the fact that people and their families have lived there a long time. (Young and Willmott, 1962, pp. 112–13).

However later studies of such urban 'villages' showed even this picture to be somewhat romanticised. Coates and Silburn's study of St. Ann's, an inner city district of Nottingham (1970) revealed mistrust and conflict as much as Coronation Street neighbourliness. The sense of community here was a very fragile one, an adaptation to stress and noise as much as mutual empathy. 'In St. Ann's, sharing an outdoor lavatory, as did many of our respondents, may be conducive to heightened social contact, but not always in an entirely happy way.' (Coates and Silburn, 1970, p. 94).

Secondly the 'Discovery of Conflict in the Country'. Studies like J. Littlejohn's of Westrigg (1963) and W. M. Williams's of Ashworthy in Devon (1963) showed that not all was peace and harmony in the village but that such communities were just as likely as towns to be divided by class and to suffer problems of isolation and powerlessness. Ray Pahl's study of Commuter Villages in Hertfordshire, ironically called *Urbs in Rure* (1965) revealed the clear split between locals and newcomers whilst Oscar Lewis's restudy of the Mexican village of Tepoztlan (1951) a village Robert Redfield depicted as idyllic and harmonious – revealed intense distrust, tension and conflict. Lewis had simply looked at this village through less 'rose tinted' glasses than Redfield. Further the work of Raymond Williams (1973) in particular helped shatter the myth of village life in Olde England being a Golden Age of Community. His studies revealed instead a life of poverty and exploitation for the mass of the population, the peasantry. They were subjected not only to the whims of nature but those of their master, the Lord of the Manor. The so called harmony and order of the medieval village was an imposed one, a 'mutuality of the oppressed'. The Enclosure Movement of the 18th century offered the peasant the chance to flee to the city and though there the yoke of the Factory Owner replaced that of the Gentry and Landlord at least he was more his own man. As Raymond Williams argues it was the urban Ruling Class that revived the 'ideology' of community as a way of controlling the new working-class by giving the impression that they were part of the larger society. After the French Revolution the urban 'mob' was greatly feared by the European aristocracies. Howard Newby's studies in East Anglia (see p. 56) reveal similar rural poverty and class division today.

Thirdly the 'Destruction of the Myth of Suburbia'. Just as the Rural-Urban Continuum portrayed distinctly urban and rural ways of life so a stereotyped picture of 'Suburban Man' emerged depicting the typical suburbanite as a young executive reaching for the top of his particular career ladder living with his wife and two children on a private housing estate, surrounded by material possessions and desperate to 'keep up with the Joneses'. Herbert Gans study of Levittown (1967) and Bennett Berger of a 'Working Class' suburb in Detroit (1969) shattered this image, by revealing a wide variety of types of suburban lifestyles and that even on a middle-class estate not everyone was from the same 'mould'.

Fourthly, the 'Academic Burial of the Rural-Urban Continuum' was completed by two sociological articles. In 'Urbanism and Suburbanism As Ways of Life' (1968) Herbert Gans argued that the key factors determining people's lifestyles are not the locality they live in but their social class and their stage in the family life cycle. The higher up the social scale a person is, the greater his choice of housing and place of residence. Such choice however is limited by a person's position in the family life cycle. A young couple with two children cannot move as easily as a retired couple of similar social class background. Thus the similarity of lifestyles found on many housing estates is not the result of the area but of the housing market creating clusters of households of similar background and ages. Ray Pahl went a stage further in his essay on this thesis.

> Any attempt to tie particular patterns of social relation-
> ships to specific geographical milieu is a singularly fruit-
> less exercise. Some people are of the city but not in it,
> whereas others are in the city but not of it; the Gemein-
> schaft exists within the Gessellschaft and the Gesellschaft
> within the Gemeinschaft. (1970, p. 88)

Possibly this is going too far. Obviously where you live – in a village, city, highrise bloc, mass estate – must have some effect on people's relationships and behaviour but as R. Dewey argued such differences are 'real but relatively unimportant'.

> There is no such thing as urban culture or rural culture,
> but only various culture contents somewhere on the
> rural-urban continuum. The movement of zoot suits,
> jazz and antibiotics from city to country is no more a
> spread urbanism than is the transfer or diffusion of blue
> jeans, square dancing and tomatoes to the cities a
> movement of ruralism to urban centres. (1960, p. 65)

In Raymond Williams' view the key differences are not those of locality or a particular 'way of life' but capitalism which has a more pronounced and pervasive influence on the city than a remote country village.

Thus the basic framework of Community Studies was undermined. Its conclusions were increasingly rejected because of their innate conservatism and anti-urban bias. They looked for consensus in the village and conflict in the City and found them. They failed to even define the term Community properly. As Bell and Newby (1974) argue the only real legacy of this tradition was its Methodology. At its best argued Maurice Stein (1960) the 'Community-Study' offers a 'Closeness to human experience and human problems of a kind rarely captured in the confines of the small-group laboratory'. But whilst sociologists might have given up the 'quest for Community', the public has not. Such a search is evident not only in the growing fashion of the urban middle-class to move into commuter villages and of the retired to dream of a home in the country but in the often grandiose schemes of Town Planners for Garden Cities, New Towns and Skyscraper Parks (see p.268). Possibly a classic example of this quest for community, of the urge to escape the urban 'Rat Race' was the Communal Movement of the 1960s – young, mainly middle-class students who tried to set up an alternative society free from materialism and competition in which people were not only in communion with nature but free from their traditional roles. Unfortunately as Phillip Abrams and Andrew McCullough's study (1976) showed, it is very difficult to build anew amongst the old, using people steeped in existing values. As one commune member so poignantly put it 'I still believe in communes; it's just that I am completely pissed off with the people living there.'

(5) Community Power

However the Community Studies tradition did not die completely. Much more specific studies of the urban environment like Young and Wilmott's (1962) survived to become classics and contribute to a range of sociological debates. Moreover this tradition also gave birth to a series of detailed analyses of local power structures. Robert Lynd's re-analysis of Muncie (1937) for example exposed the power over the local community of one particular family and Floyd Hunter's study of Atlanta (1953) revealed a Power Elite dominated by local businessmen. Robert Dahl's study of decision making in New Haven, Connecticut (1961) however revealed no such concentration of power but a constant competition between a plurality of pressure groups trying to influence an essentially impartial local government. So began what has come to be known as the **pluralist-elitist** debate over the distribution of power at both local and national levels in advanced industrial societies. Such a debate has become the focus of analysis more of political scientists than urban sociologists and is outlined in detail in the parent volume to this book (M. Haralambos, *Sociology: Themes and Perspectives*, 1980). But as chapter 3 shows, it has again become a topic of urban analysis.

Radical Perspectives in Urban Sociology

Thus by the mid 1960s both the Ecological and Community Studies traditions were under increasing criticism. Like their parent paradigm, Structural Functionalism, they were essentially conservative theories that were unable to explain rapid social change and conflict. Their depiction of urban inequality as natural not only ignored the power of some groups to run the City or village in their own interests but helped justify it. Under the guidelines of these frameworks urban and rural sociology had drifted into an academic backwater.

In the late 1960s the cities of America and Western Europe exploded. They became the scenes of destruction, violence and rebellion as the Blacks of America vented their anger and frustration with the American Dream on the ghetto environments of Harlem, Watts and Detroit. They turned to Black Power as the only means left to solve the poverty, decay and racism that surrounded them. This period also saw massive demonstrations over Vietnam and Civil Rights, over Women's

Lib and Student Power. In Paris in May 1968 students and workers joined together to help depose the government of Charles de Gaulle. Danny 'the Red' Cohen, Bendit and Rudi Deutske became household names and urban guerilla groups like the Bader-Meinhof gang, the Red Brigade and the Black Panthers took the class and race war onto the streets. The great cities of the West, the 'crown jewels' of western civilisation seemed to be disintegrating physically, socially and morally and with them people's faith in liberal democracy and welfare capitalism. The urban was in crisis and the post-war consensus seemed to have given way to the politics of conflict and confrontation.

The Ecological and Community traditions could not explain such conflict so like sociologists in other fields at this time, urban sociologists turned back to Marx and Weber. It became one of the 'new' sociologies and attracted to its ranks some of the ablest and most critical rising 'stars'. Such a paradigm revolution however was not without its problems. Both Marx and Weber had rejected the idea of a separate urban sociology. Both Marx and Weber saw the city merely as an expression of capitalism at large. As Professor Pahl put it: 'The fundamental error of urban sociology was to look to the city for an understanding of the city. Rather the city should be seen as an arena, an understanding of which helps in the understanding of the overall society which creates it' (1970, pp. 234–5). This left the problem – one that continues to bedevil this discipline – of what makes urban sociology so special. Moreover in the absence of specifically urban theories from such Founding Fathers, these new sociologists had to develop their own. By and large the Neo (or New) Weberian tradition originated in Britain; the Neo-Marxist in France following the 1968 Revolution and was later imported into Britain and America.

(a) Neo-Weberians

(i) **John Rex and Robert Moore.** The Neo-Weberian tradition, in fact the whole 'Radical' approach, is said to have originated from the publication of Rex and Moore's book *Race, Community and Conflict* in 1967. Their study of the inner-city area of Sparkbrook in Birmingham had tried to explain why black groups in particular tend to end up in the twilight zones of our major cities. They argued that such segregation was not only the result of low income and racial discrimination but the result of the way the rules and regulations of the city housing market were operated. Blacks were not offered mortgages to buy their own homes because they lacked secure employment; they could not get on council housing lists because they had not lived locally long enough. So Rex and Moore proposed the idea of housing classes as a key factor in urban society 'Membership of a housing class is of first importance in determining a man's associations, his interests, his life-style and his position in the urban social structure'. Using Burgess's concept of the zone of transition and Weber's theory of social classes Rex and Moore claimed that housing was not distributed by 'Market Forces' but by a 'class struggle' between different **housing classes,** a competition for the most desirable form of housing, that in the suburbs. Whilst a social class is usually based on occupation, a housing class in their analysis was based on a group's ability to satisfy the rules and regulations of either the Building Societies (in the private housing market) or the Local Authority (in the public housing market). Thus for example the middle-classes find it easier to get a mortgage than the working-class and the skilled working-class find it easier to get onto a 'good' council estate than the unskilled – irrespective of income – because such private and public bureaucracies have an inbuilt bias towards 'respectable' workers. Rex and Moore initially identified 5 Housing Classes but later extended this to 7.

1. the outright owners of large houses in desirable areas;
2. mortgage payers who 'own' whole houses in desirable areas;
3. local authority tenants in houses built by the local authority;
4. local authority tenants in slum houses awaiting demolition;
5. tenants of private house owners;
6. house owners who must take lodgers to meet repayments;
7. lodgers in rooms.

Like Park and Burgess, Rex and Moore saw the continuous growth of the city as a sort of 'urban leapfrog' as all classes tried to achieve the ideal of a house in the suburbs. Left behind in the twilight zones and ignored by the Building Societies and Housing Departments, the only way immigrants can own their own home is to buy a tenement at high rates of interest and let out rooms. Such multi-occupation leads to a further deterioration of inner city housing and so the Local Authority enacts new laws to stop such 'landlordism' spreading. Thus black communities become completely trapped in their ghettos and as Rex and Moore predicted 'Any attempt to segregate the inhabitants of this area permanently is bound to involve conflict. The long term destiny of a city which frustrates the desire to improve their status by segrega-tionist policies is some sort of urban riot.'

Now the city was being analysed in terms of power, class and conflict instead of environment, community and market forces and this brilliant analysis sparked off a wave of studies into urban and racial conflict. It also aroused a wide variety of criticisms.

First and foremost as R. Haddon (1970) argued, Rex and Moore seemed to have confused cause and effect. The house you own or occupy is not the cause of your position in the social hierarchy but the effect. If you are rich you can buy a big house but buying a big house does not make you rich. Thus the unequal distribution of housing in society is a result not a cause of the inequal distribution of wealth. Moreover a person's present housing position is not necessarily the same as that in the future. As people's income changes so may their housing. Your occupation or income, rather than your house, determines your class position and chances in life. Your house is merely an index of 'achieved life chances not primarily a cause'.

Secondly, since no two individuals are ever in exactly the same position in the housing market, Rex and Moore's typology is open to an infinite variety of housing classes. They themselves added to their list twice. It is more a description of struggles within than between classes because generally different classes compete in different housing markets – the middle-classes for private housing, the working-classes for council housing. Thirdly a variety of studies showed that not all social groups aspired to a house in the suburbs. Some positively preferred to live in the Inner City. Davies's study in Newcastle (1970) showed that lodging house landlords often bought tenement housing not as a last resort but as a way to make a profit. Couper and Brindley's (1975) study in Bath showed council tenants often preferred renting to buying and the convenience of living close to the city centre.

In the face of such criticism John Rex eventually gave up the idea of Housing Classes and went on to describe the social position of Blacks rather as that of an 'Underclass'.

(ii) R. E. Pahl. Rex and Moore's theory did however show that the distribution of urban resources is the result not just of market forces but the actions and decisions of a wide variety of urban managers in both the private and the public sector. Such a revelation led Ray Pahl to propose the **managerial thesis**, the theory that the key people controlling the distribution of such urban resources as housing, are building society managers, bankers, planners, etc.

> Thus there can be a sociology of the organisation of urban resources and facilities; the controllers, be they planners or social workers, architects or education officers, estate agents or property developers, representing the market or the plan, private enterprise or the state all impose their goals and values on the lower

> participants in the urban system. We need to know not only the rates of access to scarce resources and facilities for given populations but also their determinants of the moral and political values of those who control these rates. (1970, pp. 207–8)

Such distribution argued Pahl generated new forms of class conflict, new types of protest group – over housing and education rather than wages and conditions. Like Rex and Moore's thesis, Managerialism put power and conflict at the centre of urban analysis and it inspired a host of studies into the decision making processes of housing officials, town planners, estate agents and the like, into the values, biases and ideologies behind such decisions as to who gets what, when and how.

The Managerial Thesis was however increasingly criticised for concentrating on the 'middledogs' of the urban power structure and ignoring those at the top, those who laid down policy. It failed to ask why such resources were scarce in the first place (why for example housing is in such short supply) or to clearly identify which type of urban manager was most important in such allocation decisions – those in Head Office or those on the counter. In the light of such criticisms Pahl raised his sights and in collaboration with Jack Winkler began analysing the role of the State in advanced industrial societies. They proposed the **corporation thesis** but this was more a study of national economy than of the urban one.

Such Weberian studies pioneered the new urban sociology in Britain but by concentrating on the politics of consumption they tended to ignore those of production. They offered only a political picture of modern class conflict. Neo-Marxism claimed a more comprehensive analysis.

(b) Neo-Marxists

The 'New' urban sociology of the French Marxists was introduced into Britain through collections of essays like those by Chris Pickavance (1976) and Michael Harloe (1977 and 1981). Neo-Marxism sought to extend traditional Marxist analyses of class conflict to incorporate the new urban protests of the 1960s, those of blacks, women, students, tenants and environmentalists. It made the role of the state and of the City in advanced capitalist societies the focus of its attention and it promoted an interdisciplinary approach combining economic, political and social interpretations called **political economy**. Such a framework however developed along three main paths.

(1) Analyses that focused specifically on the urban environment as a whole.

(2) Analyses that like Marx and Engels simply concentrated on specific urban issues like housing and property development.

(3) Analyses that took a world perspective and saw the City as the crucial link in the long chain of dependency and exploitation that makes up international capitalism.

(i) The leading figure in the new urban Marxism was **Manuel Castells**. In a series of writings – in particular the *Urban Question* (1977) – Castells attempted to lay the foundation for a new 'scientific' urban sociology. He contemptuously dismissed all previous theories as little more than ideology because they failed to fundamentally challenge the capitalist system. By concentrating on such social problems as poverty or crime, such 'bourgeois' analyses tended to 'blame the victims' or the environment or urban managers but never the true cause, the capitalist system and its relentless pursuit of profit. Worse by categorising poverty and deprivation merely as 'social problems' and by suggesting possible solutions, such analyses helped strengthen, even legitimise capitalism. The only theories Castells did praise were those of the Human Ecologists and Louis Wirth because at least they recognised that it was powerful social forces outside individual action that were shaping the modern city. Unfortunately, they mistook such forces for urban ones rather than those of capitalism.

Heavily influenced by the ideas of Louis Althusser, Castells's analysis focused on the traditional Marxist topic of class struggle but not on the traditional basis of such conflict, that of production. Rather he argued that the new forms of urban protest were not the traditional ones of worker and employer because the modern factory is no longer located in the city but outside it. Modern capitalism is a world system controlled not locally but internationally by multinational corporations with their headquarters in certain 'world' cities. Rather urban conflicts today are over Collective Consumption and Urban Planning.

(a) By Collective Consumption, Castells meant those goods provided by the modern Welfare State such as health, housing, education, transport and leisure that are consumed 'collectively', by us all. Such goods argue Marxists are provided by the modern capitalist state as a means for ensuring the efficient 'reproduction of labour', for ensuring that the modern worker is not only healthy, housed and rested, but materially satisfied with capitalism, feels cared for rather than exploited. Thus he will work efficiently, rarely challenge or question the inherent inequalities of capitalism but rather accept it as fair and just. Welfare therefore is a form of class control, materially and ideologically. Such goods are mainly distributed through 'local governments' particularly in the cities because this is where the bulk of the population lives.

(b) By Urban Planning Castells was referring to the way local government uses 'town planning' and other controls to create an urban environment conducive to profit-making. It builds the economic infrastructure – the roads, communications and buildings – that is vital to private enterprise. Such urban planning is also a form of class control, determining where the working-class live by controlling council house building.

Thus like other Marxists, Castells saw the State, the government in a capitalist society, not as a promoter of the public interest but as an instrument of class control. Like Nicos Poulantzas, Castells believed that the modern State is not run by the Bourgeoisie directly but has a certain independence or **relative autonomy**. This allows it to protect the long term interests of capitalism without appearing to do so, to allow it to keep the various 'fractions' of capital (the businessman, financiers, property developers, etc.) together and the proletariat divided.

However in the late 1960s and 1970s Western societies faced a major economic crisis – a fall in profits and a massive rise in bankruptcies and unemployment, which in turn generated an urban crisis as governments drastically cut public spending – especially on Welfare – at the very time that such services were increasingly needed. The continuing 'flight' of the well-to-do further cut local government revenue and western cities generally were increasingly unable to provide basic local services, to maintain roads, repair houses and some like New York went bankrupt. As unemployment grew and welfare and the environment declined, more and more protest groups emerged forming what Castells believed was a new type of class struggle involving a wide variety of groups and classes – the poor, blacks, women, the middle- and the working-class.

At the centre of this urban crisis, at the forefront of such urban protest, is the capitalist state. No longer able to afford to 'buy off' the workers with welfare, the state has to show its true face and resort to repression.

> The monotonous rumble of city traffic is suddenly drowned by a confused din of shouts, footsteps, screams, the clash of metal and breaking glass. The flow of traffic

stops; crowds gather; banners, placards, posters proclaim the crowd's discontent with their town. Blocking their path the ever-present helmeted heads, order at the end of a truncheon; soon comes the slow advance, and then the charge, the violence, the rebuff. Sometimes there is gas, sometimes blood, sometimes the dull crack of firearms; but inevitably, in some form or another, there is a confrontation. (Castells in Cowley 1977, p. 46)

Such use of force however tends only to increase the militancy and class consciousness of ordinary people, to increase urban protest and class conflict. Castells was not arguing that the City caused such conflict but merely that it was the main arena for the modern class struggle. Similarly he did not see the urban system as separate from capitalism at large but did argue that it too had a certain autonomy. He therefore believed that if such urban protests could be fused into full 'social movements', such power on the streets might generate an urban crisis of such proportions that western capitalism would collapse from within. 'A spectre haunts the world: will the urban crisis become an "urban revolution"?'

Such a radical analysis gained immense support in the late 1960s especially amongst more militant groups because it both justified their protests and offered theoretical guidelines for the future. However criticism was also widespread. Firstly of the often obscure language Castells used – 'Verbal Pollution' one reviewer called it (Ruth Glass in *New Society*, 29.9.77) and of the contemptuous way he dismissed all other 'urban' theories.

Secondly his claim to universal applicability, that his theories explain all cities, though research increasingly showed that his analysis was more of French cities than capitalist ones generally.

Thirdly, his concept of collective consumption. Ray Pahl in an essay in R. Scase (ed.) *Industrial Society: Class, Cleavage and Conflict* (1977) criticised this concept because of its vagueness. It is not clear whether Castells is referring to goods provided by the Welfare State or only those collectively consumed. Housing in Britain for example is provided by both the government and privately owned and how would you define a private car on a public road. Moreover such welfare goods are also provided in socialist cities so what makes capitalist ones so different?

Fourthly his definition of Protest Movements is equally vague and seemed to include in its ranks all and any forms of protest that occur in urban areas from those of Women's Lib to Tenants' Associations. He ignored the differences between such groups, hoping they would all unite together to overthrow the State. Rather as happened in practice such groups stayed very separate and few aimed to promote revolution. Moreover many of these protests were over national not urban issues. They simply took place in the city because this is where their support was greatest and their publicity maximised.

Fifthly as Peter Saunders argued Castells' theory was 'telelogical and tautological. It encompasses every eventuality and explains none' (1981, p. 210). He seems to argue that whatever the state does – whether repressing the working-class or granting them concessions – it does in the interests of the Bourgeoisie. Moreover his analysis virtually ignores the major agent of urban control – the Police. Finally fellow Marxists were especially scathing because his version of the class struggle was based on Collective Consumption rather than as Marx and Engels decreed the Mode of Production. He highlighted urban conflicts over housing and ignored those over plant closures and redundancies. Castells in fact recognised the importance of such struggles but argued that they were not urban issues in the way housing and planning were and so could not form the basis of a new urban sociology.

Nevertheless Castells' work in the late 1960s was of immense significance. It helped break the 'mould' of traditional urban sociology and establish the paradigm for a new one. It inspired new ideas not only in sociology but in urban studies generally (see Chapter 3).

(ii) Amongst Neo-Marxists who analysed specific urban issues rather than urban-society, the work of the geographer **David Harvey** is seen as particularly important. In such studies as *Social Justice and the City* (1973) Harvey, like Castells sought to identify the sources of the economic crisis of the late 1960s and 70s and explain why it seemed to centre on 'urban space', why it happened mainly in the city. He sought to show that the physical layout or geography of the city was not the result of natural or market forces but the power of Big Business in its pursuit of profit. For Harvey the present crisis of capitalism was the result of increased competition between individual firms which resulted in the cutting of prices which in turn cut profits and investment, led to some firms going out of business and to an increasing squeeze on the labour force, its wages and social benefits. In the face of such exploitation the workforce grow more class conscious and militant so the 'class struggle' becomes more visible. This also leads to an over accumulation of capital in the economic system as a whole. Too many goods are being produced, profits are falling and so capitalists look for alternative sources of investment. Some goes into new plant (factories, offices, etc.) some into new research and technology, some into such safe investments as property. The 'property boom' of the 1970s was an example of what happens when a lot of investors pour money into one particular field and in the resultant collapse of this market, several fringe banks went bust. Pressure also grows on the state to 'create' new demand and an example of this was the encouragement of the growth of the suburbs by western government after World War II, by various forms of tax relief for home owners. This created a whole series of new markets for industry – builders, car firms, electronics, DIY etc. – and a new breed of home owners well pleased with capitalism. The State also, according to Harvey, provides industry with such basic infrastructure as transport and telecommunications, such social facilities as health, education and housing to 'reproduce' the workforce and by urban planning keeps the masses fragmented – into middle-class suburbs and working-class council estates.

Harvey's analysis is thus very similar to Castells. He too sees the City as crucial to modern capitalism in both creating new markets and controlling the workforce. Unlike Castells though, he sees the urban protests of the 70s merely as part of the traditional class struggle of labour and capital and has little faith in the power of such conflict to bring down capitalism. His faith rather rests in the internal contra-dictions of the economic system, especially the over-accumulation of capital caused by competition between capitalists. Inevitably other Marxists have attacked Harvey for putting the class struggle on the sideline, rather than in the centre, of his analysis.

The French Marxist François Lamarche (1976) similarly highlighted the way the search for profit shapes our cities and he focused in particular on the activities of property developers and speculators. Such capitalists do not invest in housing which has a low profit margin but in offices, shopping centres and new urban developments that produce high rents because of their central location. Studies by Oliver Marriot (1967) and Ambrose and Colenutt (1975) have shown the way such speculators have bought up sites cheap in the belief (or knowledge) of local authority plans for a new precinct or car park and made fortunes from the resultant sales or rents. Such 'white elephants' as Centrepoint in London were the result of allowing such private profiteering. Other Marxist writers in this tradition have focused on the activities of town planners or housing officials, local councillors or estate agents and such studies are discussed in detail in chapter 3.

(iii) Finally there are those writers – mainly Marxist – who have sought to apply theories and concepts developed by analysts in the Sociology of the Third World to the study of the City. These ideas are outlined in detail in Aidan Foster-Carter's section *The Sociology of Development*, included in this book. Very briefly such writers tend to see capitalism today as a World System and some like Immanuel Wallerstein (1974) trace its origins back to the 16th century and the great Empires of Britain, France and Spain. Colonies in parts of the world we now call the Third World (Latin America, Africa and Asia) became an integral part of such European economies, supplying their industries with raw materials and providing ready markets for the 'Mother Country's' manufactured goods. There thus developed, according to Wallerstein, an international 'division of labour' by which the colonial powers made 'their' colonies specialise in one or two primary products, on terms highly advantageous to the mother country and through this system of Unequal Exchange (Amin 1976) western economies became developed and Third World ones underdeveloped (Baran 1957). A. G. Frank has turned such ideas into a formal theory of Dependency and Underdevelopment (1967) arguing that core nations like Britain exploited peripheral ones in a chain-like system of expropriation in which such satellite countries become totally dependent on the metropolis. The key link in this chain was (and still is) the City. The colonial powers used existing cities – or built their own – as the main means not only for governing such areas but for draining them of their surplus. The elites of such colonies lived in the cities and generally collaborated with the colonial powers, using their control of local markets (and after independence, their control of the government) to exploit the peasants in the countryside, to buy up their produce cheaply and export it to the West. Thus whilst cities exploited the countryside, the urban elites and ruling classes of the Third World became more closely linked to the West than to their own people – even after such colonies gain independence. They adopt western ways, are often educated in the West and generally copy the affluent lifestyles of their counterparts in Paris and New York. They depend on the West for a continuation of such lifestyles, for the maintenance of their rule and so will often use the military to protect western interests and factories against their own people. Thus the chain of dependency reaches across the world and deep down into the Third World as the West exploits such countries and the cities exploit the countryside. The development of Western capitalism depends in turn on the underdevelopment of the Third World; the development of the City on the underdevelopment of the village. As A. G. Frank (1969) summed it up, 'That in chain-like fashion the contradictions of expropriation/appropriation and metropolis/satellite polarization totally penetrate the underdeveloped world creating an internal structure of underdevelopment.' (p. xxi). Today with the decline of colonialism, it is the multinational corporations who provide the dynamic for this system. In their relentless pursuit of profit they search the world for cheaper labour and raw materials and new markets. They can move their operations across the globe if necessary as Volkswagen has from Germany to Brazil. The profits, however, always go to the West. Dependency is also based on the Third World's reliance on the West for aid – to attempt to keep above the poverty line as much as to develop industrially. But such aid does not come cheaply. Interest charges have to be paid and/or western technology or factories bought with the money. Such debts can reach such a burden on Third World economies that they default, creating a world financial crisis as with Mexico and Brazil at present. Moreover the western powers tend to control the world prices of the raw materials such regions produce and so, by keeping such prices low, keep Third World countries poor. The only successful attempt to overcome such price controls has been that of the oil producing countries who formed OPEC. As President Nixon put it in 1968: 'Let us remember that the main purpose of American Aid is not to help other nations but to help ourselves.' Thus the cities of the Third World have come to symbolise not only the division between the 1st World and the 3rd but the gap between urban elites and the urban poor of such countries. Whilst the city centres house the rich of both the West and the Third World in the most modern and luxurious of buildings, the Shanty Towns house the poor. Whilst the wealth of such countries circulates through the formal economy, the poor scavenge around in the 'informal'. Whilst such urban elites of the 1st and 3rd Worlds intermingle, the urban poor are marginalised, socially and economically caught between the rich and the peasantry, left to fester on the fringes of their own societies. Yet it is here, in the Shanty Towns, that many Marxists see the future, see the seeds of a Third World Revolution as the crisis of the world economy squeezes the Third World to the point of bankruptcy, as the urban elites increasingly have to resort to outright repression as in Chile and Brazil. Other writers like Peter Lloyd (1979) doubt the revolutionary potential of the Shanty Town yet acknowledge the value of the Dependency framework for highlighting the exploitation produced by world capitalism.

Writers like Rosemary Mellor (1977) and Robert Moore (1982) have attempted to apply such an analysis to the cities and regions of Britain and in particular to show that the decline of the North, Scotland and Wales and even of the 'inner cities' is closely related to the prosperity of the South East and of London in particular. London is the core, the Metropolis of an economic chain that reaches up to the oil of Aberdeen and creates peripheral regions in the North. Behind this chain are the Multinationals. Most of these have their headquarters in London, their branches in Glasgow, Liverpool or Newcastle and it is these outposts that get closed down first in a recession. In turn, Britain is part of a worldchain and increasingly becoming an American satellite with approximately a quarter of British industry being US owned. As A. D. King (1983) has commented:

> The economic fortunes of Tyneside depend on decisions taken in Tokyo just as those of urban Scotland are affected by policies made in corporate headquarters in New York. As a contributor commented at the 1982 World Congress of Sociology in Mexico City, Germany's largest industrial city is Sao Paulo, Brazil. As a place of production, consumption, administration or culture, the city is embedded in a global economy. (p. 7)

The decline of the North, Scotland and Wales can be thus seen as a form of underdevelopment and certainly they depend heavily on the aid provided by the Government in London. It is government aid and the cheap labour of such areas that is now attracting the big corporations back.

Urban Sociology in the 1980s – New Agendas, New Directions

Thus the Radical perspectives of the 1970s created a 'paradigm revolution'. The Ecological and Community frameworks were replaced by that of political economy as the means to analysing the city both internally and as part of a world system of class conflict. As R. E. Pahl (1977) has argued the only real difference today between Neo-Weberians and Neo-Marxists is the Marxist insistence that the present crisis in Western cities is caused by capitalism. As Pahl points out even socialist societies suffer such problems as traffic congestion and urban planning. The 1980s thus involves a period of reflection and consolidation in this field, the testing out of this new framework on the ground and across the whole spectrum of urban analysis from local government to town planning, from the informal economy to rural sociology. The breadth of today's urban studies is illustrated in chapter 3. The following briefly outlines such new agendas and indicates some new directions in a field that has adopted a world perspective as the only way to understand what is happening in our cities as the world recession deepens and spreads, as the structure of work and our whole way of life is fundamentally changing.

(a) New Agendas

A major step forward in the consolidation and co-ordination of the new urban sociology was the establishment of the *International Journal of Urban Regional Research* by such leading figures as Manuel Castells and Ray Pahl. In the 1981 edition Ivan Szelenyi outlined what has proved to be one of the most influential of new agendas. Whilst acknowledging the debt this field owed to Neo-Marxism, he also outlined its limitations arguing for more empirical and comparative research to show what was really happening in the city in the face of today's slump and to develop alternatives to the policies of the New Right. In particular he suggested research into:

(i) The Domestic and Informal Economies, into the way both men and women are adapting to the recession, the way the 'household' is changing shape in the face of male unemployment and how more work is done at home and informally than in the formal economy.

(ii) The modern capitalist state and how amid this crisis of capitalism it manages. Will the anti-collectivist policies of Mrs. Thatcher and President Reagan solve the crisis or will a popular backlash see a return to Corporatism?

(iii) The Socialist City. What shape will it take, how will it develop in transition from capitalism to socialism?

(b) New Directions

As both the following brief outline and chapter 3 will show such appeals did not go in vain. R. E. Pahl has undertaken work into the informal economy (p.273) Szelenyi himself is developing work on the Socialist City, Peter Saunders and others have analysed urban politics (p.265). Friedman and Wolff, 'World Cities' (IJURR, Vol. 4, 1980), feminists the Domestic Mode of Production and writers like Gregory and Urry (Macmillan forthcoming) the Sociology of space. But probably the most significant study published to date though is that by Manuel Castells *The City and the Grassroots* (1983). It is a dramatic reassessment of his earlier work, a critique of scientific Marxism and a shift from theoretical to empirical analysis. His book is a highly detailed (and in contrast to his earlier work immensely readable) set of case studies of urban social movements, outlining the reasons for their success or failure. He sees the main characteristic of urban social movements as protests over either

(i) Collective consumption (goods and services provided by the State)

(ii) Cultural identity associated with and organised around a specific territory or

(iii) The state, in particular local government.

A successful urban social movement must combine all three goals, be politically conscious of its role as such a movement, be connected to the social and political system through the media, professionals and political parties and yet be 'organisationally and ideologically autonomous'. Of the four case studies Castells cites – Paris, San Francisco, Santiago and Madrid – in his view only the urban social movement in Madrid was successful because it combined the above elements. 'It improved the quality of urban services, resuscitated local cultures, asserted a new set of principles regarding the meaning of the city and contributed to the eventual restoration of democracy in Spain.' However, Castells is no longer 'Utopian'. He no longer believes such limited protests will cause the collapse of capitalism. Such protests are merely 'local utopias'. Unable to fight against the State, Big Business or the Media, people withdraw and attempt to regain some control over their 'local turf'. 'When people find themselves unable to control the world, they simply shrink the world to the size of their community.' Though such movements may not be part of the class war, may not alter capitalism, they do at least give local life more meaning and possibly 'nurture the embryos of tomorrow's social movements'.

Conclusions. Thus as the next chapter illustrates urban sociology today has matured, established a new framework and gone off in a variety of directions. Has it yet though established its own separate identity?

Chapter Three

Urban Studies

Modern urban sociology has fragmented into a wide variety of themes and perspectives, some directly concerned with the city, others more with changes in society at large. It has moved from theory to practice, from general theses to empirical analyses. It has become part of Urban Studies, a multi-disciplinary approach that seeks to combine the perspectives of the whole range of the social sciences, from geography to economics, political science to anthropology, as a means to obtaining an overall picture of how the city today works and is changing. The following is a brief outline of a few of the areas that urban sociologists are contributing to.

(1) Urban Politics

Stimulated by both the Community Power Tradition and the Radical perspectives of the seventies, a number of urban sociologists have tried to determine who runs our cities and in whose interests.

(a) Peter Saunders for example made an important contribution to the Pluralist-Elitist debate with his study of Croydon (1979) one of the few 'community power studies' in this country. He found the structure of power in this particular town to be highly elitist with local business-men especially influential.

(b) The urban managerial tradition inspired a variety of studies into the power of local officials, leading some to claim that there was virtually a 'dictatorship' of the official in local government, a dictatorship based on bureaucrats' power of information, their full-time expertise and their ability to manipulate and out-manoeuvre amateur and part-time councillors. They seemed to run local authorities yet be neither elected nor accountable. More recently Elliot and McCrone (1982) related bureaucratic power to the politics of collective consumption and urban protest identified by Castells. They argued that officials' control over the allocation of such welfare goods as housing and education has made them into a new 'Urban Ruling Class'. Ironically however such bureaucratic power, by its very impersonality, unaccountability and apparent unfairness stimulated the growth of local protest movements by all classes evident in the late 1970s. The rise of younger more militant councillors in the 1980s determined to stamp their authority and their radical policies on such cities as Liverpool, Sheffield and London however has severely undermined such theses.

(c) Patrick Dunleavy (1980) used Castells concept of 'collective consumption' as a means to analysing the growth of cross-class voting evident in the 1979 and 1983 General Elections. He argued that such issues are fragmenting the traditional social divisions. The working-class today for example can be divided into those owning their own homes and those in council housing; the middle-classes likewise into those sending their children to state schools and those using the private sector. Hence the shifts in recent voting behaviour, of the skilled working-class to the Conservatives, and many middle-classes to the Liberal-SDP Alliance.

(d) Peter Saunders (1982) has tried to use the concept of Relative Autonomy to explain the relationship between local and central government in a capitalist society. He argued that the modern capitalist state operates at two levels the 'Corporate and Non-Corporate'. The Corporate is at the national level and is concerned with production, general economic planning and infrastructure. It would therefore need to be kept out of the public eye and controlled by central government. The Non-Corporate is concerned with consumption and the distribution of resources such as housing and health provision, issues not so vital to the structure and ownership of capitalism. Therefore this level of government can be open to public pressure at the 'local' level. By such a division he argued the state can protect the long term interests of capital (at the national level) and yet appear to be democratic (at the local level).

(e) Cynthia Cockburn's study of Lambeth Council in London (1977) was one of the very few attempts at a Marxist study of local government. In her view such 'local states' are part of an overall system of class control that operates either directly through the police and courts or indirectly through the welfare services.

> The state in capitalism is an instrument of class domination; in the modern state the bourgeoisie, the dominant class who own capital and employ workers, holds political sway. As such, the state is at the heart of the perennial struggle between the bourgeoisie and those it exploits – the working-class. (p. 42)

Local government is the 'human face' of the capitalist state ' "Local government" is a face-to-face affair. The rent officer, the social worker, the school teacher – these represent the government to the man, woman and child in the "client" population' (p. 58). Ironically as the Local State in the 1970s sought to increase its control and efficiency by adopting the techniques of 'Corporate Management', it also stimulated the growth of local protests over the resultant cuts in welfare and the lack of public consultation.

Many of these sociologists have moved deeper into what might strictly be called political science especially as their studies now are more of national than local politics – Dunleavy (1985) on voting and the media, Saunders (1984) British Politics generally, Cockburn (1983) the trade unions.

Ironically however over the last few years local government has returned to the centre of modern politics as a result of:

(a) The apparent take-over of many big city councils by younger, more radical politicians prepared to use such local bases to change the face of British Society.

(b) The election and re-election of a Conservative government under Mrs. Thatcher (1979 and 1983) determined to carry out a 'monetarist' programme of economic reform intended to liberate market forces and private enterprise and roll back the present Welfare State. Cuts in welfare and in the power of the government have led to a growing confrontation between central and local government especially as it is local councils who distribute most of the key welfare services (Education, etc.). Local Government has been attacked in three main ways.

(i) By cuts in Local Government finance. Local government gets its funds from three main sources – rates, local charges and central government grants (the Rate Support Grant as it is called). In 1980 the total grant to local authorities in England and Wales was £11.5 billion; in 1985 it will be about £21.5 billion. The present government has therefore made such expenditure a key target for cuts and reduced the Rate Support Grant from 67.3% in 1975 to below 50% in 1985-6. It has set complicated targets or cash limits on local government spending which involve severe 'fines' if exceeded. The 1984 Rates (or 'Rate

Capping') Bill stops local councils trying to overcome such cuts by increasing the rates.

(ii) By by-passing Local Authorities and their bureaucracies in promoting new projects. The establishment of the Manpower Services Commission and the Urban Development Corporation are two examples of the Government going outside 'local channels' and setting up independent bodies chosen and controlled from Whitehall.

(iii) By abolishing the Metropolitan Councils. These were established in 1974 to improve the efficiency of local government in the major conurbations. Though it was a Conservative government that set these bodies up, Mrs. Thatcher now sees them as the epitomy of waste and bureaucracy, especially as most of them are Labour controlled and run by such radical critics of her administration as Ken Livingstone, leader of the G.L.C. The Local Government Act to abolish them is scheduled to become law in 1986.

However local councils are resisting such attacks either directly, as in Liverpool in 1983 by refusing to cut their budgets or by campaigning against the abolition of the Metropolitan Councils, or by refusing to supply the information Whitehall needs to assess next year's Rate Support Grants. 1985-6 seems likely to see an explosion in 'urban politics'.

(2) Urban or Town Planning

Planning is obviously a central feature of any analysis of the structure and development of the modern city. What is less obvious, and what sociologists have helped to highlight, is the Power of such urban managers over our cities and the way we live; the extent to which their apparently impartial judgements and technical plans really represent a variety of ideologies about how they think we ought to live. Such studies have revealed the way their conservatism is an important factor in maintaining the existing structure of power and inequalities of wealth.

Such studies arose out of the growing criticism of post-war town planning – the New Town, the Tower Bloc, the motorway network, the one-way system, the slum clearance programme, the shopping precinct. Many of these schemes were very successful, others have made the Town Planner 'just about the most unpopular of all the professional groups in Britain today' (Broadbent 1977). From the slums of the 1930s, they helped create those of the 80s – mass complexes, concrete jungles which lacked both heart and soul. They seemed to believe that buildings alone created a community; they forgot about the people. By the 1970s there was what Hugh Stretton (1978) has called 'some return to sanity' (p. 168). High-rise buildings were replaced by low-rise, slum clearance by urban renewal. But the damage had been done. The public's faith in such experts had been shattered and as such criticism grew so a closer examination of the ideologies behind town planning took place.

Studies of these 'urban managers' showed that many of them saw themselves not as servants of the local council but as men with a mission. 'Evangelistic Bureaucrats' as Jon Davies (1972) called them as they sought to change society, reform human behaviour by redesigning the physical environment and they weren't above using their expertise to manipulate and bedazzle local councils into financing their pet schemes. As Benington argued (1975) the term 'Community' came to be used as a kind of 'aerosol word to be sprayed on to deteriorating institutions to deodorise and humanise them. At a stroke, schools were transformed into community schools, doctors into community physicians and approved schools into community homes' (p. 8). Marxist analyses went further and highlighted the extent to which Town Planning is part of the overall system of power, inequality and class control in a capitalist society. As American Marxists Norman and Susan Fainstein (1982) put it:

> Class domination expresses itself in space most obviously in the greater amenities enjoyed by the rich than the poor. The spatial isolation of income and racial groups simultaneously insulates the bourgeoisie from rebellion and sharpens and mobilises class and racial conflict. The concentration of poor people and racial minorities threatens American central business district investments and fosters unrest, albeit often without an available target.

The very image of Town Planners as impartial professionals helps maintain the State's image of being above the class struggle and so helps deflect criticism and opposition.

Studies of town planning have also highlighted the power of those who control and distribute that most crucial of urban resources – Land – the banks, the builders, the government and big business. Studies like Oliver Marriots (1967) and Ambrose and Colenutt's (1975) have particularly exposed the often invisible power of property developers, individual firms or conglomerates like Trafalgar House that specialise in fixing land deals and promoting redevelopment schemes – at a profit.

It is companies like these that have been behind the trend towards shopping precincts, conference halls and pedestrian walkways that have become a feature of virtually every city and town centre, all housing the same mixture of major chain stores like Boots and Smiths. Such entrepreneurs, however, have come under increasing criticism as the search for quick profits or high rent sites has often distorted urban development. Whilst such companies promote the redevelopment of one side of town, other parts are left to decay, whilst their activities have helped direct shops, housing and industry to the South of England, the North has been left behind. Moreover such power to influence the life and death of a town or neighbourhood is both invisible and unaccountable, often beyond the control of local government and town planners. Rather in their desperation to attract new jobs and industry, such authorities often find themselves forced to grant developers special concessions on the rates and bend local regulations. Whilst such companies may help generate new life into wasteland areas like the old docklands, they more usually concentrate on safe, high profit areas like city centres, often to the detriment of local residents and small businesses who get pushed out.

(3) Urban Housing

Housing is possibly the major resource in the urban distribution of wealth – at least as far as the mass of people are concerned. Not only is a house a home but for most people it is their major capital asset. Not only is the ownership of housing a major party political issue but it is a key source of the economic and social division between the middle- and working-classes. However with over 60% of people in Britain today owning their own home such a class borderline is increasingly less clear.

The key influence on the production and distribution of housing today is the Government. The Conservative Party is traditionally associated with the homeowner, the Labour Party with the council tenant and so generally with a change in the party in power there has been a corresponding increase or decrease in council house building and incentives to private builders. Local government is especially important here because it is at this level that actual house building takes place. The present Conservative government has put its faith in the virtues of private ownership, promoting the sale of council houses (1980 Housing Act), shifting the balance of government subsidy from the council tenant to the mortgage holder in the ratio of £1 billion to £5 billion respectively (1984) and bringing both council housing building and maintenance to a standstill with its cuts.

However, as sociological analyses have shown government is not the only agency controlling housing. Studies in the 'urban managerial' tradition highlighted the power of such groups as estate agents, solicitors and housing managers in both the private and public housing markets.

(a) Building Societies for example tend to dominate the private housing market because most people need a mortgage to buy a house. Studies have shown, however, a tendency to discriminate in favour of the middle-class applicant with a secure career and against those in unskilled work. Studies like Rex and Moore's (1967) and Elizabeth Burney's (1967) further revealed evidence of racial discrimination whilst Shelter's 1975 report highlighted the building societies' practice of **red-lining**, of drawing red lines around districts in the town or city (especially the inner city) that they would not lend in.

(b) The officials who run local housing departments have similar power over the public market. Though the distribution of housing here is based on an apparently fair system of allocating points according to need (income, length of time on waiting list, years of residency, etc.) as John Lambert and his colleagues (1975) discovered few tenants see it in this way. The whole process is extremely secretive, certain families and individuals seem able to jump the queue, a lot seems to depend on the social worker's evaluation of a family's character as to whether they get onto a good or a bad estate and many applicants complain of the arrogant and dismissive manner in which they are treated. As one council tenant, a Jamaican, explained to John Lambert (1975),

> Well, to me, it's like this. These blokes [officers in the housing department] who hold these positions, they must be all right because they're not complaining. They are in what you call a high society and we who are in the low society suffer more. If we were in the high society, then they would help us straight away. But being as we are the low-class people then they don't want to know. (p. 56)

Recent studies of such housing departments as Hackney (CRE 1984) further found strong evidence of racial discrimination.

Thus 'urban managers' in both the private and public housing markets have enormous power over people's lives and homes and yet are accountable to no one. Moreover as Peter Saunders (1984) has gone on to argue, as more and more skilled workers buy their own homes and the cuts in council housing grow deeper and deeper, Britain will increasingly be divided into an affluent majority enjoying good quality housing and private services and a poor minority increasingly dependent on inadequate state provision and living on delapidated council estates. Thus Saunders hoped to explain the present changes in voting behaviour and the fear that the present government policy of selling council houses is helping split the working-class and creating a group of unskilled and unemployed workers who feel marginalised, segregated and powerless and who may well react by outbursts of sporadic violence against private property.

Neo-Marxists have analysed the role of housing in a capitalist society in three main ways:

(i) As Manuel Castells argued, as a key element in the politics of collective consumption and reproduction of labour.

(ii) As a classic example of the way the State creates new demand and profits for Big Business (Harvey). The government inspired growth of the suburbs in the post-war era not only stimulated the building industry but such associated ones as home furnishings, electronics and car manufacturers. Its slum clearance programmes opened up city centres for redevelopment. Its mass housing programmes of the 1950s and 60s reaped huge profits for the seven top building contractors in this period and helped increase their monopoly power. It further generated huge profits for the financial institutions who lent local authorities the money and such debt charges are still being paid – even where the tower blocks they financed have been pulled down.

(iii) As a means of class control. By encouraging both public and private housing the State keeps the workers divided at home as at work; on the different and segregated worlds of the private and council estate. With the middle-class generally well satisfied with capitalism, it is the working-class which requires stricter control and here Marxists have argued, the managers of council housing play a crucial role. It is they who decide who gets council housing, who gets onto the good respectable estate and who is put with the other 'problem' families. It is they who apply the strict rules on council home tenancy which prohibit individuality even to the point of the colour of the front door. They are a form of social 'policemen', part of a highly authoritarian and bureaucratic system that leaves tenants and applicants feeling dependent and powerless. The very facelessness of such officials prevents collective protest and each case is treated as an individual one so preventing organised opposition. It is a form of 'ideological control'. As Lambert et al (1975) argued, such officials appear to be in control but in reality they are merely agents of the Ruling Class and the State.

(4) The Urban Economy

Studies in this field have tended to concentrate on the **informal economy**, on both the rise in illegal economic activities (the Black Market, moonlighting, fiddling) and on the growth of unpaid 'work' associated with the boom in DIY industries and other household activities. The growth of this 'hidden' economy seemed to correspond very closely to the growth of mass unemployment in the 1970s and guesstimates of its size varied enormously. The British Inland Revenue for example put it at $3\frac{1}{2}\%$ of GNP (about £7 billion p.a.) a recent American Treasury estimate (1985) at $90.5 billion whilst unofficial estimates ranged from $176 to $369 billion p.a.

Some sociologists began to see such growth in the informal economy as a sign of a revolution within modern capitalism. Scott Burns for example (1977) suggested that a new form of 'household capitalism' was emerging 'which must inevitably result in the reordering of society' Jonathan Geshuny (1978) proposed the idea of a new 'self-service economy', of people increasingly turning to DIY and the Black Market for the goods and services they (especially the unemployed) could no longer afford from the formal economy. It seemed that capitalist societies, like those in both the Second and Third Worlds were increasingly dependent on the 'hidden economy'. Thus whilst Professor Lipson (quoted in Pahl, 1984) could argue 'I believe the second economy (in the Soviet Union) is an indispensable auxiliary to the first . . . and not only planned for by the regime but planned by the regime' and studies of Third World countries like India showed that it was only the Informal Economy that kept them going. Western societies like Italy seemed to be in a similar situation: 'We have come to the conclusion that the so called invisible economy is what makes the country as such tick. The invisible economy, the hidden economy is responsible for Italy's survival.' (Ferrarotti, 1978.) As indicated on page 43 Ivan Szelenyi made this topic one of the main issues on his 1981 Agenda for urban sociology. One who took up this lead was Ray Pahl as he sought to determine whether the informal economy was directly related to mass unemployment whether it was a central feature of today's urban society. His recent book (*Divisions of Labour*, 1984) however casts severe doubts on many of the above claims.

Whilst agreeing that the 1970s saw the growth of 'black, white, red, green and mauve economies' Pahl argues that these have now declined. There are fewer self-employed today, fewer manufacturing and retail jobs and so fewer opportunities to fiddle. Moreover both the social security and tax officials are more efficient and with the growth of DIY there is an increase in self-provisioning rather than employing others on the side. Therefore in his view there is still only one economy and the key factors determining the distribution of wealth and the divisions of domestic labour today are not variables like social class but the **household and the family-life cycle** (the age of the parents and of their children). A household with only the husband working and two dependent children is likely to be far less well off than one where both husband and wife work and there are no children or they are grown up and bringing money in themselves. In his view, it is this structure that is the basis of the new divisions and inequalities in our society – in particular the growing gap between the employed and the unemployed. 'A process of polarisation is developing with households busily engaged in all forms of work at one pole and households unable to do a wide range of work at the other.' Households of multiple earners versus ones in which no-one works producing 'a division between the more affluent home-owning households of ordinary working people and the less advantaged underclass households', a division that is becoming more significant than the conventional manual/non-manual one. 'The new line of class cleavage is now between the middle mass and the underclass beneath it'. Moreover contrary to popular opinion it is the employed, not the unemployed, who are most active in the informal economy because they have the money to buy DIY tools or employ people on the side. Thus argues Pahl, what is happening today is not a collapse of work – there are plenty of jobs that need doing in the home and in the community – but a decline in formal employment. We are returning to the traditional situation of under-employment and of dependence on the Household as in the past. The period of full employment in the 1950s and 1960s was an exception. 'Historically to be unemployed for a period was the normal experience of working people.' Pahl's study, though, was of the rather isolated Isle of Sheppey. Whether studies of the economic life of today's cities will reveal similar conclusions has yet to be seen.

(5) Urban Social Science

As explained in the Introduction, virtually every social scientist has attempted to explain the City, each has added a new piece to the 'urban jigsaw' but none has completed it. Each has come up against the problem of defining urban; each has undergone something of a 'paradigm revolution'.

Equally most of them have been at least touched by the new theories of urban sociology. In the 1983 Urban Yearbook for example A. D.

King argued that urban historians should adopt a world perspective along the lines advocated by Immanuel Wallerstein:

All cities today are 'world cities', yet they have not just assumed that role over-night. The agenda for urban history which perceives them in this way is clearly vast. Yet such a perspective would enable urban problems, economic, social and physical, to be seen in a much more realistic light ... The cosy viewpoint of looking at our cities from within must be replaced by the more uncomfortable view of seeing them from outside. (p. 15)

Whilst in urban geography, as Professor Herbert so clearly outlines (1981) the ideas of Marxists like David Harvey have had a significant impact and forced geographers to look beyond the physical layout of the city to the economic and political forces behind its shape. Many geographers are now developing explicitly political or sociological analyses as reflected in the work of Andrew Kirby (1982), R. J. Johnston and Derek Gregory (1978). Two areas that are particularly close to urban sociology though are urban anthropology and rural sociology.

(a) **Urban Anthropology** as Ulf Hannerz argues (1980) is a relatively recent extension of anthropology whose traditional focus has been on the culture and way of life of 'primitive', small-scale societies. However both in terms of its methodology (ethnographies based on participant observation) and its perspectives, urban anthropology can be dated back to the Chicago School's microscopic studies of deviant groups and areas and to such community studies as Young and Wilmott's (1962) of E. London and Herbert Gans' of Boston (1962). Though such studies fell out of academic favour in the 1960s and 70s, they have recently enjoyed a revival with such classics as Gerald Suttles' study of the down town areas of Chicago (1968) and Peter Lloyd's vivid and moving depiction of the Shanty Towns of the Third World (1979). From a British point of view, though Ken Pryce's study of the black, inner city, ghetto area of St. Pauls in Bristol (1979) was especially timely coming as it did just before this area exploded into the first of the 1981 Riots. Pryce explains that in such areas not only is there discrimination, racial prejudice and segregation but a general atmosphere of **endless pressure** – the pressure of unemployment, poor housing, divorce, police harassment and social stigma to the point where 'holding one's pressure' becomes an essential element of surviving in such environments, of staying sane.

The most awful plight that can befall a man in the eyes of
the people of Shanty Town is madness or insanity. When
this happens the verdict always turns out to be: 'life in
Shanty Town was too strang for him', 'the stress was too
great'; 'him couldn't hold the pressure'; 'him wasn't
strang enough'; 'him didn't know how to play it cool.'
(Pryce, 1979, p. 96)

There is therefore a great need to 'let off steam', hence the cycle of
weekend 'blues' parties, drink and marijuana. The ability to 'play it
cool', of 'doing your own thing' becomes a major source of status. The
most exaggerated example of such arrogance and independence is the
Hustler, who refuses to do the white man's shit work and who expresses
his manhood and toughness by dressing in style, living off his wits (and
off women) and by being his 'own man'. Others like the Saints and
Proletarians, as Pryce calls them, survive this 'Black Jungle' by
conforming and working hard. Such a detailed, inside description
greatly aids understanding of inner city life and the 1981 Riots.

(b) **Rural Sociology**   Traditionally the village has been seen as the
ideal 'community' the epitomy of the Good Life. However whilst
studies of rural life abounded in the 1930s and 50s, with the death of the
Community Studies tradition Rural Sociology in Britain (but not
America) became something of an academic backwater, isolated from
the newer radical perspectives of power and conflict. However the
application of such concepts to rural analysis has produced a revival of
this field and much of this is due to the work of Howard Newby and his
colleagues in East Anglia. Such studies have shown that far from being
idyllic enclaves of peace and harmony, many English villages suffer
from:

(1) Poverty as bad as that in the Inner City. Farm workers are
consistently at the bottom of Low Pay Reports with fewer perks or
pensions and very long hours. In areas like Cornwall unemployment is
as high as any major city's and so is the proportion of slum housing
(6.6% 1981). Rural communities already suffer from poor public
services (buses, shops, doctors, chemists, etc.) and amidst the cutbacks
of the 80s they often come off worst.

(2) Class Divisions and Exploitation. Despite its image of social
harmony, rural society is very much one of two classes, of two 'faces of
power':

(i) The visible face of the countryside, the owners of the means of rural production are the farmer, the landowner and less visibly the financial institutions of the City.

(ii) The invisible face, those with only their labour to sell, is the farm worker. Thus the apparent sense of community is an imposed one, based on the power of these landowners to:

• Control local politics in rural areas and so protect their rule by excluding new developments (industries or housing) that might help the farm worker and suppressing 'party' politics. Few country areas have a Labour Party so that there is no party to stand up for such workers.

• Control the local economy, employment and housing. The main source of work in such areas is farming, the main source of housing the 'tied' cottage. Unions are discouraged and 'rebellious' workers black-listed so the farm worker has to accept low wages and tied housing. Hence too the enormous inequalities of wealth in rural societies with millionaire farmers and low paid workers.

• Control of the Rural Culture. Such ideological control is based on such rural traditions as Paternalism, Deference and Community, of the farm worker deferring to his 'natural' and social superior the farmer, of the ties of family and kinship that bind such workers to village life and make it difficult to leave for the big, open city. However as Newby (1977) shows such deference is more apparent than real, more an adaptation to the powerlessness of his situation by the farm worker than a 'genuine endorsement of his own inferior position in society'.

Nevertheless change is coming to the countryside due to the growth of:

(i) Agribusinesses – commercialised and factory farming is replacing the small farm. Farms are increasingly owned or controlled by such outside interests as financial institutions or major food producers like Birds Eye and Ross. Modern farming is Big Business and, with the influx of EEC grants and British subsidies, very lucrative.

(ii) Rural Migration – the young are drifting out of the village to the jobs and bright lights of the city, the urban middle-class is moving in.

The social structure of the village has thus been radically reshaped and redivided. The locals, mainly older folk, have withdrawn in face of the newcomers' invasion and so become invisible, ignored and increasingly poor.

They don't have the cars or money to get to the services of the city and often they have turned to the farmer and local gentry for protection. But this Rural Ruling Class also feels threatened. The newcomers challenge their power and privilege, their control of local politics, their control of the countryside.

(iii) **Urban Politics** - central and even European government is increasingly intervening in agriculture and the running of the countryside. New regulations and controls pour forth and the rise of environmental pressure groups attacking such practices as the destruction of hedgerows and burning of straw severely checks the farmer's power of 'divine right' in his own rural domain.

Thus the face of the English Countryside is undergoing radical change as urban influences move in. Its traditional two class structure has been overturned by a new middle-class, its traditional sense of community based on the power of the farmer over his workers has been replaced by one of fear in the face of the 'common enemy'.

Conclusions These are just a few examples of the way urban sociology has developed, of its contribution to our understanding of today's cities and to the broader field of urban studies. Similar analyses could and have been made of such urban topics as transport and education.

Chapter Four

Urban Policy-Making: The Inner City

In the summer of 1981 Britain's cities exploded, just as the Inner Cities of America had in the 1960s, just as writers like Manuel Castells had predicted. It seemed that the British Government had learnt nothing from the American experience, nothing from the forebodings of academics. This chapter will attempt to outline the problem of the Inner City and the policies of the British Government over the past twenty five years. The devotion of a whole chapter to only one aspect of the modern city is justified by the fact that it is in the Inner City, rather than the suburbs or outer fringes, that the life and death struggles of urban survival are most clearly fought out, here that the forces of modern capitalism most clearly expressed, here that the rather abstract theories of urban sociology and government officials most clearly tested.

Defining the Inner City

The 'Problem' or 'crisis' of the Inner City is a fairly recent discovery, yet one that has existed since the birth of the industrial town. Compare for example Friedrich Engels description of Manchester Old Town in 1844 with that of the Liverpool Inner Area Study in 1977.

> Everywhere, half or wholly ruined buildings, some of them actually uninhabited, which means a great deal here, rarely a wooden or stone floor to be seen in the houses, almost uniformly broken, ill-fitting windows and doors, and a state of filth. Everywhere heaps of debris, refuse and offal; standing pools for gutters, and a stench which alone would make it impossible for a human being, in any degree civilised, to live in such a district. (Engels, 1969, p. 84)

279

In 1975, eleven per cent of land in the study area was lying vacant, much of it the cleared sites of terraced houses. For those who have to live with the day to day reality of large, rubble-strewn sites the impact is immediate, unsavoury and depressing. Packs of half wild dogs scavenge among bags of abandoned household refuse. Pools of water collect where badly filled cellars have subsided. Children build fires with cardboard cartons and the abandoned timber from demolished houses and play among the piles of brick, rubble and broken glass. Half bricks provide a ready and almost endless supply of ammunition for the frequent destruction of the windows of surrounding houses. Mattresses, furniture, gas cookers, prams and even cars that have outlived their usefulness are dumped. (Liverpool Inner Area Study, 1977, p. 47)

The term 'inner city' is therefore much more than a geographical description. It is a social and economic one representing:

(a) A Decline of Population. London's population has fallen by over $1\frac{1}{2}$ million since 1939 and is likely to be down to $6\frac{1}{2}$ million by 1991. Inner Liverpool has fallen from 700,000 to 300,000 in a similar period.

(b) A Decline in Jobs – Between 1961 and 1971 London lost 243,000 jobs, inner Manchester 84,000, inner Glasgow 60,000 and this loss accelerated in the 1970s.

(c) A Decline in Housing. By its age and quality (the tenements of the 1930s, the high rise blocks of the 1960s) Inner City housing tends to be poorly maintained and designed and in a state of decay and neglect. Slum clearance programmes have left a mess of rubble and disused land, building societies are reluctant to lend mortgages for housing in such areas and local authorities tend to dump 'problem families' on such estates.

(d) A Decline in Social Organisation. Such areas seem to have especially high rates of crime, vandalism, divorce, suicide, truancy and drug taking. They tend to have a higher than average concentration of isolated or 'problem' groups – single parent families, students, the old, tramps and prostitutes. They seem to attract a wide variety of ethnic groups not only because of cheap housing but as a form of self-help, self defence even, in a society whose language and customs they do not know. As Rex and Moore (1967) explained, such groups all too easily get 'trapped' in Inner City Ghettoes and develop a 'siege mentality' an alienation from society at large.

The Inner City thus has a concentration of deprivation and poverty. 'With 7 per cent of the British population in the 1970s, the inner cities contain 14 per cent of the unskilled workers, 20 per cent of the households in housing stress, 33 per cent of the Commonwealth immigrants, twice the national rate of unemployment, up to ten times the national proportion of people living below the Supplementary Benefit poverty line, up to four times the degree of domestic overcrowding found elsewhere in cities, over twice the national average of single-parent families, and less than half the national rate of car ownership.' (Hall *et al*, 1981, p. 2) And a general atmosphere of what Lyn Davies (1981) has called 'collective deprivation', a general sense of fatalism, alienation and powerlessness engendered by living in such conditions, a sense of being trapped.

The 'Problem' of the Inner City therefore seems to be the Inner City itself. Such areas seem to 'breed' problems and such an 'area approach' was the basis of most academic and government analyses in the 1960s. Probably the most effective and authoritative attempts to define the Inner City in this way was that by Sally Holterman at the Department of the Environment in 1975. Using data from the 1971 Census she constructed a wide variety of indicators of deprivation and drew up maps of multiply-deprived households and areas. She used Enumeration Districts (EDs) as her basic units of area and from 18 indicators of deprivation covering housing, employment, assets, socio-economic structures, special needs and housing tenure, she created three indicators of multiple-deprivation 1) male unemployment, 2) overcrowding and 3) lack of basic amenities. Her examination of all urban areas in Britain revealed 2415 EDs suffering severe multiple deprivation with the greater concentrations of such areas in Glasgow (578) Greater London (466) Birmingham (170) Edinburgh (101) Manchester (93) Dundee (73) and Liverpool (60). These cities had 63.7% of the multiply-deprived EDs in Great Britain. Similar indicators were used in the 1981 Census – unemployment, overcrowding, single-parent households, pensioners living alone, lack of basic amenities, ethnic origin, population change and standardised mortality rates.

Government Policy on the Inner City can be divided into three main phases

   i   An area-based approach between 1966 and 1977
  ii   An environmental approach between 1977 and 1979
 iii   A free market approach between 1979 and today.

(I) The Area-Based Approach

This approach derives not only from analyses like Holterman that Inner Cities are areas of a concentration of problems but from a variety of influences in the 1960s that increasingly forced politicians and officials to recognise this problem.

(a) **The Rediscovery of Poverty.** Up until the 1960s, it was generally assumed that poverty had been eliminated from the face of modern Britain with the growth of affluence, of the Welfare State and full Employment. Such complacency was shattered by the publication of such studies as Richard Titmus's *Income Distribution and Social Change* (1962), Abel-Smith and Townsend's *The Poor and the Poorest* (1960) and by such official reports as those by Crowther, Newsom and Plowden all revealing considerable social inequality and millions of people living in poverty. Michael Harrington's book *The Other America* (1962) had a similar effect in the United States.

(b) **The American Experience.** In the wake of the Race Riots of the 1960s President Johnson inaugurated a War on Poverty, a plethora of urban programmes to breathe life back into inner America. The programmes that probably most influenced British policy makers were those of 'Headstart' whose policies of positive discrimination inspired the British Educational Priority Areas and those on Community Action.

(c) **The Culture of Poverty Thesis.** The American programmes were heavily influenced by the idea that poverty breeds a cycle and a culture of its own. In the words of the 1964 Economic Advisers' Report to the President '. . . poverty breeds poverty.' A poor individual or family has a high possibility of staying poor. Low incomes carry with them high risks of illness, limitations on mobility, limited access to education, information and training. Poor parents cannot give their children the opportunities for better health and education needed to improve their lot. Lack of motivation, hope and incentive is a more subtle but no less powerful barrier than lack of financial means. Thus the cruel legacy of poverty is passed from generation to generation. Oscar Lewis's concept of a Culture of Poverty – that the poor tend to adapt to poverty by adopting a set of attitudes, a sub-culture of fatalism, apathy and aliena-tion that prevents them from even trying to break out of the cycle of poverty – was especially influential.

(d) The Concept of Multiple Deprivation, outlined above, originated in this period based on the view:
(i) that certain areas especially the inner cities of the major conurbations, contain concentrations of poverty
(ii) that such areas 'breed' poverty through the cycle and culture of poverty
(iii) that the inhabitants of such areas were in some way inadequate.

(e) The Concept of Positive Discrimination, of pouring extra resources and social workers into such areas to break the cycle of poverty, to stir such people out of their fatalism, to give children in particular a headstart, an equal opportunity, became the main form of solution from such analysis. The Plowden Report on Primary Education in 1967 exemplified this approach.

(f) Race and Immigration. Race became a major public fear after the Notting Hill riots in London in 1958 and those in America in the 1960s. Growing public concern over the apparent flood of black immigrants into British cities in this period fuelled such fears and gained public expression in Enoch Powell's famous 'Rivers of Blood' speech in April 1965 which forecast race riots and a dilution of the British character and culture.

The actual policies of the British Government in the 1960s and 1970s involved pouring a generally limited amount of money into particular projects, in particular areas, by say declaring General Improvement Areas (1969) or Housing Action Areas (1974). Various grants were offered for example to improve housing or the Environment. Certain areas were declared Educational Priority Areas and given extra teachers to give the young there a better start in life. Teams of community workers were sent into various areas to break the cycle of poverty and encourage community self help. But increasingly it became obvious that such programmes were inadequate and only scratched the surface. By the late 1970s the whole idea of an area-based approach was under attack.

(i) The Concept of Multiple Deprivation was increasingly shown to be inaccurate because:

(a) deprivation often does not occur in multiples but is due to one or two isolated factors like unemployment.
(b) deprivation outside the Inner City is often as great as that inside. Even Sally Holterman's analysis showed that only 23% of those sharing or lacking a bath live in the worst 5% of EDs and only 16% of

male unemployment is so located. Thus policies concentrating only on Inner City areas are likely to miss their target. As Professor Peter Townshend put it 'However economically or socially deprived areas are defined, unless nearly half the areas in the country are included, there will be more persons or poor children living outside them than in them.'

(ii) The Culture and Cycle Poverty. Such arguments also undermined the idea that poverty is inherited or breeds. Sir Keith Joseph was one of the earliest proponents of the cycle of poverty thesis and yet it was his department's own research that in 1976 showed that not only was it difficult to identify areas where the culture of poverty was evident but that its transmission from one generation to the next did not necessarily occur 'Many children born into disadvantaged families tend not to repeat the pattern' (Paul Lawless, 1981). In fact official interpretations of Oscar Lewis's work on both sides of the Atlantic was a severe distortion. Although Lewis identified a sub-culture of poverty, he was referring to Third World not advanced societies. Moreover his analysis was a radical critique of inequality, a criticism of the stratified nature of capitalist society, not of the inadequacies of the poor. 'The culture of poverty is both an adaptation and a reaction of the poor to their marginal position in a class stratified, highly individuated society. It represents an effort to cope with feelings of helplessness and despair which develop from the realisation of the improbability of achieving success in terms of the values and goals of the larger society.' (Lewis, 1967, p. xxi) Officials and politicians however ignored this part of this analysis and instead used his thesis to blame the poor for causing their own poverty.

(iii) Positive Discrimination therefore increasingly made little sense because it directed resources to many in the Inner City who did not need them and away from those outside the Inner City who did.

(iv) Race. Moreover, not only are ethnic groups not necessarily concentrated in the Inner City but often they are neither poor nor alienated. Many like the Chinese and Indians live out in the suburbs and own prosperous businesses. Many suffer discrimination in jobs and housing but as a recent Home Office Report showed do not feel alienated. The Report states that ethnic minorities do not lack self-respect, they do not have unrealistic job expectations, they are not generally hostile to mainstream British institutions, they do not excessively blame career failures on discrimination and they are less hostile towards white people than white people are towards them.

The one glaring exception to this general similarity is the hostility of many black people towards the police.

More recent analyses of the Inner City therefore now see the main causes as lying outside such areas rather than within them – out in the new council estates, new towns like Kirkby or the high rise blocks of Glasgow and Manchester. 'The inner areas are not a cause of deprivation found within them; responsibility for this must lie in the structure of our society, its economic relationships and institutions. They do not even contain a majority of those who are deprived. But they do contain the greatest concentrations of deprivation in Britain today.' (Liverpool Inner Area Study, 1977, p. 95). In particular such critics see the problems of the Inner City as caused by:

(a) Economic factors such as the very high unemployment rates of such areas. The Inner City areas of the major conurbations – mainly in the North – used to house the traditional heavy industries such as coal, shipping, textiles and iron and steel, industries that depended on cheap unskilled labour. Such industries declined in the face of foreign competition and the restructuring of British industry. Many firms have moved out to the suburbs or industrial estates and today's big multi-nationals operate on a world scale moving the plants to wherever the labour is cheapest. In periods of recession they tend to shut down their oldest, least profitable factories and move South or abroad. Half of all the manual workers in inner Liverpool for example are employed by just 12 major corporations. When they leave – as Dunlops and Massey Ferguson have – the whole area dies.

However not only has Big Business left the Inner City but the small firms have been pushed out by government policies, slum clearance programmes, or competition from large companies. Yet as David Birch's (1979) work in America illustrates, it is the small firm that holds the best hopes for an Inner City revival. They are the source not only of most new jobs but of the types of jobs needed in the Inner City where most workers are unskilled and lack the resources to travel out to work in the suburbs.

(b) Government Policies. The flight out of the Inner City since World War II has not only been encouraged but occasionally even created by government policies. By its use of Industrial Development Certificates, tax incentives and subsidies, government encouraged the growth of industrial estates and discouraged the growth of small firms. Its slum clearance programmes tended to relocate the young and skilled in the New Towns and greenbelt estates leaving the weakest – the old and unskilled – behind. Such estates and New Towns have bred their own problems and become the new slums of the 1980s, the new high-spots of unemployment as industry has left there too.

Similarly it was the governments of the 1950s that brought black immigrants into Britain as cheap labour to do our 'dirty jobs' – on the buses, cleaning the streets. Their numbers haven't exploded but stabilised at just over two million and many of these are now second or even third generation – born and bred British.

Government attempts at rent control are seen by many experts as a major cause of the decline in housing: 'the most efficient technique known to destroy a city – except for bombing' argued Swedish economist Assar Lindbeck. Attempts to keep rents down to help low income families have in effect drastically cut the amount of housing offered for rent and so those that do still take in lodgers or tenants can pick and choose and ignore maintenance. The blacks and single-parent families tend to lose out.

Recent cuts in public spending and the flight of the middle-classes to the suburbs have meant that even if a local authority wanted to stem the decline of the Inner City, it lacks the resources to do so.

Finally even the policies that the government of the 60s and 70s did implement have lacked the resources and political will necessary to be really effective. Studies like Edwards and Batleys (1978) from 'inside' the Home Office have shown not only that official analysis of the Inner City was faulty but that the organisation was weak and poorly co-ordinated. Even Joan Higgins' book (1983) which is more sympathetic to government action, agreed that 'bureaucratic ineptitude has been compounded by Ministerial indifference'. Whilst pouring money and community workers in on the one hand, governments were encouraging industry and the skilled out with the other. Whilst giving small amounts to Inner City housing and education, it has drastically cut public spending generally.

As Professor Peter Hall concluded in 1981:

> By and large, therefore, most of the specific inner city policy initiatives were little more than minor and peripheral experiments. They did not attempt much and they did not achieve much, however much they may have been oversold by politicians anxious to prove their bona fides to the electorate. Ironically, the main gain was in understanding that the problem has much deeper roots than we imagined before – but armed with the understanding we can see just how much more difficult it is to do anything about it. (p. 110)

More radical writers have gone further and analysed government inadequacy as deliberate. Much of such radical criticism has ironically come from some of the governments' own workers, those on the Community Development Projects. The CDPs were the largest ever government funded experiment in social action. In 1969 12 CDPs were set up in such Inner City areas as Hillfields, Coventry and, as already explained, largely rested on the idea of a cycle and culture of poverty. As the 1977 CDP report argued:

> Firstly, that it was the 'deprived' themselves who were the cause of 'urban deprivation'. Secondly, the problem could best be solved by overcoming these people's apathy and promoting self-help. Thirdly, locally-based research into the problems would serve to bring about changes in local and central government policy. (CDP, 1977, p. 4)

Action teams were sent in to promote community participation in local government, to mobilise local tenants and action groups and to provide research data for central government. This programme was largely the brainchild of Derek Morrell, a senior official in the Home Office and was initiated by the Children's Department as a means of bringing stability to such communities. These community workers however increasingly became frustrated at the slow progress being made and their analyses increasingly reflected a Marxist perspective that:

(i) The real cause of Inner city poverty was the capitalist system itself and the powerful in society at large. Coventry CDP for example began analysing the role of local officials and Benwell CDP sought to identify the Ruling Families of the North East.

(ii) The real aim of the CDPs was not to alleviate poverty but to control the poor. As Paul Corrigan has put it 'Throughout the Western World, states are characterised by one of the two major symbols of control in capitalist society – the tank or the community worker.' What the government really feared was the other side of Oscar Lewis's thesis, '. . . the poor have a critical attitude towards the basic institutions of the dominant classes, hatred of the police, mistrust of government and those in high position, and a cynicism which extends even to the church. This gives the culture of poverty a high potential for protest and for being used in political movements aimed against the state.'

As evidence of such claims, CDP workers asked why such projects were run by the Home Office, the government department responsible for law and order and not the Social Services; why the police took so much interest in their work. They felt that the government was 'blaming the victim' of Inner City poverty, the poor as a means of diverting attention from the real causes – capitalism. Inevitably such analyses antagonised local and central government officials and with the death of Morrell in the early '70s so the whole scheme soon died too. However the influence of the CDPs was extensive not only through their multitude of reports but because many of these activists got posts in local government in areas like Knowsley and Sheffield.

(II) The Environmental Approach

This policy developed out of the economic analyses outlined above and was encapsulated in the 1977 White Paper on the Inner Cities drawn up by the 1974–79 Labour Government. It was the result of five years of Inner Area Studies by the Department of the Environment and was influenced by both Liberal and Marxist-CDP arguments that Inner City decline was mainly the result of the investment strategies of the multinationals and the government's own economic policy. The aim was to integrate existing programmes on education, housing, etc. into a broad economic strategy. As the new Labour Secretary of State for the Environment, Peter Shore put it in a speech to the 1977 Save our Cities Conference organised by the *Sunday Times* 'If we are to get to grips with the underlying economic and social forces, we must deploy the major instruments of public policy.' The White Paper announced considerable increases in urban spending and offered a number of local authorities 'partnership' status. However, in April 1979 the Labour Government lost office to a radical right wing Conservative Administration.

(III) The Free Market Approach

As in other areas of government policy, the election of Mrs. Thatcher has seen a dramatic shift away from government intervention, bureaucracy and high spending towards policies designed to free 'Market Forces'. To date such an approach has affected the Inner City Programmes in the following ways:

(a) Severe cut-backs on local government spending and urban aid. The Rate Support Grant has been cut from 61% in 1978–9 to below 50% (1985–6) and councils who overspend are not only liable to fines but Rate Capping. The urban 'partnership' authorities lost £166 million in grants, £104 million in housing subsidies and £5 million in urban programmes in 1981–2 alone.

(b) An increase in central control and move to direct intervention through organisations appointed by the Government and by-passing local authorities such as the Urban Development Corporations.

(c) A shift from 'social' programmes to wealth creating ones as in the idea of Enterprise Zones.

(d) A return to social pathology and social control analyses of the Inner City problem as in the Government's handling of the 1981 Riots.

(i) **The Urban Development Corporations.** These are an adaptation of the New Town Development Corporations and have been applied to inner Liverpool, Glasgow and the London Docklands. Such bodies aim to assist industry not only by making land, premises and finance available but by having a fully integrated policy for housing, transport and other urban facilities. The aim is to make such Inner City 'Wastelands' productive and to generate new employment without the usual local authority 'red-tape'. The International Garden Festival in Liverpool in 1984 was one example of this policy.

(ii) **Enterprise Zones.** This idea originated from a speech in 1977 by the socialist, Professor Peter Hall advocating the introduction of Freeports as in Europe and abroad to revitalise Inner City and Dockland areas by giving private enterprise a 'free hand', free from taxes and controls, free to experiment. 'In other words, we would aim to recreate the Hong Kong of the 1950s and 1960s inside inner Liverpool or inner Glasgow.' (quoted in S. Butler, 1982, pp. 96–7).

Sir Geoffrey Howe picked up the idea and proposed in a speech on the Isle of Dogs (June 1978) the establishment of four or five such zones to generate an atmosphere for new ideas and as Chancellor of the Exchequer set up 11 such zones by 1981 ranging from Clydebank and Swansea to West Belfast and Corby. There was to be a minimum of bureaucracy, firms would not have to pay rent, rates or even customs duties and a range of tax allowances were made available. Such experiments have however, been criticised from both sides.

(a) The Labour Party and the left wing generally see such zones as attracting the 'unacceptable faces of capitalism' – the property shark, the tax fiddler and the 'bent' used-car salesman. They fear the growth of 'sweatshops' and the exploitation of cheap labour. Radical critics like Bennet Harrison, Doreen Massey and William W. Goldsmith see them as an excuse for Right-Wing Governments 'to unravel the social safety net' by cutting welfare payments, reducing minimum wages and relaxing health and safety regulations. New areas of blight and unemployment would appear just outside such zones because firms there – still having to pay taxes and rates – would be unable to compete and so go out of business (IJURR, 1982).

(b) Right-Wing Conservatives however felt such schemes did not go far enough towards free enterprise and the C.B.I. pointed out the lack of incentives for the small businessman. The large corporations and the property developers seem to be the ones most likely to profit and there is a very real danger that instead of such firms creating new jobs they will simply close down existing plants and move their existing work-force into such zones. As Stuart Butler (1982) concluded in his study of Enterprise Zones,

> . . . the door has only been opened partly to one segment of free enterprise, and it is far from clear that it is the right segment to achieve an economic rebirth of the inner cities. The door still appears to be firmly closed against the small entrepreneurs who offer the best hope for the innovative ideas and jobs that are needed.
>
> As has happened elsewhere large corporations may move in, grab the grants available and then move out again when such concessions run out leaving such areas even more unstable than before. (p. 127)

Moreover this return to a 'piecemeal' approach again fails to tackle the real problems of the Inner City. It allows the government to claim they are doing something but without spending any real money ' "Experiments" are now an established tradition in the inner city as a substitute for actually spending the money required to deal with these problems' (Anderson, 1980).

Alternatives

But what alternatives are there? The far-left and even liberal writers argue for a massive influx of government money and tight controls on the Multinationals. Limited area-based approaches are not enough. As David Smith (1979) puts it,

> The fundamental problem facing the inner city is, thus, that it is not ultimately within the power of the planners to counteract the major structural forces operating in a largely free-enterprise economy. Area-based policies of social regeneration or economic revival may help some people in some places. More spending on schools, housing, roads and paths may help. But unless fundamental changes are made in institutions, especially the labour and housing markets, it is hard to see much real impact being made on localised deprivation in Britain's urban areas. Inner-city deprivation may thus

have to be accepted as one of the inevitable consequences of the maintenance of capitalism in Britain in this particular period of its historic evolution. (p. 213)

Others like the Town and Country Planning Association argue instead for a policy of **decentralisation**. They see the flight from the Inner City' as natural and inevitable. It is a waste of public money to try and stop or stem it. It would be better to use such funds to help relocate and retain those trapped in the Inner City. As Paul Lawless (1979) and several of the Inner Area Studies argued the plight of the Inner City has been 'grossly exaggerated'. Nevertheless the Inner City is a problem and as Professor Hall (1981) argues a serious indictment of a civilised society, '. . . there is a very real prospect of the development, within a predominantly affluent and also enlightened society, of a substantial minority of poor, frustrated, alienated and dysfunctional groups who could present a source of grave social malaise.' (p. 130)

The 1981 Inner City Riots

The riots were to prove such predictions tragically correct and they revealed the final strand to the Conservative Government's strategy – that on Law and Order. Between May and June 1981 riots broke out in St. Pauls (Bristol), Brixton and Southall (London) Toxteth (Liverpool) and Moss Side (Manchester). The frustration and hatred they expressed stunned politicians and the public alike. This is how the Scarman Report described one such riot,

> During the week-end of 10–12 April (Friday, Saturday and Sunday) the British people watched with horror and incredulity an instant audio-visual presentation on their television sets of scenes of violence and disorder in the capital city, the like of which had not previously been seen in this century in Britain. In the centre of Brixton, a few hundred young people – most, but not all of them, black – attacked the police on the streets with stones, bricks, iron bars and petrol bombs, demonstrating to millions of their fellow citizens the fragile basis of the Queen's peace. The petrol bomb was now used for the first time on the streets of Britain (the idea, no doubt, copied from the disturbances in Northern Ireland). These young people by their criminal behaviour – for such, whatever their grievances or frustrations, it was – brought about a temporary collapse of law and order in the centre of an inner suburb of London. (p. 1)

Explanations poured out fast and furious.

(a) The Prime Minister Mrs. Thatcher blamed a breakdown in social order and control. She blamed 'naked greed' (*Times*, 9.7.81) and appealed for 'parents, grandparents, teachers, with a job or not, black and or white, to teach their children "to obey the law" (*Mail*, 9.7.81). In the areas where violence and rioting has occurred, a good deal of it has been carried out by children of school age... That has nothing whatsoever to do with the dole queue.'

(b) Others blamed outside agitators 'HUNT FOR MASKED RIOT LEADERS' (*Mirror*, 11.7.81) and the Media (copycat riots) whilst Councillor Trevor Jones, the then leader of the Liverpool City Council, called for the Army to be put on standby.

(c) The Labour Party blamed the Government's policies and in particular the massive rise in unemployment (nearly 3 million by mid 1981). But such a view failed to explain why other unemployment 'black spots' did not explode and conveniently ignored the fact that it was Jim Callaghan's administration that started the cuts in public spending.

(d) The Police were a central part of most analyses. Many saw recent policing policies – the use of the 'SUS' laws, the Deptford Fire Inquiry and the use of the Special Patrol Group – as the spark that set the riots alight and certainly as the Scarman Report showed, it was incidents with the police that started the unrest in St. Pauls and Toxteth. Several police committees complained of their lack control over police tactics and John Alderson, Police Chief of Devon and Cornwall spoke out against the growing use of tactics and weapons developed in Northern Ireland. However as Margaret Simey chairwoman of Merseyside Police Committee, argued 'For too long, instead of action on our part... we have relied on the police to "keep the lid on the dustbin".' And as Lord Scarman concluded:

> The Police do not create social deprivation though unimaginative, inflexible policing can make the tensions which deprivation engenders greatly worse. Conversely, while good policing can help diminish tension and avoid disorder, it cannot remove the causes of social stress where these are to be found as those in Brixton and elsewhere are deeply embedded in fundamental economic and social conditions. (p. 100)

As outlined above, the real roots of the 1981 Riots were laid years before by successive governments and private enterprise. P. J. Waller's article is a vivid description of Toxteth, Liverpool, the scene of some of the worst violence. Inner Liverpool still looked as though the war had just finished and what the Luftwaffe had failed to destroy, the actions of the Multinationals did. 'In 1966 about 51 per cent, and in 1975 about 70 per cent of people employed in manufacturing in Liverpool worked in multi-plant or international companies like GEC, Dunlop, Courtaulds, Lucas, Plessey, British Leyland and Vauxhall, whose controlling agency was situated elsewhere, and indifferent to local sentiment.' By 1981 several of these firms had left. Under the new Tory Government, Liverpool City Council had lost £14 million in grants and under the Liberal Administration of Trevor Jones whilst the rates were reduced by a penny, public services and the local environment continued to deteriorate.

The Government's response to the Riots was firstly to send in the police to restore law and order, secondly Lord Scarman to investigate and thirdly Michael Heseltine to organise a Task Force of businessmen in Merseyside. As Roy Hattersley wittily remarked 'the Government is throwing Ministers at the Inner Cities instead of money'. The Scarman Report emphasised the immediate need to restore community policing and re-establish public confidence in the Police but concluded that 'The only genuine, long range solution for what has happened lies in an attack – mounted at every level – upon the conditions that breed despair and violence. All of us know what those conditions are: ignorance, discrimination, slums, poverty, disease, not enough jobs.' (p. 136)

Michael Heseltine set up the Merseyside Development Corporation which to date has promoted the International Garden Festival and the Merseyside Docklands Scheme but as he himself admitted Liverpool's economic problems can only be solved in the context of national economic policy; a policy to date that has seen a further rise in unemployment, further cuts in public spending and no significant impact on Inner City problems – until the next riot?

Postscript. The Government is at present (January 1985) planning to set up five new Task Forces along the lines of the one sent into Merseyside in 1981 as a means to tackling the Inner City Problem in a way that co-ordinates both government departments and central and local government and directs resources to the areas most in need. The areas chosen besides Liverpool are the 'partnership areas' at the top of the 'league table' for urban deprivation – Birmingham, Manchester/Salford, Newcastle and Inner London (Lambeth, Hackney and Islington). However as a recent *Guardian* leader article (Jan. 3rd, 1985) pointed out these are also those authorities scheduled for the heavier cuts in their spending – very much a case of giving with one hand and taking with the other. Moreover in the light of past experience over such 'area-based approaches', why is this attempt any more likely to succeed than earlier ones?

Conclusions

The Future

What then is the future of the city? Will present trends continue or be reversed? Will the city finally die or are there signs of new life. Press and Smith (1980) provide a summary of the main possibilities.

> The field seems divided between those who think there will and those who think there won't be an urban future. On the negative side are arguments both of doom and salvation. The city will become unliveable, a jungle, insupportable, unserviceable, and certainly unfuelable. It will be so regimented or anarchistic as to drive its inhabitants away. Where the exurbanities will live is still unclear. On the other hand, anti-urban optimists envision a return to dispersed, small, and personal communities as inevitable and desirable; back to a 'natural' life, perhaps in communal rural contexts.
>   Those who see an urban future are also divided. Pessimists envision horrendous city sprawls, megalo-politan cancers upon the disappearing countryside. Trapped within them by the lack of space outside (all available land being devoted to hyperintensively mechanized agriculture), the inhabitants tumble upon one another, fighting for space, privacy, and even the legal right to marry or reproduce. Optimists see the future as a time of urban experimentation. Aesthetic and psychoemotional needs will be anticipated. Planned, human-serving cities will offer up a cornucopia of benefits and services undreamed of today, all efficiently supported by a foundation of climactic technological wizardry. (p. 454)

As Gary Gappert and Richard Knight (1982) argue, as advanced industrial societies are going through a 'post industrial transition' so too are our cities. Whilst cities in the West are being 'evacuated', those in the Third World are still growing – upwards and outwards. They represent the new sources of social division, the new extremes of wealth – between the city and the countryside, the city centre and the Shanty Town, the formal and the informal economy. They are a dual society in a dual world in which the gap between rich and poor, between the First and Third World continues to grow.

If the future of the City is so uncertain, what of that of Urban Sociology? Does its future lie in the wide variety of urban pathways discussed in chapter 3 or as part of an urban studies 'conglomerate', amalgamating the wide and varied urban disciplines of geography, economics and the like? Has it yet solved its central problem of self identity, have the new radical perspectives given it a clear and distinct foundation. It seems not; it seems that urban sociology is still as sprawling, still as multi-faceted, still as shapeless as its subject matter and to try and predict its future would seem just as pointless, save to say that its present 'world' perspective, like Peter Hall's analysis of 'World Cities', does provide a framework for more clearly understanding and comparing both its internal dynamic and external pressures. Yet as Rosemary Mellor argues (1977) the city depicted by urban sociologists still often bears little resemblance to that experienced by the general public.

> Towns are too familiar, the grey muddle of the older areas, the redbrick geometry of the new estates are as interesting as our breakfast toast, and as such disregarded. The general public's blindness to the urban environment is something academics, professional students of the cities and the regions they dominate, are unable to grasp. And yet specialization of study can render the professional equally blind – with intensity of observation, a spotlight on a few themes – and very soon we are dealing with a different world from the one known to the layman.

The present empirical work of Pahl, Castells, Szelenyi and Saunders is helping to put flesh on the 'urban skeleton'.

Bibliography

Abel-Smith, B. and Townsend, P. *The Poor and the Poorest* (Bell, London, 1960)

Abrams, P. and McCullough, A. *Communes, Sociology and Society* (C.U.P., Cambridge, 1976)

Abu-Lughod, J. and Hay, R. (eds.) *Third World Urbanization* (Methuen, N.Y., 1977)

Ambrose, P. and Colenutt, B. *The Property Machine* (Penguin, Harmondsworth, 1975)

American National Resources Committee (1973) in B. J. L. Berry 'The Counter-Urbanization Process. How General? in Hausen, H. M. (ed.) *Human Settlements Systems* (Ballinger, Cambridge, Mass., 1978)

Amin, S. *Unequal Development* (Harvester, London, 1976)

Arensberg, C. M. and Kimball, S. T. *Family and Community in Ireland* (Harvard University Press, Boston, 1940)

Baran, P. *The Political Economy of Growth* (Penguin, Harmondsworth, 1957)

Bater, J. *The Soviet City* (Edward Arnold, London, 1980)

Batley, J. and Edwards, R. *The Politics of Positive Discrimination: An Evaluation of Urban Programmes 1967-77* (Tavistock, London, 1978)

Bell, C. and Newby, H. *Community Studies* (Allen and Unwin, London, 1971)

Bell, C. and Newby, H. (eds.) *The Sociology of Community* (Frank Cass, London, 1974)

Bennington, J. 'Strategies for Change at the Local Level: Some Reflections' in D. Jones and M. Mayo (eds.) *Community Work One* (R. & K.P., London, 1975)

Berger, B. *Working Class Suburbs* (C.U.P., Cambridge, 1969)

Berry, B. J. L. 'On Urbanization and Counter Urbanization' in B. J. L. Berry (ed.) *Urbanization and Counter-Urbanization* (Sage, Beverley Hills, 1976)

Birch, D. *The Job Generation Process* (M.I.T. Press, Cambridge, 1979)

Blair, T. L. *The International Urban Crisis* (Hart-Davies MacGibbon, London, 1974)

Briggs, A. *Victorian Cities* (Penguin, Harmondsworth, 1968)

Broadbent, T. A. *Planning and Profit in the Urban Economy* (Methuen, London, 1977)

Brunn, S. D. and Williams, J. F. *Cities of the World* (Harper & Row, N.Y., 1983)

Burgess, E. 'The Growth of the City: An Introduction into a Research Project' in R. Park and E. Burgess *The City* (University of Chicago Press, London, 1967)

Burney, E. *Housing on Trial* (O.U.P., London, 1967)

Burns, S. *The Household Economy* (Beacon Hill Press, N.Y., 1977)

Butler, S. *Enterprise Zones: Greenlining the Inner Cities* (Heinemann, London, 1982)

Castells, M. *The Urban Question* (Edward Arnold, London, 1977)

Castells, M. 'The Class Struggle and Urban Contradictions: The Emergence of Urban Protest Movements in Advanced Industrial Societies' in J. Cowley *et al. Community or Class Struggle* (Stage I, London, 1977)

Castells, M. *City, Class and Power* (Macmillan, London, 1978)

Castells, M. *The City and the Grassroots* (Edward Arnold, London, 1983)

Coates, K. and Silburn, R. *Poverty: The Forgotten Englishman* (Penguin, Harmondsworth, 1970)

Cockburn, C. *The Local State* (Pluto, London, 1977)

Cockburn, C. *Brothers: Male Dominance and Technological Change* (Pluto, London, 1983)

C.D.P. *The Costs of Industrial Change* 1977

C.D.P. *Gilding the Ghetto* 1977 (C.D.P. Interproject editorial team)

Committee for Concerned Asian Scholars *China: Inside the People's Republic* (Bantam Books, N.Y., 1972)

Couper, M. and Brindley, T. 'Housing Classes and Housing Values' *Sociological Review* vol. 23, 1975

Davies, J. and Taylor, J. 'Race, Community and No Conflict' *New Society* vol. 9, 1970

Davies, J. *The Evangelistic Bureaucrat* (Tavistock, London, 1972)

Davies, K. 'The Urbanization of the Human Population' in *Cities: A Scientific America Book* (Alfred Knopf, N.Y., 1973)

Dewey, R. 'The Rural-Urban Continuum; Real but Relatively Unimportant' *American Journal of Sociology*, vol. 66, 1960

296

Duncan, O. and Schnore, L. 'Cultural, Behavioural and Ecological Perspectives in the Study of Social Organization' *American Journal of Sociology*, vol. 65, 1959

Dunleavy, P. *Urban Political Analysis* (Macmillan, London, 1980)

Dunleavy, P. and Husbands, C. *Democracy at the Crossroads: Voting and Party Competition in the 1980s* (Allen & Unwin, London, 1985)

Dunning, J. H. *Economic Analysis and the Multinational Enterprise* (Allen & Unwin, London, 1975)

Economic Advisers Reports to the President 1964 U.S. Government Printing Office, Washington, D.C.

Elliot, B. and McCrone, D. *The City: Patterns of Domination and Conflict* (Macmillan, London, 1982)

Engels, F. *The Condition of the English Working Class* (Panther Books, St. Albans, 1969)

Fainstein, N. I. and S. S. (eds.) *Urban Policy under Capitalism* (Sage, N.Y. 1982)

Firey, W. 'Sentiment and Symbolism as Ecological Variables' *American Sociological Review*, vol. 10, 1945

Frank, A. G. *Latin America: Underdevelopment or Revolution* (Monthly Review Press, N.Y., 1969)

Frankenberg, R. *Village on the Border* (Cohen and West, London, 1957)

Frankenberg, R. *Communities in Britain* (Penguin, Harmondsworth, 1966)

French, R. A. and Hamilton, F. E. I. The *Socialist City* (John Wiley and Sons, N.Y., 1979)

Friedland, R. *Power and Crisis in the City: Corporations, Unions and Urban Policy* (Macmillan, London, 1982)

Friedman, J. and Goetz, W. 'World City Formation: An Agenda for Research and Action' *International Journal of Urban and Regional Research*, vol. 6, No. 3, 1982

Gans, H. *The Urban Villagers* (Free Press, Glencoe Illinois, 1962)

Gans, H. *The Levittowners* (Allen Lane, London, 1967)

Gans, H. 'Urbanism and Suburbanism as Ways of Life' in R. E. Pahl, 1968

Gappert, G. and Knight, R. V. *Cities in the 21st Century* (Sage, Beverley Hills, 1982)

Geshuny, J. *After Industrial Society: The Emerging Self-Service Economy* (Macmillan, London, 1978)

Geshuny, J. and Miles, I. D. *The New Service Economy* (Frances Pinter, London, 1983)

Gilbert, A. and Gugler, J. *Cities, Poverty and Development: Urbanization in the Third World* (O.U.P., Oxford, 1982)

Gregory, D. *Ideology, Science and Human Geography* (Hutchinson, London, 1978)

Gregory, D. and Urry, J. *Social Relations and Spatial Structures* (Macmillan, London, Forthcoming)

Haddon, R. 'A Minority in a Welfare State Society'. *New Atlantis* vol. 2, 1970

Hall, P. and Hay, D. *Growth Centres in the European Urban System* (Heinemann, London, 1980)

Hall, P. *The Inner City in Context* (Heinemann, London, 1981)

Hall, P. 'Enterprise Zones: A Justification' *International Journal of Urban and Regional Research* vol. 6, no. 3, 1982

Hall, P. *World Cities* (Weidenfeld and Nicolson, London, 3rd Edition 1984)

Haralambos, M. *Sociology: Themes and Perspectives* (U.T.P., Slough, 1980)

Hannerz, U. *Exploring the City* (Columbia University Press, N.Y., 1980)

Harloe, M. (ed.) *Captive Cities* (Wiley, London, 1977)

Harloe, M. (ed.) *New Perspectives in Urban Change and Conflict* (Heinemann, London, 1981)

Harrington, M. *The Other America: Poverty in the United States* (Penguin, Harmondsworth, 1962)

Harrison, B. 'The Politics and Economics of the Urban Enterprise Zone Proposal: A Critique' *International Journal of Urban and Regional Research* vol 6, no. 3, 1982

Harvey, D. *Social Justice and the City* (Edward Arnold, London, 1973)

Hawley, A. *Human Ecology: A Theory of Community Structure* (Ronald Press, N.Y., 1950)

Helmer, J. and Eddington, N. A. *Urbanman: The Psychology of Urban Survival* (Free Press, N.Y., 1973)

Herbert, D. 'The Spatial Dimension – Geographers and Urban Studies' in V. Pons and R. Francis (eds.) *Urban Social Research: Problems and Prospects* (R. and K. P., London, 1981)

Higgins, J. et al. Government and Urban Poverty: Inside the Policy Making Progress (Blackwell, Oxford, 1983)

Hillery, G.A. 'Definitions of Community' Rural Sociology vol. 20, no. 2, 1955

Holland, S. The Regional Problem (Macmillan, London, 1976)

Holland, S. Capital versus the Regions (Macmillan, London, 1976)

Holterman, S. 'Areas of Urban Deprivation in Great Britain: An Analysis of 1971 Census Data' Social Trends no. 6, 1975

Hunter, F. Community Power Structure (Chapel Hill Books, N.C. 1953)

Jones, C. (ed.) Urban Deprivation and the Inner City (Croom Helm, London, 1979)

Kettle, M. and Hodges, L. Uprising (Pan Books, London, 1982)

King, A.D. 'The World Economy in Everywhere: Urban History and the World System' in the 1983 Urban History Yearbook (Leicester University Press, Leicester, 1983)

Kirby, A. The Politics of Location (Methuen, London, 1982)

Kirk, G. Urban Planning in a Capitalist Society (Croom Helm, London, 1980)

Lamarche, F. 'Property Development and the Economic Foundations of the Urban Question' in C. Pickvance 1976

Lambert, C. and Weir, D. Cities in Modern Britain (Harper & Row, London, 1982)

Lambert, J., Paris, C. and Blackaby, B. Housing Policy and the State (Macmillan, London, 1978)

Lansley, S. Housing and Public Policy (Croom Helm, London, 1979)

Lawless, P. Urban Deprivation and Government Initiative (Faber and Faber, London, 1979)

Lawless, P. Britain's Inner Cities (Harper Row, London, 1981)

Lebas, E. 'Urban and Regional Sociology in Advanced Industrial Societies: A Decade of Marxist and Critical Perspectives' Current Sociology vol. 30, no. 1, 1982

Levinson, C. Capital, Inflation and the Multi-nationals (Allen and Unwin, London, 1971)

Lewis, O. Life in a Mexican Village: Tepotzlan Restudied (University of Illinois Press, Urbana, 1951)

Lewis, O. Five Families Mexican Case Studies in the Culture of Poverty (Basic Books, N.Y., 1959)

Lewis, O. La Vida: A Puerto Rican Family in the Culture of Poverty (Secker and Warburg, London, 1967)

Lipton, M. Why Poor People Stay Poor: Urban Bias in World Development (Temple Smith, London, 1977)

Littlejohn, J. Westrigg: The Sociology of a Cheviot Parish (R.K.P., London, 1963)

Liverpool Inner Area Study, Change or Decay (H.M.S.O., London, 1977)

Lloyd, P. Slums of Hope (Penguin, Harmondsworth, 1979)

Loney, M. and Allen, M. The Crisis of the Inner City (Macmillan, London, 1979)

Loney, M. Community Against Government (Heinemann, London, 1983)

Lukes, S. Power: A Radical View (Macmillan, London, 1974)

Lynd, R.S. and H.M. Middletown (Harcourt Brace and World, N.Y., 1929)

Lynd, R.S. and H.M. Middletown in Transition (Constable, London, 1964 edition)

McKay, D. and Cox, A. The Politics of Urban Change (Croom Helm, London, 1979)

Mann, P. An Approach to Urban Sociology (R.K.P. London, 1965)

Marriot, O. The Property Boom (Penguin, Harmondsworth, 1967)

Martindale, D. (ed.) Max Weber: The City (Gertrude Neuwirth/Free Press, N.Y., 1958)

Matthews, M. 'Social Dimensions in Soviet Urban Housing' in R.A. French and F.E. Ian Hamilton 1979

Mazumdar, D. 'The Urban Informal Economy' World Development 4 1976

Mellor, R. Urban Sociology in an Urbanized Society (R.K.P., London, 1977)

Moore, R. The Social Impact of Oil: The Case of Petershead (R.K.P., London, 1982)

Newby, H. The Deferential Worker (Allen Lane, London, 1977)

Newby, H. et al, Property, Paternalism and Power (Hutchinson, London, 1978)

Newby, H. Green and Pleasant Land (Penguin, Harmondsworth, 1980)

Newby, H. and Buttel, F. The Rural Sociology of Advanced Societies (Croom Helm, London, 1980)

Nixon, R. (President of the United States) quoted by R.B. Sutcliffe in the Introduction to P. Baran, 1957

Nyrere, J. *Ujaama. Essays on Socialism in East Africa* (O.U.P., Oxford, 1968)

Pahl, R. E. *Urbs in Rure* (Weidenfeld and Nicolson, London, 1965)

Pahl, R. E. 'The Rural-Urban Continuum' in R. E. Pahl 1968

Pahl, R. E. *Readings in Urban Sociology* (Pergamon, Oxford, 1968)

Pahl, R. E. *Whose City?* (Penguin, Harmondsworth, 1970)

Pahl, R. E. 'Collective Consumption and the State in Capitalist and State Socialist Societies' in R. Scase (ed.) 1977

Pahl, R. E. and Geshuny, J. 'Work Outside Employment. Some Preliminary Speculations' in S. Henry (ed.) 1981

Pahl, R. E. *Divisions of Labour* (Blackwell, Oxford, 1984)

Park, R. *Human Communities* (Free Press, N.Y., 1952)

Perlman, J. E. *The Myth of Marginality: Urban Poverty and Politics in Rio de Janeiro* (University of California Press, Berkeley, 1976)

Pickvance, C. G. *Urban Sociology: Critical Essays* (Tavistock, London, 1976)

Press, I. and Smith, M. E. *Urban Place and Process: Readings in the Anthology of Cities* (Macmillan, N.Y., 1980)

Pryce, K. *Endless Pressure* (Penguin, Harmondsworth, 1979)

Redfield, R. *Tepotzlan: A Mexican Village: A Study of Folk Life* (University of Chicago Press, Chicago, 1930)

Redfield, R. 'The Folk Society' *American Journal of Sociology*, vol. 52, 1947

Rees, A. D. *Life in a Welsh Countryside* (University of Wales Press, Cardiff, 1951)

Rex, J. and Moore, R. *Race, Community and Conflict* (O.U.P., London, 1967)

Richardson, J. 'The Evolving Dynamics of American Urban Development' in G. Gappert and R. V. Knight, 1982

Roberts, B. *Cities of Peasants* (Edward Arnold, London, 1978)

Rose, A. *The Power Structure* (O.U.P., N.Y., 1967)

Saunders, P. *Urban Politics: A Sociological Interpretation* (Hutchinson, London, 1979)

Saunders, P. *Social Theory and the Urban Question* (Hutchinson, London, 1981)

Saunders, P. 'Beyond Housing Classes. The Sociological Significance of Private Property Rights and Means of Consumption' *International Journal of Urban and Regional Research* vol. 8, no. 2, 1984

Saunders, P. and Dearlove, J. *Introduction to British Politics* (Blackwell, Oxford, 1984)

Sawers, L. 'Cities and Countryside in the Soviet Union and China' in Tabb and Sawers, 1978

Scarman Report. *The Brixton Disorders*. Report of an Inquiry by the Right Honourable Lord Scarman O.B.E. (H.M.S.O., London, 1982)

Scase, R. (ed.) *Industrial Society: Class, Cleavage and Control* (Allen and Unwin, London, 1977)

Sidel, R. *Families in Fengsheng: Urban Life in China* (Penguin, Baltimore, 1974)

Simmel, G. 'The Metropolis and Mental Life' in K. H. Wolff (ed.) *The Sociology of Georg Simmel* (Free Press, Glencoe, Illinois, 1903)

Sjoberg, G. *The Pre-Industrial City* (Free Press, N.Y., 1960)

Smith, D. M. *Where the Grass is Greener* (Penguin, Harmondsworth, 1979)

Sorokin, P. A. and Zimmerman, C. C. *The Principles of Rural-Urban Sociology* (Henry Holt, N.Y., 1929)

Souza, P. R. and Tokman, V. 'The Informal Urban Sector in Latin America' *International Labour Review*, 114, 1976

Spence, N., Gillespie, A., Goddard, J., Kennet, S., Pinch, S. and Williams, A. *British Cities an Analysis of Urban Change* (Pergamon, Oxford, 1982)

Stacey, M. 'The Myth of Community Studies' *British Journal of Sociology* vol. 20, no. 2, 1969

Stein, M. *The Eclipse of Community* (Princeton University Press, New Jersey, 1960)

Sternlieb, G. and Hughes, J. W. *Post Industrial America* (Rutgers Centre for Urban Policy Research, 1975)

Stretton, H. *Urban Planning in Rich and Poor Countries* (O.U.P., London, 1978)

Shuttles, G. *The Social Order of the Slum* (Chicago University Press, Chicago, 1968)

Szelenyi, I. 'Housing System and Social Structure' in P. Halmos (ed.) *Hungarian Social Studies* (Keele University, The Sociological Review Monographs, 1972)

Szelenyi, I. 'Structural Changes of and Alternatives to Capitalist Development in the Contemporary Urban and Regional System' *International Journal of Urban and Regional Research*, vol. 5, 1981

Szelenyi, I. *Urban Inequalities Under State Socialism* (O.U.P., Oxford, 1983)

Tabb, W.K. and Sawers, L. (eds.) *Marxism and the Metropolis* (O.U.P., N.Y., 1978)

Titmus, R. *Income Distribution and Social Change* (George Allen & Unwin, London, 1962)

Tonnies, F. *Community and Society* (Harper Row, N.Y., 1957)

Townshend, P. 'Area Deprivation Policies' *New Statesman*, Aug, 1976

Underwood, J. 'Town Planner in Search of a Role' School for Advanced Urban Studies, Bristol University Occasional Paper No. 6, 1980

Wallerstein, I. *The Modern World System* (Academic Press, 1974)

Warner, W.L. and Lunt, P. *The Social Life of a Modern City* (Yale University Press, New Haven, 1941)

Warner, W.L. *Yankee City* (Yale University Press, New Haven, 1963)

Williams, O.P. *Metropolitan Political Analysis* (Free Press, N.Y., 1971)

Williams, R. *The Country and the City* (Chatto and Windus, London, 1973)

Williams, W.M. *A West Country Village* (R.K.P., London, 1963)

Winkler, J. 'The Corporate Economy' in R. Scase (ed.) 1977

Wirth, L. 'Urbanism as a Way of Life' in P. Hatt and A. Reiss (eds.) *Cities and Society* (Free Press, N.Y., 1957)

Young, M. and Wilmott, P. *Family and Kinship in East London* (Penguin, Harmondsworth, 1962)

Zorbaugh, H.W. *The Gold Coast and the Slum* (University of Chicago Press, Chicago, 1929)

Section 4
The Sociology of Youth
Simon Frith

Chapter One

Definitions

Is it necessary to devote a chapter to definitions of youth? Don't we all know who young people are? 'Youth' is not a term of sociological jargon. It is a common sense word, one we can find every day in the newspapers, hear every day in conversation. 'Youth', the dictionary says, 'is the state of being young'. What more do we need to know?

The sociological problems arise when we try to make such common sense thinking more precise. The dictionary provides a starting point – 'youth' describes an **age group**. People of a certain age are young and can be distinguished from people in other age groups – children, on the one hand, and adults, on the other. Theoretical sociologists don't often divide societies into age groups – they more often group people in terms of class and status, look at divisions of race and gender – but age categories are used in sociological research. Pick up books which use tables from social surveys, for example, and you will find people divided in terms of age: under 16, 16–24, 24–35, 35–45, and so on. So sociologists do draw on the common sense belief that people of different ages behave differently. There are problems though: aren't these age groupings arbitrary? Do 35 year-olds really have more in common with 25 year-olds than with 36 year-olds? Age differences are important but can they be treated so precisely?

This is the first question raised by the sociology of youth. Young people are people of a certain age, between childhood and adulthood, who form a significant social group, but it is difficult to define this age group precisely. At what age do children stop being children and become 'young people'? At what age do people become adult? It is tempting to lay down an arbitrary rule as in survey research: 'youth' means everybody between the ages of 11 and 20. But to proceed on the assumption that everyone in this age group behaves youthfully, is part

303

of 'youth culture', brings us against valid common sense objections. Many 15 year-olds 'behave like children', many 18 year-olds behave like adults (are married and have children, for example).

'Youth', in other words, describes aspects of people's social position which are an effect of their biological age but not completely determined by it. If, for example, the end of youth is marked by our taking on an adult role – marriage and children, work and a career, our own household – then people stop being young at a great variety of ages.

The picture is even more complicated when we compare similar age groups in different societies or at different historical times. Everyone has to make the move from child to adult, but different societies at different times organise the move differently. The transition can take days or years, can mean being collected together with people of the same age or being kept apart from them; it can be a time of relative social freedom or repression. The task of the sociologist of youth is to show how particular societies organise the process of growing-up. For us, youth is not simply an age group, but **the social organisation of an age group**.

Dependence and Independence

One useful way of thinking about what it means to be young in Britain today is through this class exercise: write three headings on a piece of paper – child/youth/adult – and list underneath the social characteristics of each group. What becomes apparent immediately is that while it's easy enough to distinguish children and adults, it is less straightforward to differentiate young people from either. Young people **begin** not to be treated like children, **begin** to take on adult responsibilities, but this transition from child to adult doesn't happen evenly and is full of contradictions. The best way to think about young people is in terms of **dependency** and **responsibility**. I'll discuss dependency first. On the one hand, there are children, who are dependent, on the other hand, there are adults who have achieved independence. Youth describes the movement between the two – from dependence to independence. Young people have more independence than children (hence their common complaint to their parents: stop treating me like a child; I'm old enough now to choose my own clothes/go out by myself/come in late/have a boyfriend) but they are still dependent on adults for subsistence and knowledge, for love and security.

The concept of 'dependence' has to be related to particular insitutions:

a) **The Family**

'Youth' describes a family position and the central experience of growing up is that of becoming less dependent on our family (whatever form that family takes). The assumption in Britain is that children will eventually leave home, have families and households of their own. It follows that as the shape of the family changes so does the meaning of youth.

b) **Education**

The first obvious social move towards independence from their families comes when children go to school – whether play school, nursery or infant school. Schools are the only institutions which give people of the same age a common experience formally, which treat age with biological precision – we have to attend school from age 5 to 16 whatever the differences between us otherwise. But school life does change as pupils get older, it does involve their being given increasing individual responsibility for their school work and success or failure. Sixth-formers, attending school 'voluntarily' and organising their work around individually chosen A-Level subjects are more independent even at school than primary age children.

c) **Work**

Common sense suggests that school-leaving means the end of youth. When people enter the labour market, earn a wage of their own, aren't they taking on adult status? Young workers certainly have more independence than school pupils (or the young unemployed) but they are still involved in the move **towards** adult status. This is partly a matter of money – young people are paid less than adults; it is assumed that they still live with their parents, have no 'dependents' of their own. And it's partly a matter of the work-place itself. Young people going into skilled crafts need to be trained and as trainees or apprentices they remain under particular sorts of adult authority. Unskilled young workers too come under strict forms of discipline as they are 'socialised' into work habits. The young worker is regarded by employers as less reliable than the adult worker, more likely to misbehave, to change jobs out of boredom and restlessness – even at work there is a period of 'settling down'. Adult workers are not exactly 'independent' (and most young workers don't expect to become bosses) but young workers are, on the whole, more clearly subordinate.

d) **Leisure**

Youth culture, as we'll see, is particularly associated with leisure activities. It is how young people enjoy themselves (with clothes and music and dancing and hanging about) that makes them a distinct social group, and so most sociology of youth is, in fact, a sociology of youth leisure. This concentration on leisure can be misleading – how people enjoy their 'free time' can't be understood apart from their experience of family, education and work. Why, then, do sociologists of youth focus on leisure? Because it's in their free time that young people most **visibly** behave independently, express non-adult tastes and values. Leisure is, therefore, the most **accessible** site for research into youth behaviour – I'll discuss the methodological implications of this later.

Changing Responsibilities

The second important aspect of the transition from childhood to adulthood concerns the idea of 'responsibility'. Young people are often described as 'irresponsible' but youth is, in fact, the time when new responsibilities are continually being taken on – responsibilities for homework, for evening and weekend employment, for child-minding, examination study, leisure behaviour, and so on. This reflects young people's changing institutional roles, but it reminds us too that 'growing up' has psychological implications, involves intellectual and emotional developments. Young people are expected to 'mature', and if maturity is an even vaguer concept than youth, it lies, nevertheless, behind the most precise way in which society defines the youth/adult divide, with **the law**.

The law defines adulthood in terms of responsibility – people are legally adult when they are regarded by law as being responsible for their actions, when they are treated as mature enough to make certain sorts of decisions for themselves. The complication here is that different responsibilities are associated with different ages. As a class exercise, find out, for example, at what age people may legally:

- leave home
- leave school
- buy cigarettes
- buy alcoholic drinks
- drive a motor cycle
- drive a car
- marry
- consent to heterosexual activity

- consent to homosexual activity
- vote
- draw social security
- be charged in an adult court
- stand for parliament
- join the army
- go on a council house waiting list

Laws regulate all these activities and in doing so lay down precise legal distinctions between adult and youthful responsibilities. To be young, in other words, is partly a matter of legal definitions, and when the law changes (with the raising of the school leaving age from 15 to 16 or the lowering of the voting age from 21 to 18) so does the meaning of youth. But there's a final point to make: the law decides when we are **capable** of certain actions (and has to treat biological age as the best measure of this) but does not compel us to **accept** adult responsibilities. Most people marry, for example, several years after it is legally possible. This suggests a gap between legal and social definitions of adulthood and I'll return to the implications of this in chapter 4.

Youth and Social Differences

So far I've been discussing what young people have in common, but while they may therefore share problems of dependency in family, school and work, may be defined as equally responsible (or irresponsible) in legal terms, they face these problems from different institutional positions.

The most important difference among young people is the gender difference – growing up male and growing up female involve different activities, different constraints, different patterns of socialisation. This is not just a result of the sexual differences focused by puberty, but is a consequence too of boys' and girls' different roles in the family. As long as adult men and women are not equal (in terms of job opportunity and wages, for example) so women will be in some respects 'dependent' on men, and this obviously has consequences for girls' movement towards 'independence'. Similarly, men and women are seen to have different adult responsibilities which makes for different legal treatment of boys and girls, as I'll describe in chapter 4.

The second obvious difference among young people is in terms of social class which, in particular, affects people's experience of school and work. Sixteen year-old working class school leavers looking for jobs or places on Government training schemes are 'young' in different ways than sixteen year-old public school pupils getting ready to do A-Levels, to go to university, to get professional qualifications. The differences lie not just in day-to-day experiences but also in people's expectations about the future – young people cannot ignore the structure of power and wealth in our society and nor should we.

There are other significant social differences – racial differences, ethnic differences, even regional differences – consider the different effects on growing up of town and country life. They all raise the central question of the sociology of youth: what is the relative importance of the **similarities** between young people (in terms of dependency and irresponsibility) and the **differences** between them (in terms of gender, class and race). Is there one youth culture or are there many? I'll come back to this in chapter 2.

The Experience of Generation

The importance of the term 'generation' (as used by the sociologist Karl

Mannheim) is to draw attention to the fact that people grow up at particular historical moments and may, therefore, share crucial historical experiences with fellow members of their age group – experiences which then differentiate them, as a generation, from both older and younger generations. War is the most commonly cited experience that may bind a generation together, but rapid technological change and a boom/slump cycle in the economy may also have the effect of making an age group differentiate itself from older and younger people. Thus Britons who grew up in the depression years of the 1930s brought up children who took the boom years of the 1950s and 1960s for granted, but are now bringing up children to join the youth unemployment statistics of the 1980s. Such different experiences make for different assumptions and expectations about how society can and should work, and these differences may, in turn, be expressed in social conflicts, in a 'generation gap'.

Adolescence – Biology vs Sociology

If growing up is a psychological as well as a sociological process, it follows that youth, 'the state of being young', is a psychological as well as a sociological state. The concept of 'adolescence' was introduced by the American educational psychologist G. Stanley Hall at the beginning of this century to describe the emotional problems young people may face in managing the transition to adulthood, the break from their families, the development of independent personalities, and so on. Hall, like many other psychologists, believed that adolescence meant a period of particular 'storm and stress' emotionally, and while there is little sociological evidence to support this, it is worth noting the effects of the increasing **length** of adolescence. There is tension, for example, between the biological and sociological aspects of growing up – people are physically capable of sexual activity and enjoyment several years before this is socially acceptable, and one important function of youth culture is to manage the resulting problems, the issues of sexuality, attractiveness, friendship and love (think of the 'problems' that are addressed on the 'problem pages' of teenage girls' magazines).

The History of Youth: Industrialisation and the Separation of Home and Work

Why have the social and psychological conditions of youth become an issue in the last hundred years? The answer obviously lies in the increasing length of time of the transition from childhood to adulthood, but the question remains: why has the time of transition increased? The common sense answer to this is that as the division of labour has become more complex, the production process more technologically advanced, so adult roles need more preparation, more schooling. But in thus tracing the emergence of youth back to the Industrial Revolution, we find that the key to the need for a longer period of transition was not technology as such but **the separation of home and work** embodied in the factory system. This meant, first, that becoming adult involved leaving home, having an independent position in the labour market, and, second, that adult success rested on the possession of **formal** skills and qualifications. Peasants' children may expect to work on the family land, their occupation determined by their family position; factory workers' children have to find work for themselves. This was the setting in which childrens' education was taken out of their parents' hands, organised in schools. Historically as well as sociologically, then, youth, as an institution, is the product of the shifting relationships of family, school and work. With this in mind I want to turn now to the subject of this section: the sociology of **youth culture**.

Chapter Two

The Concept of Youth Culture

What is Culture?

'Culture' is a problematic word for sociologists and often seems to have as many meanings as there are people using it. Sociologists of youth tend to give it its most general sense, meaning 'a way of life'; youth culture is thus defined as 'the way of life shared by young people'. Having said this, though, it is important to add that such a definition of youth culture has been approached in two ways.

Youth culture can describe the particular pattern of beliefs, values, symbols and activities that a group of young people are **seen** to share. The starting point of this description is the empirical observation of young people's social life. Sociologists observe that certain youth groups – punks, for example – have distinct ways of dressing and doing their hair, listen to a particular form of music, develop their own slang and tastes, gather in particular places. The assumption is then made that shared activities reflect shared values, and the sociological task is to reveal these values, to get at the **meaning** of the observed behaviour. This has been, on the whole, the British approach to youth culture and I'll go into its methodological problems in my discussion of sub-cultural theory in chapter 5.

Youth culture can, alternatively, be approached in 'functionalist' terms. The starting point here is young people's shared institutional position, their consequent shared social problems. 'Youth culture' refers to the way these problems are solved in day-to-day practice, describes the values and activities that young people develop to make sense of and cope with their shared experiences – it has a 'problem-solving' function. This has, on the whole, been the American approach to youth culture and I'll examine its theoretical assumptions in more

310

detail in the next chapter. Here I will outline how the empirical bases of both these approaches were established by sociologists in the 1950s.

Britain and the Discovery of the Teenage Consumer

The first influential sociological study of youth culture published in Britain was Mark Abrams's *The Teenage Consumer*, which appeared in 1959. Abrams was a market researcher and his book was an empirical survey of a new **consumer group**, which had emerged almost imperceptibly in the 1950s but was, by the end of the decade, vitally important for a wide range of companies making youth products. The importance of Abrams's book was that it described a distinctive form of youth behaviour that was not, in itself, delinquent – previously, 'youth culture', if used at all, carried intimations of street gangs and trouble. As a consumer group, young people were distinguished from other age groups not by their 'bad' behaviour, but simply in terms of their market choices, and it was these choices that revealed a new 'teenage culture'. This culture was defined in terms of leisure and leisure goods – coffee and milk bars, fashion clothes and hair styles, cosmetics, rock 'n' roll records, films and magazines, scooters and motorbikes, dancing and dance halls.

The definition of youth as a consumer group had two consequences. First, youth culture was interpreted as a form of **mass culture**. 'Mass culture' was a term developed by social commentators in the 1920s and 30s to describe the effects of the 'mass media' (large circulation newspapers and magazines, radio and gramophone records, cinema and advertising). It was a critical term, used by people hostile to the mass media for two reasons: first, because the media meant that people no longer made entertainment for themselves but relied on businessmen to provide it for them; second, because the media sought to appeal to the mass of the British people regardless of their particular local concerns and thus offered not accounts of people's real lives, but rather, empty fantasies that could appeal to everyone. Mass culture, in short, meant a form of culture in which people were **manipulated**, as consumers, by big business, and Abrams's research raised a question that is still often asked: is 'youth culture' really just the product of shrewd marketing men and advertisers?

Mass culture implies classless culture, a way of life (or consumption) that is shared by people in different social positions, but Abrams's research showed that the consumer habits of youth (which he defined as the period between school-leaving and age 25 or marriage) were dominated by its most affluent section, working class males. 1950s youth culture was thus interpreted as a form of **working class mass culture**. A distinction had to be made, in J. B. Mays' words 'between a culture largely based on working class peer group solidarity and the commercialised entertainment world, on the one hand, and the individualistic, middle class, school and university career system on the other'. 'Youth culture' referred initially, then, to 'working class peer group solidarity'.

Abrams's findings posed further problems for British sociologists. Why had teenage culture developed now, in the 1950s? The answer, it seemed, lay in the relative affluence of the decade. Young people were fully employed and had less obligation than previous generations to contribute their wages to the family income (their parents were in steady employment too). They had, in other words, a much greater 'disposable income' than people of their age had ever had before, and it was their disposable income that gave them their market power.

But a question remained: why did teenage spending take its particular form? Why did young people use their money differently from adults? Again, the answer seemed straightforward. The difference between adult and youthful consumers was that the young devoted their wages to 'short term hedonism', to leisure and pleasure. Their spending habits were a market expression of their lack of adult responsibiltiies and dependents.

The third issue was more complicated. Did young people's 'hedonism' mean that they had different values than their parents? Abrams's surveys showed that young people didn't just spend relatively **more** of their incomes on fashion clothes and pop records, but also that they spent their incomes on specifically **youthful** fashion clothes and pop records. Part of the pleasure of youth spending seemed to lie in its assertion of youth identity; it expressed the pleasure of **not being grown-up**! And this was why 'the teenage consumer' could be taken to be part of a 'teenage culture'.

What was the social importance of this culture? For some sociologists (including Abrams), youth spending revealed a distinct leisure group but didn't reflect any sort of 'rebellion'. Teenagers were still embedded in the key institutions of home, school and work; their central values remained those of their parents and workmates. As the National Children's Bureau's surveys have shown repeatedly since, 'the archetypal 16 year-old is a long way from the idle anarchistic teenager of legend. There is little evidence for the generation gap ... Britain's future, in fact, appears to be in the hands of a remarkably conventional generation of young men and women not markedly different from the parents who worry about them'. (This was the *Observer*'s summary of the NCB's findings in 1976.)

For other sociologists, though, the development of a specific teenage market revealed the growing importance for young people of a **peer**

group world, unpenetrated by adult authority, dominated by group pressures and easily manipulated by commercial interests. This was the way that young street gangs had always been described, and the 1950s fear was that 'ordinary' youth might be drawn into such delinquent groups via teenage culture. Teddy Boys, the first spectacular post-war youth sub-culture were, then, a new sort of social problem. They were delinquents with a glamourous style – they offered **all** working class boys a desirable image. Observers concluded that teenage culture reflected not just relative affluence but also the decomposition of the pre-war working class community. From this perspective the social changes in post-war Britain – the rebuilding of slum neighbourhoods as housing estates, the increasing difference between the places where people lived and the places where they worked, the greater time young people spent at school – involved a weakening of the authority of working class parents over their children, of the old over the young.

Teenage culture thus filled the gap left by the decreasing relevance of traditional norms of youth behaviour. Parents couldn't give their children convincing advice on how to behave as teenagers because they'd never been teenagers, in this affluent, consumer sense, themselves. And so, as I've already suggested, Mark Abrams's market research measured a mass teenage culture, a pattern of tastes and expenditure which went beyond neighbourhood and community ties and traditions. Working class teenagers in Sunderland, it seemed, wore the same styles, listened to the same records, had the same day-dreams as working class teenagers in London or Scotland or South Wales. 'Teenage' culture was, indeed, a form of American culture. Even Teddy Boys combined their Edwardian look with fashions taken from Hollywood – the city slicker's string-tie, the Western gambler's sideburns and frock coat. And they (like all other British working class teenagers) listened to American music, to rock 'n' roll. The very idea of the 'teenager' was, for many British adults, an alien, American idea, involved American myths, American idols, fantasies of American life.

The USA and the Discovery of an Adolescent Society

The image of American youth culture that British teenagers got from rock 'n' roll records and films was first formed, in fact, in the 1920s. It was then, for example, that motor-cars began to be used by wealthy youngsters as a way of escaping family supervision, that courting became 'dating', no longer directly chaperoned by adults, that the use of make-up and cigarettes ceased to be the mark of the 'bad girl', that the mass media (Hollywood films, in particular) began to shape young people's sense of their social possibilities.

What lay behind these first intimations of a youth culture was the accelerated separation of home and work. Middle class parents' influence over their children's decisions about careers and education, sex and marriage, leisure and consumption, declined. The high school and college began to replace the family as the centre of middle class youth's social life, the source of their moral values. By the late 1930s American sociologists like the Lynds were observing in small town high schools 'a self consicous sub-culture of the young'.

At this time a clear distinction could still be drawn between middle class school culture and working class street culture, but in the 1950s the high school became the social centre of the lives of most young Americans and the resulting concept of the 'teenager' blurred class distinctions. In Britain in the 1950s, as we've seen, 'youth culture' meant working class youth culture, but in the USA the term covered **both** 'rough' street group activities **and** 'respectable' school group activities (so that, for example, in the television series *Happy Days*, which looks back to 1950s youth culture, The Fonz is a street figure **within** the school). The adult worry was that teenage culture would dissolve not just class distinctions but also the differences between 'conformist' and 'delinquent' youth of both classes, and American sociologists concentrated research on this problem. 'Youth culture' was seen to be the setting for both deviant and conformist teenagers, for both 'corner' and 'college' boys (I will discuss this further in chapter 4) and it became too the setting for attempts to **control** the young.

Adults – teachers, parents, religious leaders, social workers, the police – sought to counter juvenile delinquency not by competing with youth culture but by institutionalising it, using the rules of conduct first developed by middle class teenagers in schools and colleges in the 1920s and 1930s. One result of these attempts to **intervene** in youth culture was that American sociologists developed a much more complex understanding than British sociologists of 'the adolescent society' (the title of James Coleman's definitive study which came out in 1961). Their focus was not consumer choice but the ways in which adolescent behaviour was a response to specific problems posed at home and school and work. Youth culture was understood not as an expression of **autonomous** teenage values, but as something which could be used by adults to promote the **right** attitudes.

In both sociological and popular literature on 1950s American teenagers a confused picture began to emerge. On the one hand there was the **teenager-as-rebel** – captured in films like *Rebel Without A Cause, The Wild Ones* and *The Blackboard Jungle*, in rock 'n' roll stars like Elvis Presley, Gene Vincent and Jerry Lee Lewis, in the ubiquitous image of the slouched, leather-clad, mumbling street corner gang. On the other hand there was the **teenager-as-all-American**, drinking Coca-Cola on the beach, dancing at the high school hop, playing football and cheer-leading, clean-cut and cheerful. If the delinquent image had the exaggerated lines of a 'moral panic' (see chapter 4), the high school image was equally a stereotype, an attempt to make teenagers **nice**, to control their culture by encouraging the right sort of competition (football games not gang fights), fun (cruising to the drive-in rather than getting drunk or drugged) and sex (which was regulated by elaborate codes of 'dating' and 'petting'). This teenage ideal didn't spring to life spontaneously but was deliberately fostered in a plethora of magazines, songs and television programmes which clearly placed teenagers' short-term pleasures in the long-term framework of middle class family life.

What is most striking about such 1950s teenage ideology is its concern with rules. The joy of teenage life was said to be its 'freedom' (and that television series is, after all, called *Happy Days*). A typical 1950s book for girls, Connie Francis's *For Every Young Heart*, thus begins, 'Have a ball – no strings attached! That's privilege number one in the Teenage Bill of Rights!' But the rest of the book consists of rules of dress and make-up, family and sexual behaviour (rules which can still be found laid out in the pages of British girls' magazines, like *Jackie*). What American writers realised was that youth culture wasn't **static** (a set of values to be read off teenage goods) but **dynamic** – young people had to **learn** to be 'teenagers' (and adults could therefore help teach them). As the British sociologist Tom Kitwood has argued more recently, 'becoming a teenager' can be an anxious and unhappy process. If there are rules of teenage behaviour then they can be inadvertently broken. Young people grow up by making mistakes; they can feel themselves oppressed by their peers as well as supported by them. I'll return to the implications of this in chapter 6.

Adults and Teenagers: Anxieties and Envy

Sociologists in both Britain and the USA in the 1950s found that adults had an extremely ambiguous attitude towards teenage culture. They were remarkably tolerant of their own children, asserting that youth was a time 'for sowing wild oats', that 'boys will be boys', telling their daughters 'to have a good time while you can'. But they were decidedly intolerant of other people's children, dismissing the young as 'undisciplined, oversexed layabouts'.

This confusion of attitudes has a long history. Even in the nineteenth century youth was both **celebrated** – as a time of innocence and idealism, when all life's choices can still be made – and **condemned** – as a time of anarchy and hysteria, irresponsibility and selfishness. The 1950s rise of a commercial teenage culture focused these contradictions. As teenagers developed their own distinct **public** institutions and means of expression, they became more feared and more envied. By the end of the decade, indeed, young people had become, in themselves, **symbols** of certain sorts of general pleasure (and risk). To be young was to be associated with consumption, fashion, pop and fun. The implication was that adults could be young this way too – by equally committing themselves to consumption, fashion, pop and fun. 'Youth' became a sales ideal for grown-ups. In advertisements and films and music young people were used to stand for 'freedom' to represent 'good times'. By the mid-1960s, as American sociologists like Bennett Berger began to observe, 'youth culture' had become as much a product of adult as of teenage concerns. It was an **ideological** concept, defining an **ideal** 'way of life'.

The Rise of 'Youth Culture'

In 1950s Britain the terms 'youth culture' and 'teenage culture' were pretty much interchangeable – both referred to working class youngsters. Middle class youth were thought to make sense of their lives by reference to a longer-term idea of career and achievement. But as youth culture became increasingly an ideological matter, referring to leisure ideals as well as realities, so it became attractive for middle class teenagers too, and it was the gradual appropriation of the trappings of working class teenage consumer culture by the middle classes which quickly came to be thought of as British 'youth culture' (often, understandably if misleadingly, described in terms of **classlessness**).

This was most obvious in the development of pop music – a development neatly symbolised by the sleeve covers of the Beatles' first two LPs: on the first they are obviously working class, chirpy in their best suits, on the second they have become solemnly middle class, dressed in student sweaters. By the end of the 1960s British record companies divided their market into 'pop' and 'rock' – pop records still played their traditional role in working class teenage leisure, but they were outsold now by rock LPs, and 'youth culture' no longer meant the pop scene but, rather, the rock world of 'progressive' musicians, student audiences, 'serious' fans. Abrams's affluent school leavers no longer dominated the youth market. Youth culture increasingly meant student culture – by 1967 the Beatles, still the British youth model, were hippies, part of the psychedelic underground.

Middle class youth culture was, from the start, more **self-consciously** 'rebellious' than working class youth culture. Even in the 1950s American sociologists had suggested that in becoming rock 'n' roll fans middle class children were often deliberately adopting what they perceived as lower-class values – 'toughness, excitement, chance-taking, indulgence' – and were, thereby, consciously **opposing** their parents. Working class children, by contrast it seemed, were simply enjoying themselves before settling down conventionally. They might **drift** into delinquency but such 'rebellion' was a matter of confusion, the **lack** of adult discipline. The solution to this youth problem was to regulate peer group culture, to provide the missing norms. 1960s youth culture, by contrast, increasingly articulated the **rejection** of such norms.

Student Movements and Counter-Cultures

The argument that middle class youth were intrinsically more 'political' than even 'deviant' working class youth was challenged by sub-cultural theorists in the 1970s (see chapter 5) but in the late 1960s it seemed common sense. For middle class teenagers – sixth formers and college students, trainee professionals and managers – to indulge in 'short term hedonism' was to challenge their parents' commitment to career planning and 'deferred gratification' (working hard in the present for rewards in the future). For middle class children to engage with 'pop culture' was to threaten their parents' carefully guarded status and 'respectability'. Not surprisingly, young people in both Britain and the USA experienced youth culture as a form of 'liberation' – liberation from the stuffy expectations of their teachers and families (and the resulting 'generation gap' was reinforced by the availability of the contraceptive pill, which gave young women a new sort of sexual freedom). Youth, in short, were the vanguard of the 'permissive' society.

Middle class youth culture didn't develop in an institutional vacuum. 1950s youth culture was rooted in young workers' leisure behaviour; 1960s youth culture was set in the schools and colleges which 'successful' children could expect to attend into their twenties. This had two political consequences.

First, students are in more formally organised age groups than other young people; they have more formal means of expression – student unions, student newspapers, student representatives. Colleges provide too an immediate **target** for student politics. 1960s youth culture involved, then, student campaigns against school rules, against college discipline and control of leisure activities. But attention soon shifted to more important matters, to the organisation of knowledge and educational power itself, as students demanded some influence over their curriculum, over examinations. What emerged from such demands was an explicit **student movement**. This took different forms in different places, but all Western countries (and some Eastern ones) had 1960s experience of student sit-ins, demonstrations, campaigns and protest.

Middle class young people became, in a sense, the political conscience of their countries, protesting against adult activities in which they were not yet implicated (even if their parents were) – thus it was **young** people who marched with Civil Rights demonstrators in the US South, **young** Britons who demonstrated their support of CND or the anti-Vietnam War movement.

The second political consequence flowed from this. Middle class youth culture involved older, more articulate people than working class youth culture, expressed a specific **refusal** to settle down, to behave like adults. This refusal increasingly took the form of a **counter-culture**, as young people not only rejected adult institutions but practiced **alternative** ways of growing up – play not work, drugs not drink, communes not marriage. The hippies became the symbols of the counter-culture, and in hippies' 'underground' activities we can see the seeds of 1970s 'alternative' politics – women's, gays' and animals' liberation, squatting and do-it-yourself entertainment, ecology and Greenpeace. But the immediate impact of hippie culture (which was, in important respects, developed as much on the streets as on the campuses) was on working class youth. By the end of the 1960s, 'youth culture' seemed to have moved full circle: working class youth behaviour had 'radicalised' middle class youth attitudes and now middle class youth behaviour was radicalising working class youth attitudes. In Paris in May 1968 it was the **combination** of students' and young workers' protests that faced the French government with a political crisis.

The Politics of Age: Is Youth an Interest Group?

1968 events, not just in France but around the world, raised pressing sociological questions. Was there now a youth **interest** group? Was there now a set of activities and values which, on the one hand, distinguished young people from adults and, on the other hand, gave them an identity that transcended their own class differences? Had youth culture become a **political** force?

The positive answer to these questions – the answer yes – rested on a historical argument. Young people, it was suggested, had been drawn together politically by economic affluence, by an expansion of higher education which involved more and more of them in technical training and bureaucratic routine. All young people, it was suggested, faced adult constraints over their use of drugs and noise and public places; all young people resented the attempts to turn them into well-regulated producers and orderly consumers.

Such arguments didn't long survive the 1970s recession and rise of youth unemployment. Systematic rather than impressionistic sociological surveys quickly confirmed that there were important cultural differences between young members of different social classes whatever their shared interest in personal freedom. In retrospect it seems clear that the brief 1960s moment of cross-class youth solidarity has to be related to more specific historical factors than 'affluence'. In the USA, certainly, the Vietnam War was something that affected all young people one way or another via the draft (and the efforts to avoid it). More nebulously, 1960s young people had expectations (and this was an effect of the relative economic prosperity) which gave them a shared interest in change for its own sake, a shared excitement at the feeling (whether in France or Czechoslovakia) that power structures could be broken. When they weren't, the excitement faded.

One sociological conclusion can be drawn from this, though. Arguments about the politics of youth must be given a proper context. The question 'is youth an interest group?' raises different issues in the 1980s than it did in the 1960s. Now we'd have to look at cross-class experiences of unemployment (not full employment), at new forms of education and training. I will do this in chapter 7. Next I want to outline an alternative approach to youth as an institution, an approach which considers these issues in terms not of social history but of social **function**.

Chapter Three

Functionalist Explanations of Youth Culture

What is Functionalism?

The functionalist approach to sociology begins with the idea that a society, a social structure, is like a body, a biological structure. Social institutions can then be explained in the same way that biologists explain parts of the body: by reference to their **function** in keeping the society (the body) alive. Biologists assume that every part of the body – the liver and the kidney, hair and toe-nails – has, or has had, a vital function. Organs may lose their function (and eventually wither away) as biological structures evolve, but nothing exists for no biological reason at all. Functionalist sociologists assume, similarly, that every social institution has, or has had, a social function, that history is best understood in terms of social evolution. Social structures change by becoming more complex, social institutions change by becoming more 'specialised'.

The most controversial of the functionalists' arguments is that social institutions must be explained in terms of their contribution to social stability. Biologists explain parts of the body in terms of the maintenance of life and so, following the biological analogy, functionalists relate social institutions to the maintenance of society. The implication is that an institution that was not functional in these terms, that disrupted social life and was **dysfunctional** would not survive for long. The converse also applies: an established social institution that appears disruptive must, in fact, help to maintain the social order (thus Durkheim argued that crime, as a 'normal' social phenomenon, must have a social function).

320

In the 1950s functionalists studied American teenage culture with these arguments in mind. They began with the assumption that youth culture (however delinquent some of its forms) had a social function, had appeared because changes in the American social structure had posed new problems that youth culture solved. The sociological task was to describe **what** function youth culture played in the maintenance of social order and to show **how** it performed that function. But there was also a further question implied: for **whom** was this function performed?

Functionalist sociology usually describes institutions as functioning for 'society' but we can also look at the way in which institutions function **for their members** – marriage, for example, contributes to the maintenance of social order, but also has a function for the people who get married (which is why they do so). The same point can be made about youth culture. The functionalist approach means explaining its function not just for society as a whole but also for the young people who live the culture for themselves.

Youth and the Social Structure: On the Margins

The functionalist approach to youth was first sketched out by the American sociologist Talcott Parsons during the Second World War, in a discussion of the role of age groups in society. However it was given its most systematic treatment in S. N. Eisenstadt's 1956 book, *From Generation To Generation* and it is his argument that I'll summarise here.

Eisenstadt begins by pointing out that in all societies children have to be 'socialised' before they can attain full adult status. They have to be taught their society's moral code, its common sense, its rules of behaviour; they have to be given the skills and knowledge necessary to perform their adult roles (and so socialisation may vary according to children's gender and class). In 'primitive' societies the values that inform the lives of children within their families are much the same as those that will organise their adult lives and so the change of status from child to adult is not particularly problematic. Even adult skills and knowledge are acquired 'naturally', as part of the experience of growing up, and so the moment of transition to adulthood is just a matter of ritual – a puberty or initiation rite. 'Youth' doesn't really exist.

In modern industrial societies, by contrast, there is a significant structural gap between the family in which children are brought up and the economic and social system in which they must eventually take their place. The shift of status from child to adult is neither quick nor easy, it means a lengthy period of transition and youth becomes an important structural position. Society has become more complex (the necessary consequence of social evolution) and new specialised institutions are needed to maintain it. As the family unit becomes concentrated on emotional and sexual (rather than economic) functions, so new institutions are necessary to handle other aspects of socialisation, to manage the move **out** of the family. Youth culture, in short, has to be understood by reference to the process in which a modern industrial society detaches children from their families and places them in/prepares them for the wider social system.

Eisenstadt emphasises two aspects of this process. First, the young have a **marginal** social status. Young people at school or college, in apprenticeships and as trainees, in and out of unskilled work, are not yet fully integrated into the economic structure; they have emerged from one family but not yet formed another, they are not yet fully integrated into the social structure. Their legal status (as we saw in chapter 1) is confused; even their 'free time' is regulated by adult authorities.

Second, industrial societies have developed a series of formal training institutions to control the transition period: not just schools, apprenticeships, colleges, and other overt forms of education, but also organisations, like youth clubs, and media products, like youth magazines, to train people in the norms and expectations of adult 'private' life, to prepare people for marriage and parenthood, for being householders and citizens. Whatever the differences between them in other respects, all young people have to be socialised, find themselves in socialising institutions and they share, consequently, a sense of subordination. These institutions may be **for** the young but they are not controlled **by** them. They are run by adults; young people are central to their purpose but marginal in terms of power.

The Function of Youth Culture: Managing Transitions

Shared experiences make for shared needs. Eisenstadt argued that young people seek a sense of stability to offset the experience of change, a sense of self-esteem to offset the experience of powerlessness. Youth culture is the result. It provides a clear set of values, attitudes and behavioural norms to follow whatever else is going on; by acting on youth cultural rules young people can feel good whatever anyone else thinks of them. Punks, for example, may look funny to passers-by or *News of the World* photographers, but to become a punk is to achieve a measure of success and status which is **under one's own control**.

Functionalists explain social institutions in terms of social problems and cultural solutions. The problem is described with reference to strains within the social structure; the solution is described in terms of the easing of such strains. The youth 'problem' lies, then, in young people's marginal status; youth culture eases the resulting anxieties and uncertainties. The sociological importance of youth culture lies in their **codes** of conduct and dress. The significance of punk, for example, is less its content – **what** people wear and do – than its form – the fact that there is a punk uniform, a punk version of success and prestige. From this perspective, **all** forms of youth culture (student rugby clubs as well as skinhead football gangs) have the same function.

The 'problem solving' approach to youth culture is used by many sociologists who would not consider themselves functionalists. Sub-culturalists, for example, also explain youth culture in terms of its solution to young people's problems (see chapter 5). They place a different emphasis, though on the question of for **whom** the culture is functional. For sub-culturalists, some young people are clearly **more** powerless than others, **more** marginal to the social order. Children who are school failures are more committed to alternative sources of status than school successes; youngsters in boring jobs are more committed to the leisure pursuit of risk and excitment; teenagers who don't expect to have much economic or cultural power when they become adults are more committed to the control now of whatever space they've got. The youth 'problem', in other words, can't be divorced from adult problems; youth cultures don't all have the same relationship to the social structure.

I'll come back to this point, but first it's worth stressing that Eisenstadt's position reflects his starting question: how does youth culture work to maintain social order? His argument is that in meeting young people's needs (which may well vary across classes) youth culture has the **general** function of smoothing the transition from child to adult. The important point for Eisenstadt is not that some young people become 'deviants' (punks, for instance), but that most 'deviant' youths become 'normal' adults. On the whole youth marginality has **not** been the cause of either political rebellion or lasting psychological problems. Despite moments of riot and counter-culture, contemporary industrial societies do succeed in socialising each new generation, in keeping society going as its members change.

Eisenstadt argued that youth culture's most important function for its members was emotional – it mattered in psychological rather than economic or political terms (he was writing before the rise of the student movement). This was the clue to its social function. The primary importance of 1950s youth culture, he suggested, was not to provide teenagers with a set of **norms** (which may or may not accord with adult values) but was, rather, to give them a set of **relationships**. Youth culture was a way of managing the psychological tensions involved in adolescence, a way of coping with the emotional shifts made necessary by the movement out of the intimate world of the family into the public world of school and work. The most significant aspect of youth culture, then, was its basis in the activities of **peer groups.**

The Importance of Peer Groups

Peer groups are so taken for granted by sociologists that it is sometimes easy to forget that references to youth culture are usually references to people of the same age doing things in groups – whether those groups are described as gangs or cliques or sub-cultures. Youth cultural activity means group activity. The sociological assumption is that young people develop their tastes in clothes and music **in groups,** that they watch football matches and go dancing, hang around the bus stop and 'do nothing' **in groups.** In the 'adolescent society', argued Coleman, people belong to very clearly defined social networks; they organise their behaviour round these networks' rigid systems of value and prestige.

Eisenstadt, though, was less interested in the content of peer groups – what particular norms they adopted – than in their **form,** in the **sort** of social interaction they involved. A peer group, he suggested, is charac- terised by friendship and loyalty, by people's commitment to each other because of **who** they are rather than because of **what** they represent. In social psychological terms, the peer group lies somewhere between the family (with its ties of absolute emotional commitment) and the economic system (with its formal contracts, its organisation of roles by reference to achieved skills and qualifications). To use Eisenstadt's language, the peer group manages the move from 'particularistic' to 'universalistic' values, from a social world in which decisions are made by reference to parental authority and family tradition to a social world in which decisions must be referred to universally agreed rational principles.

Peer groups, in short, support young people's initial steps out of family life, give them their first introduction to other ways of treating the social world. At the beginning this may simply be a matter of comparison (which leads children to argue with their parents – 'But *Karen's* mother lets her go to discos . . .') but as peer group activities become the centre of young people's social life, so they become the chief reference point for young people's behaviour. Peer groups enable their members to assert their independence of their families while still being able to depend on friendship and emotional support whatever they do. The functionalists' point is that peer groups matter as a source not of new **values** but of a new way of **placing oneself in the world.** They cease to matter once adult status is achieved. People 'grow out' of youth culture as they establish a new, exclusive form of emotional tie (marriage, their own families) and as they become identified with an occupational or career position. The social and psychological problems of growing up cannot be separated from each other. Youth culture itself only becomes a problem when people refuse to grow up and this (as sociologists like Talcott Parsons argued in the 1960s) needs a psychological rather than a political explanation.

Critiques of Functionalism: Are All Young People The Same?

Eisenstadt's argument is a general argument. It refers to the problem of transition that faces **all** young people in industrial society. The most telling criticism of his approach addresses this assumption. Are young people really all the same? Can 'youth culture' be used to describe a single institution, one that includes **everyone** in the relevant age group?

In an important article published in 1968 ('Some theoretical problems in the study of youth'), Sheila Allen argued that in capitalist societies, at least, the experiences of different **classes** occupying different economic situations, with different amounts of power, different sorts of access to educational reward, cannot be the same **at any age.** Sociologists would, these days, extend the argument. In patriarchal societies, at least, the experiences of different **genders** occupying different economic situations, with different amounts of power, different sorts of access to educational reward, cannot be the same at any age either. Growing up middle class is still a different process than growing up working class, and growing up male is a different process than growing up female. The sociology of youth culture must be able to make sense of these differences. Functionalists, Allen suggests, cannot.

The point is that if we examine youth cultures carefully we find not only sharply contrasting consumer tastes and choices, but also, more importantly, contrasting **constraints** on people's cultural activities. These constraints reflect people's class and gender positions as well as their age. Leisure activities, in short, are not really 'free' – they relate to people's position in the family and in the labour market. Leisure patterns, to put it another way, reflect leisure opportunities, and different groups of young people have different opportunities. Boys and girls use their 'free' time differently partly because they are 'free' in different ways. Girls have greater domestic obligations than boys, for example, and they seem to have a greater interest in using leisure as a means to marriage, as a way of 'finding the right boy'. I'll return to the implications of this in chapter 6.

Sociologists have, in general, shown that there are patterned differences in youth behaviour between students and young workers, between the skilled and the unskilled, the employed and the unemployed, between blacks and whites and Asians. To treat all these groups as part of the **same** youth culture is to argue at a high level of abstraction – what these young people all share are the 'psycho-social' problems of making the transition from childhood to adulthood in an industrial society, as Eisenstadt argued. But the **differences** in how such problems are experienced and resolved (or not resolved) are just as important, and it is such differences I'll be considering in the rest of this book. One particular contrast needs a note here, though.

Growing up British vs Growing up American

In recent years Kings Road, Chelsea, has become a favourite spot for American tourists. They go there to take pictures of Britain's 'youth tribes' (*Time* magazine's description) – punks, skinheads, teds, rockers, mods, rockabillies, new romantics. These tribes have members in the USA (and the rest of Europe), but they are a peculiarly British phenomenon and point to an interesting paradox: in the 1950s the USA was clearly the model for teenage fashion, teenage music and teenage culture, now Britain seems to set the styles. How can we explain youth cultural history in these two 'modern industrial societies'? Why have the British produced such a dramatic series of spectacular youth sub-cultures?

There are two obvious reasons. First, a much higher proportion of American youth continues in full time education after the age of 16. Their activities have a formal, student setting. British school leavers, by contrast, have to create their own youth spaces and identities. Second, social mobility is greater (or is thought to be greater) in the USA. American teenagers seem to believe in the possibility of changing their lives (if only by moving across the country) for much longer than British teenagers, who thus, again, have a greater need to dramatise their duller local identity. It is noticeable that the American youth groups which do put a premium on style and fashion, the blacks and the hispanics, are the American youth groups with the most restricted educational and occupational opportunities.

I'm mentioning this here in order to make my final point about the functionalist approach to youth culture. Like all sociological theories it must be related to its historical circumstances – in this case the 1950s. It was explaining youth culture in a time of relative affluence and optimism. If youth culture was, therefore, 'functional' this was, in part, because growing up wasn't a particularly problematic thing to do – people looked forward to the future. In other circumstances youth cultures carry different meanings, raise different problems. It is to these which I will now turn.

Chapter Four
Youth as a Social Problem

Hooliganism – The History of a Moral Panic

In his important book, *Hooligan*, Geoffrey Pearson tells the story of juvenile delinquency backwards, focusing on **reactions** to young criminals. He begins in the present, quoting contemporary newspapers' and politicians' arguments that delinquency is getting out of hand, that tough forms of discipline and punishment are urgently needed. These editors and MPs remember the law abiding 1950s, a time before youth culture, the permissive society and comprehensive education had undermined traditional family and school discipline. The problem, it seems, is that in the last twenty years the young have lost their 'respect for authority'.

Curious about this, Pearson turns to newspapers' and politicians' 1950s discussions of delinquency and finds exactly the same arguments! Then, too, it was believed that there was a hooligan crisis, that the young lacked discipline, that war and the welfare state had undermined the moral certainties of the 1930s. In search of a time when delinquency wasn't a problem, Pearson moves back to 1930s discussions and finds the same fears much in evidence, 'good behaviour' now being referred to the turn of the century, while at the turn of the century people referred back to the 1850s as the golden age of law and order, agitated about the new 'hooligan' problem.

Pearson takes his history back even further, but this summary does enough to establish two important sociological points. First, youth has been seen as a 'social problem' for at least a hundred years, certainly since groups of working class boys were first observed hanging around the streets, getting into 'trouble' with the police and other passers-by. Second, in describing youth as a problem, we are describing not just youth behaviour but also adult responses to it. We have to be able to make sense of 'respectable fears' (Pearson) and 'moral panics' (Stanley Cohen).

Delinquency, Disorder and Contamination

If we look back at the nineteenth century response to juvenile delinquency, examine the offences for which young people could be sentenced to periods in reform schools, it is clear that while the young were often criminal in adult ways (were robbers, for example) there were also offences that were exclusively youthful, that called forth a distinctive legal response.

The young, for example, were seen to be the source of a particular sort of **disorder**. Gangs of boys on the streets engaged in destructive and violent behaviour ('hooliganism' and 'vandalism') that had no apparent material ends, that didn't provide the boys with goods or cash. Hooliganism seemed to be enjoyed for its own sake, and hooligan gangs were a source of **contamination** – innocent youngsters were being drawn into their activities, cut off from adult influence and criminalised. Put these two problems together and it seemed obvious to nineteenth century politicians that the state had the right to control youth behaviour, to break up gangs, put 'idle' youths into custody **even if they hadn't actually broken the law**. The streets were a breeding ground for crime and criminals and the state therefore had the right to remove young people from them, to **reform** gang members.

From the beginning, then, 'juvenile delinquency' described a law and order problem that was different from the law and order problem posed by adult criminals. Three issues were involved in particular.

First, is delinquency a **collective** or an **individual** problem? The law defines crime in individual terms – this is the logic of arrest, trial and sentence – but much juvenile delinquency takes place in groups. Football hooliganism, for example, is a problem because of the activities of **groups** of people, but the law can only deal with those individuals 'unlucky' enough to be picked out of the crowd by the police.

Second, is delinquency a **rational** or **irrational** activity? Vandalism, for, example, is usually described by newspapers as 'mindless', football hooligans are called 'animals'. How can a 'rational' legal system respond to irrational behaviour?

Third, should the treatment of delinquents emphasise **punishment** or **reform**? Do young people need a clear **deterrent** from delinquency, 'a short sharp shock'? Or is the problem one of poor socialisation so that what is necessary is re-education?

These issues have particularly concerned sociologists and if, as a result, the sociology of youth has been dominated by studies of problem youth, then this is because such studies are seen to have **practical** implications. If sociologists can explain juvenile delinquency then they can have a direct influence on the state's youth policy.

Explaining Juvenile Delinquency – The 'Psycho-Dynamic' Approach

Juvenile crime was first seen as a problem when criminology was dominated by **positivism**. Positivist criminologists like Cesare Lombroso believed that 'criminality' was an inherent quality of criminals who were different sorts of people than non-criminals. He suggested that the inherent, genetic, **disposition** towards crime must have physical signs too, which could be discovered by **measuring** every aspect of convicted criminals and seeing what they had in common. It would then be possible to reduce the crime rate by recognising people with criminal tendencies even before they did anything wrong.

There are two difficulties in applying this approach to juvenile crime. First, delinquency involved group behaviour – could criminal groups be treated as 'diseased' in the same way as criminal individuals? Second, there was a political reluctance to treat children and young people as **doomed** to crime by their genes. Couldn't they be re-socialised and reformed? The positivist criminologists soon combined their biologistic approach with a concern for the role of the **social environment** in causing (and curing) criminality.

The most influential of these theorists in Britain was **Cyril Burt**, whose mammoth study, *The Young Delinquent*, was published in 1925. His starting point was that delinquency was a form of **moral subnormality**, but he concluded from his survey of delinquents in London that such subnormality had 'a multiplicity of contributory factors', varying from criminal parents to spending too much time in the cinema. Burt sought to organise these factors in order of importance and the result was a **psycho-dynamic** explanation. If delinquency reflected people's inability to follow rules and act responsibly, then this inability had to be referred to people's emotional and moral development. Genetic factors were certainly relevant to this, but the key to healthy moral growth was the **family** – Burt's study provided the evidence for the common sense view that juvenile delinquency is caused by 'bad families' and 'broken homes'.

Burt's approach was immediately influential and it continues to be applied in general terms by both criminologists and educational psychologists. What has changed is the definition of 'delinquency' involved. D. J. West's *The Young Offenders* (1967), for example, concludes that 'most convicted youth are ordinary youth', and that 'since so many delinquents are quite ordinary youngsters, it is reasonable to suppose that their behaviour represents the normal response of their age group to everyday circumstances'. Most delinquents, in short, are **not** morally subnormal. But West does then refer to 'the hard core of highly persistent delinquents with repeated convictions' (the 'nutters', to use youth's own term), and he still accounts for them in psycho-dynamic terms, by reference to emotional development and family history.

West, in other words, redraws the line between morally normal and morally subnormal youth. Subnormality, at least for boys, is no longer equated with **a** criminal conviction but with **persistent** criminal convictions. (I'll discuss the implication that all **girl** delinquents **are** abnormal later.)

Explaining Juvenile Delinquency – The Sociological Approach

The psycho-dynamic approach to delinquency leaves a number of sociological questions unanswered. How can we explain the **normality** of delinquency for some young people in some places? Where do delinquent norms come from? How should we explain the **collective** aspect of youth crime? What is the significance of the gang? Why does delinquent behaviour take the **form** it does? What does it **mean** to the delinquents themselves? People don't have emotional urges to break milk bottles or go for joy-rides – these are **cultural** events.

American sociologists began the detailed study of delinquent **culture** in the 1920s. They argued that the psycho-dynamic approach was too negative, explained delinquency by reference to what **hadn't** happened, to the **lack** of healthy socialisation. The way forward theoretically was to look at what **had** happened, to discover how some young people **learnt** to be delinquent. Thus the criminologist **Edwin Sutherland** developed the theory of **differential association**. He argued that criminal behaviour is learnt and that the learning of criminal skills and values occurs primarily within 'intimate personal groups'. To become criminal, then, young people must value their associations with criminal groups more than their associations with non-criminal groups. Sutherland's point was that the choice of delinquent behaviour depended as much on the available patterns of social life as on people's 'dispositions'.

The 'Chicago School' of Sociology (based in Chicago University) elaborated this 'sub-cultural' approach to delinquency in a series of detailed studies of delinquents' social settings. One strategy was to analyse the delinquent group itself, **the gang**, describing its social organisation, its rules, its methods of recruitment, its power structure. To understand how delinquent gangs worked was to understand their appeal, their **function** for their members. This enabled social workers to develop their own boys' clubs and youth clubs as legitimate ways of fulfilling the same functions. Another group of researchers developed a broader **ethnography**, analysing the local and ethnic communities in which Chicago's youth gangs were based, tracing their patterns of socialisation so that delinquent **sub-cultures** could be related to the particular shape of their **parent cultures**.

These 1930s approaches were developed theoretically after the Second World War and I'll outline them in more detail in the next section. First I need to mention the most important pre-war 'cultural' account of delinquency, which came not from Chicago but derived from the work of the nineteenth century French sociologist, Emile Durkheim – **Robert Merton** applied Durkheim's concept of 'anomie' (normlessness) to American crime patterns and, in doing so, suggested an approach to youth crime that was to be extremely influential. The rising crime rate in the USA in the 1930s was the result, Merton argued, of an increasing disjunction between the American ideal of the equality of opportunity, the American definition of success in terms of material wealth and power, and the Depression reality of poverty and material failure, of 'blocked access' to educational and business opportunities for most lower class Americans.

Crime, Merton argued, signalled not the **rejection** of dominant American goals, but the adoption of **illegitimate means** to the pursuit of those goals. Juvenile delinquency, from this perspective, was thus best understood as reflecting a **confusion** about norms, about the relation of legitimate and illegitimate means and ends. Such 'anomie' had to be understood in terms of the wider society rather than by reference to inadequate socialisation within the family. The solution to delinquency, in other words, lay in economic and social change rather than in moral reform.

Gang Cultures and Street Corner Societies

The importance of Merton's work was to define delinquency as a problem of society, not the individual. It followed that the 'normality' or 'abnormality' of delinquents needed a socio-historical rather than a psychological explanation. Merton, though, like other pre-war sociologists, treated juvenile delinquency as the first move into a life of adult crime, and so reinforced the tendency to treat juvenile gangs as criminal in the same sorts of way as adult gangs. Post-war sociologists changed this tendency.

A. K. Cohen's study of delinquent boys, for example, concludes that juvenile gang delinquency was essentially 'non-utilitarian'. Most gang activities did **not** involve the pursuit of material goals but were, rather, 'maliciously' destructive (i.e. violence against people and property) and enjoyed for their immediate excitement – youth gangs, for example, stole cars not to resell but simply for the fun of joy-riding and crashing them. Crimes were committed for the hell of it, because they gave gangs and individual members of gangs status and prestige. The pleasure taken in trouble making and law breaking for their own sakes suggested to Cohen that delinquent gangs deliberately **reversed** social norms. Young people, Cohen argued, did not join gangs and therefore become anti-social, but, rather, 'anti-social' people got together in gangs because only such small, autonomous groups could sustain anti-social norms and status.

The question then became, why were some young people anti-social to begin with? Cohen suggested that this was a 'reaction formation' to their institutional experiences: 'certain children are denied status in the respectable society because they cannot meet the criteria of the respect-able status system. The delinquent sub-culture deals with these problems by providing criteria of status which these children **can** meet.' The roots of delinquency lie, then, in children's failures at school and work, in their lack of social achievement and prestige in 'respectable' terms.

Cohen took from W. F. Whyte's classic study, *Street Corner Society*, a division in lower class youth culture between **college boys** and **corner boys**. College boys sought middle class status using middle class norms – an **individualistic** stress on education, qualifications, respectability, marriage. Corner boys developed a **collective inversion** of middle class norms, a stress on immediate pleasures, on rough activities, on celebrations of toughness and excitement that offered no future rewards. This corner/college boy distinction clearly reflected the tension between street and school values in 1950s teenage life that I discussed in chapter 2, and Cohen's argument was not that all corner boys necessarily became delinquent, but that delinquency could only be understood by reference to corner boy society. The question became why, given their shared social environment, some working class boys conformed to and some rebelled against the middle class norm.

Where Do Delinquent Values Come From?

The flaw in Cohen's approach to delinquency was his equation of 'middle class values' with the American norm – non-middle class values were therefore deviant, non-respectable, by definition. What this left out of account was the relationship of the corner boys to **working class values** (Cohen, like previous sociologists, assumed that juvenile delinquency was primarily a working class phenomenon).

This point was taken up by **Walter Miller**, who argued that young delinquents were best understood not in terms of their inversion of middle class values but as **conforming** to the norms of their 'lower class milieu'. What made them delinquent was not their 'deviant norms' but the **intensity** of their concern to conform to such lower class values as toughness and excitement and the resulting **conflicts** with middle class authority (in school, for example). The problem facing the corner boys, according to Miller, was not their failure in middle class terms but their **marginality**, as youth, in their local working class community. Young delinquents certainly resented having to engage with middle class authority, but their experiences at school and work were less important than their feelings of insignificance among their immediate neighbours and friends. And this milieu, Miller suggested, treats delinquency with tolerance and even respect. 'Getting into trouble' is accepted as a normal hazard of growing up working class and can, indeed, be a source of local prestige.

The flaw in Miller's approach was that it implied that **all** working class boys should be delinquent – it couldn't explain working class 'college boys' who were **deviant** in their cultural milieu. Subsequent studies have tried to address this issue, to explain different youth responses to the same cultural environment. **Cloward and Ohlin**, for example, suggested that working class teenagers have available a variety of ways of dealing with their marginal status – even the term 'delinquent' covers quite different sorts of behaviour. Whether people get involved in thieving, fighting or drug-taking depends, in part, on available **opportunities**. Young people don't make a firm, clear decision either to be a delinquent or a non-delinquent (to be a corner or a college boy), but, rather, respond to opportunities, find themselves engaged in particular sorts of conflict with various forms of authority. And what the authorities do (police and parents, courts and teachers) is as important in the production of 'delinquency' as what young people do.

David Matza developed this point by studying young people's own accounts of their activities. He discovered that they did not make any clear distinction between their 'delinquent' and 'non-delinquent' behaviour. Delinquents justified their 'deviant' acts by reference to the same 'respectable' norms which organised the rest of their lives. Delinquent acts occurred because the 'delinquents' believed that in certain circumstances 'normal' judgements could be suspended – to use a British example, skinheads justify 'Paki-bashing' and 'queer-bashing' by **excluding** Asians and gays from the community in which, as the skinheads themselves agree, hitting people for no reason is wrong. Matza concluded that 'becoming deviant' involves learning not deviant values but deviant **justifications**. As Sykes and Matza put it: 'It is our argument that much delinquency is based on what is essentially an unrecognised extension of **defences** to crimes in the form of justifications for deviance that are seen as valid by the delinquent but not by the legal system or society at large.' Hence the familiar excuses offered by young delinquents on arrest and in court – 'we didn't really hurt anybody', 'everyone else was doing it', 'the police started it'.

In his later work, Matza argued that just as deviants have their own sort of commitment to conformist values, so conformists have their own sort of commitment to deviant values. 1950s and 1960s USA had a **subterranean** as well as a dominant value system, a shared if furtive commitment to personal violence, non-conformity, rule-breaking and sexual adventure. Subterranean values are expressed through fantasy (all those Clint Eastwood films, for example) or in carefully demarcated times and places (on holidays, on the sports field, in red light districts), and what juvenile delinquents do wrong is bring subterranean norms to the social surface, acting out violent fantasies in real gang activities, being destructive and disorderly daily on the streets.

Explaining Juvenile Delinquency – Labelling Theory

Matza's argument made clear that 'delinquency' is the result of the **interaction** of people behaving in certain ways and other people responding to that behaviour. To call an **action** delinquent is also to describe the social **reaction** to it. This approach to deviance, as developed by **Howard Becker** and his colleagues, is known as 'labelling theory' although, as Becker argues, it should be called **the interactionist theory of deviance**.

It's a theory which raises a number of important points. First, labelling theorists explain delinquency as a **process** (not a state). What sociologists have to make sense of are situations in which delinquency may or may not be constructed – not every football match leads to 'trouble', not every football hooligan gets into a fight. Reactions by the police and passers-by and the media are as important for the occurrence of 'delinquency' as actions by delinquents. Delinquency is often experienced therefore as accidental, a matter of chance not choice – which both adds to the excitement of delinquent occasions and explains why young people feel so aggrieved when they are confronted – 'why pick on **me**?'

It follows too that if action and reaction are equally significant for the making of delinquency then they should be paid the same amount of sociological attention. Becker and his colleagues were thus able to show how **deviancy amplification** works: being labelled as a deviant can intensify someone's commitment to deviancy. The most obvious British example of this process is the police labelling of black youth – by treating black teenagers as 'trouble' just because of the 'deviant' colour of their skins, policemen both encourage and legitimate the black youth rejection of 'white' law and order.

Labelling theory, then, has changed sociologists' ideas about **who** should be studied in the analysis of delinquency – the labellers need as much study as the labelled. We must, for example, be able to explain the **moral entrepreneurs** (the newspaper writers and moralists and political speech makers) who defined the 'problems' of teddy boys and punks and Hell's Angels, dope smoking and glue sniffing, football hooliganism and mugging. The labels applied to delinquents have their own sociological, historical and cultural meanings – why have they developed the way they have? To go back to the beginning of the chapter, why have people thought for so long that hooliganism is a 'new' problem, that young people were once well behaved?

These questions became particularly important for sociologists in the 1960s when some youth deviants claimed a political justification for their deviance, when the moral certainties of the labellers were put into doubt. Thus, in his influential study of the mods and rockers phenomenon, **Stanley Cohen** focused on press, political and court **responses** to the seaside battles. He was interested in how 'moral panics' worked. And, in general, sociologists now include discussion of police and media behaviour in studies of juvenile delinquency as a matter of course – even Lord Scarman's report on the 1981 'riots' paid attention to police and press contributions to the trouble.

Female Delinquency

I'll return to the general implications of labelling theory for the sociology of youth in chapter 5. Here I want to draw attention to some of the gaps and weaknesses of delinquency theory itself.

Most obviously and most seriously, 'delinquency' studies have focused almost exclusively on **male** behaviour. Sociologists have accepted the statistical indications that delinquency is an aspect of growing up male (about ten boys appear in court for every one girl) without considering what they really mean. Are such statistics the best measure of 'delinquency'? Isn't labelling theory relevant here? Policemen faced with a football crowd, for example, are more likely to pick on boys as the trouble makers, to tell the girls to go home, so maybe girls' absence from the courts the next week tells us more about police attitudes to women than about girls' attitudes to crime.

Even if girls aren't as delinquent as boys (or are delinquent in different ways) we still need to be able to account for such differences, and it's not clear that existing sociological approaches can. After all, girls also experience blocked access to material rewards, they too fail at school, have a marginal status in the community. And girls also become punks and skinheads, share lower class and subterranean values. So why don't delinquency theories discuss them? None of the theories I have summarised presents itself as an explicitly **gendered** explanation of delinquency; the theorists refer to class rather than to male values.

The fact is that male sociologists have, on the whole, shared the attitude of police and courts that female delinquency is unusual. This statistical conclusion conceals a theoretical assumption, as feminist sociologists have more recently pointed out – girls can't be brought into sociological accounts of delinquency and so explanations of their behaviour can be left to the social psychologists. Thus D. J. West's *The Young Offenders* moves from the finding that girls are far less delinquent than boys to the conclusion that girls who are delinquent are **abnormal** – their behaviour has to be explained in psycho-dynamic rather than cultural terms. West notes that 'wayward girls are worse than delinquent boys', are more likely to come from 'disordered' homes, to show 'neurotic symptoms' and 'psychopathic traits'. But the most significant aspect of West's conclusions is that they relate female delinquency to **sexual** misbehaviour: 'girl thieves are often, but not always, sexual rebels'. Other criminologists have taken this suggestion even further. Cowie, Cowie and Slater's 1968 survey, *Delinquency in Girls*, for example, linked female delinquency to abnormal 'hormonal balance' – 'sex chromosome constitution is one of the basic factors determining the liability to delinquency'.

This is to return explanations of delinquency to nineteenth century assumptions, and it is a measure of the inadequacy of sociological accounts of delinquency that such a biological approach still had credibility at the end of the 1960s. Two points about this should be stressed, in particular. First, the idea that female delinquency is 'abnormal' and likely to be linked to sexual activity has material consequences for the girls who are brought to court. They are more likely than boys to be declared 'in need of care, protection or control', more likely to be given custodial sentences, even if these sentences are passed 'for their own good'. As Cowie, Cowie and Slater explain magistrates' actions: 'these girls have to be removed from society into the security of a residential school much more for their own sakes than to protect society'.

Second, there is an obvious double standard at work here: girls' sexual activity is treated as 'problematic' in a way that boys' sexual activity is not (boy shop-lifters who come to court are not usually questioned about their sex lives). This double standard is not just applied by courts and criminologists; within youth cultures themselves female behaviour is judged differently than male behaviour; girls are labelled by boys on the streets (as 'slags' or 'drags', for example) as well as by police and social workers in court reports. Sexual assumptions and gender divisions are built into youth sub-cultures, and the real problem of delinquency theory is not that it ignores female delinquency, but that in doing so it provides only a partial and inadequate account of male behaviour. I'll return to this point in chapter 6.

Race and Crime

Black youth has become a 'problem' in Britain in the last twenty years, in much the same way that white working class youth became a 'problem' in the nineteenth century. The sight of male teenagers hanging around public places in groups, dressed in distinctive clothes, 'doing nothing' and getting into trouble triggers off press and police suspicions now as it did a hundred years ago – then the youth problem was labelled 'hooliganism'; in the late 1960s the black youth problem became encapsulated in the headlines about 'mugging'.

In the most important sociological study of youth, race and crime, *Policing The Crisis*, Stuart Hall and his colleagues show how mugging (meaning robbery from a person in a public place involving assault or the threat of assault) was a label developed to refer to more general fears about **law and order** and about **race relations**. Mugging is not a legal category ('muggers' are actually charged with a variety of robbery or assault offences) but it does carry a common sense meaning. It describes, for example, an offence that is seen to be essentially **irrational**. Mugging means random violence, an attack that could be experienced by any law abiding citizen. Mugging, unlike vandalism, may have a material 'reason' – it is a form of theft – but press reports concentrate on its most pointless examples: 'Pensioner Beaten For Fourpence!' And mugging is a crime that is seen to make particular **places** dangerous – areas of cities, tube stations, underpasses. In the headlines, then, mugging stands for a **breakdown** of law and order – in certain places, in particular communities.

This relates to the second aspect of mugging as a label: its association with **race**. The places and people linked to mugging become the places and people linked to certain sorts of social change, certain sorts of 'strangeness' – people and places linked, that is, to 'immigration' and 'immigrants'. By the 1970s black muggers had become the symbol (in both Britain and the USA) of white fears (made public by racist organ-isations like the National Front) of black neighbours and black neigh-bourhoods. Hall and his colleagues conclude that we can't understand the 'problem' of black youth without understanding the political and cultural activities of white adults.

There are several sociological studies now showing how this sort of labelling affected policing and sentencing, how black youth culture was 'criminalised' (this is, as I have suggested, a clear case of 'deviancy amplification'). Other researchers have examined the crime statistics themselves, showing that mugging is not a very serious problem (people are far more likely to be burgled than mugged), that the young are more likely than the old to be attacked, that racial identities of muggers and victims fall into no neat patterns. But, as *Policing The Crisis* suggests, while it is important for sociologists to replace the myth of mugging with rational analysis, this should not be done by ignoring black youth culture altogether. Nineteenth century 'hooliganism' was a myth too, but the label did refer to something of the shifting experience of working class boys in the big cities, and the mugging label too refers to a real aspect of black youth culture, its **street** presence, its organisation of black Britons from West Indian family backgrounds around certain sorts of leisure **style**.

Sociological arguments about black youth culture draw on the theories developed to make sense of white youth sub-cultures, relating their developments to boys' failures and lack of status in middle class institutions, to the rejection of middle class values, to the celebration of subterranean norms. The difference between black and white youth cultures is that black youth have to deal not simply with 'middle class' values, but with **white** middle class values. School failure involves a discrediting of black culture and language; work failure involves racial discrimination. For black youth, too, a job is not necessarily a desirable mark of adult status; it may involve commitment to an apparent lifetime of subservience to white authority. Hall and his colleagues argue that this has two consequences. First, black youth culture has a tendency to forms of cultural **nationalism** – middle class norms are rejected via an assertion of pride in black identity. Second, black youth culture involves, more clearly than white youth culture, a rejection of a simple work ethic, a stress on self-employment, on 'hustling' as a means of getting by. Black youth, in short, use local streets and other public places as the setting for work as well as leisure, politics as well as pleasure. It is not surprising that they get associated with 'street crimes' like mugging, that they come into conflict with the police – the conflict that lay behind the 1981 'riots'.

Explaining Juvenile Delinquency – Begged Questions and Unresolved Issues

One of the complaints facing sociologists is that in seeking to **explain** behaviour, they are actually trying to **justify** it. This is a particularly vigorous complaint about the sociology of deviance and delinquency: sociologists, by the very nature of their work, are thought to be 'on the side of the criminals'. This is, in practice, a matter of sociologists' individual political and ethical positions. A more important sociological problem, it seems to me, is that in developing general explanations of why some young people **are** delinquent, sociologists are in danger of leaving it unclear why most young people **are not**. In focusing on 'problem youth' sociologists have contributed to the idea that young people are, in themselves, 'a problem'. I have already suggested that this means ignoring girls, who don't fit the various deviancy models (so that accounts of black youth culture too leave it unclear whether there are female muggers, what their behaviour means), and it has other obvious consequences – Asian youth are neglected in the literature, for example, they are not 'problems' in the right sort of way.

At the beginning of this chapter I cited Geoffrey Pearson's study of the 'respectable fears' adults have had of youth for at least a hundred years. Why have adults so consistently 'over-reacted' to juvenile delinquency? Why does reasonable concern about teenage bad behaviour so often take on the exaggerated form of a 'moral panic'? Stanley Cohen suggests that moral panics reflect adult attempts to cope with certain sorts of social change, to deal with anxiety about a society's economic or moral stability. Young people become the target for such anxiety because they are highly visible (their leisure behaviour is on public display) and relatively powerless (the forces of moral order, police and social workers, teachers and courts can do things to them, can be seen to **act**).

The 'problem' of youthful deviancy is, thus, in many ways, a projection on to the young of adult concerns, and this goes too, for the sociology of youthful deviancy. Sociologists have also slipped from explanations of specific delinquents into the suggestion that all young people are deviant, have begged the question of the relationship between deviancy and conformity, between growing up working class, or male or black and growing up 'normal'. And sociologists too have projected on to youth their own political concerns. This is particularly the case with British sub-cultural theory, which I will discuss in the next two chapters.

Chapter Five
Sub-cultural Theory

Youth Groups in Britain

Passers-by were first startled (and frightened) by the Edwardian cow-boy look of the Teddy Boys in the early 1950s, and ever since then British youth cultures have been associated in the public's mind with bizarre street styles. The Teds were followed in the 1960s by Mods and Rockers, in the 1970s by Skinheads and Punks. Youth styles change but rarely vanish. Saturday afternoon shopping in most provincial towns still means watching a spectacular parade of the main youth styles of the last thirty years (not to mention the more specialist displays of the Rockabillies and Bowie Boys, the Heavy Metal Kids and Soulies, the New Mods and Ois).

Such youthful identity is a matter of looking right (clothes, shoes, hairstyles) and sharing tastes (for styles of music, ways of having fun), and however different such youth groups are from each other (differences which have sometimes involved ritual fights – mods vs rockers, teds vs punks) they equally outrage 'straight' society – grown-ups, shop keepers, the police, teachers, newspapers quick to use such peculiar images (girls with rings in their noses, boys with tattooed heads) for their shock value. In Britain the general fears about young people – what are our children coming to? – have been focused on the public eccentricities of working class youth styles. The sociological question is: what do these styles **mean**?

The sociological answer to this question rests on the concept of 'sub-culture'. In dictionary terms, a sub-culture is 'a social, ethnic or economic group with a particular character of its own **within** a culture or society', and this was how the term was first used by sociologists – to draw attention to the distinctive cultural patterns of minority groups within 'plural' societies (thus we might talk of Mormon sub-culture in the USA or Chinese sub-culture in Britain).

At first glance British youth groups, however distinctive their look, don't fit this model. Young people of all styles are still defined by the dominant cultural institutions of family and school, class and work place; their styles are not ways of life but aspects of leisure. On the other hand, these leisure groups (which seem to be a uniquely British phenomenon) can't be accounted for in terms of other theories of youth either. They're 'deviant' but not necessarily delinquent – it's not a **crime** to dye your hair green. Their styles depend on commercial teen culture (pop music most obviously) but weren't created by it – ted and mod and punk and skinhead styles certainly weren't dreamed up by businessmen. The young people involved aren't 'classless' – they seem to be working class in social origin and setting – but neither are they obviously embedded in their parent cultures. British youth styles appear as bizarre in their local communities of family and neighbours as they do to middle class and media observers. Sub-culture does seem an appropriate term to get at these youth groups' sense of **difference** from society, as long as we continue to be clear that youth sub-cultures are, at the same time, embedded **in** society.

Sociologists developed the sub-cultural theory of youth, then, to show how young working class 'deviance' is, in fact, an effect of dominant cultural patterns. In the words of *Resistance Through Rituals*, the classic study of youth style published in 1975:

> We have tried to dismantle the term in which this subject is usually discussed – 'Youth Culture' – and reconstruct in its place a more careful picture of the kinds of youth sub-cultures, their relation to class cultures and to the way cultural hegemony [domination] is maintained structurally and historically.

The Origins of Sub-cultural Theory

As this quote from *Resistance Through Rituals* makes clear, the sub-cultural approach to youth is not easily summarised. It marked a new perspective on youth culture, but one which wove together strands of other approaches, and developed a particularly opaque theoretical jargon. In this chapter I will try to provide a 'simple' account of sub-cultural theory while using direct quotations to give an idea of the woolliness of much of the finished product. The most useful starting point is the American delinquency theory discussed in the last chapter. The aim of the Chicago School in the 1920s and 1930s was to outline a sociological alternative to criminologists' positivist accounts of delinquent behaviour, to provide social rather than individual explanations of juvenile crime. The empirical basis of this was ethnography, detailed observation and description of teenage gangs, which attempted to get at the group values which justified individual delinquent acts. The argument was that, in its cultural context, delinquency was 'normal', determined by cultural norms, and not a symptom of psychological deficiency. Even apparently 'non-rational' delinquent behaviour (like vandalism or street fighting) could be understood from this perspective. It might not bring material benefits (like robbery) but it did win status and prestige according to gang values of risk and toughness. The Chicago sociologists understood juvenile delinquency as **collective** behaviour organised around gangs' 'focal values'. Youth deviance had to be explained, in short, in terms of young people's membership of delinquent sub-cultures, and the question became where did these sub-cultures' values come from? How did they relate to the USA's dominant value system?

Over the last fifty years American sociologists have come up with various answers to this question. The most important were outlined in the last chapter:

a) delinquency is the result of blocked access to social rewards, both material (wealth and power) and cultural (status and prestige). Sub-cultures are deviant not in their ends but in their means to those ends (Merton).

b) delinquents deliberately reverse dominant social values in order to legitimate and cope with their 'failure' according to those values (A. K. Cohen).

c) delinquency is an aspect of 'lower-class culture' – it is deviant only according to middle class norms (Miller).

d) delinquency involves the 'inappropriate expression' of widely shared but 'subterranean' social values (Matza).

e) deviance is an effect of labelling – youth groups are 'delinquent' because of the reactions to them by societies' moral authorities (teachers, police, courts, social workers, mass media) (Becker).

Each of these arguments was developed in response to the explanatory weaknesses of the others, and British sub-cultural theorists too began by taking what they could from these positions to make sense of the history of British youth cultures. The general sociological tasks were the same: to explain deviant behaviour by reference to sub-cultural values, to show that the most irrational styles (shaved heads, ripped clothes) were 'normal', to tease out the relationship between sub-cultures and society. What British theorists added to the argument was a Marxist perspective. American youth theorists were concerned with the social production of norms in the immediate circumstances of collective behaviour (in gangs and on street corners) and with the relationship of 'deviant' and 'normal' values but didn't pay much attention to where these norms came from. British youth theorists wanted to develop a wider social structural perspective. Influenced in part by the emergence of a Marxist 'new criminology' in the late 1960s, which related crime to the **class** structure, they sought to link youthful deviance too to class **conflict**.

Youth and Class Conflict

British sociologists of youth (like their American counterparts) are agreed that deviant youth sub-cultures are working class sub-cultures. The young people concerned come from working class families and neighbourhoods, have a working class experience of growing up – they're in the lower streams at school, leave as soon as possible to look for a job, they're unemployed or passing through a succession of dead end tasks and training schemes. The sociological questions follow from these empirical observations: what is the relationship between such young people's class-based experiences and their sub-cultural styles? How do deviant groups express **working class** 'values'? What is their connection to working class parent culture? Why are such styles adopted by only a minority of working class youngsters? Are the Teds and Mods, the Punks and Skinheads, more or less 'class conscious' than their 'normal' peers?

British sub-cultural theory began from the answer to this last question. Deviant styles are, obviously, non-conformist and such non-conformity is, according to *Resistance Through Rituals*, not simply a gesture of adolescent rebellion against parents but involves, more importantly, a confrontation with middle class authorities, a statement of working class identity. A skinhead gang is an 'us' against 'them' gesture writ large in class rather than generational terms. The shock value of deviant styles, their effect in making people jump, getting boys and girls sent home from school, turned down from jobs, picked on by the police, is essential to their meaning. Young people in the late 1970s, for example, didn't just dye their hair green because they liked the colour, but also because they knew what effect this would have on other people. They wanted to **parade** their rebellion, and this was a rebellion not against working class experiences as such but against middle class attempts to define and confine those experiences.

American sociologists like Miller had argued that young delinquents expressed lower class culture 'naturally' – they articulated in intense and public but spontaneous ways the beliefs and values they had grown up with (notions of masculinity, what it means to be a 'real man', in particular). British sub-cultural writers developed this argument with the suggestion that deviant stylists weren't simply reflecting, unconsciously, existing working class norms (though macho values were an obvious part of British youth cultures too) but using them as the basis of a form of **resistance** to the expectations of school and leisure and workplace. It is their visible, public, **collective** commitment to such resistance that differentiates these youth groups **both** from conforming 'normal' working class youngsters **and** from A. K. Cohen's 'corner boys'. The latter may 'reverse' bourgeois norms in order to generate immediate social status from their 'failure' but they're not concerned to **symbolise** their position, to publicise their revolt by turning it into a public style.

Resistance Through Rituals

To define sub-cultural style as 'working class resistance' is to make two sociological assertions: first, that the style relates to specifically working class experiences (and not just to general adolescent concerns for fashion and peer group solidarity) and, second, that the style is a 'political' response to those experiences, works, that is, to give the stylists some sort of power over their situation, a way of confronting authority. Neither claim rings immediately true in common sense terms, if only because the various youth uniforms, in their very precision, seem so 'irrational'. The Marxist New Criminologists linked crime to class via a straightforward materialistic argument. To put it crudely, if you're in a low paid job or unemployed, with no prospects or qualifications, then robbery is an obvious way of making money and gaining social status. But what does putting on crepe soles or having a mohican haircut achieve? If the underlying cause of deviance is young people's class position, their relationship to the means of economic production, then why do styles change (when material conditions don't)? Why did people become Teds in the 1950s, Mods in the 1960s, Punks in the 1970s? What does it mean to choose to become a Skinhead rather than a Rocker?

What's at issue in such choices is not a change in material circumstances but a use of symbols, and in trying to explain how **symbolic behaviour** was a form of class resistance sub-cultural writers drew their arguments directly from labelling theory. Labelling theorists had argued that social deviance is an effect of the activities of labellers, but left it rather unclear why the labellers, the moral entrepreneurs in society, acted the way they did. American labelling theory, in particular, was essentially pluralistic in its assumptions. It described society in terms of a value competition in which the labellers (because of their social position) had the power to make their labels stick, while the labelled, low status minority groups, hadn't. Sub-culturalist theorists rejected this idea of a free competition of ideas and argued, instead, that 'labellers', particularly as they are organised in state institutions (the police force, schools, the law, the social services), are the bearers of **bourgeois** values. They don't just happen to have different attitudes from deviants; their values (and the labelling process itself) derive from the problems of maintaining an orderly capitalist society.

The difference between the pluralist and Marxist use of labelling theory is clear from a comparison of Stan Cohen's account of the media responses to mods and rockers, which he describes in terms of a 'moral panic', something essentially irrational, and Stuart Hall and his colleagues' analysis of the media responses to mugging, which they related to a **political** crisis such that problems of law and order and race couldn't be separated from an analysis of class relations (see the discussion of these books in chapter 4). The point to be taken from the latter argument is that disputes about youth styles (and mugging as a social issue, as I've already suggested, raised the particular problem of black youth style) are **real** disputes. There may be no obvious material stakes (as in a strike over wages) when skinheads are sent home from school or banned from football grounds, when the police stop and question anyone with dreadlocks, but such confrontations do concern the way in which the social structure is 'reproduced'. What's going on, from this theoretical perspective, is **class struggle at the ideological level** (and in 1981 no-one could deny that the youth 'riots' in Brixton, Toxteth and Bristol were **political** events).

Resistance and Ideology

The crucial distinction between American delinquency theory and British sub-cultural theory lies in the latter's use of the concept of ideology. Both approaches agree that deviant behaviour is best understood as a form of problem solving. In Mike Brake's words, 'subcultures arise as attempts to resolve collectively experienced problems arising from contradictions in the social structure'. Working class youth are in a marginal position in contemporary capitalist societies. They lack power, status and wealth now, and they already know that they will have extremely limited access to power, status and wealth in the future. Youth deviance is thus a way of generating alternative forms of success and reward. This was the great insight of American sociology, and British writers' problem was to apply it to deviant styles.

In what way do they **solve** youth problems? Skinheads still lack power and property however short their hair and frightening their appearance, and the argument became, then, that deviant styles are solutions to ideological problems, a response to the gaps and contradictions in the set of **ideas** that young people are offered (by parents, by the media, by the teenage consumption industry, by the state) as a way of **making sense of their marginality.**

If we want to explain the emergence of skinheads in the late 1960s, in other words, we should examine not their material conditions (experiences at home and work didn't change much in this period) but their cultural conditions; we should analyse the available ways of interpreting the world. Youth sub-cultures solve ideological problems and to make sociological sense of them we must begin by understanding their 'ideological conditions of existence'. Thus *Resistance Through Rituals* provides a history of British youth groups not in terms of wages or job opportunities or educational organisation but in terms of changing **ideas** about youth and leisure and style. Phil Cohen summed up this approach in his pioneering study of skinheads:

> the latent function of sub-culture is this – to express and resolve, albeit 'magically', the contradictions which appear in the parent culture. The succession of sub-cultures which this parent culture generated can thus all be considered as so many variations on a central theme – the contradiction, at an ideological level, between traditional working class puritanism and the new ideology of consumption . . .

For Cohen, then, the 'problem' facing young people in Britain since the war had been to make sense of competing systems of meaning and morality – traditional working class emphasis on the importance of workplace solidarity, community and family life, middle class emphasis on educational opportunity and individual ambition, media emphasis on consumption and fun. The 'magical' solution was to develop a style, a form of group leisure that negotiated a path between such competing values by presenting individual prestige in terms of collective consumption. Cohen suggested that sub-cultures should be seen as **ritual** solutions to cultural contradictions, and the question became how such rituals worked as forms of 'resistance'.

The Concept of Hegemony

The argument of 'resistance through rituals' rests on the concept of **hegemony,** which was first developed by the Italian Marxist, Antonio Gramsci, in the 1920s. Hegemony means leadership or domination, and Gramsci's purpose in using the term was to draw attention to the role of cultural institutions (the church, the family, the law, education, the arts, the media) in the organisation of power in class societies. He argued that the bourgeoisie in capitalist societies is the ruling class (is 'hegemonic') not just because it controls the 'repressive' state forces (the police and military) and owns the means of economic production, but also because it dominates the 'civil institutions', the way people organise their 'private' lives and their 'common sense', the ways in which they each understand their situation, decide what's right or wrong, possible or impossible, natural or unnatural. To be 'hegemonic' a class has to impose its ideology, its particular organisation of values, beliefs and symbols, on everyone else, and class conflict thus involves a struggle for ideas as well as a struggle for state power and economic resources. It follows that ideological resistance is a key form of political activity – all challenges to a ruling class depend on people who are convinced that society could be organised otherwise, that present social arrangements aren't 'necessary' or 'natural'.

Deviant youth styles are a real threat to the ruling class, then, because they challenge dominant **ideas** – which is why they provoke 'panics'. And even struggles over ideas have material effects. In the words of *Resistance Through Rituals*:

> sub-cultures are not simply 'ideological' constructs. They, too, **win space** for the young: cultural space in the neigh-bourhood and institutions, real time for leisure and recreation, actual room on the street or street-corner. They serve to mark out and appropriate 'territory' in the localities. They focus around key occasions of social inter-action: the weekend, the disco, the bank-holiday trip, the night-out in the 'centre', and 'stand-about-doing-nothing' of the weekday evening, the Saturday match.

Sub-cultures and Style

I think anybody reading this description will be struck by the gap between the sociologists' abstract account of youth sub-culture and the explanations for their behaviour one would be likely to get from the sub-cultures themselves. Punks and Skinheads and Mods and Teds are unlikely (unless they've done Sociology A-Level) to talk about 'winning cultural space', 'resistance at the ideological level' or the 'magical reclamation of community', and an obvious comment to be made on sub-cultural theory is that it reads into youth styles meanings that aren't there. There has always been a tendency for sociologists (who usually come from middle class, bookish backgrounds) to celebrate teenage deviancy, to admire the loyalties and excitement of 'street life', to forget the painful problems that cause street life to be like that in the first place. If for American delinquency theorists this meant romanticising gang life, have Marxist sub-cultural theorists romanticised 'resistance'?

This is an aspect of youth culture – the way it is used by other people, sociologists included, to symbolise certain values, to carry certain messages – that I'll come back to. The sub-cultural theorists them-selves, while acknowledging that their conclusions don't derive from questionnaires or interviews, claim, nevertheless, to be using an objective approach. Their interpretations of sub-cultural styles are ordered by **semiology**, the science of signs. Theorists have drawn particularly on the work of the French semiologist, Roland Barthes, whose work was full of suggestive comments about the ways 'signs' work in everyday life. The significance of people's clothes, the meanings of advertisements, the implications of the names and shapes of, say, motor-cars, are all socially constructed even if we normally take them for granted. How such images work depends on their organ-isation of cultural elements whose resonance comes from their meanings in other settings, from their contrast to 'opposing' signs. Thus a skinhead's short hair takes part of its meaning from other images of short hair (on a Borstal boy or army recruit), part from its opposition to long hair (on a hippie). Sub-cultural styles in general depend for their effect on 'bricolage', the accumulation in one uniform of signs taken from all sorts of context (the union jack moved from the flag-pole to a skinhead T-shirt, the swastika moved from a nazi uniform to a punk ear-lobe, and so on). Youth sub-cultures **take-over** signs – from respectable society (the mods' suits and ties), from disreputable society (the punks' bondage gear), above all from commercial teenage culture, and reassemble them in images which shock not just because they are unusual but because they also threaten the usual stability of imagery. Think, for example, of people's unease, anger even, at seeing boys with long hair and 'dresses' (hippies in the 1960s or Boy George followers in the 1980s) and girls (skinheads, punks, feminists) with short hair and 'masculine' work clothes. Such deviant use of clothing becomes a challenge to dominant conventions of sexuality.

According to sub-cultural theory, then, youth styles are a form of resistance not because the stylists are consciously challenging 'bourgeois ideology' but because in using social signs to give themselves a sense of control over their own lives, group members simultaneously draw public attention to the contradictions in the dominant ideology as it relates to their lives. In the words of *Resistance Through Rituals*, 'the Teddy Boy expropriation of an upper class style of dress "covered" the gap between largely manual, unskilled, near-lumpen real careers and life-chances, and the "all-dressed-up-and-nowhere-to-go" experience of Saturday evening', while 'in the expropriation and fetishisation of consumption and style itself, the Mods covered the gap between the never-ending-weekend and Monday's resumption of boring, dead-end work'.

Sub-cultural Theory: Does It Make Sense

We can summarise the sub-cultural argument like this, then. Youth groups use their own area of power – their 'free time' – to make a gesture against their lot. Their material situation (school failure, unemployment, no future), is, at one level, accepted – there is nothing they can do about it – but, at another level, rejected – deviant styles symbolise a refusal to accept dominant accounts of their position. Youth sub-cultures can only cast spells against the boring powerlessness of the daily routine, but such magic does have cultural consequences. It challenges the ideology that normally keeps the social machinery working.

The sub-cultural approach to youth culture is complex, sometimes confused, and overtly Marxist but it has become, nonetheless, a central strand in the British sociology of youth. All other theorists have had to take account of it and the next chapter will examine their responses. A final point needs to be made here, though.

Sub-cultural theory rests on remarkably limited empirical research. The readings of youth styles in *Resistance Through Rituals*, for example, are based not on direct observation but on media sources – youth styles are analysed according to the ways they've **already** been labelled. This gives the description of style as conflict a certain conviction – the media do set up sub-cultures as 'threats' to society – but it also raises doubts about the real extent of those threats. In the two important empirical studies that have emerged from the sub-cultural school the doubts become pressing. Thus Paul Willis's *Learning To Labour* shows clearly enough that the 'lads' sub-culture is a form of resistance to schooling, but he also makes it plain that it exactly fits the lads for their future as workers, as unskilled manual labourers. Angela McRobbie's interviews with teenage girls show, similarly, that their 'feminine' style is both a form of resistance in the class room **and** a way of preparing themselves for their future roles as housewives, as domestic labourers.

The 'resistance' displayed by sub-cultures, in short, may be exaggerated by sociologists' concentration on the most spectacular aspects of youth culture (the aspects that interest the media). Willis and McRobbie, in placing such spectacle in its 'ordinary' context of work and leisure, school and family, make clear that the line between 'conforming' and 'non-conforming' youth is, in practice, hard to draw. If there are elements of resistance in sub-cultures, there are also elements of incorporation (and, indeed, some sub-cultures seem over-conformist to dominant norms, in their racial and sexual attitudes, for example). If youth cultures pose, in Dick Hebdige's words, 'an oblique challenge to hegemony', might they not also represent an equally oblique form of acquiescence to dominant social norms?

Chapter Six

Critiques of Sub-cultural Theory

The Feminist Critique

The most telling criticisms of sub-cultural theory concern its account of girls, or, rather, its lack of an account of girls. This point was made by Angela McRobbie and Jenny Garber in the *Resistance Through Rituals* collection itself. Why, they asked, were girls absent from the accompanying analyses of Teds and Mods and Skinheads? Were girls really absent from sub-cultures (and if so, why)? Or were they there but not noticed by sociologists (and if not, why not)? What was apparent was that in ignoring girls, sub-culturalists were ignoring boys' relationships with girls, were ignoring sub-cultural sexuality, the groups' attitudes to marriage and the family. Boys' 'masculinity' was taken for granted; 'resistance' was defined solely in terms of class and race; sub-cultures' political complicity with dominant sexual norms was not discussed.

Angela McRobbie has followed up these points in her subsequent research. Her empirical studies confirm that girls **are** members of sub-cultures but in marginal, 'feminine' positions that reflect the boys' 'normal' sexual expectations. Girls are defined as 'girl friends', for example. Female skinheads and punks are certainly rebelling against the mainstream culture of femininity, but within the sub-culture themselves traditional working class gender divisions still seem to hold.

McRobbie also suggests that there is not really such a thing as a **female sub-culture**, a way in which working class girls can resist dominant cultural norms collectively, as a group of girls. Young teenagers do share a 'teenybopper' or 'bedroom' culture, female friendship groups based on the home, on girls' magazines like *Jackie*, on pop stars and pin-ups, but these friendships become less significant as girls grow older, as their lives become defined by their marginal status in sub-cultures or by their incorporation into the commercial culture of femininity.

The implication of this sort of research is that the teenage activities analysed in sub-cultural theory, the activities that are described as 'resistance through rituals' or 'winning cultural space', are **male** activities. If girls do 'win space' or 'resist through rituals' they do so differently than boys, in ways that male sociologists haven't noticed. Why are there such differences between male and female teenage behaviour?

One still influential answer to this derives from the social-psychological approach to youth developed at the beginning of the century. This explains the cultural differences between boys and girls in biological terms. Girls are said to be 'naturally' passive, conformist and uninterested in joining groups. Puberty thus marks the onset of psychological as well as physical differences between the sexes. G. Stanley Hall's *Adolescence*, the source of this sort of argument, suggested that 'adolescence' actually meant quite different things for boys and girls. Adolescent boys became ambitious, curious, in need of mental growth and challenge; adolescent girls became emotional, prone to weepiness and giggling, flirtatious, in need of social protection as their maternal instincts emerged.

Such attempts to explain cultural norms in terms of hormones and instincts are no longer sociologically credible, but they do, to an unfortunate extent, still inform the common sense of parents and teachers, social workers and magistrates' courts. As I have already mentioned (see chapter 4), girls who do get involved in aggressive, gang activities are treated not as naughty but as abnormal. Female delinquency is still interpreted as the mark of a sexual problem; girls are still thought to be in special need of social protection.

The central feminist criticism of sub-cultural theory (particularly now that it is dominant in the British sociology of youth) is that in failing to account for the gender differences in youth culture, it has left common sense assumptions about sexuality unchallenged.

The Liberal Critique

The liberal critique of sub-cultural theory has been argued most passionately in Britain by David Marsland, who objects to the theory of 'resistance through rituals' because of its **Marxist** assumptions. I'm labelling Marsland's argument 'the liberal critique' (it's not his own term) because his underlying explanation of how British society does and should work is an essentially liberal position. He opposes the

Marxist model of classes in conflict with a liberal model of individuals pursuing and negotiating economic, social and moral freedom.

Marsland's liberal starting point has a number of implications for his sociology of youth. He rejects, for example, the sub-cultural suggestion that 'youth', as an explanatory concept, is meaningless, must be subordinated to the concept of class. The sub-culturalists argue that the activities and values of sixteen year-olds must be explained, in the end, by reference to their class position. The differences between growing up working class and growing up middle class are far more significant than the fact that members of the different classes all have to 'grow up'. Marsland retorts that youth culture does have some autonomy, refers to sets of beliefs that young members of all classes relate to. He suggests that in the explanation of why sixteen year-olds act and behave as they do, class is only one variable among many. Its relative importance can only be assessed empirically, will be different for different groups in different situations. As an age group, young people of all classes do share the structural problems of the transition from childhood to maturity; they are well aware of their difference from the other age groups in society.

Marsland's own conclusions from this are paradoxical. He begins by stressing how much cultural 'freedom' young people have (he's not willing, therefore, to interpret sub-cultural styles as **determined** by people's class position). Teenagers are relatively free of adult responsibility and control; they are institutionally separated from adults and have the market power to develop their own cultural symbols; they are in a strong position to **reject** adult norms and assumptions. Youth culture is, therefore, an expression of **autonomy**. But Marsland goes on to argue that precisely because teenagers are so free, adults have a duty to guide them. Sub-cultural theory suggests that official adult interference in youth cultures (via the Youth Service, for example) is a form of **social control**, an aspect of class struggle. Marsland argues that the Youth Service is necessary for young people's own good. He accepts that 'through the medium of youth culture young people are substantially involved in resistance and challenge to many of the fundamental features of modern society', but suggests that 'the Youth Service cannot allow themselves to collude in phony dreams'.

Marsland's overall approach to youth is best summarised in his own words: 'This freedom that they have is authentic, and at the same time terrible. For they must navigate its open seas without charts; live out a life in it without a structure of beliefs; be themselves while pursuing an identity without which they cannot yet be themselves at all; travelling here, since only here in leisure are they free, towards adulthood with only childhood to guide them; wishing for adult guidance and support and finding precious little. It is a painful privilege indeed, from any perspective, and from some perspectives manifestly a punishment rather than a privilege at all.'

I'm not sure that Marsland's arguments amount to a **theory** of youth, but they do, at least, remind us that while the problems of being young may be shaped **by** class position, they are not simply problems **of** class position. As the feminist critique also made clear, youth cultures are not **just** class cultures.

'Ordinary' Youth

Marsland's work makes a regular rhetorical appeal to the lives of 'ordinary' youth. The priority of the Youth Services he suggests, for example, should be 'the ordinary problems of ordinary young people of all social types in their transition out of childhood into adulthood'. He neglects, though, the most detailed sociological accounts of such ordinary lives, those produced by **ethnographers**. The ethnography of British youth, the painstaking description of how young people organise and make sense of their daily lives, has a long history (Pearl Jephcott's pioneering study of *Girls Growing Up* was published in 1942; Peter Willmott's classic description of *Adolescent Boys of East London* came out in 1966) but its recurrent finding is that young people are more aware of **constraints** than **freedom**. Ethnographers have therefore been concerned to show how the **rules** of teenage life are constructed and learnt.

Analysing youth cultures in terms of rules of behaviour helps us to clarify the differences between boys and girls – they are subject to different rules. In *Disclosures to a Stranger*, for example, Tom Kitwood shows how class and sex differences affect teenagers' negotiations with their parents about 'going out'. Middle class boys have to persuade their parents that going out won't interfere with their studies or bring them to harm; working class boys have to persuade their parents that they won't get into trouble; girls, of both classes, have, in addition, to convince their parents that they won't be at risk of **sexual activity.** The problematic relationship between leisure and sexuality is thus built into the ways in which girls are expected to regulate their 'free time'. Boys are protected by the sexual double standard – parents are much less concerned about their sons' sex lives. The contrast is indicated by the different implications of saying 'he got into trouble' (with the police) and 'she got into trouble' (she's pregnant).

Different sexual rules thus affect the meaning of 'free time' itself. Empirical evidence suggests, for example, that boys have **more** free time than girls. Girls take on domestic obligations from an early age, have to help their mothers and contribute to household tasks. As Kitwood puts it: 'There is a continuity in home life, between the roles of schoolgirl, daughter-who-goes-out-to-work, wife and wife-who-goes-out-to-work.' And different norms within the family shape leisure possibilities outside it. Boys' free time is mostly enjoyed outside the home; girls, even in their leisure time, come under continuing family authority – have to say where they are going, be back at earlier times, and so on. Given that youth sub-cultures are usually described as street cultures, it is, again, worth noting the conventional implications of saying that a girl or woman is 'on the streets'.

Even in leisure time, then, there are different social constraints acting on boys and girls. They are expected to enjoy themselves in different ways (which are certainly not the results of different biological or psychological needs). Ethnographical studies suggest, in particular, that a highly important aspect of girls' leisure is **having or not having a boy friend**. As girls grow up, they break with 'teenybop culture', shift interest from sports and hobbies to the pursuit of 'femininity', a concern with clothes and make-up and display. Boys don't seem to experience the same sort of break. Their interests remain much the same through puberty; they still go out and about with their mates. If boy friends are central to girls' interests, girl friends are marginal to boys'. Being 'a girlfriend' means being on the fringes of male activities (watching them play football or rehearse with a band, hanging on to the back of a bike, cheering-on a fight), while also being excluded from leisure activities of one's own – 'a girlfriend' is not supposed to go out with anyone else.

Even girls without boyfriends are constrained by the need to have one – which may rule out some activities because they are seen as 'unfeminine' (like getting drunk) or 'childish' (like being involved in hobbies, youth clubs or even school-work). As Diana Leonard observed in her study of girls in Wales, *Sex and Generation*, 'They give up going to youth clubs because their interests are not catered for, because they feel they are under instruction ("and they can't teach you kissing there") and because boys who go to youth clubs are either not interested in girls, or not interested in them in the context of the youth club'.

It is important to stress that ethnographic studies don't suggest that teenagers always obey these rules or agree to these expectations. The point is, rather, that they know that they exist and have to take account of them. Of course the rules can be and often are broken, but such rule breaking is a source of anxiety, can mean teenagers feeling isolated, treated as 'weird' by their peers. To grow up 'extraordinary' needs political (as well as sub-cultural) support (a feminist group, for example). Growing up 'ordinary', by contrast, is growing up according to the pervasive **commercial** and **media** ideas of masculinity and femininity. Even Abrams's original market research showed that boys spent their money on immediate pleasures – cigarettes, drink, travel, while girls saved up for more substantial 'feminine' goods – clothes, shoes, cosmetics, hair-dos. A more recent market research study, Susie Fisher and Susan Holder's *Too Much Too Young?* explains this with this quote: 'Boys, everything you do is for boys, you don't want spots for boys, you want to look nice for boys and you take more care over yourself when there's a boy you fancy.'

Boys, it seems, are much less anxious about attracting girls. Even the sub-cultural stylists, who do pay detailed attention to how they look, are primarily concerned to impress their male friends. In the words of a 1960s mod: 'When you were at work you were a nobody. So when you put on your suede or mohair suit and Desert Boots and go to the dance hall, you want to be a somebody to your mates. It's your mates you want to impress, not the girls. You make a statement through your clothes, or your dancing, or your scooter. You had to be cool. To be chasing birds was seen as soft, a bit sentimental. You didn't want to lose face with the other guys.'

One conclusion from this sort of evidence is that peer groups, which are central to sociological accounts of youth, actually play quite different roles for boys and girls. The tension between peer group activities and courtship or sexual pairing is thus resolved differently for the different sexes. Males remain committed to their friendship groups, only have special nights out 'with the girlfriend'; girls 'grow out' of peer group activities and develop instead intense friendships with just one or two other girls. 'Best friends' support each other in the tricky negotiations about leisure and sexual behaviour with both parents and boys.

There is a paradox in the apparent subordination of female leisure to the 'boyfriend problem'. Boyfriends don't seem to be enjoyed much (sexually or otherwise) for their own sake. As Leonard puts it: 'For girls there is little sense of enjoying the time **when one is young and free**, or enjoying a relationship for what it is at a particular time – there is always a concern with where a relationship is leading, and with getting **married**.'

It follows that getting and keeping a suitable boyfriend is a matter of hard work and considerable worry, involves the recurring problem of managing sexuality, deciding 'how far to go'. Boys are (publicly, at any rate) exempted from such anxiety. Not having a girlfriend is less of a social stigma than not having a boyfriend; teenage culture still treats male sexuality as unproblematic: 'boys are after only one thing!' What ethnographic studies show, in short, is that while having a boyfriend is the focus of female leisure activity, it is not a source of much pleasure. What girls say they most enjoy is 'having a good laugh, just doing what you want to do', and that means enjoying oneself **without boys** (disco dancing in female groups, for example). As one of Angela McRobbie's teenagers told her: 'Well, if I had to choose between a boy and me mate, I'd choose her anytime. You know, all they're interested in is if you'll give it to them – and when you don't they pack it in.'

Learning To Be A Teenager

Detailed studies of teenage leisure suggest that many of the activities that are described as 'fun and freedom' are experienced in terms of anxiety and constraint. Most boys do, though 'choose' to behave like boys (even if they're therefore frightened or bored), and most girls do 'choose' the effort of getting and keeping a boyfriend over the pleasure of having laughs with their girl friends. Why?

The issue here is youth culture as a form of **socialisation**, as the setting in which girls and boys learn to be 'feminine' and 'masculine' in preparation for their adult roles. Why, then, are supposedly 'autonomous' or 'deviant' youth groups the setting for such conformist norms of behaviour?

In answering this, most sociologists have examined the ways in which young people are manipulated **ideologically**. Feminist writers like Germaine Greer, Sheila Rowbotham and Sue Sharpe have paid particular attention to the ideology of romance and femininity. The fashion industry, for example (boutiques and chain stores, cosmetics and clothing corporations) invests millions of pounds every year to hard-sell the latest versions of 'glamour' and 'attractiveness'. However female fashions change, their purpose doesn't – to make women desirable to men. Girls' books and magazines like *Jackie* and *Honey* combine this presentation of feminity with the enticement of romantic fictions, which suggest that the purpose of life is the emotional charge provided by 'falling in love'. Youth cultural activities themselves, music making for example, situate the sexes differently: boys become musicians, technicians, experts; girls are fans.

The ideology of femininity suggests that to be a desirable, successful or even recognisable woman means looking, acting and thinking in certain ways. It is such an overwhelming ideology in our society that to preserve some sense of their social significance girls have to collude with the ideology, to make decisions about themselves that go along with the suggestion that to be a teenage girl means to attract teenage boys. The ideology of femininity is, in short, a **patriarchal ideology**. It supports men's power over women and there is little evidence that sub-cultures **resist** such power.

This approach to youth culture implies that ideology is something which is applied 'from the top down' – young people's values derive from the influence of the mass media, parents, adult common sense. But we can approach teenage ideology from the opposite end, as a system of ideas generated by young people themselves in response to their **material** conditions. Thus, even as teenagers, girls and boys are placed differently in social institutions because of the projected division of their adult roles – boys as breadwinners, girls as wives and mothers. Equalities of opportunity legislation may change some of the more obvious school differences (girls doing domestic science, boys doing woodwork and so on) but they remain crucial in the youth labour market. For example, the few girls who get apprenticeships are likely to get them in hairdressing; the few girls who get professional qualifications are likely to get them in nursing. Unskilled girls are more likely to be unemployed than unskilled boys. Unskilled girls who do get jobs get jobs without training, with sparse prospects of career advancement or the acquisition of authority.

In the light of this sort of evidence, it can be argued that, at least for unskilled female school leavers, marriage and motherhood are crucial **occupations**, involve girls' most important **career** choices – marriage will determine both their likely standard of living and their adult status (and, indeed, marriage and motherhood are 'solutions' to girls' experience of unemployment – they offer an instant adult position). The pursuit of boyfriends, potential husbands, is not, therefore, the **result** of romantic ideology, but, rather, romantic ideology is a way of handling the **necessity** of finding 'the right man'. Romance invests the material basis of marriage with a degree of fun and fantasy.

Leisure, Work and Family

I've focussed on studies of female youth in this chapter in order to make a general point. Most sociologists define youth as a **leisure institution**. The analysis of youth cultures and sub-cultures thus focuses on values, on explanations of why young people **choose** to act the ways they do. Descriptions of girls growing up show very vividly, however, that youth cultures are equally a matter of **constraints**. Leisure has to be related to people's situations at work and in the home. Teenagers certainly have possibilities to behave in ways that will be closed off by adult roles and responsibilities, but their leisure is not entirely free, and this has three implications for sub-cultural theory.

First, young people's 'class position' is not just a cultural (or ideological) matter, a question of values. Young people also have specific material positions in the labour market and work place. Even school children are acquiring forms of knowledge and qualification that will determine what sort of jobs they will do, and, in general, there are significant differences in work experience between the employed and the unemployed, the skilled and the unskilled, students and workers. The differences that concern me here are not those between wage rates and leisure resources, but between different sorts of work commitment, satisfaction and expectation, between different sorts of workplace status and discipline. How people experience work (and prepare themselves for it) has significant effects for how they experience leisure (and use it). To make an obvious point, people go out on Friday and Saturday nights because they don't have to go to work on Saturday and Sunday mornings – rhythms of work (student patterns of reading, lectures, seminars and exams vs worker patterns of clocking in, the assembly line, rigid tea and lunch breaks) affect rhythms of leisure. And differences in the 'domestic labour market', the household, equally structure the sexual differences in leisure use.

There is a pressing need for sociologists of youth to follow up Paul Willis's thorough study of unskilled boys (*Learning to Labour*) with equally thorough studies of other social groups (skilled boys, students, young women). How do **they** relate work position, family position and leisure? Are their ideas of fun and pleasure the same as those of Willis's 'lads'?

My own belief is that the deviant/conformist distinction that sub-culturalists took from delinquency theory (it is used by Willis too) may not be the best way of understanding youth politics. 'Naughty' teenagers are not the same thing as 'rebellious' teenagers. Sub-culturalists followed the mass media in focusing on **spectacular** youth, but in doing so they missed the subtler ways in which young people resist and seek to **change** their situation.

This leads to my second point. In common sense terms, political 'resistance' refers to the activities of **organised** groups, with **explicit** demands and arguments and structures. Sub-culturalists made the important point that, in youth culture, resistance can also have a symbolic dimension, involve **implicit** gestures of style. But they seem then to imply that this is the **most** significant form of youth politics. It appears that non-political stylists like mods 'resist' dominant norms, while counter-cultural stylists like hippies do not. But this is to discount not just middle class youth politics, but also those youth struggles (round issues like housing, work, student rights, women, CND, the police, drug laws) which involve **cross-class** alliances. Is **organised** politics middle class (and therefore part of the dominant ideology) by definition? Political youth groups may or may not be important, but we certainly need to be able to analyse their relationship to sub-cultural styles.

Finally, a word on **fantasy**. In reading youth styles for signs and symbols of **collective** consciousness, the sub-cultural approach under-estimates the **individual** joy of dressing up, inventing an image, striking poses. This is a point made in the most entertaining of the sub-cultural studies, Dick Hebdige's *Sub-Culture: The Meaning of Style*. Hebdige suggests that styles are as much gestures of individual imagination as of class expression, relate to people's fantasies as well as to their reality. Thus suburban sixth formers dress up in the imagery of street gangs and play punk and reggae records; working class youth idolise David Bowie, invent their own night clubs, act out scenarios of art and bohemia, dress up as the 'new romantics'.

Sociologists can't, despite the sub-culturalist efforts, judge a style by its cover. Leisure is an alternative to reality as well as a way of expressing it, involves magic for its own sake as well as 'magical solutions to ideological problems'. Young people certainly do seek to inhabit worlds (the pub, the club, the disco floor) in which they are in control. But so do adults, who also indulge in leisure, use it as a source of fantasy, a place to act out 'subterranean values'. The distinctive nature of youth culture must be explained, then, not by reference to leisure itself, but to young people's position in work and family, to the 'reality' from which leisure is, on occasion, an escape.

Chapter Seven

The Future of Youth

The Consequences of Youth Unemployment

In the last chapter, I suggested that one of the limitations of the sociology of youth is that it has been, predominantly, a sociology of youth leisure. There have been numerous theoretical disagreements about what youth leisure means, but empirical studies have focused on young people's free time activities. There are good methodological reasons for this: teenagers' public, collective behaviour (and misbehaviour) is easier to observe systematically than their individual dealings with people at home and work. But the focus on leisure has obvious drawbacks. In the last decade, for example, the most important youth issue in Britain (and most other capitalist countries) has been **youth unemployment**. What can leisure sociologists say about this?

Some writers have been tempted simply to equate unemployment and leisure, to conclude that worklessness will intensify young people's commitment to youth culture. This conclusion is, indeed, reflected in successive British governments' policy responses to youth unemployment. The Youth Opportunities and Youth Training Schemes were designed, at least in part, to keep young people occupied, to meet the fear that 'idle' youth are 'mischievous' youth (although there is little statistical evidence for this). It is assumed, in short, that without work school leavers are trapped in their marginal social status. The anxiety is that they will become so embedded in youth cultural pleasures that they'll never be willing to grow up.

There are two immediate problems with this argument. First, leisure has to be defined in **contrast** to work, 'free' time is experienced in contrast to disciplined time (whether in school or occupation) – no work doesn't mean all play. Second, unemployment is not experienced

361

collectively like leisure. Social psychological research suggests that even though most young unemployed people know that everyone around them is out of work too, they still regard their own situation as an **individual** problem (and certainly not a matter of 'free' choice or 'free' time). Unemployment means staying in bed, hanging around the house, watching day time television or the video, kicking a ball against the wall, boredom; it does not mean spreading into weekday time peer groups' evening and weekend public jaunts.

The sociological implication of this is that the consequence of mass youth unemployment is **not** the intensification of previous youth cultural patterns but **a redefinition of working class youth experience** such that the traditional concept of 'youth' may cease to be relevant to it. In the 1950s and 1960s, when sociological theories of youth were first developed in Britain, the majority of young people left school at 15, went straight to work, earned relatively good money and had a marked degree of independence in both the home and the labour market. In the 1980s the majority of young people leave school at 16, become unemployed or enter short-term training schemes, have a relatively low income and a marked degree of dependence on both their parents and the welfare state. What does this shift in experience mean sociologically?

Youth as an Institution

Sociologists have, conventionally, focused on the 'subjectivity' of youth; they've been interested in how and why young people **construct themselves** as a particular group or culture or style. But youth is also an **effect** of other people's activities, is constructed as a particular role or structural position or institution in society by market forces, state policies and family expectations. Mass youth unemployment, in particular, can't be understood in terms of young people's own choices or even as just a statistical effect of the general economic recession. Young people seem to be specifically unemployable, and in understanding why we can also understand how 'youth' is constructed as a particular category in the labour market.

The question is simple. Why don't employers want 'young workers'? Why, given the choice, do they employ adults? One common answer is that young people these days don't have the right skills and aptitudes. This leads on to a critique of the school system (hence the call in the last few years for a more 'relevant' school curriculum and exam system) but a close inspection of the skills required by industry and instilled in school leavers by Manpower Services Commission (MSC) training schemes suggests that what's at issue is not really formal knowledge or a specific craft. One feature of youth unemployment is, indeed, the decline in the number of apprenticeships, and what employers seem to want is a set of **personal qualities** – responsibility, self-discipline, flexibility, punctuality and so on. These are the 'life skills' which adult workers have acquired through experience. In the labour market, then, a 'young' worker means an **inexperienced** worker.

The contemporary emphasis on experience needs to be understood in its historical context. In the 1960s industrial sociologists carried out a number of empirical studies of 'the transition from school to work'. One of the objects of this research was to improve the careers service, to make job placement more efficient, but even these sociologists were surprised by how long it took school leavers of both sexes to settle down into a particular job or workplace. The transition from school to work meant, in practice, a couple of years of continuous labour movement. Young people left jobs (and were sacked) for essentially trivial reasons; employers took it for granted that to be a young unskilled worker was to have a **casual** attitude to employment (trainees and apprentices were, by contrast, committed to their position). Becoming an adult worker meant, then, a period of **experiment** in the workplace itself.

From this perspective, the rise of youth unemployment means a decline in the demand for 'casual' labour, a decrease in the opportunity for school leavers to experiment with work. The reasons for this must be found in changes in the production process itself. I can only indicate these here but think, for example, of current shifts in the overall shape of the British economy – the decline of steel manufacture and the shipyards, the slump in construction, the expansion of the service sector and micro-electronics business. Even within established companies, technological change, the increasing use of computer-based processes, means a declining demand for **purely** manual skills, for workers with sheer physical strength, courage and stamina. What's happening is a process of 'semi-skilling', a declining demand for traditional crafts (and apprentices) but a rising need for workers who can be trusted with and adapt themselves to expensive electronic machinery. The only employer left, it seems, who still needs unattached, physically fit, 'macho' young labour is the army.

To be a worker now means to be an adult worker, an experienced worker. Employers almost exclusively want settled, responsible employees who can adapt to change on the job and don't require the expense of training (and thus girls find themselves losing in the job competition to the increasing number of married women returning to work). And if school leavers can no longer acquire work discipline simply by getting a job, then state agencies have to step in to provide it – hence the development of Youth Training Schemes.

The most significant consequence of youth unemployment, in short, is the reorganisation of the transition from school to work. If to become a 'young worker' once meant to take an important step towards adult status, now it means increasingly to be a trainee, one's adult status clearly postponed. Two aspects of this should be stressed in particular.

First, the sharpening differentiation between adult and young workers has a significant economic effect. The assumption now is that employers will only take on school leavers (whose inexperience supposedy makes them less productive and more troublesome than adult workers) if they are much cheaper. One purpose of the MSC training policy is to feed young people into the labour market (via state subsidies and the various work experience and job opportunity programmes) as **cheap** labour.

Second, as trainees, young workers have a distinctively low status in the work place itself. They are excluded from trade unions and collective bargaining, they are subject to school-like forms of discipline and control, they are, indeed, dependent on the state for work in the first place. Such 'work experience' is **not** a source of adult status.

To summarise: the direct consequence of wide-scale youth unemployment is to give school leavers a new institutional position, as cheap, dependent labour, clearly demarcated from both adult workers and their peers in further and higher education. This seems a very different position than that occupied by 1950s and 1960s working class teenagers, who had money in their pockets, jobs to choose from, were irresponsible and cocky as they set the leisure pace for everyone else.

Youth as Ideology

What are the implications of changing youth experience for the ideology of youth? In some respects youth unemployment simply widens the existing gap between the commercial image of youth (the poster pictures of freedom, mobility and affluence) and most young people's day-to-day experience of the constraints of work and home and neighbourhood. As David Downes showed in *The Delinquent Solution,* there was always a sector of working class youth for whom 'teenage culture' was inaccessible. Such young people lacked the resources for 'success' in teenage terms as well as for success in school or work terms, hence their 'delinquent solution' to the problems of prestige and self-esteem.

But it can also be argued that the public concern about youth unemployment (reflected in successive governments' youth policies) has had an effect on media images of youth more generally. The established tension between youth as ideal and youth as threat has been overlaid by a new awareness of youth as victim. Press and politicians refer routinely, for example, to 'a wasted generation', to young people being 'thrown on the scrapheap'. It is interesting to observe how young people are addressed as an audience (and as an interest group) by television's increasing number of 'youth programmes', which try to be both entertaining (in their emphasis on pop music and fashion and dance) and serious (in their concern with young people's difficulties in getting jobs or housing or leisure resources). The 1981 'riots', to cite another example, were interpreted not just as an extreme form of delinquent behaviour but also as an understandable, **political** response by young people to their economic and social situation. From being an object of adult envy, youth have become, it seems, an object of adult pity.

The End of Youth Culture?

The concept of 'youth culture' has always had a wider function in society than as simply a term of sociological description. It has acted too as a sort of public fantasy, a model for everyone of leisure consumption, of **how to have a good time**. This idea of youth culture has its origins in the 1920s when the middle class youth world of flappers and jazz and dance was first established as a media image. The youthful interest in fashion and change and up-to-dateness, young people's use of style to establish in-group membership, became themes for all consumption. Advertisers used youthful images of sexiness, sophistication and carelessness to sell goods which in reality had nothing to do with youth culture at all.

Youth culture, in short, is an aspect of a more general consumer culture in which people are encouraged to buy goods with the suggestion that their possession can keep you young. People have no real human or subsistence **need** to buy fashion clothes or furniture, to drink cocktails or Coca-Cola, to smoke or make-up, to choose one particular make of car rather than another. The purchase of such 'luxuries' is thus seen by advertisers as essentially irrational, based on fantasy not reason, and so, for the last fifty years, the 'irrationality' of adult pleasure has been sold in association with the spontaneity and **fun** of being young. This was the flappers' message in the 1920s and it was a message that spread down the social structure to the 'affluent 50s' and 'swinging 60s'.

The question is what happens to such advertising imagery when the meaning of youth as a social category shifts from irresponsibility and **choice** to uselessness and **constraint**, when the young are widely thought of not as an enviable consumer group but as a disturbing labour problem?

It's too soon to answer this question sensibly (and for the moment the commercial image of youth is still obvious in magazines and on advertising hoardings). But some people within the teenage industry itself (the pop and fashion business) are talking about 'the end of teenage' or 'the death of youth' and so one sociological comment should be made. As long as young people are defined and treated as a specific social category, so they will develop (according to their class and gender positions) a 'youth culture', a way of making sense of their situation. What, if anything, will change is that this youth culture will no longer play the part it has in the past for adults too.

Final Questions

Sociologists are no more able than anyone else to ignore common meanings of youth culture, and so it is not surprising, perhaps, that in Britain so much of the academic work on youth has been done by people (like myself) who were teenagers in the late 1950s and early 1960s, who grew up on rock 'n' roll and had their own fantasies of teenage life. But history doesn't stop for sociologists' convenience and it is worth remembering that the 'youth' who feature in the sociology books, the delinquents and affluent teenagers of the 1950s, the sub-culturalists of the 1960s, are now parents, as little able to help their children cope with youth unemployment as their parents were able to help them cope with teenage affluence.

Sociologists can learn from such parental doubts and anxieties. It is always tempting to take a set of categories developed to make sense of one historical moment and to apply them to another historical moment, as if sociological concepts had a permanent, ahistorical power. The implication of this approach to youth is that rising unemployment means rising sub-cultural activity, an increase in delinquency, a dole-queue version of traditional teenage culture. Is there evidence for such conclusions? On the whole (and despite the riots) Britain has absorbed the fact of permanent mass youth unemployment with remarkably little public difficulty (though what goes on within the privacy of the family is another question).

This doesn't mean, though, that there aren't significant changes going on in how young people interpret their situation. It can be argued that one effect of the recession has been to sharpen the class differences among the young. The 1960s notion of the 'classless' youth culture certainly seems irrelevant to the increasing educational gap between those young people who are being made 'relevant' to industry and those who are preparing for higher education, for professional, career qualifications. But it is also true that middle class youth, university and polytechnic graduates, are experiencing unemployment too. The 60s hippie ideal of a classless bohemia, a street culture of squats and music making, hustling and the black economy, political and social action, does still have an inner city presence and may, indeed, be growing. And precisely because working class school leavers don't now achieve adult status directly, through their individual efforts in the labour market, but have to move through the collective experience of training, so their lives are beginning to become more like those of students (one effect of unemployment is that more people than ever before are studying, in one way or another, in technical colleges). Such 'student' experience makes possible new sorts of youth organisation, new definitions and demands from youth as an interest not a consumer group. Is it in the 1980s that youth will become, finally, a **political** category?

Bibliography

Abrams, M. *The Teenage Consumer* (Routledge & Kegan Paul, London, 1959)

Allen, S. 'Some theoretical problems in the study of youth', *Sociological Review* 16, 1968

Becker, H. *Outsiders – Studies in the Sociology of Deviance* (Free Press, New York, 1963)

Berger, B. 'On the Youthfulness of Youth Culture', *Social Research*, 30, 1963

Brake, M. *The Sociology of Youth Culture and Youth Subcultures* (Routledge & Kegan Paul, London, 1980)

Burt, C. *The Young Delinquent* (University of London Press, London, 1925)

Casburn, M. *Girls Will Be Girls* (Women's Research and Resources Centre, London, 1979)

Cloward, R. and Ohlin, L. E. *Delinquency and Opportunity* (Free Press, New York, 1960)

Cohen, A. K. *Delinquent Boys – The Subculture of the Gang* (Collier-Macmillan, London, 1955)

Cohen, P. 'Subcultural Conflict and Working Class Community', *Working Papers in Cultural Studies* 2, 1972

Cohen, S. *Folk Devils and Moral Panics* (Paladin, London, 1973)

Coleman, J. S. *The Adolescent Society* (Free Press, New York, 1961)

Cowie, C. and Lees, S. 'Slags or Drags', *Feminist Review* 9, 1981

Cowie, J., Cowie, V. and Slater, E. *Delinquency in Girls* (Heinemann, London, 1968)

Downes, D. *The Delinquent Solution* (Routledge & Kegan Paul, London, 1966)

Eisenstadt, S. N. *From Generation To Generation* (Free Press, Chicago, 1956)

Fass, P. S. *The Damned and the Beautiful. American Youth in the 1920s* (Oxford University Press, New York, 1977)

Fisher, S. and Holder, S. *Too Much Too Young?* (Pan, London, 1981)

Frith, S. *Sound Effects. Youth, Leisure and the Politics of Rock'n'roll* (Constable, London, 1983)

Gillis, J. R. *Youth and History* (Academic Press, New York, 1974)

Greer, G. *The Female Eunuch* (Paladin, London, 1970)

Hall, S. and Jefferson, T. *Resistance Through Rituals* (Hutchinson, London, 1976)

Hall, S. et al *Policing the Crisis* (Macmillan, London, 1978)

Hebdige, D. *Subculture: The Meaning of Style* (Methuen, London, 1979)

Jephcott, P. *Girls Growing Up* (Faber, London, 1942)

Kitwood, T. *Disclosures to a Stranger* (Routledge & Kegan Paul, London, 1980)

Leonard, D. *Sex and Generation* (Tavistock, London, 1980)

McRobbie, A. 'Settling Accounts With Subculture', *Screen Education* 34, 1980

McRobbie, A. 'Working Class Girls and the Culture of Femininity', *Women Take Issue* (Hutchinson, London, 1978)

McRobbie, A. and McCabe, T. *Feminism for Girls* (Routledge & Kegan Paul, London, 1981)

Mannheim, K. *Essays in the Sociology of Knowledge* (Routledge & Kegan Paul, London, 1952)

Marsland, D. *Sociological Explorations in the Service of Youth* (NYB, Leicester, 1978)

Matza, D. and Sykes, G. M. 'Juvenile Delinquency and Subterranean Values' *American Sociological Review* 26, 1961

Matza, D. *Delinquency and Drift* (John Wiley, New York, 1964)

Matza, D. *Becoming Deviant* (Prentice-Hall, New Jersey, 1969)

Mays, J. B. *The Young Pretenders* (Michael Joseph, London, 1965)

Merton, R. K. 'Social Structure and Anomie' *American Sociological Review* 3, 1938

Miller, W. B. 'Lower Class Culture as a Generating Milieu of Gang Delinquency' *Journal of Social Issues* 14, 1958

Nagel, J. *Student Power* (Merlin, London, 1969)

Parker, H. *View From The Boys* (David and Charles, Newton Abbott, 1974)

Parsons, T. 'Age and Sex in the Social Structure of the United States', *American Sociological Review* 7, 1942

Pearson, G. *Hooligan: A History of Respectable Fears* (Macmillan, London, 1983)

Rees, T. L. and Atkinson, P. *Youth Unemployment and State Intervention* (Routledge & Kegan Paul, London, 1982)

Robins, D. and Cohen, P. *Knuckle Sandwich* (Penguin, London, 1978)

Rowbotham, S. *Woman's Consciousness, Man's World* (Penguin, London, 1973)

Sharpe, S. *Just Like A Girl* (Penguin, London, 1976)

Smart, C. and Smart, B. *Women, Sexuality and Social Control* (Routledge & Kegan Paul, London, 1978)

West, D. J. *The Young Offenders* (Penguin, London, 1967)

Whyte, W. F. *Street Corner Society* (University of Chicago Press, Chicago, 1943)

Willis, P. *Learning to Labour* (Saxon House, London, 1977)

Willmott, P. *Adolescent Boys of East London* (Routledge & Kegan Paul, London, 1966)

Section 5

The Sociology of the Mass Media

David Glover

Chapter One

Media Effects

The Martians Are Coming

> The girls... huddled around their radios trembling and weeping in each other's arms. They separated themselves from their friends only to take their turn at the telephone to make long distance calls to their parents, saying goodbye for what they thought might be the last time... Terror-stricken girls, hoping to escape from the Mars invaders, rushed to the basement of the dormitory.
>
> (Cantril, 1940, p. 53)

With these words an American college student, a victim of one of the most extraordinary collective delusions ever to have taken place, recalled her experience of a notorious radio broadcast and the fears it provoked in her and her family and friends. Over a million people were frightened or disturbed by Orson Welles' 1938 radio play *War of the Worlds* which dramatised an H. G. Wells' tale of an invasion from outer space with such terrifyingly convincing effect that people fled for their lives. So devastating was its impact that the rules governing broadcasting in the United States were changed to prevent anything like it from happening again.

This story symbolises much of our thinking about the influence the media have upon us. Many believe that television or the printed word can mould individual personalities or completely transform society like some genie in a magic bottle that has escaped our control. Orson Welles' power over his audience seems to sum up this feeling of impotence and it is hardly surprising that the story of the radio invasion is now deeply lodged in our folk-memories.

How and why so many people came to believe that they really were

371

being invaded by a strange race of creatures armed with heat ray guns and poisonous black gas is a question to which I will return later in this chapter. For the moment I simply want to note that the Welles' broadcast raises in a peculiarly vivid form the whole issue of the media's effects upon us. Like the Martians in the play, the media often appear in public debates as a kind of alien force poised to take over our lives and acting upon us without our being able to resist. Nowadays radio is seldom perceived as a very dangerous medium, but it is worth remembering that the fears which are currently voiced about television or video were once associated with the 'wireless'. The 'invasion from Mars' helps alert us to the fact that anxieties about the media have a history, and that the notion of their having powerful and all-pervasive effects upon us is far from new. To emphasise this point, consider the following:

> One powerful agent for the depraving of the boyish classes of our towns and cities is to be found in the cheap shows and theatres, which are so specially opened and arranged for the attraction and ensnaring of the young . . . it is not to be wondered at that the boy who is led on to haunt them becomes rapidly corrupted and demoralised, and seeks to be the doer of the infamies which have interested him as a spectator. (quoted in Murdock & McCron, 1979, p. 51)

Although the language is old – this passage was written in 1851 – the argument is still around today. Only the media have moved on. Instead of the theatre, our worries now focus upon television or video, though the corruption of the young continues to be a key theme.

What has tended to happen is that the arguments and anxieties associated with the culturally dominant media of the past have been re-directed as new media have come into existence. This pattern is reflected in the history of research into media effects. As we will see in the next section, the earliest mass media research reflected these long-standing fears.

The Hypodermic Syringe Model

The first studies of the mass media were based on the theory that their effects upon our lives were very simple and direct. For example, it was assumed that the mere portrayal of criminality by the media was enough to stimulate a rise in criminal behaviour amongst a vulnerable audience. This perspective came to be known as the 'hypodermic' theory. It saw media effects as like an injection into the veins of the audience, an injection that was usually harmful, though occasionally beneficial. Much of this research was preoccupied with the impact of the cinema, particularly on the young. Most famous of all were the studies financed by the Payne Fund, a body set up in New York in 1928 to look at the relationship between film-watching and the attitudes, emotions and behaviour of young people, especially the phenomenon of juvenile crime. Yet although these studies were very detailed, they were rather inconclusive. It was hard to demonstrate any consistent causal connection between cinema attendance and delinquency, and where links were found they were far from simple and were difficult to explain.

Despite its weaknesses the hypodermic syringe model has been extremely influential. Part of the reason for its appeal lies in the fact that its roots are to be found in ideas that have become deeply ingrained in modern societies. In the first place, the hypodermic model drew upon assumptions about social change that went back at least as far as the nineteenth century and which can be seen in the passage about the corruption of young boys by cheap popular theatres quoted above. It was assumed that the social upheavals associated with industrialisation had made people extremely vulnerable so that they were easily swayed by any attempt to grab their attention or provide them with novel experiences. Thus they were prey to political demagogues and readily duped by the new mass media. The reason for this vulnerability was that industrialisation had broken down the older, more settled communities in which people had a sense of belonging, but had failed to put anything in their place to recreate a feeling of order and identity. Instead society was increasingly becoming a mass of isolated individuals cut adrift from local social ties and with little to channel their energies or hold their desires in check. Hence it was called a 'mass society'. Echoes of this view can be found in social theorists as different as Alexis de Tocqueville and John Stuart Mill, and later Vilfredo Pareto and Karl Mannheim. Similar ideas can also be detected behind Durkheim's concept of anomie, with its notion of appetites and aspirations that are no longer restrained by society. In a mass society in which traditional forms of social control were seen to be breaking down, the mass media appeared as a powerful force controlling behaviour.

A second source of the hypodermic theory derived from the rise of behaviourism in psychology in the early years of this century. This school of thought saw all human action as modelled on the conditioned reflex so that one's personality consisted of nothing more than responses to stimuli in the individual's environment which formed stable and recognisable patterns of behaviour – hence the name 'behaviourism'. It therefore seemed to provide strong grounds for thinking that social action was heavily determined by external forces rather than being a matter of personal choice based upon social beliefs and knowledge. The mass media appeared to be an obvious candidate for any theory of the powerful stimuli to be found in modern society. Behaviourism thus dovetailed neatly with the pessimistic assumptions of the earlier 'mass society' theorists.

The weakness of this way of thinking about the media will be readily apparent. Audiences are assumed to be manipulable and dependent while the mass media's capacity to influence them is seen as enormous, the two being connected together by a relatively simple one-way mechanism of social learning. However the mass media affect us, it is clearly more complex than was ever imagined in the early days of research. Hypodermic theories are rarely found in their pure form today and current work which springs from this tradition has considerably modified the original model by bringing in more subtle social psychological processes of attitude formation, as in the theories of the American researcher Melvin DeFleur. Where this sort of thinking does survive is in public discussions about the media which are often haunted by the ghosts of theories that have long since passed away. There is a certain irony in this for, as two of its critics were quick to point out, the hypodermic theory was partly developed in the first place 'from an image of the potency of the mass media which was in the popular mind' (Katz & Lazarsfeld, 1955, p. 17). The hypodermic syringe model had a very narrow view of the media's audience. People were seen as passive receivers of the media's message. They had little or no say in the matter. They appeared to be overpowered by a mass media which simply injected its message. Yet audiences are made up of people who select and reject, make judgments and communicate with each other. These observations formed an important part of the 'two-step flow model' which will now be examined.

The Two-Step Flow Model

If the hypodermic theory was flawed by an unsophisticated and un-sociological view of the media's audience it was this major defect that its principal challengers set themselves to remedy. This point was emphasised from the very beginning when Elihu Katz and Paul Lazarsfeld gave their path-breaking book *Personal Influence* the sub-title *The Part Played by People in the Flow of Mass Communications*. They altered the whole direction of media research and founded a theoretical tradition which was to dominate media sociology in the post-war period and was still being described as 'the dominant paradigm in the field' as late as 1978 (Gitlin, 1978, p. 207). The origins of the paradigm go back to a study of the 1940 American presidential election carried out by Paul Lazarsfeld, a German émigré and a former mathematician who had switched to sociology and whose work was to revolutionise the analysis of social survey data. What the election study showed was that the impact of the media upon people's votes was far less than the hypodermic theory would lead one to expect. Only a quarter of the voters made up their minds during the campaign itself, and as many as 50% of all voters had not only decided who to vote for six months before the election, but had maintained their preference right up to polling day. Amongst those who did decide which way to vote during the campaign period it was not the political discussion in the media which influenced them so much as the opinions of what the study called 'molecular leaders', individuals whose views and ideas were respected and important in the voters' immediate social circle. Lazarsfeld believed that this finding warranted further investigation and so the election survey, appropriately entitled *The People's Choice*, was followed up with a study of how opinions were formed in 'a middle-sized American city' in Illinois, the results of which appeared in Katz and Lazarsfeld's *Personal Influence*.

The book confirmed and considerably refined Lazarsfeld's earlier discovery. Far from being an atomised mass of isolated individuals, society was pre-eminently a matter of *group* life (indeed Katz and Lazarsfeld wrote enthusiastically of 'the "rediscovery" of the primary group'), and it was how these groups were organised that counted in the formation of social attitudes. In other words, we are influenced by members of our family, our friends and co-workers and therefore those who direct and help form opinions are not special high status individuals but are found at every level of society. As Katz and Lazarsfeld put it 'opinion leadership is an integral part of the give-and-take of everyday personal relationships' and 'an opinion leader can best be thought of as a group member playing a key communication role' (p. 33).

This seems to leave the mass media out in the cold, almost a complete reversal of the hypodermic theory. However, the media were found to be important, but in a different way than had been previously thought. It was the opinion leaders who tended to be susceptible to the media and it was through them that the media's effects were transmitted. In the two-step flow model of mass communication ideas and attitudes are said 'to flow *from* radio and print *to* opinion leaders and *from them* to the less active sections of the population' (p. 32). This process is by no means automatic however, and Katz and Lazarsfeld had a far more modest conception of media effects than earlier theorists, one which emphasised personal *decisions* made by opinion leaders as a result of their greater *exposure* to the media than non-leaders. In practice the link between exposure and decisions was quite complex. While opinion leaders usually devoted more time to books and magazines, radio and the cinema, they differed in the extent to which they gave credit to these experiences in making up their own minds. In each of the four main areas in which opinion leaders influenced the attitudes and choices of others – in the buying of food and household goods, in fashion, in going to see a film, and in judgments about current affairs and politics – the results suggested that there was a unique pattern of interpersonal contact with distinct leaders in each sphere. Opinion leaders typically saw their decisions as the outcome of other influences besides the mass media, and only in the area of fashion did they self-consciously rely upon the media in forming their ideas. In short, this research suggested that the impact of the media was far from being as straightforward and direct as previous theories had claimed.

Whereas the hypodermic model saw the media as decisively shaping the ideas and behaviour of an audience made up of individuals who were easily swayed, the two-step flow model revealed the importance of the social relationships amongst audience members in determining their response to the mass media. Katz and Lazarsfeld identified opinion leaders whose views were said by others to be particularly influential. They showed that these key individuals were more exposed to the media than the rest of the population, and that the effects of this exposure were both varied and subtle.

This two-step model has been criticised for dividing media audiences too readily into active and passive members, and also for simplifying the process of influence unnecessarily. As one critic has pointed out 'there is absolutely no reason why there should not be a three-, four-, or five-step flow of communications or more' (Howitt, 1982, p. 21). Against this it should be remembered that opinion leaders only lead on specific issues so that the distinction between leaders and non-leaders is a very fluid one; in fact, this did prompt Katz and Lazarsfeld to suggest that the chains of influence might be even more complex than their evidence was able to show.

A more damaging criticism of this approach is that the authors narrowly equated power with one person's influence over another. A different view of power would stress the importance of political and economic institutions like the State and big business. Radical critics of the two-step flow model have argued that it ignores the fact that the ownership and control of the mass media have become more tightly concentrated than ever before and thus are a potent instrument of class domination (Gitlin, 1978). These questions will be examined in Chapter 3.

The Uses and Gratifications Approach

The two-step flow model did open the way for a better understanding of audiences in the study of media effects, and this was taken up in greater detail by subsequent researchers. In an aside Katz and Lazarsfeld had suggested that it would be worth investigating 'the different kinds of "uses" to which the media are put by leaders . . . as compared with non-leaders' (p. 320). They argued that people actively draw upon the media in order to satisfy various needs and interests – thus, for example, reading popular fiction was particularly marked amongst women who led narrow social lives and this served as 'a substitute for socializing' (p. 378). Later writers tended to abandon Katz and Lazarsfeld's focus on opinion leaders and instead concentrated solely upon the uses made of the media and the satisfaction derived from them by audiences as a whole. Although there are several distinct versions of this theory all of them start from a view of human beings purposefully striving to shape their lives in accord with the needs which they have. A complex psychological make-up is usually assumed, with lower level needs, such as the need for safety and security, and higher level ones like the need for love, acceptance and self-realisation. It is the latter which figure most prominently in people's relation to the mass media. For example, McQuail, Blumler and Brown (1972) have argued that soap operas like *Coronation Street* meet the social need of companionship for some people. 'You feel you know them' was a typical comment from one of the women interviewed about the serial's characters, a remark which suggests the close interweaving of fiction with real life.

Some of the uses made of the media might seem very humdrum but are nevertheless important to the individuals involved: buying and reading a newspaper is a ritual which organises and structures the beginning of one's day, as well as providing up-to-the-minute information and an interpretation of public events. In addition the purchase of a paper like *The Times* might be used to confer social prestige upon the reader. To take another example, Radio Three might be used as musical wallpaper, a background to one's daily tasks, or alternatively as a source of relaxation giving a deep aesthetic experience. The same medium may have different *functions* depending upon the kind of person who is using it and what his or her motives are.

Some critics have argued that uses and gratifications models represent a retreat from the original gains of the two-step flow approach since they are concerned so much with the individual psychology of audience members that they are in danger of losing the social dimension altogether. Not all uses and gratifications models can be dismissed in this way, however. For example, Rosengren and Windahl's (1972) study of media use in two southern Swedish towns tried to test the idea that newspapers, radio and television were turned to by some people as a 'functional alternative' when the possibilities for 'face-to-face interaction with real, living human beings' were either blocked or reduced. This meant extensive investigation into the life-styles and behaviour patterns of audiences. Yet even where this is the case it can be argued that such models are far too speculative to be of much value. They usually take the results of audience interviews as evidence of basic, underlying human needs as if this was all the proof that was necessary. That this is not so is shown by the wide variety in the lists of needs that researchers have produced, there being little agreement about what these basic needs are. Again, users of the mass media are said to be extremely purposeful in their viewing, reading or listening. However, generalisations of this kind ignore the extent to which activities like watching television are often casual and un-planned. And where particular programmes are sought out it may be more a matter of their general popularity and reputation (as reflected in TV audience ratings) than of individuals with certain specific needs trying to gratify them with appropriate programmes.

The uses and gratifications approach was, however, a new departure in the study of the mass media and their audiences. It emphasised the selective way in which people make the media a part of their everyday lives and by so doing are able to satisfy a variety of social needs and desires.

Effects? What Effects?

Both the two-step flow model and the uses and gratifications approaches arose in reaction to the hypodermic syringe theory and, as a result, they share certain common features despite their differences. Where the hypodermic theory overstated the media's impact by con-ceiving of effects too simplistically and was easily discredited by a lack of evidence, its two successors tended to lose sight of the media having any real effect at all. In the two-step flow model the media's influence was placed at one remove from the majority of the audience and even for opinion leaders the connection was a weak one, a matter of 'exposure'. By contrast, the uses and gratifications approaches put the media almost entirely at the audience's beck and call since it was for individuals themselves to determine what role the media were to play in their lives. In both cases effects coming directly from the media were seen to be on the whole negligible.

This was the orthodox view in the sociology of the mass media until the late 1960s. By this time, however, things were slowly starting to change. Quite why this happened would take another book, but certainly, as so often in scientific thinking, the accumulation of weaknesses and discrepancies in existing theories together with the rise of new styles of research combined to lead to a paradigm shift (see Kuhn, 1962). In the rest of this section, I will look at some of these weaknesses.

As Katz and Lazarsfeld themselves pointed out in their book *Personal Influence* 'there are a variety of possible effects that the mass media may have upon society'. Most research, their own included, has been preoccupied with only one: short-term changes in attitudes and opinion. In Stuart Hall's words 'switches of choice – between advertised consumer goods or between presidential candidates – were viewed as a paradigm case of measureable influence and effect' (Hall, 1982, p. 59). This gives the rather misleading impression 'that the media are quite ineffectual' which is only true for one kind of effect. There are other kinds, 'predominantly of a long term sort' which, as Katz and Lazarsfeld admit 'have barely been looked into'. These 'promise to reveal the potency of the mass media' much more than the short-run effects previously studied (p. 19).

Why is it so misleading to concentrate upon changes in attitudes? Partly this is because the concept of 'attitudes' that has been used is a very limited one, as is shown by the way in which they have been investigated. A before-and-after methodology was employed in which people were asked about their changes of mind on a particular issue, and, if so, how they had been influenced. Where their attitudes remained unaltered, the assumption was made that they had not been influenced. Not only does this ignore the possibility 'that a respondent had begun to "change her mind" on a given issue, only to be persuaded back to the original position by personal influences, or, directly, by mass media'. It also fails to consider the relationship between the media and the original set of beliefs, values and opinions which form the baseline against which changes in attitude are measured (Gitlin, 1978, p. 215).

At the very least we can expect the media to play a key role in creating a web of opinions and beliefs around new issues, especially where there are no alternative sources of information. Indeed, Katz and Lazarsfeld themselves reported findings that were quite at odds with their general argument. Thus, 58% of the changes of opinion they studied 'were apparently made without involving any remembered personal contact, and were, very often, dependent upon the mass media' (p. 142). Similar discrepancies have been detected in the earlier study of the 1940 American election. What all this suggests is that the idea of there being some kind of direct media effect was abandoned much too quickly.

Cultural Effects Theory

More recent work has led to a re-thinking of the nature of effects. Cultural effects theory leads us to see the media in a different light and to draw fresh insights from older studies (see Tudor, 1979).

This approach assumes that the media can have important effects on their audiences. However, these effects are not the immediate changes of opinion studied by earlier researchers, but rather the slow, cumulative build-up of beliefs and values through which we understand the world. For example, feminist writers have argued that the kinds of images of women with which the media surround us have had a major influence on our ideas of what women are like and how they should behave. In order to study the influence of the media in terms of cultural effects it is important to analyse the content of the media. We have to see how these images are put together or constructed: to ask, for example, how such types as 'the dumb blonde' in TV films are created out of styles of dress, speech mannerisms, and the like. To understand this fully we would also need to analyse the plot and the portrayal of characters in a story which used this kind of figure. We return to some of these issues in the next chapter.

Cultural effects theory does not look at such images in isolation. The influence of the media will also depend upon the social situation of the audience. For example, the same film shown to working class teenagers and middle class, middle-aged businessmen may well have very different effects on the two audiences. They will interpret the content of the film in terms of their social class subcultures, with reference to their social situations, and in terms of the experiences of their age group. The cultural effects approach seeks to bring together both the way in which meanings are created by the media and the way in which these relate differently to the cultures of particular social groups.

The Return of the Martians

Orson Welles' Martians have already put in an appearance earlier in the book. Now I want to re-introduce you to them in order to show how the idea of a cultural effect can be used to make sense of the way the media work.

On the face of it the story of the 'invasion from Mars' would seem to fit in well with the hypodermic theory: a single immediate and dramatic effect. Certainly at the time when Hadley Cantril's study of these events was published in 1940 this theory was still the dominant perspective, although, significantly, it was on the brink of a severe decline. It is, however, a tribute to the carefulness of Cantril's research that his book *The Invasion from Mars* shows just how complex the real explanation was. Despite the fact that the idea of a cultural effect was not developed until much later several points in his analysis seem to give support to this idea. To justify this claim I shall have to sketch in the background to the broadcast.

First of all, it is important to be clear about the scale of the panic that ensued. The Orson Welles play was part of a regular series, 'The Mercury Theatre on the Air', carried by the Columbia Broadcasting System, America's largest radio network. This meant an audience of six million people spread right across the country from California to New York State. Of these about a million, or one-sixth of those listening, believed it to be a real invasion. What we need to know, therefore, is not just why the broadcast had the effect it did, but why only some listeners were taken in and not others.

The core of Cantril's investigation was based upon detailed interviews with 135 people who had heard the broadcast, of whom over 100 had been upset by it, together with the results of two large national surveys of people who had tuned in to the broadcast. One factor seems to have been especially important in distinguishing those who panicked from those who did not: namely, that the former had a tendency to begin listening to the programme after it had started. A national survey carried out by CBS showed that only 12% of those who had listened from the very beginning were misled. Tuning in late was as commonplace then amongst radio audiences as it probably is now for television viewers. The listeners cannot choose which programmes will be made available and when, but must pick from a pre-arranged menu.

On the night of October 30th 1938 the Mercury Theatre was competing with one of the most popular radio variety shows of the week. People would typically switch stations after the act they wanted to hear had finished and the advertising jingles were just starting, so that they caught the Mercury Theatre broadcast well after the introductory announcements were over. Many of those who were alarmed at what they heard then phoned their non-listening friends who also tuned in, which meant that the panic quickly snowballed.

A second main strand in the explanation of the panic lies in the way in which the Mercury Theatre made use of long-standing cultural expectations about news. At the time of the 'invasion from Mars' nearly three times as many people believed in the dependability of radio news compared to that of newspapers, particularly because of the growing importance of the special news bulletin. Welles and his players tried to achieve an impressive and convincing realism in their broadcast: they virtually started from the question, 'How would a radio news bulletin report a real invasion if one occurred?' and constructed their programme around the answer. As Cantril notes 'the broadcast was so realistic for the first few minutes that it was almost credible to even relatively sophisticated and well informed listeners' (pp. 67–8). The technique the broadcasters used was to move gradually from statements that were quite believable to ones that would be very hard to accept taken in isolation. Thus the story started with reports of 'several explosions of incandescent gas, occurring at regular intervals on the planet Mars' and led on to an account of falling meteorites, setting the scene for the sighting of alien beings. Throughout the drama lifelike details were subtly interspersed to indicate that the narrative was situated in real time and space: references to the weather, 'eastern standard time' and well-known geographical locations. As one of those interviewed was at pains to stress '*if they had mentioned any other places but streets right around here*, I would not have been so ready to believe' (p. 73). In fact, those interviewed in the northern New Jersey area, where the towns mentioned in the broadcast were situated, were far more likely to panic than those who lived further away. To add to the realism, the events in the play were constantly being authenticated by what seemed to be expert witnesses: scientists, army officers and high-ranking government officials.

Finally, the nature of the historical moment in which the 'invasion' happened played its part too. America in the late 1930s was an insecure and anxious nation. Still recovering from the shock of the 1929 financial crash, 'probably more important than anything else' in leading to a feeling of demoralisation, Americans were beset by political worries as they watched the rise of Fascism in Europe and mentally prepared themselves for the growing international crisis to erupt into war (p. 203). Between August and October 1938 radio broadcasts were frequently interrupted by news bulletins about the increasing likelihood of war and, as Cantril comments, 'probably never before in the history of broadcasting had so many people in this country been glued to their sets' (p. 159). Not only were people expecting bad news, but some sort of foreign attack could not be ruled out. Even to those who had listened to the play from the very beginning it was far from implausible to believe that the play itself had been interrupted by a news bulletin, as many did. As a result, legislation was passed to prevent the imitation of news broadcasts for dramatic purposes.

Cantril's argument, then, is that these social factors – the manipulation of the conventions of radio news, together with a generalised sense of uncertainty and hopelessness which had been festering for a decade – combined to inhibit what he calls people's normal 'critical ability', producing a startling, albeit temporary, shock. Critical ability simply refers to the capacity for checking one's experience against other sources of information. Some people either checked badly or failed to check what was happening at all – thus they would turn to other frightened listeners for confirmation of what they had heard generating a new and more intensely collective form of fear in the process. Cantril rejects any claim that the panic can be explained by the innate stupidity or neuroticism of the audience precisely because critical ability is not something which is innate but 'is the result of a particular environment' which has formed the individual. Thus one listener who was not taken in found that the information about the army did not square with his own army experience, even though 'it all sounded perfectly real' (pp. 90-1).

Cantril's research suggests that the 'invasion from Mars' panic can be seen as an example of a cultural effect by the media. It was the life-like quality of the broadcast combined with the social and cultural situation of the listeners which brought about the scare. A panic 'occurs when some highly cherished, rather commonly accepted value is threatened and when no certain elimination of the threat is in sight'. Here the value placed on security and human life was threatened and the 'news' about the 'invasion' offered no hope of the threat being lifted. Cantril argues that the fear triggered off by the panic was 'latent in the general population, not specific to the persons who happened to participate in it'. It was intensified by 'the discrepancy between the whole superstructure of economic, social and political practices and beliefs, and the basic and derived needs of individuals' typical of the troubled 1930s (pp. 199-204). In other words, people's needs were not being met in US society of the 1930s. The tension and anxiety that resulted fuelled the panic. Thus to understand the effect of the media, the relationship between its content, its audience and the social context must be examined.

Mods and Rockers: A Moral Panic

The second example illustrating the idea of a cultural effect is a more recent one – although not recent enough to be considered truly contemporary. Stan Cohen's book *Folk Devils and Moral Panics* was already a bit of an historical curiosity when it appeared in 1972, for the youth groups of the mid-sixties which he described had long since disappeared. Nevertheless his work has become a classic study of the way in which the media contributes to the creation of deviant behaviour.

Cohen's study was inspired by those interactionist theories which draw attention to societal reaction or labelling in their explanations of deviance. Here the stress is upon the way in which deviant acts are identified and publicised by society at large, or powerful groups within it, and thus with 'the *nature, emergence, application* and *consequences* of deviancy labels' (Plummer, 1979, p. 88). Cohen is therefore less concerned with looking for the causes or motives lying behind deviant behaviour as such. Instead he is interested in trying to see how these acts are picked out for special censure and the influence which this has upon the likelihood of further acts occurring. The use and application of deviancy labels not only allows the majority of people to make sense of social life by charting the boundary between right and wrong, it also may produce the very behaviour it is used to condemn – not least by contributing to and confirming the deviant's feeling of self-identity once an initial act has been labelled.

The mass media have an important role in developing the labels by which social problems are publicly recognised. Typically such problems are conveyed to us as a conflict between 'goodies' and 'baddies', or heroes and villains. The hue and cry against such moral outcasts, which is likely to be intensified when society is undergoing a crisis, resembles the old practice of witch-hunting with its scapegoating and persecution. The result is that the social problems represented by modern 'folk devils' become magnified out of all proportion.

The beginning of the Mods and Rockers phenomenon occurred in Clacton, a seaside resort which had traditionally attracted young people from the tougher parts of London, despite the fact that the range of amenities it offered was small. Bad weather meant bad business for local shopkeepers and boredom for the young people, intensifying an atmosphere of mutual suspicion. One wet weekend in Easter 1964 trouble started when 'a few groups started scuffling on the pavements and throwing stones at each other'. Over the weekend there were broken windows, wrecked beach huts and a great deal of noisy riding around on bikes and scooters (p. 29). Though the nature of the disturbance was fairly minor the local police were taken by surprise by the sheer numbers of young people on the streets.

Cohen argues that the vocabulary used by the media wildly inflated any threat these events presented. Even the Assistant Editor of the *Daily Mirror* later acknowledged that these incidents had been 'a little over-reported'. The *Daily Telegraph's* headline proclaimed: 'Day of Terror by Scooter Groups', and the *Daily Express*: 'Youngsters Beat Up Town – 97 Leather Jacket Arrests'. Cohen attempted to gauge the accuracy of the reporting by the national press by comparing it with that of the local papers which gave more detail and avoided making statements that their readers would obviously recognise as false or misleading.

There are three main types of over-reporting: exaggeration or distortion, prediction, and symbolization. *Exaggeration* takes the form of over-estimating such features as the numbers of people involved or the scale of the damage. Emotive language such as 'riot', 'orgy of destruction', 'siege' or 'beat up the town' is used and crucial facts are misrepresented. For example, Cohen's study shows that much emphasis was given to motor-bikes and scooters, yet these were in a minority and 'the majority of young people present came down by train or coach or hitched' (p. 35). Similarly, the reports of violence and vandalism were overwritten. At Clacton just twenty-four of the ninety-seven arrested were charged, and only a couple of these were charged with offences involving violence.

These inflated accounts of specific events are also projected into the future in the form of a *prediction* that there will be a repeat performance. For example, witnesses may be asked leading questions about what will happen next time, thus helping to stimulate a self-fulfilling prophecy. Through *symbolization* a whole wealth of associations are built up around certain words and the styles and individuals to which they refer. The Mods' fur-collared anoraks and scooters became visual signs of delinquency and 'became sufficient in themselves to stimulate hostile and punitive reactions' from police and public. Because of the publicity value of labels like 'mod' or 'punk' they are often dubiously applied by the press as a technique for arousing readers' interest. For example, a 1964 headline 'Terror Comes to English Resorts. Mutilated Mod Dead in Park' actually referred to the stabbing of a man in his mid-thirties in a park in the 'resort' of Birmingham!

Cohen argues that the take-off from fairly trivial, if unpleasant, happenings to a full-scale societal alarm constitutes what he calls a 'moral panic'. This has two sides to it. The sparks of the initial deviant behaviour are fanned into something far more serious by lurid reporting which in turn generates an increase in deviance. At the same time representatives of what Cohen terms 'the control culture' – the police, the courts, and members of the local community – start to step up their response. They become less tolerant of flamboyant styles of dress and behaviour amongst young people and are sensitised to be constantly on the look-out for hooliganism. In the atmosphere of hysteria which is created innocent individuals may easily be harassed or even arrested, and the increased activity on the part of the control culture is itself taken as showing the seriousness of the problem. The control culture at such moments is likely to be extended beyond routine law enforcement as new institutions like local action committees come into being and questions about the state of the nation are asked in parliament. The spread of deviance due to the attention it receives and the escalation in the reaction to it from the control culture feed on each other to produce an 'amplification spiral' in which each new occurrence adds to the problem and confirms each of the participants in what they are doing. While a moral panic is by no means inevitable in such circumstances, once started it is difficult to stop. In this case a cycle of holiday disturbances was set in motion across England which continued until 1967 by which time Mods and Rockers as social phenomena were practically dead.

Cohen used letters to the press and the minutes of council and parliamentary debates to document the societal reaction. He also interviewed members of the public, including a survey of attitudes amongst those who were formally concerned with the problem of delinquency: headmasters, lawyers, magistrates and youth workers. As Cohen himself admits, this was the least satisfactory part of his research in that it was not a comprehensive study of public opinion, but his results do make some interesting points. The analysis of the letters suggested that the Mods and Rockers were a symbol for 'a whole pattern in which pregnant schoolgirls, CND marches, beatniks, long hair, contraceptives in slot machines, purple hearts and smashing up telephone kiosks were all inextricably intertwined' (pp. 54–5). The interviews reflected this generally negative view of Mods and Rockers, but were far less alarmist. Indeed, many people were 'explicitly critical of the role of the media' (p. 69). Cohen's samples were very small and the questions he asked were fairly limited, but they do suggest that the reactions in society at large are not all of a piece – people had reservations about the media's portrayal of young people based on their own beliefs and experiences, despite their general acceptance of media imagery.

Cohen draws the following conclusions from his research. 'Folk devils', in this case Mods and Rockers, are central to the creation of a 'moral panic'. A 'moral panic' occurs when people fear that the major values and institutions of society are under attack, as many did in Britain in the mid-1960s. Young people fit the bill as 'folk devils', 'visible reminders of what we (youth especially) should not be'. They are easy to identify, relatively powerless and it is fairly simple to exaggerate certain aspects of their behaviour so as to make them appear as a threat to society. They become scapegoats, an easy target for the fear and hate of many people in the wider society. The media play an important role in whipping up moral panics, identifying folk devils, amplifying their deviance, and providing targets for popular anxieties. Again the effects of the media are explained in terms of their audience and the social context.

So far we have looked at two examples of cultural effects: Cantril's study of 'the invasion from Mars' and Cohen's work on moral panics in the mid-sixties. Both suggest that cultural effects are far from uniform: in complex industrial societies media effects will partly be shaped by the social situation and experience of audience members. For example, our sense of identity as a man or woman, one's feeling of class membership or one's loyalty to one's town or region are all likely to colour our response to what we find in the media. Yet neither of the studies examines this source of variation in cultural effects in any detail. This suggests that a more sophisticated version of the cultural effects model is required, one which takes account of the social variety of the audience. This can be seen from the work of David Morley.

Researching Audience Response

David Morley's research is one of the best recent attempts to study the variation in audience response to the media. In a project on the reception of the TV current affairs programme 'Nationwide' he has considerably refined our knowledge of the cultural meaning of television. This returns us to a point made earlier in relation to Cantril's work on 'the invasion from Mars': that the power which a symbol or message possesses will derive from the social and cultural context in which it is seen or heard, in that case from the anxieties of a demoralised pre-war America.

In his book *The 'Nationwide' Audience* (1980) Morley shows how careful and sensitive interviewing can reveal differences in audience response that are neither random nor purely personal but systematically tied in with one's place in the social structure. Morley carried out group discussions with 29 different sets of people after letting them watch a video recording of *Nationwide* programmes. The groups were deliberately chosen to represent a wide range of social and educational backgrounds and usually consisted of between five and ten people. The decision to go for group interviews followed from the conviction that it was misleading to talk to individuals outside of any social context. The groups were made up of people who were peers in some respect and, because they were based on classes in schools, colleges or universities, the groups had been in existence for some time. They included bank managers, full-time trade union officials, apprentice printers, engineers and metallurgists and general literacy students. Morley sought to conduct the interviews in as non-directive a way as possible, allowing his respondents to define the situation for themselves and to express their views naturally. Only in the later stages did he move towards more specific and more probing questions.

A few of the group discussions can be singled out to illustrate his findings. For example, what is striking about the groups of bank managers interviewed is their complete acceptance of the content of the programme. Their criticisms were chiefly directed at the programme's style or what has come to be called its 'mode of address' – that is the way it puts its message across to us. *Nationwide's* mode of address was determinedly populist and down-to-earth in its approach, representing ordinary people against experts, officials and 'red tape'. It was precisely this to which the bank managers objected, finding it 'embarrassing' and 'patronising' and 'talking down . . . even to the lowest paid worker' (pp. 106–7). By contrast, a group of shop stewards were approving of this populist style. However, they were so incensed by the implicit assumptions behind what was being said in the programme that they produced a critical running commentary while they were viewing it. For them, *Nationwide's* treatment of the 1977 Budget made it sound 'as if everyone's aspiring to be middle management' (pp. 112–118). As a final example, a group of young black students at a college of further education found the programme irrelevant to their world. As Morley points out 'their particular experience of family structures among a black, working class, inner city community is simply not accounted for' (pp. 122). Thus, when they criticise the programme for not dealing with the average family, in terms of their experience of families this was true. Their criticisms struck out at one of *Nationwide's* proudest claims: that it represented the national community of individual citizens. The liveliness and immediacy cultivated by the language of 'Nationwide' passed these young black people by and consequently they found the programme was soporific and dull. They did not feel themselves a part of the 'people' *Nationwide* was supposedly representing. Instead they saw it as portraying a nation of 'middle class shoppers and businessmen' (p. 118).

Morley argues that the kinds of audience responses he discovered can be broadly categorised into three main types, according to how the broadcast is 'read' or understood: (i) viewers can endorse the dominant common-sense values built into the programme which tacitly justify the status quo, (ii) they can generally accept the meaning of the programme as given but seek to modify or adjust it by making exceptions or qualifications in line with their own social situation, or (iii) they can oppose it. Morley refers to these respectively as dominant, negotiated and oppositional readings or decodings of the programme. There are also variations *within* each of these types of readings. Clearly the bank managers and the shop stewards represent the extremes of acceptance and opposition, yet the black students too produced their own oppositional reading of the programme different from that made by the shop stewards. While the black students and the shop stewards can be said to share a common class position, argues Morley, the precise character of their response derives from variations in ideas and experiences, in one case from trade union radicalism and in the other from black youth culture.

Morley's work makes a number of important points. Audiences are not passive receivers of media messages. They actively interpret what they see and hear. To understand their interpretations we must analyse both the content of the media and the social backgrounds and experience of audience members. Media effects are the result of a complex interaction between these factors.

Violence and the Media

Now that I have given an outline of what is involved in talking about cultural effects and looked at some of its implications for research I want to return to an issue mentioned earlier, that of the impact of violence in the media. As I said then, this is a perennial debate. Because of the indignation it excites amongst people and because of the questions it raises about the social responsibility of the media it hits the headlines again and again, with each new research study being treated as a human interest story in its own right. Part of the problem is that there is so much research and most of it is inconclusive and contradictory. In the remainder of this chapter I want to look at some of the difficulties with this research and to see if we can use the notion of a cultural effect to help us assess its strengths and weaknesses.

Problems of Method

It is easy to get lost in the maze of research and some commentators have yielded to the temptation of supposing that it is a hopeless venture to even try to prove that such effects exist. TV campaigner Mary Whitehouse, speaking in 1970, recommended that we should trust to the certainty of commonsense instead, for it tells us 'that the screening of violence, horror, shock and obscenity into the home ... can have nothing but a destructive effect upon our sensitivities and our society' (quoted in Tracey and Morrison, 1979, p. 85). One of the reasons why this view is so appealing is precisely because research into media effects is very difficult to carry out.

Three different sources of data have been used to investigate the effects of the portrayal of violence on the screen. These are clinical case studies, laboratory experiments and field studies. None of them is foolproof and to some extent their employment depends upon the perspective from which one is working.

As Eysenck and Nias have pointed out, the clinical case study 'is popularly regarded as the most convincing and impressive, but is scientifically of least interest' (Eysenck and Nias, 1980, p. 65). This approach looks at the biographies of individuals who have been convicted of anti-social acts which seem to have been influenced by particular films or programmes. Now such a line of investigation seems to have a great deal of plausibility. When a 17-year old boy tries to murder his father with a meat cleaver after watching a film on TV in which a boy kills his father, it is hard not to be both shocked and convinced, especially when the boy confesses to the police: 'It's just that when I watch television I sometimes imagine myself committing murders and thinking I can get away with it' (quoted in Eysenck and Nias, p. 67). But a moment's reflection will make us want to ask for more proof. Might this not be a case of a seriously disturbed individual who is likely to act violently anyway, and for whom television is little more than an excuse? After all, the very fact that this is an exceptional case and that the overwhelming majority of young viewers are not influenced in this way might make us wonder whether other factors are not at work here. The case study method can assemble much interesting information but is never likely to be conclusive simply because it does not allow us to compare similar individuals and to tease out why some people seem to be susceptible while most are not.

This strongly suggests that in order to study the effect of violence in the media we need to devise controlled experiments in which conditions can be carefully managed by the investigator so as to isolate the factors in which she or he is interested and assess whether any of them is causing a change in behaviour. In other words, we try to find out what will happen in a highly specific set of circumstances and generalise from our findings to other situations. Laboratory experiments in social science have largely been the province of psychologists, and fall outside the scope of this book. From a sociological standpoint their precision of method is achieved at the cost of excluding the relevant details of real social settings so that behaviour in the laboratory is highly artificial. *The Williams Report on Obscenity and Film Censorship* which appeared in 1979 found the evidence provided by experimental studies subject to severe drawbacks. It noted that 'since criminal and antisocial behaviour cannot itself, for both practical and ethical reasons, be experimentally produced or controlled, the observations must be made on some surrogate, or related behaviour, often expressed on a representational object, in some fictional or "pretend" context' (Williams, 1981, p. 65). For example, in experimental studies of the imitation of violence by children after watching films or TV, special toys or dolls are given to the children and their behaviour towards them is used as a measure of the programme's effect. A comparison is made between the level of aggressiveness towards the dolls of those children who had been exposed to the programme and those who had not. The difficulty here is that the dolls have been deliberately designed to invite rough play and are therefore hardly a true guide to interpersonal violence. Indeed, those children who have prior experience of the dolls seem to engage in less imitative aggression than others. A further problem is that only the effect of short doses of film or TV violence can be investigated in this way if people are not to become permanent experimental subjects. Thus as Eysenck and Nias admit 'it is not ... possible to study the effect of years of exposure to television under laboratory conditions' (Eysenck and Nias, 1980, p. 75). Long-term effects could only be studied as a series of brief exposures to violent material, a solution which they accept is a compromise.

Field studies comprise a variety of methods, including the use of observation, interviews and questionnaires, but all aim at getting close to social behaviour as it naturally happens. Compared to the experiment they are very inexact since it is hard to select people for study in such a way as to be sure that the results obtained were due to one particular cause rather than a large number of other possible factors. In order to meet criticisms of this kind some of the more positivist researchers have tried to approximate to experimental rigour as closely as possible when designing their studies. An example of a field study which does this is discussed in the following section.

William Belson: TV and Teenage Violence

In his book *Television Violence and the Adolescent Boy* (1978) William Belson carried out in-depth interviews with 1,565 boys in London aged between 12 and 17 years. The purpose of this large-scale field study, which was funded by the US Columbia Broadcasting System, was to test the hypothesis that the boys' exposure to television violence was a cause of their involvement in acts of violence. The research design he used was extremely sophisticated and complex. Firstly, he attempted to eliminate alternative explanations by matching the boys in his sample on a wide variety of factors which might conceivably have caused an increase in violent behaviour, and then systematically comparing groups that were alike except for one single characteristic, much as one would do in a controlled experiment. Secondly, he gathered his data in three stages in order that the answers to his questions could be checked and cross-checked by obtaining information in different ways and under different conditions. For example, the boys were interviewed both at home with their parents and individually at a research centre. By comparing boys who had had above-average exposure to television violence with those who had only a low exposure, Belson claimed strong support for his hypothesis. Thus because 'high exposure to television violence increases the degree to which boys engage in serious violence' he felt confident in recommending that 'steps should be taken as soon as possible to achieve a substantial reduction in the total amount of violence being presented on television' (Belson, 1978, pp. 15–20).

For all the undoubtedly painstaking effort that went into this research (Belson even sees fit to mention that the interviews 'spanned both hot and cold weather'), it has attracted its fair share of criticism. Some social scientists have been frankly incredulous of Belson's finding that boys who were heavily exposed to television violence committed 49% more acts of serious violence than those who had little exposure. So strong are the claims that Belson makes that it is worth looking in more detail at the problems that his work faces.

In the first place, there are inconsistencies in his results which are never really explained. For example, not only does he show that very violent acts are correlated with watching a lot of television violence, his findings also reveal a correlation between these acts and *all* television viewing. Unfortunately we never really learn why this is so. Similarly, the link between violent behaviour and TV violence is far from being as straightforward as Belson sometimes suggests. Thus, whilst the amount of violent behaviour rises the more violent TV is watched, this relationship reaches a peak and then declines. In other words, as Dennis Howitt has pointed out, it is those who watch a moderate amount of violent TV who are actually the most violent in their behaviour, and 'heavy and light viewers of TV violence alike are less aggressive than middle range viewers'. As Howitt also notes, this means that 'it is equally logical to argue that we can reduce aggression in society by *increasing* the amount of violence watched as by decreasing it' (Howitt, 1982, pp. 98–9).

A further set of problems concern the measurements that Belson took in order to assess the violent behaviour of the boys and the level of violence in TV programmes. Murdock and McCron have argued that both are suspect, particularly because they rely very heavily on memory. To find out how exposed the boys were to televised violence Belson presented them with a list of over one hundred programmes shown between one and twelve years earlier and asked them how many times they remembered seeing them. This has the drawback of producing data that are based in several cases on recollections of viewing experiences which took place when the boys were only a few years old, even allowing for the imperfections of ordinary memory. Moreover, Belson attempted to devise an independent and objective measure of the level of violence in the TV programmes by getting panels of adults to judge them, and then turning these judgments into a ten point scale. Yet as Murdock and McCron point out, 'we know from other audience studies that there is a considerable divergence between the preferences of middle-class adults and those of teenage boys, especially those from working-class backgrounds' (Murdock & McCron, 1979, p. 57). This may explain some of the oddities in the results. For example, Westerns were found to be causally related to aggressiveness, while science fiction programmes were not, despite the fact that the judges rated a programme like *Dr. Who* as more violent than Westerns like *Rawhide* or *High Chaparral*.

The measure of violent behaviour by the boys is open to similar criticisms. It relied upon self-report data thus raising once again problems of bad memory or exaggeration. To help the boys remember,

Belson introduced details about the circumstances surrounding typical violent acts of different kinds. Unfortunately, once this data was obtained, it was categorised in a very abstract way which ignored all reference to the context which made the act of violence intelligible in the first place. Thus the category of 'serious violence' includes statements like 'I busted the telephone in a telephone box' and quite different ones like 'I deliberately hit a boy in the face with a broken bottle' and 'I fired a revolver at someone'. Questions of context and motivation are avoided and 'difference in *type* between these acts are submerged in favour of totting up the number of acts reported and grading them for seriousness' (Murdock & McCron, 1979, p. 58).

An Alternative View of TV Violence

In spite of Belson's claim that his enquiry 'would be based upon *normal* long term exposure to television violence, upon behaviour as it *normally* occurs and upon attitudes as they *normally* develop', there are serious doubts as to whether this was so (Belson, 1978, p. 10). Critics have argued that his research is insensitive to the realities of contemporary youth cultures. Indeed his method of selecting individual boys from the whole of London fails to take sub-cultural groups into account at all, and therefore makes little use of an important body of theory and research in this field. By contrast, ethnographic studies using in-depth interviews try to show how patterns of leisure amongst young people are rooted in the class cultures of local neighbourhoods. Dave Robins and Phil Cohen's work on young East Londoners, for example, begins to answer questions which only puzzle Belson. At one point Belson notes that 'parents had been full of stories about the imitation by their sons of Kung Fu type violence' but his own impression is that imitation occurs only 'under certain circumstances' which he never really specifies (Belson, pp. 524–6). Robins and Cohen in their book *Knuckle Sandwich* (1978) document the interest in martial arts amongst both boys *and* girls (the latter ignored by Belson). They show that this is no simple matter of imitation, however, particularly since this interest was shared by those who were members of fighting gangs and those who were not. Robins and Cohen argue that it is the kids' sense of being descendants of earlier youth groups like the teddy boys as well as their half-admiring relationship to the adult criminal subcultures in their locality which creates an interest in the martial arts and gives special meaning to media output. This returns us to David Morley's point that programmes are interpreted in line with social experience and social background. The effects are mediated through the culture of audience members. They are therefore 'cultural effects'. Since the culture of audience members varies, it is thus hard to support the kind of blanket assessments of media violence which are frequently given.

This chapter has reviewed the main approaches to media effects, and has suggested that it is necessary to study both the kinds of pictures of the world which are painted by the mass media, and the varied ways in which this imagery is interpreted by different social groups. In other words, it has been argued that media effects are cultural effects which shape our understanding of the social world in line with our background and experience. So far, however, only very brief examples of the actual content of the media have been given. The next chapter will deal more fully with the sociological analysis of media content.

Chapter Two

Media Imagery and Representations

The media now provide us with a continuous flow of images and information. We take this for granted, but in the early days of the mass media things were very different. When the first American newspaper appeared in Boston in 1690 its editor proclaimed his intention to publish news regularly – once a month. (Boorstin, 1962). In modern industrial societies we expect news to be up-to-the-minute and to have drama at the turn of a switch. The media are massively present in our lives and it is this that gives them their cultural effect: they feed into our world-views and our culture, and help to shape them. This chapter looks at the kinds of view of the social world offered by the media, and the questions these raise.

Representations, Stereotypes and Ideology

All human culture is based upon the use of signs and symbols, since it is these that allow us to communicate and make sense of our environment. For example, the people of north eastern Thailand classify insects into those which can be eaten and those which cannot. We rely upon such categories and imagery in order to produce, record and store information. Sociologists sometimes refer to these as *representations*. The classic French sociologist Emile Durkheim used this term to include 'drawings, symbols of all sorts, formulae, whether written or spoken', our conception of animate and inanimate objects, and even the actual objects themselves, as for instance when a goat symbolically serves as a regimental mascot. He argued that 'essentially social life is made up of representations' and that they constrain our thought and behaviour (Durkheim, 1952, p. 40). The media are an important source of these collective representations for they constantly map out for us the contours of our culture and society.

396

Durkheim tended to write as if collective representations were shared by everyone in much the same way. He stressed social integration rather than social conflict and failed to emphasise that our representations may become a matter for dispute. For example, the 'harmless fun' of page three of the *Sun* can be seen as a symbol of degradation from a feminist perspective, precisely because it conveys a view of women as mere playthings of men that is socially limited and confining. Feminist writers would argue for more positive representations of women in which they have effective control over their own bodies and are not simply used to sell newspapers to men. Representations are a necessary part of social life, but this does not prevent us from being able to choose between different kinds of representations and trying to change them.

The term *stereotype* is often used to indicate those representations which are misleading or offensive. A stereotype is a conventional way of representing someone or something so that our view of them becomes 'frozen' or fixed and may give rise to social prejudices. Stereotypes mark out the acceptable boundaries of our social world: they typically point to those who do not fully belong. Thus women, blacks and homosexuals frequently figure as stereotypes and this reflects their inferior position in society. For example, stereotypes of black characters in films as 'Uncle Toms', faithful servants, comedians or minstrels, and wild savages conjure up a whole history of slavery, discrimination and colonialism. Stereotypes like these are a potent vehicle for *ideology*; in other words, they are a source and support for ideas which legitimate powerful vested interests in society, such as the social advantages enjoyed by whites at the expense of blacks. Ideologies are sets of ideas which justify social disadvantages and injustices, whether these ideas are deliberately put forward by privileged sections of society or not. As we shall see later, a number of writers argue that ideology arises out of the structure of society itself, rather than from the self-interested designs of some of its members.

This chapter continues by looking in more detail at media representations dealing with (i) sex and gender, and (ii) race.

Representations of Sex and Gender

Studies of the ways in which women are represented in the mass media have, until recently, been few and far between. With the recent revival in feminist ideas, however, this area of research has assumed increasing importance. Its neglect is all the more surprising when one remembers that women are identified by media professionals as a specialised market for journalism and fiction. A magazine like *Woman's Own*, for example, was being read by nearly a quarter of all women in the UK in 1981, and even 13% of British men regularly look at a woman's weekly.

These publications are deeply contradictory. On the one hand they speak to women's interests – for example, by providing a forum for information and advice; while on the other, they seem to reinforce narrow and unrewarding feminine roles. Advertisements often present glamorous female images, yet their visual conventions subtly imply the disadvantaged position of women in society. Erving Goffman's study of gender representations in advertisements found that 'men tend to be located higher than women' and 'women are pictured on floors and beds more than men'. He points out that 'lowering oneself physically in some form or other of prostration' is a way of representing inferiority and subservience: it is 'a classic stereotype of deference' (Goffman, 1979, pp. 40–2).

It can be argued that women's magazines traditionally fulfil an important pastoral role by offering women solutions to the problems they experience in their everyday lives. Bridget Fowler (1979) has suggested that women's magazine stories took over one of the key tasks of religion, namely to state a moral code laying down 'how life can and should be lived'. She examined a sample of domestic melodramas taken from popular twopenny magazines like *People's Friend* and *Home Chat* between mid-1929 and the late 1930s, which were read mainly by working class women. Her aim was to see how these moral ideas were put across.

Fowler found domestic melodramas to be a predominantly optimistic genre: they centre upon the pursuit of romantic love and a number of obstacles have to be surmounted before there can be a happy ending. These obstacles often reveal the ideological assumptions behind the stories. An example of this is the treatment of bigamy in some of these tales. In a typical plot the heroine is an unhappily married woman who meets her true love and whose marriage is therefore an obstacle to her real romantic happiness. She cannot get divorced since this was unacceptable in the 20s and 30s. Later in the story she discovers that her husband has committed bigamy. The marriage is not legal and binding and she is now free to marry her true love with whom she lives happily ever after. The ideological message presented in this kind of story supports the conventional morality of the time: love finds its rightful place in a proper marriage. Indeed Fowler notes that 'in the stories bigamy is viewed as so shameful that horrific sacrifices on the part of the good are required before the social order can once again be restored' – thus bigamously-conceived children always die. The institution of marriage and a woman's place within it are reaffirmed against the unthinkable alternatives of divorce and separation.

The barriers of social class are another obstacle to romantic happiness. Yet as Fowler points out, within the class structure described in these stories there is frequent social mobility and the wealth of the rich is depicted 'more as a *decorative trimming* than a vital social difference'. As a result heroines may happily marry into a higher social class free from snobbery and social discrimination. In other words, class and gender are imagined in such a way as to legitimate each other and inequalities of wealth and position are never challenged. Because they appeared at a time when Britain was experiencing a severe economic depression, Fowler argues that the ideological view of the world contained in these stories served as a 'bulwark against despair and resentment', a kind of consolation.

Some studies of more recent examples of this kind of fiction have suggested that it puts forward simple stereotypes of women which its readers try to live up to. For instance, Adams and Laurikietis claim that representations of women in romance stories fall into two groups: 'the "good", sexually innocent woman, who gets her reward – her man' and 'the "bad" woman, who is often sexually experienced, and makes demands' (Adams and Laurikietis, 1976, p. 48). Janet Woollacott (1980) has taken issue with this argument, because it underestimates the skill and variety of much of this writing and assumes that women readers are gullible and unsophisticated. Taking the example of Georgette Heyer's Regency romance, *The Grand Sophy,* Woollacott demonstrates that this novel is a pleasurable read for women because it uses an unconventional heroine who outrages everyone around her to make fun of the stereotypes and clichés associated with this kind of story. However, this makes the ideological message of the text very subtle: to recognise this we have to become consciously aware that the admirable independence of the heroine and the equality which she enjoys with the hero is only made possible by Sophy's having her own fortune. In other words, the author makes us forget the usual patriarchal property relationships of the period: she makes her readers identify with the heroine and think of men and women as already socially equal when clearly they are not – then or now. The heroine may be a positive and therefore an enjoyable representation of a woman but it is one that is based on fantasy. Yet it is far from being a crude stereotype. Plot and characterisation can convey ideology in fiction in complex and attractive ways. Fowler and Woollacott tend to suggest that authors too are unconscious victims of the very ideology which their stories encourage, since these ideas are so widespread in modern societies.

Marjorie Ferguson's book *Forever Feminine* (1983) is the fullest account of women's magazines to date. She argues that they celebrate the fact of being a woman and also promote the ideal of the exemplary or outstanding woman. This is a sacred ideal rather like a religion with its own beliefs and rituals 'attached to beautification, child-rearing, housework and cooking'. Ferguson calls this 'the cult of femininity'. Like Durkheim she is interested in showing how collective representations hold a social group together. Yet she also recognises that women's magazines are both a social and an economic phenomenon: for the enhanced sense of female solidarity they promote is part of a profit-making exercise.

Ferguson identifies the shared values which underpin the cult of femininity by analysing the content of the three best-selling women's magazines in Britain between 1949 and 1974: *Woman, Woman's Own* and *Woman's Weekly*. She looked at a number of different types of items – fiction, problem pages, features and beauty columns – and found that they were constructed around eleven main themes. These included the importance of emotional expression in women's lives as against rationality and logical thought, feminine unpredictability and mysteriousness, and the value of youth. However, two themes turned out to be dominant time and again: firstly, the theme of love and marriage, 'getting and keeping your man', and secondly, the theme of self-improvement or self-perfection, the virtue of individual achievement. Ferguson carried out a follow-up study for the period 1979–80 to see whether this same order of dominant themes had continued. In fact, they were reversed: in the 1979–80 magazines the theme of self-improvement moved from second to first place as the chief message associated with the cult. Ferguson argues that there is a tension between these two themes since the duties of a wife and mother are not easily reconciled with 'showing you are someone in your own right'. The magazines play down this conflict. Indeed, the theme of the working wife being a bad wife, which was prevalent in the 1950s, had been over-turned by the 1970s, when a reader would be reminded that she was 'Not Just a Housewife' (pp. 54–5).

Although the late 1950s were a golden age for British women's weeklies, between 1958 and 1981 their combined weekly sales fell from 12 million to 6.1 million copies. This change is accelerating in the 1980s when women's magazines face increased competition not only from elsewhere in Fleet Street but from the expanding electronic media too. Ferguson also notes that the success of the theme of female self-perfection may carry with it its own built-in obsolescence: the more women are able to control their own lives, the less they need to rely upon the advice offered by women's magazines. Changes in values, together with social and technical changes such as the rationalisation of domestic work through the increasing use of freezers and shopping at large-scale supermarkets may, Ferguson argues, render much of that advice superfluous. Yet the magazines which have survived are those which have maintained the traditional trappings of the cult. Their message is still that 'women are uniquely different' and 'require separate treatment and instruction in ways that men do not' (p. 190). While their audience is smaller than it once was, it is no less committed.

This section has briefly outlined some of the research into the representations of women in the media, particularly those found in women's magazines. It suggests that women's views of themselves and their place in society are to a degree moulded and reinforced by such representations. This process is ideological in the sense that it supports powerful vested interests in society – those of men – and so helps to maintain the subordination of women. Ferguson, however, sees a positive side to the 'cult of femininity' presented by women's magazines. In her view it provides collective representations which contribute to a sense of self-esteem and belonging amongst women, a source of support that is often lacking in the wider society. She even goes so far as to compare these magazines with the women's movement: both are 'directed towards raising the consciousness of women', but while women's magazines aim to make their readers more aware about 'getting, if not keeping, a man', the women's movement is concerned with 'getting the better, or at least the equal, of him' (p. 187).

Race and the Media

In race relations, the media provides information where public knowledge is fragmentary. Although there are some two million black people in Britain, they live mainly in a few major population centres and therefore the white majority's contact with them is often slight. Research into the media's treatment of race over the years has suggested that its reporting has been limited in its themes and negative in its content. Hartmann *et al* (1974) in their analysis of the national press between 1963 and 1970 found that race relations coverage tended to focus upon signs of racial conflict and to give very little attention to the access of black people to housing, education and employment, 'competition for which would seem to be among the underlying roots of tension' (p. 132). Race was usually associated with trouble, as in the cliché 'race riot'. Certainly it is possible to show that the use of this kind of stereotyped language by the press has sometimes resulted in gross misrepresentations. For example, the *Evening News*' front page headline 'SCHOOL MOBS IN LONDON RACE RIOT' in July 1973 was later censured by the Press Council as 'inaccurate' and 'unjustified' following an official complaint; 'the riot' was, in fact, a fight between two rival schools and not two different ethnic groups (Braham, 1982, p. 273). Stories like this give a highly ideological and misleading view of black people as a problem and a menace, and helps to perpetuate their social disadvantages.

Troyna's more comprehensive study of the local and national press and local radio revealed that between 1976 and 1978 reporting about black people was chiefly organised around the idea of 'the outsider within' (Troyna, 1981, p. 45). Nevertheless, despite a big decline in New Commonwealth immigration into Britain, 'immigration' was the second major topic in the press reporting of race, accounting for 11.7% of all material devoted to this item. What was also striking was the convergence upon the same issues and themes by the different media. The impression created was still basically negative and ideological: in 'the media's representation of reality, cultural differences are disparaged and the black population seen as a problem to, and essentially different from the mainstream of the society' (p. 80). Editorials may emphasise the need for harmony and tolerance, but they are outweighed by the quite different treatment given to news stories. Troyna carried out a survey of public attitudes in order to see whether reporting had influenced popular opinion. His results supported the earlier work of Hartmann *et al*, since the interviews showed that the media had encouraged an ideological belief that black people were a source of trouble. However, this process of influence was a complex combination of personal experience (including gossip and myth) and media exposure.

Some of the assumptions underlying this type of research have recently been challenged by Peter Braham. Firstly, he argues that it is difficult to tell whether the media promote racial prejudice or merely reflect already existing racist attitudes on the basis of the data which have been presented. For example, he suggests that the impact of Enoch Powell's speeches on the general public is not necessarily to be explained as a result of the negative values typical of media coverage of race. Powell's popular acclaim stemmed from a failure by the media to recognise the extent of the public's fears; in other words, 'anxiety and discontent about race and immigration...had been accorded insufficient attention in the mass media' (Braham, 1982, p. 282). Secondly, Braham argues that criticism of the media for neglecting the 'underlying roots' of racial tension misses the point. It assumes that 'if you take away shortages of housing and jobs, race relations will become universally smooth' and under-estimates how deep-rooted an historical phenomenon racism may be (p. 283). Furthermore, to expect the press, radio or TV to always be concerned with lengthy in-depth reporting of the social conditions relevant to issues like race is to mistake the role of the media, since much news is concerned with capturing the short-term and the dramatic for tight editorial deadlines and easy and ephemeral consumption.

However, one reason why the reporting of race by the media can be criticised as misleading and distorted is because both newspapers and TV do claim to present information objectively. The press distinguishes between editorial statements of opinion and factual reporting and maintains that these should always be kept separate. As the old news-paper adage says: 'comment is free but facts are sacred'. Yet while the British press is free to support particular political parties and policies, broadcasters are legally required to abstain from editorial comment and taking sides. Not only must they give a factually accurate account of the news, they are also bound to balance different opinions and argu-ments from the mainstream of British life in matters of major controversy. In other words, broadcasters must be objective and impartial. The reporting of race suggests they are neither.

Industrial Relations: 'Bad News' from the Glasgow University Media Group

Industrial relations is an area where there are deep conflicts of interest over jobs, pay and working conditions. How an industrial dispute is reported will be a question of great concern to managers and workers alike. An ideological account of a dispute as the fault of one group may prejudice the way in which it is resolved, especially by influencing public opinion. Moreover, representations of workers and managers in the reporting of industrial relations in general may adversely affect their public credibility; for example, images of trade unions as greedy and selfish may undermine the legitimacy of strike action.

Amongst the most famous (some would say notorious) recent studies of media representations has been the work of the Glasgow University Media Group on industrial relations. It has been particularly controversial amongst broadcasters themselves because it challenges their claim to be impartial and objective. This section examines their research.

The Group's first book *Bad News* (1976) was concerned with television coverage of industrial relations in 1975. They found that reports of strikes and disputes concentrated unduly on certain specific industries at the expense of others. As a whole there was 'no consistent relationship between the stoppages recorded during the first five months of 1975 and those reported by television news' (p. 167). The motor vehicle industry was singled out, while other industries like shipbuilding or engineering received little attention. For example, engineering, which had well over twice as many stoppages as the motor vehicle industry, involving roughly the same number of workers and accounting for about a quarter of working days lost in *all* industries, appeared in only two news stories. In the case of one car manufacturer, British Leyland, news broadcasts frequently mentioned strikes as the key problem facing the company, despite the fact that the government-sponsored Ryder Report rejected the view that they were the major difficulty in BL and blamed lack of investment and management failings. In one example the Glasgow Group show that a speech by the then Prime Minister, Harold Wilson, which criticised both management and unions was edited in such a way as to sound like a criticism of the workforce only. However, whereas the BBC began by reporting the criticisms that had been made of both groups, later narrowing this down to only one of them, ITN completely failed to acknowledge Wilson's criticisms of management, portraying the speech as 'a blunt warning' to workers. Generally speaking, disputes were reported in terms of 'trouble' and inconvenience, as in this statement from a BBC2 news review:

> The week had its share of unrest. Trouble in Glasgow with striking dustmen and ambulance controllers, short time in the car industry, no *Sunday Mirror* or *Sunday People* today and a fair amount of general trouble in Fleet Street and a continuing rumble over the matter of two builders' pickets jailed for conspiracy (p. 23).

The authors conclude that 'viewers were given a misleading portrayal of industrial disputes in the UK when measured against the independent reality of events'. At the same time, other industrial matters such as accidents at work are considerably under-reported and usually only appear when linked to disaster stories, even though they account for many working days being lost.

A second book, appropriately called *More Bad News* (1980), continues this work and argues that there is a uniformity or 'lack of competitiveness' in broadcast news. The Group details a slanting in the presentation of arguments so that some points of view fail to gain a proper hearing. For example, in a case study of the reporting of economic affairs in 1975 the authors show that wage inflation was the dominant explanation given of the nation's problems. This was a matter of the sheer weighting given to this theme which occurred in 383 references between January–April 1975. Investment was mentioned only 89 times in spite of its importance. For example, the ITN industrial correspondent stated that 'since the war, Britain's overriding problem, almost universally agreed, has been a failure to invest adequately' (p. 24). Similarly, the language applied to industrial disputes in news broadcasts was found to be heavily stereotyped, using warlike imagery and describing workers as nearly always making 'claims' or 'demands', while employers 'offer' or 'propose'. By contrast, sentences like 'management demand higher output' rarely appeared. Language is especially significant since news film is merely used for illustration and the bulk of news consists of talk or what are known in the trade as 'talking heads' – typified by the news reader. Thus in TV news written or spoken story lines predominate over visuals. Interviews were often prejudicial, especially where these were filmed outside the TV studio. In the reporting of industrial disputes management was typically interviewed in an office and asked about the consequences of the dispute for their firm or organisation, while workers were interviewed outdoors – on pickets or after mass meetings – and asked for an explanation or justification of their position, rather than about the problems the dispute created for them. Interviews of this kind have an *agenda-setting* role – they fix and thereby limit the terms in which an issue will be thought through and discussed. Not surprisingly recent TUC guidelines have warned union representatives to avoid interviews which are structured in this manner, noting that 'a background of a busy street or factory gate with on-lookers peering over your shoulder will not help if you have a complicated case to explain'. The Glasgow Media Group conclude that broadcasters 'continually reinforce a managerially skewed view of industrial relations' (p. 189).

This research is not without its critics. One difficulty is that the authors are often relying on case studies to make their point, and this means that their evidence can be rather sketchy. For instance, as Philip Elliott (1981) has observed, their argument that the use of super-captions to identify interviewees is discriminatory (so that 'lower case is lower class') is based on just two examples taken from one sample week's broadcasting. A more damaging criticism is that the Glasgow Group have failed to see that it is not impartiality but 'due impartiality' which broadcasters have to achieve. As Tony Bennett has pointed out 'due impartiality' entails recognising 'not just the whole range of views on an issue', but also 'the weights of opinion which hold these views' (Bennett, 1982b, p. 306). In other words, it is perfectly acceptable for broadcasters to give more attention to some views than to others if they believe that these carry wider support in society. We should not be surprised if broadcasters reflect the status quo – this is what 'due impartiality' requires them to do. To suggest that there could be an absolute impartiality on our screens is to misunderstand what broadcasting in our society is really about.

   Another criticism which has been levelled at the Glasgow Media Group is that their work is fairly strong on description, but weak on explanation. While it shows us that distortions do occur in the media, that these are far from being random and have a discernible pattern to them, it does not give us a very good account of why this happens. Philip Elliott has argued that the Glasgow Group ultimately put the bias they detect down to the 'conscious product of broadcasting élites' – that is to say, they adopt a conspiracy theory in which bias is deliberate, as if TV were directly manipulated on behalf of the more powerful members of society. This criticism is not entirely fair, but it does have a grain of truth in it. The Glasgow Group do emphasise the importance of the self-conscious or 'reflexive' role of senior managers in broadcasting who enjoy real power within their institutions, backing this up with evidence from the minutes of top boardroom meetings which have been leaked to them. Yet the authors also note that much of the time broadcasters' tacitly trade upon the unspoken and dominant ideology of our society', uncritically accepting received ideas which favour those who own and control business. However, the relationship between deliberate and unwitting types of bias is not explained and we do not really learn how and why bias occurs.

   So far we have looked at representations of gender, race and industrial relations and asked whether the media present a misleading or ideological view of their place in society. The remainder of this chapter deals with a fourth topic which figures prominently in the media – that of crime. A final part reviews some problems with the claim that media representations are ideological.

The Reporting of Crime

Much of our knowledge of the everyday occurrence of crime comes from reading newspapers. In fact, the press has a near monopoly on this kind of information. But how accurate is this knowledge? Jason Ditton and James Duffy (1983) investigated the reporting of crime in six Scottish newspapers during the month of March 1981. Their analysis focussed particularly upon the Strathclyde region which has the largest number of reported crimes committed in Scotland. The press here has a very high readership with most people reading at least one newspaper per day. Yet this major source of information about crime was found to give a very inaccurate picture.

Ditton and Duffy calculated the amount of space in each paper which was devoted to crime news and also the percentage of this which dealt with Scottish crime news and crime which specifically related to the Strathclyde area. They found that the reporting of crime was only a small percentage of news coverage as a whole, making up on average 6.5% of all news, of which over a quarter was regional crime news. Although the amount of space given over to crime might not appear to be very great, it was the major source of images of crime in the locality. What was especially striking was the highly selective nature of the press reports. When compared with the regional crime statistics for the period in question less than 1% of crimes made known to the police or brought to court appeared in the newspapers. This would be defensible if the categories of crime covered in the press fairly reflected the actual incidence of crime in the region. However, Ditton and Duffy uncovered a very marked pattern of biased coverage where crimes involved sex or violence. Crimes of violence that had been made known to the police were over-reported in the papers by 19.4 times their actual occurrence, and crimes involving indecency were over-reported by 8.1 times. Similarly, violent crimes dealt with in court were over-reported by 36.2 times their real number, and crimes of indecency were over-reported by 34.3 times. At the same time, motoring offences, which accounted for over 40% of all court cases, received hardly any coverage at all.

Ditton and Duffy suggest that this kind of sensational reporting which uses scare-mongering headlines like 'ARMED BANDITS TAKE TO THE STREETS' greatly inflates people's fears of crime, particularly amongst vulnerable groups like the old. In fact this has the cultural effect of misinforming the public by a deceptive emphasis on those crimes which are relatively untypical of crime as a whole with the result 'that people's growing anxiety about crime is not commensurate with increases in crime itself' (Ditton & Duffy, 1983, p. 164).

A Marxist Perspective on Crime Reporting: The Case of Mugging

For Marxists law and order has to be understood as part of the class struggle. Marx believed that the increasingly severe crises stemming from the problems faced by the economic system would intensify class conflict between the proletariat or working class and the bourgeoisie or ruling class. On the one hand, Marx argued that this would bring members of the proletariat to organise themselves politically as they came to recognise their common interests, and their struggles would lead to a new kind of society in which classes and class privilege were a thing of the past. However, he also suggested that this process might be held back by the power of ruling class ideas in society as a whole. This was his theory of ideology. It stated that the ideas which were dominant in any historical period would always be those of the ruling class. This was not a matter of deliberately hoodwinking people; rather, the bourgeoisie would naturally expect other social classes to view society in the same way that they did and had the power and influence to promote this kind of thinking. For example, the law, in defending private property, the basis of the class structure, is both coercive and ideological, since 'laws enacted according to the dictates of a dominant ideology will appear to the members of that society as rules designed to preserve the natural social and economic order' (Collins, 1982, p. 43).

Policing the Crisis (1978) by Stuart Hall *et al* looks at the role of the media in promoting ideological representations of law and order. The authors skilfully combine labelling theory with Marxist political economy in an investigation of the moral panic surrounding the controversial crime of 'mugging' in Britain in the early 1970s. They suggest that it marked an important change in the manner in which the ruling class was able to exercise power in society, a change aided by the media.

Their explanation of what happened draws upon the work of the Italian Marxist Antonio Gramsci. Gramsci used the term 'hegemony' to emphasise that the ruling class does not merely rule, it *leads* – in other words, the bourgeoisie maintains power by persuading other classes in society to give their consent to its aims and policies. This power is both moral and intellectual – it convinces people that ruling class views are right and thus wins public arguments – and this enables it to mobilise the support of those it governs. Gramsci's concept is valuable, Hall and his associates claim, because it extends our understanding of what ideology really means in a practical sense. Using this concept they argue that by the late 1960s Britain was experiencing a crisis of hegemony in which its ruling class was finding it increasingly hard to hold on to the consent of the populace. The causes of this crisis were ultimately economic, rooted in the beginnings of the end of the successful post-war industrial boom. This had been successful not simply because it 'delivered the goods' of material prosperity – it had also brought with it an ideology of affluence and consumption, illustrated by the claim that a process of 'embourgeoisement' was taking place whereby many manual workers were adopting the values and life-style of the middle class. At the same time ruling class hegemony rested on a political consensus in which the opposing parties tended to concur in the view that the fundamental problems facing modern industrial societies had been solved and that all that was needed now were minor adjustments. Once these ideas became harder to believe as economic realities started to call them into question a new foundation for social order had to be found.

As a response to this crisis the ruling class was forced to become more coercive by strengthening the police, the courts and the law – for example, the attempt to control strikes and industrial disputes through new legislation. In ideological terms this meant that 'law and order' became a central theme of political debate. It served as a way of winning people over to the view that a stronger State was needed. Hall and his associates suggest that mugging became especially important as a symbol of the fear of a disordered, troubled society, and that the media had a crucial role in creating and sustaining this image, an image that brought together social anxieties focussed around youth, race and crime.

It is important to bear in mind that in strictly legal terms the crime of 'mugging' does not exist. As a label for crime it is an American import which only began to appear in the British press in the late 1960s in stories of urban breakdown in cities like New York, sometimes with the implication that it was soon destined to spread to England. The first report of a specifically English mugging occurred in August 1972 when a murder near Waterloo station was described by a policeman as 'a mugging gone wrong'. However, its uncertain legal status made it a term that was often difficult to apply. For example, when the Home Secretary wrote to police chiefs at the height of the scare asking for more statistical information he offered a definition of the crime which even the police found confusing. A senior officer in Southampton wrote in reply that it was 'very difficult to differentiate mugging from the old traditional crime of a seaman getting "rolled" ' (Hall *et al*, 1978, p. 5). In fact most muggings were charged as 'robberies' or 'assaults with intent to rob', well-known criminal charges covering a wide variety of circumstances. Statistics relating to mugging have always been highly contentious.

Hall and his associates suggest that if we compare the figures for 'robbery or assault with intent to rob' between 1955–1965 with those between 1965–1972 the rate of increase had fallen by well over two-thirds. Despite this, even before mugging had begun to surface as a 'new' social problem in the courts and the media, there is evidence of an increase in police activity with the setting up of special squads to deal with urban crime. This was a strengthening of the 'control culture' which actually anticipated what was to follow. Mugging was one of many themes by which the State justified its already increasingly coercive stance. This is not to deny that street crime was a problem, but it is to suggest that its significance was over-rated and its portrayal extremely misleading.

The role of the press in this process of exaggeration was vital, because of its subordinate relationship to the main centres of power in society. For reasons that will be discussed more fully in the next chapter newspapers are unusually dependent upon the police as a source of information. The police are accredited with expert status and are among those who have special access to the media. As a result the media naturally tend 'to reproduce symbolically the existing structure of power in society's institutional order' (p. 58). However, newspapers are not simply mouthpieces of the ruling class: the press takes the 'primary interpretations' with which it has been provided and turns them into items of news according to the norms and values which make up the journalists' professional culture. Stories are translated into the particular stylised version of everyday language in which each paper addresses its public. In this way the press claims to speak on its readers' behalf and at the same time its statements serve to confirm the policies and actions of the control culture so that each supports the other, a process Hall *et al* call 'taking the public voice' (p. 63). The rhetoric of police statements and courtroom verdicts is passed back and forth by the press and this focusses and channels popular opinion. The press supplies the link between those in the control culture who define and deal with social problems and the public.

Once set in motion newspaper reporting has its own rhythms and news stories follow a logic peculiar to themselves. Mugging started off as something extraordinary, what the *Daily Mirror* called 'a frightening new strain of crime'. The newness of the label was what made it frightening, for as we have seen it was arguably not new at all. Press coverage of mugging peaked in October 1972 and then began to go into decline. By August of the following year one 'cycle of newsworthiness' was over. The supposed novelty of the crime was no longer enough to keep it in the limelight. After this new twists had to be found to keep the story alive, and these usually took the form of bizarre or humorous news angles, such as that of a youth forcing 'a man, who had no money, into a bank at knife-point in order to cash a cheque' (pp. 70–4). When the next cycle of newsworthiness began in 1975 mugging was specifically identified with West Indian youth and linked to the continuing tensions between the police and the black community in areas like Lambeth and Brixton. Each news cycle presents us with a set of 'facts', and puts them into a context so that they make sense. Hall and his associates wish to dispute both the facts and the context that the press have supplied about mugging. They argue that the press helped to create a moral panic, an ideological over-reaction which served ruling class interests at a time of crisis.

Their analysis raises a number of questions. Hall and his associates may be criticised for failing to make clear why mugging was so important to the crisis they discuss – in other words, how did the image of mugging particularly come to represent the experience of social upheaval at the time that it did? Was it really a prior economic and political crisis which made it so important *ideologically*, or are other explanations possible? For example, the scepticism which the authors display towards the mugging statistics makes the relationship between the problem of crime, changes in policing, and the reports in the press seem very uncertain, especially since they insist that ' "mugging" *was* a real social and historical event arising out of its own kind of struggle' (p. 186). As John Lea and Jock Young (1982) have argued, (citing *Policing the Crisis* in support), 'the inner city crime rate is extremely high' and racial discrimination and urban deprivation 'sets the scene for the development of a vicious circle whereby relations between police and community deteriorate in such a way that each step in deterioration creates pressure for further deterioration'. If we could clarify the causal links involved here we might well have to re-evaluate our view of the role of the press.

Crime in Fiction: Thrillers

Many of our representations of crime come to us through media fictions of all kinds. These have always been extremely popular; for example, a survey of viewing habits amongst *Sunday Times'* readers carried out in October 1982 revealed that 'mysteries' were still the type of film that most people preferred watching on TV. Thrillers like the James Bond novels sell in their millions. They contain a distinctive view of the world which feeds into the reader's enjoyment of these books.

Jerry Palmer in his book *Thrillers* (1979) has tried to find out what it is about narratives like these that grip us so compulsively and why they came to prominence in the modern period. First of all, he picks out the unique formula which distinguish thrillers from other genres, and make them a special kind of fictional experience. Palmer mainly discusses literary texts, but his analysis could also be applied to film or TV. He argues that thrillers are always built around two common elements which are closely interlinked: the hero and the conspiracy. This means that the same formula actually underpins a wide range of texts including Agatha Christie's classically English detective stories, tough-guy private eye novels by Raymond Chandler and Mickey Spillane and the spy thrillers of Ian Fleming and John le Carré. In all these books what sets the story in motion is 'a mysterious conspiracy...that springs from nowhere, which produces events whose source is incomprehensible' (p. 86). The task of the hero is to unravel the mystery and so avert the conspiracy; indeed the hero is the only person with the special qualities it takes to do this. If this is the heart of the story, then everything else is, strictly speaking, secondary to it – for example, the sexual encounters in the James Bond novels are there merely to underline his status as hero and this is why women are portrayed in a stereotyped way. But such encounters are not essential to the thriller. The Sherlock Holmes stories contain few references to sexuality at all. Here the hero's status emerges through the contrast with his muddled assistant Dr. Watson or the bumbling Inspector Lestrade.

The addictive pleasure of the thriller results from our identifying with the hero as the sole point of certainty in a world that is under threat, at least for the duration of the story. Thus our 'excitement and suspense derive from wholeheartedly wanting one person to succeed and fearing setbacks to their projects' (p. 62). Once the conspiracy is under way nothing is what it seems, and this is just as true when it is the identity of the villain which is at the root of the mystery, as in an Agatha Christie novel, or when the villain's identity is known but the nature of his or her plan is not, as in most James Bond stories. Palmer's claim is that no other popular genres work quite like this, even where they make use of mystery and suspense as an added ingredient. For example, romantic love stories have heroes and heroines but their plots are dominated by the quest for happiness, and where mysteries do occur, they are only one of many possible barriers to a happy ending.

Palmer argues that the emergence of the twin elements of hero and conspiracy can be traced back to changes in ideology during the industrial revolution. Although heroism as an ideal goes back to feudal times, its modern form is the embodiment of competitive individualism. The hero is set apart from society in the thriller – so much so that ordinary laws may not apply to him. James Bond, for example, is specially 'licensed to kill'. Thus he is an exceptional individual in a male-dominated society which is represented as a collection of individuals, who constantly have to compete with each other in order to be successful and so prove themselves. This ideology legitimates the competitive behaviour required by a society which is based on the economy of the market. The hero is the successful competitor writ large. The theme of conspiracy, on the other hand, derives from a shift in attitudes to law and order in which crimes against property and crimes against the person came to be seen as the same kind of threat to the social order. This change reflected the growing importance of private property in the nineteenth century. The first thrillers therefore coincided with the founding of the modern police force, and put forward 'a paranoid representation of the world' (p. 86).

Because of the nature of this ideology, Palmer tends to see the thriller as an intrinsically conservative genre. In the thriller 'courageous intervention by one man . . . saves the Western way of life' (p. 205). This description fits the James Bond novels, but whether it can be applied to the whole range of texts that Palmer wishes to explain is more doubtful. Palmer's strict classification does not help us to understand, for example, how the Bond films evolved into the technological spectaculars they are today, nor the tie-in between the films and the books which have clearly influenced the popularity of both. As Tony Bennett has pointed out, following the first Bond film in 1961 sales of the novels in Britain rose from 300,000 the previous year to a peak of nearly 7 million in 1965. He concludes that 'for the vast majority of readers, the films . . . must be taken into account in assessing their relationship to and mode of reading the novels' (Bennett, 1982a, p. 11). A further weakness is that Palmer's stress on the conservative slant of the genre fails to account for the variety shown by thrillers: Joseph Hansen's novels, for example, consciously aim to offer positive representations of homosexual self-identity and life-style by portraying a gay detective hero. This suggests that some thrillers may use the techniques of popular writing to challenge rather than support the status quo.

The remaining sections in this chapter discuss some criticisms of the idea that the mass media promote stereotyping and ideology.

Anderson and Sharrock – An Ethnomethodological Critique of Media Studies

Some writers have been extremely sceptical of many of the analyses of news and current affairs which have been discussed in this chapter. Anderson and Sharrock (1979) base their criticisms on an ethnomethodological perspective. Ethnomethodologists argue that the main feature of social life is that it consists of orderly interaction between the members of society and that this follows unacknowledged or taken-for-granted rules. For example, ethnomethodologists have investigated the rules which make ordinary conversations possible, like those which ensure that we take regular turns when speaking to one another. Flouting such rules can bring interaction to an abrupt halt. Researchers in this tradition have been particularly interested in the use of language in the achievement of social order.

Anderson and Sharrock re-analysed a study by Graham Murdock in which he used a random selection of news stories from his local paper, the *Leicester Mercury,* to show how the press promoted ideological images of young people. Murdock argued that news stories about youth rely on two contrasting stereotypes embodied in sensational headlines: well-adjusted high-achievers – as in the headline 'BOY, 16, SWIMS THE CHANNEL' – and unruly, anti-social delinquents – as in 'YOUTH THREATENED WITH KNIFE AS GANG GO ON RAMPAGE'. These stereotypes are, according to Murdock 'typical of the routine news coverage of young people'. They exacerbate popular fears of youth whilst hiding their root causes which lie in social deprivation.

Anderson and Sharrock find this line of argument unsatisfactory because it misunderstands the implicit rules by which we read headlines in general and these headlines in particular. They claim that Murdock takes the headlines out of the practical context of reading and neglects the cues and skills that go into making sense of them; by doing so he makes readers out to be more gullible and less discerning than they really are. In any newspaper, Anderson and Sharrock suggest, headlines merely perform the task of arousing a reader's curiosity and pointing to the sort of story we are about to read – one of a series, a story with a moral, or perhaps a piece of comment. Put simply, a headline serves as a preface or signpost which directs attention to a particular story: it tells the reader what to expect, not what to believe. In the case of the boy channel-swimmer the headline announces an extraordinary and unlikely achievement in just the same way as would a headline like 'MAN WHO ONLY LEARNED TO SWIM LAST YEAR SWIMS CHANNEL' or 'EIGHTY YEAR OLD SWIMS CHANNEL'. It makes no generalisation about contemporary youth at all, contrary to Murdock's claims – 'it is Murdock that stereotypes youth not the local newspaper'. Similarly the 'rampage' headline arouses only a sense of drama and danger in the reader's locality – notice that the gang that is mentioned is not itself described as young. Whereas Murdock argues that dramatic headlines encourage ideological thought, Anderson and Sharrock suggest that they are nothing more than cues devised to guide the reader round a newspaper. These cues assist in the task of reading, but need not influence our beliefs.

In reply Murdock (1980) has cited the interviews he carried out with the parents of teenagers as evidence that the press stereotypes he has identified do influence public perceptions of young people. However, for Anderson and Sharrock this is no answer at all since they see Murdock's questions to parents as being based upon careless and unjustifiable readings of newspaper materials and therefore only too likely to confirm Murdock's own theoretical point of view by eliciting the answers he wants to hear. In summary, Anderson and Sharrock would not accept that news headlines have the ideological content it is sometimes said they do. They argue not only for greater care in the analysis of media output but also for the adoption of a new perspective – ethnomethodology. This viewpoint stresses the importance of understanding how audiences actually go about reading what is in the media. Anderson and Sharrock claim that in this case the audience – readers of the *Leicester Mercury* – use headlines as cues, guidelines and ways of making sense of newspaper content. By contrast, the so-called ideological component is really only the researcher's way of making sense of media output. One is imposing one's views upon the audience by suggesting that ideological messages are reaching newspaper readers. Anderson and Sharrock argue that such researchers have failed to discover the way readers use and make sense of newspaper headlines and media output in general.

The Problem of Ideology

Many of the studies reviewed in this chapter have used the concept of ideology critically to show that media representations serve powerful vested interests in society. The strongest version of this approach comes from the Marxist perspective which argues that there is a dominant ideology which supports the capitalist ruling class and that this is associated with its control over the means of mental production. However, the notion of a dominant ideology which somehow draws together different representations of society into a seamless web of domination is one that is fraught with difficulties.

Abercrombie, Hill and Turner (1980) have challenged the idea that there is a clearly identifiable ideology in the later stages of capitalism. They argue that business enterprises now rely much less upon the inheritance of family capital since this has been replaced by impersonal financial institutions like pension funds. As a result, the traditional ideology of property developed during earlier phases of capitalism has been weakened and it is doubtful whether any new dominant ideology has taken its place. The status quo is now secured by such factors as the mutual interdependence between different sections of the division of labour, increased material benefits enjoyed by many employees, the economic compulsion of daily work, and the threat of physical force wielded by those who hold power. Ironically, this process of ideological decline is argued to have occurred at the same time as the means of transmitting ideology have become exceptionally efficient, particularly with the growth of the modern mass media. Thus, although the media is potentially a powerful tool of domination, it lacks a central ideological vision, because ideology is not as important as it once was. Against this argument, the studies discussed in this chapter tend to suggest that media representations often present an ideological picture of people and events, which seriously distorts the knowledge which we have of them. Nevertheless, Abercrombie, Hill and Turner's work has raised an interesting and difficult question: how far do representations like these add up to a single ideological viewpoint which significantly contributes to the integration of modern societies? The authors query the assumption that the media 'do disseminate a coherent set of values which derive from a dominant ideology' (p. 130).

This chapter has considered the images and representations found in the mass media and the part they play in social life. Sometimes, as in the case of certain representations of women, they may be a source of enjoyment and pleasure, helping to define a group's view of itself. However, where representations are stereotyped they can also be a source of ideology: individuals and social situations are depicted in such a way as to confer power on some groups and deny it to others. To look at who is being represented in the media and how they are being represented is to gain a unique insight into the nature of power and conflict in contemporary society.

Chapter Three

The Structure and Organisation of the Mass Media

The previous chapter examined the images and representations found in the mass media and showed that their treatment of such topics as crime, race or gender tend to fall into recurring patterns. These contribute to our view of the social world, and are likely to be particularly influential where other sources of information are lacking – that is, they may have a cultural effect. Many writers would argue that the media help create an ideological climate which disguises the true character of society and disadvantages some social groups against others. However, we have yet to really tackle the difficult question of why these distortions occur. To do this we will need to examine how the media are organised and the kind of work that people in the media do. As Janet Wolff has argued, 'ideological analysis is insufficient if it is not supplemented by an understanding of groups, pressures, hierarchies and power relations within organisations involved in the general process of the production of culture' (Wolff, 1981, pp. 30-1).

In trying to explain the patterning of stories and images, sociologists have generally tried to avoid two equally simplistic answers. The first of these suggests that the patterns we find in the media are the result of a conspiracy, a deliberate attempt to mislead or misrepresent. Some versions of Marxism find this idea of the media as a manipulative expression of ruling class interests attractive. The difficulty with this view is that it is hard to demonstrate. It is one thing to show that some members of society consistently have greater power, opportunity and advantage than others, but quite another to prove that, say, a particular story in a newspaper is the consequence of a small tightly-knit group seeking to exercise control over the rest of us. The second answer views media output solely as a response to audience demand. However, while sales and audiences are clearly vital to the media's survival, this argument ignores the way in which the media are organised to meet, encourage and even shape that demand, and also the work that goes into making what are very stylised products. The first section of this chapter examines the question of the ownership and control of the mass media and its relation to the range of products they make available to us.

Ownership and Control in the Mass Media

One of the major trends in industry this century has been the growth of the large business corporation. Media industries are no exception to this, but it is important to bear in mind that government intervention into radio and television has meant that the shape taken by some media organisations has been influenced by considerations of national policy rather than purely commercial criteria. Even with a recent willingness to leave the media more open to market forces than before, the problem of a communications monopoly arising amongst some sections of private enterprise is still taken sufficiently seriously to warrant traditional restrictions on new developments. Thus in July 1983 the Department of Trade announced that existing local newspaper, radio and television companies would not be permitted to own or have a controlling interest (i.e. owning more than 50% of shares) in cable television companies in their own areas (*Guardian*, 19.7.83). Nevertheless, as the next section shows, the mass media are big business.

Concentration and Conglomeration

A very high percentage of what we see, hear and read during our leisure derives from a small number of extremely large companies. At least two-thirds of the British audience for daily and Sunday newspapers, paperbacks, records and commercial TV programmes are served by the top five firms dealing in these products. This domination of the market is even more striking in other media. When you visit the local cinema or buy a woman's magazine, the chances are that in each case your money will be going to one of the top two companies in that field. For instance, since the early 1940s cinema chains have been in the hands of a duopoly: Rank and Associated British Cinemas (ABC). These are only the most dramatic examples of a process that has been at work throughout the media, that of *concentration*. Concentration refers to firms in the same line of business merging with one another.

A second process which has been changing the structure and organisation of firms is potentially more significant still. The term *con-*

glomeration is used to refer to firms with different business interests coming together to form new giant corporations. There are two main forms this can take. *General conglomerates* are the result of a takeover of a company specialising in one or more branches of the mass media by another with non-media industrial or commercial interests. A case in point was the takeover of *The Observer* by the Lonrho Group in February 1981 in a £6 million deal. In such cases there may be public concern that a decline in quality will occur because the newly acquired company will be submerged in the industrial identity of the parent conglomerate. These feelings can be exacerbated by the speed and stealth with which business mergers are conducted, and the rapid changes in management which often follow. The assumption behind such fears is that the media are not like other industries and cannot be run along the same lines, an assumption which finds support in the professional self-image of media personnel.

Multi-media or *communications conglomerates* occur where companies operating almost exclusively within media or leisure industries merge. The takeover of Times Newspapers by Rupert Murdoch's News International is a good example of this. Murdoch's company also owns the *Sun* and the *News of the World* and has annual profits of around £25 million. His other business interests include Australian television and aviation firms as well as an international chain of newspapers. To take only the United States, Murdoch's News America Publishing Inc., jointly owned by News Limited of Australia and News International Ltd. of Britain, controls the *New York Post*, the *Village Voice* and *New York Magazine* and also a number of newspapers and magazines in Texas. Conglomerates often have world-wide business interests. For example, the bulk of records sold throughout the world are produced by four huge multi-national companies – two of these are American-based (CBS and WEA), while the remaining two are European (EMI and Polygram).

Many conglomerates have deliberately pursued a policy of diversification, collecting together a very varied portfolio of business interests in order to compensate for possible losses in any one field of activity. The Rank Organization met the long-term decline in cinema attendance by branching out into hotels, television and hi-fi equipment and motorway services. The Granada Group is another example of this strategy and includes cinema, bingo clubs, motorway services, music publishing and the second largest television rental chain. It was formerly Britain's fourth largest paperback publishing company (owning Panther, Paladin and Mayflower books) – although book sales never provided more than 2% of the group's total profits between 1978-83. However, in March 1983 these publishing interests were bought up by William Collins Ltd. (owners of Fontana paperbacks) in a deal which pushed that company into neck-and-neck rivalry with Pearson Longman, the publishers of Penguin books, each jointly leading the UK publishing industry with about 25% of the paperback market each. Interestingly, Collins had successfully fought off a take-over bid by Murdoch's News International Ltd. in 1981 in which Murdoch had acquired a 42.3% share in their company.

Events like these vividly illustrate the fast-moving world of takeovers and mergers. What has happened to the mass media is only one instance of a wider set of changes in corporate structure and organisation which have been gathering speed since the mid-1950s. Between 1957 and 1968 nearly 40% of all the companies with shares listed on the London Stock Exchange were swallowed up in mergers and acquisitions, and from 1967 to 1973 the number of mergers among manufacturing and commercial companies rose from 1,709 to 2,415 (Murdock, 1982, p. 119).

The Debate about Corporate Control

The sheer scale of these conglomerates obviously raises questions about the economic power which they wield. The idea that property would become concentrated in fewer and fewer hands and that society would polarize into two classes – those who own the means of production and those who have only their ability to work as a way of making a living – is, of course, associated with Karl Marx. Latter day radical writers have used the kind of evidence outlined above as proof that Marx's key predictions have been vindicated by history. At the same time, others have argued that modern industry is different from anything that Marx envisaged, and that these dissimilarities show Marx to have been wrong. Since the mass media are, in Ralph Miliband's words, 'not only business, but big business' we need to see what this debate is about (Miliband, 1973, p. 203).

Critics of Marx have argued that his account of social class was based upon capitalist private enterprise at only one stage of its development. He saw the capitalist as an entrepreneur who both owned and ran his company, and power resided in a privileged class of propertied families. However, the second half of the nineteenth century saw the family firm begin to change into the joint-stock company, or what would today be called the corporation. This was simply a way of expanding the activities of the firm by raising money from the sale of shares to outside investors, and in the last hundred years it has become 'the dominant feature of the economic landscape' (Scott, 1979, p. 15).

Writers like Ralf Dahrendorf have argued that this has resulted in the break-up of the ruling class as Marx understood it. There are two reasons for this. Firstly, with the sale of shares, ownership of the firm ceases to lie with the individual entrepreneur and belongs to the body of shareholders, each of whose shares carries with it a vote in electing the board of directors. More than this, it was claimed that as shares were made as widely available as possible in the search for capital, so share ownership would become increasingly fragmented. Some writers, like Adolf Berle, have even suggested that the outcome would be a 'people's capitalism' in which everyone would have a stake. Secondly, the decline of the owner-entrepreneur who had actively managed his own company, together with the increasing size of the corporation, meant that a new group of professional managers came to the fore, and it was they who really ran the industrial system. In short, ownership had become separated from control and a 'managerial revolution' was in progress in which managers were becoming a new ruling élite. Their professional expertise and their privileged access to corporate information allowed them to outflank the shareholders, depriving them of their power and leaving them little option but to approve the decisions the managers had already made. Indeed, the distancing of owners from managers opened up the possibility that the latter would develop a new approach to business, one less interested in profit-making for its own sake and more concerned with the social respon-sibilities of their work.

Defenders of Marx point out that in actual fact he was well aware of the new importance of the joint-stock company. In *Capital Vol. III* he also noted that it had 'the tendency to separate this function of managerial work more and more from the possession of capital'. His view was that the manager was only a 'mere manager', a functionary working for the capitalist, and the salary the manager received was 'simply the wage for a certain kind of skilled labour' (Marx, 1981, pp. 512 & 567). The capitalist class had not been dissolved because of the spread of share-ownership, nor was it being replaced by a new managerial élite.

Having sketched in an outline of this controversy, I now want to see how it relates to a specific example in the mass media: the British press.

Power and Influence in the British Press

We have already seen some evidence of concentration in the British newspaper industry in the discussion of multi-media conglomerates. Who controls the press is a crucial issue in a society which values freedom of speech. Journalists often like to present themselves as public watchdogs protecting us from the abuses of power. But how do these cherished values and ideals square with the facts about the corporate structure of the British press?

Graham Murdock (1980) suggests that sociological work on the newspaper industry has tended to divide into two camps. On the one side there are the pluralist defenders of the press who argue that it is truly independent; while on the other side stand the radical critics who follow Marx in believing that 'the class which has the means of production at its disposal, has control at the same time over the means of mental production' and is able to 'regulate the production and distribution of the ideas of their age' (Marx and Engels, 1966, pp. 64–5). Broadly speaking, then, these two different positions reflect the wider debate about the significance of changing patterns of ownership and control.

Pluralists argue that power in society is dispersed amongst a variety of interest groups which do not coincide with the property relations discussed by Marx. According to adherents of this perspective, 'pluralistic societies are dotted with a variety of pressure groups, some of them striving to promote more or less overtly political aims' (Gurevitch and Blumler, 1977, p. 286). Free competition between firms is often cited in support of this argument. For example, across the different branches of the British media some 25 companies vie for market domination (see Tunstall, 1983, p. 174). Not only is this dispersal of power true of society as a whole, it is also a feature of the communities and organisations within it, so that it is hard for any one group to gain the upper hand for long. The separation of ownership and control is just one special instance of this general principle. There is, however, one institution which does threaten the independence of the various groupings in society and that is the State, which has an unrivalled monopoly of power and may at times fail to be the servant of the people. This pluralist view finds much favour in Fleet Street and is regularly put forward by newspaper representatives. Their belief is that owners' desires for profit, editors' and journalists' professional interests and the demands of their readers are all finely balanced. Thus, according to journalist John Whale, the power of the proprietors 'where it survives at all . . . must still defer to the influence of readers' (Whale, 1977, p. 84).

The radical and Marxist opponents of this position have criticised it from two different angles. Graham Murdock labels these 'instrumentalist' versus 'structuralist' approaches. Where they differ is in the attention they give to particular aspects of the way in which corporations operate. For instrumentalists the key question for research to establish is: 'Who holds power and how is it exercised?' Structuralists, on the other hand, are more concerned with showing how the policies pursued by the corporations stem from their place in the capitalist system and follow its economic logic. Each of these approaches will now be examined in turn.

Instrumentalists like Ralph Miliband argue that the facts about concentration and conglomeration undermine the pluralist case. Far from there being a divorce between ownership and control, ultimate power resides with the owners who are effectively able to determine long-term policies such as whether to expand or invest, whether to close or to merge, and who also decide on the hiring and firing of executives. Managers only have discretion within the framework set by such policies or decisions and therefore have only a limited form of control, sometimes described as 'operational control'. It is not difficult to show that a few large companies dominate the market. 85% of the circulation of all daily and Sunday papers, whether local or national, is covered by seven major newspaper publishers. These are among the biggest companies in the British economy, with four included in the top 150 corporations and the other three in the top 500. There has also been a marked move towards diversification since the mid-1950s, and the majority now have extensive interests elsewhere in the media, most notably in book publishing and commercial television. Instead of this leading to a more dispersed form of ownership, however, 'in five out of seven leading concerns, the controlling interests remain in the hands of the original founding families and their associates', families such as the Harmsworths and the Berrys (Murdock, 1980, p. 45). Instrumentalists argue that these owners share the same social background and participate in a common way of life: they can be identified as typical members of a privileged ruling class, bending the running of the corporations to their own designs. Even where the press is run by relative outsiders like the Canadian Lord Thomson and Australian Rupert Murdoch, it is still the case that they have benefitted from an Oxbridge university education. A top public school education, followed by Oxford or Cambridge, and membership of exclusive London clubs like Whites or the Royal Yacht binds such men together into a cohesive social group and links them to their fellows elsewhere in industry and the City. This is further reinforced by the overlap between companies that occurs through interlocking directorships so that the same individuals will sit on several different boards of directors giving them opportunities for sharing business information and access to channels of influence. It is this combination of shared life-style and boardroom experience that makes newspaper owners part of a capitalist class and therefore we should not be surprised at the one-sidedness of the press and its support for this class.

Structuralists claim that this sort of argument gives us a misleading picture of the press as nothing more than a tool (or instrument) of the capitalist ruling class and that its emphasis on personal decisions and group membership draws us back to the idea of a conspiracy. Little weight is given by instrumentalists to the competition and rivalry between capitalists (as evidenced in the recent circulation 'wars' using gimmicks like bingo). Also, because power is seen as a question of personal influence, the pressure of the economic system upon the decisions that are taken is not adequately understood. Structuralists argue that we need to show how concentration and conglomeration in the newspaper industry came about if we are to explain why we have the press we do and account for its deficiencies.

The structuralist approach has been pioneered by Graham Murdock himself, in collaboration with Peter Golding. Murdock argues that 'proprietors and other capitalists do not need to intervene in newspaper production since the logic of the prevailing market structure ensures that by and large the output endorses rather than opposes their general interests' (Murdock, 1980, p. 57). If we look at the conditions under which a newspaper can make a profit it becomes clear that in order to survive it either has to attract a very large readership or a small but more affluent one. The fierceness of competition has reduced the number of titles available to consumers, and with this there has been a narrowing of the range of editorial opinion on offer, most papers identifying with the political centre or right of centre. The cut-throat economics of the business has also meant that the cost of entry into the newspaper world is now prohibitively high. For example, a plan commissioned by the TUC setting out the feasibility of starting a tabloid Labour paper estimated that it would cost some £7.7 million (*Guardian* 18.6.83). Some commentators have suggested that the situation has been worsened by the rise of the human-interest story in mass circulation papers which has led to a decline in public-affairs reporting. In order to explore the structuralist perspective in more detail, the next section will examine the growth of human-interest journalism.

The Sociology of the Human-Interest Story

James Curran, Angus Douglas and Garry Whannel have tried to trace the origins and appeal of this kind of writing. As they point out 'mass circulation papers dominate the market and contain very little about home and international news in the traditional meaning of the word *news*' (Curran, Douglas and Whannel, 1980, p. 305). They try to show how this came about.

The future of the newspaper business was in a sense decided by the industralisation it underwent in the second half of the nineteenth century. From that period on, the fixed costs of machinery and raw materials began to rise steeply as a result of technological innovation. By the 1920s the pattern was set and has continued down to the present day, interrupted only by the Second World War with its rationing of newsprint. Because of the high cost of producing the first copy, most publishers could only achieve economies of scale by pushing up the circulation of their papers. Those who failed to do this fell victim to an increase in costs and were forced to fold. Thus between 1921 and 1939 eight national newspapers closed down. At the same time the growth of advertising during this period allowed newspapers to sell at prices well below what they cost to produce, subsidising their readership through advertising revenue.

Curran *et al* illustrate the impact of these factors by the case of the re-vamping of the *Daily Mirror* between 1933–36 which turned it into a pathbreaking new enterprise at a time when it faced closure. The paper re-oriented itself to address as wide an audience as it could, bringing in new groups of readers for which advertisers were searching. One such group, according to journalist Hugh Cudlipp, consisted of 'working girls, hundreds of thousands of them working over typewriters and ledgers' who had previously read romantic fiction rather than news-papers (quoted, p. 292).

The long-term result of these market pressures has been the polarisa-tion of the press that we are familiar with today. Those papers which follow the pattern established by the *Daily Mirror* depend upon reaching a very large readership in order to remain economically viable. By contrast, 'quality' papers like *The Times* rely far more upon advertising revenue and seek to secure a small prosperous audience for upmarket advertisers – in fact, increasing their circulation may actually drive this advertising revenue away. Advertisers' satisfaction with the audience that is being delivered by a particular newspaper is crucial. Thus the *Daily Herald* closed in 1964 with a readership over five times as large as that of *The Times*, but consisting of people advertisers did not wish to reach: namely, older, male members of the working class whose purchasing power was low.

For those newspapers seeking to attract the maximum number of readers there is a need to concentrate upon those stories which represent a common denominator amongst their target audiences. As Curran *et al* point out, the evidence provided by investigations into readers' preferences have consistently shown over the last fifty years that human-interest stories 'cross the barriers of sex, class, and age, appealing almost equally to all types of reader' (p. 301). This is true for readers of quality and popular papers alike. However, the economic pressures on quality papers to maintain a small but élite audience has ensured that they have continued to deal in news. Mass circulation papers, on the other hand, have been increasingly driven to jettison this in favour of human-interest stories, a process intensified by the changes in style initiated by the *Sun* in the late sixties.

Human-interest stories are not 'news' in the traditional sense at all, because they lack any social or political context. Curran *et al* argue that they portray instead a world composed of individuals whose lives are 'strongly governed by luck, fate, and chance' and who are united in 'a community that shares common universal experiences: birth, love, death, accident, illness, and, crucially, the experience of consuming' (p. 306). Thus a typical headline would be 'MYSTERY VIRUS KILLS BOY, 3' or 'DEATH ENDS A LOVE STORY'. Indeed, the fatalistic view of life as a kind of lottery fits well with the popular papers' compulsive use of competitions, which simultaneously celebrate the virtues of conspicuous consumption in their glamorous prizes. Because their dramas are always presented in highly personal terms, the human-interest story exploits the minor doings of stars and celebrities to the full. A whole column can be written around 'the fascination David Steel has for pop stars' and his friendship with Rod Stewart. Curran *et al* argue that this type of journalism 'embodies a particular way of seeing the world', a cultural effect which is profoundly ideological in that it disguises the social and political forces that influence the shape of events (p. 306).

This study provides evidence which supports the structuralist perspective on the influence of the press. It shows that the human interest story spread because it was a formula by which newspapers could maximise the size of their readership. Although this formula tends to ignore the diversity of political beliefs amongst these readers and even to de-emphasise politics altogether, it was not introduced by capitalist proprietors as a deliberate ploy to spread ideological views but grew out of the economic necessity of reaching as big a circulation as possible.

The Problem of Choice

So far we have taken the British press as a case study of the consequences of concentration and conglomeration for the media. But how typical is the press? Do economic pressures result in restricted choice and standardised products elsewhere in the media?

The answer to this question is complex because of the differences between one medium and another. By way of a contrast, consider the case of publishing in Britain. Here, although there is free competition between firms, books are not treated like any other commodity. For one thing book prices are controlled by law. You cannot go to a big retailer like W. H. Smith to buy the latest Penguin paperback at a cheaper price in the same way that you might buy foodstuffs more cheaply at a supermarket. Also, the number of new titles published each year has continued to rise – although works of fiction as a proportion of these have tended to decline steadily since 1945, particularly novels by new authors. Fiction is however, still the largest and most popular category of book published, and in 1983 its numbers increased by 50%. It is therefore debatable whether choice has been narrowed in publishing, and media tie-ins have given quality novels like Evelyn Waugh's *Brideshead Revisited* a wider readership than they have ever enjoyed before. Nevertheless, publishing companies have been subject to mergers and takeovers in much the same way as other parts of the media and this has resulted in increased control by accountants and a greater concern with profitability and salesmanship (Lane, 1980, pp. 52–6).

Media Work and Media Organisation

The research discussed above chronicles some of the key changes in the way that the media are structured and run, and tries to show how this has affected their output. Though valuable, what these studies fail to provide is an analysis of the kind of work which goes on within the media, and the conditions under which this is carried out. This is essential if we are to have a full understanding of the factors which shape media content. We begin with some studies which look at the production of news.

News Gatekeepers

An early and influential way of looking at how potential news items come to be included in broadcasts or news pages is in terms of 'gate-keeping', a simple metaphor in which the editor is likened to a farmer standing by a gate letting some animals in and keeping others out. So, certain items are chosen while others are rejected. This idea attempts to describe some important aspects of journalistic work. The very organisation of the news room of a national daily paper is said to show the gatekeeper process in action. The news-desk receives news stories or copy and gives out the reporters' assignments each day. Once a story has been handed in it will be passed to a 'copytaster' who takes the initial decision as to whether to accept the item and forward it to a deputy editor who will give it a first title and then pass it on to be sub-edited to the required number of words. It will also be processed by specialists who look after lay-out, photographs, headlines or feature pages.

There are several criticisms of this model. Firstly, it sees news as the outcome of decisions made by individuals, notably editors, and pays scant attention to the social constraints upon journalists which stem from their sources of news. Secondly, news is seen as relatively un-problematic – it appears to be already awaiting collection, rather than having to be actively constructed or produced. As Herbert Gans has observed, 'gatekeeper theory is more easily applied to media which depend largely on wire-service news than those which also search out their own news' (Gans, 1980, p. 341).

The Routine of Newswork

The popular image of newsgathering makes it out to be an exciting business, full of drama and action, in which no one can quite be sure what is going to happen next. Dedicated to the relentless pursuit of 'hard facts', the typical news reporter is pictured as an investigator or sleuth tracking down the truth in search of the ultimate scoop.

In contrast to this rather glamorous picture, however, news is produced in bureaucratic settings which have clear hierarchies of authority and formal rules, and this has a decisive influence on the character of news. Journalists do not just search randomly for their news stories or wait for stories to break, but follow well-trodden paths and procedures laid down by the organisations to which they belong. An example of this is the 'news diary' which gives the dates of important regular announcements like the monthly unemployment figures or forthcoming visits by politicians. Journalists, in common with members of other occupations, want to be able to control their work and make it as manageable as possible and this means planning ahead. This is not to say that journalists are never faced with the sudden and the unexpected, but it does mean that a large part of the job involves the routine processing of information or stories whose general outlines are known well in advance, even it their exact details are not.

In his study of the BBC, *Putting 'Reality' Together* (1978), Philip Schlesinger points out that about 70% of the news diary is used in news bulletins so that 'most news is not spontaneous, or unanticipated' (p. 69). News is run on a daily cycle called a 'newsday' which is controlled by editorial conferences at the beginning of each cycle. These decide on how to allocate staff and resources to meet the expected flow of items for a particular day. Deadlines play a key role in organising the time of news staff and this is so marked that Schlesinger calls the TV journalists' world a 'stop-watch culture'. This obsession with time is built into the composition of the news bulletin itself, in which every picture or sentence has to be precisely timed. The bulletin is constructed around the idea of 'pace', the need (as one broadcaster put it) 'to keep the interest moving' (p. 103). This will affect the placing of individual items; stories using film, for instance, are spaced out in television news so as to guarantee variety. The requirement of pace will mean that stories will often be cut, not in order to make way for something more important, but to accommodate something shorter. Film will be used according to its availability rather than its intrinsic merit. For example, film of the assassination of the Egyptian President Anwar Sadat was very prominently featured even though it was so jumbled and chaotic that it was very hard to tell what was happening. Schlesinger also emphasises the extent to which the media is a rather closed and self-pre-occupied world. Thus the BBC makes great use of the press as a source of news items or opinion. Fishman (1978), in a study of crime reporting in New York, has suggested that this kind of mutual dependence between the different branches of the media can be an important factor in producing and sustaining exaggerated accounts of crime waves which often bear little relation to police statistics. He claims that a more accurate term would be 'media waves'.

News Values and Professional Ideologies

Like any other specialised occupation, journalism has its own beliefs and values. These provide guidelines for carrying out journalistic work and a self-image which justifies the profession as a whole. Several writers have argued that these factors are important in determining what is presented as news, as well as the form it takes.

A good example of this type of approach is the study of what have come to be known as *news values*. Galtung and Ruge (1965) in their analysis of foreign news reporting see news values as falling into two broad types: bureaucratic and cultural. Bureaucratic values are closely tied to the routine of the job and the nature of the final product. For example, in order to qualify as news an item must have a timespan that fits in with the work schedule of the medium in question. A newspaper, like TV, operates on a 24 hour cycle and will prefer stories that follow this same rhythm – thus the building of a dam would be ignored, but its public opening would not be. Also, newspapers have to fill fixed amounts of space or time allocated to different types of story (e.g. crime, foreign news, sport) irrespective of how much news is actually happening in the real world. News also tends to be based on certain cultural values: particular attention will be paid to 'the familiar, to the culturally similar, and the culturally distant will be passed by more easily and not be noticed' (Galtung and Ruge, 1965, p. 67). Thus there is a legendary journalist's rule of thumb known as 'McLurg's Law' which states that air crashes or other major accidents in Asia should normally get less coverage than those in Europe. Galtung and Ruge also mention other typical news values: these include reference to members of élites, the reporting of events in terms of personalities, and a preference for negative news.

Values like these help buttress journalists' claims to be professionals, to be 'as unequivocally recognised as members of a skilled and learned profession as those who follow medicine and law' (Christian, 1980, p. 290). As well as making a case for higher pay and higher status, this is also a claim that journalists should be given a maximum of independence in order to do their job properly. Jock Young (1981) has suggested that this self-justifying professional ideology grows out of the journalist's unique position in the production of news. Firstly, they are situated between production workers on the one side and management on the other, distanced from the main lines of conflict in industry. Secondly, the job itself involves a high degree of individual responsibility for the work that is carried out; its standards are meritocratic and individualistic. Thirdly, the variability in the work of producing news stories is unusual compared to most other jobs, and helps generate a special sense of professional identity. As Young notes, 'the only parallel to a news journalist would be if the designers in Fords made a new model car every day' (p. 418).

Part of this professional ideology is a view of what the audience wants and how to supply it. Philip Schlesinger has observed that 'newsmen do not doubt that they know what is wanted' and 'they explain their knowledge by invoking the related notions of professionalism, commitment, and experience' (1978, p. 116). Thus, although television ratings are routinely monitored, these are relatively uninformative and journalists largely rely upon their own 'news sense' rather than audience response when deciding on programme content. This may sometimes go awry – as one BBC man told Schlesinger: 'In the end it's professional judgement and we're not always right' (p. 120). As we saw in the last section, their professional judgement is reinforced by an intense awareness of what is being produced by other news media. The professional culture of journalists makes it an imperative for them to immerse themselves in news, and their work ethic requires that the good journalist keeps up with what is happening even while on holiday.

Objectivity in Practice: A Strategic Ritual

We have already seen that objectivity is one of the ideal standards of journalism. In an important article Gaye Tuchman (1972) examined the work routines of journalists on a daily city newspaper in the United States to see how they made use of it in their everyday professional lives. She studied the paper as a participant observer, following its daily round unobtrusively. Her findings suggest that while objective reporting may be an ideal, in practice it refers to a set of procedures which are used by journalists to avoid unnecessary trouble.

Tuchman argues that the norms defining objectivity are best understood as guidelines for reducing the risks of the job. Reporters have to cope with a number of pressures which could undermine their professional credibility. All journalists have to meet the demand that they adhere to daily deadlines and failure to do so can have disastrous results: the printing of the paper may be delayed, its distribution held up allowing drivers to claim overtime payments for working late, and the postponed delivery may mean that customers choose to buy a rival newspaper resulting in a squeeze on profits. At the same time, reporters have to keep an eye open for editorial criticism of the accuracy of their stories, and must always beware of leaving themselves open to be sued for libel or misrepresentation. Unfortunately, speed and accuracy are not easily reconciled demands. In the time available to gather together the basics of a good story, reporters are forced to take many items of information on trust. Although they are required to check their facts this cannot always be done. It would be impractical if they were to indicate every single unexamined statement in their stories, and it would make stilted reading. There are limits to how many questions the reporter can ask and still meet the afternoon deadline. But in order to make themselves less vulnerable they adopt a set of safeguards which allow them to claim that they really are being objective.

Tuchman argues that journalists resort to what she calls 'strategic rituals'. These are very similar to those found in pre-industrial societies: as she observes, 'newspapermen invoke their objectivity almost the way a Mediterranean peasant might wear a clove of garlic around his neck to ward off evil spirits' (p. 660). In other words, reporters have a number of tricks of the trade which allow them to hold editorial criticism at bay, even though these merely avoid the real problems of objectivity rather than solve them. Such rituals can be considered 'strategic' because they act as a means of self-defence, a symbolic way of side-stepping future censure or attack.

There are several different forms that strategic rituals can take. First of all, journalists may find themselves in a situation in which it is hard to tell that which an informant is saying is correct or not. For example, a claim by a Democratic Party senator that America is lagging behind the Soviet Union in nuclear weaponry would be difficult for a reporter to check. A way out of the difficulty is for the reporter to search out an alternative point of view – he or she could contact the Secretary of Defence from the opposing Republican Party for instance – and then set down the two contrasting statements side by side. Without trying to assess who is right, the reporter simply prints both statements and needs make no further attempt to find out the truth. This 'presentation of conflicting possibilities' gives the reporter the best of both worlds – a set of 'facts' have been revealed and the editorial deadline has been met. Yet the truth of the matter is left undecided and uninvestigated.

Another strategic ritual is the 'presentation of supporting evidence'. This involves the piling of fact upon fact in such a way as to *appear* to shed light on a topic, when strictly speaking no firm conclusions may be drawn. Tuchman gives the example of an obituary in the newspaper she studied in which a reporter referred to the deceased as a 'master musician'. When the editor questioned this he was told that the musician had once played with a famous composer, and this additional information was enough to satisfy the editor that the reporter had covered himself. Here, once again, we have something less than complete objectivity – an objective statement is implied but never really justified or proved.

A final ritual safeguard relies on the 'judicious use of quotation marks' as a way of avoiding charges of inaccuracy and bias. Tuchman cites the case of a reporter covering an anti-Vietnam War rally. Privately the reporter was very impressed by the demonstration and supported its aims, but knew that to say this would be to bring censure from unsympathetic editors. The reporter therefore wrote a column whose tone was favourable to the demonstrators, but which carefully used quotation marks in order to distance himself from what was being said. A typical sentence ran: 'some thousands of persons swarmed to a sunny City Park yesterday to an "incredibly successful" anti-draft, anti-war rally' (p. 669). Here the quotation marks are a way of saying that the words in question do not belong to the reporter. Carefully used they create an impression which colours our understanding of events, while still allowing the journalist to claim to be unbiased. Tuchman's study shows how these taken-for-granted procedures underpin journalists' conventional judgments as to what counts as news and how it is to be presented.

News as Commercial Knowledge: The Work of the Crime Reporter

In another study of journalists at work based on a series of interviews with crime reporters, Steve Chibnall (1975) has produced an important critique of the gatekeeper approach. His research suggests that instead of being determined by editorial selection, what will be in the news will have already been decided upon long before the reporter's copy has reached the editor's desk.

Crime reporters are highly specialised and rely almost exclusively upon a single source of information. Of the seventy Fleet Street journalists who regularly report on crime only about one-third are full-time crime reporters. Chibnall argues that these are really 'police reporters'. Orginally a crime reporter was merely someone who went round the London police stations in search of tit-bits of information which could be passed on to senior journalists. However, as crime stories gained in importance a Scotland Yard Press Bureau was founded in the mid-1920s to provide official statements to the growing body of crime reporters, making them a more specialised professional group than they previously were.

However, one of the problems with this Press Bureau was that it failed to meet these journalists' needs. The press officers were seen as a kind of barrier between reporters and senior policemen and often the information which was released came too late to be used by the press.

Furthermore, press releases were, by definition, given out to *all* reporters and this hindered the compiling of an exclusive news story. Reporters even doubted whether press officers could really recognise a good story. The local representatives of the bureau, the Divisional Liaison Officers or DLOs, were nicknamed the 'Don't Let Ons' by the press because of the way in which they were felt to withhold information.

Difficulties of this kind have led crime reporters to carefully cultivate close personal contacts with police officers as an alternative source of news. Status in this field of work depends upon both the number and quality of contacts at a reporter's disposal. In fact, if it is justifiable to talk about gatekeepers in crime reporting at all, those gatekeepers are the police. Ultimately the police have a strong veto power over the reporter who would be out of a job if this supply of information dried up. However, despite this asymmetry between the two parties, these relationships have a certain equality about them because both sides have something to offer. Although reporters rarely give the police cash payments, such sources may be expensive where money is lavishly spent on food and drink in order to create a sociable atmosphere for exchanging information. Most of the information received is 'paid for' by the return of favours. There are two kinds of service that the press can give. Firstly, reporters can anonymously pass on tip-offs from their criminal contacts which could not be given directly to the police for fear of incrimination. More generally, an important resource that reporters have is their discretion in handling information. The press can be used by the police as a means of appealing to the public for help, and can also take a direct part in police operations by releasing information which is deliberately misleading – for example, by 'declaring that bank raiders have stolen a million rather than half a million pounds, in the hopes of causing the thieves to fall out' (p. 56). The press can also give 'promotional aid', since crime reporters do not just deal with crime, but write on police pay and conditions and police politics. Providing a sympathetic view of police work and police causes is therefore one of the most important bargaining points that the reporter has, though it is usually part of an unspoken agreement.

Chibnall sees the reporter's news story as a product – knowledge which is bought and sold. As one journalist told him: 'I regard news as a commodity – it's there to buy, it's there to report' (p. 59). In transforming his or her material into a marketable form, the journalist is involved in the work of packaging. This is not merely a response to reader demand but is constrained by a number of other factors. First of all, crime reporters have their own specialised version of journalistic news values which give priority to some stories over others. For example, they tend to ignore certain crimes altogether. 'Company fraud is a difficult thing to write about', said one reporter in interview, 'you can't work clichés into it, there's no violence, no drama' (p. 58). Secondly, reporters are constrained by their relations with their sources. For example, a story may be held back at a sensitive moment in a police investigation. There may also be a tendency to turn a blind eye to police misdemeanours for fear of losing one's source. At times, therefore, 'the informal ethics of police work dominate the formal ethics of journalism' (p. 61).

In explaining the characteristics of news, Chibnall (1977) takes issue with Marxian approaches, which he suggests are unclear about how economic interests actually determine what appears in the press. He attacks the Marxist writer Ralph Miliband's contention that the capitalist ideology of the owners and controllers of the press is passed down to editors and journalists, limiting the range of ideas and views they express, since it tells us little about how the 'seeping downwards' of ideology happens. We should not see journalists as 'simply puppets on strings pulled by capitalists' as some instrumentalist or conspiracy theorists propose (1977, p. 224). Chibnall argues that we need instead to focus upon the day to day situation of reporters in order to understand what they write. Journalists have to negotiate the demands of four sets of people – editors, colleagues, sources and readers – all of whom have to be satisfied. Although news is 'commercial knowledge', a special kind of knowledge which has to be sold to the public, it is brought into being under a variety of constraints. None of these can be reduced to a single economic factor as writers on ownership and control in the media argue. For Chibnall 'police sources exert a more immediate influence on crime reporters' accounts than do newspaper proprietors or even, perhaps, the economic conditions of newspaper production' (p. 225). Even where they are dependent upon a single source, reporters bargain and exchange information and services, and exercise choice within the social limits that their job imposes using the received professional wisdom of their craft.

Cultural Industries and the Problem of Fads and Fashions

Other branches of the media also develop complex professional strategies in order to cope with the uncertainties of their work. Paul Hirsch's (1972) comparative analysis of American commercial publishing houses, film studios and record companies looks at the problems faced by those in the business of supplying a product that is meant to be creatively or expressively unique. If, for example, a film simply repeated other films, it would fail to find a market. At the same time, because they are operating for commercial rather than purely aesthetic motives, these cultural industries need to standardise production and distribution as much as possible in order to maximise their profits.

Although it is possible to reduce the risks involved by resorting to tried and trusted formulas or employing famous stars, no-one can be absolutely sure what will guarantee a best-seller. Cultural industries are always seeking to capitalise on fads and fashions, but these are by their very nature unpredictable. To get round this difficulty, companies have to rely upon the professional judgement of specialist personnel who operate on the peripheries of the organisation and whose work cuts across technical, artistic and managerial responsibilities. They include talent scouts, acquisitions editors, record producers and film directors, as well as promoters, press coordinators, and public relations staff. Hirsch refers to these as 'boundary-spanning roles': they link the organisation to new sources of talent and keep it in touch with potential audiences. Not only are they accorded a great deal of professional autonomy, but 'their value to the cultural organisation as recruiters and intelligence agents is indicated by high salaries, commissions, and prestige within the industry system' (p. 651).

Secondly, these industries try to deal with the uncertainty of their markets by overproducing; thus 'the number of books, records and low-budget films released annually far exceeds coverage capacity and consumer demand for these products' (p. 652). This is a way for companies to hedge their bets. The point here is that a wide spread of products will ensure that at least *some* are successful, and this is less costly than only promoting a few items which have been expensively market-researched. Finally, Hirsch notes that cultural industries need to obtain coverage by the other mass media to ensure the successful promotion of their products. Disc jockeys, book critics and film reviewers all act as 'surrogate consumers' by giving the public a guide to what is on offer. They can effectively regulate the access a producer has to an audience by influencing popular taste and buying habits. Although surrogate consumers have to be seen to safeguard their independence of judgement if they are to retain credibility with their audiences, cultural industries will seek to co-opt them. This has always been a sensitive area and one that has sometimes led to conflict. The most famous instances are the notorious American 'payola' scandals of the 1950s in which there was a public outcry against the major record companies for paying off disc jockeys as an incentive to play their new releases. In fact this practice was only officially made illegal in 1960.

The Media and Technological Change

Hirsch's concept of 'cultural industries' serves as a timely reminder that the mass media are first and foremost work organisations and depend upon the labour of technicians, engineers and workers at a variety of levels of skill. This tends to be submerged below the exciting image the media projects of itself as a world of stars, personalities and glamorous professionals. The technology underpinning the mass media has been constantly changing throughout this century, and probably never more rapidly that at present. We conclude with a comparison of two very different kinds of work within the media which have been radically altered as a result of changes in technology: the sound mixer and the printer.

The technology of sound mixing in the record industry has tended to become progressively more sophisticated since the 1940s. In the early days the recording technician's skill involved placing and balancing microphones and making best use of the acoustics of the studio in an endeavour to reproduce the sound of the concert hall. In America these studios were large and capital-intensive and this led to craft union organisation amongst these workers. This system was undermined in the early fifties by the development of tape recording which simplified studio technology and considerably lowered its cost. It became easy to set up small studios to produce records for the minority-taste audiences which the radio industry was trying to reach as it began to reorganise itself after losing its mass audience to television. These were the days of the rise of rock 'n' roll, and sound mixers began to work in small entrepreneur-run settings developing new recording skills based on echo and reverberation equipment. In the 1960s the technology of recording became considerably more complex with the advent of multi-tracking. Rock musicians themselves began to challenge the sound mixer's prerogative of control over the technical details of recording and would insist on mixing their own tapes personally. Edward Kealy (1979) has noted that this has led to a new type of studio professional which he terms the 'artist-mixer', who was often an ex-rock musician and shared in the artistic ambitions of the rock groups. Such figures free-lance and compete for bonuses and royalties, and are now awarded Gold Records by record companies for outstanding commercial success in the same way that recording artists are. Kealy argues that the evolution of this type of work is 'a counter-example to the general trend in the development of the modern work experience' which is towards routinisation and de-skilling (p. 26).

Cynthia Cockburn's book about changes in the British newspaper printing industry, *Brothers* (1983), tells a different story. Although printers' immediate influence on the content of newspapers has typically been limited to the very occasional veto on material viewed as anti-union, they have had a major impact upon the structure and organisation of the press as a whole. Now, however, the traditional technology of linotype machines, hand assembled pages and rotary letterpress printing is gradually being replaced by computer-assisted techniques of photo-composition in which newspaper copy is typed directly into a computer and printed out ready for use. Eventually whole pages could be assembled on a computer screen and then transformed by a digital typesetter into printable output. The effect of these changes upon the workforce have been twofold. On the one hand, the new technology has meant increased earnings, shorter working hours and an improved working environment without the noise, grime and sheer physical effort of the old crafts. On the other, the skills which the new technology requires are far less specific than those they are replacing, and are increasingly being found throughout industry wherever computers are introduced. Thus the scarcity value of the printer is being eroded in a period of rising unemployment and the hand of the owners has been strengthened.

Although few of the workers whom Cockburn interviewed wanted to return to the old conditions, most of them felt that something had been lost. As one said: 'I think I have gone from skilled to semi-skilled, that's what it is. And I feel a bit let down. It has been a worry in my mind all the time' (p. 118). Cockburn stresses that one important dimension of this process is the undermining of the implicitly patriarchal nature of the craft. Women have always been a more excluded or marginalised group in newspaper printing than in other branches of the trade, and men have disproportionately benefitted from this discrimination. As Cockburn comments: 'in the last resort, the craft work of composition for print was men's work *because men said it was*', and they maintained this position by actively campaigning against women (p. 152). Ironically, part of the effect of the new technology is to bring printworkers' jobs closer to the office work that has traditionally been seen as women's work, and this is very threatening to them. 'If *girls* can do it, you know, then you are sort of deskilled you know, really', commented one male printworker (p. 118).

Cockburn shows that skill is about gender as much it is about social class, since it is partly defined by ideologies of masculinity. Whether the position of women will be changed in the new large-scale union amalgamations, NGA-82 and SOGAT-82, which have been the printworkers' major response to the new technology remains to be seen.

The present is viewed as a watershed by some writers who see industrial societies as poised to take off into a novel and unprecedented phase, perhaps an era of *post-industralism* based upon the new information technology, the combination of telecommunications with the microchip. Similarly, the introduction of satellite and cable technology has led to predictions that the mass media will completely re-shape day to day life in the near future. Once familiar media may decline dramatically or even disappear altogether under the impact of new technological and cultural forms. Cinema, for example, 'could well end up confined to the larger city centres (especially London) and a small fringe of cinephiles by the mid-'80s' (Blanchard, 1983, p. 109). Whatever the future holds we can expect that it will not only raise new problems but also, as the story of the mass media to date has shown, it will re-kindle old criticisms from the past.

Bibliography

Abercrombie, N., Hill, S., and Turner, B. S. *The Dominant Ideology Thesis* (George Allen & Unwin, London, 1980)

Adams, C. and Laurikietis, R. *The Gender Trap, Book 3: Messages and Images* (Virago, London, 1976)

Belson, W. *Television Violence and the Adolescent Boy* (Saxon House, Farnborough, 1978)

Bennett, T. 'Text and Social Process: The Case of James Bond' *Screen Education* no 41, Winter/Spring 1982a

Bennett, T. 'Media, "reality", signification' in M. Gurevitch *et al*, 1982b

Blanchard, S. 'Cinema-Going, Going, Gone?' *Screen* vol 24 nos 4–5, July–Oct. 1983

Boorstin, D. *The Image* (Penguin Books, Harmondsworth, 1962)

Braham, P. 'How the Media Report Race' in M. Gurevitch *et al*, 1982

Cantril, H. *The Invasion from Mars: a Study in the Psychology of Panic* (Princeton University Press, Princeton, 1940)

Chibnall, S. 'The Crime Reporter: A Study in the Production of Commercial Knowledge' *Sociology* vol 9, 1975

Chibnall, S. *Law-and-Order News: an Analysis of Crime Reporting in the British Press* (Tavistock London, 1977)

Christian, H. 'Journalists' Occupational Ideologies and Press Commercialisation' in *The Sociology of Journalism and the Press* edited by H. Christian (Sociological Review Monograph 29, University of Keele, Oct. 1980)

Cockburn, C. *Brothers: Male Dominance and Technological Change* (Pluto Press, London, 1983)

Cohen, S. *Folk Devils and Moral Panics: the Creation of the Mods and Rockers* (Mac-Gibbon & Kee, London, 1972)

Cohen, S. and Young, J. *The Manufacture of News: Deviance, Social Problems and the Mass Media* (Constable, London, 1981)

Collins, H. *Marxism and Law* (Oxford University Press, Oxford, 1982)

Cook, J. and Lewington, M. (eds) *Images of Alcoholism* (British Film Institute, London, 1979)

Curran, J., Gurevitch, M. and Woollacott, J. (eds) *Mass Communication and Society* (Edward Arnold, London, 1977)

Curran, J., Douglas, A. and Whannel, G. 'The Political Economy of the Human-Interest Story' in *Newspapers and Democracy: International Essays on a Changing Medium* edited by A. Smith (Massachusetts Institute of Technology Press, Cambridge, Mass., 1980)

Ditton, J. and Duffy, J. 'Bias in the Newspaper Reporting of Crime News' *British Journal of Criminology* vol 23 no 2, April 1983

Durkheim, E. *Suicide: A Study in Sociology* (Routledge & Kegan Paul, London, 1952)

Elliott, P. 'Review of *More Bad News* by the Glasgow University Media Group' *Sociological Review* vol 29 no I, Feb. 1981)

Eysenck, H. J. and Nias, D. K. B. *Sex, Violence and the Media* (Paladin, London, 1980)

Ferguson, M. *Forever Feminine: Women's Magazines and the Cult of Femininity* (Heinemann, London, 1983)

Fishman, M. 'Crime Waves as Ideology' *Social Problems* vol 25 no 4, June 1978

Fowler, B. ' "True To Me Always": An Analysis of Women's Magazine Fiction' *British Journal of Sociology* vol 30 no I, March 1979

Frith, S. *Sound Effects: Youth, Leisure and the Politics of Rock 'n' Roll* (Constable, London, 1983)

Gans, H. J. *Deciding What's News: a Study of CBS Evening News, NBC Nightly News, Newsweek and Time* (Constable, London, 1980)

Galtung, J. and Ruge, M. H. 'The Structure of Foreign News' *Journal of Peace Research* vol 2, 1965

Gitlin, T. 'Media Sociology: the Dominant Paradigm' *Theory and Society* vol 6 no 2, Sept. 1978

Glasgow University Media Group *Bad News* (Routledge & Kegan Paul, London, 1976)

Glasgow University Media Group *More Bad News* (Routledge & Kegan Paul, London, 1980)

Glasgow University Media Group *Really Bad News* (Writers & Readers, London, 1982)

Goffman, E. *Gender Advertisements* (Macmillan, London, 1979)

Gurevitch, M., Bennett, T., Curran, J. and Woollacott, J. (eds) *Culture, Society and the Media* (Methuen, London, 1982)

441

Gurevitch, M. and Blumler, J. 'Linkages between the Mass Media and Politics: a Model for the Analysis of Political Communications Systems' in J. Curran *et al*, 1977

Hall, S. 'The Rediscovery of "Ideology": Return of the Repressed in Media Studies' in M. Gurevitch *et al*, 1982

Hall, S., Critcher, C., Jefferson, T., Clarke, J. and Roberts, B. *Policing the Crisis: Mugging, the State and Law and Order* (Macmillan, London, 1978)

Hartmann, P., *et al* 'Race as News' in *Race as News* edited by J. D. Halloran (UNESCO, Paris, 1974)

Hirsch, P. M. 'Processing Fads and Fashions: an Organization Set Analysis of Cultural Industry Systems' *American Journal of Sociology* vol 77 no 4, 1972

Howitt, D. *Mass Media and Social Problems* (Pergamon Press, Oxford, 1982)

Katz, E. and Lazarsfeld, P. *Personal Influence* (The Free Press, New York, 1955)

Kealy, E. 'From Craft to Art: the Case of Sound Mixers and Popular Music' *Sociology of Work and Occupations* vol 6 no I, Feb. 1979

Kuhn, T. *The Structure of Scientific Revolutions* (University of Chicago Press, Chicago, 1962)

Laing, D. 'The Music Industry in Crisis' *Marxism Today* July 1981

Lane, M. *Books and Publishers: Commerce Against Culture in Postwar Britain* (D. C. Heath & Co., Lexington, Mass., 1980)

Lea, J. and Young, J. 'Urban Violence and Political Marginalisation: The Riots in Britain; Summer 1981' *Critical Social Policy* vol I, no 3, Spring 1982

Mcquail, D. (ed) *Sociology of Mass Communications* (Penguin, Harmondsworth, 1972)

McQuail, D., Blumler, J. G. and Brown, J. R. 'The Television Audience: A Revised Perspective' in McQuail, 1972

Marx, K. *Capital Vol. III* (Penguin, Harmondsworth, 1981)

Marx, K. and Engels, F. *The German Ideology* (Lawrence & Wishart, London, 1965)

Miliband, R. *The State in Capitalist Society* (Quartet Books, London, 1973)

Morley, D. *The 'Nationwide' Audience* (British Film Institute, London, 1980)

Murdock, G. and Golding, P. 'Capitalism, Communications and Class Relations' in J. Curran *et al*, 1977

Murdock, G. and McCron, R. 'The Broadcasting and Delinquency Debate' *Screen Education* no 30, Spring 1979

Murdock, G. 'Class, Power and the Press: Problems of Conceptualisation and Evidence' in H. Christian, 1980

Murdock, G. 'Large Corporations and the Control of the Communications Industries' in M. Gurevitch *et al*, 1982

Palmer, J. *Thrillers: Genesis and Structure of a Popular Genre* (Edward Arnold, London, 1979)

Plummer, K. 'Misunderstanding Labelling Perspectives' in *Deviant Interpretations* edited by D. Downes and P. Rock (Martin Robertson, Oxford, 1979)

Robins, D. and Cohen, P. 'Enter the Dragon' in Cohen and Young, 1981

Rosengren, K. E. and Windahl, S. 'Mass Media Consumption as a Functional Alternative' in McQuail, 1972

Scott, J. *Corporations, Classes and Capitalism* (Hutchinson, London, 1979)

Schlesinger, P. *Putting 'Reality' Together* (Constable, London 1978)

Tracey, M. and Morrison, D. *Whitehouse* (Macmillan, London, 1979)

Troyna, B. *Public Awareness and the Media: a Study of Reporting Race* (Commission for Racial Equality, London, 1981)

Tuchman, G. 'Objectivity as Strategic Ritual: an Examination of Newsmen's Notions of Objectivity' *American Journal of Sociology* vol 77, 1972

Tudor, A. 'On Alcohol and the Mystique of Media Effects' in J. Cook and M. Lewington, 1979

Tunstall, J. *The Media in Britain* (Constable, London, 1983)

Whale, J. *The Politics of the Media* (Fontana, London, 1977)

Williams, B. *Obscenity and Film Censorship: An Abridgement of the Williams Report* (Cambridge University Press, Cambridge, 1981)

Wolff, J. *The Social Production of Art* (Macmillan, London, 1981)

Woollacott, J. 'Teaching Them to Read: The Politics of Imagination' *Schooling and Culture* Issue 7, Spring 1980

Young, J. 'Beyond the Consensual Paradigm: A Critique of Left Functionalism in Media Theory' in S. Cohen and J. Young, 1981

Section 6

The Sociology of Knowledge

David Glover and Sheelagh Strawbridge

Chapter One

Knowledge and Society

Asthma, Bloodletting and Witchcraft

We live in a society in which knowledge is on the increase. When the first edition of the Encyclopaedia Brittanica was being prepared in the middle of the eighteenth century, it took only one or two individuals to survey the entire field of human knowledge. Nowadays as many as 10,000 specialists are needed for this massive undertaking, and it has been reckoned that the output of knowledge in areas like medicine is so great that it would take a doctor several centuries to read it all. (Bell, 1974, p. 174.) We expect ideas to keep changing too. At the time that the first Encyclopaedia Brittanica appeared, the recognised cures for asthma were opium or bloodletting. We would be very worried if a doctor prescribed either of these treatments today, and find it hard to understand how people could ever have believed in such remedies.

While societies may differ about what is true or false, right or wrong, all of them have bodies of knowledge by which to live. Pre-modern medical opinion, like other forms of thought such as Roman law or medieval ideas about witchcraft, reveals to us not only what members of a society think, but also illuminates their actions. This has led sociologists to try to explain why people hold the ideas they do, and to see how far this can be accounted for by social factors – in other words, to develop a sociology of knowledge. As an illustration, take the case of witchcraft. Accusing women of witchcraft was often a way of providing scapegoats during times of social upheaval. However, compared to most European societies, belief in witchcraft appears to have been relatively weak in England in the sixteenth and seventeenth centuries. Why was this? According to Anderson and Gordon, a major factor here was that English women enjoyed 'a status and independence which found no parallel elsewhere'. They were gaining in income and wealth, becoming more literate, and their subordination within marriage was increasingly being questioned. This made English women seem less acceptable targets for scapegoating than was the case in Europe. They were therefore much less likely to be accused of witchcraft. As a result, English witchcraft trials tended to be rather few in number, the executions infrequent, the sentences light and the chances of being acquitted were good. By contrast, the prevalence of witchcraft prosecutions in countries like Scotland was in part a product of the low status of women within both the church and society (Anderson and Gordon, 1978).

As this example shows, the sociology of knowledge seeks to relate patterns of thought to social situations. These patterns of thought are many and varied for, in addition to the kinds of ideas and beliefs mentioned above, the sociology of knowledge also looks at concepts like space and time which are fundamental to the activity of thinking itself. Through these concepts we form our view of the natural world, the way it works, and our place within it. This chapter provides an introduction to the sociology of knowledge by considering how concepts of time arise and how and why they vary from society to society.

Time in Traditional African Society

Our own idea of time is something that we take for granted. There is a past, a present and a future, and we think of ourselves as moving forward in time without knowing exactly what lies ahead. In the here and now, though, our use of time is extremely precise. We run our lives according to the clock, marking time's passing in factories and schools by the ringing of bells, and setting a high value on punctuality. Maybe other societies are not so obsessed with time as we are, but surely all human beings share the same experience of living through a past, a present and a future? Some philosophers have even argued that this sense of time is part of the mental equipment with which we are born. If this is true, what is there to explain?

So ingrained is this view of time in the West that it takes a comparison with other societies to show how unique it is. Many tribes, like the Nuer of East Africa, have no equivalent expression which means 'time' in their language. Far from there being a single and consistent system like our own in which everything can be measured or placed along a uniform scale of years, months, days, hours and minutes, time amongst the Nuer is extremely varied and can mean many different things. According to E. E. Evans-Pritchard's classic anthropological study of the Nuer, there are two broad ways in which they reckon time. Firstly, there is 'ecological time'. This arises out of the Nuer's relationship with their natural environment. It consists of a cycle of seasons like winter and summer, but is mainly concerned with what happens within each season. For example, it dictates when fishing dams should be built or cattle camps formed. On a more day to day basis their herds of cattle serve as a 'cattle clock'. In other words, the Nuer gauge everyday time according to when pastoral tasks like milking have to be carried out. Hence 'the time of day and the passage of time through a day are to a Nuer primarily the succession of these tasks and their relations to one another' (Evans-Pritchard, 1940, pp. 101–2).

Because it centres upon activities like herding and milking, ecological time can alter its meaning depending upon who is using it. Members of a particular family will often reckon time in a way that is specially important to them. Thus they will date a key event like that of a family wedding by associating it with the time when calves were born to the herds which they own. At this point, ecological time merges with a second system of time-reckoning which is built around significant features of group life like wars, generations in a family, initiation rites and other age-specific ceremonies. Evans-Pritchard calls this way of marking past and present 'structural time', because it is based upon people's relation to each other in the tribe's social structure. Structural time provides the Nuer with a rough record of historical fact. It explains their social relationships as an outgrowth of the past, incorporating them into tribal myths. Because of this it is 'mainly a looking-backwards' (p. 108).

This emphasis upon the past is characteristic of traditional African thought. The African theologian John Mbiti has pointed out that the majority of East African languages do not even have words which refer to the distant future. Time is understood to move backwards rather than forwards, because 'people set their minds not on future things, but chiefly on what has taken place' (Mbiti, 1969, p. 17). Strictly speaking, things which have not yet happened lie outside time as they conceive it: events occur in the present and quickly recede into the past. For traditional Africans time is a thoroughly religious concept. Thus the tribal myths embodied in structural time tell them where the tribe came from and its relationship to the universe and its creator.

Notions of time vary from society to society. Certain Western concepts like that of the future, which we consider to be essential, have no real counterparts amongst many East African tribes. Time for the Nuer is closely bound up with their social organisation and patterns of work and this makes it quite unlike our own. It is part of their culturally determined stock of knowledge.

A Functionalist Explanation of 'Social Time'

So far we have shown that concepts of time reflect social and cultural differences between societies. But we have not yet tried to explain how and why this happens. In other words, we need a theory which will account for the variety found amongst concepts of time. One way of explaining these differences derives from the functionalist perspective, and we will take this as a first example of a sociology of knowledge approach, since it is also one of the earliest studies of its kind.

In an important article published in 1937, Pitirim Sorokin and Robert K. Merton claimed that we can account for variations in ideas about time by what they call 'social necessity'. Like biological organisms, they suggest, societies have 'needs' which must be satisfied if they are to survive, and which it is the function of social institutions to meet. Just as the human body is made up of a set of interlocking parts, each one maintaining the healthy organism, so a society consists of interrelated institutions, most of which work in such a way as to ensure a stable social order. Thus, following the basic assumptions of functionalism, Sorokin and Merton argued that systems of time-reckoning, like other social phenomena, can best be explained by showing how they contribute to the workings of society as a whole. The problem, then, is to identify the function that time performs. What 'needs' does it meet, and how does it help to hold society together?

Sorokin and Merton argued that concepts of time have the function of coordinating the various activities which go on within a society. Hence 'each group . . . sets its time to fit the round of its behaviour'. In other words, time has an integrative function. It blends together a whole series of individual actions so that the group can benefit from pooling its efforts. This is particularly clear when life becomes hard, for we find that the use of time changes in order to cope with adversity. To take the case of the Nuer again, during the difficult drought period the tribe shifts to a more finely graded way of marking time in order to regulate access to the short supplies of water and good pasture. Accordingly, each day is very carefully counted. Sorokin and Merton's point is that at such moments a group's chosen 'mode of life' encounters problems which can only be met by group solidarity. Systems of time-reckoning offer a solution here. They serve as a means of controlling behaviour by providing a shared calendar which dictates what has to be done and when. In short, concepts of time 'arise from the round of group life, . . . are perpetuated by the need for social co-ordination, and are essentially a product of social interaction'. Hence we should think of them as concepts of 'social time' (pp. 620–1).

But why is it necessary for different societies to have their own distinctive concepts of time? Sorokin and Merton's answer is that ideas about time are related to the size and complexity of the social group. Where societies have organised a series of days into a week, this was originally to allow them to exchange their produce regularly in a market. The days of the week distinguished when one bought and sold from days when one worked. By contrast, a tribe of subsistence cultivators like the East African Kaguru have no names for individual days, and consequently no traditional week: they merely calculate time according to what has to be done each day, adjusting this to meet the arrival and departure of the rains (Beidelman, 1963).

In a simple economy where no large stores of food are kept, a week may consist of only three or four days, whereas a large-scale complex society such as ancient Rome would have an eight day week, the eighth day being the one on which farmers came into the city to dispose of their produce. Societies like ancient Rome covered a wide geographical area within which activities like crop-growing varied from region to region. This meant an increase in the scope of the market in order to cater for a diversity of occupations, and led to a lengthening of the week. Sorokin and Merton point out that as societies increase in size 'the field of interaction expands' bringing together people from a variety of social and cultural backgrounds. If these different people are to 'synchronise and coordinate their activities', they will 'require some temporal scheme which will be equally intelligible to all' (pp. 624–6). At the other extreme, small-scale face-to-face societies like the Nuer can base the present on lessons drawn from the tribe's past experience, and this is reflected in the way in which they think about time. Everyone in the tribe shares the same mode of life, which changes very slowly. One consequence of the kind of group cohesion they have is a time scheme which looks backwards to the tribe's past. Thus their idea of time is so deeply embedded in their mode of life that it cannot readily be adopted by others.

There are however a number of problems with this approach. Like many functionalists, Sorokin and Merton over-estimate how much integration is necessary to society. Even if 'the spread of contact and organised interaction' did create a stimulus for a common standard of time to synchronise diverse social activities, this does not mean that modern pluralistic societies will rely on only one kind of time-scale. As Sorokin and Merton themselves point out, in advanced industrial societies specialised concepts of time like those found in physics or economics can co-exist with much vaguer references like 'I'll meet you after the concert'. This variety of usage does not seem to pose any threat of social disintegration.

On the other hand, the authors also fail to recognise that social groups with powerful vested interests may on occasion come into conflict over ideas about time. For example, the international conference of 1884 which eventually worked out and agreed a world-wide time system was the scene of intense imperial rivalry between Britain and France. Even today, international standard time is by no means uniformly observed throughout the globe, and is sometimes actively resisted. Moslem countries regard it as 'a blasphemous interference with the divine natural order' and disregard it when time-tabling their prayers and ceremonies. As the Iranian leader Ayatollah Khomeini once complained, 'the heads of our countries are so influenced by the West that they have set their clocks according to European time. It's a nightmare.' (see Zerubavel, 1982). This suggests that concepts of time are linked to questions of power and domination, a point ignored by most functionalists. We will return to this issue in the next chapter.

Summary

To summarise, we can say that the sociology of knowledge has two sides to it which can be summarised as follows. Firstly, it seeks to document some of the socially varied ways in which people think. Fundamental questions like 'how is the physical world made up, and why is it like this?' or 'what happens to us when we die?' or 'how do we judge a work of art to be beautiful?' have been both asked and answered very differently by other societies, and by our predecessors in earlier historical periods. Secondly, and more importantly, the sociology of knowledge tries to account for these differences in thought by relating them to key aspects of social life, particularly the way in which societies are organised.

This chapter has considered the functionalist approach as an example of the sociology of knowledge. In Chapter 2 we will explore the perspectives on the sociology of knowledge offered by classical sociological theory.

Chapter Two

Classical Perspectives on the Sociology of Knowledge

The sociology of knowledge owes its origins to three major sociological theorists: Karl Marx (1818–1883), Émile Durkheim (1858–1917), and Karl Mannheim (1893–1947). Although they were working at different times and belong to different intellectual traditions, all three writers saw knowledge as the product of social structures and social interaction. This chapter examines each writer in turn and tries to assess the current status of their work.

Marx and the Theory of Ideology

Although Marx never set out to write a sociology of knowledge as this would be understood today, he is nevertheless widely recognised as its most important forerunner, to whom it owes what has been called 'its root proposition' (Berger & Luckmann, 1967, p. 17). This states, in Marx's words, that 'it is not the consciousness of men that determines their existence, but, on the contrary, their social existence that determines their consciousness' (Marx & Engels, 1968, p. 181). In advancing this view, Marx was taking issue with the idealist inter-pretations of history which were influential at that time. These maintained that the basis of social life was to be found in the ideas which people hold and upon which they act. Thus it was the changing logic of ideas which brought about change in society.

Against this idealist position Marx argued that the way we think stems from the social conditions we experience. He wrote: 'Men make their own history, but they do not make it just as they please; they do not make it under circumstances chosen by themselves.' (1968, p. 96). His theory of revolution is a good illustration of this. Marx believed that as capitalism developed, those firms which survived on the battlefield of free competition would increase in size, and this would

451

tend to bring large numbers of workers together under a single factory roof. Sharing a common set of exploitative circumstances, they would increasingly realise that they had nothing to gain from a capitalist society, and this would lead them to organise against it. Here it is the social and material conditions associated with wage labour which will promote class consciousness as capitalism lurches from crisis to crisis. Marx was not saying that ideas are unimportant in social change, but he did insist that 'when people speak of ideas that revolutionise society, they do but express the fact, that within the old society, the elements of a new one have been created' (1968, p. 51).

However, because societies are split along class lines, Marx also argued that it is possible for people's thinking to become distorted rather than clarified by their experience of social divisions. If one class is more economically and politically powerful than another, then this makes it likely that its vision of society will be more intellectually powerful, precisely because of the material advantages it enjoys. This is the core of what is now known as Marx's 'dominant ideology thesis', according to which 'the ideas of the ruling class are in every epoch the ruling ideas', since 'the class which has the means of material production at its disposal, has control at the same time over the means of mental production'. The capitalists or bourgeoisie do not just own industrial property; they dominate politics and the State, communications, the arts and education, and this enables them to 'rule also as thinkers, as producers of ideas'. Those within the ruling class who specialise as thinkers Marx terms its 'ideologists' (Marx, 1971, pp. 47–9).

Why does he describe these ideas as ideological? Marx gives two main reasons. Firstly, ideologies are ideas which enable a class formed by new economic conditions to win and consolidate power. To do this it has to portray itself as acting on behalf of everyone in society in order to rally other social groups to its side. This portrayal may indeed be convincing, but it in fact gives a distorted picture of what society is really like. For example, it may disguise or downplay the existence of class conflict, or present social classes in a misleading light by claiming that they can co-exist in harmony with each other. Marx's second point about ideology, then, is that it covers up social contradictions.

Marx was not, however, claiming that ideologies were cynically created in a deliberate endeavour to deceive and manipulate. When he spoke of them as 'illusions' he emphasised that they were illusions that a class had 'about itself'. Why this self-deception? To answer this question we have to return to Marx's contention that ideas have to be explained by social conditions. In its ideology the ruling class shows both the strengths and weaknesses of its own position in society. On the one hand, ideology offers a justification for the conditions under which the ruling class holds power; yet, on the other, because of this self-justification it is unable to recognise itself as a class which stands in the way of further social advances, defending its privileges like the ruling classes which preceded it.

Although ideology primarily derives from the ruling class and is then spread throughout society, other social classes may also develop forms of thought displaying the limitations which class domination imposes upon their social lives. Where a society is divided into classes, Marx believed that the impossibility of solving the social problems this created without far-reaching social change could give rise to ideas which simply added weight to the status quo. The continuing existence of poverty in the midst of plenty may, for instance, encourage the response that 'the poor are always with us', since life just is inherently unfair and as a result little can be done about poverty. This ideology of fatalism on the part of the subordinate classes defuses support for action which would bring the extremes of wealth and poverty and its causes to an end. Though they originate outside the ruling class, ideas like these strengthen it. However, as we have already seen from Marx's theory of revolution, workers are increasingly placed in a position which enables them to see that they have common interests and this undermines the credibility of the bourgeoisie's view of society. Thus, as *The Communist Manifesto* points out, 'the dissolution of the old ideas keeps even pace with the dissolution of the old conditions' (Marx & Engels, 1968, p. 51).

To sum up: Marx, in claiming that ideas are socially determined, also held that in a class society ideas could often be ideological, giving a one-sided, inadequate guide to social reality which reinforced ruling class domination. This was part of the power of one class over another. Yet by no means all ideas that are socially conditioned are ideological; this depends upon their role in society. Proletarian class consciousness is a case in point. According to Marx, the working class's changing social situation gives it a clearer view of capitalist society as old social structures are being swept away.

Time and Industrial Capitalism

In the last chapter we suggested that time was often closely linked to issues of power and domination. The social historian E. P. Thompson has examined this from a Marxist perspective. In his article 'Time, Work-Discipline and Industrial Capitalism', Thompson sets out to examine how changes in the way in which people thought about time came about as a result of changing patterns of work, bringing in 'a severe restructuring of working habits' (1967, p. 57). We tend to assume that our modern use of time is simply an outcome of technological progress; to argue, for example, that 'the use of the telegraph signal in 1852 made possible the synchronisation of local times with Greenwich Mean Time' (see Lowe, 1982, p. 38). Thompson, however, observes that changes in attitudes to time depend first of all upon how it is embodied in social relationships, especially where these are based on economic power.

He begins by examining the use of time common in peasant societies typified by the medieval village. Here, as we saw in the case of the Nuer, time is related to the tasks that have to be done. It has two main characteristics. Firstly, 'the working-day lengthens or contracts according to the task' and work is therefore integrated with the social life of the community. And secondly, by the standard of the clock, work of this kind often seems to be inefficient and leisurely. The picture starts to alter once labour develops into employment, since this begins to establish a link between time and cash-payments. Put simply, time is equated with the employer's money. Thus 'as soon as actual hands are employed the shift from task-orientation to timed labour is marked', and time is now split between that which belongs to the employer and that which is 'free' (Thompson, 1967, pp. 60–1).

Although clocks date from the second half of the thirteenth century, their role in time-keeping was initially fairly limited. 'Many of the early church clocks did not strike the hour' and a bell-ringer was employed to signal the hours of curfew, while 'the sundial remained in use (partly to set the clock) in the seventeenth, eighteenth and nineteenth centuries' (p. 63). Similarly, the possession of watches had other, more important purposes than simply telling the time: they served as status symbols and ornaments amongst the gentry, and, for artisans, were an investment which could be pawned in times of hardship. Hence the custom of rewarding years of long service with a gold watch.

Clocks began to take on a different meaning once the small workshop was eclipsed by large-scale industry with its elaborate division of labour. Not only do the different branches of work have to be synchronised, but employees must also be habituated to the continuous running of the new machinery. It was no longer enough to roughly reckon days worked; hours and minutes had to be recorded too. Thompson quotes from the rule book of the Crowley Iron Works in 1700 which paid wages only 'after all deductions for being at taverns, alehouses, coffee houses, breakfast, dinner, playing, sleeping, smoaking, reading of news history, quarelling, contention, disputes or anything forreign to my business, any way loytering' (Original spelling, p. 81). Here we see the origins of modern time-and-motion studies.

Industrial capitalism was introduced in the face of great resistance for it involved rooting out old working practices and replacing them with a new sense of self-discipline. This process was greatly assisted by the Puritan religious ideology of such figures as John Wesley with his exhortations to keep 'all the time you can . . . out of the hands of sin and Satan'. Thus the old habit of observing 'Saint Monday' as a day when one did not go into work, a custom which went back to the pre-industrial market days and holidays, was attacked as wasteful and irresponsible. In order to break such practices industrialists in the mills and factories sought to keep strict control of time. As one early workman recounted: 'there was nobody but the master and the master's son who had a watch, and we did not know the time. There was one man who had a watch . . . It was taken from him and given into the master's custody because he had told the men the time of day' (p. 86).

Thompson's study shows how the introduction of clock time into capitalist production brought about a new stress on punctuality and industriousness which enabled the new ruling class to discipline and control its social inferiors. This was justified by moral and religious criticisms of earlier routines of work as mere idleness and time-wasting. As a result, there was a change in what Thompson calls 'the inward apprehension of time of working people'. He notes that similar struggles over time are currently occurring in the industrialising Third World where employers complain of the peasant's inability to adhere to a 'regular pace of work' (p. 92). Although he does not actually use the term 'ideology', Thompson's study is a good illustration of the Marxist proposition that 'the ideas of the ruling class are in every epoch the ruling ideas', and that ideas about time are no exception. As Marx once put it, for the worker in the modern factory, 'Time is everything, man is nothing' (Marx, 1955, p. 47).

A Critique of the Dominant Ideology Thesis

In the years that have followed Marx's death, Marxists have tended to put much greater emphasis on the theory of ideology than he himself did. Many writers have argued that one can explain why revolutions in the West have been either unsuccessful or have failed to occur by the hold which ideology has upon us. More recently, this view has been strongly questioned. In their book *The Dominant Ideology Thesis*

(1980), Abercrombie, Hill and Turner have concluded that it fails to square with the facts. Put simply, their argument is as follows. Looking at any class society to see whether 'the ruling ideas of each age have ever been the ideas of its ruling class' entails addressing four distinct issues. Firstly, one has to show that there is indeed a dominant ideology for the society in question. Secondly, one needs to be able to identify those institutions which transmit that ideology. Thirdly, the ideology has to be shown to exert an influence over the subordinate classes. And finally, the impact of the dominant ideology on the ruling class itself must be considered.

Abercrombie, Hill and Turner examine the evidence on three historically significant types of society, concentrating mainly on British examples. These are feudalism, early capitalism and late capitalism. The authors suggest that only in the first two types of society is there a well-defined dominant ideology. Under feudalism this centred around the Catholic religion, while in early capitalism it derived from 'the fundamental value of individualism', which justified the virtues of self-improvement, *laissez-faire*, and the inheritance of private property. However, in neither case were the means for inculcating this ideology into the ruling class's social inferiors very highly developed. Much of the evidence we have about feudalism implies that rulers and ruled had quite separate cultures, and, far from being devoted adherents to Christianity, 'the majority of the population was cut off from the church by language, literacy, learning and liturgy', preferring their own folk-belief in witchcraft, magic and demonology instead (p. 78). In early capitalism too there was little social contact between the major classes, and institutions like compulsory education or the mass media were mere shadows compared to today.

By the time we reach the 'late capitalism' of our own period with its powerful new forms of mass communication like radio and television, and its expanded education system, the capacity to promote a dominant ideology has been enormously increased. Paradoxically, however, there is no longer any coherent set of ruling ideas; what we have in its place are a series of ideological themes which are often in contradiction with each other. For example, support for the welfare state clashes with a belief in free market forces. The old ideology of individualism has been undermined by the rise of giant corporations and finance houses, and the private property of family capitalism is being replaced by complex, impersonal forms of ownership and control. Even the patriotic fervour of nationalism is at odds with the economics of the multinational conglomerate.

This suggests several conclusions. Perhaps the central point is that, where a dominant ideology does exist, it is of less importance in managing the behaviour of the lower classes than many Marxists would have us believe. Instead, other factors such as force of arms and force of law, the economic compulsion of keeping one's job, and the interdependencies of the division of labour may be more significant in maintaining the power of the ruling class. A dominant ideology is probably of greatest importance in providing the ruling class itself with a shared set of beliefs and values. Those who hold power in a class society can have divergent aims and objectives. For example, under capitalism those who control the banks do not necessarily see eye to eye with those who run their own firms. A dominant ideology can serve to remind the various competing sections of the ruling class that they do have common interests and so reduce its internal splits and conflicts. Yet, as we saw a moment ago, the authors argue that in late capitalism there is no clear dominant ideology to unify the ruling class, as there was in early capitalism.

These criticisms by no means apply to all versions of Marxism. Nor do the authors deny that beliefs are socially determined in the way that Marx suggested. In fact, they admit that in late capitalism some of the ideological themes found in ruling class thinking are successfully passed on to the working-class, even though these do not add up to a dominant ideology. For example, many members of the working-class accept the ideology of the nation state and patriotically support the political status quo, despite the fact that the ruling class has a very divided view of nationalism because of its multinational business interests.

Durkheim's Sociology of Knowledge

For an alternative perspective on the sociology of knowledge, we turn to the French sociologist Emile Durkheim. Throughout his life Durkheim sought to establish a science of the social world. He argued that society is more than just a collection of individuals. It consists of institutions and established patterns of behaviour like fashions in dress, a system of currency, or a shared language which derive from society rather than the individual and shape the way we live. For example, we need a common set of signs and symbols in order to communicate with each other, and these form the basis for a public world of beliefs and ideas which Durkheim termed 'collective representations'. Collective representations provide a framework and vocabulary of ideas without which individual thinking would not be possible at all. In other words, there exist 'social states of mind ... qualitatively different from individual ones' (Durkheim, 1952, p. 313). Durkheim's sociology of knowledge explores the social origins of these collective representations.

In an essay written jointly with Marcel Mauss and published in 1903 under the title *Primitive Classification*, Durkheim tried to demonstrate that the way we order, arrange, and make sense of the things we perceive in the world around us derives from the kind of structure our society has. For instance, the ability to think clearly and logically is not an innate feature of the human mind. It has only emerged quite recently in history. Durkheim and Mauss suggest that it grew out of older, pre-scientific ways of classifying and understanding 'things, events, and facts about the world', some of which can still be found in modern societies. As an example they cite the survival of the Christian idea that the bread and wine in the eucharist turn into the body and blood of Christ. Here 'images and ideas...are not separated from each other...with any clarity', and seem to defy our ordinary sense of cause and effect. Durkheim and Mauss point out that this apparently disordered kind of thinking is extremely common in other societies. Thus some clans amongst the Sioux Indians symbolically associated themselves with certain colours and animals. Elks, mountain lions, buffaloes and the colour red seem to have no intrinsic connection to us, yet to the Sioux they are signs or badges of the clan, and therefore belong in the same category. The sheer historical and cultural variety of such schemes of classification make Durkheim and Mauss doubt that they can be in any sense innate, and this leads them to seek a sociological explanation.

Though different in detail from the Sioux, many societies have systems of thought which link places, animals, plant-life, the weather, and human beings in odd juxtapositions. These range from the Australian aborigines, who classify everything in the natural environment as part of one of their clans, to traditional Chinese civilisation with its complex philosophy of Taoism. Durkheim and Mauss claim that 'the most rudimentary classifications made by mankind' are found amongst the Australian aborigines and that these categories give rise to religious beliefs because they tell each clan which things are sacred and worthy of worship. This is why these bodies of thought have such a powerful hold over the minds of group members. By associating the clan with certain material objects which have a ritual significance, 'primitive classifications' serve to define the clan's place in the world and give it an identity. Durkheim and Mauss believed that these beliefs, known as totemism, were the earliest type of religion.

Although group identity appears to come from the sacred object or totem, Durkheim and Mauss contend that 'the classification of things' was founded on 'the classification of men'. In other words, groups were not organised on the basis of the tribe's view of the world; instead 'it was because men were grouped, and thought of themselves in the form of groups, that in their ideas they grouped other things'. Put simply, it was group structure which determined tribal thought. This means that 'the first logical categories were social categories' and 'the first classes of things were classes of men, into which these things were integrated' (p. 82). To back up this claim Durkheim and Mauss compare simply-organised societies with more complex ones, claiming that complexity of social structure is always associated with complexity of thought. For example, they argue that the Zuni Indians have a more complex social structure than the Australian aborigines and as a result their view of the world is more complex. The Zuni see the universe as consisting of seven regions of space, roughly following the four main points of the compass plus an 'above', a 'below' and a centre, to each of which particular plants and animals permanently belong. These seven regions of space correspond to the seven clans which make up the pueblo or town, which is regarded as the centre of their universe.

Durkheim and Mauss believed that complex societies are always the outcome of simpler societies growing in size and then sub-dividing, so that it is always possible to discern amongst a tribe like the Zuni traces of an earlier and more elementary social structure than that of the seven clans. Hence 'the Zuni system is really a development and a complication of the Australian system' (pp. 54–5). In fact, Durkheim and Mauss argued that modern science was the eventual result of these classificatory schemes becoming more subtle and complex. Originally, the totems into which the natural world had been divided were heavily invested with emotion because of their importance to the group. However, as systems of classification grew more complicated it became difficult to associate them with strong emotional feelings, thus allowing thought to become more objective and rational. This prepared the way for modern science. Durkheim was later to incorporate many of these insights about 'primitive classification' into his sociological account of religion.

Durkheim Today

Few sociologists would accept Durkheim and Mauss's theory today. For one thing, their essay was based upon evidence which others had collected and some of this was very weak. Anthropological fieldwork has advanced enormously since they wrote and we now have far more information about tribal societies. Much of this invalidates Durkheim and Mauss's ideas. For instance, Peter Worsley's work on the Groote Eylandt aborigines suggests that totemic thought is often rather haphazard and fails to classify everything in the natural world. Furthermore, totems may be shared by groups, instead of belonging exclusively to one as Durkheim and Mauss supposed. Worsley found three kinds of totems, each of them based upon different principles, and their origins were hard to pin down. Sometimes they were related to historical events, as in the case of the airbase totem, which reflected the impact of the Second World War. But they were certainly not modelled on group structure.

Because totemic classification is so arbitrary, Worsley regards it as the enemy of logical thought. Side by side with it, however, was another quite independent ordering of the natural environment, developed for essentially practical purposes. This was 'rational, ordered, consistent and systematic . . . with objective analysis of natural phenomena' (Worsley, 1956, pp. 60–1). For Worsley this is the true ancestor of science, whereas Durkheim and Mauss assumed that this kind of pragmatic knowledge, unlike totemism, would be too piecemeal to lead to scientific theorising. Worsley's evidence suggests that the reverse is actually the case.

Despite these criticisms Durkheim and Mauss's ideas have been very influential. Their thesis that it is the form that social relationships take which explains the character of our collective knowledge of the world remains a provocative one.

The Sociology of Karl Mannheim

Karl Mannheim did not coin the term 'sociology of knowledge', but he probably did more than anyone else to make sociologists aware of it as a subject; so much so that he is often taken to be its founder. His most famous book *Ideology and Utopia* (1929) is an attempt to work out a method which will illuminate 'the social roots of our knowledge'. This was no mere academic exercise. Mannheim believed that only if we correctly understood the influence of the lives we lead upon the ways we think would it be possible to run society properly. In other words, the end-product of the sociology of knowledge was to be 'the scientific guidance of political life' (1960, pp. 4–5).

Mannheim took as his point of departure Marx's theory of ideology. However, although this provided the first systematic statement of the social determination of beliefs and ideas, Mannheim saw it as restricted to an exposé of their distortion by class interests. He argued, therefore, that it needed to be broadened in two ways. Firstly, Mannheim proposed that the sociology of knowledge should be concerned not 'with distortions due to a deliberate effort to deceive', but with 'the varying ways in which . . . mental structures are inevitably differently formed in different social and historical settings' – an alternative he termed 'the total conception of ideology' (pp. 238-9). As we have already seen, Mannheim's criticisms of Marx are not really accurate here, because for Marxists ideology does not stem from one class intending to hoodwink another. Secondly, Mannheim asserts that our ideas are not conditioned by social class alone, even though this tends to be the major factor; we are also influenced by belonging to groups based upon age, status, religion, occupation or ethnicity. As he notes, 'even the categories in which our experiences are . . . collected and ordered' vary with the social position of such groups (p. 130).

However, a look at the relationship between one group and another reveals that their most striking characteristic is that they are constantly coming into conflict. Each is engaged in a struggle for domination, and this affects the kinds of ideas that they will develop. Mannheim argues that inter-group competition creates aspirations that either go beyond the immediate situation in which a group finds itself or beliefs which fall short of it. These 'situationally transcendant' ideas are of two main types. On the one hand, there are what he calls 'ideologies' (using the term in a slightly different sense from that cited above). Ideologies are said to be out of step with social reality because they consist of outmoded forms of thought that are defended in order to block social changes that are actually occurring. Mannheim gives the example of the ban by the medieval church on charging interest on loans. This was enforceable in a society 'based upon intimate and neighbourly relations' such as feudalism. But as capitalism began to emerge this taboo failed to reflect the social structure of the time and degenerated into 'a weapon in the hands of the Church' to preserve its established position against its new rivals (p. 85).

The second type of thought is the mirror-image of ideology: 'utopia'. A utopia is a set of ideas embodying an alternative view of what society could be like, and which a social group tries to bring into existence. In other words, it is a special kind of wishful thinking. As Mannheim notes, 'as long as the clerically and feudally organised medieval order was able to locate its paradise outside of society, in some other-worldly sphere', this posed no threat (p. 174). Utopias only come into being when people start to compare such ideals with their own society and try to put them into practice. Mannheim sees this as the true beginning of modern politics, since it tends to draw all sections of society into the struggle for a say in how society is run. The ideal of a perfect world is sometimes taken up by oppressed social groups, who no longer fatalistically accept their traditional place in society. Unfortunately, Mannheim is not entirely clear about what brings social groups into conflict in the first place. Sometimes, as we have seen, he cites specific economic factors like the emergence of capitalism; at other moments, he makes vague references to 'the unrealised and unfulfilled . . . needs of each age' (p. 179); and at still others, he describes revolutions as being fuelled by deeply-rooted emotional energies which society has somehow repressed (p. 192). This imprecision is never really clarified.

How are we to study such modes of thought? Mannheim argues that we need to grasp what he calls their 'documentary meaning'. This is not simply a description of a set of ideas nor is it an account of the motives of the people involved; rather, it is an attempt to analyse the essential features of a body of thought by placing them in their full social and historical context. An example of this approach is Mannheim's study of modern conservative thought. He argues that this came into existence in the nineteenth century as a reaction against the political demands of the French Revolution and the economic upheavals associated with the rise of capitalism. Thus he notes that 'conservatism' is a word 'of comparatively recent origin' (1953, p. 98). Its 'documentary meaning' is an 'inner core' of values exemplified in 'the way in which it clings to the immediate, the actual, the concrete', virtues embodied in the life-style of traditional landed communities, from which the early supporters of conservatism were drawn (p. 102). This 'inner core' of thought is partly defined by those notions it opposes – thus a concept like 'equality' (central to the French Revolution) was attacked by conservatives as either a cloudy, philosophical idea or a mere abstract slogan. Getting to this kind of 'documentary meaning' is the work of painstakingly and sensitively sifting through the evidence. This task may be made easier if the sociologist has been involved in similar circumstances to those being studied, because this gives an insight into how people might have thought and behaved. However, this kind of empathy is not always possible.

Mannheim identified five major world-views in the modern era: bureaucratic thought, conservatism, liberal-democratic bourgeois thought, socialist-communist theory, and fascism. He believed that it was possible, however, to advance beyond these alternative perspectives. The sociology of knowledge could demonstrate how each of these world-views was limited by the social circumstances in which it had arisen, but, by the same token, it could show how, if brought together, each could contribute something to an understanding of the problems facing modern societies. Thus a science of politics could be achieved. This task of synthesis would be carried out by a special social group, the modern intelligentsia, whose members were recruited on the basis of merit and who had no firm ties to any particular section of society. Indeed, for Mannheim, the conditions which brought this group into being were precisely those which made the sociology of knowledge possible: namely, the decline of traditional society, an increase in social mobility, and the development of a large-scale pluralistic society in which people's horizons were widened as they came into contact with different points of view.

The irony of Mannheim's work is that, having put the sociology of knowledge on the map, he inspired no Mannheimian tradition of sociology resembling those of contemporary Marxists or neo-Durkheimians. While his writings have been extremely influential, few writers have applied his major concepts in empirical investigations. One noteworthy exception is Kurt Danziger's 1970 study of ideologies and utopias in South African society. Although Danziger was able to show a link between social position and world-view, however, in no case did this form an entirely consistent pattern, so that Afrikaners, for example, were not invariably conservative. Most damagingly, Danziger found no evidence to suggest that South Africa's intelligentsia had developed an independent, constructive political solution, unattached to any of the main conflicting social forces. But, as he wryly comments, 'it would require an extraordinary intellectual feat to arrive at some synthetic perspective which combines the partial historical insights of Afrikaner nationalists, English liberals and African revolutionaries' (Danziger, 1973, p. 377).

Instead of following Mannheim, the sociology of knowledge has gone in other directions. It has breached the barrier he tried to erect against the possibility of a sociology of natural science, and it has found new ways of defining what the sociology of knowledge should be about. These departures will be the subject of the following chapters.

Chapter Three
Modernity and Everyday Life

The first sentence of Karl Mannheim's *Ideology and Utopia* declared it to be 'concerned with the problem of how men actually think'. But, as we saw in the last chapter, Mannheim's sociology of knowledge deals chiefly with certain kinds of thought, such as legal doctrines, political ideologies and religious creeds. What he really meant by the phrase 'how men actually think' was the practical role played by these ideas in social life. He believed that they could be traced back to the position in society of particular social groups, each with their own distinctive way of looking at the world, and hence ideas could be said to be 'socially determined'.

However, if we consider how people do 'actually think', it is clear that they typically think religiously, politically or legally only on specific occasions. Subtract these ideas from the sum total of human consciousness, and it is at once obvious that a great deal is left unexplained. Mannheim himself deliberately excluded mathematics and natural science from his sociology of knowledge because he argued that they could not be said to be founded upon group interests. What is an even more glaring omission from his book is any account of human consciousness in ordinary, everyday situations. This would truly show how people 'actually think'.

'The Social Construction of Reality'

This is precisely the issue addressed by Peter Berger and Thomas Luckmann's innovative book *The Social Construction of Reality*. According to them 'the sociology of knowledge must concern itself with everything that passes for "knowledge" in society' (Berger and Luckmann, 1967, p. 26). Berger and Luckmann therefore recommend that sociologists define 'knowledge' much more broadly than they have

464

in the past. It should refer to the ways in which people organise their day-to-day experiences of the social world. For instance, we 'know' what to do in a wide range of social settings without even thinking, and it takes a new experience to reveal to us just how much we take for granted. Thus a society in which people push and fight their way on to buses reveals to us how disciplined our concept and practice of queueing really is. Similarly, we base our face-to-face encounters on the knowledge we have acquired about individuals and about social types. It is this knowledge which gives us our understanding of society, and this is as apparent in our dealings with the postman as it is from a party political broadcast.

There are many possible social worlds we could learn to 'know', a fact vividly displayed by the variety of societies that have come into being in human history. Berger and Luckmann argue that this variety results from a unique characteristic of human beings. They are far less limited by their biology and their environment than other species, and this has enabled them to dominate nature the world over. Like all species humans have a need for an ordered, patterned way of life, but what is unusual about them is that neither their biological make-up nor their environment pre-determine the form this will take. Instead they collectively produce institutions which organise behaviour, shaping it into socially predictable routines. Put simply, human beings construct a social world of their own, and carefully seek to maintain it against disruption and uncertainty.

Not only must this social world be orderly, it must provide meaning too. That is to say, it must supply definitions of what social reality is like for its members. The ability to create a meaningful human world rests upon the possession of language and its social uses. It is by means of language that we are able to impose culturally significant distinctions upon our experience and so make sense of things. Aboriginal totemism and modern science may be very different, but they share this common feature. In any culture such systems of meaning are embodied in language or in related signs like gestures, bodily movements or even material objects (for example, Christian crosses). These acquire subjective importance for the individual. However, language is also detachable from the immediate situations in which it originates. It can retain or store meanings, and individuals can speak of things they have not experienced directly. Because language serves as a kind of reservoir, preserving meaning over time, we as individuals are born into cultures which consist of institutions whose patterns of meaning are already structured in language. Thus, although we 'make' meaning through our use of words, we also 'take' meaning by sharing in the knowledge of a particular social world or culture through its language. As Berger and Luckmann note 'man . . . and his social world interact with each other' in a dialectical process of reality construction. That is to say, the social world is 'a humanly produced reality', but one which then 'acts back upon' and influences its human producers (p. 78).

Berger and Luckmann's sociology of knowledge combines Max Weber's stress on the subjectively meaningful nature of social behaviour with Émile Durkheim's view of society as an objective structure which constrains and confines our actions and beliefs. At the same time Berger and Luckmann owe a great debt to phenomenological sociology with its insistence that all social institutions involve human consciousness. They believe that it is one of the key tasks for the sociology of knowledge to describe and account for the different forms that consciousness takes. The following section looks at Peter Berger's attempt to apply a sociology of knowledge perspective to the study of marriage.

Re-constructing the Social World: Marriage and the Sociology of Knowledge

At first glance marriage might seem to be an odd topic for the sociology of knowledge to investigate. After all, there are now well-established traditions in the study of the family and sociologists have amassed a lot of information about who marries whom and why, and about the different ways in which the roles of husband, wife or parent have been performed. So what could the sociology of knowledge tell us that we do not already know? Peter Berger suggests that we should see marriage as a vital ingredient in our knowledge of everyday life.

In an article written in 1964 with Hansfried Kellner, Berger points out that the most important feature of marriage is that it creates a social world for the individual, 'the sort of order in which he can experience his life as making sense'. In marriage two people engage in the task of building a life together, re-defining themselves in the process. As Berger and Kellner note 'the partners construct the present, reconstruct the past and develop a commonly projected future'. Language, in the form of daily conversation, is the main resource which makes this possible. It replaces the earlier conversations from the family life they had each individually known before, but which they could not fully share, and marks the transition from one social world to another.

However, despite the fact that the two partners usually come from similar (if separate) backgrounds, this process of world construction is fraught with difficulties. The couple must adjust their previous experiences and biographies so that these are in harmony. A good example of this is the way in which their circle of friends and acquaintances is re-assessed. Former friends can no longer be accepted on the strength of old personal ties, but must be viewed in the light of the new marriage. An old friendship will become a topic in the marital conversation, and its status may change as a result. As Berger and Kellner point out, even if a wife does not accept her husband's image of someone, the very fact of being aware of his response is likely to have a strong influence on her attitudes. Thus the marital conversation produces a shared understanding of people known in common. Such 'joint images' serve to define the world of the marriage itself. Along with major events like holidays, illnesses or moving house they add to the stock of knowledge and experience around which the relationship is built.

Berger and Kellner stress that this accumulation of knowledge is not usually recognised by the husband and wife for what it is. This is because everything is evaluated from the standpoint of the marriage and it is difficult for the two partners to be objective about it. For example, we typically talk about 'tensions with in-laws' or 'friends disappearing', seeing these things as difficulties faced by a marriage, but impinging on it from outside. We fail to notice the part played by the shared reality of the marriage itself in producing and defining them as problems. One of the reasons for the invisibility of this process of reality construction is our subjective involvement in it. This is particularly marked in the case of the modern family because it is seen as an institution which provides a private haven from the anonymity, impersonality and competitiveness of the more public realms of work and politics. Marriage is perceived as a kind of refuge, a 'little world' in which people can 'discover who they really are' or 'really be themselves'. In fact, this belief is part of the family ideology in our society, 'a taken-for-granted image of marriage' into which we are socialised.

It is tempting to react to Berger and Kellner's account of the family by pointing out that the marital conversation is often a marital argument. However, Berger and Kellner do emphasise that the construction of the marriage relationship is a task requiring 'considerable effort', whose results are always of a 'precarious nature'. Nevertheless, what is missing from their picture is any analysis of the different lives men and women lead, both within and outside a marriage, and the inequalities which stem from this. As David Morgan has observed, Berger and Kellner never ask: 'whose marriage?' They fail to see that different experiences at work and in the labour market will 'have consequences for the perception and experience of marriage on the part of the spouses' (Morgan, 1981, p. 23).

Marilyn Porter's study of working-class families suggests, for example, that men and women live 'worlds apart', despite the fact that 'both sexes regard the home as the primary locus of their lives'. Even if they went out to work women basically saw themselves as homemakers, whereas for men it was their identity as breadwinners that was most important. Porter shows that this was 'the organising principle' behind their ideas. The work men did was seldom discussed at home and as a result their trade union consciousness was never understood by their wives, which could lead to tension when industrial disputes took place. The women, on the other hand, tended to make judgments in terms of values derived from the home. Thus the sexes had rather different responses to the political events presented by the mass media. As one woman said: 'If women ran their homes the way men run the country there wouldn't be any happy homes.' This indicates that men and women do not define social reality in quite the same way and that marriage is not always the mutually shared social world portrayed by Berger and Kellner (Porter, 1978).

It also points to a more general problem with Berger and Luckmann's argument in *The Social Construction of Reality* that it is our human freedom from biology and environment that creates the need to construct orderly social worlds. As the above account of marriage illustrates, it is far from clear that human beings either require or actually achieve social order to the extent that Berger and Luckmann claim. In other words, Berger and Luckmann have failed to show that the claims they make about the human condition have the social consequences they say they do.

Modern Consciousness: A Sociology of Modernity

Much of the force of what Peter Berger has to say about marriage comes from the fact that he is talking about the modern family. Indeed, he claims to be describing a new 'global marriage type' which is now gaining prominence in industrial societies. His arguments here illustrate one of his main preoccupations, namely the sort of experiences we have in the modern world. What fascinates Berger is the way in which people's everyday consciousness is changing under the impact of modern social conditions. This theme is explored most fully in his book *The Homeless Mind*, written with Brigitte Berger and Hansfried Kellner.

Once again their work is squarely in the sociology of knowledge tradition. As the authors emphasise, their aim is not only to describe the styles of thought which are typical of modern social life – it is also to show how consciousness is rooted in the institutions which form its 'social base'. Thus 'the sociology of knowledge always deals with consciousness in the context of a specific social situation' (Berger *et al*, 1974, p. 21).

Berger *et al* start from the fact that the world is being transformed by technological innovation. This marks a major break between our own societies and those of the past, because this technology requires an appropriate set of institutions if it is to be applied successfully. The authors use the term 'modernisation' to refer to this process of technologically-based institutional growth which includes the rise of the bureaucratic state, the market economy, mass education, and the urban way of life. Although they see technological change as fundamental to modernisation, their's is not a Marxist approach. They argue that social change could not have occurred 'without antecedent processes that were neither technological nor economic', such as the spread of new religious beliefs like the Protestant ethic (p. 16). Technology is therefore not a final cause of modernisation, but is part of a complex chain of cause and effect in which it both influences institutions like the bureaucratic state and is in turn influenced by them.

Modern institutions are closely linked to patterns of consciousness and together these form what the authors call 'packages', in which specific beliefs and behaviours are intertwined. Some of these packages cannot be undone without social disruption. For example, factory machinery cannot be properly run without regular time-keeping and self-discipline. One has to keep one's emotions in check and accept a narrowing of one's attention so that it focuses upon the essentials of the job in hand. As the authors point out 'an artistically inclined worker on an assembly line who, smitten by his muse, loses himself in contemplation of the unique and irreproducible features of a particular screw' would probably be unable to get the job done (p. 33). There has to be a willingness to work in an environment which is quite impersonal in the sense that its tasks are standardised so that anyone can do them, its limits firmly fixed by the division of labour. Certain forms of consciousness are therefore unacceptable in such a context.

Nevertheless, not all packages are as tightly wrapped as this. Bureaucracy is a case in point. Like technological production it too demands orderliness, set procedures, anonymity, and the involvement of only a part of one's self-identity in its routines. It classifies and files, dealing with clients as 'cases' rather than as uniquely individual persons. Yet tied in with this stock of knowledge defining how a bureaucracy operates are ideals and standards against which it can be judged and held to account. These centre upon the right of the individual to receive fair treatment and redress from injustice. Berger *et al* note that these values derive from the political beliefs historically associated with liberal democracies. For example, these standards were absent from the bureaucracies of Nazi Germany. Thus the relationship between ideas and social structure may be of two kinds: either necessary and unavoidable as in the link between the assembly line and technological consciousness, or, as in the case of bureaucracy and accountability, the result of purely historical factors which are far from inevitable and may vary.

The other major feature of modernisation which has implications for consciousness is the fragmentation of society into separate compartments – what the authors term 'a pluralisation of social life-worlds'. As Benita Luckmann has put it, in earlier societies 'the tribe, the clan, the village, the small town represented kinds of small worlds within which all of man's living was done' and of which 'man possessed detailed and intimate knowledge' (Luckmann, 1978, p. 276). What we now experience, by contrast, is a social world which is so highly specialised and divided that we only fully comprehend our own particular bits of it. Similarly, modern cities contain such large and diverse populations that our knowledge of how people live is often very restricted and based upon ideas drawn from the mass media rather than direct experience. We typically have contact with only a limited number of enclaves which make up the wider social world and we seek to model our lives in relation to them. Because modern society 'confronts the individual with an ever-changing kaleidoscope of social experiences and meanings', it forces us to continually make choices, decisions and plans in order to cope with them (p. 74). At the same time, this experience of variety and diversity undermines any feeling of certainty, since 'what is truth in one context of the individual's social life may be error in another' (p. 165). This places an immense burden upon the individual for, unlike previous eras, there is no common religion to provide an overarching framework of meaning which puts everything into perspective. Not only are we aware of many competing religions, but religion figures as merely one belief amongst others. It is in this sense that Berger *et al* refer to our lives as 'homeless', passing through many social worlds, but being settled in none.

De-modernisation

However, modernisation is no one-way street. Probably modern consciousness reached its peak of self-confidence in the nineteenth century when people believed that industrial society offered a future of boundless progress. Few would subscribe to such optimism today. More importantly, there has been a reaction against modern society and some of its central values have been rejected. This desire to roll back the achievement of modernity is described by Berger *et al* as 'de-modernisation'. It gives rise to its own peculiar forms of thinking which offer alternative definitions of reality and styles of life.

Most industrial societies have in fact experienced 'an astonishingly powerful resurgence of de-modernisation' (p. 169). According to the authors this has been due to a speed-up in the rate of technological change, together with the ever more rapid bureaucratisation, urbanisation and pluralisation of social life. It is therefore far harder for the individual to feel at home in the social world than has previously been the case. Moreover, industrial societies now contain some disruptive new features. Berger *et al* single out the changing character of childhood and youth. For now the majority of children survive into adulthood, thanks to improved living standards and medical advances. They spend an increasing amount of time in education or training which effectively excludes them from full participation in other spheres of social life. Child labour has been replaced by pupil and student sub-cultures. As a result of these changes, young people have experienced very protected lives and this has given them high and idealistic expectations of society. Their subcultures provide a social base for discontent.

In making this last point, Berger *et al* were perhaps over-impressed by the college campus revolts of the sixties. Nevertheless, it is true that many of the themes which they cite as belonging to de-modernising consciousness, such as ecology or environmentalism and communal living have been primarily found amongst the young. In Berger *et al*'s view what unites the various strands of de-modernising thought is that they are all responses to the alienating experiences of modern life. Put differently, they seek to provide a 'home' where none is available by offering a sense of group belonging and commitment which is attractive to frustrated youthful ideals. In consequence the key ideas of de-modernising consciousness offer a mirror-image of their society. For example, the authors argue that many members of new political and social movements like women's liberation or black nationalism disavow claims to individual human rights typical of liberal democracies, and prefer to make demands on behalf of themselves as particular groups. This rejection of individualism is also shared by the commune movement and by the newly popular religious sects like the

Moonies, which proclaim the virtues of group identity. Similarly, both ecology and occult religions are defined by their critical attitude to technological rationality. They aim to replace it with more fulfilling or more humane bodies of knowledge.

Leaving aside the problem of whether Berger *et al* are right to lump together such different ideas in this way, we can question their argument on other grounds. Take the rise of belief in magic and the occult. For Berger *et al* what lies behind this development which ranges 'from fascination with ancient Chinese divination techniques to the revival of faith-healing practices' is an endeavour 'to cope with the discontents of modernity' associated with technological production. However, as Clive Ashworth has pointed out, such approaches tend to disregard the content of these ideas and merely look at the way they allegedly satisfy social needs, in this case the need for an orderly social world.

Ashworth argues that in order to account for the spread of these beliefs we have to consider both what they have to say and the way in which they relate to other bodies of knowledge. He notes that the occult is part of a massively popular field which includes interests like alchemy, spoon-bending, UFOs, and transcendental meditation. It focuses upon phenomena which seem to reveal the deficiencies of orthodox religion and science, those anomalies which neither can successfully resolve or upon which they are silent. Ashworth terms this field 'popular science' because it is concerned with explaining unusual facts and relating them to the many other features of the known world, however bizarre. Thus, the occult, for example, 'concerns itself with the psychic force, or forces, to which all things belong'.

Ashworth's analysis draws upon the structuralist perspective of French writers like Claude Lévi-Strauss. According to Lévi-Strauss, it is possible to explain the variety of existing social customs and institutions by uncovering deeper, underlying regularities which are normally hidden from full awareness. He compares the social scientist to the geologist who accounts for 'the tremendous diversity of landscapes' by 'a finite number of geological layers and of geological operations' (Lévi-Strauss, 1978, p. 8). Similarly, the basic structures of society, like the inner logic of kinship rules and mythological thought, lie beneath its surface and are a social expression of the way in which the human mind works. From this view, our knowledge and beliefs should be seen as part of the human mind's innate propensity to combine opposing categories and ideas into understandable structures. These form myths or stories we tell ourselves about the world in order to explain it. 'Popular science' takes off where religion and science end.

Religion, particularly since the Darwinian theory of evolution, offers us a moral code which is no longer clearly linked to what we know about the universe. By contrast, science gives us isolated facts and theories, but cannot tell us what life is all about. 'Popular science' fills the gap between the two, resolving them into a hybrid which provides a satisfactory social myth. In other words, it is the shortcomings of religion and science as socially acceptable ideas, rather than a dissatisfaction with modern life, which explains the success of 'popular science' (see Ashworth, 1980).

Ashworth's study leads us to the very edge of the sociology of knowledge, for the social myth of 'popular science' he identifies is said to derive from the logical operations of the human mind which, according to French structuralists, are genetically based. Whether or not we accept his claims for the ultimately biological basis of myth, Ashworth has thrown a new and different light on the social factors underlying some of our strangest modern beliefs. Rather than being a general reaction against modernisation, Ashworth shows them arising in response to the specific limitations of science and religion as social bodies of knowledge.

It is worth emphasising the point that science can be seen as a social body of knowledge. The classical perspectives on the sociology of knowledge gave scant recognition to this, believing that natural science could not be explained sociologically. In re-directing us to the world of everyday life, Peter Berger and his colleagues have also given little attention to the possibility of a sociology of science. Having concluded this chapter with a brief look at the sociology of 'popular science', we now turn to the sociology of science proper.

Chapter Four

The Sociology of Science

R. K. Merton and the Development of a Sociology of Science

The original concerns of the sociology of knowledge centred on sets of ideas embodied in legal doctrines, political ideologies, religious creeds and the like. In the last chapter we saw how a strong interest in 'everyday knowledge' and popular beliefs has developed in recent years. In this chapter we shall begin to explore a contrasting concern with scientific knowledge.

It is perhaps not too difficult to accept that political and legal ideas, religious beliefs and everyday knowledge are shaped by social forces. However, it is more difficult to see the natural sciences, and particularly physics, in these terms. They seek knowledge of the material world which appears untouched by human social concerns. Certainly Durkheim, Mannheim and, to some extent, Marx, felt that the natural sciences produced knowledge which was free from social influences. However, we shall see that, quite justifiably, the sociology of scientific knowledge has become a flourishing area of research.

The work of Robert K. Merton has been more influential than that of any other single sociologist in establishing the sociology of science as a specialist area of study. He drew attention to science as a social institution with its own form of organisation and ethos and analysed it from a functionalist perspective. Merton's earliest work in this area in the 1930s was concerned with science and its social context. He argued that science, like all other social activities, needs the support of the values of the group if it is to develop and flourish. He focused on the emergence of science as a social institution in seventeenth century England (Merton 1938a). In particular he examined the relationship between the values of ascetic Protestantism, which Weber had linked

474

with the development of capitalism, and the development of experimental science. However, he was also concerned with the response of science to other social interests such as those related to economic development and military power.

As science develops as a fully fledged autonomous social institution, an identifiable 'scientific community' is established. The actual concept of a 'scientific community' as 'a collectivity which evolves its own norms, policies and patterns of behaviour' owes much to the work of Michael Polanyi and that of Edward Shils (see Joseph Ben-David 1971, pp. 3–4). This internal structure of the 'scientific community' formed the second and major focus of Merton's work on the sociology of science.

The Social and Cultural Contexts of Science

Merton argued that it is only in societies which provide suitable cultural and material conditions that science develops substantially. Before science becomes widely accepted and valued in its own terms it must be justified by values external to itself.

He argued that the rapid development of science in seventeenth century England was spurred by the powerful social movement of Puritanism. Catholicism had come to terms with science but merely tolerated it whereas Puritanism embraced and advocated science. Many of the prominent scientists of the day made explicit connections in their writings between Puritan beliefs and values and their scientific work. Merton lists a number of these scientists including Robert Boyle, John Wilkins and Isaac Newton, and states that a complete list, 'would comprise a Scientific Register of the time'.

Central to the ascetic Protestantism of the Puritans was the conviction that a religious life did not entail a turning away from the affairs of the world. Rather, it required diligent labour in the worldly calling for the Glory of God. Also as God's Power, Wisdom and Goodness could be seen in His creation it was argued that the study of nature led to a fuller appreciation of God's works. Moreover, mere contemplation was identified with idleness and industrious practical activity was encouraged as the way to express faith. This was in tune with the contemporary emphasis on empiricism and active experimentation was seen as the proper way to study nature.

A further aspect of Puritanism stressed social welfare, the good of the many, as a goal to strive for. In this connection, the power of science to facilitate technological invention and contribute to the improvement of the material conditions of life was acknowledged.

However, this did not imply any narrow restriction to research that was directly connected to technological developments. It was recognised, for example, that experiments into the nature of light had led to such things as improved telescopes and other optical instruments. So technological benefits were seen to come from the encouragement of what we would now call 'pure science'.

Because science was seen to be useful in this way, it attracted economic and military support, in addition to the ideological support it was gaining from religious beliefs and values. It was viewed as providing knowledge that would help to solve problems involved in mining to increased depths, navigation and military technology. Although Merton found that the research interests of scientists in the seventeenth century were often dictated by intellectual developments in their fields, external forces were also at work. He found a complex interrelationship between economic and military concerns and scientific interests. Merton's main theoretical point in this work is that for science to develop as a new social institution in any society there is a functional requirement of support from other social and cultural values and institutions. In seventeenth century England it happened to be Puritan values which largely supplied this support. These combined with economic conditions and military aspirations to boost the development of science to the point where it could function as a social institution in its own right.

The Ethos of Science

Just as science requires favourable cultural and material conditions in which to develop, its healthy functioning and even its continued existence can be threatened by hostile conditions. In a paper read to the American Sociological Society in 1937 (Merton 1938b) Merton argued that hostility towards science may arise if either the methods and results of scientific research appear to undermine important social values or the sentiments embodied in the scientific ethos conflict with those found in other institutions.

For example, he argued that one sentiment central to the ethos of science is its 'purity'. It should not become the tool of theology, the economy or the state lest research be inhibited or distorted. However, this can be a source of hostility as it also implies that the scientist, as a scientist, should not be concerned with the social consequences of his or her research but only with its scientific significance. So when, for example, a line of research improves weapons of destruction science itself may be held responsible even though this was not the intention of the research.

Another source of potential hostility is the scientifically necessary attitude of 'organised scepticism' or the systematic questioning of traditional beliefs, values and authority which may lead people to resent science as a subversive force in society.

Merton argued that the situation in Nazi Germany after 1933 provided a clear illustration of how several factors may combine to impede scientific activity. Scientific work which promised direct practical benefit to the Nazi Party or the Third Reich was favoured and funds were allocated in accordance with this policy. Moreover, the ethos of science demands that theories are evaluated in relation to evidence and, that a scientist's work is taken on its merits, irrespective of his, or her, race, politics or religion. In Nazi Germany, however, loyalty to the political creed took precedence. This meant, for example, that any research carried out by members of so-called inferior races and any research which threw doubt on the idea of a superior 'Aryan' race would be discredited. Non-Aryans were dismissed from universities and scientific institutions and German scientists were forbidden to collaborate with Jewish and other non-Aryan scientists. Werner Heisenberg, for instance, was declared a 'White Jew'. This was because, despite Einstein's Jewishness, Heisenberg insisted that the theory of relativity was an obvious basis for further research.

In general, Merton argued that science is more likely to flourish in liberal democratic than in totalitarian societies. The former are not so centrally controlled and have a greater tolerance of cultural variety and divergent ideas, which is more compatible with the scientific ethos.

Having raised the question of the relationship between the scientific ethos and the wider social context, Merton set about examining the character of that ethos in more detail (Merton 1942). He viewed it as being composed of a set of norms, values and rules which are legitimised by the scientific institution. They are held to be binding and scientists are emotionally as well as rationally committed to them. The ethos of science is functional in that it serves the goal of the scientific institution. That goal is to add to and develop the body of tried and tested knowledge. However, the values and norms are felt to be binding not simply because they are functional but because they are right and good; they have a moral force.

Merton identified the ethos of science in terms of four sets of institutional imperatives:

1.   Universalism

The purpose of universalism is to guarantee that new knowledge is evaluated solely in terms of objective, impersonal criteria and that such things as career advancement are determined by talent alone. Knowledge cannot be invalidated by decree and the race, sex, nationality and so on of scientists are irrelevant to the truth of their findings.

2.   Communism

The point of communism is to ensure that scientific knowledge – the product of science – is subject to common or public ownership. Science advances as a co-operative enterprise so knowledge must be held as the property of the whole community and the only 'property rights' of the individual scientist are those of recognition and esteem for good work. This right to be acknowledged is highly regarded but, on the other hand, secrecy is forbidden and it is the scientist's duty to communicate his or her findings in order to promote the extension of knowledge.

3.   Disinterestedness

Scientists are supposed to take a deep but detatched interest in their work and to be interested in the workings of nature for its own sake. Moreover, they are expected to make discoveries available for public scrutiny so there is little scope for fraud or irresponsibility.

4.   Organised scepticism

No aspect of the world is considered 'sacred' or worthy of uncritical respect and all aspects of the world can be open to objective scientific study.

It is this 'normative structure' of science that has made it possible to claim science as the yardstick against which any claim to knowledge can be tested.

The Reward System of Science

Merton's interest in the ethos of pure science reflected his developing interest in wider questions concerning the internal structure and dynamics of the scientific community. In 1957 he read a very influential paper, as his presidential address, to the American Sociological Society (Merton 1957). In it he discussed the reward system in science. He outlined the motivations, produced within the scientific institution itself, that could account for the willingness of scientists to accept and adhere to its very demanding norms and values.

Merton noted the enormous number of disputes, 'often sordid disputes', in the history of science, over who first made a discovery. He argued that this was not purely egotism on the part of individuals. Frequently scientists not directly involved in the discoveries raised such questions of priority. For example, Henry Cavendish and James Watt, both unassuming men, were embroiled in a great controversy over who first discovered the compound nature of water. This 'Great Water Controversy' was instigated and largely carried on by other scientists who had nothing to do with the discovery. Merton contended that such controversies can be explained in terms of the sociological theory of institutions. The expression of moral indignation by disinterested bystanders indicates the violation of a social norm. The disinterested scientists wish to see fair play and the very fact of them entering into the fray shows that science is a social institution with a distinctive body of norms exerting moral authority. Fights over priority are not just expressions of hot temper. They are responses to what are taken to be violations of the institutionalised norms. Recognising a scientist's claim to be the first to make a discovery is important to the functioning of the reward system of the scientific institution.

In science value is placed on originality as this is what advances knowledge. So scientists are under pressure to be original and make new contributions to knowledge. Their only 'property claim' on this knowledge is recognition. Moreover, recognition of originality is the symbol and reward for having done their job well. The reward system consists of the bestowal of honours for originality. The highest honour is to be deemed the 'father' of a new branch of science. For instance, Robert Boyle was called the father of chemistry and Auguste Comte the father of sociology. Then there is the honour of associating the scientist's name with his or her discovery as in 'pasteurisation' and 'Brownian movement', prizes such as the Nobel prize, various medals, fellowships and memberships of prestigious societies like the Royal Society and so on.

With the production of this paper Merton completed the functionalist model by interrelating the normative structure of science with a model of motivation. His approach contributed greatly to the rapid growth of the sociology of science after 1957. A good deal of work draws on his model and from it an identifiable 'functionalist school' developed.

Barnes and Edge (1982) list a range of studies in this tradition. W. O. Hagstrom, for example, elaborated upon Merton's work on the motivations of scientists. He took up Merton's point that the out-standing motivation of pure scientists is a desire for recognition by their peers. He argued that in order to achieve this they offer 'gifts' to the scientific community in the shape of publishable information. Status is achieved in the first place by such 'gift-giving'. The publication of papers indicates the attainment of the standards of the community because journals select only a proportion of the papers that they are offered. More tangible recognition, such as invitations to speak at conferences, elections to specialist societies and ultimately the higher forms of recognition noted by Merton, may follow.

Criticisms of the Mertonian Tradition

Within the functionalist framework it is assumed that conformity to the institutional norms is an essential feature of modern science. The central idea is that actions which contravene the norms will clearly detract from the development of scientific knowledge. For instance, if scientists become too committed to their own ideas they will cease to be disinterested and emotionally neutral. They will then tend to overlook inconsistencies between their ideas and the evidence. Similarly, if they adopt personal non-universalistic criteria in assessing claims to new knowledge, their judgements will be biased and lack objectivity. It is also assumed that deviance from the norms is rare because control is exerted and conformity maintained through the reward system.

However, the British sociologist M. J. Mulkay (1969) argued that the reception of Immanuel Velikovsky's book *Worlds in Collision* (1950) casts doubts on the extent to which scientists do conform to Mertonian norms. Velikovsky blatantly challenged many of the fundamental assumptions of biology, geology and astronomy. Had the Mertonian institutional imperatives been effective, Velikovsky's claims would have been subjected to detailed, disinterested and critical evaluation. Instead there were vicious attacks on Velikovsky as an individual. Attempts were made to prevent access to his data and research papers and highly emotional judgements were made about his work. Indeed, one prominent scientist, Harlow Shapely, wrote a damning critique of the book, after refusing to read it, because its 'sensational claims' violated the laws of mechanics. Mulkay noted that it is these 'laws' which are operating here as norms themselves. He contended that in science it is the dominant theories and methods which act as norms and command the allegiance of scientists rather than Merton's institutional imperatives. He suggested that Merton's norms act rather as a kind of moral rhetoric that scientists can draw upon when they wish to justify their own behaviour or characterise that of others as improper.

The work of Mitroff (1974) similarly throws doubt on scientists' adherence to Mertonian norms in practice. His studies suggest that scientists often have great emotional commitment to their theories; that they are frequently secretive concerning their research findings; and that their judgements are commonly based on personality and prestige rather than on objective assessment.

Mulkay and Mitroff tend to confirm Kuhn's argument that during periods of what he calls 'normal science' scientists are deeply committed to established theories and methods. Indeed, he argues, contrary to Merton, that the successful development of science requires this commitment. Kuhn's work will be discussed in more detail in the next chapter. Most of the later work in the functionalist tradition focussed on the internal structure of the scientific institution and tended to ignore problems concerning the relationship with the wider culture. Nevertheless, its contribution has been very valuable. If the 'institutional imperatives' identified by Merton have drawn a good deal of criticism his identification of an 'ideal type' in the form of academic science has been particularly useful. It has been a major achievement of the Mertonian tradition to explore how the academic scientific community operates as an institutionalised system which is both a system of communication and a reward system. As we have seen, the system rests on peer judgement. The contribution of a scientist is assessed by an audience of colleagues. If they judge it to be original and significant they allow it to be published and may draw upon it, and refer to it, in their own work. The scientist thus receives the reward of recognition which brings enhanced reputation, perhaps promotion, and so on. The reward system, through the process of recognition, also significantly affects the allocation of resources, in the form of research grants, etc., and hence future directions of research. The reward, communication and resource allocation systems in science are, therefore, closely bound together, and their operation tends to produce social stratification amongst scientists.

Pure and Applied Science and Technology

Within the functionalist tradition a close connection is perceived between the growth of knowledge and the social organisation of the scientific community. Joseph Ben-David has worked independently of the Mertonian school. However, his research on the ways that the growth and organisation of academic institutions such as universities affected the development of the scientific community can be seen as complementary to the work of the school.

It is the internal structure of the scientific community that is seen as responsible for sustaining the social processes which maintain order, confer rewards and allow for the exercise of control over the quality of certified scientific knowledge.

This academic community of 'pure' scientists is viewed as being largely free from external interference and, therefore, able to acknowledge the advancement of knowledge 'for its own sake' as its central institutional goal. Consequently, academic or pure science is seen as the fullest embodiment of scientific ideals and practice and the ultimate source of intellectual authority.

This view is still widely accepted. Scientists doing 'pure' or 'basic' research are frequently distinguished from researchers carrying out work in an 'applied' context. So called 'applied' scientists are generally held to be subject to different social constraints. Their goals will, at least in broad terms, be set by their employers. The employers are the judges of success and the sources of reward. In such circumstances the control of the 'academic community' and the rewards it offers are of secondary significance.

Distinctions are frequently made between 'pure science', 'applied science' and 'technology'. A publication of the Organisation of Economic Co-operation and Development entitled *The Measurement of Scientific and Technical Activities* (1970) makes them in the following way:

a) Pure or basic research is undertaken primarily to gain new knowledge or understanding. It is not directed to any particular application.

b) Applied research is also undertaken to gain new knowledge but it is directed towards a particular practical goal.

c) Technological or experimental development is the use of existing knowledge to produce new or improved materials, processes, products and the like.

Distinctions such as these draw attention to contrasting emphases on 'knowing' and 'doing'. Stewart Richards (1983, p. 111) suggests that it tends to be the communities that support science on the one hand and technology on the other, which have contrasting values. Science carried out in academic institutions is primarily directed at an audience of other research scientists. Technology, however, is supported by communities of businessmen, politicians and the military who primarily value practical results.

There is a related difference between pure science and technology reflected in patterns of publication. Price (1969) draws attention to this. Technologists tend not to publish publicly accessible papers in the scientific sense because they are often trying to gain a commercial advantage over competitors. Consequently, they are far more eager to scan whatever literature is available to gain useful information, frequently by reading 'between the lines'. Price says, 'the scientist wants to write but not read, the technologist wants to read but not write'. He defines technology as 'that research where the main product is not a paper, but a machine, a drug, a product or a process of some sort'.

Richards is, however, careful to warn against placing too much weight on such distinctions. Pure and applied science and technology are closely interwoven and have increasingly become so. No one disputes that the origins of the nuclear power industry, for example, lies in theories about the fundamental nature of matter and energy. Einstein's equation $e = mc^2$ was a product of pure and highly theoretical research yet it led to the development, amongst other things, of nuclear weapons. On the other hand, much fundamental knowledge about the nature of biological organisms such as bacteria and viruses has been produced by workers in the 'applied' field of medical research.

Nevertheless, although they are ultimately somewhat arbitrary the distinctions are worth making, partly because they are connected with certain worries about the changing character of science. The changes are seen to be related to the enormous growth of science particularly since World War 2.

The Growth of Science

Derek de Solla Price has been influential in drawing attentions to the rate of growth of science. Price argues (1963) that science has shown an 'exponential' growth since the seventeenth century. In other words it grows, he says, at 'compound interest', multiplying by a fixed amount in equal periods of time.

He measured this growth in terms of such things as the number of new scientific journals and the memberships of scientific institutions. According to Price the amount of scientific activity has doubled every 15 years from about 1665 when the *Philosophical Transactions of the Royal Society* first appeared. This is greater than the rate of world population growth. The population doubles about every 50 years.

Science grows in this way partly because answers to questions often pose new questions and open up new directions for research. However, its growth is also the result of external support. Particularly since the Second World War this external support, from industry, government and the military, has increased enormously. Growth has been accompanied by a change in the character of science, from what Price calls 'Little science' to 'Big science'.

Pure scientists are now strikingly outnumbered by applied scientists and even pure research has often expanded in scale, scope and expense and become 'Big'. Whereas Little science is performed by individuals or small groups, Big science involves large teams working on long-term planned programmes and is frequently carried out by large research organisations sponsored by industry or government (e.g. ICI and Harwell). There are aspects of this new situation that have aroused both interest and concern. First of all, as the scientific community has increased in size, highly specialised skills have been developed. This has led to an increased differentiation or division of labour amongst scientists and this often means that quite large teams are required to carry out simple experiments. Moreover, as journals multiply and become more specialised they can be understood by a smaller proportion of the scientific community.

Secondly, the team research of Big science requires senior scientists to spend much of their time as administrators or 'entrepreneurs'. Their junior colleagues, on the other hand, become mere employees working in a 'conveyor-belt' atmosphere. They become 'proletarianised' – a scientific working-class prone to trade union organisation.

Thirdly, the whole research community becomes orientated towards applied concerns. The increasing reliance on large funds which can only be provided by government and large scale industry enhances this tendency as funds can be ear-marked for specific projects by their providers.

Considerations of this kind have led Ravetz (1971), amongst others, to argue that we are witnessing 'the industrialisation of science'. Concern about this process is linked to the loss of what was seen as the controlling influence of the ideals and norms of pure science. In a sense the concern is that the ethos of applied research and technology is taking over from that of pure science. The emphasis on practical applications of this applied ethos is often linked directly to the economic, political or military goals of the funding organisations. The worry, therefore, is that the aims of science will be distorted and progress in areas of knowledge where practical gains are not immediately obvious will be impeded.

The Politics of Science and Technology

Perhaps the major concern then, about the way the growth of science and technology has meant a closer interrelationship of science with industry and government, is political. What is at issue is the way in which political and economic power, through the resources it commands, can exert a strong influence over the direction in which knowledge develops and even over the kinds of knowledge that are allowed to develop.

Traditional values emphasising the disinterested pursuit of knowledge, 'for its own sake' and for the benefits it brings to humankind as a whole, seem to have been undermined as knowledge has become more subject to the control of powerful interest groups.

In America 'mission orientated' research (that is research related to some identifiable social purpose) has generated huge and expensive projects. These have been funded either by large private foundations such as Ford and Rockefeller or by government. For example, after the USSR launched Sputnik I in 1957 the American government put a priority on space research and funds for the space programme increased by a factor of 17 in only 10 years. It also fostered a new federal agency NASA and established a government advisory post on science and technology.

The military nature of much 'mission orientated' research, together with the degree of research funding by large private corporations, has led to the rise of what has become known as the 'military-industrial complex'. President Eisenhower, on his retirement, cautioned Americans on the threat this presented to democracy. C. Wright Mills (1956) writing on power in America supported this line of argument and suggested that power is concentrated in three crucial sectors (i) the large corporations; (ii) the military leaders and (iii) the political executive.

Although the military–industrial complex has been most studied in America, similar connections operate elsewhere, including China and the Soviet Union.

Close relations between the latest technological expertise and military requirements have always been a feature of a nation's preparation for war. In modern powerful nations the so-called permanent-arms economy has served to emphasise this connection. Daniel Greenberg (1967) carried out a detailed study of the inter-relationship between basic scientific research and the American government since the Second World War. An index of the significance of this relationship is given by the increase in expenditure on research and development by major government agencies such as the Atomic Energy Commission, NASA, the National Science Foundation and the Department of Health, Education and Welfare. The total expenditure in 1954, according to government sources, was 3,148 million dollars. It reached a peak of 17,030 million dollars in 1968 and the estimate for 1971 was 15,696 million dollars (Appendix: Greenberg 1970 edition).

A good example of the effect of economic power on scientific research is provided by the drug industry. No one could deny that modern drug companies have sponsored research which has produced enormously beneficial drugs. Nevertheless, these companies are essentially profit making organisations and questions arise about the effects of this on the development of medical knowledge.

The drug industry is highly research intensive. Most drug companies spend approximately one-tenth of their turnover on research and development and this is often used to justify their high rates of profit.

However, Doyal (1979) points out that most of the drugs produced as a result of this expenditure are not fundamentally new drugs. They are developed to compete with drugs of rival firms which are protected by patents and are only slightly different from them chemically. They are not, therefore, socially useful products but are developed entirely for profit in order to gain a share of the market. This process explains the very large numbers of drugs (approximately 7,500) available and prescribed by doctors in the NHS.

So, Doyal argues, high profits, which mean expensive drugs, are justified by research which is for the most part unnecessary on medical grounds. Much of this research aims merely to duplicate competitors' products.

Furthermore, drugs are aimed at curing diseases rather than preventing them. Hence drug companies have an interest in promoting curative rather than preventative medicine. They attempt to maximise the use of drug therapies presenting them as the best means of dealing with most of the problems doctors have to face. This is reflected in the continuing rise in the volume of drugs prescribed in the post-war period. This increase has been especially significant in the prescribing of drugs, particularly for women, for psychological problems such as depression.

Energy research is another example of the link between economic and political power and science. Without a large and steady supply of energy modern industrial societies could not function. It is, of course, to science and technology that we owe the concept of energy itself, and the practical means of generating, distributing and using it in various forms.

There are great contemporary controversies over the kinds of energy that governments and industries should invest in. Energy research and development is beset by competing economic and political interests. There is much concern, for example, over the adoption of nuclear or non-nuclear energy policies. Questions are being raised about resources for research into renewable sources of energy such as wind and wave power, as known deposits of fossil fuels threaten to run out, and further exploration and development becomes increasingly costly.

Decisions on issues such as these have implications for the futures of whole industries, some of which are very powerful, and involve enormous investment programmes. It would be very naïve to imagine that in such circumstances disinterested research could be the basis of such decisions.

The above examples serve to illustrate the very real nature of the concern expressed over the post-war growth in science and the related changes in its character.

Technology and the Sociology of Science

In addition to causing concern over the increasing interconnections between the political and economic institutions and the scientific institution, the industrialisation of science has generated the related sociological interest in the supposedly conflicting cultures of science and industry.

The background and training of the modern industrial scientist is usually the same as that of the pure scientist. Consequently, a number of American sociologists in the Mertonian tradition, have assumed that he or she is the victim of conflict between two opposing cultures. According to this view the industrial scientist, like the pure scientist, has been socialised during his or her training into the norms of pure science.

The 'management culture' of industry emphasises loyalty to the company. This is at odds with the notions of common ownership of knowledge and the general cosmopolitanism of the ethos of science. Furthermore, values such as financial soundness are placed above those concerned purely with the advancement of knowledge, and the hierarchical organisation of industrial corporations conflicts with the egalitarianism of science.

The work of N. D. Ellis (1969) has, however, cast doubt on the view that the opposing cultures cause stress in scientists. Ellis conducted an empirical survey of both academic and industrial scientists and technologists. He asked them directly what they thought about their conditions of work. The following table summarises the results:

Item	Scientists		Technologists	
	University	Industry	University	Industry
A Salary	55 (31)	77 (50)	81 (40)	76 (52)
B Quantity and quality of assisting personnel	79 (47)	78 (38)	65 (40)	63 (39)
C The amount of free time available for private research	90 (74)	38 (49)	73 (66)	38 (65)
D Opportunity for gaining experience in administration	20 (64)	63 (37)	32 (64)	55 (41)
E Prestige of this dept. in the scientific/technical world	60 (51)	43 (50)	67 (37)	51 (60)
F Prospects for promotion up a research career ladder	60 (49)	75 (44)	70 (38)	91 (54)
G Extent my qualifications and experience are fully utilised	81 (84)	94 (47)	95 (70)	85 (65)
H The opportunity to pursue basic research in my field	90 (83)	33 (60)	70 (85)	49 (65)
I Freedom to choose my own research projects	88 (96)	51 (49)	80 (85)	54 (56)
J The degree of freedom I have to manage my own work	96 (93)	91 (63)	88 (93)	90 (79)
K Opportunity to attend scientific/technical meetings/conf.	72 (60)	65 (51)	70 (45)	60 (67)
L Opportunity to work with highly reputed technologists/scientists	63 (77)	44 (49)	72 (38)	50 (61)
N =	50	118	40	75

Note: In the above table the first figure is an index of 'importance for overall work satisfaction' (Question 1); the second figure (in brackets) refers to 'present level of satisfaction' (Question 2). A high figure indicates that the item is of high importance to work satisfaction.

(from N. D. Ellis 'The Occupation of Science', in *Technology and Sociology*, Vol. 5, No. 1, 1969, pp. 33–41)

The scientists and technologists were asked to answer two questions about the conditions listed A–L:

1) How important do you feel that condition is for your overall work satisfaction? They rated degree of importance from 0–100.
2) How satisfied are you at present with each condition? They rated the degree of satisfaction similarly from 0–100.

There is a good deal of information contained in the table. For example, the high ratings by university scientists of conditions C, E, H, I and L seem to confirm their attachment to the ethos of pure science as described by Merton.

However, in contrast, the low ratings given by industrial scientists suggest that, no matter what their views were when they left university, they were quite happy with the industrial ethos. On the other hand, industrial scientists rated the opportunity to gain administrative experience highly, whilst academics rated this very low. For the former this presented a more obvious path to promotion than for the latter.

Ellis's survey then, did not support the theory that a conflict is felt by scientists in industry as a result of their attachment to the so-called ethos of pure science. Industrial scientists, who after all are in the great majority, do not act according to any code of conduct arising from this ethos. The explanatory value of Merton's view that scientists are socialised into the norms and values of pure science and that this ethos exerts a moral force was thus thrown into question.

This chapter began with an examination of Merton's view of the nature of science, scientific research and the scientific community. It then examined studies which argued that Merton's picture of science was idealised and that the real world of science is rather different in character. The following chapter begins to explore some new directions in the sociology of scientific knowledge which diverge further from Merton's model and which rest on alternative views of science.

Chapter Five

Changing Perspectives on Scientific Knowledge

Introduction

In the 1970s new sociological approaches to the study of scientific knowledge were emerging. Functionalist sociology preferred a 'macroscopic' or large scale approach in considering the conditions under which scientific knowledge is produced. It focused on science as a social institution and examined its interrelationships with other, particularly economic and military, social institutions. It attempted to define the general characteristics of the scientific community and show how these served the institutional function of producing tried and tested knowledge.

In contrast, the newer approaches favour more 'microscopic' analyses. They tend to involve detailed empirical research into the activities of practising scientists in industrial as well as academic situations. The emphasis is on what scientists actually do and how they interact with each other in particular situations; how they communicate with each other; how they negotiate; and how they interpret their results. The focus is on the detail of specific research activities in specific situations though some of the studies do employ more generalised explanations in conjunction with detailed analyses.

Functionalist sociology made a distinction between the technical and social aspects of science and concentrated on the social conditions under which scientific knowledge is produced. The newer approaches, on the other hand, include the technical content of scientific knowledge within their enquiries. For the first time social scientists are engaged in a systematic investigation of the technical activities, the judgements and theoretical interpretations of scientists.

The sociologist who studies the detailed practices of scientists is in much the same position as one who studies religious practices. In order to understand the meaning of much that is going on he or she has to understand something of the shared knowledge or beliefs of the group being studied. This means that these detailed studies of scientific practices involve understanding something of the science that is going on. These studies can, therefore, be quite technical themselves.

The inclusion of the technical content of science within the scope of sociological enquiry was very controversial at first and is still questioned. This is because it tends to reject the traditional view of scientific knowledge as 'uncontaminated' by social factors. The traditional view, in the philosophy as well as the sociology of science, held that, no matter how much the amount and kinds of research done might be affected by social factors, the knowledge produced was tried and tested against impersonal criteria and rigorous observation. Nature itself was seen as the yardstick by which the truth of scientific knowledge was measured.

However, more recent conceptions of the nature of scientific knowledge have tended to undermine this traditional picture. We shall now need to consider how views of scientific knowledge have changed. This will help us to understand why some sociologists think that it is important to study the effects of social conditions and relationships on the technical content of scientific judgements and theories.

Scientific Theory and Observations

Traditional views of scientific knowledge, rather like our commonsense view, have assumed that the goal of scientific theories is to describe and explain the natural order of the material or physical world. Nature behaves in an orderly way and the stability that we observe and rely upon in natural phenomena and natural relationships is due to the underlying structure and order of the natural world itself. Scientific theories, according to this view, are held to be true when they accurately describe the structure of relationships to be found in nature. They are known to be true because they account for the regular patterns of behaviour that we can observe amongst natural phenomena.

For example, early astronomers carefully noted the regular patterns of movement of the planets and searched for the correct way to describe this and the 'mechanism' that could explain it. At first it was thought that the planets moved around the earth, which was the centre of the universe. The universe was seen as being made up of concentric, rotating, crystalline spheres and this accounted for the movement which was described in terms of perfectly circular orbits. The

Alexandrian astronomer Ptolemy worked out a very complex system of circles to account for the observed variations in the positions of the planets. Copernicus was later able to account for the observed positions much more simply by arguing that the earth itself was a planet and that all the planets moved around the sun. He still held a version of the crystalline spheres theory and the view that the orbits were circular.

Copernicus' theory, which was simpler, and made calculations of the orbits easier and perhaps more accurate, was eventually accepted. We cannot here go into the repercussions, far beyond the realms of astronomy, of removing the earth from its central position in the universe. Later developments in astronomy involved the acceptance of Kepler's equally disturbing theory that orbits were elliptical rather than circular and Newton's theory of gravity as the mechanism which accounted for the motion.

Traditional views of science have tended to see later theories over-throwing earlier ones because they more simply describe the observations that are made, and provide more effective bases for making predictions. They are, therefore, thought to be nearer to explaining the true structure of the material world. The theories are thus held to be derived from and can be tested against observations that, in principle, anyone can make. New theories gain acceptance when they are proved superior in the light of observations of natural phenomena. This whole process is obviously facilitated when science is not held back by theological world views as it was in the early days of astronomy. As science freed itself from the shackles of theology it was able to devote itself dispassionately to discovering the natural laws of the physical world.

It is, I hope, clear from this rather over-simplified account, that if theories are held to be tested against observations the observations and the descriptions made of them must be independent of the theory which is supposed to explain them. For example, suppose the measurements required to describe the varying positions of the planet Venus in the night sky depended on Kepler's theory of elliptical orbits. These observations could not then be said to count in favour of that theory and against circular orbits.

Unfortunately, the idea that scientific theories are derived from and tested against observations which are independent of theory has been shown to be over-simple. The relationship between theory and observations is a complex one and all observations are based on theory – they can be said to be theory-laden or theory dependent.

The Theory-dependent Nature of Observation

Let us first consider an illustration used by Michael Polanyi in his book *Personal Knowledge* (1973).

Polanyi asks us to think of a medical student attending a course in the X-ray diagnosis of lung diseases. The student watches and listens whilst the radiologist points to significant features of the X-ray picture and comments upon them. At first the student is completely puzzled and can see only shadows of the ribs and a few meaningless blotches. However, after a few weeks, understanding begins to dawn. The student begins to see lung scars, signs of infection and patches of diseased tissue. The X-ray picture begins to make sense and the student begins to see what the expert can see.

The commonsense reaction to this is to say that the student sees the same things as the expert from the start but has to learn to interpret what he or she sees. But does the expert see something and then interpret it? In Chapter 3 we saw how Peter Berger stressed the importance of language in constructing social reality. It is perhaps less obvious that the natural world is also structured, classified and made sense of by language. We have to learn to see the world and learning to see is closely connected to learning a language.

Consider how, as children, we learned, for example, to distinguish dogs from other furry creatures. Young children watch and listen whilst parents point and say 'doggy', 'pussy-cat', 'moo-cow' and so on. Gradually they begin to understand that not all furry creatures are the same. Although they make mistakes at first, they begin to make the same discriminations as their parents. Eventually these discriminations are taken-for-granted. We just look and see dogs, cats, cows and so on and it is easy to forget that we had to learn to distinguish them.

The medical student in the illustration learns to see the X-ray picture in much the same way. In learning the technical scientific language of medicine the student learns at the same time to distinguish the blotches on the X-ray plate. He or she gradually makes sense of them and eventually just sees patches of diseased lung and so on.

Our observations of the world are always described in some language and languages, even everyday languages, embody theories about how the world is organised and classified. Think of the terms flower, petal and fruit. Botanists, like everybody else, use these terms to describe observations. However, their meanings in botany are derived from theories about the structure of plants. For the botanist the magnificent petals of the clematis are not petals at all but sepals, the poinsettia flower is not a flower but a cluster of bracts and what we see as the luscious fruit of the strawberry is merely a swollen receptacle. For the botanist the true fruits are the 'seeds' that get between our teeth. The theories that we use to classify the world of plants are not so well worked out as those of the botanist, but they are, nevertheless, theories. Our theories are more likely, however, to relate to what is good to eat or what makes an attractive garden rather than to the structure of plants.

The important point is that there is no neutral language, free from the differing theories of botanists, gardeners and cooks, etc., in terms of which they can all describe their observations of plants. All statements about observations depend on some theory or other and this presents serious difficulties for the view that scientific theories are derived from and tested against independently made observations.

Observations cannot simply be collected and stored as un-controversial 'facts' to be explained. They are always guided by some theory, no matter how simple or vague, which not only tells us what to look for but very often tells us how to look for it as well.

The above example suggests that, unlike most of us, botanists, guided by a theory of plant structure, will carefully observe such characteristics of plants as the number of petals and sepals, the arrangement of leaves and so on. These characteristics are used to classify plants, to place them in relation to each other and group them into species, genuses and families. However, there are rival botanists who, committed to an alternative theory, argue that different characteristics should be observed. Furthermore, these characteristics require special techniques of observation and experimentation developed in the newer disciplines of genetics and cytology. The rival botanists claim that plants cannot be correctly classified unless various breeding experiments, and analyses of chromosomes are carried out. When these alternative techniques are used they do not simply result in more precise classifications. For some groups of plants at least, they produce competing alternative classifications. The botanists here disagree about which theory to employ in classifying plants. The rival theories consider quite different kinds and methods of observation to be relevant. So there is no straightforward way of choosing between them on the basis of observation (see J. Dean 1979).

This example illustrates the close connection between theory and observation in science and perhaps the more science uses specialised techniques of observation the more obvious this becomes. The following photograph is of the tracks made by alpha particles (atoms of helium gas) passing through moist oxygen. However, before we can see this we have to take-for-granted quite a lot of theory. For example, the

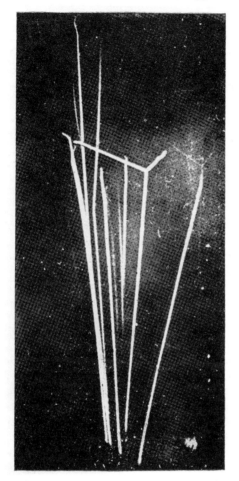

(from W. C. Dampier *A Shorter History of Science*, Cambridge University Press, 1944)

photograph was taken using a 'cloud chamber'. This is a piece of apparatus that works on the theory that under certain conditions moisture will condense around particles and leave 'cloud-tracks' as the particles move.

Falsification of Theories

We can see then that observations of the world are always made from a particular point of view and involve theories. As the interrelationship is complex, theories cannot be said to be derived from observed 'facts' or tested against them in any straightforward way.

Nevertheless, Karl Popper, in his very influential book *The Logic of Scientific Discovery* (1934), argues that the testing of scientific theories is through observation and experiment. However, because observations depend on theory there is no solid bedrock, no point at which theories can be said to have been finally proved true by observation. He says:

> The empirical basis of objective science has thus nothing 'absolute' about it. Science does not rest upon solid bedrock. The bold structure of its theories rises, as it were above a swamp. It is like a building erected on piles. The piles are driven down from above into the swamp, but not down to any natural or 'given' base; and if we stop driving the piles deeper, it is not because we have reached firm ground. We simply stop when we are satisfied that the piles are firm enough to carry the structure, at least for the time being. (Popper, 1959, p. 111)

So according to Popper scientific enquiry stops, at least temporarily, when scientists reach a large measure of agreement about their observations and about the theories they support. There is, however, nothing final about this.

Nevertheless, Popper contends that scientific theories, unlike everyday theories and other sets of beliefs, have a special status because they are rationally tested. He argues that scientists do not collect observations and develop theories about them. Prompted by difficulties encountered by previous theories they dream up new theories in an imaginative way. Guessing and quite wild speculation may be involved in this process. However, once a theory has been arrived at it must be expressed in a very formal way which will allow it to be rigorously tested by systematic observations and experiments.

A very important aspect of Popper's view is that, although we can never know conclusively that a theory is true, we may be able to prove it false. Science, according to Popper, involves a systematic and rigorous testing procedure involving a wide range of observations that are especially designed to try and prove a theory wrong. Theories which gain acceptance have been subjected to this procedure. They can never be said to be finally proven and may eventually be overturned by new theories but, if they have withstood vigorous attempts to disprove them, they can be widely accepted.

Good theories on this view, which is often referred to as

'falsificationism', make definite claims about the world. They also predict observations that can be made that could show them to be false. The more a theory claims the more potential opportunities there will be for disproving it. A very good theory is one which makes wide-ranging claims, and is therefore highly falsifiable, but nevertheless resists falsification whenever it is put to the test. For example, Newton's theory of gravitational attraction was a very good theory because it was highly testable. The theory claimed that all material bodies in the universe attract each other with a force related to their masses. This meant that a very wide range of precise predictions could be made about the orbits of planets as well as about the ways in which objects would fall to the earth. Scientists could, therefore, make a wide variety of observations based on these predictions. As the theory would be proved wrong if any of these predicted observations failed, there were many opportunities for falsifying it. The more it resisted attempts to falsify it the more likely it was to be true. If Newton's theory had only referred to the gravitational effects of the earth it would have predicted less and would, therefore, have been less testable.

Popper's view of science has been widely accepted both as a description of what scientists actually do when they accept and reject theories and as a model of good scientific practice. It has been the basis on which many people have argued that science is a highly rational process which results in well tested theories about the world.

Unfortunately, there are rather serious objections to falsificationism. First of all, the close interrelationship between theories and observations that presents an obstacle to conclusively proving theories also prevents them from being conclusively falsified. An observation which was thought to falsify a theory could at some future time, perhaps using different techniques of observation, be rejected itself. A second, though related, objection concerns the complex nature of real theories and real test situations. Theories are themselves complex and if they are to be tested they must be supplemented by statements concerning the conditions under which observations may be made or experiments carried out. Furthermore, whenever specialised instruments of observation are used, additional theories concerning their operation will be involved. Even simple telescopes and microscopes are constructed according to the theories of optics. Electron microscopes and the cloud chambers, used to detect alpha particles in the experiment mentioned earlier, involve the theories of particle physics and so on.

Because of this complexity, observations which seem to count against the theory under test may be dismissed as due to the conditions.

of the experiment or faults in the instruments or in the theory behind the instruments.

The following imaginary example illustrates the point.

The story is about an imaginary case of planetary misbehaviour. A physicist of the pre-Einstein era calculates the path of a newly discovered small planet, A. To do so he applies Newton's laws of mechanics and his theory of gravitation. Using the accepted methods of observation, he finds that the planet deviates from the calculated path.

Does the physicist, therefore, conclude that Newton's theories have been falsified? No. He suggests that there must be another, as yet unknown, planet, B, which affects the path of planet A. He calculates the mass, orbit, etc., of this unknown planet and with the help of an experimental astronomer attempts to observe it.

However, the hypothetical planet is so small that existing telescopes cannot observe it. The astronomer, therefore, applies for a research grant to build a more powerful telescope. When the new telescope is ready he tries to observe planet B but fails to do so.

Do the scientists then conclude that Newton's theory is false after all? No. They suggest that a cloud of cosmic dust hides the planet from us. They calculate the size and location of the cloud and apply for a research grant to send up a satellite to test the calculations.

When the satellite fails to locate the cloud they still do not reject Newton's theories but argue that satellite instrumentation, still in its infancy, must be at fault . . . and so on (adapted from Lakatos, 1970, pp. 100–101).

Although this is an imaginary example, the history of science is littered with examples of 'falsifying' observations which have been rejected and favoured theories held on to. A. F. Chalmers (1982, pp. 66–67) points out that if 'falsificationism' had been strictly adhered to some of the most respectable scientific theories would never have been developed. For example, both Newton's gravitational theory and Bohr's theory of the atom conflicted with observations that should have falsified them early in their careers.

Paradigms and Revolutions in Science

In 1962 Thomas Kuhn published a book, *The Structure of Scientific Revolutions*, which caused a storm of controversy. In it he put forward a view of science which seemed fundamentally to challenge its rationality. His account was very much at odds with Popper's falsificationism and presented a picture of the scientific community which contrasted sharply with Merton's.

Kuhn began his career as a physicist but had his pre-conceptions about the nature of science shattered when he became interested in the history of science. His theory, based on historical examples, suggests that science is characterised by phases of very conservative practice followed by periods of revolutionary upheaval. The sociological characteristics of communities of scientists play a very important role in his account.

Kuhn argues that scientists, far from being open-minded and dis-passionate, are strongly committed to their theories. Instead of trying hard to falsify them they defend them against attack. When necessary they will make all sorts of ad hoc modifications to theories rather than give them up.

This is largely because of their apprenticeship and training in an established scientific discipline. Scientists are socialised into the academic cultures of scientific communities. Unlike Merton, Kuhn does not refer to 'the scientific community' which includes all academic scientists irrespective of their particular disciplines or research areas. He talks instead of communities in the plural which are centred on particular disciplines and areas of research. These communities work mostly in consensus groups basing their work on a shared 'paradigm'. In the dictionary the word paradigm is said to mean a model or example. However, in Kuhn's sense it means much more than this. It refers to a research tradition, a whole way of thinking and working within an established framework of theories, ideas and methods. Young scientists are trained in these methods and ways of thinking. They carry out standard experiments under the guidance of experts. Young physicists, for example, learn the accepted laws and mathematical formulae of mechanics and apply them to problems set by their teachers and text-books. Far from questioning the paradigm they must learn to take it for granted. The process is much the same as that whereby we are all socialised into the taken for granted framework of beliefs and patterns of behaviour of our everyday lives.

Once socialised in this way scientists find it difficult, if not impossible, to describe their paradigm in any detail. Again, this compares to our difficulty in describing and explaining our everyday social reality to a stranger. Try, for example, describing exactly what you do when you ride a bicycle, drive a car, write an essay or solve a maths problem.

According to Kuhn, all mature sciences have a paradigm and this is necessary if progress is to be made within the science. If young scientists are forever questioning the fundamental theories and methods of their discipline very little empirical research would ever get done.

The paradigm sets the framework within which research problems are posed and it guides the designing of programmes of experiments and observations. 'Normal science' or science within such a paradigm is a kind of puzzle solving activity. Kuhn compares it to the attempt to complete a jigsaw or a crossword puzzle. Failure to solve such puzzles does not reflect on the paradigm but on the scientist. In this way the bare-bones of the paradigm are fleshed out with detailed knowledge.

The firm commitment of scientists to their paradigms during periods of normal science is borne out by the work of Mitroff mentioned earlier (p.481) and by Mulkay's paper on the highly emotional reaction of scientists to Velikovsky's book *Worlds in Collision*.

Research within 'normal science' inevitably produces observations and experimental results which conflict with the paradigm. These anomalies may be dealt with in a variety of ways such as those outlined on p.498. However, in the course of time they accumulate or a particularly significant one proves difficult to deal with. Under these circumstances the paradigm will become unstable and enter a state of crisis. Professional scientists will become insecure and inclined to engage in philosophical disputes about the nature of their science. Kuhn quotes Einstein, commenting on the upheavals in physics in the 1920s:

> It was as if the ground had been pulled out from under one, with no firm foundation to be seen anywhere upon which one could have built.

and Wolfgang Pauli, just before Heisenberg published an important paper leading to the development of quantum mechanics:

> At the moment physics is again terribly confused. In any case, it is too difficult for me, and I wish I had been a movie comedian or something of the sort and had never heard of physics.

Only a few months later, after the publication of Heisenberg's paper, he began to see the light and said:

> Heisenberg's type of mechanics has again given me hope and joy in life. To be sure it does not supply the solution to the riddle, but I believe it is possible to march forward. (Kuhn 1970, ed. pp. 83–84)

The seriousness of a crisis deepens when a rival paradigm makes its appearance. The new paradigm will have a very different picture of the world and will think of it as being made up of different things. It will regard different kinds of questions as appropriate and meaningful and will apply different and incompatible standards.

The following examples illustrate the enormous differences that can be involved between incompatible paradigms:

Consider the difference between Ptolemy's universe with the unmoving earth at its centre and Copernicus' universe in which the earth, with the other planets, moves around the Sun.

Chemistry, before Lavoisier, claimed that a substance called phlogiston was driven out of burning materials. Lavoisier proposed the existence of a gas called oxygen, which played a quite different role in burning, and implied that phlogiston did not exist. Questions about the weight of phlogiston, which had previously produced a good deal of research, were meaningless in Lavoisier's paradigm.

Maxwell's paradigm assumed that electromagnetic waves travelled through the aether which filled space. Scientists spent a good deal of effort trying to work out the velocity of the earth relative to the aether, as this was a very significant problem given their assumptions. Einstein's new paradigm did away with the aether; and so on.

When scientists switch their allegiance from one paradigm to another Kuhn likens the process to a religious conversion. There are no compelling rational grounds for such switches. New paradigms cannot be tested by old methods and at first they will not be supported by many experiments and observations of their own. Once converted a scientist will understand the world in a quite different and incompatible way. The kind of difference involved can be illustrated by optical illusions such as the one on the following page.

However, with such illusions we are capable of switching from one to the other image more or less at will. Once scientists have adopted a new paradigm they cannot revert to their old ways of seeing the world. The earth centred universe was a very different one from the sun centred one in all respects and Newton's universe can never be recaptured by scientists committed to relativity theory and quantum mechanics. Kuhn refers to the incompatibility between paradigms as 'incommensurability' and a switch from one to another involves enormous and wide-ranging changes in a scientist's whole way of thinking and working. He or she has to learn to live in a completely different world.

Why then do individual scientists abandon old and tried ways of thinking and working for strange and unfamiliar ways? Kuhn argues that many scientists brought up in one paradigm are never converted to a rising new one. Newton's theories were not generally accepted for more than half a century. Darwin wrote, at the end of the *Origin of Species*:

This picture cannot be a picture of a young girl and an old woman at the same time but it can be either.

(from F. R. Bradbury (ed.) *Words and Numbers*, Edinburgh University Press, 1969)

Although I am fully convinced of the views given in this volume..., I by no means expect to convince experienced naturalists, whose minds are stocked with a multitude of facts all viewed, during a long course of years, from a point of view directly opposite to mine...but I look with confidence to the future – to young and rising naturalists, who will be able to view both sides of the question with impartiality (Kuhn 1970, p. 151).

And Max Planck remarked in his *Scientific Autobiography*:

...a new scientific truth does not triumph by convincing

its opponents and making them see the light, but rather because its opponents eventually die, and a new generation grows up that is familiar with it (Kuhn 1970, p. 151).

Scientists who do convert, do so for a variety of reasons that are more social than rational. The younger ones with their productive careers ahead of them are more likely to convert than their older more established colleagues. Mulkay (1969) argues that those scientists who occupy more than one role, such as practitioner-scientists in medicine, are more likely to be active in the process of innovation in science. Also those who have a peripheral status in their scientific groups or who have contact with other fields and disciplines will be more involved in innovation than central figures in a research field.

The triumph of a new paradigm constitutes what Kuhn calls a scientific revolution. Such a revolution is complete when the relevant scientific community as a whole becomes committed to it and the old paradigm is finally abandoned. A new period of normal science then begins during which the detailed work necessary to flesh out the new way of understanding the world is carried out. Young scientists socialised into the new ways will have great difficulty imagining the old world before the revolution.

Kuhn then, in contrast to Popper, does not see science as a highly rational activity. Scientists are not viewed as dispassionate people concerned only to test their theories rigorously by doing their best to disprove them. His work in the history of science led Kuhn to develop a very different picture. He emphasises the fundamentally social character of science and the importance of the communities in which scientists work. Such communities are based upon shared paradigms to which their members are deeply committed and do their best to defend. Switches from one paradigm to another are strongly resisted and when they occur social forces are central to the process of change.

So Kuhn holds that social factors do not merely affect the conditions under which scientific knowledge is produced, they also affect the theoretical judgments of scientists. This view has done much to pave the way for the new approaches to the sociology of scientific knowledge mentioned at the beginning of this chapter. It has also raised in a very acute form, the problem of 'cultural relativism'. If all knowledge is shaped by social and cultural forces, can we distinguish between genuine knowledge and mere belief? Can what is true in one society be false in another? In the final chapter we shall consider this problem together with these new approaches.

Chapter Six

New Sociologies of Scientific Knowledge and the Problem of Relativism

The Sociology of Knowledge and the Problem of Relativism

As we have seen, Thomas Kuhn has suggested that the rationality of science has been greatly over-estimated. Other recent work, in the field of social anthropology, indicates that there has been an opposite tendency to under-estimate the rationality of traditional belief systems. Robin Horton (1967), in particular, has drawn a number of parallels between western science and traditional African systems of belief. The overall effect of such work is to lessen the distinctions that we commonly make between scientific knowledge and other sets of ideas and beliefs.

Science, due to its apparently rigorous, rational testing procedures, is often taken as the ideal model against which all forms of knowledge might be judged. Kuhn's work has been fiercely attacked because it calls into question the rationality of science. In doing so, along with work such as Robin Horton's, it seems seriously to undermine the view that real knowledge, as opposed to culturally defined sets of beliefs and ideas, is possible. If Kuhn and Horton are right scientific knowledge can no longer be set clearly apart on the grounds of its superior rationality from such things as political and moral beliefs and traditional and religious views of the world.

As indicated at the end of the previous chapter this raises the question of 'cultural relativism' as a very serious problem. This problem centres on the question of whether we can ever confidently distinguish between true and false beliefs, genuine knowledge and ideology. It arises from the recognition that ideas are shaped by social and cultural forces and are therefore 'culturally relative'. As Pascal once said, 'What is truth on one side of the Pyrenees is error on the other'. The idea that there might be different truths in different places and at differing times in history seems to contradict the very notion of truth itself. Truth is something that we normally consider to be timeless and cultureless. If something is true it must be true at all times and in all places.

This problem of cultural relativism is posed, to some extent, by the very idea of a sociology of knowledge. All approaches to the sociology of knowledge examine the ways in which ideas are shaped by social forces. Marx and Mannheim were, for example, concerned with the ways in which class interests affect ideas about social relations. However, one sided class viewpoints may be seen as ideological distortions and distinguished from genuine scientific descriptions of social relations.

Traditionally, sociologists of knowledge have tended to exclude certain kinds of knowledge from their inquiries. We have already noted that Durkheim, Mannheim and, to a lesser degree, Marx considered scientific knowledge to be free from distorting social influences. Merton, and the structural functionalist school in general, examined the social conditions under which scientific knowledge is produced but, nevertheless, considered that the theoretical judgements of scientists are governed only by rational procedures.

As long as such exclusions are made, it is possible to avoid the full force of the problem of relativism. Political, religious and moral ideas may be viewed as being socially conditioned. We may consider the world of everyday reality to be socially constructed as Peter Berger suggests and we may explore how popular beliefs arise in relation to social experiences. However, once it is argued that all sets of ideas and beliefs, including all scientific theories about the world, are culturally relative, then it seems that all possibility of achieving genuine knowledge is lost.

Fortunately perhaps, there seem to be limits built into the very idea of relativism. We shall return to this question after discussing some of the new approaches to the sociology of scientific knowledge which have been opened up by these bold challenges to the superior rationality of science.

Strong and Weak Programmes in the Sociology of Knowledge

If the work of Kuhn, Horton and others has posed problems, it has also made legitimate the question: In what sense and to what degree is scientific knowledge rooted in social life? In doing so it has eased the development of research into the detailed practices and decision making procedures of scientists. The technical content of science and the working methods of scientists are now being researched in ways which would not have been possible, if questions about the rational status of scientific knowledge had never been raised.

The so-called 'strong programmes' in the sociology of knowledge quite explicitly adopt a form of relativist viewpoint. They seek to link all knowledge and beliefs, including scientific knowledge, to social conditions in a causal way. In other words they are interested in how particular social conditions bring about, or cause, people to hold particular ideas and beliefs. Their central concern is to explain why someone or some group of people holds a particular belief or set of beliefs or why they have changed beliefs. In doing so the strong programmes make no distinction between true and false beliefs, or reasonable and unreasonable ones.

A strong programme was advocated by Barnes (1974) and Bloor (1976) and their 'Edinburgh School' has produced a range of empirical case studies of a largely historical nature. A similar programme has been adopted by H. M. Collins and a group of colleagues at Bath and they have produced complementary work focusing on modern case studies. Advocates of the strong programmes consider various kinds of social interests, including political, economic and professional interests, to be amongst the most significant causes of people holding the beliefs they do. These interests, however, rarely figure in people's own accounts of why they believe as they do.

John Dean, for example, argues that it was the rival professional interests of the two groups of botanists, mentioned on p. 50, that determined their commitment to one or the other method of plant classification. The two groups worked in different kinds of institution, museums and herbaria on the one hand and research laboratories on the other. They had learned different skills and belonged to different scientific communities with distinct professional goals. The museum and herbarium workers considered experimental methods of plant classification to be irrelevant. The experimental botanists, on the other hand, who had learned the methods of genetics, considered their opponents to be out of date and old fashioned. All the arguments between the two groups were couched in terms of the scientific merits of the two opposing methods however, and they did not recognise the effects of their career interests in their professional rivalry.

Within the strong programmes there have been case studies of pure and applied scientific research in academic and industrial settings. The methods of study are basically microscopic and interpretative. They involve detailed analyses of scientists' activities, interactions and decision making processes and they take account of scientists' own descriptions of their activities. As far as the modern studies are concerned, Collins (1983) advocates a form of participant observation research as far as possible and at least a series of in-depth interviews. However, the strong programmes differ from some of the other new sociologies of scientific knowledge, in adopting a framework of causal explanation in addition to these 'microscopic' levels of analysis.

The strong programmes have attracted a good deal of criticism partly because they make no distinction between reasonable and unreasonable beliefs. They hold that all beliefs are caused in basically the same way. Newton-Smith (1981), however, argues that the reasonableness or unreasonableness of a belief makes an important difference to the kind of explanation we give for it. He agrees with Bloor that our own judgments about a belief's reasonableness are irrelevant. Nevertheless, we do need to take into account, whether or not the belief was reasonable, given the culture and experiences of the believer.

For example, if a doctor in our own society started to practise exorcism in an attempt to cast out demons from patients, we should count this unreasonable. It is likely that we should seek causes for the doctor's behaviour in terms of his or her own mental health. However, when the belief in demons as a cause of ill-health was widespread in our society, it would have been perfectly reasonable to attempt to cure diseases by casting them out. An explanation of the practice of exorcism would need to go no further than the general framework of social belief.

The rationality, or reasonableness, of particular beliefs and actions may be judged in relation to a general framework of beliefs. Within science this is provided by the current paradigm. For example, it was just as reasonable for scientists to believe in the 'aether' before Einstein as it is now for quantum physicists to believe in anti-matter. The existence of such a paradigm or framework of beliefs is often a quite sufficient explanation for holding a particular belief and acting in accordance with it.

We encounter more serious difficulties when the question of the rationality of a whole framework of belief or a whole research paradigm is raised. It is here where we run into the real problem of relativism because, if there are no rational criteria for judging between paradigms, then we have no grounds for believing, for instance, that Einstein's physics was an improvement on Newton's. The whole notion of progress in knowledge must be abandoned. Questions of truth and falsity can only make sense within a paradigm or some framework of socially sanctioned beliefs.

The strong programmes in the sociology of knowledge appear to deny that there can be any general criteria for comparing and choosing between whole frameworks of belief or alternative paradigms in science. However, the strong programmes seem to require such criteria. They claim that all beliefs, ideas and theories can be explained in much the same way, by causes, many of which are social. If this claim is true, then the theories of the strong programmes can equally be explained in terms of social causes, such as the professional interests of Barnes and Bloor and their Edinburgh School. In which case there would appear to be no good reason to take the explanations they put forward seriously. They have no greater claim to rationality than the theories they seek to explain. We shall return to this point, as all extreme claims about the cultural relativity of beliefs and theories fail in the same way.

Taking up this criticism Chubin and Restivo (1983) argue that, so long as the strong programmes claim the status of scientific research projects, this trap cannot be avoided. They agree that conflicts between scientists, about their theories and research programmes, have more to do with conflicting interests and values than with the purely intellectual merits of the theories. However, sociology is not some kind of super-science, uninfected by interests, that can stand outside such conflicts and explain them within a causal framework. The proponents of the strong programmes are wrong in claiming impartiality.

Chubin and Restivo propose instead what they call a weak programme. The central focus of their weak programme is on how theories are translated into social policies. They argue that theoretical conflicts in science are not just of academic concern. They have the character of political struggles. Moreover, successful theories are translated into policies which are designed to change the world.

For example, consider the effects on social policies of competing claims to know the risks involved in nuclear reactors like that at Seascale in Cumberland. Scientists with different view points calculate the actual risks differently and disputes about acceptable risks (however calculated) are potentially endless.

The task of the weak programme is to make explicit the interests and value assumptions involved in scientific struggles and controversies and subject them to criticism. The aim of such value criticism is not merely one of understanding but of influence. Whereas the proponents of the strong programmes claim impartiality, those of the weak programme are intentionally partisan. They accept that their own position will be as value-laden as any other and they set out to clarify and criticise the values and interests of disputing parties including their own. Their aim is to make explicit, as far as possible, what is at stake as a means of influencing the outcomes of struggles and their effects on social policies. They see their role as that of critical participants in conflicts rather than detached observers who seek to explain them 'scientifically'.

Laboratory Studies and the Social Construction of Scientific Knowledge

The strong and weak programmes involve detailed case studies of research programmes and scientific controversies. Scientists' ideas and beliefs are related to their interests and, in the case of the weak programme, the effects of the outcomes of particular controversies on social policies is the primary focus.

A range of studies which can perhaps best be seen as complementing rather than competing with the strong and weak programmes is concerned with a somewhat different level of analysis. These studies are often described as laboratory studies. They share, with the strong and weak programmes, the belief that scientific knowledge is socially constructed. However, they are not concerned to relate this process to questions of interests, values and social policy. Rather they are concerned with even more detailed microscopic analyses of the social interactions between scientists through which knowledge is actually generated. The studies are referred to as 'ethnographic', 'constructivist' or 'ethnomethodological' depending on differences of theoretical detail and methods of analysis. However, they share the view that the specific situations and circumstances and the particular scientists involved affect the nature of the knowledge produced.

Knorr-Cetina (1983) emphasises that at every point in the process of construction of scientific knowledge, decisions have to be made. She argues that particular situations and circumstances are so important that it may be doubted whether any general rules governing these decisions could be found. She claims that the activities observed in laboratories involve tools and materials that are highly pre-constructed. Nowhere in the laboratory do we find the 'nature' or 'reality' it is often assumed that scientists describe. They use complex instruments that depend on theories which relate to past decisions about what is real. For example, they use all kinds of complicated measuring devices, cloud-chambers, mass-spectrometers and so on. Their raw materials too are often carefully grown plants, specially bred animals, highly purified chemicals and sterilised water.

What is eventually agreed upon as knowledge will have involved choices concerning such things as which raw materials to use, which measuring instruments and how to set up experiments as well as negotiated decisions about the interpretation of results. Moreover, the personalities, relative statuses and particular relationships of the scientists involved will all affect these decisions.

The construction of scientific knowledge according to Knorr-Cetina can be thought of as a 'world-making' process. Reality is not just interpreted but 'manufactured'. What emerges from scientific work is 'the known world' but 'this known world is a cultural object, a world identified and embodied in our language and our practices' (p. 136). We have to think of science as a world-producing activity not simply as an attempt to know a world which exists independently of our activities.

Knorr-Cetina and a whole range of ethnographers and ethnomethodologists then are concerned with the detailed practices and processes of social interaction to be found in laboratories.

Michael Mulkay and his colleagues (Knorr-Cetina and Mulkay, 1983, pp. 171–203, and Gilbert and Mulkay, 1984) have recently argued the need to focus on the language that scientists use in their interactions and interpretations. Mulkay draws on the insights of sociolinguistics and the methods of discourse or conversation analysis. He argues, for example, that a number of studies have shown that scientists portray their actions and beliefs differently in their formal literature and their informal conversations. They write in a conventionally impersonal manner but in less formal contexts they tend to emphasise social and personal factors. Mulkay also draws attention to the way scientists have been found to present their current beliefs in a way which emphasises their relationship to experimental evidence whilst accounting for discarded beliefs by reference to the distorting effects of personal and social factors.

Mulkay argues that language analyses will not only help us to understand scientific practices, they may also explain some other sociological findings. For example, studies which have examined informal interaction between scientists in laboratories have not surprisingly placed greater emphasis on social factors in knowledge construction than those which have examined the formal literature of science.

The new sociologies of scientific knowledge then have focused on the detailed practices of scientists in constructing knowledge. They have questioned the idealised traditional conceptions of science which over-emphasised its rationality. The alternative image of science which they have presented suggests sets of cultural practices similar to other cultural practices. In this process the problem of relativism, to some extent side-stepped by previous approaches to the sociology of knowledge which excluded scientific knowledge, has been thrown into sharp focus.

The Limits of Relativism

In the opening section of this chapter it was suggested that there are built-in limits to the cultural relativist position. That is, there are limits to the notion that all beliefs and theories about the world, all knowledge claims, are determined by the cultural contexts in which they arise. This is fortunate because, were it not so, there could be no possibility of distinguishing truth from falsity, genuine knowledge from ideology.

What is meant by a built-in limitation was illustrated by the criticisms of the strong programmes in the sociology of knowledge. The claim, that: 'all knowledge is constructed by social forces', must either be immune from those forces or it must itself be relative to a particular social context. It contradicts itself because it claims to be true of 'all' knowledge. If it is, then it cannot be known to be true because it will be just as infected by interests and other social forces as all other 'knowledge'.

The recognition of this built-in limitation offers some comfort. However, it does not take us very far. We are still left with the problem that our theories about the world cannot simply be tested against observations. As we have seen, observations are dependent upon theories. Moreover, there is an increasing amount of evidence, from the Edinburgh School, laboratory studies and the like, which must be given serious consideration. All this evidence points to the importance of social factors in constructing even scientific knowledge and in defending and rejecting competing theories.

We can confidently assert that there are built-in limits to relativism. However, we are still a long way from being able to say what criteria may be used, in judgeing one set of beliefs about the world to be better or more rational than another set, at the same time as giving due weight to social factors in the construction of knowledge. The reasonableness or rationality of a particular idea or belief can be judged in relation to a general framework of socially sanctioned beliefs such as a scientific paradigm. The larger question though, as to whether there are any universal criteria of rationality against which whole belief systems may be judged, remains unanswered. This is not to say, however, that the question has not been explored. It is a question which has wide ramifications and far reaching implications. Two collections of essays, Wilson (1970) and Hollis & Lukes (1982), have done much to clarify the issues and provide an essential starting point for further study.

A discussion of these essays would take us well beyond the scope of the present book. However, in the context of our discussion of the sociology of knowledge it is perhaps worth introducing, very briefly, two contrasting lines of argument that have had a significant impact on social scientific thinking. These two lines of argument have been developed in interesting ways by French 'structuralists' on the one hand and 'critical theorists' on the other. In different ways they both point beyond relativism.

Structuralism

Although 'structuralism' can be identified as a broad tradition there are important theoretical differences between structuralist thinkers. Nevertheless, they all owe a great debt to Ferdinand de Saussure (1857–1913), a Genevan linguist who instigated a revolution in the study of language. Saussure argued that language should be understood as a structured system of signs with a set of rules governing their relationships with each other. The pattern of relationships could be discovered by studying the language itself rather than particular bits of conversation or writing. Indeed, conversation and writing are only possible because we understand how to relate the various elements of language, combining sounds into words and words into sentences and so on. In other words, we somehow understand the structure of the language. Saussure concentrated on the rules for combining sounds. Later linguists, such as the very influential American Noam Chomsky, have worked on the rules for combining words into sentences or 'syntax' and so on.

Placing stress on the structure of language in this way focuses attention on the pattern of relationships between elements in the system rather than on the separate elements. What is more the various elements are defined in terms of their relationships. For example, verbs are only defined as verbs because of the way they combine with nouns, etc., to make grammatical sentences.

Rather than emphasising cultural diversity and the differences between languages, 'structural linguists' point to the fact that human languages translate from one to another remarkably well. This translatability would seem to suggest a basic set of rules common to all languages – a universal structure. If there is a universal structure underlying the superficial differences between languages then, it is argued, it must be somehow biologically given. Furthermore, as there is a very close relationship between language and thought, a universal language structure suggests some more general universal mental structure. The possibility of discovering a basic, biologically given, universal structure of the human mind has seemed very exciting to a number of thinkers in other areas of work besides linguistics.

Jean Piaget (1896–1980) a Genevan like Saussure, took up this quest through the study of the development of thinking in children. Piaget claims that there is a universal pattern of development which cuts across cultures and which relates to the developing structure of the mind. Claude Lévi-Strauss (b. 1908) the French social anthropologist has explored aspects of human cultures by treating them as patterned systems like languages. He argues that underlying the wide superficial variety between cultures a relatively few basic patterns can be discovered. Lévi-Strauss investigated kinship early in his career and, despite an apparently wide range of customs governing marriage in differing cultures, he worked out that just a few sets of basic rules are involved. His later work explores the range of myths that are found in human cultures. Myths are stories which answer fundamentally important questions such as, Where did we come from? and they often have a moral content. They are essentially sacred stories. All human cultures have myths and they appear in rich variety. Nevertheless, Lévi-Strauss argues that there is a great deal of 'repetition' and certain elementary themes repeatedly occur, for example, mother/son and brother/sister incest, patricide and fratricide. Rather like Agatha Christie's detective stories the whole variety of myths share a few basic plots. Lévi-Strauss considers that these plots reveal a universal logic shared by all human beings and which is concerned with resolving certain basic contradictions. For example, the concept of life entails the concept of death. This apparent contradiction is resolved in myths either by stories which present death as the gateway to eternal life or by stories which tell of the origin of death.

Both Piaget and Lévi-Strauss are highly original and very controversial thinkers. Their work illustrates an alternative preoccupation to that of sociologists of knowledge. The latter are fascinated by differences between cultures and the ways in which what is taken as knowledge varies relative to cultural contexts. Piaget, Lévi-Strauss and other structuralist thinkers, on the other hand, are struck by certain fundamental similarities in human thinking which underlie surface differences. They believe that such similarities derive from the basic structure of the human mind. Such a structure would define the limits of cultural relativism by imposing certain universal patterns on human thinking.

Critical Theory

We have seen that a recurring theme in the sociology of knowledge is how human interests are involved in the construction of knowledge. Marx and Mannheim were both very concerned with the effects of class interests and the way these produced one-sided viewpoints or ideological distortions, particularly in the context of social relations. Barnes and Bloor have drawn our attention to the operation of competing professional interests in the construction of scientific knowledge. Critical theorists too are concerned with the interconnections between knowledge and interests and have also addressed the problem of whether knowledge, undistorted by interests might be possible.

The development of critical theory was linked to the establishment, in 1923, of the Institute of Social Research, linked to Frankfurt University. Critical theorists are also, therefore, sometimes referred to as the 'Frankfurt School'. The Institute was originally a centre for the study of Marxist theory and critical theorists all owe a debt to Marx. However, they have also been deeply influenced by other thinkers including Freud and Weber. To what extent their work can be considered Marxist is a debatable point. The focus of their work, however, is to develop a thoroughgoing critique of the bourgeois culture and ideology of capitalist societies. Some of the better known critical theorists were Max Horkheimer, Theodore Adorno and Herbert Marcuse.

At present the most significant thinker in the tradition is probably Jurgen Habermas who is very concerned with the question of the relationship between interests and knowledge. He argues that so long as there are conflicts of interest in human societies knowledge will remain infected by them and distorted. Habermas is particularly concerned with the distortions produced as a result of class conflict in the sphere of human economic activity. When people stand in relationships to each other which are characterised by economic exploitation and political oppression, they will inevitably develop distorted one-sided viewpoints.

It is only as conflicts of interest are overcome, and relationships of exploitation and oppression are replaced by relationships based on mutual interests and the common good, that knowledge undistorted by conflicting interests will become possible. Undistorted or competent communication, which is necessary for the development of undistorted knowledge, is linked with the development of societies free from class conflicts, and for that matter any other fundamental conflicts of interest.

Habermas then, proposes one interesting answer to the problem of ideology, where differences in viewpoint can be related to conflicting interests. He does not, like Mannheim, and later Barnes and Bloor, propose a sociology of knowledge as a way of revealing ideological distortions and perhaps of mediating between conflicting viewpoints. On the contrary, Habermas argues that such distortions cannot be overcome except by removing the conflicts of interests that produce them.

Like Marx, Habermas sees human thinking and practical activity as intimately linked. Human activity is conscious activity and is rooted in solving problems posed by nature and by human conflicts. Ideas and theories will inevitably be distorted so long as they arise in situations characterised by conflicting interests. Like Chubin and Restivo, Habermas sees no possibility of standing outside such conflicts. However, in so far as conflicts are resolved through struggle a common viewpoint or consensus may be reached. The possibility of truth is linked to such a notion of consensus. It is far from being a purely theoretical consensus as it involves overcoming one-sided interests and moving towards societies based on mutual interest and the common good.

Within the context of world development and world history, there exists a future possibility of a universal consensus. However, this again is capable of being realised only when conflicts of interest are overcome and human beings can direct their activities by general human interests. Critical theory then points beyond the relativity of viewpoints linked to conflicting interests by looking forward to a society free of such conflicts. This is a position which seems to echo a conception developed by Marx, in his early works, of human beings as beings capable of becoming 'species-beings'. In other words, they are capable of realising themselves as members of the human species as a whole and of developing the potential of the species.

In Conclusion

During the course of this section we have explored some of the ways in which sociologists have tried to understand how what is viewed as knowledge varies between human cultures. We have seen that the very idea of a sociology of knowledge raises the problem of relativism in differing degrees. Indeed, some of the bold new philosophies and sociologies of science raise the problem in such an acute form that the possibility of saving rationality is in doubt. However, we have seen that some limits to relativism may be drawn and we have briefly explored two strands of thinking that propose ways beyond relativism.

We have raised many questions and posed many problems. However, we have not proposed any conclusive answers. As a field of enquiry, the sociology of knowledge is relatively new and has far to go. It is also an area which poses very difficult theoretical problems. Nevertheless, it is an exciting and rapidly developing field and we hope that we have been able to communicate some of that excitement to you.

Bibliography

Abercrombie, N., Hill, S. and Turner, B. S. *The Dominant Ideology Thesis* (George Allen & Unwin, London, 1980)

Anderson, A. and Gordon, R. 'Witchcraft and the status of women' *British Journal of Sociology* Vol. 29, No. 2, June 1978

Ashworth, C. E. 'Flying Saucers, Spoon-Bending and Atlantis: A Structural Analysis of New Mythologies' *Sociological Review* Vol. 28, No. 2, May 1980

Barnes, B. *Sociology of Science: Selected Readings* (Penguin, London, 1972)

Barnes, B. *Scientific Knowledge and Sociological Theory* (R. K. P., London, 1974)

Barnes, B. and Edge, D. *Science in Context* (Open University Press, Milton Keynes, 1982)

Beidelman, T. O. 'Kaguru Time Reckoning: an Aspect of the Cosmology of an East African People' *Southwestern Journal of Anthropology* Vol. 19, 1963

Bell, D. *The Coming of Post-Industrial Societies* (Heinemann, London, 1974)

Ben-David, J. *The Scientist's Role in Society: A Comparative Study* (Prentice-Hall, Englewood Cliffs, N.J., 1971)

Berger, P., Berger, B. and Kellner, H. *The Homeless Mind* (Penguin, Harmondsworth, 1974)

Berger, P. and Kellner, H. 'Marriage and the Construction of Reality: an Exercise in the Microsociology of Knowledge' *Diogenes* No. 46, 1964

Berger, P. and Luckmann, T. *The Social Construction of Reality* (Penguin, Harmondsworth, 1967)

Bloor, D. *Knowledge and Social Imagery* (R. K. P., London, 1976)

Chalmers, A. F. *What is This Thing Called Science?* (2nd ed., Open University Press, Milton Keynes, 1982)

Chubin, D. E. and Restivo, S. 'The "Mooting" of Science Studies: Research Programmes and Science Policy' in Knorr-Cetina and Mulkay, 1983

Collins, H. M. 'An Empirical Relativist Programme in the Sociology of Scientific Knowledge' in Knorr-Cetina and Mulkay, 1983

Danziger, K. 'Ideology and Utopia in South Africa: a methodological contribution to the sociology of knowledge' in G. W. Remmling (ed.) *Towards the Sociology of Knowledge* (R. K. P., London, 1973)

Dean, J. 'Controversy over Classification' in Barnes, B. & Shapin, S. (eds.) *Natural Order* (Sage, London and Beverley Hills, 1979)

Doyal, L. with Pennell, I. *The Political Economy of Health* (Pluto, London, 1979)

Durkheim, E. *Suicide* (R. K. P., London, 1952)

Durkheim, E. and Mauss, M. *Primitive Classification* (Cohen & West, London, 1963)

Ellis, N. D. 'The Occupation of Science' *Technology and Society* Vol. 5, No. 1, 1969, abridged in Barnes, 1972

Evans-Pritchard, E. E. *The Nuer* (Clarendon Press, Oxford, 1940)

Gilbert, G. N. and Mulkay, M. *Opening Pandora's Box: A Sociological Analysis of Scientists' Discourse* (Cambridge Univ. Press, Cambridge, 1984)

Greenberg, D. S. *The Politics of Pure Science* (The New American Library, New York, 1967)

Hollis, M. and Lukes, S. *Rationality and Relativism* (Blackwell, Oxford, 1982)

Horton, R. 'African Traditional Thought and Western Science' *Africa* Vol. 37, Nos. 1 & 2, 1967, and in Wilson, 1970

Knorr-Cetina, K. D. 'The Ethnographic Study of Scientific Work: Towards a Constructivist Interpretation of Science' in Knorr-Cetina and Mulkay, 1983

Knorr-Cetina, K. D. and Mulkay, M. (eds.) *Science Observed: Perspectives on the Social Study of Science* (Sage, London, Beverley Hills and New Delhi, 1983)

Kuhn, T. S. *The Structure of Scientific*

517

Revolutions (Univ. of Chicago Press, Chicago and London, 1962, 2nd ed., enlarged, 1970)

Lakatos, I. 'Falsification and the Methodology of Scientific Research Programmes' in Lakatos, I. and Musgrave, A. *Criticism and the Growth of Knowledge* (Cambridge Univ. Press, London, 1970)

Lévi-Strauss, C. *Myth and Meaning* (R. K. P., London, 1960)

Lowe, D. M. *History of Bourgeois Perception* (Univ. of Chicago Press, Chicago, 1982)

Luckmann, B. 'The Small Life-Worlds of Modern Man' in T. Luckmann (ed.) *Phenomenology and Sociology* (Penguin, Harmondsworth, 1978)

Mannheim, K. 'Conservative Thought' in *Essays in Sociology and Social Psychology* (R. K. P., London, 1953)

Mannheim, K. *Ideology and Utopia* (R. K. P., London, 1960)

Marx, K. *The Poverty of Philosophy* (Progress Publishers, Moscow, 1955)

Marx, K. 'Existence and Consciousness' in K. Thompson and J. Tunstall (eds.) *Sociological Perspectives* (Penguin, Harmondsworth, 1971)

Marx, K. and Engels, F. *Selected Works* (Lawrence & Wishart, London, 1968)

Mbiti, J. S. *African Religions and Philosophy* (Heinemann, London, 1969)

Merton, R. K. *Science, Technology and Society in Seventeenth-Century England* (Saint Catherine Press, Bruges, 1938a). See also Merton 1973

Merton, R. K. 'Science and the Social Order' *Philosophy of Science*, 5, 1938b, reprinted in Merton 1973

Merton, R. K. 'Science and Technology in a Democratic Order' *Journal of Legal and Political Sociology*, 1, 1942, later published as: 'Science and Democratic Social Structure', in Merton 1949 and reprinted in Merton 1973

Merton, R. K. *Social Theory and Social Structure* (The Free Press, New York, 1949)

Merton, R. K. 'Priorities in Scientific Discovery: A Chapter in the Sociology of Science' *American Sociological Review*, 22, Dec. 1957, reprinted in Merton 1973

Merton, R. K. *The Sociology of Science* ed., Storer N. W. (Univ. of Chicago Press, Chicago, 1973)

Mills, C. Wright *The Power Elite* (Oxford Univ. Press, Oxford, 1956)

Mitroff, I. I. *The Subjective Side of Science* (Elsevier, Amsterdam, 1974)

Morgan, D. H. J. 'Berger and Kellner's Construction of Marriage' *University of Manchester Sociology Occasional Paper* No. 7, 1981

Mulkay, M. J. 'Some Aspects of Cultural Growth in the Natural Sciences' *Social Research* Vol. 36, No. 1, 1969, abridged in Barnes 1972

Newton-Smith, W. H. *The Rationality of Science* (R. K. P., London, 1981)

Popper, K. R. *The Logic of Scientific Discovery* (Hutchinson, London, 1959: German original 1934)

Porter, M. 'Worlds Apart: the Class Consciousness of Working Class Women' *Women's Studies International Quarterly* Vol. I, No. 2, 1978

Price, D. J. de Solla *Little Science, Big Science* (Columbia Univ. Press, New York, 1963)

Price, D. J. de Solla 'The Structure of Publication in Science and Technology' in Gruber, W. and Marquis, G. (eds.) *Factors in the Transfer of Technology* (MIT Press, 1969) and in Barnes, B. 1972

Ravetz, J. R. *Scientific Knowledge and its Social Problems* (Oxford University Press, Oxford, 1971)

Richards, S. *Philosophy and Sociology of Science* (Blackwell, Oxford, 1983)

Sorokin, P. A. and Merton, R. K. 'Social Time: a Methodological and Functional Analysis' *American Journal of Sociology* Vol. 42, No. 5, 1937

Thompson, E. P. 'Time, Work-Discipline and Industrial Capitalism' *Past and Present* No. 38, Dec. 1967

Wilson, B. R. *Rationality* (Blackwell, Oxford, 1970)

Worsley, P. 'Emile Durkheim's Theory of Knowledge' *Sociological Review* Vol. 4, No. 1, 1956

Zerubavel, E. 'The Standardization of Time: a Sociohistorical Perspective' *American Journal of Sociology* Vol. 88, No. I, 1982

Section 7
The Sociology of Health and Medicine
Nicky Hart

Chapter One

Health and the Mythology of Medicine

The Relationship between Health and Medicine

In present day Britain, it is difficult for most people to separate their ideas about health from their ideas about medicine. This is because the medical profession has successfully persuaded us that our personal health depends upon high standards of medical care. As a result, the National Health Service (NHS), has been designed as a national medical service. It consists almost entirely of surgeries, clinics and hospitals and it is the mainstay of government policy for health. In maintaining it as a system of free medical advice and almost free treatment, at an annual cost of more than 5% of national income (£15 billion in 1982), the government reckons that it has discharged its duty to protect the nation's health. In fact so complete is the grip of the medical profession over both popular and political consciousness that to most people medicine is synonymous with health.

What's wrong with this state of affairs? Surely the medical profession has every right to monopolise national health policy? Have they not earned it through the demonstrable effectiveness of their knowledge and skill? Surprisingly, the answers to these questions are all in the negative. Medicine has not made a significant contribution to improving people's health in the past and much of the treatment carried out in the NHS today has never been carefully evaluated. Obviously some forms of medical intervention are highly successful. But because they cannot be separated from unsuccessful techniques, we cannot measure the contribution of medicine to contemporary levels of health. An example may help to clarify this point. Every year in Britain, thousands of people suffering from lung cancer are treated in the NHS. The consultants responsible for them are well aware that probably less than 5% will derive any benefit from the treatment which for the majority might even be worse than the effects of the disease itself in what is likely to be the final year of the person's life. This is why some people reject the offer of medical help. But because treatment is not evaluated, we do not know how many people survive and for how long. Some routine treatment, e.g. the repair of fractures, is self-evidently beneficial. But in the absence of statistical records of the outcome of all treatment, we have no way of knowing the value of resources expended in the NHS, both in the financial sense and in terms of their contribution to the nation's health. The remainder of this chapter will be devoted to proving the truth of these statements. But before going on to examine the evidence, we should clarify what we mean by *health*.

The Concept of Health

The concept of health is difficult to define and measure. Although we associate it with the activities of doctors, it is only indirectly linked to medical treatment. Doctors deal primarily with disease and not with the promotion of health in any positive way. The knowledge of medicine is a catalogue of disorders implying that when none are present people are healthy. But to promote health involves the prevention of disease, not merely its treatment. Given that limited scope exists to restore or repair damaged health (see pp.527–529), there is little to be learned about health as such in medical literature.

So what is health and what are the factors that protect it or put it at risk? At a personal level we all know the answer at least to the first of these questions. We know from personal experience of feeling well and feeling ill how to distinguish health and ill-health in subjective terms. But converting subjective knowledge into a standard measure which applies to the whole population is by no means easy. To begin with, not everybody has the same threshold of pain or the same expectations about what counts as abnormal symptoms. Some people go to the doctor for complaints which others may not even notice and yet the latter include people who spend a whole lifetime apparently feeling healthy only to die at an early age of a preventable or treatable condition. The problem is finding a definition for health which covers these variations and permits the measurement of health experience in the population as a whole.

The World Health Organisation (WHO) defines health as, 'Not merely the absence of disease and infirmity but complete physical, mental and social wellbeing'. (WHO, 1955). This definition emphasises the interdependence of physical and mental welfare, stressing that feeling well is not just a physical experience. But how can these different dimensions be converted into a measure which can be used to study the distribution of health in one society or to compare standards of health between societies? In the absence of any universally valid measure, most surveys of health rely on one or other of the health status indicators of *morbidity* and *mortality*.

The first of these, morbidity, which means quite simply sickness, is an indicator not of health but of its absence. It is measured either through self reported illness in health surveys or from the statistics of time off work. Alternatively it may be constructed from the records of consultation between doctors and patients. The statistics of morbidity in any of these forms represent health negatively as a state of illness at one point in time. As such they tend to convey the impression of ill-health in episodic terms as something that happens suddenly and then goes away, rather than as a continuous dimension of experience. They also pose a number of problems of interpretation when applied for the purposes of comparing health experience within a population. Self reported sickness has the shortcoming already mentioned of being based on subjective judgement. Thus statistics of sickness absence can only represent the experience of people at work, while those of medical treatment are as much a measure of availability of, as demand for, services. Given the substantial variation found all over Britain in the length of waiting lists for different kinds of treatment, records of medical consultation and treatment provide a limited picture of the extent of morbidity in the population, and an even more limited indicator of its health in any positive sense.

What of the other health status indicator, mortality? This measure of health is constructed from mortality statistics. It can provide information about the risk of death at any age and from any particular cause. Its great limitation is that it only represents forms of ill-health that are ultimately fatal and not all those other forms of pain and suffering that do not result in loss of life. However it is not influenced by the processes of subjective judgement in the way that morbidity is and, being a more objective measure, it can be used to study changes over time. In fact the incidence of mortality is the only means of studying health in earlier times before the introduction of the NHS, national insurance schemes and the questionnaire survey. Age at death provides a measure of the length of the human lifetime. It indicates, in other words, the durability of the human body, the time it takes to wear out. In this sense mortality is a particularly useful indicator. It captures the positive dimension of health and it avoids the trap of presenting ill-health as an episodic event.

Life expectation is the only means of making any sense of what people's health was like in the nineteenth century and before. In the remainder of this book, we shall make extensive use of this measure to study (1) the contribution of medicine to improvements in health in both the past and the present, (2) the impact of social and economic change on health in the nineteenth and twentieth centuries and (3) the extent of social inequality in health.

Health and Medicine: The Historical Balance Sheet

During the last 150 years the causes of death in Britain have been gradually transformed. Before 1900, infective diseases like tuberculosis accounted for most deaths at every age, yet today they have virtually disappeared. Their place has been taken by accidents among young people and by heart disease and cancer among middle-aged and older people. These changes are examined in more detail in chapter 2 (p.540). The elimination of fatal infections has been associated with a 'leap forward' in life expectation. People live longer today than they ever did in the past and the fact that human bodies have become more durable, is the most important evidence of better health in the modern world.

Table 1.1 gives changes in life expectation since 1830 and reveals the improvements that have taken place especially at birth.

Table 1.1   Expectation of Life at Selected Ages by Sex

Period	Birth		Age 15		Age 65	
	Male	Female	Male	Female	Male	Female
1838-1854	39.9	41.8	43.2	43.9	10.8	11.5
1891-1900	44.1	47.8	45.2	47.6	10.3	11.3
1950-1952	66.5	71.5	54.4	58.9	11.7	14.3
1974-1976	69.6	75.8	56.2	62.1	12.4	16.4

Source: *The Demographic Review* 1977 p.19 (England and Wales)

The increase in life expectation at birth from around 40 years in the first half of the nineteenth century to 70 and over in the mid 1970s, means that the majority of babies born today can expect to live to the age of 60 and beyond. During the same period, an increase of 13 and 18 years for males and females respectively at age 15 has been achieved.

When and why did the decline in mortality come about? Most observers agree with McKeown that the fall began around 1830. It was made up of a combination of causes but more than 60% of the total decline between 1850 and 1970 was due to a reduction in infective conditions. Among them, the most important single cause was tuberculosis or as it was popularly known in the last century, *consumption.* The decline of this disease is shown in Figure 1.1 From an annual level of more than 4000 per million population in the second half of the nineteenth century, the incidence of TB had fallen to less than 500 by the time that drugs became available for its treatment in 1947. As figure 1.1, demonstrates the bulk of the decline took place well before this time and the slope of the gradient is only slightly altered by the introduction of effective medical treatment. The reductio threat of TB in Britain must therefore have been stimulated by other than medical factors and there is no reason to suppose that these same factors did not continue to account for most of the further decline of the disease after the introduction of chemotherapy - in plain language, antibiotics.

Figure 1.1 Respiratory Tuberculosis: The Decline in England and Wales, 1840-1970

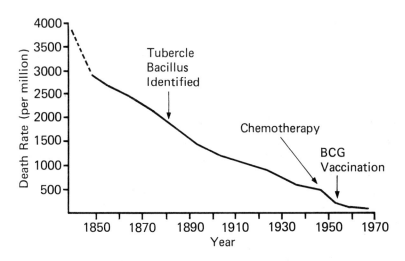

Source: McKeown, T., *The Modern Rise of Population,* Edward Arnold, London, 1976, p.81.

All of the other *major* diseases that declined, measles, scarlet fever, pneumonia, bronchitis and whooping cough, tell the same story - a steady decline beginning well before the introduction of effective treatment leaving only a relatively small residue of cases by the time vaccination or effective drugs become available. From then on it is difficult to separate the impact of medical treatment from the continuing influence of the factors which began the decline in the first place. It all suggests that the threat of infective micro-organisms (viruses) to human health was being systematically swept away not by improvements in medical science but by other events and processes which are new to the nineteenth and twentieth centuries.

It is important to recognise that the fall in the death rate that occurred in the last century was not merely the result of the disappearance of a series of different diseases, it was rather the disappearance of the whole class of disease that had afflicted human beings and curtailed the human lifespan from time immemorial. Improvements in life expectation are largely the product of this revolutionary change in human health and medicine played a very peripheral part in bringing them about. But what of the other causes of death that have declined - is the record of medical achievement any better there?

The eighteenth and nineteenth centuries saw a tremendous growth in the number of hospitals in London and the provinces. It was during this period that many of the famous teaching hospitals were established. On the face of it, this must surely have had some effect on the health of the population. But did it? It is difficult to find evidence to assess the effectiveness of hospital treatment on individual patients because few records were kept. This is also true for the present day; rates of survival following hospital treatment are not recorded by the NHS. But we can get some idea of the contribution of hospitals by estimating the adequacy of their methods of treatment in the light of present day knowledge. Proceeding in this way McKeown is led to the conclusion that hospitals could not have made an appreciable impact on the population's health before the twentieth century. Techniques of surgery were very primitive by modern standards and death rates from it were very high. Like heart transplants in the present day, surgical intervention, in the absence of anaesthesia and antiseptic methods, was a rather experimental affair and only attempted when the patient was likely to die anyway. At this time too, what Illich has called *iatrogenic* conditions (see p.566) i.e. sickness brought about by medical treatment itself, were widespread. In the lying-in hospitals (predecessors of today's maternity hospitals), maternal death rates from puerperal fever were much higher on wards where infants were delivered by doctors. Doctors ignorant of the risk of infection, examined patients with hands smothered with the debris of postmortem examinations. As McKeown concludes,

> ... on balance the effects of hospital work in this period were probably harmful ... any patient faced the risk of contracting a lethal infection up to the second half of the nineteenth century ... and it was not until much later that hospital patients could be reasonably certain of dying from the diseases with which they were admitted. (McKeown 1976, 150).

What about the period since then? Standards of health have continued to improve in the last eighty years and it is natural to assume that this has been influenced by the growth of access to medical treatment, especially since 1948 when the NHS was established. The next section will consider the value of medicine in our own times.

The Effectiveness of Medicine in the Twentieth Century

What credit can doctors claim for their part in the continuing improvements in life expectation that have been achieved in the twentieth century? In attempting to answer this question, we come up against the problem of how to separate the possible contribution of medicine from all the other beneficial influences which have helped to reduce premature death by raising standards of health in the population. The case of falling rates of infant and maternal mortality illustrates these problems well.

Since the beginning of this century, there has been a continuous decline in the risk of death at birth for mothers and babies. There are a number of possible reasons for this trend. Of certain importance is declining fertility. The risks of childbirth for both mothers and infants increase substantially when the mother has already had several previous births. This suggests that falling family size is one of the most important reasons for reducing the risks of childbirth. Another important factor is diet. Infant survival is closely correlated with birthweight which is itself linked to the diet of the mother during pregnancy. This is a further beneficial effect of smaller households, their members are likely to be better fed for the simple reason that they are fewer in number. The research of Winter (see p.553) shows that between 1900 and 1930, infant mortality fell most sharply during the First World War (1914-1918). The most important reason was rising living standards in the poorest section of the community during the war, brought about by direct government intervention to ration food and control its price, to set minimum wage levels and to offer employment either in uniform or out of it. The most interesting of Winter's conclusions from the point of view of the present discussion is that medical treatment could not have made any positive contribution to the decline. This is because over 60% of the profession were in uniform. Some have inferred from this wartime shortage of medical care that the decline may have reflected a reduction in the use of instruments like forceps which often lead to birth damage. Whatever the truth of this, one thing is quite clear. In the first thirty years of the twentieth century, infant and maternal mortality rates fell most sharply at the time when the British population was starved of medical services because the majority of doctors had been 'drafted'.

How do we separate the effects of rising living standards, improved nutrition and reduced family size from other factors that might have helped to bring down mortality rates? Obstetricians have drawn on the evidence of decline to persuade governments that hospitalised childbirth is safer. This is despite the fact that there is no evidence to show that domicilliary childbirth (i.e. at home) carries more risk. In fact the opposite is true, the statistics show that babies born at home have a lower death rate. Doctors explain the greater safety of home birth by pointing out that more than 90% of babies are born in hospital including those most at risk. It is because only risk-free cases are permitted the option of a home delivery that they appear safer. The problem of testing the competing claims of the obstetrics lobby and those who support the call for more freedom of choice in childbirth is that it is no longer possible to carry out a test of which is the safer venue. This would involve the comparison of randomly selected mothers giving birth either at home or in hospital to see which is the safer. Because most births (over 95% in 1982) take place in hospital this test of effectiveness cannot be carried out.

If we look at the pre-war period, when most babies were born at home and when the mother being delivered in the maternity hospital was rather more likely to be from a higher social class, the evidence suggests that the hospital may well have been more dangerous. Death rates among rich women being delivered in hospital were actually higher than those of poor women being delivered at home! The trend of hospitalised childbirth has continued since then in the absence of any systematic evaluation of its relative effectiveness and without any attempt to test the ever more complex technological gadgetry applied to childbirth as part of the same process. So we do not know what part, if any, the machinery and drugs of modern obstetrics has played in reducing the risks of infant and maternal mortality although doctors are apt to claim credit for them. The same problem crops up when we look at other areas of treatment.

Intensive coronary care units for treating the victims of heart attacks were introduced into the NHS at great expense and without evaluation. Since then research has shown that the chances of recovering from a cardiac arrest are just as good, if not better, if the victim remains quietly at home in the bosom of family life. Nevertheless, the expansion of intensive care units in the NHS has continued. The reason that expensive methods of treatment come to be implemented without careful evaluation is that doctors are principally merchants of hope and their ethic is to try everything in their power to save their patients even if this involves new untested treatments. Even where it is clear that the chances of recovery are almost nil and where the treatment is more devastating than the disease, powerful therapies are still applied in the hope that 'this time it might just work'. In this doctors must often find themselves giving in against their better judgement to a desperate patient's need to try anything to keep hope of survival alive.

It would be wrong to suggest on the basis of this, that all medical treatment is useless. The problem is rather one of not knowing the relative merits or risks attached to different medical procedures and practices. This was the conclusion reached by Cochrane, in a book which called on his own profession to adopt a more scientific approach when introducing new forms of treatment. He argued that the value of most treatment routinely carried out in NHS hospitals had never been established and that consequently, doctors were more prone to act on the basis of 'medical opinion' rather than their knowledge of scientific fact. If so, this may go some way towards explaining why so few statistics are available to study the rate of recovery from various conditions among patients treated in NHS hospitals. The most striking example of this is the Hospital Inpatient Enquiry. This massive annual survey does not even bother to differentiate discharges where the patient is alive or dead.

In conclusion therefore, there is a shortage of evidence on which to reach a careful judgement about the contribution of medicine to general improvements in health in post war Britain. What we can say however is that medical science itself concedes that its theoretical knowledge of the aetiology (causes) of the two major diseases of the present day, cancer and heart disease, is underdeveloped. In each of these diseases the available medical treatment has a negligible impact on the chance of survival.

But if medicine cannot cure the major diseases of contemporary civilisation, what can be done about them? The realization that attempting to 'cure' degenerative disease is like trying to turn the clock back, has highlighted the importance of *prevention* and *care* in recent years.

Preventive approaches to health care are aimed at delaying the onset of disease by slowing down the ageing process of the human body. Preventive health care has little to do with the practice of medicine. It is much more concerned with the risks to health that are encountered in modern society, in diet, in work, in the environment and in behaviour. In some ways it constitutes a rediscovery of ideas widely prevalent at the turn of the century that the causes of disease are to be found in social arrangements and that social rearrangement is both possible and desirable if disease is to be prevented.

Growing recognition of the importance of *care* as opposed to *cure* is symbolised in such trends as the hospice movement. Hospices have been designed as places which provide a supportive and humane environment for the relief of pain in people suffering from incurable terminal disease. They have emerged in reaction to the impersonal and bureaucratic order of the modern hospital which is incapable of providing an environment where people can die with dignity and the support of their families. The aim of the hospice is to care for, not to cure the sick, reflecting a willingness to concede that medicine has no effective means of restoring health to many cancer patients. Similar 'winds of change' are blowing through the professional training of nurses. The rediscovery that the vocation of nursing has its own particular contribution and is not merely an adjunct to medical treatment, is witnessed in the emergence of the *Nursing Process,* a new conceptual model for improving the quality of nursing care.

As yet, these trends could scarcely be said to present a fundamental challenge to organised medicine's control over the direction of health policy and the disbursement of national resources. 'High Tech' medicine with its emphasis on drugs, machinery and the drive to master disease remains the dominant feature of the NHS. The question of how the medical profession, despite its very limited record of achievement, became entrusted with the guardianship of the nation's health, will be taken up in chapter 7. In the present context, the question that remains to be answered is why the message that it is more useful to see the causes of disease as lying outside individuals in their living environments somehow got lost during the course of the last century as the emphasis on treating disease by treating the individual became the more prevalent approach.

Contemporary Medical Practice and the Bio-mechanical Model

What is contemporary medical practice like? The following brief summary may help to describe its principal features. Modern medicine is *cure* oriented. The primary goal is treatment and medical consultation starts with the description of symptoms. These are all the reported deviations from normal health, the clues needed for diagnosis and the application of the correct remedy. The patient's own feelings and impressions of what is wrong are less important than any organic signs that may be felt, observed or tested. If necessary, samples of the patient's body such as urine or blood may be taken or more complicated mechanical tests such as X-rays or ultra-sound scans might be carried out to find a medical label for the problem. The objective is the identification of organic causes beyond the patient's comprehension. This is why the sufferer's own account of what is wrong is largely irrelevant to diagnosis.

It would be unjust to suggest that doctors only treat the symptoms that patients bring to the consulting room. These may be only superficial signs of more serious underlying disorder. But by the time a patient consults a doctor, the option of prevention is already ruled out because the disease has advanced to the point of damaging the human body. Sometimes doctors are able to cure the patient by reversing the disease process. They may even be able to repair the organic damage by employing miraculous techniques which 'take the breath away'. Unfortunately, this is not a realistic possibility for most major degenerative conditions so that medical treatment can only hope to manage an irreversible disease by suppressing the continuing effects of its symptoms. From this it can be appreciated that medicine intervenes late in the development of disease. Doctors are not present when a disease starts, they wait for patients to present themselves for treatment. Consequently their primary interest is focused on the end point of the disease process not on its root causes. Like the efforts of witchdoctors, medicine is therefore primarily a pragmatic activity, oriented to answering the immediate needs of individual patients. This contrasts with its public image as a scientific activity oriented to the discovery of the true causes of disease.

Medical practice is also organised in such a way as to obscure clues about the root causes of disease. The doctor/patient relationship is highly confidential and surrounded by an atmosphere of anonymity. The preferred place of consultation or treatment is deliberately set apart from the normal living environment of the sufferer, thereby blinding the doctor to any clues it may contain about the causes of illness. Furthermore, since the content of consultation is ideally restricted to the description and examination of organic symptoms, information about the patient's social identity: occupation, marital status, workplace, income etc. only comes up incidentally, if at all.

From this brief summary of contemporary medical practice, a number of distinctive features stand out. They are as follows:

(1) A dominant concern with the *organic* appearances of disease combined with a tendency to ignore, if not dismiss, the link between mind and body, between physical and mental well-being. Even psychiatry, the medical speciality devoted to mental illness,

predominantly seeks organic causes for the conditions it treats.

(2)   An orientation towards *cure*, towards the manipulation of organic symptoms with the intention of effecting their disappearance if at all possible. In this medicine shares certain parallels with magic and religion. All seek to perform their own style of conjuring trick.

(3)   A perception of *disease* as an autonomous and potentially manageable entity which threatens personal health in temporary or episodic fashion. Disease is the alien intruder which needs to be expelled. This is in contrast to the view of disease as an integral product of the person/environment relationship.

(4)   A focus on the isolated *individual* as the site of disease and the appropriate object of treatment.

(5)   A belief that the most appropriate place for treatment is a *medical environment,* the consulting room or the hospital, not the environment where symptoms arise.

These combined features of modern medicine have been summed up by some contemporary critics under the heading of the *bio-mechanical model.* This metaphor emphasises the shortcomings of restricting attention to the biological dimensions of disease and treating the individual sufferer as a mindless object whose physical body can be engineered like a machine. The doctor appears as a 'body mechanic', insensitive to the spiritual welfare of the patient, oblivious to the injury that medical treatment may itself inflict and ignorant of the wider environment in which disease originates.

McKeown's summary of the negative influence of the bio-mechanical model is as follows:

> Medical science and services are misdirected, and society's investment in health is not well used because they rest on an erroneous assumption about the basis of human health. It is assumed that the body can be regarded as a machine, whose protection from disease and its effects depends primarily on internal intervention. The approach has led to indifference to the external influences and personal behaviour which are the predominant determinants of health. It has also resulted in the relative neglect of the majority of sick people who provide no scope for the internal measures which are at the centre of medical interest. (McKeown 1976, XIV).

As he points out, the singular emphasis on the nuts and bolts of treatment pervades even the theoretical knowledge of medical science. This emphasis, perhaps inevitable in the consulting room or operating theatre, where the desperate patient needs immediate relief, quite wrongly dominates almost all medical research. University medical schools and research institutes, instead of searching for the fundamental causes of disease in the relationships between people, their behaviour and their environments, remain fascinated by the organic end-products of disease in human tissue. While their funds are used up on experiments into the chemical basis of inheritance or the immunological response to transplanted organs, major questions about how disease starts in the first place, are not merely left unanswered, they are not even asked. The result, in the words of one of the profession's own most celebrated scholars: '. . . almost none of the modern basic research in the medical sciences has any direct bearing on the prevention of disease or on the improvement of medical care'. (Sir Macfarlane Burnett 1971, 218).

These are devastating criticisms of medicine's approach to health in contemporary society advanced by some of the profession's own most respected members. They point to serious shortcomings in the ethos of medical science which are manifested in the organisation of medical research, in the training of doctors, and in everyday treatment. How could a misdirection of medical science on this scale come about?

Certain elements of contemporary medical practice arise necessarily in consultation and treatment and have probably been a typical feature of the relationship between healers and their clients from time immemorial. Among these we might include the one to one relationship, the emphasis on cure and the tendency to view illness as a temporary phenomenon. Like the client of an Azande witchdoctor, the typical patient has a pressing desire for the symptoms of illness to disappear. If treatment appears like a 'medical conjuring trick' this may have as much to do with the emotions of patients as with any deliberate design on the part of doctors. But some of the features identified above belong to a more recent phase of the history of western science. They are part of the legacy of two important developments: the 'Cartesian' revolution and the discovery of 'Germ Theory'.

How Medicine Mislaid the Real Nature of Health: The Mind Body Dualism and the Doctrine of Specific Aetiology

The 'Cartesian' revolution refers to the impact of the philosophy of René Descartes on social morality and via that on the development of science in the seventeenth century. Descartes insisted on the independence of mind and body. He saw the physical substance of the body as subordinate to the mind, a machine to be activated at the will of the human spirit. His ideas had a profound influence on the development of positivist science (logical thought based upon empirical observation) and they acted as a liberating force in medicine. Before Descartes and the advent of the *mind/body dualism*, the development of medicine was severely constrained by a religious embargo on the study of human anatomy. The orthodox Christian view held that body and soul were one and the same thing and, if the human body was not preserved intact, the soul could not ascend to heaven. As a result, human dissection was virtually impossible and without knowledge of anatomy, the development of medical science was severely retarded. Descartes paved the way for the development of a medical science oriented to the physiology of the human machine. The mind remained the seat of the soul, the province of religion while the body was handed over to new positivist science. In consequence, the foundations of medical science as it is practised today, were laid in the seventeenth century with an emphasis on the separation of physical and mental life which in its own way has been as confining as the influence of the medieval church on the physicians of pre-renaissance days.

The discovery of germ theory came much later and was itself a product of positivist science. It was discovered late in the nineteenth century through the research of Louis Pasteur in France and Robert Koch in Germany. Each succeeded in showing that infection occurs through the action of invisible micro-organisms. At the time, infective disease was still the major cause of death among all ages, as it had been for centuries. The orthodox medical view held that these diseases were caused by *miasmata* or bad air arising out of filth and lack of hygiene. Operating on this false premise, the sanitary reformers of Victorian England (see p.550) had implemented a series of public health measures which substantially reduced the risk of diseases like cholera and typhus. After Pasteur, the true nature of the infective process was understood. Infection does not arise spontaneously out of bad air but occurs though the invasion of one living organism by another. It happens when people eat infected food, drink infected water, get bitten by infected insects or animals and get close enough to inhale the infected air expelled through coughs and sneezes. The result is a struggle for survival between the human host and the virus (remember Darwin was around at this time too). In 1882, Robert Koch isolated and grew the tubercle bacillus in the laboratory. This meant that he could demonstrate that tuberculosis, the most virulent disease of the day with a reputation similar to cancer in our own times, was caused by a specific micro-organism. From this emerged the *Doctrine of Specific Aetiology:* a specific disease always has a specific cause.

This doctrine has been the most influential force in medical research for over a century. It implies that the way to understand disease is to create it in the laboratory and that the ingredients for explanation are found through minute observation of its bio-chemical appearances. In other words it proposes that the symptoms of disease tell their own story. Where Pasteur and Koch searched for the specific germs which caused each infective disease, medical scientists in laboratories all over the world today search for the specific *carcinogens* which they believe cause malignant tumours. Even the same idea of disease being caused by a noxious foreign body invading the healthy person, is retained.

The major shortcoming of this interpretation of disease applied as much in Koch's time as it does today. What Koch could not explain despite his ability to create disease at will in experimental conditions, was why *disease is rare, when infection is the norm*. To the city dwellers of nineteenth century Europe, lethal micro-organisms were no strangers. Most of the population would have been exposed to the tubercle bacillus and many probably retained the virulent infection in their bodies. Yet only a small proportion developed and suffered from tuberculosis. In fact during the course of his researches, Koch discovered that he had an immunity to TB which meant that he must have been exposed to the infection earlier in his life. Nevertheless he lived to a vigorous old age and died of a stroke. So the ability to create disease in an artificial environment, does not explain how and why the disease strikes living people in the real world outside the laboratory.

The arrival of germ theory has been hailed as a scientific revolution and many have concluded from this alone that it was responsible for declining mortality throughout the last century. But although they provided a reinterpretation of the major health problems of their day, the discoveries of Koch and Pasteur had no impact on the rate of death. The assumption that they did, arises from a confusion of pure knowledge and its application. Mortality from infective causes had been in steady decline for several decades before scientists were awakened to the existence of micro-organisms. The subsequent course of this decline was unaffected by the new knowledge. The reasons why health improved in the nineteenth century are the subject of the next chapter and we can only briefly anticipate them here. Death rates fell principally in response to rising living standards and to public health measures inspired by the movement for sanitary reform. The sanitary reformers, while they may not have understood the correct details of infective processes, knew well enough that their fundamental causes were poverty, overcrowding, and pollution. In 1849, John Snow, had proved that cholera was caused by impure water. He noticed that the risk of death from this disease was much greater in a part of London supplied with water by a particular company. By the simple expedient of removing the handle of the 'Broad Street Pump', he cut cholera death rates at a stroke and earned his place in epidemiological history.

Although germ theory filled in more accurate details of the transmission of infection, the basic proven methods of its prevention remained unaltered. Mortality from infective causes kept on falling at the same rate before and after the scientific breakthrough and it was to be another 70 years before effective treatment in the shape of penicillin was discovered. By then (1947), death from infection had become quite rare. So despite the ingenuity of Koch and Pasteur, the impact of germ theory on health has been limited. Its main influence has been on the theoretical development of medicine. In concentrating attention on the miniscule details of what disease does in the human body, Koch's *doctrine of specific aetiology* has deflected attention away from its *prior* causes in the environment and the individual's relationship to it. This is why modern medicine is dominated by the concern to explain and treat organic symptoms in individuals.

It also throws light on the removal of medical treatment from the patient's home to the consulting room or the hospital. In the nineteenth century most doctors treated their patients at home. Founded on charity, hospitals were primarily places of training where pauper patients received free treatment in exchange for acting as 'guinea pigs' for medical students. Those who could afford to pay were not eligible for free hospital treatment, and consequently it was stigmatised. In any case, before germ theory finally established the crucial importance of hygiene, hospitals had a quiet deservedly dangerous reputation. It took several decades to expunge the negative image of the hospital. The process was aided by germ theory in a number of ways. The most direct effect was on standards of hygiene and the realisation that infective patients constituted a risk to people suffering from other conditions. The isolation of contagious patients made hospitals much safer places. Furthermore, given the idea at the heart of germ theory that disease itself is best understood when isolated in laboratory conditions, it makes more sense to investigate symptoms in a specialised medical environment where tests can be undertaken in hygienic conditions. This helped to make the hospital more acceptable, even necessary for good results. As a further consequence, the process of diagnosis came to rely less and less on the verbal reports of patients and more and more on technological machine and drug-aided tests for symptoms. As Reiser (1979) shows, patients today have become objects in treatment, onlookers who may even be kept in the dark about what is happening to their bodies. The combination of the mind/body dualism and the doctrine of specific aetiology have helped to shape the five principal features of contemporary medical practice identified on page 11: the emphasis on *(1) curing, (2) individuals of (3) episodic* bouts of *(4) organic* disorder in a *(5) clinical environment.* Some of these were reinforced rather than invented for the first time in the healing process. People suffering from an illness are inevitably predisposed to think of it as a temporary phenomenon and to seek out healers who are prepared to offer a cure. The concern with organic symptoms inside the individual and the rise of hospitals as 'high tech' disease palaces are newer features of the healing relationship. Their dominance in modern medicine may be due to the fact that they fit more easily with a curative focus. It is easier to treat one individual at a time and the reduction of illness to visible organic symptoms offers more scope for immediate remedial action. That patients attend doctors on medical premises in the present day rather than on their own home ground reflects the greater prestige of the profession and the growing, if somewhat misplaced, confidence of the public that effective cures are available.

Medicine as a Social Ideology

It is easier to see why medicine developed in the way it did than it is to explain the success of the profession in persuading us to believe in its version of what is good for our health. Public confidence in medical care has not been built on a sound record of achievement and it is in large degree nurtured by myths about the past. In the light of this it is easier to appreciate the role that medicine plays in contemporary society as *a social ideology.* In modern times doctors have taken over some of the social functions that priests played in the past officiating at birth and at death and determining the morality and ethics of human conduct in such spheres as reproduction and parent/child relationships. Medicine has become like a secular religion, a view reinforced by the knowledge that belief in its powers is based on myths about the past and faith in the present.

In portraying medicine as a social ideology, the intention is to stress that it should not be thought of as a body of scientific and apparently neutral truths about the nature of existence. Medicine presents an image of health which fits with the culture of industrial capitalist societies. The most important parallel is between the ethic of individualism in modern society and the focus of medical treatment on individuals. The modern way of life is more privatised and impersonal and these tendencies pervade all aspects of experience including health care. In these terms we can more readily understand why it is that medicine has become so influential in the determination of health policy in the advanced capitalist societies. Equally the reliance on machine technology and the belief that empirical science holds the key to human welfare both stem from the same self confident source.

This picture of medical science as a social ideology shaped in large degree by the social forces of our age, provides the rationale for the sociological study of health and of medicine. By demystifying the real process of how human health improved in the past and how it is promoted in the present, a whole new area of study is opened up. If medicine is not responsible, what is? This is the principal question addressed by the sociology of health. At the same time there is the question of how the medical profession succeeded in 'pulling the wool over everybody's eyes' including their own by all accounts. Explaining just how a profession succeeded in claiming the right to an exclusive monopoly of health care in the advanced industrial societies and with what consequences for human experience is the subject matter of the sociology of medicine. These questions will be addressed in the remaining chapters of this section.

Chapter Two

Human Health and Society

Health as the Product of Society

The evidence that health is the product of society rather than nature or medicine comes in a number of forms. To begin with there is historical evidence that patterns of disease change systematically over time in relation to social and economic development. We shall be reviewing this in the pages that follow drawing particular attention to the way in which the process of industrialisation eliminated the major diseases of the nineteenth century. This process was accompanied by the modern rise of population. Starting about 1830, the rate of death in Britain began to fall and it kept on doing so throughout the rest of the century. It led to a massive increase in the size of the population. The process was not confined to Britain although it does seem to have happened here first. But as methods of capitalist industrialisation spread elsewhere in Europe and beyond, population growth followed leading in the present day to the global population explosion.

The fall in the death rate occurred in all age groups and among both sexes. But it was most concentrated among females and, especially after 1900, among children. It had two effects. One is that the risk of death has become systematically linked to age, it increases as people grow older. Today a premature death is no longer, as it was in our great grandparents' day, that of a child. It is now a death before the retirement age of 65 years, an age which most people living before 1900 did not expect to reach. The other effect is the sexual division in the ageing population. The growing divergence of male and female life expectation means that after 65, there are almost twice as many women as men in the population. These demographic shifts have accompanied changes in occupational and domestic life. Women and children were gradually expelled from the workforce in the nineteenth century to become dependant housewives and schoolchildren. The coincidence of these events suggests that the influence of society on health includes the impact of changing age and sex roles. The following sections of this chapter will examine these demographic changes in detail and their possible causes.

Social Change and Patterns of Disease

As we saw in the previous chapter (p.524), the last 50 years has witnessed a gradual transformation of the profile of fatal disease. The direction and character of this change is illustrated in Figure 2.1. Figure 2.1 shows the distribution of death between different causes and by age. The most striking divergence between 1931 and 1973 is the virtual disappearance of deaths caused by infective disease. In the pre-war period this accounted for more premature death than any other single cause making up 40% of the total for both sexes before middle age. By 1973 they have almost disappeared from sight to be replaced among males by accidents and violence and among females by a combination of causes. Other distinctive changes include the reducing significance of respiratory illness especially among people below the age of 50, and the growing significance of cancer (neoplasms) particularly among women. In 1973 circulatory diseases (heart attacks and strokes) become the dominant feature of male mortality after the age of 30 accounting for well over 50% of the total. Among women, cancer is a more numerous cause in middle age although diseases of the heart and circulatory system become the chief cause of death in old age. There has been less change in the pattern of mortality among the elderly. In both periods the two major causes are the same, but they do not dominate the picture quite so much in the earlier period, accounting for about 60% of the total in 1931 and 80% in 1973 among people over 60.

These changes, which appear to have been gradually taking place during the pre- and post-war period in Britain were part of a much longer run change which began in the first half of the nineteenth century. Then infective disease accounted for an even larger share of total mortality especially among babies, children and young adults. They are often called the diseases of poverty because most of their victims were poor and malnourished. In contrast, the diseases that have taken their place in the twentieth century are called the diseases of *civilisation* or *affluence.* This is because they are thought to be the result of eating too much, taking too little exercise and abusing the body by smoking or drinking too much. They are also referred to as degenerative conditions, a term which links them to the gradual decay of the body's organs. An example is arterio-sclerosis, the 'furring up' of the arteries which carry the blood around the body. In plain language they imply that the human body is wearing out and it is ironic that they should be linked to a lack of moderation in consumption when they occur earliest among the section of the community who have the least income to spend.

Figure 2.1 Mortality by Cause, Age and Sex, 1931, 1973

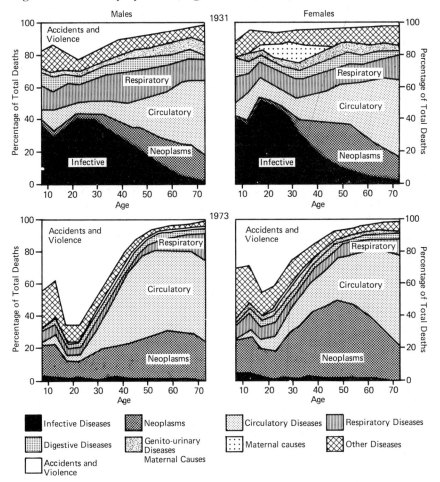

Source: OPCS *Trends in Mortality*. (HMSO, London, 1978). Reproduced with the permission of the Controller of Her Majesty's Stationery Office.

Today's major diseases are not new. It is of course extremely difficult to assess the relative contribution of different causes of death in the distant past. But fossil and bone remains suggest that the condition of arthritis, so prevalent from middle age onward in Britain today, is a form of suffering which unites our own experience with that of the early cave men and even the dinosaurs. The mummified remains of the pharoahs have proved to be a particularly valuable source for the investigation of disease among the ancients. From this source we find evidence of cancer, heart disease, pneumonia, kidney stones, cirrhosis, as well as a host of infections including many such as malaria, tuberculosis and schizosomiasis, which are still prevalent in Third World countries like Egypt, more than 2000 years later.

Nevertheless the comparative prevalence and severity of various diseases has changed greatly in the course of history and there is little doubt that in the centuries before 1900, infective disease was the main cause of death. Infection in human beings occurs when a bacterium or virus invades the human body. Although such organisms are by no means foreign to human beings, the arrival of a novel species creates a disturbance among the trillions already present causing an infection which could be fatal. If the individual recovers, future encounters with the same organism will be less severe because the body will have acquired an immunity. This is the reason why children were most at risk in the nineteenth century and before, and why today most infectious diseases like measles, chicken pox and whooping cough are childhood conditions to which the vast majority of adults are immune. However, in earlier centuries, as people from different continents met each other for the first time through voyages of exploration and conquest, unknowingly an exchange of micro-organisms also took place, often with literally devastating consequences. In these circumstances, when a previously unexposed population was introduced to an infection like measles for the first time, the result might be a catastrophic epidemic which was fatal for almost any contact irrespective of age.

The bubonic plague which wiped out about a third of the population of Europe in the space of little more than a decade of the fifteenth century, is a good example of this process. But equally instructive are the epidemics of smallpox which helped to destroy the populations and with them the civilisations of Central and South America (Aztecs and Incas) after the arrival of the Spanish conquistadors in the sixteenth century. According to McNeill, the population of central Mexico fell from 30 to 3 million in the space of less than 50 years from the time when Cortez and his hundred or so troops landed there and 'inaugurated epidemiological as well as other exchanges between the Amerindian and European populations'. As he wisely continues:

> In an age of almost world-wide population growth it is hard for us to imagine such catastrophies . . . Faith in established institutions and beliefs cannot easily withstand such disaster; skills and knowledge disappear. This indeed is what allowed the Spaniards to go as far as they did in transferring their culture and language to the New World, making it normative even in regions where millions of Indians had previously lived according to standards and customs of their own. (McNeill 1977, 205).

This is how infective disease contributed to the European conquest and colonisation of peoples and territories all over the globe.

In *Plagues and Peoples* McNeill describes how, in the centuries before 1800, the population of Europe developed a level of immunity to a variety of infections. In his words they became 'disease scarred'. Each century had a different disease. Leprosy in the fourteenth, plague in the fifteenth, syphilis in the sixteenth, smallpox in the seventeenth and eighteenth and tuberculosis and scarlet fever in the nineteenth. This epidemiological sequence gave Europeans a 'physiological superiority' which greatly aided their bid to colonise aboriginal peoples all over the globe. And, since disease was thought to be an instrument of divine will, it also gave the illusion of moral superiority: it was a sign that God was on their side when their enemies were wiped out by 'pestilence'.

Nevertheless, even among less susceptible European populations, mortality from infections remained high until the second half of the nineteenth century. From then on death rates began to tumble in a process known as the *modern rise of population*.

Health, Population Growth and Industrialisation

The nineteenth century witnessed many revolutionary changes of social organisation. These involved a spectacular growth of large towns and cities, the removal of work from the home to the factory, the growth of the state and of democratic politics and the beginnings of dramatic technological changes, which in the twentieth century would prove capable of putting men on the moon. Among these great transformations of human experience must be counted the modern rise of population. Figures 2.2 and 2.3 display the scope of the demographic revolution that began in the early decades of the nineteenth century.

Figure 2.2 The Modern Rise of World Population

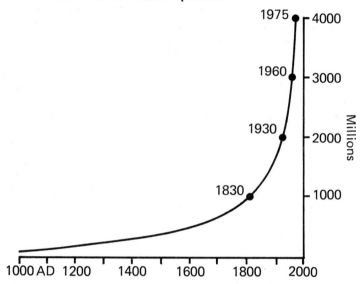

Source: McKeown, T., *The Modern Rise of Population,* Edward Arnold, London, 1976.

Figure 2.3 The Modern Rise of Population in England and Wales

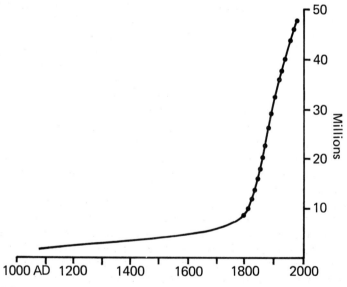

Source: McKeown, T., *The Modern Rise of Population,* Edward Arnold, London, 1976.

The increase of population that took place in the nineteenth century is called the 'Modern Rise' to distinguish it from previous periods of demographic growth. Unlike earlier periods when demographic increase was part of a cycle of growth and decline, the modern rise is unique because, as McKeown puts it, 'of its *size, duration and continuity'*. What this basically means is that it just went on rising and rising. Moreover it was not just a British phenomenon, it was global. How did it come about?

Population growth is determined by the combination of three factors, fertility, mortality and migration. Throughout the period in question, there was a net loss to the population of Britain from migration, so we may leave it out of any calculation of the reasons for population growth. Of the other two factors, some commentators, notably Wrigley and Schofield, have argued that the seeds of the modern rise were sown in the eighteenth century through an increase in fertility. But, since the period after 1870 has seen a fall in the birth rate, there can be little doubt that the most important mechanism of the change and its continuity is falling mortality particularly among the young.

The coincidence of:- (1) the modern rise of population; (2) the transformation of the nature of fatal disease; and (3) the rise of industrial capitalism constitutes powerful circumstantial evidence that the three processes are causally linked. Before we examine the evidence of their association and the possible directions of causal influence, we should first exclude one other possible reason for mortality decline. Is it conceivable that the human race, starting with the British, began to develop a spontaneous natural immunity giving protection from *all* infective micro-organisms? Could this be the explanation for the progressive disappearance of infective disease in the nineteenth and twentieth centuries.

We have already noted the way in which natural immunities develop in a population (p.542). Infections do not generally disappear completely, they usually survive as childhood diseases. But some are eliminated altogether. This happened to leprosy. Before 1400, it was an endemic disease in Britain, but then it disappeared from our shores and has never returned. But what needs to be explained in the nineteenth century is the disappearance not just of one infective condition, but all of them. Moreover these diseases which, even in a relatively immune population, survive to cause substantial mortality in childhood, no longer do so to anything like the extent they did in the past. And we must stress that the past means time immemorial. Infective disease has almost certainly been the main restraint on population growth since human beings first began to adopt a settled way of life thousands of years ago. If spontaneous natural immunity was the main reason for their sudden disappearance in the nineteenth century, we still need to explain why it happened when it did and not some time earlier.

The case of respiratory TB, the major cause of death during the period, provides a good example for illustrating the limitations of the natural immunity thesis. Because of population density, town dwellers developed more immunity to TB than people from the countryside. After 1830, the rapidly growing urban centres of Britain saw a continuing influx of rural migrants who ought to have been prime targets for infection. But instead of seeing an increased mortality from this disease amongst this unexposed rural population, the opposite occurred. The rate of death began to fall before the urbanisation process reached its peak and it kept on falling in the face of increasing migration from the countryside to the towns. So there can be little reason to conclude that the decline of TB was brought about by the development of natural immunity. If the resistance of the population improved it was more likely to be due to social or economic rather than natural causes.

Changes in the Risk of Death and the Social Division of Labour

The idea of *the social division of labour* was employed by the French sociologist Emile Durkheim to portray the source of reciprocity in social life. He wanted to explain how society could remain stable despite the tremendous social and economic upheaval of industrialisation. These changes meant the end of self sufficiency for the majority of households. Men, women and even children had to enter the expanding labour market to earn a wage to purchase the subsistence needs they previously produced directly for themselves. He argued that industrialisation created greater diversity in occupational life which might have been a source of social instability had it not also involved a higher degree of social co-operation. This was the result of the specialised nature of industrial production. Each firm produces only one type of commodity and people must necessarily enter into exchange relationships with one another to acquire the basic necessities of life. This promotes a network of interdependency with the market as its focal point.

The transition from a peasant household economy to a factory based industrial one did not occur overnight. In Britain, it gathered pace over several centuries in response to the enclosures of the land

and the introduction of capitalist methods of agriculture. In the nineteenth century the speed of change accelerated.

The redrafting of the social division of labour created a distinctive pattern of age and sex roles. This is what happened. In the first half of the century women and children were just as likely as men to be wage earners. But by the end of it they had been pushed out of the labour market via a programme of 'protective' parliamentary legislation which barred them from working underground and restricted their opportunities for factory work. Compulsory primary education (through a series of Acts from 1870), helped complete the process of turning adult males into breadwinners and females and children into their dependents. These changes, usually interpreted as part of a humanitarian struggle to improve the conditions of life of the working class, appear to feminist historians as evidence of the struggle between the sexes over rights to monopolise opportunities for paid employment.

The awful conditions of working class life whether in the factory or the home, had been brought home to the Victorian middle classes through surveys and reports like those of Edwin Chadwick, the Poor Law Commissioner. Through his surveys he came to believe that high rates of disease and death among working class parents and children were caused by their living conditions. Later, as an influential figure in the movement for sanitary reform, he drew on this knowledge to press for public health legislation. A primary aim of the factory acts was therefore to protect and promote maternal and child health. What was their impact?

One indication that the rise of the male breadwinner may have influenced the distribution of health, is found in the changing pattern of sex differences in mortality in successive periods since 1850. These are depicted in figure 2.4. Death rates by age are shown at 4 successive periods 1846, 1900, 1946 and 1973. At each period male death rates are expressed as a proportion of female rates.

There are only two instances in figure 2.4 when the female death rate is greater than that of males. These are in 1846 among 25-34 year olds and in 1896 among 5-14 year olds. These apart, the evidence points to a growing divergence in the risk of death between men and women which began sometime in the early part of the twentieth century and which has continued, opening up an enormous gap in early adulthood and middle age. These developments should not be interpreted as an increase of magnitude since 1946. In fact death rates for both sexes fell over this period. It is because the female rate has fallen faster and lower than the male rate that the gap between the sexes has widened so much.

Figure 2.4 Historical Change in the risk of Death for Males and Females throughout the Lifetime

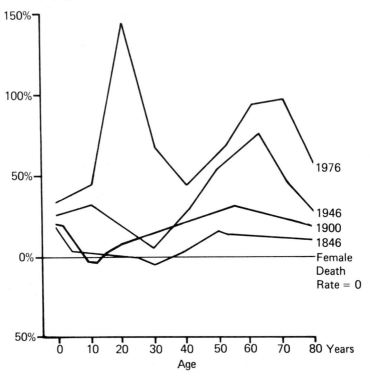

Source: OPCS *Trends in Mortality* (HMSO, London, 1978). Reproduced with the permission of Her Majesty's Stationery Office.

Is this picture the result of general social change and the recasting of male and female roles? The fact that the gap between the sexes was so much narrower in 1846, that it remained at the same level for the rest of the century, and then diverged so dramatically through the course of the twentieth century suggests that there is nothing 'natural' about the trend. If it were the product of genetic differences between the sexes then we might have expected more of a gap to be evident a century ago. So it looks as though the reason must lie in the changing social relationships of men, women and children.

A possible reason for these trends is the emergence of the male breadwinner and the retreat of his wife into domesticity. But even there things have not been static. Another important area of social change with direct implications for health, is the decline of marital fertility beginning after 1870. This had a direct impact on women's lives. It reduced the twentieth century family to a fraction of its nineteenth century size, transforming the routine experience of motherhood. In the last century this role involved a continuous cycle of pregnancy and childbirth which literally filled women's lives from marriage to old age. The reproductive career of a Victorian mother might involve a dozen or more pregnancies, several miscarriages and/or stillbirths and the quite likely prospect that one or more of her children would not survive infancy, childhood or adolescence. The expectations of her twentieth century sister could hardly be more different. With an average of only two children who are both likely to outlive her, a modern mother will complete her maternal duties well before she reaches middle age. This leaves almost half of her life still ahead for other social responsibilities. This change has come about through the desire for smaller families. It was made possible by changes in the moral climate surrounding contraception and by technological advances in the methods. The impact has been considerable both in improving standards of maternal and child health and in raising women's expectations of the part they may play in the social division of labour. Since the war the proportion of married women who work outside the home and whose wages contribute to the household income has risen to 60%. It is a trend that has done much to raise working class aspirations for home ownership as well as the means to pay for it.

These are fairly recent trends whose impact on sex differentials in mortality are yet to be felt. The situation before the Second World War was rather different. Then, apart from the war, the vast proportion of married women seemed content to remain at home. So it appeared that following soon after their expulsion from the labour market, the maternal dimensions of their roles were also diluted with beneficial effects on their health. Combined with the male monopolisation of breadwinner responsibilities, a fact later to be enshrined in welfare state and divorce legislation, this surely played some part in the growing divergence in the risk of premature death. The general picture then of improving health for both sexes but increasing inequality between them suggests that society influences health through the social division of labour and its gendered structure.

Standards of Living and Standards of Health

At the beginning of the twentieth century people were more sceptical about the value of medical treatment than they are in general today.

They could see more clearly why health was improving. Prominent social reformers like Beatrice and Sidney Webb had been alive in the nineteenth century to witness public health initiatives implemented often in the face of opposition from some sectors of the medical profession. Beatrice Webb had been one of Charles Booth's interviewers in his surveys of the labouring classes of London. Her experience had taught her that good health was built upon decent living standards not only in the form of adequate income, food, warmth, clothing and shelter, but also a clean and safe environment. This knowledge had been impressed upon the Victorian middle classes by the movement of sanitary reform. To them it was self evident that the maintenance of good health lay in high standards of public hygiene in the way of pure drinking water, efficient sewerage, safe working conditions, paved streets and highways and even public control over the standard of rented housing. These measures had gradually been implemented since 1834, culminating in the 'Great Public Health Act' of 1875. This legislative achievement was the reward for a 40 year struggle waged by people quite self conscious about their aim to make British towns and cities healthier places to live.

Today, we tend to equate the word sanitary with hygiene, but, strictly speaking, it is another word for health. Drawn from the latin 'sanitas' meaning healthy it is also linked to the word sanity. Sanitary reformers like Edwin Chadwick, who masterminded the 1842 *Report of the Sanitary Conditions of the Labouring Classes of Great Britain,* were pledged to the creation of healthy living conditions. One element was the provision of clean water and safe drainage, but other important goals were the reduction of overcrowding, the availability of work and free elementary education. The report contains a series of 'sanitary' maps showing a strong correlation between the social class of a district and its mortality rate. These maps reveal that the average age of death for the gentry was 42 years while for tradesmen and labourers it was 30 and 22 years respectively. Chadwick argued that the most effective way of reducing the poor rate, a tax levied for the support of the destitute, was to improve the health of the population and thereby reduce the numbers of unsupported widows and orphans. To this end he advocated new central powers to clean up the environment and supply clean water and safe drainage. His proposed reforms, like the 1834 *Poor Law Amendment Act,* in which he had also played a leading role, represented a high degree of state intervention in private affairs. Inevitably they invoked strong opposition. It was to be several decades before comprehensive public health measures of the kind he envisaged were implemented, and by that time the principle of state intervention in private life in the name of public health was well established. In the present day the same principle is even more powerful giving to public authority the right to intervene even in matters relating to the conduct of marriage and the treatment of children by their parents.

In the establishment of the singular importance of rising living standards for improving the health of the Victorian generation and its descendants, the work of one scholar stands out. The name of McKeown has already cropped up in this text. He is important in the debate about the causes of the modern rise of population for a number of reasons. He has brought together the empirical evidence and presented it in a particularly striking and accessible way. But equally significant, his critical assessment of the role of medicine has come from within the profession and has therefore been less liable to be dismissed as a 'doctor bashing' heresy.

McKeown's search for the major determinants of health in the nineteenth century is structured around an attempt to eliminate factors which were least likely to have made a significant contribution. Proceeding in this way he concludes that only three factors were important, nutrition, public hygiene and contraception. They were the principal agents in the decline of water- and food-borne plus airborne infections which formed 60% of the total reduction from 1850 to 1971. But, it is nutrition which McKeown picks out as having made the most significant contribution to the overall decline. He stresses that being well fed is the most effective form of disease prevention. This is seen today in less developed societies where vaccination programmes are not as successful as they should be because children are so malnourished. In effect he argues that the diseases we think of as the causes of death are really no more than an intermediate mechanism of high mortality resulting from food shortage and starvation.

McKeown concludes that the high mortality of the pre-industrial era was either the direct result of starvation or a function of decreased resistance to infection brought about by hunger and malnutrition. By 1900 the population of Britain was better fed through a combination of increased food production and a reduction of family size. This meant that the average household had more to eat and fewer mouths to feed. This explains how the spread of contraception, from 1850 onwards, helped to improve health. It also had a more directly beneficial effect on rates of maternal and infant mortality. Parity, i.e. the number of births in a woman's reproductive history, is strongly correlated to both rates. The more children a woman bears the greater the risks both for herself and the baby. Falling fertility probably made the most important contribution to improvements in survival prospects at childbirth.

McKeown goes further. He argues that much of the very high mortality of our own pre-industrial past was the direct result of starvation particularly among infants. In the absence of effective contraception, unplanned birth and unwanted children were commonplace. In such circumstances very high infant mortality must in some degree have been the result of parents being forced to neglect or even abandon babies that they could not afford to feed. The nineteenth century saw the growth of a concerted effort to save unwanted children through the creation of orphanages and foundling hospitals and by banning women from work. This was the publicly visible sign of a change in social morality encouraged by the increasing productivity of the British economy and the greater availability of resources to support human life.

Where did the resources come from? The answer to this question must undoubtedly be found in the rise of industrial capitalism. In the space of these pages we cannot enter into a discussion of why and how this economic revolution took place. But it is clear that the development of a fully fledged market economy in nineteenth century Britain, for all the human exploitation and social upheaval that it entailed, led to an enormous increase in human productivity and national wealth. The social distribution of the benefits of this economic miracle was very unequal but nevertheless it can hardly be disputed that by the end of the century the population in Britain was better fed, better educated and better clothed because of it.

Among the components of rising living standards, McKeown isolates diet as the principal determinant of increasing life expectation. But he also draws attention to the importance of improvements in communication, technology and hygiene as background factors which were necessary to enable the larger volume of food produced to be made available to the population in a state fit for human consumption. Nevertheless, his tendency to single out food as the principal reason for the reduction of risk to infection has led one observer to dub his approach as that of a 'nutritional determinist'.

This mild rebuke is issued by Winter, in an article which largely endorses McKeown's main thesis and which is concerned to investigate the impact of the First World War on infant mortality. From 1914 to 1918, a period when the British economy was put on a war footing, the decline in infant mortality was greatly accelerated. In an examination of possible reasons, Winter concludes that it was the war itself, and its effects on the economy, that led to an above average improvement in the health of the population. There are three main grounds for this conclusion:-

(1) Access to medical care during the war years was greatly reduced because more than 60% of the medical profession was drawn into military service. For this reason it seems most unlikely that the recorded improvements could be due to medical treatment.

(2) Local authority services were cut back by the need to economise so that improvements to housing, sewerage and health clinics were at a standstill.

(3) Unemployment and casual employment among men were virtually eliminated, and women were drawn into the labour market in large numbers because of the extra demands of wartime production. This together with a whole host of other specific economic measures like rent control, food rationing and minimum wages in agriculture. introduced as part of the war effort, ensured that a substantial decline in poverty took place during these years.

His conclusion, that rising living standards amongst the poorest section of the community explains the precipitous fall in infant mortality, is reinforced by the fact that those same county boroughs of England, Wales and Scotland that registered the highest pre-war rates of infant mortality, experienced the greatest decline during the wartime years. These areas were concentrated in the industrial Midlands and the North containing urban areas with high concentrations of semi and unskilled manual workers. In the more affluent county boroughs of the southern England, the war made little impact on the course of infant mortality rates. The ironic conclusion therefore was that the health of the working class in this country benefited more from the 1st World War than it did from any other event in the first thirty years of this century.

Winter's analysis of why health improved shares much in common with McKeown. Both stress diet and rising living standards as the principal determinants of health. But Winter goes beyond this to emphasise wider societal mechanisms. For the period he studied the most significant of these was the interventionist role of the state in controlling the level of demand in the economy, the price of goods and services, the rationing of scarce commodities and the distribution of income. He deals with the period in which the scope for state intervention was enlarged as a result of the efforts of the movement for sanitary reform. The most important lesson from his work, is that access to work, to a stable and sufficient income, to decent housing, to family planning, to a clean environment and safe food and drink are more the product of government intervention than of individual initiative.

State Intervention and Human Welfare

The scope for government intervention to improve the health of the population was understood quite early in the nineteenth century as the struggle for sanitary reform testifies. The story of this movement illustrates the way in which the state came to assume a more direct responsibility for the lives of ordinary people. Sanitarianism represented the self confident beliefs of the Victorian middle classes that they possessed the right, the means and the power to shape their own and their fellow citizens' health. This was all the more significant as a social trend when one remembers that the movement developed in a society where the belief that God was the originator of life and decision maker about death, was still widespread. Preceding generations had accepted the ravages of disease as part of the normal order of human relationships with a divine authority. When Simpson introduced chloroform as an anaesthetic in childbirth in 1852, he was denounced from the pulpit. The pain of childbirth was the pre-ordained lot of mankind (or rather womankind). To prevent it was a sacrilege. As one clergyman of the time put it, 'Chloroform is a decoy of Satan, apparently offering itself to bless women, but in the end it will harden society and rob God of the deep earnest cries that arise in times of trouble, for help'. Simpson was accused of challenging the express command of the scripture 'In sorrow shalt thou bring forth children', and of usurping God's right to control life, death and the reproductive process. The same reasoning lives on in the continued opposition of Catholicism to contraception.

Strangely enough some of this self confidence has been eroded in contemporary times. The divine authority over human welfare today is not God, but the *market*. Those responsible for running our society have become fearful of interfering with the market mechanism which they see as a self-regulating phenomenon, best left to its own devices. This view is a throwback to a primitive phase of industrial capitalism. It denies the power of human beings to control their affairs through rational and intelligent methods, preferring the idea that a 'hidden hand' guides human beings to their material destiny. These ideas were quietly dispensed with by the Victorian middle classes. It remains to see how long their late twentieth century descendants will take to make the same discovery.

The recognition of the power of public authority to prevent disease was aided by, and helped stimulate, the development of statistics or 'political arithmetic' as it used to be called. This provided the knowledge for understanding the totality of disease, its distribution and its social correlates. Without this, there would be no grounds for rational public action. The series of sanitary maps in the 1842 report are an early example of these techniques used to accumulate evidence that would strengthen the appeal for public intervention. Armed with this innovative 'data base', Sanitarians like Chadwick, set out to persuade the government of the day that they could improve the health of the people by planned intervention in the environment. By 1875, as a result of their efforts, legislation had been passed which controlled the hours and conditions of work, ensured hygienic conditions in the production and sale of food and drink, empowered landlords to keep their tenancies in good repair, and local authorities to maintain high standards of public hygiene. These public health measures helped to create a healthy urban environment in Britain and they must be counted among the factors which raised the standard of living in this country before the end of the last century.

The concept of the standard of living therefore has two distinct dimensions. One consists of the personal resources available to individual households to provide for subsistence needs. The other comprises the social resources gathered and used by public authorities (central and local) for collective purposes. Political opinions differ as to the appropriate balance to be struck in dividing national income between private income and the 'social' wage. Those to the right of the political spectrum favour a redistribution of resources to private households letting them decide for themselves how much education or health care they need. Those to the left believe that this would lead to a deterioration of standards and to greater inequality and injustice. Whatever the virtues of these opposed perspectives, one thing that stands out from nineteenth and early twentieth century history is that the standards of health and welfare of the most vulnerable people in the community have risen most when the state played a more active and interventionist role in the economy and society.

This raises the question of the relationship between standards of health and the power of the state in different societies, one of the themes of the next chapter.

Chapter Three

Capitalism, Socialism and Health

Human Health and the Rise of Capitalism

The last chapter argued that human health was revolutionised by the development of industrial capitalism. Indeed the last 150 years have been the most dynamic period for human health in the whole of recorded history. Improvements appeared earliest in Britain, the first industrial nation, but they soon spread to other industrialising parts of the world. Today the modern rise of population is a worldwide phenomenon, a global explosion which, some people find as threatening to the future of humankind as a nuclear holocaust. The material fruits of capitalism, measured by rising living standards and improved life expectation, are not equally shared. Enormous inequalities exist between different nations in the developed and the less developed world and between classes within individual nation states (see chapter 4). Even so, industrial capitalism ushered in new material conditions for human life witnessed in population growth on a scale never previously encountered.

How did industrial capitalism revolutionise human health? Marx provided the answer to this question when the new economic system was still in its infancy. He recognised its enormous potential for expanding the productivity of human labour and for bringing the forces of nature under human control. Marx had a love/hate relationship with the capitalist economic miracle. He saw clearly and prophetically its progressive character, but he also knew that while for some it represented civilisation, for others it equalled class exploitation. Marx anticipated that capitalism would ultimately give way via a process of class struggle, to a socialist version of industrial society. Socialism would retain the best features of capitalism while sweeping away its exploitative class structure. The private ownership of productive property would be abolished, leaving the workers' state

556

to control the use and allocation of economic resources in the interest of everyone. The standard of health of the whole population would then be raised to that enjoyed by the ruling class because protecting health would be a fundamental goal of socialist industrialisation, replacing the profit motive as a means of gauging the value of human labour.

Has Marx's prophecy come to pass? In general the answer is no. Since the First World War, his model of political economy has inspired the formation of a number of socialist industrial states in Eastern Europe, although the manner of their appearance has not been exactly as he envisaged. They have generally been born in a pre- or early capitalist phase of development and inaugurated by war rather than through explosive economic contradictions. In each of these societies, the power of the state is much greater than it is in the liberal democracies of Western Europe and North America, and central planning has replaced the market in the allocation of scarce resources. At the same time the original capitalist states have themselves introduced substantial reforms. Like their Eastern European neighbours, societal reform has been stimulated by the events of war as much as through economic struggles between classes. The effect of the two world wars in the twentieth century on the politico-economic map of Europe, has been to bring about social revolutions in the losing nations while promoting welfare state systems among the victors. In Britain the development of the welfare state was largely the product of the second world war. During the 1920s and 30s the shortcomings of market capitalism were revealed in stark fashion with mass unemployment and deteriorating living standards providing almost perfect conditions for organised labour to rise up and overthrow the system. Yet, compared to the war years of 1939-45, this was a slack period for reformist legislation. It was at the height of hostilities in 1942 that the Beveridge report appeared with its detailed design for a comprehensive welfare state including full employment, an overhaul of secondary education, the national health service and the social security system.

Health in Contemporary Capitalist and Socialist Societies

So the historical events of the twentieth century gave the modern world a number of more or less capitalist and more or less socialist states in various stages of economic development. All vary internally in the degree of social and economic inequality and in the comprehensiveness of their welfare legislation. In general those societies which have retained the market as the means of allocating economic resources have been more successful in raising living standards. This is reflected in higher standards of health. Even so within the category of welfare state capitalism there are marked variations. At one extreme is Sweden with the lowest infant and adult mortality rates anywhere, the product of wide ranging and generous welfare provision. At the other is the United States, where mortality rates would be much lower were it not for massive social and economic inequalities between black and Hispanic and white Americans perpetuated by the relative absence of comprehensive welfare state provision. Even so, by 1975, the US recorded lower overall mortality than England and Wales despite the latter's more developed welfare provision.

Table 3.1   Trends in Mortality in Selected Industrial Societies

Country	1916	1926	1936	1946	1956	1966	1971-5
Czechoslovakia	316	248	180	152	109	108	108
Hungary	367	265	201	167	118	107	108
Italy	314	225	184	133	108	96	90
Japan	385	358	334	197	129	97	84
Spain	386	274	264	160	110	92	90
Sweden	170	137	125	103	89	82	73
UK (England & Wales)	222	167	146	114	102	97	93
USA	255	192	156	97	102	98	90

Source: Adapted from *International Mortality Statistics,* Alderson 1981. Based on SMRs (all persons) calculated from a base of England and Wales 1951-1975 = 100.

Table 3.1 compares mortality trends in a number of countries since 1916. Czechoslavakia, Hungary, Italy, Japan and Spain are included to represent a variety of market and planned economies in the present day whose mortality rates at the beginning of the period were broadly similar. They therefore provide some clues on the impact of different pathways to industrialisation on health. Sweden, USA and the UK are included to show variation between the mature capitalist societies. The evidence suggests that societies which have retained the market as the means of organising economic production have experienced more substantial reductions in mortality, especially since the war. Take for example Czechoslovakia and Italy. In 1956, the mortality rates of each stood at 109 and 108 respectively. By 1976 the rate in Czechoslovakia remained static while that of Italy had fallen to 90. Even more striking is a comparison of Hungary and Japan. In 1956, their rates were 118 and 129 respectively. Twenty years later the relative position was reversed following a dramatic fall in Japanese mortality. There can be little doubt that this trend is closely associated with the spectacular growth of industrial capitalism in Japan.

Is Modern Capitalism bad for your Health?

These trends indicate that health is primarily the product of social and economic development. Since the highest living standards have been achieved in contemporary capitalist societies, this is where people enjoy the highest standards of health. Nevertheless some writers insist that the capitalist version of industrialisation is extremely harmful to health. Drawing on Marxist concepts and categories, these critics assert that the capitalist mode of production damages health in two specific ways. First they point to the dangers inherent in capitalist commodities themselves and in the manner of their production. The very goods and services which contribute to high living standards, together with modern methods of production, are held up as sources of health risk in themselves. It is alleged that people are led to desire and therefore to consume hazardous goods like refined and processed foods, cigarettes and motor cars because they are profitable. The implication is that healthy commodities are less profitable and could be manufactured with less risk to health.

The second target is the manner in which the capitalist labour market erodes social relationships based on kinship, neighbourhood and community. This occurs through the necessity for the labour force to be semi-nomadic, obliged to move wherever work is to be found. This negative theme is reminiscent of Louis Wirth's image of the rootless and anonymous state of humanity in modern urban communities.

In these critiques, the process of class exploitation in mature capitalism does not take the form of what Marx called immiserisation: ruthless profiteering at the expense of wage levels and living standards. This process, called absolute exploitation, belongs to an earlier more primitive phase of competitive capitalism where small enterpreneurs struggle with one another for a larger share of the market. In the advanced capitalist societies characterised by large monopoly corporations, exploitation takes a relative form. It consists of the imposition of methods of organising work which are alien to human beings and of commodities which do more harm than good. The latter theme, which draws on the Marxist concept of *commodity fetishism,* has the unfortunate tendency of depicting ordinary people as the dupes of capitalist advertising, unable to recognise their real material interests and dependent on radical intellectuals for a true understanding of their basic needs. Let us examine each of these two themes in more detail.

The first theme has a number of strands. The goods produced by capitalist industrialisation constitute one set of risks to health. Many popular capitalist commodities are said to be not useful and some positively lethal. High on the list of offenders are tobacco products. The mass consumption of cigarettes is perpetuated despite the established health risk through largely uncontrolled advertising. Other dangerous commodities include some everyday staples such as white bread and artificial baby milk. They constitute health risks because they are highly processed, the result of modern methods of production. These regressive features of commodity production under capitalism come about because exchange value dominates use value in determining what goods and services will be produced. The foods available on the supermarket shelf are there not because consumers prefer them to healthier alternatives but because they have higher profit margins. Thus capitalism is responsible for a diverse range of modern 'ills' from obesity to women's desire to liberate themselves from breastfeeding.

A second set of risks is encountered directly in the form of industrial injuries and diseases and indirectly through the dehumanising nature of work itself. It is argued that they are worse under capitalism because productivity is measured by the profit motive and not by criteria which include the welfare of workers. The dehumanisation of work occurs through the substitution of machines for human skill leading to a deskilling of the workforce. Even worse is shiftwork necessary to keep the machines going night and day. As a result, work carries no intrinsic satisfaction. It becomes no more than a means of earning a livelihood. On the other hand, being out of the labour force is also seen as a source of deprivation. Doyal and Pennell in *The Political Economy of Health* depict housework as a deprived form of work because it is menial on account of being 'undercapitalised and isolated' (p.74). What the term undercapitalised means is unclear. One interpretation would be that there is a lack of machinery to substitute for human labour. This however, would stand in contradiction with arguments elsewhere in the same text linking deskilling to the very same process. The argument is unsupported by empirical evidence, which makes it difficult to take issue with it. However it is hard to agree with the claim that the modern home is undercapitalised. Trends in personal consumption in the last decade would point to the opposite conclusion, showing working class households striving to both own and improve their own homes. Home improvement firms have been a growth area of capitalism and household commodities like built-in kitchens, washing machines and freezers have been acquired by more and more families. In these circumstances it seems that housework in modern times is only menial where the household is poor and cannot afford the modern housewives' basic tools. From this perspective it is difficult to sustain the image of depressive illness as the occupational disease of housewives brought on by the repetitive, isolated, exhausting and demoralising task of looking after home and children. More persuasive and closer to the empirical reality would be a linkage of poverty and powerlessness as sources of stress-related symptoms in housebound women.

The other charges against the capitalist mode of production in the sphere of work, are less clearly linked to capitalism. Tendencies to fragment the production process and to substitute machines for human labour are a feature of industrialisation as a whole and it is not clear that a transition to socialism would necessarily make work processes themselves any more intrinsically satisfying. Moreover it may be that some of the most important features of modern occupational life are underestimated in Marxist accounts. This is revealed, for example, in the dual attitude to labour force participation among women and men. For women paid work represents a solution to 'housewife blues', yet for men it equals alienation, boredom and a psychological if not a physical health risk. What is underestimated is the importance of work for both sexes as a means of participating in the public sphere of society, of being *seen* making a contribution to the division of labour and to the process of production itself. The wage packet and access to a job may be as important as symbols of social citizenship as they are of direct material benefit. This maybe why women themselves have come to perceive of entry to the labour market as a means of personal liberation. The post-war era has seen a steady growth in female participation and today more than 60% of married women work for wages outside of the home. This suggests that there is no functional link between the oppression of housewives and the capitalist market making it incorrect to see female depression as an occupational disease *caused* by capitalism. Some might go even further and argue that under capitalism, the liberation of women has gone further than it has in any previous form of civilisation. Certainly in terms of life expectation women have benefited disproportionately to men.

The idea of work as a symbol of social participation owes much to Durkheim's model of the social division of labour as the principal mechanism of social integration in modern society. From this perspective it is immediately evident that unemployment would constitute a threat to health. This is another theme in the portrayal of capitalism as a threat to health. The fact that rates of mortality and unemployment tend to rise and fall together adds weight to this idea and a number of studies have sought to investigate it. Fox and his colleagues offer strong evidence linking job loss to increased mortality among both breadwinners and their wives but it is unclear how this comes about. Brenner argues that unemployment causes stress-related disease because it is a disruptive life event (see p.603). Stern and others have contested this, showing that those at risk of unemployment are the same people who are at risk of premature death because of their poverty. They argue that it is the poverty rather than the stress caused by unemployment which increases mortality risk (see p.613). In either case it is likely that an unfettered system of free enterprise capitalism would cause the rate of unemployment and of poverty to fluctuate in accordance with market forces. In such circumstances unemployment as a cause of stress or poverty-related disease can be directly linked to capitalism. However unfettered market forces are not inevitable. To assert otherwise is a misconstruction of both Marxism and Thatcherism. Since the Second World War, most capitalist societies have sought to regulate the level of unemployment through a variety of Keynesian economic policies. As a result the volume of unemployment tolerated, along with the level of social security paid to the jobless, are both matters of political choice subject to the decision of the ballot box. If a minority of unskilled and semi-skilled people can be made to bear the brunt of economic recession or industrial restructuring, why should the survival of capitalism be threatened? The welfare of the weakest members of the society depends on the compassion of the rest of the electorate and on the skill of political parties in representing their case. In these circumstances allocating blame for the insult of unemployment is complicated by political and ideological considerations and cannot be simply reduced to being an inevitable or unmanageable feature of the capitalist mode of production. The wide inequalities in health in advanced capitalist societies do not take the form of a simple polarised division between haves and have nots. As chapter 4 reveals, they take the form of relative deprivation, a series of layers of advantage and disadvantage which do not provide a clear basis for collective identification and action. For this reason a specifically Marxist analysis of class offers no more insights on the causes of inequality in health than any other sociological model.

Is Socialism any Healthier?

The argument that the profit motive increases the risk of industrial accidents and injuries is surely correct. Many industrial processes are inherently dangerous and some should probably be banned altogether. If the relationship between an industrial disease or injury can be established, then a worker or a union can use the courts to gain compensation. In these circumstances the market itself may outlaw the production of certain commodities because the cost of compensating victims makes the enterprise unprofitable. This has been the fate of asbestos companies in the United States. But for most industrial diseases, the risks are not established as clearly as for asbestosis, making the market effects of legal compensation an ineffective mechanism for protecting workers' health. Nevertheless the influence of market forces in determining the health risks of work should not be overstated. Since 1900 the incidence of industrial accidents has fallen considerably and comparisons between contemporary capitalist and socialist states in the modern world do not suggest that market forces encourage more accidents than the forces of central planning. Table 3.2 provides evidence of mortality risk from a number of causes in Czechoslovakia, Hungary, Italy and Spain selected because of their similar levels of economic development in the pre-war era. The UK data is given as a point of reference.

Table 3.2   Selected causes of death in some contemporary industrial societies, 1971-75

Country	Czechoslovakia	Hungary	Italy	Spain	UK (England and Wales)
All causes	108	108	90	90	93
Lung Cancer	200	148	140	97	222
Stomach Cancer	195	218	161	151	117
Circulatory Disease (males)	128	238	98	107	102
Accidents (males)	240	230	200	179	119
Accidents (excluding traffic)	242	236	136	177	102
Suicide	240	374	59	46	76

Source: Adapted from *International Mortality Statistics,* Alderson 1981.-SMRs derived from a base of England and Wales, 1951-1975 = 100

Each of the causes in table 3.2, has a higher incidence in the planned economies of Eastern Europe. The one exception is the elevated risk of lung cancer in the UK, one of the few areas where Britain still leads the world. The causes are chosen to represent the so-called diseases of civilisation which Doyal and Pennell link to the consumption of capitalist commodities. It is clear however that the chances of dying from circulatory disease or lung cancer are no less in Czechoslovakia or Hungary suggesting that exposure to risk factors in diet and smoking is much the same in all industrial societies regardless of their political character. Furthermore the higher rate of accidents among men under Eastern European socialism offers no support to the argument that the workplace is safer in societies where the central planning bureaucracy has the opportunity to treat occupational health as a major priority of the productive process. Why is this so?

The most probable answer is the drive to industrialisation in socialist societies. Translated at factory level into a race to meet central planning goals, this pressure on the production line may be just as destructive to human health as the profit motive in capitalism. Another factor likely to be of major importance is the absence of participatory democracy as a means of safeguarding the workplace and the environment. In Western Europe and North America, this is achieved through the activities of political organisations, pressure groups and trade unions. In Eastern Europe, there is less countervailing power to regulate the activities of those who control the means of production and this may help to explain the greater risk of accidental death (see Table 3.2).

Individualism, Stress and the Capitalist Way of Life

The other theme in the Marxist critique is that the capitalist way of life is stressful. This is because it is highly individuated. The labour market is oriented to individuals not to families or kinship groups and because people are forced to leave their communities in search of work social networks and ties binding people together are destroyed.

> The basic social process of capitalism is itself the source of increased stress. The very same social changes which increased agricultural productivity and made possible a large non-agricultural labour force are also the fundamental causes of the health risks that increase with capitalism. These changes can be summarised as the uprooting of people from stable communities and the subjection of life to the constantly changing demands of the market for labour. (Eyer 1984, 28).

This assessment of social disorganisation under capitalism is reminiscent of Durkheim's concept of anomie: the breakdown of the normative structure of relationships in the transition from mechanical (pre-industrial) to organic (industrial) social solidarity. It was a feature of the capitalist mode of production which Marx particularly admired. The destruction of traditional paternalistic ties binding people to particular communities was for him one of the pre-conditions for the growth of a new *social* consciousness. However research on diseases of stress (see p.600) suggests that social support is important in the maintenance of self esteem which in turn enables individuals to handle stressful experiences without ill-effect. The problem is how to create social support outside of the enduring bonds of kinship or community of birth.

Another dimension of stress induced by capitalism is the encouragement of individualistic, selfish attitudes in which people are only concerned with the acquisition of material possessions. This egotistic and materialistic orientation to life further serves to undermine the individual's access to social support. The role model for this is the so-called *type A personality,* particularly prone to coronary disease. This personality type has not been found to predominate among stroke and heart attack victims in Britain, although research indicates that it is prevalent in the USA (see p.608). Eyer argues that the rise of possessive individualism and the destabilisation of traditional communities explains class differences in health, rural/urban differences and the relationship between rates of mortality and the changing rate of unemployment.

There is a fundamental flaw in this argument stemming from a failure to examine the empirical realities of disease and premature death in modern capitalist societies. The sort of person held up as the most likely victim of disease, the striving materialistic nomadic worker, has better than average chances of surviving to retirement age and beyond. Those at the greatest risk of early death are people in social class IV and V, whose occupational prospects scarcely make it either worthwhile or even possible for them to kick over the traces and seek their fortunes in a new locality. In contemporary Britain the highest death rates are found among low paid manual workers whose major resource is likely to be the tenure of a council house which ties them to a neighbourhood for life (see p.575). Their health is principally at risk through long term economic deprivation, the product of being stuck on the lowest rung of the socio-economic hierarchy.

The general impression left by Marxist writers is that capitalism is disastrous for human health. The argument is advanced from the position of a socialist utopia undefined beyond the identification of certain negative features of capitalism such as the profit motive that would be abolished. From this hazy perspective, capitalism is treated as a blanket category with no account being taken of the substantial differences between contemporary market societies in standards of health and welfare provision. Doyal and Pennell develop their case through a process of theoretical logic which is only reinforced by evidence where it fits the desired construction of reality. Hostile evidence is avoided. There is no reference to the societies of Eastern Europe which have attempted the socialist experiment. Not even the usual disclaimer of modern Marxism that these societies have nothing to do with the kind of socialism Marx anticipated. This means that an opportunity to use material relating to alternative models of industrialisation (where the market has been eliminated) is missed. This partiality of approach belongs to an analysis primarily oriented to political persuasion rather than to understanding the real nature of the relationship between health and societal development. It is further reflected in the imbalance of the critique as a whole. Doyal and Pennell do not concede that many of the commodities of advanced capitalism are very beneficial and have transformed human experience in positive ways. Instead everything is lumped together in equally negative terms. Eyer commits the same mistake when he implies that the destruction of traditional close knit communities and the freeing of the individual from the interpersonal ties of kinship and community is a wholly negative process. What he fails to recognise is that these very same communities have operated cruel restrictions of personal freedom and development. If capitalism has helped to break up stifling and repressive social norms such as those surrounding the oppression of women, this may be one of its finest achievements.

Utopian Models of Health

The singular emphasis on the negative dimensions of contemporary capitalist civilisation, unites the Marxist perspective with the anti-industrialisation stance of Ivan Illich. Illich picks on over-industrialisation, not capitalism as the principal cause of ill-health in contemporary society. The main butt of his attack is medicine and in his book *Limits to Medicine,* he identifies three ways in which modern medicine is pathogenic to human health. His theme is *iatrogenesis* meaning something having its origin (genesis) in doctors (iatros). Its three forms are clinical, social and cultural. Clinical iatrogenesis constitutes the risks to health contained within medical treatment itself: the application of dangerous experimental techniques, the prevalence of unwanted side effects, medical drug addiction and treatments that are more painful and disfiguring than disease itself. Social iatrogenesis refers to the wider influence of medical ideology in society at large, to the process whereby diverse areas of human experience such as birth and death have become medicalised. In the medicalisation of social problems, their political nature is stripped away as they become neutral objects for technological treatment. Cultural iatrogenesis is the process whereby individuals relinquish the will to take care of themselves to professional experts. It results in a form of personal paralysis, a loss of control and of self confidence in dealing with a whole range of personal and emotional problems. Via these three forms of iatrogenesis, Illich accuses medicine of expropriating health for selfish professional interests. This is what constitutes the major threat to health in advanced industrial societies.

His critique is part of a wider reaction against the dependence of modern society on science and technology and the neglect, even abandonment, of spontaneous natural human capacities. Human beings have lost control over their destiny and even the natural environment of the world is at risk from the technological monster out of human control. The remedy proposed is a retreat from advanced industrial society to small scale intimate communities liberated from the tyrannies of machine, factory, bureaucracy and scientific expertise - back to a world where human beings experience direct control over their circumstances and destinies. No detailed proposals for the reconversion of the massive urban communities of the modern world are offered.

There are several parallels between Illich and Marxists like Eyer and Doyal and Pennell. Both emphasise negative dimensions and neglect the dialectical interplay of good and bad in the modern way of life. In each there is a strong theme of dehumanisation; alienation for the Marxists, expropriation for Illich. The reactions against advanced technology and machines usurping natural human capacity and skill is common to both. It implies that a return to an earlier technological phase of economic life would represent an improvement in the human condition. Allied to this is the idea of false needs. Human beings are seen as being tempted, bought off, by commodities which do them more harm than good. Finally both Eyer and Illich react against the urban migration promoted by industrialisation. They share the view that people would be better off if they stayed put in small scale, close knit communities. What seems to unite these two pessimistic accounts is an element of romantic idealism. Each promises a vision of better health under new social conditions — de-industrialisation for Illich and socialism for the Marxists — but neither offers any guidance on how their model societies could be made a reality.

Despite the common ground, Marxist writers specifically reject the views of Illich. Navarro in a spirited challenge, accuses him of mistaking industrialism for the pattern of class dominance in capitalist society. He argues that the road to better health is paved with the process of democratic control over the productive system. But although, he carefully avoids much of the romantic idealism of fellow Marxists, he does not specify how his model of democratic socialism would work. The unanswered question is how a complex industrial economy can be controlled and managed by everybody without bureaucratic power structures. In other words, he does not face up to the problem posed by Max Weber, that bureaucracy is the fundamental mechanism of legal rational authority and the most pervasive form of power in modern society. In particular he does not answer Weber's challenge that bureaucracy is even more of a constraint in socialist society where public officials rule in the name of collective welfare.

Concluding Remarks

Let us be clear in concluding this chapter that the capitalist mode of industrialisation is far from perfect as a form of social organisation and there are many ways in which it is corrosive of human health. Among the different varieties of welfare state capitalism that exist in the world today some are far more effective than others in promoting and protecting human health. Equally amongst the same family of capitalist nations, levels of social and economic equality or social citizenship vary considerably. But whatever its shortcomings there are no signs to indicate that the majority living under the capitalist version of industrial society would wish to roll back the tide of either capitalism or industrialisation. Consequently there is a credibility gap between the vision of human welfare presented by writers like Illich and Doyal and Pennell and the everyday experience of real people. The picture they draw makes it difficult to see why the Western working class have put up with capitalism for so long given the damage it is supposed to do to their health. The reason for the continued popularity of the capitalist system, is that the majority of people do quite well out of it. They know from direct experience that living standards have improved and this may be why they are unwilling, in the absence of more persuasive reasons 'to sacrifice a bird in the hand for two in the bush'. In Marxist terms their pragmatism is an example of false consciousness: a sign that people do not realise their true material interests because the exploitative nature of capitalism is obscured by ideological processes. In Marx's own day, religion was the opium of the people, today it is medicine. In this way, Marxist critics create a further problem for explanation. How does capitalism mystify its negative effects on health? How, in particular, does it succeed in retaining popular loyalty despite all the suffering it causes? This theme, prominent in the work of Navarro, we will leave to chapter 7.

Chapter Four

Social Inequalities in Health

The Duration of Life as a Measure of Social Welfare

We have seen how the development of industrial capitalism in Britain in the nineteenth and twentieth centuries was associated with a continuous decline in the death rate and consequently with an increase in the average length of life. This represents an improvement in human health, brought about by the process of industrialisation and the social and economic changes which it entailed. It means quite literally that human bodies are more durable than they used to be and that people consequently tend to live longer than their parents or grandparents. Improvements in health are thus embedded in the general rise in living standards which began in the nineteenth century and which continued at an accelerating pace in the twentieth.

This extension of the length of life is the best measure of health available (see p.523) and it is also a good indicator of *social welfare*. This last point deserves special emphasis. We have seen in chapter 2 that the increased life span of British people in the twentieth century is a product of a change in the way society is organised. It is therefore a form of welfare produced by society: hence the term *social* welfare. This leads to an obvious sociological question: how equally is this particular form of social welfare i.e. health, distributed among the British population? The answer to this question is found through an examination of social inequalities in health and it is worth emphasising that the existence of differences in health between socio-economic groups, shortly to be examined, is further evidence of the fact that health is a product of society.

The Measurement of Social Inequality in Health

The analysis of social inequality is a predominant concern of sociology and social class is without doubt the discipline's master concept. But sociologists differ in the way they use this concept. Some employ it in a purely theoretical way to convey the nature of social conflict as a force for societal change. Others use it as a distributional measure. They divide the population into a series of layers each representing different degrees of social and economic power. In this book social inequalities in health will be examined in the latter sense, as a hierarchical distribution of advantage and disadvantage. We will employ the Registrar General's classification of social class. This choice is largely dictated by the form in which the official statistics of mortality are published. Every decade the Registrar General (RG) carries out a study of variations in mortality among people engaged in different occupations. These data have provided the most clearcut evidence of the extent of social inequality in health. The RG's social class sorts all the occupations in the labour market into six broad groups arranged hierarchically according to their 'social standing in the community'. It is therefore a measure of occupational class. Although, as critics often observe, the basis of the classification has never been systematically evaluated, it has proved to be a remarkably powerful discriminator of life chances not only among male wage and salary earners but also among their wives and children. It is made up as follows:-

Social Class		Percentage of Workforce (1970)
I	Professional e.g. Doctors, Lawyers	5%
II	Managerial and Lower Professional e.g. Teachers, Sales Managers	18%
IIIN	Non-Manual Skilled e.g. Clerks, Cashiers	12%
IIIM	Skilled Manual e.g. Bricklayers, Underground Coal Miners	38%
IV	Semi-Skilled e.g. Bus Conductors, Postmen	18%
V	Unskilled e.g. Porters, Ticket Collectors, General Labourers	9%

In this scale, there are three manual and three non-manual classes. It would be possible to analyse health inequalities between two classes: manual and non-manual workers. However to do so would be to obscure the substantial differences which are found within these two broad categories as the following pages will indicate.

The Extent of Inequalities in Health

Official statistics for England and Wales clearly indicate that the risk of premature death is systematically related to social class (cf. OPCS 1978). Inequalities are found at birth, in childhood and adolescence and throughout adult life. Figure 4.1 illustrates the consistent way in which the Registrar General's scale identifies the pattern of class differentials in mortality.

Figure 4.1 Mortality by Social Class, Age and Sex

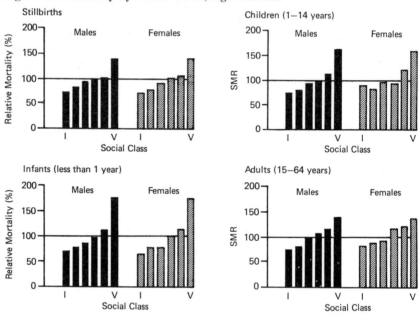

Source: *Occupational Mortality: 1970-72* (HMSO, London 1978). Reproduced with the permission of the Controller of Her Majesty's Stationery Office.

In figure 4.1 the incidence of mortality is represented by the standardised mortality ratio (SMR) which is a measure of the extent to which the mortality rate of each social class deviates from the average (100) of the age group as a whole. How much inequality in health in total is represented by this continuing pattern of class differentials in mortality risk from birth to retirement? One way of answering this question is to compare the life expectation of infants born to parents in social classes I and V respectively assuming that they remain throughout their working lives in the same social class. Proceeding in this way we would find a life expectation for a male infant in social class I of 72.19 years compared to 65.02 years for his counterpart in social class V. Thus a professional man's son is likely to live 7 years longer than the son of an unskilled worker.

Is the Gap in Life Chances between the Classes Increasing?

In chapter 2 we saw the way in which the general decline in mortality was associated with an increase of inequality in life chances between men and women. Now we must ask whether the same trends are found between the social classes. Answering this question involves the comparison of class gradients in mortality over time.

The study of trends in health inequality is complicated by shifts in the occupational structure during the course of this century which have led to a reduction in the percentage of the workforce in semi- and unskilled manual work and an expansion in non-manual jobs. A further complication is introduced by modifications that have been made to the RG scale which means that some occupations have been moved from one class to another thereby invalidating the practice of making comparisons between classes over time. For these reasons, questions about trends in the extent of health inequality can only be answered for the period since 1950 shortly after the introduction of the National Health Service. In the period since 1950, fewer changes have been made to the RG scale and those that have, can be offset by grouping together the adjacent classes between which most classificatory swops have been made. The period since 1960 is particularly instructive since this is one in which no changes were introduced.

Figure 4.2

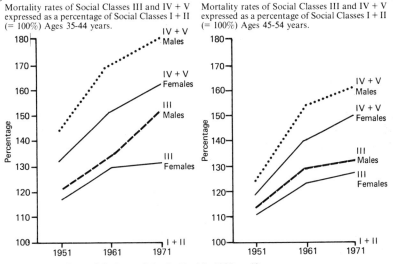

Mortality rates of Social Classes III and IV + V expressed as a percentage of Social Classes I + II (= 100%) Ages 35-44 years.

Mortality rates of Social Classes III and IV + V expressed as a percentage of Social Classes I + II (= 100%) Ages 45-54 years.

Source: Based on Table 3.3, *Inequalities in Health*, 1980, p.68.

In figure 4.2, social class I and II have been grouped together as have classes IV and V. The death rates for III and IV and V respectively have been expressed as a percentage excess of I and II. It can be seen immediately that, relative to social class I and II, the position of each of the other two grouped classes has deteriorated in each age group. On the basis of these data, the answer to the question 'Is health inequality becoming worse in England and Wales?' is yes.

Alternative Dimensions of Socio-Economic Inequality

The Registrar General's scale provides a means of approximating the extent of inequality between six broadly based occupational groups. In so doing it implies that the social and economic circumstances of the people who comprise each class are relatively homogeneous. But occupation is only one possible indicator of the distribution of power and resources stratifying life chances and we can safely assume that *within* occupational class, inequalities in health will also be found. Evidence of the kind of factors which produce variation within each class is found in the OPCS Longitudinal Survey. This survey, which is a sample of 1% of census returns linked to the system of death registration, provides a record of the census characteristics of people dying. From this source the relationship between education, region of residence, employment status, occupation and housing tenure with the risk of death in any age group can be examined.

Housing tenure provides a useful tool for exploring the extent of variation in health within each class. This is because it represents other aspects of socio-economic status. Apart from home ownership, it also stands for all the factors which enable people to acquire and maintain their own homes, including inheritance of property, stability of employment and income and credit-worthiness with the building societies. It is not surprising therefore that tenure proves to be a powerful tool for discriminating life chances *within* each occupational class. As figure 4.3 reveals, within each social class, the mortality of owner occupiers is substantially below that of people who rent their homes. Indeed there is more variation *between* owner occupiers and council tenants than there is between the social class divisions among home owners. This serves as a striking reminder that social and economic well-being can be measured in a number of ways and that any single variable like education chosen to indicate the extent of inequality provides only a partial guide to the full picture.

Another variable which performs the task of differentiating life chances within any of the six occupational classes is sex. In all age

Figure 4.3 Social Class, Tenure and Mortality, 1970-1975 (males aged 15-64)

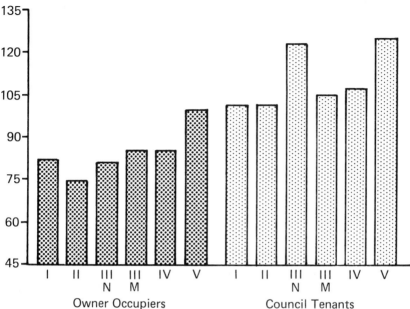

SMR

Source: Based on Table 13.5 in *Longitudinal Study*, OPCS, 1982.

groups, the risk of premature death for men is in excess of that for women. This is not revealed in figure 4.1 because the SMR has been calculated for men and women separately. When actual death rates within each sex and age group are compared directly, as they are in table 4.1, the full extent of sex inequality is revealed.

The following table shows two forms of inequality in health: occupational class and gender. For both sexes there are two and a half deaths among unskilled manual workers (V) for every one in the professional class (I). At the same time male death rates are almost double those of females in every class. This is indicated by the sex ratios for each class in column C. Indeed, apart from social class I, male death rates in every social class are consistently above even the highest rate recorded by women in social class V. The sex differential in mortality risk tends to increase with age whereas class differences become less significant as people get older. Among pre-school children, sex differences are somewhat less evident, but they become more marked as children grow into adolescence and adulthood (see figure 2.4 p.548).

Table 4.1 Death rates by sex and social class

Social Class	(A) Males	(B) Females	(C) Ratio Male to Female
I	3.98	2.15	1.85
II	5.54	2.85	1.94
IIIN	5.80	2.76	1.96
IIIM	6.08	3.41	1.78
IV	7.96	4.27	1.87
V	9.88	5.31	1.86
	2.5	2.5	

Source: Adapted from *Occupational Mortality 1970-72*
Females = Married women classified by their husbands occupation. Death rates per 1000 population

Sex and Class Differences in Mortality and Morbidity

Should we conclude from the foregoing picture of sex differences in mortality, that women are healthier than men? Certainly, if mortality is our measure there is little doubt that men are the disadvantaged sex. But when we examine other evidence of sickness and ill-health, a rather more complicated picture of sex-based health inequality emerges. This alternative indicator of health status is conventionally known as *morbidity*. It is usually measured through self reports of sickness and through records of medical consultation and treatment. Neither form of measure is entirely satisfactory. The former depends on individual judgement and action, while the latter besides being influenced by these subjective processes is also dependent on the supply of facilities for medical consultation and treatment. Neither type of measure can therefore be assumed to represent either a full or a standardised record of the extent of sickness in a population.

The reasons for adopting mortality to measure health were given in chapter 1 (p.523). Mortality is a more objective indicator of health status, it is easier to interpret and to apply to the analysis of trends in health over time. But is mortality a good substitute for morbidity including the subjective experience of ill-health sickness and disease? A comparison of the two among men and women, suggests that the answer to this question is no. Those whose lives are most likely to be prematurely brought to an end (i.e. men) do not seem to *experience* as much ill-health as those who live longer (i.e. women).

The following table compares sex and age differences in self reported morbidity and medical consultation from the General Household Survey (GHS) with mortality. For simplicity, the data are expressed in the form of ratios. Any figure above 1 means an excess of male morbidity or mortality and vice versa. By comparing the ratios in columns A to D with E, it is possible to see the extent to which the various measures of morbidity correlate with the relative risk of mortality. Thus, for example, among pre-school children, mortality rates are 34% higher among males but this greater vulnerability is not reflected in medical consultation where there is a slight female excess. The gap between the different types of health status indicator is at its widest between the ages of 65 and 74 where the mortality risk among men is almost double even though women make more frequent use of medical services.

Table 4.2 Sex Ratios in Self Reported Sickness, GP Consultation and Mortality
(Females = 1)

Age	(A) Consultation	(B) Chronic Illness	(C) Chronic Handicapping Illness	(D) Acute Illness	(E) Mortality
0-4	.97	1.13	1.5	1.13	1.34
5-14	1.01	1.38	1.67	1.10	1.36
15-44	.56	1.01	1.01	.92	1.67
45-64	1.01	1.05	1.13	1.00	1.83
65-74	.83	.91	.88	.74	1.93
75+	.99	.86	.90	.79	1.35

Source: Adapted from *General Household Survey 1974*
England and Wales

The tendency for mortality ratios to substantially exceed self reported morbidity is encountered in every age group over the age of 14. So it appears that although men consistently outnumber women in the risk of premature death, their vulnerability is not reflected in self reports of symptoms and medical consultation. While men die early, women suffer more sickness. Why should this be so? Is it because women are more vigilant about possible threats to their health, a fact reflected in their tendency to notice symptoms and resort to medical treatment? It seems doubtful that this could explain their lower mortality rates, since there is no effective therapy for most of the diseases which account for excess male mortality before retirement age. How else might we explain these sex differences in experience, behaviour and survival?

We have already considered some of the possible reasons for the increasing survival of women in the twentieth century in chapter 2 (pp.547–548). There we concluded that a persuasive reason for the dramatic divergence between male and female mortality rates since 1900 was found in the changing pattern of male and female domestic and occupational roles. These changes which have tended to make women more dependent both as housewives and clients of the welfare state, may also provide some clues to sex differences in mortality and morbidity.

It is possible that the phenomenon of morbidity in its various forms reflects a much broader range of social circumstances and experience than merely the symptoms of organic disorder that doctors treat? It is well known for example, that women are more likely to consult general practitioners about emotional, psychological, social and economic problems even though doctors feel ill-equipped to deal with them. Why are men more selective in their reasons for seeking medical advice? Is their need less because they experience greater autonomy over everyday life through work and the wage packet? If so, the gap between mortality and morbidity no longer seems paradoxical since the two measures reflect different dimensions of social inequality.

Inequalities in Health Care

The National Health Service (NHS) in Britain was established in 1948 by the post-war Labour government to provide a comprehensive system of health care with free access to everyone irrespective of the ability to pay. The implicit aim was to bring about equality of health in the population by making health care free. In its first thirty years the NHS has clearly not achieved this aim. Inequalities in health have persisted and worsened in the post-war period. There is nothing particularly surprising about this. As chapters 1 and 2 make clear, health is not determined by medical resources, it is the product of social and economic welfare. As long as inequalities of property, income, education, occupation and social privilege persist in a society, so will inequalities in health. The continuing picture of inequality in health in Britain is therefore like a barometer of socio-economic inequality in general.

Interestingly enough the NHS is also something of a barometer of the extent of inequality in the wider society. Despite the aim of its founders, the distribution of resources in the NHS is so unequal that one observer concluded it conformed to 'An Inverse Care Law' (Tudor-Hart, 1971). This law states that health care resources tend to be distributed in inverse proportion to need or put more simply, that those whose need is less get more resources, while those in greatest need get less. In practice this means that poor working class communities tend to have the shabbiest and most over-crowded facilities in the NHS. This happens because general practitioners prefer to work in more prosperous communities and consequently those who serve the poor have larger numbers of patients and less time for each consultation. The result is that the better off, whose need for health care is less, get a better deal out the NHS than the poor who have the highest rates of mortality and morbidity combined with a poorer standard of service.

How are these differences expressed in doctor/patient relationships? Studies of consulting room behaviour reveal that doctors spend more time with their middle class patients even within the same practice. Cartwright and O'Brian found that, while the average consultation with a middle class patient took 6.2 minutes, the working class equivalent took only 4.7 minutes. This time difference helps explain another finding that middle class patients get more information from their doctors, ask more questions and prove less easily satisfied with advice or treatment. And this was not all. Even though working class patients had been with the doctor for an average of 4 years longer, they were less well known. General practitioners had a better knowledge of their middle class patients and they were more likely to recognise them by name. This study suggests that medical consultation varies according to the social class of the patient. Treatment for the middle class appears to be more patient-centred (see p.624), focused on the needs of the consuler, while in the working class, it tends to be more doctor-centred, geared to the needs of the doctor. This may be the result of differences between patients. Middle class patients are probably more articulate and confident in reporting symptoms, and if they get better treatment, perhaps it is because they demand it. Could this also explain a further finding of Cartwright and O'Brian that, despite the fact that doctors have 'less sympathetic and understanding relationships with their working class patients', their consultations with them tend to be more satisfying?

> Our analyses show that doctors seemed to be more satisfied with consultations at which the conversation time was less than five minutes, where the patient asked not more than one question, and also possibly those at which fewer problems were discussed. (Cartwright and O'Brian 1974, 92).

Inequalities of treatment at the level of verbal exchange are probably equally prevalent when patients meet specialists in hospital, but it is not clear whether they influence the outcome of treatment. There are few up to date statistics available to study class differences in the benefit derived from hospital treatment. Cancer registration data suggest that middle class patients have better survival prospects, but this is probably the result of social class itself rather than anything encountered in treatment. One of the few studies that attempted to follow up patients discharged from a district general hospital, found marked differences in rates of survival by social class. Two years after discharge, less than 50% of patients could be described as 'cured' or improved of whom the majority were in non-manual occupations. The authors conclude:

> The transition from the sheltered atmosphere of the modern hospital ward to the icy chill of the workaday world, is indeed a testing time and it is not surprising that many soon break down. The ex-patients who showed the heaviest mortality at early ages, the strongest tendency to relapse and the poorest record in point of early return to work, were the group of unskilled labourers . . . In many cases early recurrence of breakdown came from bad social conditions rather than any inevitability on medical grounds. (Ferguson and McPhail 1954, 137).

It is obvious that the NHS cannot compensate for the structure of social and economic inequality in the community at large. But has it even tried?

In 1976 the government adopted the recommendations of a report on the reallocation of resources in the NHS. The 'RAWP' report recommended that there should be a redistribution of the NHS budget to areas which had never received a fair share of available resources. These areas included some with the highest mortality rates in Britain. The report showed that the areas best endowed with health service facilities had the lowest mortality rates. Even so these areas in south-east England had been allocated a much larger than average per capita share of the NHS budget every year since 1948. Table 4.3, summarises the lack of fit between indicators of need for health care (infant and adult mortality rates) and the distribution of health care resources.

Table 4.3   Regional Inequalities in Health and Health Care in the UK, 1977

Region	Males	Females	Infants	Hospitals	GPs	Nurses
		Mortality		NHS Expenditure		
ENGLAND	99	99	13.7	61.76	4.84	73.5
Northern	111	109	14.9	56.19	4.55	71.4
Yorkshire	105	105	15.5	56.86	4.70	73.6
Trent	103	102	13.9	50.9	4.54	66.1
East Anglia	89	96	11.2	53.83	4.85	65.6
NW Thames	89	90	11.8	74.91	5.48	75.4
NE Thames	94	92	14.0	76.35	5.10	76.6
SE Thames	95	92	13.1	73.61	5.01	80.5
SW Thames	90	95	11.6	67.00	5.17	76.5
Wessex	92	92	13.1	52.44	4.98	68.5
Oxford	90	96	12.7	53.18	4.73	62.3
South Western	93	97	12.5	57.58	5.17	74.7
West Midlands	103	103	15.0	52.65	4.56	67.9
Mersey	110	109	14.4	62.16	4.60	80.6
North Western	113	111	14.8	57.63	4.55	75.0
WALES	108	106	13.5	61.50	5.05	79.0
SCOTLAND	112	109	16.1	78.10	5.98	102.2
N. IRELAND	112	115	17.2	83.07	4.98	77.1

Source: Adapted from *The Report of the Royal Commission on the National Health Service,* 1980 (Tables 3.1, 3.2 & 3.3). GPs and Nurses per 10,000 population. Hospital Expenditure = £ per capita. Mortality = SMRs for males and females. Infant mortality per 1000 live births.

This inequality is a built-in feature of the NHS. It results from the tendency to allocate resources on the basis of what already exists rather than on the basis of need in a fundamental sense. The technical word for it is incrementalism. The principal reason for the continued overfunding of the richest parts of the country at the expense of the poorest, was simply that most of the prestigious teaching hospitals are in London and these absorbed a large and, in the past, generally unquestioned share of available resources. As a result people at greater health risk in heavily industrialised parts of the country had worse medical facilities than their fellow citizens in London and the home counties. It is unlikely that this would explain the reasons for unequal mortality risk. Most premature death is incurable and as table 4.3 shows there is no correlation between mortality risk and share of the NHS budget. The healthiest part of Britain, East Anglia, has never received a fair share, while Scotland, with the worst record of health, gets 50% more per head of population that England and Wales as a whole.

Since the implementation of RAWP, a process of reallocating the NHS budget has been underway. Coming at the same time as public expenditure cuts, it has led to the closure or threatened closure of a large number of hospitals in London. One unfortunate result has probably been to make access to medical care in poor inner city areas even worse. The prevalence of 'shut-up shop' style general practices manned by deputising services out of hours made the local hospital the best hope of emergency treatment for many people. Their closure will mean that the cost of any redistribution that takes place from London to the rest of the country will be born by the poor rather than the better off.

The evidence in table 4.3 also serves to illustrate another dimension of health inequality to contemporary Britain. This is inequality based on region. People resident in the north of England, Scotland, Wales and Northern Ireland live shorter lives. Regional differences have been evident ever since statistics were kept. It used to be thought that they were no more than an expression of occupational class, since areas of high mortality have a larger preponderance of manual workers whose average mortality would tend to be higher. However this is not the case. Controlling for the class composition of each region makes very little difference to mortality risk. What this means is that death rates within each class are lower in London or Brighton than they are in Manchester or Sheffield. The exact causes of regional inequalities remain obscure.

Explaining Class Inequalities in Health

Class inequalities in health have been accounted for in a number of different ways. The report of the DHSS *Inequalities in Health Working Group* ('The Black Report'), lists four types of explanation. These are:- (1) Inequality as an artefact; (2) Inequality as natural selection; (3) Inequality as material deprivation; (4) Inequality as cultural deprivation. How does each account for the evidence of health inequality surveyed above?

(a) Health inequality as an artefact

The artefact explanation argues that inequalities in health are not real but artificial. They are an *effect* produced in the attempt to measure something which is more complicated than the tools of measurement can appreciate. More an expression of scepticism than a theoretical explanation, this view is held by statisticians who claim that the evidence of health inequality is so complicated by changes of classification etc. that it is impossible to tell whether things are getting better or worse. Furthermore it is argued that changes in the occupational structure are likely to combine with age to confound *any* attempt to measure inequality in mortality even at one point in time. It is suggested that the age structure of social class V is likely to be biased towards older workers because younger recruits to the labour force will have entered better paid, more skilled occupations, that have expanded since the war. Since mortality risk increases with the age, this effect is likely to enlarge the rate of social class V as a whole. If so, the observed gradient is really caused by the skewed age structure of the unskilled manual class rather than by the poorer health of its members. Age specific mortality differences cast doubt on the validity of this explanation for they show that inequality tends to reduce with age and that it is among younger people that inequality is most pronounced and moreover increasing. (See figure 4.2). This means that the evidence of inequality in mortality risk is not an artefact, but a real phenomenon of class advantage and disadvantage which must be explained in other ways.

(b) Health inequality as a selection process

The most persuasive attempt to explain health inequalities as the outcome of a process natural selection, has been put forward by the statistician, Jon Stern. He argues that observed inequalities in mortality between socio-economic groups like the Registrar General's social classes, reflect a process of social mobility in which individuals with better health move up the social hierarchy, while those in poorer health move down. Paradoxically this exchange of people up and down the socio-economic hierarchy, reflecting as it does an open class structure, creates an effect of worsening inequality in measured differentials. His argument can be illustrated by way of a hypothetical example. Let us assume two social classes which we will simply call the rich and the poor. Stern argues that the exchange of people between these classes will take the form of upward mobility on the part of the healthy poor and downward mobility on the part of the unhealthy rich. This means that the rich class sheds its unhealthy members and gains new healthy recruits from the poor, while the poor lose their most healthy people and get as replacements people who cannot hold on to their wealth because of poor health. The overall result of this two-way exchange is to improve measurements of *average* health status among the rich while depressing those of the poor. Social mobility therefore reinforces any health inequality in this imaginary two class society by widening the gap in survival chances between rich and poor. This leads Stern to conclude that the measurement of change in class gradients in health should be conducted on the basis of class of origin rather than achieved social class. This is a good example of an important *methodological* problem in sociological research. The survey method, the sociologist's primary instrument for gathering data produces a vision of the individual as a snapshot, a collection of social attributes at one point in time. This has the effect of disguising the historical dimension of every human lifetime and variation in personal experience over time is lost to sociological view.

To support his argument, Stern draws on the research of Illsley (1950) which linked the upward and downward mobility of women at marriage to their health status and intelligence. Illsley concluded that the lower infant mortality of higher social classes was the result of better maternal health indicated by such factors as the height of women. Of particular interest was the fact that women from lower social classes who had been upwardly mobile, were very healthy and their inclusion in the higher class improved its average as a whole. From this evidence Stern is led to conclude that observed class differences in health, far from showing that trends in social and economic deprivation are worsening, are actually compatible with greater fluidity in the class structure and hence greater opportunity in society. As he argues, if social mobility were more difficult or even impossible as in a caste system, inequalities in health would disappear since the poor would retain those in good health and the rich those in bad health thereby maintaining parity in average health status.

In effect Stern defines health as a fixed or genetic property of individuals largely independent of their immediate social and economic circumstances. This view is contrary to a sociological account which sees health as primarily a product of the social and economic environment. His argument rests on the assumption that health itself increases the probability of social mobility and that the class structure permits movement up and down. This means that no matter how deprived the social background, a genetic potentiality for good health will enable a person to overcome material disadvantage and 'climb out' of poverty. To prove or disprove this thesis would require data which trace the progress of individuals throughout the course of their lives. Since most sociological and statistical data lack this biographical dimension, it is impossible to settle the claims of this thesis one way or the other. Its plausibility depends on the extent to which people can insulate their health from material disadvantage during the course of their lifetimes. This leads to a consideration of the importance of material deprivation in shaping health and survival prospects.

(c) Health inequality as material deprivation

Material deprivation means a shortage of the material resources on which healthy human existence depends. In less developed societies its effects may appear in very high death rates from diseases primarily caused by malnutrition and exposure. The poorest sections of the community simply lack adequate resources to maintain the material substance of their bodies or to protect them from the natural environment. In this form, material deprivation may be accepted as a fact of life only surfacing to remind the better off that it is the result of material inequality when deaths from starvation-related disease occur in epidemic proportions. In earlier centuries in our own society, massive mortality from 'pestilence' occurred frequently against the background of war and bad harvest. The heaviest toll of death was amongst the poor, whose inadequate nutritional state made them the easiest targets for infective organisms (see p.551). In modern times death on this scale is only encountered in the Third World and then not often on the scale of the Ethiopian 'Human Tragedy'.

Where material deprivation has an immediate, visible impact, it seems to constitute an absolute shortage of essential needs. One might imagine a dividing line of economic welfare called basic subsistence below which human survival is put at risk. However in practice it is not possible to define a minimum subsistence level in this way because rates of human survival are not fixed. When living standards rise, both rich and poor improve their life expectation and the gap in life chances is maintained. But if life expectation can be extended even for the poorest members of the community, then there can be no *absolute* standard of subsistence that ensures good health. The definition of deprivation is always relative to social and economic norms. In these terms inequality in survival rates between the social classes is the product of fundamental inequalities in the distribution of wealth and income. This was the explanation favoured by the DHSS chief scientist and other members of the Working Group on Inequalities in Health.

Table 4.4   Social Class, Average Weekly Income and Standardised Mortality Ratios

Social Class	Average Weekly Income (£s)	SMR
I	44.14	77
II	34.02	81
IIIN (non-manual)	24.12	99
IIIM (manual)	27.05	106
IV	22.46	114
V	22.09	137

Source: Adapted from *Occupational Mortality 1970-72*, p. 151
   (men aged 15-64)

Table 4.4 displays the relationship between mortality risk and one dimension of material deprivation, inequalities in weekly income.

Average weekly income is closely related to the risk of dying before retirement. Only among clerical workers (IIIN) is the gradient disturbed. Their average income is below that of IIIM, yet their SMR is lower. Apart from the incorporation of overtime earnings in the average for IIIM, this divergence is likely to reflect the greater safety of the work environment of social class IIIN and the relative youth of non-manual workers. Among men, social class IIIN tends to be a transient phase in the career, a mid-point on the way up the occupational ladder. This is generally not the case among skilled manual workers for whom IIIM is lifetime class location. This serves as a reminder that income is only one dimension of occupational class. Other dimensions include prospects for personal development and the nature of the work people carry out in order to earn their livelihood. The greater hazards of manual work are reflected in the risk of accidents at work. (Figure 4.4). In sociological terms this means that, in their contribution to the *Social Division of Labour*, manual workers must systematically expose their health to greater risk.

Figure 4.4 Mortality by Social Class for Accidents at Work (men aged 15-64)

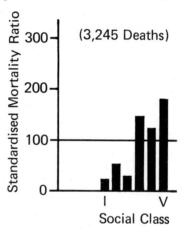

Source: *Occupational Mortality: 1970-72* (HMSO, London 1978). Reproduced with the permission of the Controller of Her Majesty's Stationery Office.

Income and work conditions are two possible indicators of material welfare and deprivation in contemporary Britain. Other important dimensions include: being employed or unemployed, security of tenure in employment, job satisfaction, expectation for retirement pension and not least important, the possession of wealth and property itself. We have seen some of these factors at work producing variation in mortality risk according to house ownership (p.575). Another dimension also of relevance is ownership of society's productive system: the land, large corporations and firms, factories, banks, insurance companies, even the means of communication themselves, newspapers and commercial television companies. How might this form of private wealth ownership, literally of Britain's economy itself, play a part in determining the distribution of life chances in society?

In Britain the ownership of private wealth is highly concentrated in a relatively small sector of the community. In 1972, according to the Royal Commission on the Distribution of Income and Wealth, 89% of the private wealth ownership was in the hands of 20% of the population. Within this group, the richest 1%, 5% and 10% respectively owned 30%, 56% and 72% of wealth accounted for in Inland Revenue returns. This highly unequal concentration of property ownership is, in Marxist theory, *the axis* of class stratification in capitalist society. It gives rise to two classes: those who own the means of production and those who are propertyless. The owners, the capitalist class, run the national economy in their own interests according to the rules of profit and loss. Profits are generated through the accumulation of surplus value. This is the value produced in the labour process after costs including wages have been deducted. Capitalism is an exploitative economic system according to Marx, because workers are alienated from what they produce and because they do not receive its full value as wages. In the middle of the nineteenth century, when Marx was developing his theories, the working class was, by any standard, terribly exploited. The working week was seven days and the working day was ten hours long. The employment of small children in mines and factories, which is illegal today, was commonplace. It was against this background that Marx identified the processes of *immiserisation* and *polarisation,* integral features of the capitalism of his day. They are manifested in the drive for profit which leads to a lowering of wages and to a worsening of work conditions finally leaving the worker with insufficient resources to maintain bodily health or, as Marx put it, 'to reproduce his labour power'. The fall in wages and living standards affects the whole workforce with the result that *all* workers become more impoverished. This has a unifying effect. It leads to the polarisation of owners and workers into two distinct classes with opposed economic interests.

The advent of Keynesian economics cast these processes in a rather different light. Keynes argued that economic growth and the profitability of firms depends primarily on the level of consumer spending. In this light forcing down wages is a shortsighted route to capital accumulation since it has a negative effect on the economy as a whole. Keynes provided a rationale for government intervention in the management of the economy to regulate the supply of money and maintain high levels of demand in order to protect firms and their employees from the periodic cycle of boom and recession. From a Keynesian perspective it is not so clear that the interests of workers and owners are fundamentally opposed and in the post-war era the adoption of Keynesian policies has brought about substantial improvements in living standards.

In consequence the population has not been polarised in the way Marx predicted. As the evidence presented earlier testifies, it is more instructive to see the structure of inequality as a stratified hierarchy rather than a two class division. For this reason, the concepts of immiserisation and polarisation appear irrelevant to the circumstances of modern capitalism. This is why modern Marxists refer to **relative** as opposed to **absolute** exploitation (see p.559). The modern mode of exploitation is to foist unnecessary commodities on people creating a materialistic society where things become more important than human relationships. The drive to consumption leads people to make money and work their main priority, which in turn undermines the social relationships which make life meaningful and worthwhile. In general the statistical evidence of health inequality suggests that poverty, defined relative to prevailing living standards, is more closely correlated to premature death than is the accumulation of modern commodities. This seems paradoxical because as we saw in chapter 2, infective diseases caused by poverty and malnutrition have been replaced by degenerative diseases associated with smoking, rich diet and inactivity. In these changed circumstances, the idea of health inequality being due to material shortage seems less persuasive. This is why some observers have been persuaded by the idea that cultural divisions between the classes determine health and survival. In what follows the scope of cultural deprivation as an explanation for health inequality will be explored and further consideration will be given to the role of poverty as a source of ill-health in contemporary society in chapter 5 (p.613).

(d) Health inequality as cultural deprivation

Part of the culture of any social group is concerned with ideas and practices about health. In earlier centuries it was believed that sickness and disease were the product of supernatural causes, the work of either

God or the Devil. The medieval man of God doubled as healer and monasteries were also pharmacies. As medical treatment was on balance rather dangerous, faith healing with its potential *placebo* effect, probably offered the most effective response to sickness. The incorporation of healing within religion therefore had a certain rationality. With the development of science and technology in the wake of industrialisation, these cultural beliefs about the impotence of human intervention in matters of health were gradually swept away. It took a long time. The history of the incorporation of contraception, abortion and artificial insemination as acceptable cultural practice, is an interesting, topical case study of the continuing hold of religious morality over the rights of human intervention in bodily processes. Today there is little doubt that contemporary cultural beliefs about health and disease have been captured by medicine. We shall have more to say about the culture of modern medicine and its role in present day society in chapters 6 and 7.

The culture of an advanced industrial society is heavily influenced by science and technology and by universal literacy. It is moreover much less stable than the systems of belief of earlier times. By its very nature, it is subject to a continuous process of reappraisal and modification; it reaches out and communicates with larger and larger populations through media of its own creation. Advanced technological media such as the television, the computer, or the intercontinental communication satellite are examples. The script of modern culture therefore requires individuals to be flexible. Nothing is fixed, knowledge and skill are continually on the move and individuals must be prepared to adapt their ideas, behaviour and relationships to keep up. The resulting instability is offset by advanced forms of communication such as the telephone, the television and the motor car, basic possessions of the average household. They allow individuals to get in touch with people easily and rapidly, to keep up to date with what's new, and to move about at will. In this way modern men and women are able to experience a sense, at least, of control over their immediate circumstances. This, in part, is what is meant by an individualistic way of life.

These tendencies of modern culture are beginning to be expressed in beliefs about the causes of disease. The major causes of death today are increasingly thought of as the outcome of degenerative processes, of human bodies literally wearing out. Given that nobody lives forever, this must happen to everyone sometime in their lives. But, the message goes, people should be capable of regulating the life of bodies in some degree, by looking after them properly. The scope for personal health care includes diet, exercise, the effective use of medical services and the avoidance of bad habits like smoking. In this way the life of organs like the heart, can be prolonged and the onset of disease prevented or rather put off. Naturally, people who do not heed the advice, are likely to die earlier.

The need to teach the public how to look after itself, has given rise to a new profession. The ethos of health education work is that the secret of good health lies in the hands of individuals themselves. This leads to a tendency to locate the causes of premature death at the same door. Lower class people therefore are sometimes seen as the victims of their own cultural backwardness, being either ignorant of good health practice or too inert to do anything about it. This was how Brotherston (1976) explained the greater mortality of babies in social class V households — their mothers came too late for ante-natal care. He drew this conclusion in the absence of evidence proving that ante-natal care made any difference to the survival prospects of infants. Since then research has questioned its value by showing that it is not effective at identifying mothers and babies at risk *(Hall et al* 1980). Nevertheless, to Brotherston, the problem seemed to be one of lower class women clinging to their own culture of childbirth and resisting, and therefore losing out on, the benefits of medical technology.

If this situation is one of cultural deprivation, then the source of the problem should be located not in the individual but in the failure of new cultural practices to penetrate the lives of lower class people. Culture is a concept which embraces a collectivity, it is the ideas and practices of a *group* and to survive, it must be interwoven in the beliefs of a community. This was how Oscar Lewis employed the concept to describe the mechanisms which perpetuated poverty in the Mexican families he wrote about. His *Culture of Poverty* consisted of the ideas, behaviours and strategies, poor people adopt in order to cope with the perpetual material deprivations of their lives. Their methods of surviving in a harsh environment, by infiltrating their culture, take on a life of their own. As a result, they are likely to persist even if the economic environment changes for the better. This leads to the Community being imprisoned in poverty by its beliefs and its habitual behaviour. This is what constitutes *cultural deprivation.*

Can this explain the excess mortality of the working class? Could it be the product of outmoded and redundant cultural norms, the result not of their relationship to the means of production but to the shifting cultural norms of advanced capitalist societies? Let us explore the scope of this 'poverty of health culture' thesis with a concrete example.

Among causes which contribute to the higher mortality of manual workers, the most important is lung cancer. In 1970-72, this cause accounted for 40,000 deaths of men aged 15-64 years (40% of all cancer mortality in the age group). Although the aetiology of this disease remains poorly understood, it is well known that heavy smokers carry five times the risk of non-smokers. In the last 15 years smoking has become strongly class-related. In 1960, there was little difference between the social classes in the consumption of cigarettes. Since then, consumption in the middle class has fallen off substantially, leaving a class gradient in tobacco consumption which closely reflects the gradient for lung cancer mortality.

Figure 4.5

Cigarette consumption by Social Class (males aged 15-64).   Deaths from Lung Cancer by Social Class (males aged 15-64).

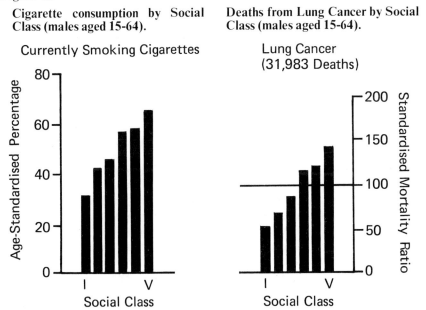

Source: *Occupational Mortality: 1970-72* (HMSO, London 1978). Reproduced with the permission of the Controller of Her Majesty's Stationery Office.

The general correspondence between these gradients implies that higher death rates are largely due to heavy smoking. This leads to the question why the people most at risk of premature death, have failed to take heed of the message that smoking is bad for your health. Could it be ignorance? Is it possible that manual workers have not understood the warning on each deadly packet? Since this is hardly likely to be the reason, we must look elsewhere for an explanation of this apparently dangerous class-related behaviour.

Remember that the behaviour in question is not a series of random individual acts. It is a group phenomenon, a cultural norm rather than a personal habit. This raises the possibility that the failure of health education to make the impact on manual workers as elsewhere in the population, is because smoking remains closely interwoven with the culture of everyday life. In the past, smoking has been a socially valued behaviour. It was deliberately encouraged in two world wars when cheap cigarettes became one of the perks of being in uniform. Among the young, smoking has long been a significant symbol of the transition from school to the labour market and from childhood to adult independence. Increasing consumption among women perhaps testifies to its continuing importance as a symbol of personal independence, of 'growing up' into adult (labour market) social roles. Giving up therefore involves more than overcoming what is in any case an addictive habit. It also requires a cultural redefinition of the behaviour. Why should this be more difficult in working as opposed to middle class circles? It is easy to see how a declining rate of smoking would serve to reinforce a negative sanction against the behaviour and vice versa. As smoking becomes a culturally despised habit among the middle classes, those who persist become exposed to group pressures to give up. Meanwhile continued high consumption among manual workers positively reinforces and perpetuates the habit. But how does the cultural redefinition of smoking begin and flourish in one section of society and not in another?

It must be said that the cultural 'recoding' of smoking, a pleasurable habit, will be more easily achieved if there are substitutes to satisfy the physical and cultural needs it fulfills. This may require for example the identification of other symbols of impending adult status to denote social independence. Manual workers make the transition from school to work earlier, when they are still quite young. This may be why they have more need of external symbols of the status change. Middle class lives are in any case less uniform and the transition is less likely to be a one-off but a continuing development involving further education or training and occupational career developments. No wonder then, that the symbolic value of smoking is less. What of the physical needs that smoking satisfies? Here we must ask whether the seeming reluctance of manual workers to take the health warning seriously, is because of its narcotic value as a means of reducing the sheer physical stress of manual work. If so the problem is one of material not cultural deprivation. On the other hand if smoking is not a pacifying drug but is really just a pleasurable activity, then giving up may simply denote the availability of a wider range of other sources of enjoyment.

Another possibility is that middle class men and women have responded more rapidly to the idea that smoking is bad for your health because their socialisation leaves them better equipped to adapt to the shifting character of modern culture. Group solidarity is less important in their lives because they experience more social and geographical mobility. Individualism is not merely an ideological banner, they have direct experience of it in their personal lives in the absence of any lasting attachment to particular groups or communities. Consequently the redefinition of a cultural norm in terms of everyday behaviour may gather momentum more rapidly because it depends more on individual initiative. Furthermore behavioural innovation, in this more privatised world, is less subject to negative group sanctions.

Giving up cigarettes is a form of deferred gratification, a valued social activity is sacrificed in order to reap some future benefit. As with all preventive health care measures nobody can be completely sure that the sacrifice will pay off. Like the Calvinist entrepreneurs who inspired Max Weber, one only discovers if one is among the elect at the end of the road and the best insurance meanwhile, is to act as if one were. Preventive strategies, in the absence of hard evidence stem from hope and conviction, but they still imply that the individual possesses some sense that the course of life is something over which a degree of control may be exerted. This sense of 'self mastery' over personal circumstances is also a more prevalent middle class expectation.

This fits with research findings from the United States linking class differences in ageing to outmoded cultural norms. Blue collar workers are said to *feel* old at a younger chronological age than white collar age peers. Because white collar workers expect to survive to a healthy old age, they take steps in advance to preserve their looks and their bodies. The more limited survival horizons of blue collar workers, on the other hand, leads to a fatalistic approach to the ageing of the body. They literally 'let themselves go' to an early grave. This suggests that people who try to become the architects of their own health by regulating consumption, by jogging etc., can actually influence their life expectation. This portrayal of a person's *sense* of being in control, as an important factor in the ageing process might be called a *poverty of health culture thesis*.

The problem with research like this however is that it is very difficult to determine whether subjective individual assessments of health actually reflect the *material* realities of growing old. Perhaps the *sense* that nothing can be done to slow down the 'clock of life' is a rational response to poverty and powerlessness. Equally, the expectation that the future is within personal control may arise because to some extent it is among those who possess a larger share of power and resources to plan their lives. A sense of self mastery in these terms is not so much a product of the imagination as one of pension rights, bank balance and property ownership. At this point, cultural deprivation shades into a material form and leaves open the question of how useful the distinction between the cultural and material dimensions of life is to the analysis of social inequality.

Health Inequality: Questions and Answers

The explanations for health inequality, discussed in the last section, differ in their assumptions, their conclusions and in the way that questions are posed. Artefact explanations tend to be favoured by statisticians and by sociologists who reject statistical data altogether on the familiar grounds that 'There are lies, damn lies and statistics'. It is not a theoretical explanation on a par with the other three. It consists of a set of negative conclusions emerging from attempts to test theory with available data: the data are not adequate for the task of theoretical evaluation. This conclusion can be expressed with a number of different emphases which have different implications. On the one hand it might be concluded that *There is no evidence of health inequality in present day Britain.* On the other, it could be said that *The available statistics leave the question unsettled one way or the other.*

It might be thought unfortunate that difficulties of interpretation makes the task of choosing between competing theories well nye impossible. In practice, however, in both medicine and social science, it is very often the case that empirical data leave plenty of room for controversy. Research findings can all too often be stretched to support a number of even opposed theoretical explanations. In consequence theoretical evaluation usually turns out to be a rather complicated task requiring judgements about the structure of a theoretical argument including its assumptions as well as the fit with empirical proof. As we have seen (p.573), despite problems of reclassification etc., the statistics of class-related mortality give grounds to believe that during the post-war era social class mortality gradients were still very much in evidence and more seriously so among younger age groups.

The other explanations identified by the Black Report have theoretical aims. Our attention has already been drawn to the fact that two of them are essentially sociological explanations and that the other is not. What difference does this make?

The argument that inequality in health reflects material or cultural deprivation is a sociological position. It states that health is the product of social forces whether these take a material (economic) or a cultural (normative) form. Health is *assumed* to be a property of the social environment and of the individual's relationship to it. In sociology therefore health is defined in *relational* terms. It is *relative* to place, time and class. At the same time inequality is also located as a property of structures and forces ultimately beyond individual characteristics and control. It also has a *relational* form. From this perspective, economic or cultural well-being has little to do with personal initiative, energy or skill, and everything to do with the inheritance of wealth, education and social privilege including their influence on socialisation. It is the individual's *relationship* to the distribution of these valued social resources that determines the socio-economic course of his or her lifetime. While some may escape from a poor social background up the ladder of social mobility, the structure or framework of class inequality persists from one generation to the next to determine the welfare of the majority who are left behind.

How does the other type of explanation differ from this? The alternative thesis, at its crudest level, traces inequalities in life expectation quite literally to the 'survival of the fittest'. Health is conceived as an integral property of individuals which enables them to escape from a low social class to a higher one. Indeed it implies that the whole hierarchy of social class is itself strongly influenced by the tendency of the 'fit' and the 'unfit' to exchange positions on the social ladder. Class differences therefore arise from the sum of the personal attributes of the people who occupy each rank and any social structure of inequality contained within social institutions, recedes into the background. A dominating feature of this approach therefore is the emphasis on the individual and the role of personal attributes in the process of social stratification be it health or wealth.

The ingredients for each type of explanation are therefore quite different. The explanatory problem is shaped in each case by a distinctive set of assumptions which in turn help to influence any conclusions reached. The natural selection thesis provides a plausible account of the mechanisms which may translate social mobility into a deceptive picture of health inequality. Its validity depends on the extent to which its key assumption, that health itself is an independent and determining factor in social mobility, is accepted. In the alternative approach, the problem to be explained is defined differently. With health now appearing as a dependent variable, a product of social and economic life, the question at issue is whether *the structure of inequality* is getting better or worse. It is taken for granted that the distribution of life chances in the population will reflect the level of inequality in society. As with the selection thesis, the validity of any conclusions depend upon the soundness of initial assumptions.

Proponents of most theories can usually find some modicum of empirical support for their favourite conclusions and for this reason it is seldom possible to choose between competing explanations on the grounds of evidence alone. Whether a theory is accepted or rejected has as much to do with whether the assumptions and hence the whole tenor of the argument are in tune with whoever is listening. The natural selection thesis starts with the advantage of a definition of health which fits well, with, is perhaps even drawn from contemporary medical practice. Doctors focus on the *socially anonymous individual,* the patient. Given that popular knowledge about health is generated through encounters with doctors, the assumption that it is a natural biological feature of individuals may be widely acceptable. Against this, in any careful analysis, must be weighed the historical evidence which shows that health status is highly sensitive to material living standards. This evidence reinforces the argument that correlations between income, property and the risk of death in the present day, follow the pattern of the past.

Is it either necessary or possible to choose between these types of explanation? Can the pattern of health inequality be the product of both processes acting together, so that the tendency for healthy people to improve their social status actually increases measured differentials which are already shaped in large degree by social class in its various dimensions. If this happens then it must mean that upward mobility on account of health occurs despite, even in the face of, socio-economic deprivation. But how can personal health be insulated for some people in a harsh environment but not for the majority? Or to put it another way, how does the genetic health potential of an individual, destined for social mobility, escape the systematic and continuous environmental processes that shape the experience of everyone else in the same community?

These crucial questions about the nature of health cannot be satisfactorily answered because of a lack of empirical evidence. They involve the investigation of individual life careers from birth to death, tracing all critical points of change in both socio-economic and health circumstances. General Practitioners are probably the best placed to accumulate the necessary evidence. But because they are socialised within the bio-mechanical model, they tend to favour more individuated explanations of health focusing on personal biology and psychology. The next chapter will introduce further evidence relating to sociological approaches to understanding how health develops through the course of life, in response to social and economic circumstances.

Chapter Five

Becoming Ill as a Social Process

The most obvious symptoms of disease in the human body are physiological in form. They are tangible biological phenomena — tumours, blood clots, burst arteries, kidney stones, congested lungs — and it is only natural to assume that they are caused by the same kind of organic material or that their formation is stimulated by biological processes. In this chapter we will examine the evidence for the claim that the roots of organic disease are to be found in social life itself, in personality, in behaviour, and in social relationships. By this account the physical manifestations of organic disorder, while real enough, are in effect no more than the end product of social and psychological experiences encountered in everyday life. In short, disease is a case of mind over matter.

Life Events and Illness

Does personal anxiety arising out of unhappy experiences in the course of the lifetime hold vital clues about the causes of organic disease? This line of theorising, although novel in scientific circles, is by no means new. The belief that worry leads to illness or even death is a longstanding tradition in our own society. Certainly in other cultures, the causes of sickness and disease are thought primarily to lie in troubled social relationships. The Azande of the Sudan studied by Evans-Pritchard, believe that organic illness is the result of witchcraft directed at the sufferer by some unknown person who 'wishes him ill'. Likewise among the Nuer, another Sudanese tribe, studied by the same anthropologist, sickness is liable to be explained by such events as sexual infidelity. These forms of belief are dismissed by Western science as being irrational and mystical. But there is evidence in our own advanced industrial civilisation, that personal crises prompted by disruptive social relationships lead to disease.

In a study published under the title of *Broken Heart,* Rees and Lutkins demonstrated that, in the year following the death of their wives, widowers were subject to an increased risk of dying themselves. When compared to a control group matched for age and occupation, newly widowed men were 40% more likely to die of a number of causes, the most frequent being heart disease. After the first year of bereavement the excess mortality of the widowers fell back to the level of the control group. The authors concluded that the stress of losing their wives was a serious risk factor for heart disease and that there might be some truth in the old belief that people die of a broken heart. The increased susceptibility of the widowed to heart attacks is well documented in other research as is their greater vulnerability to that other great killer of modern civilisation, cancer. Similar results have also been found for the divorced and separated suggesting that the loss of a marriage partner poses a particularly important threat to health.

This fact was noticed more than eighty years ago by the French sociologist Emile Durkheim, who pointed out that suicide rates were systematically linked to social variables like religion and marital status He insisted that this was a function of social integration. The lives of married people are more subject to normative regulation which strengthens the will to survive. The single and the formerly married on the other hand, lead a more 'anomic' existence which weakens it. This protective feature of being married is not restricted to the risk of suicide. As figure 5.1 reveals, the risks of premature death from *all* causes are closely correlated with marital status, suggesting that having a partner enhances survival prospects and that being without one exposes people to greater risks of all kinds. These data support Durkheim's contention that people bound together in supportive social relationships find everyday life more meaningful. Following him even further we could go on to argue that premature death is a social phenomenon, or as he would have put it a *Social Fact.*

Durkheim's interpretation of the correlation between marriage and the risk of suicide presents individual motivation as a socially constructed phenomenon. The individual's sense that life is worth living is not a matter of personal psychology, it is a reflection of the circumstances of married life, of moral regulation and mutual support. Anticipating the ideas to be examined in the next chapter, we could infer that marriage is a social role which involves a number of normative rights and duties. This creates a sense of obligation and belongingness which not only strengthens the individual's will to live, in a subjective sense, it actually appears to protect the very physical substance of their bodies.

Figure 5.1 Death Rates by Sex, Age and Marital Status

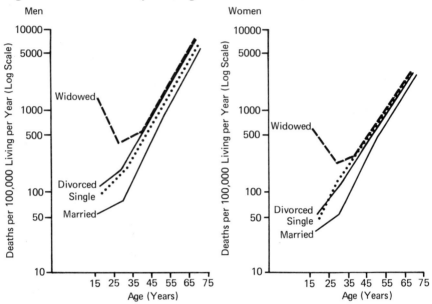

Source: *Occupational Mortality: 1970-72* (HMSO, London, 1978) Reproduced with the permission of the Conrtoller of Her Majesty's Stationery Office.

Meanwhile other research suggests that the loss of all kinds of important social relationships and valued social statuses increase the individual's susceptibility to a wide range of diseases. In his book, *The Social Causes of Illness* Totman reviews the evidence linking disruptive life events such as widowhood, separation, adultery, divorce, job change, unemployment, migration, retirement and eviction to a multitude of conditions including leukaemia, tuberculosis, pernicious anaemia, heart failure, asthma, multiple sclerosis, breast and cervical cancer and even the common cold. The array of evidence supporting this so-called *Loss/Disease Hypothesis* is impressive but most of it is surrounded by a methodological controversy. Many of the studies which report an association between life events and disease have been retrospective in design relying on the reconstructed reports of personal crises of people already suffering from a particular disease. Such evidence is of dubious validity for as Totman observes:

> Human memory, in particular, the memory of emotionally charged events, is not like a passive store. Its contents become distorted and elaborated with the passage of time. Thus when someone is asked by an

interviewer to recount past events which have distressed him, he cannot be relied upon to produce an 'objective commentary'. (Totman 1979, 113).

Attempts to overcome this methodological objection have led to the development of more objective methods for recording life events in the individual's past. One of these is the Holmes-Rahe Social Readjustment Rating Scale (the SRRS), a series of experiences involving the loss or rejection of a single social relationship, a set of relationships, or a valued part of the personal identity. This scale is made up of 42 events which are all held to require some degree of social adjustment when they happen to a person. The events are arranged hierarchically according to how they were scored by a sample of 400 healthy Americans who were asked to judge how much 'life change' each was likely to involve. A high degree of agreement about the relative severity of each event was reported by Holmes and Rahe who then used the results to derive a scale of measurement for life crisis based on life change units (LCUs). The top of the scale (100 LCUs) is the death of a husband or wife, divorce scores 73, while getting the sack or retiring gets a score of 45. The idea is to obtain an objective count of the incidence of life events in the subject's experience, (usually over a specified period of the recent past) and not to rely on the individual's own selected reconstruction of past problems in order to predict which people are most at risk to serious disorders. It has been used in both prospective (i.e. predictive) and retrospective studies but with only moderate success in identifying the most vulnerable. It appears that threatening experiences are most dangerous to health when they are perceived as such and the attempt to eliminate subjectivity in the SRRS diminishes the predictive power of recent life events as indicators of stress.

Before going on to explore in more detail the sociological literature in this area, it will be useful first of all to clarify the physiological link in the chain of causation leading from life events to disease.

Stress: A Physiological Link in the Social Process of Disease

The simplest biological version of the causal sequence from a state of health to one of illness involves, the invasion of a virus, the response of the body's immune system and the appearance of physical symptoms (see p.534). This aetiological chain could be elaborated to take account of the susceptibility of the potential victim on account of genetic characteristics or acquired immunity. But basically the individual sufferer is, to use Totman's phrase 'A biological black box'.

Everything that affects the sequence is contained in the individual's own physiological condition.

The research that we have just described clearly represents a challenge to this orthodox medical version of how disease happens. It does not fit easily into the usual causal chain because there are no obvious mechanisms for relating social and psychological threats in the production of organic damage and physical disorder. The exception to this is the medical category of *psychosomatic* disease.

The idea of psychosomatic disease depends on the concept of *stress*. This word has become something of an umbrella category covering a wide range of threatening phenomena as well as individual reactions to them. But in its early usage by Selye, it meant an adaptive response in the human body to a stressor, i.e. a threatening stimulus. The response takes the form of a spontaneous secretion of adrenalin, the hormone produced by the pituitary gland. It is easy to appreciate Selye's argument because we are all probably aware from personal experience that threatening situations are likely to produce involuntary physical reactions. In fact the word adrenalin has entered everyday language as a term to depict the felt sensation when stressful situations make greater demands on our bodies. Stress is not necessarily pathological. Stressful stimuli can be quite positive calling up more resources to improve individual performance in a whole range of activities. But if the exposure to a stressor is too prolonged or too strenuous, then the stress adaptation may be dangerous. It was to describe this negative scenario that Selye introduced his concept of the General Adaptation Syndrome: GAS. This is a three step process. Beginning with the excessive secretion of hormones, a build up of corticosteroids in the blood stream occurs to a level which eventually disturbs the correct functioning of the body's immune system and directly damages body tissue. The organic damage which Selye envisaged as the outcome of the GAS, was the bleeding stomach ulcer and this image has filtered down into contemporary popular belief. We have come to see ulcers as *the* typical organic manifestation of stress. But there is growing evidence that stress leads to other kinds of organic damage. It seems that the immune system plays a vital function in restraining the development of tumours in the body, a function that is impaired by the presence of an excess of corticosteroids.

The GAS as Selye described it, has been reproduced in experimental conditions with both animal and human subjects. Following the introduction of a number of different threatening physical stimuli: heat, cold, hunger and electric shocks, a wide range of individual response has been recorded. A major finding of these experiments is that perception and emotional arousal are a key feature of the stress reaction. When the same physical stressor is disguised to make it appear more or less threatening, the response varies according to the degree of mental anxiety that is aroused. Furthermore, researchers have also shown that the GAS is initiated not only in response to physical stressors but to psychological stimuli on their own. So it appears that thought processes are a necessary mechanism of stress, acting as the intermediary between the external stimulus and the body's system of defence.

The discovery of the importance of subjective perception in highlighting stressful experiences opens the door to a much larger range of potential stressors. Among these, we can include the personal crises that sociologists have called life events. From this broader conceptualisation, it is possible to begin to understand why certain biographical experiences seem to be associated with illness and disease. Social mobility, changes of marital status, unemployment and even promotion, have all been identified as risk factors for life threatening disease and it is possible that the causal mechanism is stress. Here we find the missing link between life events and the onset of physical symptoms. The process begins through individual exposure to a stressor which may take a variety of basic forms: physical, psychological or social. To be threatening it must be perceived and defined as such by the subject whose emotions are then aroused, triggering off the stress reaction. This alters the balance of hormones in the body and interferes with the capacity of the immune system to protect the individual. In this state of heightened susceptibility the individual exposed to a disease agent is more likely to succumb. The chain of causation in this version of the disease process is more complex than the model depicted at the beginning of this chapter. It begins with the relationship of the individual with an environment full of potential stressors in a variety of different forms. From there it proceeds in the following hypothetical way:-

Figure 5.2 Stress and Illness

1 **Stressor:** e.g. redundancy.

↓

2 **Cognition:** Loss of job equals loss of:- income, means to pay bills and mortgage, status of breadwinner, contact with workmates, everyday routine.

↓

3 **Stress:** Excessive secretion of adrenalin and release of dangerous
│   volume of corticosteroids.
▼

4 **Organic State:** Increased susceptibility through damage to
│   lymphatic system.
▼

5 **Environmental Exposure:** e.g. to disease agent line influenza virus.
▼

6 **Body's response:** Weakened immune system means no resistance.
▼

7 **Symptoms:** Flu.

This stress model of disease finds powerful support in the research of Hinkle who has shown that unrelated episodes of illness in the same person are clustered in specific phases of the lifetime. This suggests that people are more susceptible to disease at particular periods of their lives which may be the critical points of biographical experience when disruptive life events make them more susceptible to disease agents.

This sequence of interactions between social and psychological experience and the material fabric of the body itself undermines the idea of mind and body being separate and autonomous entities. It recalls ideas about the nature of health and human wellbeing which were prevalent before the Cartesian revolution which, as we saw in chapter one (p.533), laid the foundations for the development of the modern bio-mechanical approach with its emphasis on the organic properties of disease (p.531). The model of the disease process in figure 5.2 identifies an important potential role for individuals themselves in the aetiology of disease. It is through the mechanism of individual perception that threats become real suggesting that disease may be prevented if people are prepared to manipulate their ideas about the significance of threatening events and situations. Equally, it implies that potential stressors may be found in the social and economic environment such as, in the above example, the risk of unemployment.

What can people do to protect themselves from stress in the course of everyday life? This question can be approached in two different ways. On the one hand there is the question of whether individuals, given the right frame of mind, can either avoid a potential stressor or lessen its impact by changing the way they *think* about it. On the other is the question of what scope exists for people to take direct action themselves to either escape the threat posed by a stressful event like redundancy or to get over it once it has happened. Each of these different responses, one based in cognitive processes, the other rooted in social action, have been identified as devices for *coping* with stress.

Coping: The Individual Response to Stress

The concept of *coping* was first introduced by Richard Lazarus to describe the psychological efforts individuals make to adapt to stressful experiences. It proved attractive to others working in the field of stress research and has been applied in a number of different ways. As a result the concept of coping cannot be defined unambiguously. In general it refers to the part individuals themselves play in mediating the relationship between stress at source and the risk of impact on their bodies. Among the diversity of applications, two are of particular interest to the sociological reader. They are:- *coping* as a mental and emotional activity, and *coping* as purposeful action. These two alternative uses of the concept will be referred to as *psychological* coping and *social* coping. This distinction also highlights important variations in the degree of self-consciousness in individual attempts to cope with stress. More self-conscious coping strategies are likely to be initiated at an earlier phase in the potential disease process increasing the chance of preventing any physiological manifestation of stress. Less self-conscious coping is more likely to be defensive in character oriented to the suppression of stressful sensations in the body or to minimising organic damage.

The distinction between psychological and social coping is also associated with other differences of meaning. Conceived of as a strictly mental process, coping tends to carry an implication of personal adequacy or even moral correctness. People who cope do not get ill. Those who succumb to stress, falling prey to illness are by definition non-copers. The event of illness therefore reveals a failure to cope with problems in emotional terms, suggesting a lack of personal control. Social coping does not have this tendency of moral valuation because it is applied to all efforts to deal with stress irrespective of how they turn out. For this reason coping may be initiated at any point in the potential disease process and it may succeed or fail. In terms of the chain of causation in figure 5.2, psychological coping would prevent the onset of disease altogether. Social coping on the other hand points to personal efforts to deal with stress at any of the seven stages in addition to any action taken before onset and afterwards in recovery or adaptation to a chronic condition. It describes all the ways people *try* to overcome their difficulties before symptoms develop, during the course of an illness episode and after it, should it lead to a permanent state of disability.

Coping with Stress: Personality

Lazarus also drew attention to the importance of subjective perception in determining the level of stress attached to any life event. In a famous experiment he demonstrated that the physiological impact, (e.g. increased heart rate), of a disturbing set of visual images of circumcision rites varied according to the sound track which accompanied the film. More soothing music produced lower measurements of physiological stress in the audience and vice versa. It was this that led him to emphasise the role of subjectivity in judgements about stressful experience. He described coping as a secondary psychological device, adopted in the face of a stressful event and designed to reduce stress in the human body and thereby prevent the onset of disease. In his interpretation coping is a summary of the psychological properties of individuals who do not develop disease following exposure to threatening events. Prominent among these, is a sense of self confidence and self esteem. Protected by this psychological armour, individuals overcome events which threaten to overwhelm them because they are willing to redefine them as less significant. Antonovsky, who studied concentration camp survivors, uses coping in a similar way. He defines the capacity for coping as a personal sense of social coherence which enables people to insulate themselves from a stressful environment. For Antonovsky coping is a psychological process in which individuals draw on 'resistence resources' to prevent stressful events from overwhelming them. Resistance resources are made up of flexibility of response in awkward situations and access to close relationships and supportive community.

A central element of psychological coping appears to be the capacity to adapt to change. People who are heavily committed to the status quo and who respond to stress in a 'clinging' fashion are most at risk. Those, on the other hand, who can relax their attachment to any valued dimension of their current circumstances, are better equipped to search for and secure alternative sources of personal identification. Inserting this flexible response into figure 5.2 might take the form of an attempt to rationalise the impending redundancy so it no longer appears threatening to the individual: 'It was an awful job anyway' or 'They did me a good turn forcing me to find some other job better suited to my talents'. Here the threat of job loss is diluted by a reassessment of its value to the individual. The sign that individuals have failed to cope, would be an inability to relinquish the high value they placed on the job about to be lost. Instead of acknowledging the reality of threat and setting about the task of 'neutralising' it, the individual tries to deny it. Knowledge of the impending threat is suppressed and feelings about it are bottled up in a vain attempt to pretend it either will not or has not happened. When the inevitable can no longer be resisted, the individual is left demoralised, depressed and defenceless in the face of whatever agents of disease may be lurking about.

Psychological coping appears as a process of dealing with the stresses and strains of everyday life that is more or less determined by fixed attributes of individuals. The ability to cope by acting creatively to redefine personal circumstances so as to minimise threat is made up of personality traits that have been developed in the past rather then constructed in an impromptu fashion out of whatever resources are encountered in the present. These personality traits are acquired in the process of growing up as people learn to respond to particular situations in particular ways. The part they play as coping mechanisms has been widely researched on both sides of the Atlantic and a number of personality based risk factors for disease have been identified. The most famous example is the so-called 'Type A Personality' possessed by people who are prone to coronary disease. Type A behaviour, originally described by Freidman and Rosenman in 1959, has the following typical characteristics:- over-commitment to work, perfectionism, competitiveness, impatience, aggressiveness and intensive striving for achievement. These forms of behaviour have been repeatedly shown in American studies to be more prevalent among people who develop heart and circulatory conditions: hence the label, the *coronary-prone* personality.

The combined characteristics of this personality type bear more than a passing resemblance to the ideal norms of the protestant work ethic whose adherents are the folk heroes of capitalist civilisation. This suggests that the set of behavioural norms held up as *the* role model for the successful businessman, is actually pathological. The idea that competitive entrepreneurs are more prone to disease is quite a well established folk belief. The most typical candidates for stress-induced ulcers and premature heart attacks, are thought to be 'workaholic' businessmen who sacrifice their health by striving after wealth. The evidence reviewed in chapter 4 casts some doubt on the validity of this belief and in fact research in Britain on the risk factors in heart disease lends no support to the 'Type A' hypothesis.

Marmott's study of heart disease in the British Civil Service, clearly shows that those at greatest risk are the lowest grades of manual workers whose occupational lives offer little scope for the development of 'Type A' traits and who achieve negative ratings on the personality inventory designed to measure them. Marmott concludes that the 'Type A' syndrome probably only applies to middle class white American males.

Even so there have been a great many studies in the United States which identify certain personality traits as risk factors in disease. Some show parallels with 'Type A' behaviours, others seem rather different. Those which conflict despite having also been identified among heart disease patients include, rigidity, overconformism and the tendency to be self-sacrificing. These traits are also found among sufferers from lung cancer, rheumatoid arthritis and digestive disorders and among women with breast cancer strong tendencies to emotional inhibition have been uncovered. While much research remains to be done in this area, it does seem that certain modes of response to stressful events may themselves help to increase rather than diminish the risk of disease.

These various attempts to identify personality traits as risk factors for degenerative disease imply that coping and non-coping are habitual responses invoked day in day out to deal with life in general not just with occasional crises. The scope for personal creativity depends on more or less fixed personal characteristics. A flexible and resourceful attitude to both minor and major life events helps people survive them without 'ill-effect', but survival is largely a matter of personality, not the character of the crisis. This raises the interesting question of how fixed these coping responses may be and what scope exists for training individuals to change the way they handle problems through, e.g. psycho-therapeutic methods.

Coping with Stress: Social Action

The best known British study of coping with disease presents a somewhat less deterministic view of the process. In trying to link life events to the onset of depressive illness in women, Brown and Harris concluded that certain factors mediate between potential stressors (life events), and the risk of disease, acting either to increase or decrease individual vulnerability. Four sources of vulnerability are singled out in the onset of depressive illness. These are:- death of a mother before the age of 14, the absence of close and confiding relationships, the lack of a paid job and the presence of dependent children in the home. Three of these are linked to the stage of the life cycle, while one of them, the loss of the mother in childhood, is a more fixed characteristic of individual women. These vulnerability factors predispose a women to depressive illness only when triggered by disruptive or distressing life events. The process of causation is depicted in figure 5.3.

Figure 5.3 The Link between Life Events and Clinical Depression

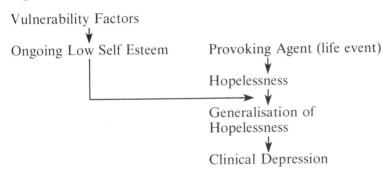

Source: Brown and Harris, 1978, p.238.

For Brown and Harris the factors which weaken the capacity for successful coping are not so much descriptions of individual psyche as descriptions of difficult social circumstances or situations. The four vulnerability factors listed above lead to low self esteem which in turn creates a sense of hopelessness. When a person in this situation is confronted with a difficult life event, the reaction is demoralisation and the inability to cope. Low self esteem is not presented as an invariable feature of the woman's personality. It is the product of her current social situation or, in other words, it is a situational phenomenon and not a personality trait. It is encountered in both working class and middle class women but more frequently in the former. The depressed woman in the Brown and Harris study might, in other circumstances e.g. with a job and a supportive partner, experience a greater sense of self assurance enabling her to handle life crises which could lead to depression.

This study stands at the interface between psychological and sociological coping. Its authors emphasise that the origins of disease are largely found in social and economic circumstances. These circumstances have a double edged effect - they determine both the flow of disruptive life events and personal vulnerability. Working class women experience more depressive illness because of relative social and economic deprivation in general (i.e. more life events) which leaves them more vulnerable (i.e. with fewer material and emotional resources). The focus on self esteem as the key mechanism of coping links this study to the psychological approach, but it also shares much common ground with a social action approach.

Apart from psychological adaptation by what other means can individuals avoid or reduce their exposure to stress? This leads us to the other major application of the concept: to individual efforts to manipulate the environment itself rather than merely trying to manipulate ideas about it. This form of coping is an example of social action. It goes without saying that the initiation of action to cope with the problems of everyday life depends on what people perceive and define as problematic in the first place. What this means is that it is subjective understanding which defines whether the individual is inspired and propelled to act. This is how Weber defined social action as behaviour guided by the meaning that individuals attach to it. The social action perspective must be contrasted with the more purely psychological perspective which restricts the process of stress-adaptation to one of only rethinking events.

Coping as social action unites mental, emotional and behavioural reactions into a single process. Although it may be initiated as a thought process, it will only run to successful completion if it results in effective action to neutralise threat. This implies that mental processes on their own, i.e. redefining a threatening event as non-threatening, are unlikely to constitute a sufficient protection for the individual. Reverting to the example of redundancy in figure 5.2, this would imply that the threat of job loss cannot be made to go away purely through an act of mental will, it will only be removed by individual action to get another job. The willingness to be flexible, to view the redundant job as something that can be replaced becomes converted into a successful coping strategy only if this frame of mind leads to energetic job search activities. All this implies the existence of some sense of personal control over immediate circumstances. The redundant worker has sufficient self-confidence to believe that all is not lost, that other labour market opportunities are available. This fits with the focus on self esteem in the Brown and Harris approach. At the heart of successful coping is an image of self as a valuable worker that another employer will want. But what if there are no vacant positions in the economy? In this situation no amount of vigilant social action in pursuit of self interest may be enough to enable the unemployed to protect themselves from the stress of this life event. Indeed the more the unemployed person strives to replace what has been lost in the context of a deteriorating economy, the more stressful the life event becomes. The alternative option, available to a redundant worker in circumstances of high unemployment, is to come to terms with unemployment as a perpetual state of existence. This involves a redefinition of self as a retired person, but it can offer only a limited refuge from the stress of job loss. Quite apart from the economic losses associated with being jobless, there is the normative pressure of the work ethic which makes the unemployed man below retirement age, feel devalued, obsolete and parasitic, if denied the opportunity to work. The individual in these circumstances is caught in a 'double-bind'; whatever he chooses to do, he cannot win. This is because the solution to the problem lies outside of individual control.

Class and Coping in the Negotiation of Stressful Life Events

The last section introduced a new dimension into the process of coping. It revealed that the backdrop to coping activity, conceptualised as it is in highly individual terms, is the structure of society itself. This structure is made up of an unequal distribution of income, property, educational opportunities and qualifications and occupational rights and privileges which favour some sections of society at the expense of others. This patterned inequality shields the more privileged from the worst effects of stress, it leaves some better equipped to cope with events like redundancy, while leaving others totally exposed. This is the link between the management of stress as an individual preoccupation and the pattern of class inequality in the wider society. Coping in sociological terms can now be seen to be a function of social forces and of social structure. It depends on access to resources which can be employed to soften the impact of disruptive life events and provide a breathing space to give individuals time and opportunity to rethink and if necessary reorganise their lives. People best placed to handle transitions of this kind are in any case least likely to experience them. The risk of unemployment is not randomly distributed in the population, it is concentrated among semi- and unskilled workers, the very same groups who are least well equipped in terms of material resources and qualifications, to cope effectively with it. This was the conclusion of Dohrendwend and Dohrendwend in their study of class and race as sources of stress. They argue that the most important determinant of the capacity to cope with life crises is the context in which coping takes place and this is shaped by factors external to the individual which come from the structure of social and economic inequality.

Coping as social action offers important insights into the pattern of health inequality surveyed in chapter 4. It suggests that stress arousal and capacities, strategies and resources for dealing with it must be seen in the context of poverty and material deprivation. Stated in these terms, the concept of the life event seems to lose some of its explanatory power. It does not capture the *pervasive* prospect for stress arousal in contexts of relative social and economic deprivation. A more apt term for the enduring potential for stress in the everyday experience of working class life is *long term difficulties*. Gerhardt following Brown and Harris, argues that it is necessary to distinguish between *loss events* which are essentially personal and involve emotional adaptation, and *long term difficulties* which can only be resolved by purposeful human action.

> In general, psychological and social coping seem to relate to two types of aetiological event: *loss events* which deprive the individual of a loved object or role seem to call for the reconstitution of the person's perception that the world is meaningful, i.e. 'grief work' is required as an adequate form of dealing with the loss. The second provoking agent-*long term difficulties* - seems to call for a different type of coping. Manipulation of and appeal for help to outside sources such as friends, welfare agencies, employing organisations, etc., are required, i.e. attempts at changing one's social rather than one's psychological world. (Gerhardt 1979, 208).

This means that life events are not all of the same character and that differences between them may require different types of coping. From what we know about the distribution of social and economic welfare, long term difficulties can be expected to predominate as sources of stress for working class people while loss events will loom larger (proportionately) for the middle-classes. Even so, loss events would still feature prominently in working class experience.

The concept of long term difficulties appears more persuasive as a means of depicting the onset and development of degenerative illnesses like heart disease and cancer. To explain the pattern of class inequality in age-specific mortality from these causes, involves putting the question not in the terms of: 'Why did X get this disease?' but, 'Why did X get it so early in the lifetime?' In other words why is a member of social class V likely to die of a heart attack a decade before an age peer in social class I; or, why does this body wear out more rapidly than that one? If stress is the physiological link between organic disease and class inequality, then it is much more likely to be an ever present feature of working class experience, whittling away at the fabric of the human body rather than a one-off bout of anxiety triggered by a disruptive life event. This conclusion was reached by DHSS researchers studying the link between unemployment and mortality. Official government statistics provide clear evidence that unemployed men and their wives suffer an increased risk of mortality (see Fox *et al*, 1984). These findings match the observations of Brenner that trends in mortality and unemployment since the beginning of this century are related, that the rate of each rises and falls together. In studying these statistical correlations Stern and others were led to the conclusion that mortality and unemployment are linked through poverty. The people most at risk of losing their jobs in an economic recession are the poorest members of the community who have the highest death rates at every age. The same group experiences the longest duration of unemployment and this means more or less persistent economic insecurity. At times of economic recession this group is disproportionately represented in the ranks of the unemployed which in turn swells its mortality rate as a whole. However it is economic insecurity as a continuous fact of life rather than unemployment as a temporary disruption that it is the primary cause.

Nevertheless it is important to be aware of the fact that loss events are likely to constitute periodical crises for individuals in all social classes requiring varying degrees of emotional adjustment. A typical example of a loss event is death of a close relative or friend. Given the much higher probability of premature mortality in social classes VI and V (p.572), bereavement events are clearly not free of the influence of social class in their incidence. The research of sociologists like Brown and Harris makes it clear that personal vulnerability to, and the distribution of resources for coping with, loss events are highly class related. Figure 5.4 identifies these links.

Figure 5.4 Social Class, Life Events and Coping

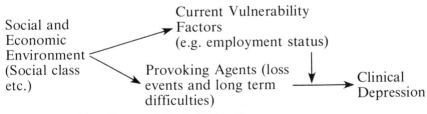

Source: Adapted from Brown and Harris, 1978, p.48.

Coping as social action carried out in the context of a society stratified by class inequalities is likely to mean different things according to where people are located in the social hierarchy. Those with most resources will face fewer life events and have more scope to handle them effectively. Where stressful experience is a much more pervasive feature of everyday life and where opportunities to overhaul everyday circumstances are more restricted, long term adjustment is likely to be rather more defensive in character. Coping may be reduced to rearguard actions designed to ameliorate the effects of stress or even just suppress its physical sensation through resort to medical drugs like tranquillisers or non-medical ones like tobacco and alcohol.

Coping with Stress: Concluding Remarks

The word coping implies that people themselves either consciously or unconsciously, influence their own state of health and even contribute to the onset, progress and outcome of diseases which afflict them. The two major versions of this concept however differ in the extent to which individual motivation is seen as being capable on its own of changing the course of an individual health career. Psychological coping is a mental activity, while social coping unites thought and action into a single activity. In each case there is an implication that ordinary people are not the passive victims of a disease process but may help to bring illness upon themselves by inappropriate responses to stressful circumstances. This chapter has argued that coping should not be analysed in a socio-economic vacuum. The capacity to cope at any level is very largely a product of access to the kind of resources which enable people to exert some degree of control over their circumstances. In this broader sense, the process of coping with stress which threatens to damage the body, offers important insights on the pattern of class inequalities in health examined in chapter 4.

Meanwhile the idea that individual motivation is an important element in outbreaks of disease, has also emerged from an entirely different source in sociology. Talcott Parsons, the most famous American theorist, began his sociological career doing empirical research on medical care. In his book *The Social System* he selects health and medicine to illustrate his ideas on mechanisms of social control. His conclusions on how medicine *functions* to uphold the spirit as well as the physical substance of health will be the theme of the next chapter.

Chapter Six

Medicine as an Institution of Social Control

Medicine and the Social Construction of Illness

What is illness? In chapter 5 a sociological account of the process of illness was presented focusing on personality, behaviour, life events, and class position. This account of how illness happens is of course, only one version of reality drawn from a sociological view of human experience. A medical account of the same process would pick out and emphasise different dimensions. We can predict in a general way what these would be from the bio-mechanical model of illness discussed in chapter 1. It would highlight its organic features, the physical symptoms which prompt the individual to seek out a doctor. The social factors which have priority in a sociological account would fade into the background as attention and effort are directed to the manipulation of visible organic damage.

These alternative accounts, arising from the different disciplinary bases of sociology and medicine, are two versions of the same reality. Neither can claim to capture the whole process of disease or the subjective experience of it. But of the two, medicine is likely to make a much greater impression on what appears real at first hand to the sufferer. This is because people go to doctors to get their symptoms treated and they do not go to sociologists. From the experience of going to the doctor, people learn that sickness is principally a matter of organic disorder because this is what captures the doctor's attention. In this way the *reality* of the illness is interwoven and informed by the experience of being a patient. We have seen in chapter 1 that the effectiveness of medical treatment is generally over-rated. Yet, when things go wrong with our bodies, it is to doctors that we automatically, even 'naturally' turn to for help. We do so because the medical profession occupies a strategic position in society. It is *the* recognised authority on illness and it possesses a virtual monopoly over the practice of healing. This exclusive right, enshrined in Britain, in the Medical Act of 1858, means that only licensed members of the profession may be employed by the state. In the twentieth century, with the growth of the NHS, this monopoly has delivered to doctors almost complete control over all aspects of health care.

In the NHS, the profession has established a network of clinics and hospitals within reach of the whole population and these stand out like the churches and cathedrals of that other once powerful profession, the ministry. Indeed medicine's rise to preeminence has in many ways been accompanied by the social descent of the clergy. Occupying this strategic position in modern society, and surrounded by the symbols of its occupational craft, the medical profession has achieved an unchallenged right to literally define what health and illness are like. In other words our knowledge about health and disease is obtained from medicine, not because it is the scientifically correct version, but because it has secured a position of social influence which has made its own version of what is good for our health *the* orthodox version. This is what is meant by the statement that the social reality of illness is constructed by medicine. Medicine is a social ideology underwritten by the 'neutrality' of science which quite literally defines our understanding i.e. our social ideas, about what health and illness are like. The occupation of doctor therefore is not just a job or a means of income, it is an important social status with power over people and their behaviour. It is in this sense that we may speak of medicine as an institution of social control.

The Sick Role

Going to the doctor is a learning experience. It is the means of transmitting the bio-mechanical model of disease to everyday life. Through the routine contact of doctors and patients in hospitals and surgeries, medical ideology penetrates the subjective experience of illness and herein lies the scope for social control.

> . . . by virtue of being an authority on what illness really is, medicine creates the social possibilities for acting sick . . . its monopoly includes the right to create illness as an official social role. (Freidson 1970, 205-6).

This official social role for the sick person which arises out of the very existence of the medical profession was recognised by Talcott Parsons in *The Social System*. As a systems theorist, Parsons' primary interest was to explain the stability of society as a system of interlocking social roles. The equilibrium of the social system depends on everybody doing a fair share of role playing to keep the system ticking over. Consequently people must be *strongly motivated* by a sense of duty and obligation to their social relationships. Parsons identified sickness as a threat to this sense of interpersonal responsibility because it provides a legitimate reason for people to withdraw from role obligations. For this reason it requires systematic regulation to prevent it being used as an excuse for getting out of customary duties.

This regulation is achieved through the appointment of doctors as (unselfconscious) agents of social control in a process which simultaneously creates an officially sanctioned *Sick Role*. By embracing the sick role, i.e. going to the doctor, the individual sufferer is able to gain social recognition for any symptoms and at the same time society is able to isolate and regulate what might become an outbreak of 'role obligation evasion' which could 'infect' other people. The sick role therefore is an example of *motivated deviance*, a social invitation to temporarily withdraw from role obligations and submit oneself to the officially recognised treatment. In this way Parsons identified in the doctor's role, the important function of maintaining social responsibility among the ill. The silent directive is 'get better quickly because the stability of society depends upon you'. If outbreaks of sickness were left to the whims of individuals in the private sphere of domestic life, they might gradually corrode people's sense of duty to work, to family life, to the community. Only by bringing sickness into the public sphere and encasing it in a system of social control would the risks of role evasion be kept to a minimum.

Vulnerability and Deviance: Two Dimensions of the Sick Role

The sick role is testimony to Parsons' insight on the penetration of social processes into all spheres of human experience. Most people see sickness and disease as biological events somehow apart from societal influence. Parsons' originality in suggesting that they are in essence social phenomena is akin to that of Durkheim when he insisted that suicide was not a matter of individual psychology, but a social fact (see p.599). Nevertheless the sick role has been a controversial concept in the sociology of medicine. This is because of its functionalist character. Parsons implies that the power of professions like medicine to shape ideas and knowledge and to dictate behaviour, are necessary, even good for the maintenance of social stability. He appears to accept the professions' own altruistic propaganda that they are first and foremost oriented to the service of the community not to self interest and that they can be entrusted with monopoly privilege on this account. In his view the necessity for the social control of sickness derives from the needs of the social system and the medical profession is the most appropriate and trustworthy candidate for the guardianship of this function. By other accounts, and Freidson is the leading exponent, the drive to control and dominate the sphere of health and sickness, is found in professional ambition itself and the selfless ideology of community service is little more than a means to this end (see p.632).

The incumbent of the sick role is a patient and, as the word suggests, the expectations of the role are passivity, trust and a willingness to wait for medical help. In other words the sufferer is not held responsible for illness and it is up to others to care for and cure the condition. These expectations arise from the obvious incapacity of the sufferer but also from bio-medical imagery which depicts disease as something that happens to people and not something that is within their control. Getting better therefore cannot be achieved by individuals of their own accord. It involves medical guidance and the requirement that individuals submit their bodies to medical inspection and intervention. This latter necessity is one reason medical work needs social regulation. Quite apart from the awkward necessity to expose one's nakedness to a stranger — a transgression of normal rules of social interaction — treatment itself could lead to irreversible damage, or even death. Combined with the personal insecurity, which the sick already feel on account of worrying symptoms, this makes patient-hood a particularly vunlerable social status. In such circumstances, how can people be expected to reach rational decisions about who to consult and what to pay? How, moreover, can society protect the sick from the risk of exploitation by unscrupulous practitioners who might take advantage of their vulnerable position? This is one theme of the social construction of illness. It stresses the innocence of the sick, their passivity in the onset of disease and in treatment, and their vulnerability in the marketplace as consumers of medical therapy.

In contrast to this image of sickness as a status which may be exploited, is one in which it appears as a means of exploiting other people. Since sickness allows people to withdraw from normal social obligations, it provides both opportunity and grounds for the evasion of social responsibilities. This theme is epitomised in the image of the 'malingerer' who fakes illness in order to get out of doing things or the 'hypochondriac' for whom sickness is a permanent but imaginary state of invalidism. These stereotypes of the 'misuse' of illness, are a disguised form of deviance. This is the second theme in the social construction of illness. It stresses the difficulty of identifying genuine sickness and the importance of not leaving it to ordinary people. These elements of the patient role emphasising the need for external intervention and surveillance, give rise to the other theme in the social construction of illness.

Vulnerability and *deviance* are twin dimensions of the sick role and they call for social regulation in two simultaneous directions. On the one hand it is the patient who requires some degree of social protection on account of weakness and vulnerability. On the other, what needs to be guarded against is the risk that the sickness might become a device for evading role obligations thereby weakening the 'motivational' structure of the social system.

Parsons identifies four normative expectations which attach to the *sick role:* two rights and two duties. They are as follows:-

Rights

(1)   Depending on the severity of the illness, an entitlement to some exemption from normal social activities including in extreme cases a requirement to curtail them completely.

(2)   Freedom from personal responsibility for the illness and for recovery. The misfortune of sickness is not the patient's own fault and recovery is not expected to occur through an act of personal will. The patient cannot help it and needs to be taken care of.

Obligations

(1)   Being sick must be viewed as undesirable. This means that the patient must strive to get better. There should be no resignation to the illness state, nor should any advantage be taken of any secondary gains which arise out of being the centre of attention and concern.

(2)   An obligation to seek technically competent help and to co-operate in the process of treatment.

The rights and the obligations are conditional upon one another. The sick cannot expect to be granted time off with sympathy and support if they do not communicate a desire to get well by seeking out the appropriate treatment.

Note how the image of passivity and innocence attaching to the sick person is emphasised as a device to control deviance. By removing individual initiative from decisions about the reality and severity of symptoms, the risk of their being used for subversive purposes can be minimised.

This interpretation of medicine as an agent of social control *functioning* to maintain the stability of society has emerged in some more recent Marxist accounts (see p.642). Naturally they take a more negative view of social stability, i.e. the capacity of industrial capitalism to perpetuate itself without the revolution Marx predicted. To explain the absence of revolutionary fervour in the working class, modern Marxists have unwittingly followed Parsons in a search for the mechanisms of social control which *they* see as necessary to reduce the ideological contradictions of the capitalist system. Medicine is depicted as a means of disguising the unacceptable face of patriarchal capitalism (see p.641). By organising health care around 'atomised' individuals and by focusing attention on the organic dimensions of disease, its real social nature is disguised. Medicine is presented as producing the illusion that capitalism has a progressive technological solution to all ills and it even serves to quell symptoms of rebellion at the kitchen sink through modern wonder drugs like Valium. In consequence ill-health does not become a political issue in the society at large nor is it recognised as the product of conflicting interests in the privacy of family life.

Similar themes are at the heart of Illich's critique of medicine's role in contemporary society. He also focuses on medicine's capacity to deprive people of responsibility for their own health and to stultify personal initiative and willpower for self care. For Illich though it is over-industrialisation and not merely its capitalist variety that is the root cause (see p.567).

Patienthood in Practice

Common to functionalist accounts of medicine's role in society is an image of the sick person as a highly conditioned, passive social actor who has learned to respond obediently to the medical script of illness. The patient looks like the epitome of what Garfinkel called the *Cultural Dope,* an object of manipulation who lacks the will to resist or the imagination to innovate in social relationships. How does this image measure up to the way people actually behave when they get sick? The sick role has proved to be a fertile stimulus to research in the sociology of medicine whose findings suggest that contact between doctors and patients is not quite as Parsons envisaged.

The sick role presents the therapeutic relationship in an aura of harmony and co-operation where the ideal patient is compliant, submissive and co-operative. Consulting room tales tell a different story of conflict, anxiety and tension. Perhaps this is unsurprising given the gap in expectations on each side. As Freidson points out, the typical consultation brings together committed involvement and casual detachment. To the patient the reason for consultation may be pressing, intimate and personally crucial, to the doctor it represents no more than a brief exchange, a drop in an ocean of symptoms to be dealt with as a part of routine work. Given this divergence, disappointment seems inevitable with the doctor appearing impatient and unsympathetic while the patient looks agitated and demanding. Conflict between doctor and patient is widespread. Anne Cartwright in one of her many studies of medical care, reveals that it is doctors rather than patients, who are the most likely to voice dissatisfaction. She found that more than 25% of general practitioners in a survey, complained that over half of their patients consulted for trivial reasons and 56% complained about their lack of humility. It seems that patients do not respect medical judgement as much as they should and they demand treatment as of right instead of requesting it in a deferential manner. This reveals an interesting conceptual contradiction in the sick role. The patient is supposed to defer to the technical expertise of the doctor, to be passive in the process of diagnosis and treatment. Yet, it is patients themselves who have to make the initial decision that their symptoms are serious enough to warrant the call on expert help. The ideal patient from the perspective of Cartwright's dissatisfied GPs, would seem to be resourceful and well informed about symptomatology outside the consulting room, but willing to abandon his fate to medical authority once inside it.

Another conceptual problem of the sick role is the difficulty of identifying the transition between health and illness. It assumes that the transition, while not unproblematic, nevertheless has relatively clear boundaries. Much empirical research on the other hand suggests otherwise. Becoming ill can be an unpredictable, attenuated process in which the difference between being well and unwell is unclear. This means that the sick role is an uncertain status, to be negotiated rather than simply adopted. This is a familiar criticism of the tendency of *structural functionalist role theory* to ignore the problems of entry and exit to new social roles. In this case the issue of role transition is complicated by the fact that it is not at all easy to agree on what constitutes illness. While some sociologists researching the sick role seem to accept the bio-mechanical model with its assumption of the existence of a class of organic illness with identifiable symptoms, others do not. They insist that illness is itself a matter of societal definition much influenced by value judgements about what is normal or abnormal. From their perspective doctors arbitrating the individual entry to the sick role are liable to find themselves exercising moral rather than medical judgement.

The argument that the sick role oversimplifies the nature of the transition between health and sickness is highlighted in research on chronic illness. This is illness which is acknowledged to be long-standing, requiring adjustment to disability and infirmity rather than leading simply to recovery. As a type, long term or chronic illness is much more widespread than the acute type implicit in the sick role. The idea of illness as an acute crisis rather a chronic and persisting state, incorporated in the sick role suggests that Parsons identifies with the professional rather than the lay viewpoint. The bio-mechanical model favoured by the medical profession portrays disease as temporary phenomena, disorders which ought to go away if properly treated. This episodic view reflects more than anything else the episodic pattern of treatment and the profession's indifference to the need to follow up patients who do not return for further treatment. Most degenerative conditions treated in the acute wards of general hospitals are in every sense chronic from the viewpoint of the sufferer.

Chronic illness poses particular problems for the smooth performance of both parties to the sick role. At one level it implies more serious and longer term interference with customary role performance and therefore presents precisely the kind of potential deviance that Parsons saw as threatening to the social system. But equally it leads to difficulties in the therapeutic relationship with which doctors are ill-equipped to deal. By the fact of its persistence, chronic illness has proved resistant to treatment and, by exposing the limitations of medicine, it undermines the technical superiority of the doctor. As a result the therapeutic relationship is likely to be transformed in two ways. Against the shifting background of medical knowledge, the patient may well become more of an expert on his own specific condition than the doctor for whom it is but one of many to be treated on a given day. Secondly, given the failure to find a cure, the only resource the doctor has to offer the patient in exchange for consultation may be a signature on an invalidity certificate, in other words, long term permission for role deviance. Hardly what Parsons had in mind for the purposes of social control. Alternatively, therapy might take the form of counselling, aimed at maintaining the patient's motivation to conquer disability and 'get on with life'. This would fit with Parsons' idealisation of the social control function of medical work but it would hardly fit with the organic ethos of orthodox medicine which leaves doctors ignorant and suspicious of treatment oriented to a mind over matter focus. So it appears that the sick role seriously misconstrues the real nature and duration of sickness as it is subjectively experienced and what medical treatment would look like if it were to be seriously oriented to social control,

Another difficulty lies in the assumption that sickness, venereal disease apart, is a morally neutral category and not the responsibility of the individual sufferer. This is another legacy of the bio-mechanical model with its image of disease being caused by invading alien micro-organisms. In the history of popular ideas about health and illness, this notion is definitely a minority viewpoint. The much more prevalent view has been that victims themselves are partly to blame for their own misfortune. Before germ theory, disease and disability were quite likely to be seen as a divine judgement or as punishment visited upon a sinner. Knowledge about the true mechanism of infection undermined these beliefs in the late nineteenth century. But today the model of the innocent victim is becoming tarnished once more by the growing belief that the onset of degenerative disease linked to smoking or diet is the sufferer's own fault. To the extent that these beliefs penetrate medical treatment they must negate that basic right of Parsons' sick role, that the individual is held blameless.

The lack of fit between the ideal norms of the sick role and research findings on doctor/patient interaction has prompted the development of a number of classificatory schemes designed to explain the variation that has been found in practice. Szasz and Hollander suggest that the relationship of doctors and patients varies according to where it takes place and to the nature of the medical problem involved. They identify three types of therapeutic relationship:-

(1) Activity/passivity: where the doctor dominates an asymmetrical relationship. This pattern is the role model for the medical emergency where the patient may even be unconscious.

(2) Guidance/co-operation: the most prevalent pattern where problematic symptoms predispose a co-operative response to medical advice. This is closest to the ideal expectations of the sick role.

(3) Mutual participation: marked by equality between doctor and patient and found where patients suffer from chronic conditions which involve a great deal of self care.

These three types form a continuum in which the guidance/co-operation model is the mid-point. Clearly where doctor/patient interaction takes the form of mutual participation, the asymmetry which Parsons saw as paramount to the social control function of medicine will be absent.

An alternative classification, developed by Byrne and Long, arranges doctor/patient communication on a continuum of doctor-to-patient-centred treatment. This classification, depicted in figure 6.1, was based on an analysis of a large number of tape recordings of patients consulting doctors. Four styles of communication were uncovered.

Figure 6.1. Doctor/Patient Communication

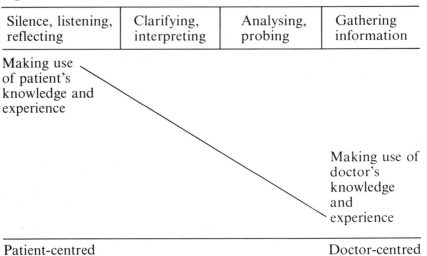

Silence, listening, reflecting	Clarifying, interpreting	Analysing, probing	Gathering information

Making use of patient's knowledge and experience

Making use of doctor's knowledge and experience

Patient-centred   Doctor-centred

Source: Adapted from Byrne and Long 1976, p.91.

Most studies, including that of Byrne and Long, find that doctor-centred interaction is by far and away the most prevalent form. In the words of one of their doctor respondents,

> The doctor's primary task is to manage his time. If he allows patients to rabbit on about their conditions, then the doctor will lose control of time and will spend all day in his surgery listening to irrelevant rubbish. Efficient doctoring is characterised by a quick clean job.

Getting a 'quick clean job' done in the Byrne and Long survey meant an average of five minutes for each consultation varying from six to four minutes for middle and working class patients respectively. This time difference helps explain why middle class patients were more likely to get patient-centred treatment while their working class counterparts put up with the doctor-centred variety.

It appears then that time as much as anything else constrains the possibility for mutuality in the therapeutic relationship. But there are other obstacles. Another constraint which stands out from research is that doctors deliberately try to keep patients in the dark to make their own job easier. They do so by employing what Goffman called *information control*. By restricting the flow of information about diagnosis and treatment, doctors can cover up uncertainty on their own part, while inducing anxiety and helplessness in their patients. The use of this method for managing patients has been reported by a number of studies. Millman, in a survey of medical errors and their impact on patient trust, concludes that withholding information is the principal means doctors adopt to protect themselves from the possibility of error. The more ignorant the patient about diagnosis and treatment, the less his or her ability to detect mistakes if and when they occur. The reluctance on the part of doctors to provide a free flow of information about treatment is signified by the profession's unwillingness to evaluate the work of colleagues even to the extent of withholding vital evidence about possible negligence.

In studies of satisfaction and dissatisfaction among patients, non-disclosure of information stands out as the running sore of the sick role relationship. Where, it occurs it has the effect of alienating patient from doctor and reducing the likelihood that recommended treatment will be followed. This helps to illuminate the reason why, when the doctor respects the patient's feelings, taking what they have to say seriously and sharing information, compliance with 'doctor's orders' is more forthcoming. In more doctor-centred relationships on the other hand, the submissive and compliant posture of patients while on medical premises, may turn into a refusal to 'take the medicine' when they get home. But of course, depending on where treatment takes place, patients do not always have the same degree of choice about whether or not to obey the doctor. The hospital is one site for treatment where opportunities for patient resistance are much less and no account of social control and medicine would be complete without some consideration of this.

The Hospital and the Mortification of Self

The patient's freedom to negotiate a tolerable relationship with the doctor in pursuit of medical advice and treatment, is linked to the power and resources that each can muster. In the community a person has much more freedom of manoeuvre to decide how much time and energy to devote to the sick role. Inside the hospital, the sick role comes to dominate the identity of the person and all thoughts, behaviour and access to other people becomes oriented to the demands of medical treatment.

In a hospital setting doctors possess much more power to make patients conform to their ideal requirements of unquestioning, passive obedience. The rituals of admission seemed designed to communicate this change in the balance of power in the sick role. Goffman, in his study of the manner in which *total institutions* reprogramme their inmates, describes this initiation process as a *mortification of self*. This means quite literally the death of the self. How is it accomplished?

Changes of social status are often accompanied by ceremonies designed to emphasise the transition taking place. An obvious *public* one, marriage, has a clear *rite de passage* which openly displays the change of circumstances of the newly-weds. Other ceremonies are more private experiences, designed to communicate and enforce a change of circumstances to the person directly involved rather than to outsiders. These social transitions are less easily distinguished because they are embedded in things that people take for granted. The process of being admitted to hospital is one of these. It is characterised by a number of procedures designed, in Goffman's words to 'trim and shape' the new inmate for life on the ward. On admission, the person is delivered by kin into the hands of a uniformed member of staff who directs the initiation. Forms must be filled in to create a dossier of personal details — the case notes — open to inspection by staff but not to the patient. Everyday clothing and personal possessions must be removed and taken away to emphasise that escape is impossible. An identity bracelet is attached to the body as a mark of the impersonality of the new environment in which the person will not be automatically recognised. The institution may insist on certain 'cleansing' procedures such as shaving, enemas and bathing which serve to introduce the newcomer to the fact that everyone in white has the right to manipulate the body and marking loss of personal control over it. The whole experience may be summarised as one in which the old identity is taken off and a new one installed marked by an intermediate point of physical and psychological nakedness.

When the patient's kin depart carrying away any personal belongings for which there is no room on the ward, the new patient experiences a sense of being cut adrift in an alien environment in which everyone is a stranger. There may follow, as Coser suggests, a sense of personal betrayal. The family was complicit in the act of incarceration. They co-operated in the removal of personal effects and the new inmate may realise that admission represents a release from the onerous duties of caring for the sick person at home. This may be communicated to the patient emphasising the isolation of the new status and the absence of allies. The asymmetry between staff and patients is marked by the contrast of the starched uniforms and insignia of office of medical and nursing staff to the patient's state of semi-undress. Being perpetually dressed for bed stresses the irrelevance of time, while the scantiness of patient clothing highlights diminishing control over the body.

Goffman stresses that the key feature of a total institution, is the barrier between self and the outside world. As long as a person is at home, even if bedridden, there is some control over daily routine. In the hospital all vestiges of personal power are removed as the person becomes subject to the unpredictable whims of staff. The patient may be left in suspense waiting hour by hour for a chance to speak to the consultant physician, who knows all the secrets of the case and who will determine his or her fate on the ward. The unpredictability of the great one only serves as a reminder that the patient's time does not matter, he or she is at the disposal of medical staff who turn up at their own convenience and not at the convenience of the patient. Daily personal routines, which give structure and meaning to everyday life in the outside world, lose significance inside a total institution. Being an inmate is a twenty-four hour a day preoccupation and the only basis for social interaction. The patient is dissociated from previous sources of social identification. Attempts to draw on past biography, to restore a sense of personal identity, are shunned by staff who are only interested in physical symptoms and have little time to listen to personal reminiscences or look at photographs. As a result the patient is rendered socially anonymous, no more than a bundle of organic symptoms ready for bio-medical processing.

Admission to hospital therefore, by isolating the individual from a community of social support and by systematically denying the relevance of previous bases of social identification, strips the social identity leaving the individual socially naked. As a result, to the fears and anxiety already aroused on account of threatening symptoms a new and equally threatening transformation of self is added which robs the individual of self esteem. It is a process which fits with, even if it is not specifically designed for, the bio-mechanical model of treatment. This model, oriented to the physiology of anonymous human beings and hospital routines, seems designed to sweep away personal social characteristics which get in the way of diagnosis. What are the implications of this process of mortifying the self for recovery and/or the need to adjust to a more permanent state of disability?

From a non-medical perspective the mortification of self would appear to make an illness worse because it heightens the sense of anxiety. Furthermore, by denying the relevance of the patient's social identity in the world outside, treatment in hospital may actually obscure important clues to diagnosis. Elements of self wiped out by the process of conditioning people for life on the ward, may be the very means of understanding how the illness started in the first place. The process could hardly be considered productive in terms òf the intended socialisation functions of the sick role, since the patient, deprived of a sense of personal identity and of role obligations, may need resocialisation on discharge in order to pick up the threads of previous life. This might prove even more problematic if, as is often the case, treatment has not been particularly successful and adaptation to a more permanent state of disability is necessary. In these circumstances, the hospital experience may have the effect of adding to the sense of physical disability, a permanent disability of *self*.

Some Concluding Remarks on the Sick Role

Parsons saw the sick role as a means of stabilising society by upholding the sense of duty and obligation that individuals feel towards one another. This is achieved through the institutionalisation of sickness as an official social role to be monitored and controlled by doctors. It means that medical treatment has the object of making the symptoms disappear, not only in the physical sense but also in a motivational sense. The doctor's social control function is to guide the patient back to full participation in society as soon as possible, thereby reducing the length of 'absenteeism' from customary social roles. If Parsons is right, we would expect the medical model of treatment, i.e. the bio-mechanical approach, to be implicitly, if not explicitly tailored to this social control function. This would require that doctors be willing to recognise the importance of the mental as well as the physical dimensions of illness and to extend their therapeutic approach to counselling their patients and encouraging them to conquer physical disability. There is little to indicate either in the structure of the bio-mechanical model itself or in reports of doctor patient interaction, that this is a feature of medical treatment. On the contrary, the strategy of the physician is to emphasise the organic dimensions of illness. Patients are encouraged to wait for the doctor to make them better rather than take any personal initiative themselves. Any counselling performed in primary care in the NHS is carried out, if at all, by social workers attached to clinics and health centres. In the hospital sector which consumes three quarters of the NHS budget, the effects of treatment seem to be designed to destroy self respect rather than to uphold it. Moreover, in judging the achievement of the medical profession in the role envisaged for it by Parsons, we would have to conclude from statistics of sickness absence that it has failed. Since the NHS was established in 1948, the number of days lost through certified sickness, has increased every year and greatly outnumbers those lost on account of industrial disputes (see p.641). Whatever the achievements of the NHS therefore, improvements in 'health' as witnessed by motivation of the workforce, is not one of them.

At the very least this suggests serious flaws in any sociological explanation of the social role of medicine as a means of either upholding the work ethic or, for that matter, the productivity of workers or the profits of their employers. This leads us to consider just whose interests medicine does serve in contemporary society, the subject of chapter 7.

Chapter Seven

The Power of Medicine in Society

Profession or Class: The Roots of Medical Power

What is the source of the power of medicine in society? Among sociologists the answer varies according to which major theoretical tradition they favour. Those influenced by Marx, see power as ultimately rooted in economic relationships. All power in capitalist society flows from the ruling class who own the productive resources of society. By controlling the economy on which the whole population depends for survival, the capitalist class dictates the shape of social institutions and ideas to suit its own interests. Medicine is one such institution. It exercises power over the cultural definition of health and disease; as orthodox treatment it shapes the personal experience of illness and it takes the form it does because it suits the purposes of capitalism.

Marxist theory is sometimes described as economic reductionism. This means that everything to be explained is ultimately reduced to an economic source. A basic distinction is made between the base and the superstructure. The base is the foundation of society. Everything depends upon it. It consists of economic institutions and relationships: private property, the market and classes. Resting on the base are the other social institutions that sociologists study, law, religion, the family, education and so on. In calling these a superstructure, the intention is to convey their superficial nature in relation to the base. They are, moreover, not merely less important than the economic institutions in determining what a society is like, they are actually shaped by the economic base. The family for example, with its gendered social roles, is presented as a development that has come about in response to the logic of capitalism. Similarly medicine is presented as a tool of the ruling economic class. Each is a part of the superstructure, tailored to the needs of capital accumulation, with little autonomy of its own.

630

This means that medical care, far from being a humanitarian, philanthropic activity, is actually geared to the business of class exploitation. It performs two different kinds of function for capital. Its ideological function is to disguise the true nature of disease and how it is caused. For some Marxists, e.g. Navarro and McKinley, it also plays a more direct part in the process of capital accumulation. It is itself a form of profit making commodity production and, by maintaining the health of the workforce, it also improves productivity and therefore profits. As servants of the ruling class, the medical profession enjoys high economic rewards in return for exercising delegated power. As long as doctors remain loyal to their paymasters, medicine, as a social institution, is secure. The power and privilege of the medical profession results from its value to the capitalist class in maintaining the status quo. But this does not give the profession control over its work: doctors remain the puppets of those who own the commanding heights of the economy.

Other sociologists, less inclined to accept the existence of only one source of power in society, are more likely to trace the power of medicine to other social institutions. For them, politics and ideology are equally important means of generating and exercising power and cannot be reduced to a veneer of capitalist economic interests. This viewpoint is influenced by the theories of the German sociologist Max Weber who, while accepting the power of economic institutions to help determine social organisation, laid equal stress on politics, religion and other social institutions. Contemporary sociologists who take their cue from Weber, are more likely to see the source of medicine's power lying within its political organisation as a profession rather than in any allegiance to the ruling economic class.

Weber was particularly concerned to distinguish what the exercise of power looks and feels like in practice, particularly from the subordinate perspective. He emphasises the difference between the legitimate and the non-legitimate domination by one person or group over others. When the exercise of power carries social legitimacy, it is invested with authority and those on the receiving end are likely to accept their subordination as quite right and proper. When social legitimacy is absent on the other hand, the powerful cannot count on the willing submission of the people they dominate and may well need to resort to naked coercion to get their way. Clearly non-legitimate domination is a much less stable form of power and unsuited to the long term maintenance of social order. How is the means of legitimate domination generated and sustained? Weber identifies three ways:- (1) tradition, (2) charisma and (3) rational-legal authority. The third predominates in modern industrial society. Rational-legal power is the power of office. Its rise to pre-eminence in contemporary society is connected to the growth of bureaucracy, in which power is exercised according to written rules and regulations. It is to this kind of power base that sociologists like Freidson, have traced the origins of medical authority. By this account the power of medicine lies in its political organisation as a profession.

Professional Power and Medicine

Freidson defines a profession as an occupation with a special form of organisation, a special form of legal power (analogous to that of bureaucratic officials), and, in the case of medicine, a special position of dominance in the set of occupations that provide health care in modern society. Unlike many sociologists before him, who were prone to define the professions in terms of the altruistic claims they made for themselves, Freidson argues that the professional ethic of community service should be seen as a device used by occupational groups to obtain exclusive rights to practice. The power of the medical profession lies in its success in having secured, by political means, a legal monopoly over the practice of healing in contemporary industrial society. This made the doctor *the* official expert on health and illness in modern society, a title enshrined in written law. This is the legal-rational base of medical power. It consists of a monopoly, granted by the state, giving the profession exclusive occupational rights, freedom to control the process of recruitment, training and practice and control over the conduct of individual members who each enjoy the right of clinical autonomy. Clinical autonomy means that no lay person can look over the shoulder of the doctor to judge the quality of work and in practice it means that no doctor will ordinarily judge the quality of a colleague's work or even release information that would allow such an evaluation to be made. It is autonomy over the technical aspects of work that Freidson picks out as the essential element of professional power which gives the doctor, in societies as diverse as the USA and the Soviet Union a similar degree of occupational freedom and control over the content of work. For the same reason he suggests that the medical profession is largely autonomous of the ruling class in any society and would be likely to survive any revolutionary social change. What the state has given therefore, it cannot necessarily take away.

Some observers have doubted Freidson's claim that the profession of medicine enjoys similar privileges in the Soviet Union and the United States. They point to the fact that most doctors in Russia are women. This is claimed to be a sign of its weakness. If it were as privileged in the Soviet Union, as Freidson makes out, more men would pursue it. Furthermore, doctors in the Soviet Union are part of the state salariat, they are like civil servants with much less control over the conditions as opposed to the content of work. This suggests that the power of the profession depends upon the relationship of medicine to the state. In both societies the state grants doctors their monopoly of practice but, in the USA, the provision of medical care is largely left to market forces. On this basis we might predict that when medical care is a citizenship right and the direct responsibility of the state, the profession will be less autonomous and more dependent on the political elite for resources. However the situation in Britain would not offer much support to this conclusion. Although more than 90% of medical care is paid for by government, state control over the profession is in some ways less than in the USA. Organised medicine had an outright victory in their struggle with Aneurin Bevan when the NHS was introduced and governments of both right and left have learned to be wary of making it a political enemy. Certainly there is much less scope in Britain for doctors to be held legally accountable for negligence than there is in the United States.

In other ways the situation in Britain is more like the Soviet Union. Compared to other advanced industrial societies, Britain spends less of her national income (approx. 5.5%) on medical care. The government has more control over the total volume of resources devoted to the NHS, because it is directly funded out of taxation revenue. In societies where medical care is paid for through state subsidised insurance such as France (6.9% GNP) or Sweden (7.3% GNP), costs have risen more and consume a larger share of gross national product (GNP). However within the NHS budget, doctors have retained considerable influence over how much goes to specific specialities. Most resources are spent on acute hospitals, the 'high tech' sector. The 'Cinderella' services are the same in all societies. They include services for the mentally ill, the mentally handicapped, the elderly and the chronically sick.

Freidson does *not* pick out technical expertise or esoteric knowledge as a basic source of medical power. Unlike Parsons, who took the technical expertise of the medical profession for granted as a self evident reason for their occupational privilege in the labour market, Freidson argues that a special body of professional knowledge can be generated just as easily after, as before a monopoly of practice has been obtained. If one thinks about it this is necessarily the case. If outsiders were capable of judging the technical merits of the profession's case there could be no claim to autonomy of technique. Both lay public and the political elite alike must take on trust the profession's claim to *know* best. This is why Weber pointed to *legal rights of office* as the source of professional power rather than scientific or technical expertise. The power of medicine is a part of the tendency to bureaucratisation in modern life. It is part of the drive to subject all areas of human experience to rational order and discipline. This leaves us with the question of how an occupational group like doctors was so politically successful?

The Social Rationale for Professional Privilege

We have already hinted, in chapter 6, at the rationale for subjecting the healing craft to professional control. The sick role it will be remembered has two dimensions, deviance and vulnerability (see p.618). It is mainly on account of the second of these that doctors have based their successful appeals for professional monopoly rights.

The sick are vulnerable to exploitation in a number of ways. To begin with techniques of healing are often physically invasive, breaching social taboos of every kind. The doctor claims the right of privileged access to the private body space of the client in order to conduct examinations and carry out treatment which could lead to irreversible damage or even death. This underlines the necessity for some degree of regulation to ensure minimum standards of competence. Equally, given the potential for intimacy in the therapeutic relationship, there is a need for high ethical standards to prevent practitioners from divulging personal information entrusted to them or from getting emotionally or even sexually involved with their clients.

A further problem lies in the asymmetry of the relationship. Patients are supposed to give consent to treatment but in reality they are so dependent on the doctor for guidance that their decisions can seldom be more than rubber stamps of medical advice. Given this asymmetry, patients could be exposed to experimental or risky techniques without even knowing it. This difficulty is magnified by the fact that most forms of treatment carry no absolute guarantee of success so patients seldom have any come back if things go badly wrong. In consequence a high degree of trust is inherent in the relationship. This means that medical treatment is not well suited to being bought and sold in the marketplace, because its customers cannot be expected to exercise the 'natural instinct' for striking a good bargain that they use when purchasing other forms of personal service. This explains how doctors succeeded in obtaining a public monopoly over the treatment of sickness. The key to their political success was to join together into a single profession which could be clearly identified and which claimed to offer a uniformly high standard of competence and ethical conduct. By sheltering under the reputation of their profession, doctors appear to the public as a standard product, equally skillful and equally trustworthy. Given the absence of any systematic evaluation of medical technique, it is virtually impossible to demonstrate medical incompetence, and the occasional expulsion of deviants who break the medical code of practice serves to uphold the fundamental integrity of the profession as a whole. In Britain, the medical profession has shown itself more willing to punish unprofessional behaviour than its sister profession the law. This pragmatism is a sign of political skill. The law society, by defending indefensible cases of malpractice, has made the legal profession vulnerable to its critics, with the result that some of its privileges e.g. the conveyancing monopoly, have been put at risk.

The interpretation of professional power and privilege as the outcome of political action, must be clearly distinguished from structural functionalist explanations which accept the profession's benign self image as well as the claim that public and professional interest are one and the same thing. For Freidson, the first and foremost goal of the profession is to serve the interests of its members and there is no necessary identity between these and those of the general public. This contrasts with Parsons' vision of the patient as the prototype of the professional client, a classic case of vulnerability and dependency whose needs cannot be catered for in the context of open-market competition. From this viewpoint the inherent risk of granting monopoly rights to an occupational group (that their prices will rise in the absence of competition) is offset by the fact that doctors, like all professions have a vocational orientation that is altruistic. This means that they are basically oriented in their work to serve the community rather than to personal gain. In medicine this means the Hippocratic Oath which enjoins doctors to do all in their power to help the sick irrespective of material interest. This selfless quality of putting the client first, is in addition to the other occupational attributes which Parsons argued were a general feature of the division of labour of industrial societies. These include: achievement values, universalism, functional specificity, and affective neutrality. Borrowing Freidson's translation of these, what this means in terms of medical practice is that:-

> . . . it is expected that physicians be recruited and practise on the basis of ability rather than ascribed characteristics, that they rely on generally accepted scientific standards rather than on particularistic ones, restrict

their work to the limits of their technical competence, work objectively without emotional involvement, and finally, put the patient's interests before their own. (Freidson 1970, 159).

These are the reasons doctors themselves advance in defence of their exclusive rights to practice. Some economists, notably Milton Friedman, have argued that professional claims to protect clients are fraudulent. They make the practice of medicine inefficient and non-accountable, in short, the best closed shop in the labour market. The experience of the NHS suggests that there is some force to this criticism given the many forms of treatment which are not properly evaluated either before being introduced or even after they have been in use for a long time (see p.529). This points to a problem in both Parsons' and Freidson's explanation of the power of medicine. One would expect that in granting a legal monopoly the state would expect the profession to demonstrate some degree of occupational competence and effectiveness in practice. Yet, if medical opinion rather than scientific fact (see p.528) is how the profession operates today, over a century ago when it obtained its legal privileges from the British State, there would have been even less to go on in terms of effective therapy.

Freidson argues that a *consulting* profession must be capable of demonstrating some degree of effectiveness with a lay public in order to sustain professional integrity and public confidence. *Scholarly* professions like university professors are insulated from the public and do not need to justify their privileges in the same way. In the light of present day knowledge, it is difficult to see how the proven effectiveness of medical expertise could have formed any part in the profession's bid for legal privilege.

However treatment is only one aspect of the medical task. An equally important goal of medical consultation, for both doctors and patients, is diagnosis. People in the throes of a health crisis need to know what is wrong even though they may be disappointed when the medical judgement is announced. In this respect, the limitations of treatment itself are less relevant than professional skill at description and classification.

In Britain the period in which the profession was consolidated was one characterised by substantial social and economic change. Industrialisation had led to the growth of a new class of middle-income occupations which provided an enlarged clientele for doctors. It was also a growth period for hospitals which at the time were primarily places for medical training and the care of the destitute sick. The spread of hospitals and institutions like them for incarcerating the sick and needy, led to a growing need on the part of the state for trustworthy employees who could supervise them, which in turn expanded occupational opportunities for doctors. How was the state to distinguish the trained doctor from the quack? The 1858 Medical Act by insisting that only members of the profession need apply for state salaried positions, provided the answer to this question.

The period was also one of great optimism about science and technology. Even if medicine had yet to find a means of converting new scientific knowledge into effective therapy, as the standard bearer of science in the field of health care, it was probably assumed that it was just a matter of time. As the Victorian middle classes began to realise the scope for taking their future into their own hands, they would naturally believe that health was a suitable sphere for professional intervention and should not be left to divine fate. The profession also undoubtedly benefited from being associated with public health innovations which, although they had nothing to do with medical treatment as such, were nevertheless sometimes due to the inspiration of medical practitioners like Snow (see p.535). It was in this historical context that the British medical profession 'earned' its legal monopoly of practice.

Is there a Link between Medical Power and Capitalism?

In the twentieth century, doctors have become the most powerful, the most respected and the best paid professional group. In terms of their economic position, their education and life style, they seem to be part of the richest and most privileged class in society. This has led some writers to conclude that medical power itself derives from the profession's membership of the ruling economic class.

McKinley, in an analysis restricted to the organisation of health care in the USA, argues that medicine is a fully fledged part of commodity production under capitalism. He asserts that the *logic of capitalism* i.e. the drive to accumulate profit, has penetrated and overwhelmed the delivery of health care. The lack of demonstrable effectiveness of treatment, discussed in chapter 1 is a direct outcome of this. Treatments on offer in 'high tech' hospitals are there because they are profitable and any benefit to the sick person is quite coincidental. 'Consequently the House of Medicine under capitalism will never contribute to improvements in health unless such improvements facilitate an acceptable level of profit'. (McKinley 1977, 462).

For McKinley then, there is no difference between the production of the usual capitalist commodities, cars, washing machines, hot dogs, hairdressing and open heart surgery. The underlying logic of the manufacture of all these goods and services is the search for and seizure of profit. The real profit of medical practice is creamed off by:- (1) the large corporations which manufacture medical supplies, (2) the insurance companies which insure people against the potential 'misfortune' of both disease and treatment and (3) the owners of private hospitals who charge exhorbitant rates for in-patient treatment. This is why McKinley defines the majority of doctors as workers who are 'productive for capital'. Although their labour is 'socially wasteful' in that it does not fulfill real needs or contribute to human welfare, it is highly profitable. Doctors are therefore part of the subject class. They are there because they '. . . return even more value in the form of social surplus than they receive in the form wages'.

McKinley's thesis is directed as a critique of Freidson. His object is to show that medicine has no autonomy, that it is under the thumb of capitalist interest. Because medical treatment is so attractive to capital, doctors lose control and autonomy over the content of their work, finding themselves obliged to devote *most* effort to ineffective but profitable treatment. This means that medical science itself comes to neglect the most important health problems of the population. McKinley's model of the forces dictating the character of modern medical treatment depicts medicine as a dependent client of capital, a relationship negotiated by the state which grants the profession its monopoly.

Figure 7.1 Forces Determining the Character of Modern Medicine

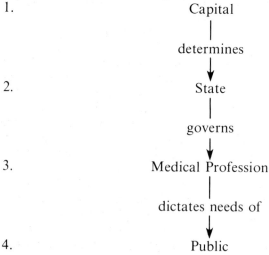

1.   Capital
                              |
                          determines
                              ↓

2.   State
                              |
                          governs
                              ↓

3.   Medical Profession
                              |
                         dictates needs of
                              ↓

4.   Public

Capital is the principal factor determining the nature of medical care in modern society. The other three levels are ranked hierarchically in order of decreasing importance. At the bottom, we find the dependent and guileless public who are presented as the willing human sacrifices on the alter of profit-oriented medical care. The medical profession are also a subject class in this model. Their control over their work conditions which features so prominently in Freidson, is illusory. Their work is ultimately just another form of commodity production subject to the logic of capitalism.

McKinley supports his account by pointing to the enormous profits generated from medical treatment in the US. He quotes the figure of $139 billion (8.9% GNP) as the total output of the medico-industrial complex in 1976. With all this money swimming around, McKinley finds the appeal of a Marxist interpretation irresistible. That medicine in the US is highly profitable is indisputable, but does this mean that that profitability is the principal force shaping what treatment is like?

The view of the medical profession as part of the subordinate class whose rewards do not represent the full value of their labour, is certainly novel. But in McKinley's application of Marxism to the medical industry in the US, the site of exploitation is not so much the human labourer as the human consumer. In other words the patient seems more exploited than the doctor. Nothing could be further from Parsons' view of this most vulnerable of social statuses requiring special protection in market society. In McKinley's account, the state acting as the executive of the ruling class, turns this vulnerability into a profitable business angle corrupting the healing profession into the bargain.

Can we accept this argument that the logic of capitalism determines every aspect of social organisation to the extent in this case of completely distorting the entire healing art/science? Certainly the USA provides the best example for the elaboration of the case. Other varieties of capitalism where the distribution of medical care has not been left to market forces, offer much less support. In Britain, virtually all investment in medical treatment comes from public funds and the scope for profiteering is very much less. Even so, the character of medicine is much the same in both societies suggesting that the criterion of profitability is not the major determinant of medical knowledge and technique. Doubting the validity of McKinley's position does not involve the denial of the existence of a profit orientation in the manufacture of medical supplies. But saying that profits can be made out of medicine does not lead to the conclusion that the businessman's greed for profit ultimately determines medical judgement and the treatment of patients. In McKinley's own words, 'the game would have little public appeal and could even be cancelled if the star players were absent' (p.467). This underlines the need to distinguish the real sources of the power of medicine from the mere fact that capitalist enterprise can cash in on it. Where health care is left to free market forces, medical work will undoubtedly favour forms of treatment which offer the highest rewards to the profession. But just because doctors can demand high salaries or fees does not mean that medical power is economic rather than political or ideological in *origin*.

Furthermore, to accept McKinley's case involves agreeing with an extremely pessimistic view of humanity. In his model, the consulting public are presented as a manipulated mass, hardly promising material for the fulfilment of the historic proletarian mission of liberating humankind through the inauguration of democratic socialism. This portrait of individuals painted by McKinley, is 'over-socialised' man, programmed to think and act in ways dictated by society. What it fails to take account of is the tendency of contemporary capitalism to raise individual consciousness and make people believe that they can and ought to exert more control over their circumstances and destines. The growth of individualism is the reason that challenges to the medical domination of ideas about health have begun to take shape in capitalist rather than collectivist or socialist societies.

In a classical Marxist sense, the capitalist class is distinguished by its ownership of the means of production and its economic position is sustained by making profit out of the labour of the working class. Clearly the medical profession does not fit easily into the picture of class relationships in this orthodox sense. They do not own productive property as such nor do they extract surplus value (i.e. profits) from workers in any direct way. However, Navarro argues that medicine aids the process of capital accumulation in an indirect way. By improving and maintaining the health of the workforce, medicine expands the productivity of human labour and thereby increases the volume of surplus value that may be extracted from it. Ironically the working class itself is seen as helping this process along. In making free medical care an object of class struggle, workers themselves have persuaded the state to subsidise wages and increase profits by relieving the employer of the burden of compensating workers directly for the damage to their health incurred by capitalist production.

A shortcoming of this interpretation is the false assumption that medicine has been and is responsible for improving human health. We have seen that there is no evidence to support this assumption. If anything, there is more evidence to support the opposite conclusion that medicine has helped reduce the productivity of the labour force in their official capacity as gatekeepers to the social security system. Since 1948, general practitioners have certified an ever increasing volume of 'time off' for sickness suggesting that the NHS has undermined the health of the workforce rather than improved it.

Table 7.1 Certified Sickness Absence in the UK

Year	Days Sickness Certified Per Man.
1954	12.8
1960	12.8
1962	13.2
1964	13.9
1966	14.5
1970	15.8
1973	16.2 (As % of 1954 = 127%)

Source: Adapted from *On the State of Public Health (1976)* HMSO, 1977. Adapted from table 2.5, p.30.

A more persuasive interpretation of the link between professional and class power sees medicine as acting as an ideological support to the capitalist system. Navarro calls medicine 'an ideological state mechanism' serving to mystify the real exploitative nature of capitalism and allowing the system to perpetuate itself. This interpretation, in common with other modern Marxist attempts to elaborate a *political economy of health,* starts from the premise that capitalism is the source of most if not all of the afflictions of human beings in the advanced industrial societies. From this perspective, what needs explaining is why the working class have not figured out how awful the system is and embarked upon the process of overthrowing it. The answer is provided by the Marxist concept of false consciousness. The working class have been lulled into a false sense of security which prevents them from recognising their true material interests. Medicine appears as an instrument of class rule in this explanation. It creates the illusion of a clever and caring society which is oriented to save human life. In focusing on the organic end product of disease, medicine deflects attention away from its causes in economic life. It thereby prevents health from becoming the political issue and potential force for social change that it would otherwise be.

All theoretical explanations have their limitations and this is no exception. The political economy of health thesis has a tautological character. This means that its conclusions are fashioned to provide a solution to a problem of its own making. The problem is: why is there so little class consciousness about the damage to human health caused by capitalist methods of production and distribution? The answer is: the capitalist class have incorporated the dominant healing profession within their ranks in order to use them as a means of disguising the way in which human health is corroded by a market society organised around the profit motive. But does capitalism have that much to hide? In relative terms, health has improved continuously under capitalism so that an alternative explanation might be that the ruling class has undersold itself. It has been duped by the medical profession along with most people into believing that doctors were responsible for bringing about improvements in health. In fact as we saw in chapters 1 and 2, the reduction of mortality in the nineteenth century was more likely to be linked to the growth of industrial capitalism in Britain than it was to anything connected to medicine as individual therapy.

This version of the political economy of health thesis suffers from a basic inability to show that capitalism as such is the cause of disease in modern society. There is no evidence to show that health in capitalist society is systematically worse than it is in socialist societies or any other kind of society for that matter. If anything, advanced capitalist societies have a better record in the post-war era than their collectivist neighbours in Eastern Europe (see p.558). While rates of mortality have continued to fall in most European societies, those in the West have fallen faster and further than those in the East. An exception to this is the Soviet Union, the only industrial society to actually witness increases in the mortality of citizens of all ages including infants. Since 1976, when the upward trend was clearly evident, the USSR has declined to supply any further statistics to the World Health Organisation (cf. Davis and Feshbein, 1981).

This suggests that the ruling class in capitalist society is not on the defensive to the extent that writers like Navarro presuppose. This in turn means that the need for agents of mystification, a role in which, by all accounts, the medical profession is in a class of its own, is overrated. This is not to argue that there is not an accommodation between the ruling profession and the ruling class. It is quite evident, for example, to take the case of the drug companies, that massive profits can be made out of the medical monopoly. But a handy alliance does not reduce professional power to an offshoot of capital. This leads us back to the possibility that the power of medicine in contemporary society is not just an adjunct of capital but has an autonomy all of its own.

Professional Autonomy and Health Policy

Freidson argues that *occupational autonomy* is the key to understanding the power of the medical profession in contemporary society. All occupational associations including trade unions seek to secure greater autonomy for their members. Few, if any, have been as successful as the medical profession in capturing complete control over the conditions of work, including a virtual guarantee of non-interference from outsiders. This occupational privilege is further strengthened in most industrial societies by the fact that medical care has largely been removed from the cash nexus. In consequence most patients do not pay the doctor directly for services provided. The paymaster is either the government or an insurance company with the result that there is less scope for accountability in the case of unsatisfactory treatment. In Britain the state pays for medical care mostly from taxation revenue. Treatment is free and general practitioners receive an annual capitation fee for each patient, irrespective of the quantity or quality of treatment provided. This tends to convert the delivery of medical care into a sort of free gift passing from the doctor to the patient in a manner which underlines the subservience of the recipient and the autonomy of the donor. The separation of the client from the process of payment may help to explain why the costs of medical care have rocketed well above the inflation rate, particularly in those societies where the insurance principle prevails.

In most advanced industrial societies, standards of health and health care are in part the responsibility of government, and political parties seeking election include health policy in their manifestos. However the existence of powerful professional interests severely restricts the room for political manouvre. How can politicians judge what is best for the nation's health? They lack the means to evaluate the prevailing claims of medicine and the absence of any independent evidence for assessing the effectiveness of treatment (see p.528) makes them dependent on the members of the profession for advice and guidance. The scope for conflict between politicians and the profession is minimised by the fact that medicine exerts great influence over popular ideas about the nature of health and illness so that professional aspirations tend to be synonymous with those of political parties. Debate takes the form of how much GNP should be spent on health (i.e. medical care) rather than focusing on issues which present any serious challenge to the status quo. This means that political parties seldom question the wisdom of tying up most resources earmarked for health in curative medical treatment. But when struggles over the use of resources do arise, the profession usually emerges victorious. The history of the NHS provides some illustrative examples of the triumph of professional autonomy in practice.

The introduction of the National Health Service in 1948, was the culmination of a bitter struggle between the Minister of Health, Aneurin Bevan, and the medical profession. The idea of a comprehensive system of health care had gained credibility during the war through the formation of the Emergency Medical Service and the publication of the Beveridge Report (1942). Before the end of hostilities, a number of discussion documents and proposals had been put forward by Liberal and Tory health ministers in the coalition government. These early plans included the proposal that doctors become salaried employees of the state. This was rejected by the profession who saw it as a threat to autonomy. The National Health Service Act of 1946, the enabling legislation for the new service, deliberately left vague the question of how doctors would be paid. Bevan favoured the idea of medical state salariat but knew it would be the major sticking point for the profession. According to Michael Foot, his biographer, he always intended to let the profession have their way, but judiciously left the question open so that it could be a point for negotiation and compromise on his part.

In the ensuing struggle Bevan allied himself to the most prestigious spokesmen for the profession, the leaders of the Royal Colleges, who represented the interests of the consultants in hospital. This elite section of the profession was not opposed to the idea of salaries which they had become used to during the war. Their recent experience of greater state intervention in the hospital sector enabled them to see the direct benefits to be gained from a stable source of finance. At this time many of the hospitals in Britain were funded by a mixture of charity and public funds. With the growth of new technology this source of finance was proving to be precarious and insufficient. During the thirties a number of financial crises had only been averted through the intervention of the state and many hospital specialists realised that a general take over was only a matter of time. In consequence they were natural allies for Bevan in his task of persuading the whole profession to come into the NHS. In the final compromise, the hospitals were taken into public ownership and the consultants became either full or part-time employees of the state. They even enjoyed the privilege of being able to use the enhanced resources of the publicly owned hospitals for private fee-paying patients. In addition a system of secret merit awards was introduced to provide some means for the leaders of the profession to reward what they took to be high standards of excellence. The general practitioners remained as fee-paid independent contractors: free to decide where they would practice, to arrange their own hours of work and to provide their own premises.

This agreement left the medical profession with a great deal of control over, not only their immediate conditions of work, but also over the definition of the priorities of the new service. It is unclear how far Bevan was aware of the power he had surrendered to the profession in 1948. At the time he declared, 'My job is to give you all the facilities, resources, apparatus and help I can and then to leave you alone as professional men and women, to use your skill and judgement without hindrance'.

In practice this meant that the National Health Service became a comprehensive medical service or, as some critics have put it, a national disease service, oriented to the treatment of symptoms and not to preventing disease or promoting health in any positive sense. The profession retained substantial control over the management of the service and inequalities in the provision of services between different parts of Britain which were evident before the war remained just as marked thirty years later (see p.580). These inequalities were the product of the haphazard development of voluntary hospitals set up on the proceeds of charitable trusts and bequests. A nationally organised system of medical care ought to have equalised variations over the country, but it did not. The budget for the service instead tended to be allocated according to historical precedent, so that areas best endowed in 1948, continued to be so when the government took over responsibility for finance. Bevan's aim was to provide equality of access to medical care across the country as a whole, but he did not establish a central means of control that was capable of resisting the profession's desire to maintain things the way they were. In effect, by gaining control of the NHS in this way, the profession consolidated its power making it virtually unassailable.

It is interesting that Bevan, the health minister of the 1946 Labour Government, recently elected in a landslide poll, did not question the assumption that health care was synonymous with medical treatment. He seemed to share the belief of Beveridge, that there is a finite quantity of disease in the population. In 1948, it was anticipated that the high initial costs of the NHS would gradually fall as people became healthier under its influence. This forecast proved to be disastrously incorrect and within a few years, a Royal Commission was set up to inquire into the reason for rising costs. Since then the same trend has continued despite government economies. The continued growth of expenditure reflects the expansion of the medical profession, the introduction of new specialisms and forms of treatment often involving expensive technological equipment and, not least important, demographic trends (in particular an ageing population). The impact of advanced medical technology on the health of the population as a whole is not understood with any precision. What can be said is that it is not very great (see chapter 1). Nevertheless, according to the distribution of merit awards for excellence of achievement, high technology medicine appears to be the area the most valued by the leaders of the profession. Merit awards are secret payments made to selected consultants in the NHS on the advice of a professional committee. In 1977, while more than 60% of cardiologists and neuro-surgeons received these awards, effectively doubling their salaries, less than 30% of specialists in geriatrics or mental health were so lucky. The greatest rewards in terms of both salaries and resources for practice, go to the sector where the feats of 'heroic' surgery take place. Perhaps the profession has realised that there is nothing like an occasional mircale for sustaining public confidence in routine medical treatment.

However, there are signs of an increasing awareness of the limitations of medical treatment. These have come from within the profession as well as from outside of it. Critics accept that most serious disease afflicting people after the age of 50 is more amenable to prevention than to cure. Equally the disabling conditions of old age which increase as the population ages, require nursing and counselling rather than medical attention. But redirecting the priorities of the NHS has proved to be a near impossible task. Successive priority documents published by the DHSS (Department of Health and Social Security) have called for a redistribution of the budget to favour community care for the 'cinderella services'. They argue for the contraction of the hospital sector and an expansion of domicilliary care, enabling people to be cared for in their own homes instead of being incarcerated in long-stay hospitals. But they have never been put into effect by the regional and district health authorities directly responsible for NHS expenditure. In the period since 1970, the hospital sector has continued to expand at the expense of the underprivileged community sector as Figure 7.2 reveals. Alaszewski and Haywood, in a study of how these national priorities get subverted in the process of local decision-making, conclude that the blockage is to be found in the principle of *clinical autonomy*. District treasurers and administrators faced with powerful local consultants who insist that their resources be maintained or even increased, have no means of challenging 'clinical judgement'. To do so would be tantamount to claiming that they know better than the doctor.

Figure 7.2 Selected Health Service Labour Power Statistics, 1959-1973

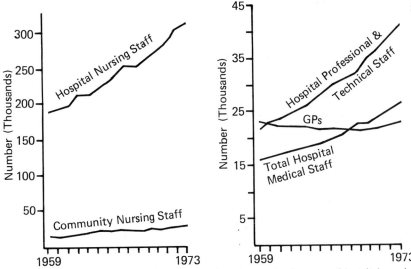

Note: Whole-time equivalents are used throughout except in the case of hospital nursing staff and GPs where actual numbers are given.

Source: *Health, Money and the National Health Service* by P. Draper, G. Best and J. Dennis, p.34 (Unit for the Study of Health Policy, Guy's Hospital Medical School, April 1976).

These national statistics indicate the increasing share of the NHS budget consumed by the hospital sector. The tale they tell is of a decentralised system of decision-making in the NHS, heavily influenced by powerful clinical interests, who get their own way despite central directives from the DHSS.

Concluding Remarks: Whose Interests does Medicine Serve?

In every advanced industrial society, the medical profession enjoys monopoly privileges in the labour market. These privileges have been secured from the political elite of each nation state with the result that medicine is, in large measure, an international profession. Its practitioners are highly paid, highly respected and they enjoy a great deal of control over the conditions of their work, even to the point of being insulated from criticism and accountability. The power of the profession in society at large is not merely the sum of the occupational privileges of each doctor. Individual privilege flows from the position medicine occupies as a social institution in contemporary society. As a social institution, medicine is rather like a secular religion. It is the received wisdom on matters of life and death as well as on physical and spiritual welfare. Its esoteric knowledge has the characteristic form known as the 'bio-mechanical model' and because of the power of the profession, it is *the* orthodox way of thinking about health and organising the delivery of health care. Naturally this means that in Britain, the medical profession has captured the National Health Service. Control over the NHS gives doctors 5.5% of GNP to spend on their professional activities. This has meant that the development of health care over the post-war era has been dominated by cure-oriented, hospital centred treatment, with a corresponding neglect of prevention and a devaluation of the caring dimensions of healing relationships.

The power of the profession has an explicit legal form. It is enshrined in the statutes of each separate nation state and this implies a certain level of dependence on political elites. In other words, medicine got its exclusive mandate from the state, and what the state has given, the state could conceivably take away. However, the prospect of the ruling elite in any society attempting to withdraw the exclusive license it issued in the past, is not very great. In Britain, the profession has enjoyed its monopoly for over a century and during this time it has gradually imposed its own version of the meaning of health and health care on the population. This book has argued that there are a number of regressive features in modern medicine: the singular focus on cure rather than care or prevention; the mind/body dualism; the tendency to ignore the influence of behaviour and environment in preference for taking the abstract individual as the site of disease; the obsession with the manipulation of organic symptoms through chemical and mechanical means; and the treatment of patients in the isolated, even mortifying, environment of the hospital. Remember these negative dimensions of contemporary medicine are not the unfortunate but unavoidable side effects of successful treatment. They are the core of the profession's occupational skill and the NHS is organised to deliver health care according to this professional recipe whose contribution to present standards of health has never been carefully evaluated but is known to be very limited.

Nevertheless the profession's version of what health and disease are like, is written into our culture. The bio-mechanical approach is literally interwoven with everyday beliefs about why sickness occurs and what must be done about it. This means that the profession has greatly consolidated its power base in society. Skilfull political organisation was its original route to power, but in becoming an orthodox body of cultural belief, a new ideological dimension has been added which makes the profession virtually immune to outside interference. It is possible that doctors are more powerful in Britain than in other industrial societies which have continued to allow the market to intervene in the provision of treatment. By gaining control of the NHS, doctors find themselves offering free services to people in need. The gift-like dimensions of the professional art in this country must also serve to build public support for the profession and to further weaken the scope for any government to take back any part of the medical monopoly. Medicine's power in contemporary society is therefore built out of a combination of political organisation, ideological domination, and control over the infrastructure of public resources for health. To reform health care would involve action to weaken the medical power base on each of these fronts and the most important preliminary would be to dilute the power of medical ideas in our culture by exposing their limitations. Herein lies the real message for health education.

This explains how doctors sustain their powerful position in society, but in whose interests do they exercise their power? This chapter has provided three possible answers to this question. Parsons sees the medical profession acting to protect the public interest by upholding high standards of treatment. We have seen in earlier chapters that health care fashioned according to the bio-mechanical model has serious limitations and, in this chapter, that attempts to reform it in the direction of prevention and domicilliary care, are invariably blocked by professional autonomy. It is clear from this that the promotion of better health in the population is not the profession's overriding concern. If it was, the NHS would devote far more resources to disease prevention than it currently does (less than 1% in 1982). This suggests that altruism towards fellow human beings is not a particularly important force behind the development of professional medicine. This in turn means that it is inappropriate to locate the objectives of the profession's bid for power in something called community service.

More significant for Parsons, is medicine's role as an agency of social control. Good health is a functional pre-requisite for society and 'health' for Parsons, means the satisfactory performance of social roles. Medical treatment is presented as a mechanism for maintaining the individual's sense of commitment to social roles and of responsibility to other people. It therefore helps to maintain the high levels of social co-operation which are necessary in advanced industrial society. To Parsons therefore, medicine exercises its power in the interests of society as a whole.

We saw in chapter 6 that empirical studies of doctor/patient relationships offer little support to Parsons' typification of the sick role. Moreover, the statistics of sickness absence suggest that access to free medical care has, if anything, led to an increase in absenteeism rather than acted, as Parsons would predict, to uphold the work ethic. There is an important sense in which organised medicine serves as a preservative of social solidarity, but it is not the one which Parsons had in mind. Since the war, the NHS has been the primary symbol of citizenship in Britain. By promising to treat everyone in an equal fashion, it stands as a testimony to the idea of social equality in a democratic society. This was an explicit intention on the part of its founders and like other features of the welfare state, it has helped to bind the political consensus that our own form of society is the best currently an offer.

Navarro's view of the objects of medical power shares certain similarities with Parsons, although in other ways, it is radically different. Like Parsons, he sees medicine performing a conservative social *function*. It is principally designed to preserve the social system. The explanation of social institutions in functionalist terms is the hallmark of Parsonian social theory. In Navarro, we see a Marxist inspired version, an example of what Mishra calls 'left functionalism'. Navarro finds medicine serving to maintain the stability of the capitalist system, by maintaining the health and productivity of the workforce while dampening down social protest. This last function sees medicine as an 'ideological state mechanism', with the profession acting as the public relations arm of the ruling class, obscuring the real causes of disease in order to make the system appear more attractive than it really is. This view echoes the memorable pronouncement of Balfour at the turn of the century that social legislation is not merely different to socialist legislation, it is its most direct and effective antidote.

Navarro's interpretation of the purposes medicine serves makes use of the fit which exists between high technology medicine and the dominant character of industrial capitalist civilisation. He draws out the essential features of the bio-mechanical model and uses them to show how the profession disguises the real environmental and occupational nature of disease under capitalism in a false model of individual pathology. The bio-mechanical model is not an isolated feature of contemporary culture. As chapter 1 argues, it reflects the individualistic and technological ethos of advanced industrial civilisation. For this reason it could be argued that there is a natural fit between contemporary medicine and industrial capitalism. While this may be correct, it does not explain why professional medicine fits perfectly well, and for that matter helps to sustain, other kinds of social organisation which are far more collectivist than capitalist in character.

Both Navarro and Parsons provide 'functionalist' accounts in which medicine appears primarily as an institution of social control maintaining the stability of society. Where Navarro and Parsons part company is over the purpose of theory. For Navarro the purpose is not just to explain social order and stability but to disturb it. By his account, medicine only serves the public interest to the extent that this is defined by the ruling class. The issue therefore is not whether professional interests are in line with those of the general public, it is whether the 'public interest itself' represents the true needs of the people. Navarro identifies an antagonism between the *real interests of ordinary people* and the stability of the capitalist system. In his view, people would be better off if the system fell apart. He makes the presumption that the collapse of Western capitalism, would usher in a better socialist system and not fascist or totalitarian regimes of the extreme right. But the antagonisms he identifies in capitalist society are so disguised and imprisoned by powerful institutional devices that they do not appear to pose any particular threat to the survival of the system. The inherent contradictions of capitalism, which were the seeds of its downfall for Marx, appear to have been so securely 'packaged' in Navarro's theory, that there is little chance of their seeping out to damage society. This underlines a fundamental difficulty of all 'functionalist' theory. If everything functions together to maintain the stability of the whole, how does change come about? It is ironic that contemporary Marxist interpretations of the *political economy of health* should find themselves so closely allied to the mainstream of conservative American social theory.

This leaves us with Freidson's view of medical power and influence in society. His answer to the question, 'Whose interests does medicine serve?' is quite clear. The profession is primarily devoted to serving its own interests. According to Freidson, doctors have secured such an extraordinary degree of control over the conduct of their work that they are in a class of their own — in short they are socially autonomous. This autonomy has delivered to the profession the unquestioned right to literally define what is health and what is illness, nothing less than a direct participation in the social construction of cultural knowledge. But Freidson is not tempted to elaborate this into a grand theoretical design in which doctors either consciously or unconsciously devote themselves to the preservation of the status quo. His theoretical aims are more modest. He seeks primarily to understand of the role of professions in the labour market and the wider society. His choice of medicine as a case study of professional organisation stems from its contemporary preeminence in the social division of labour. As he notes, among the traditional professions only medicine has developed a systematic connection with science and technology. This has led to the development of a complex division of labour in medical care which is orchestrated and controlled by doctors. Here is further evidence of medical autonomy. The profession not only controls its own conditions of work, it is also in charge of a whole army of helpers ranging from the unskilled to lesser professions.

The source of medical power and autonomy is located by Freidson in political action. It was through collective organisation that the profession was able to successfully negotiate with the state for monopoly rights in the labour market. Esoteric knowledge and technique, are also important and this chapter has argued that there is an ideological dimension to medical power which develops in the aftermath of the profession's successful efforts in the political arena. Freidson's approach emphasises the significance of political and ideological power resources. While he does not deny the existence of capitalist enterprise organised to cash in on medical treatment, he sees no evidence that the character of treatment itself is dictated by it.

It is easier to accept the arguments of Freidson, not least because they are more modest in their scope. Freidson remains sceptical of reductionist explanations, for, as he points out, individual capitalist and socialist countries develop their own highly variable and particular character so that: 'Neither the logic of capitalism nor the logic of socialism can thus get realised in anywhere near a "pure" form.' (Freidson 1977, 486). It is in this spirit that he insists that the autonomy of the medical profession sets its members apart from other workers, bestowing a type of power of much broader social relevance which is quite simply different from economically determined power, or power flowing from an imaginary functional logic of social stability.

Bibliography

Alaszewski, A. and Haywood S. *Crisis in the Health Service* (Croom Helm, London, 1980).

Alderson, M. *International Mortality Statistics* (Macmillan, London, 1981).

Antonovsky, A. 'Conceptual and Methodological Problems in the Study of Resistance Resources and Stressful Life Events' in *Stressful Life Events: Their Nature and Effects* edited by Dohrenwend, B.P. and Dohrenwend, B.S. (John Wiley & Sons, New York, 1974).

Brenner, M.H. *Estimating the Social Cost of national Economic Policy: implications for mental and physical health, and criminal aggression* (Joint Committee of the US Congress, Washington DC, 1976).

Brotherston, J. 'Inequality: Is is Inevitable?' in Carter C.O. and Peel J., eds. (1976).

Brown, G. and Harris, T. *Social Origins of Depression* (Tavistock, London, 1978).

Burnett, M. *Genes, Dreams and Realities* (Medical and Technical Publishing Company Ltd., Aylesbury, Bucks. 1971).

Byrne, P.S. and Long, B.E. *Doctors Talking to Patients* (HMSO, London, 1976).

Carter, C.O. and Peel, J. *Equalities and Inequalities in Health* (Academic Press, London, 1976).

Cartwright, A. and O'Brian, M. 'Social Class, Variations in Health Care and the Nature of General Practitioner Consultations' in *The Sociology of the NHS* edited by M. Stacey (Sociological Review Monograph No. 22, Keele University, 1976).

Cartwright, A. *Patients and their Doctors* (Routledge and Kegan Paul, London, 1967).

Cochrane, A.L. *Effectiveness and Efficiency: Random Reflections on Health Services,* (Nuffield Provincial Hospitals Trust, 1972).

Cooper, R. 'Rising Death Rates in the Soviet Union: The Impact of Coronary Heart Disease' in *New England Journal of Medicine* (Vol. 304: 21: 1259-65, 1981).

Coser, R.L. *Life on the Ward* (University of Illinois Press, East Lansing, 1962).

Davis, C. and Feshbein, M. *Rising Infant Mortality in the USSR in the 1970s* (Government Printing Office, Washington, D.C., Series P.95, No. 74, 1980).

DHSS *Report of the Resource Allocation Working Party* (DHSS, 1976).

DHSS *Inequalities in Health: Report of a Research Working Group* (1981).

Dohrendwend, B.P. and Dohrendwend, B.S. (eds). *Stressful Life Events. Their Nature and Effects* (John Wiley and Sons, New York, 1974).

Doyal, L. and Pennell, I. *The Political Economy of Health* (Pluto Press, London, 1979).

Dubos, R. *Mirage of Health* (Harper & Row, New York, 1959).

Durkheim, E. *The Division of Labour in Society* (The Free Press of Glencoe, Collier-MacMillan Ltd., London, 1964 Ed.)

Durkheim, E. *Suicide* (Routledge and Kegan Paul, London, 1952).

Dutton, J. 'Changes in Soviet Mortality Patterns, 1959-1977' in *Population and Development Review 5* (pp.267-69, 1977).

Evans-Pritchard, E.E. *The Nuer* (Clarendon Press, Oxford, 1940).

Evans-Pritchard, E.E. *Witchcraft, Oracles and Magic* (Oxford University Press, Oxford, 1978).

Eyer, J. 'Capitalism, Health and Illness' in *Readings in the Political Economy of Health* edited by McKinley J. (pp.23-59) (Tavistock London, 1984).

Ferguson, T. and McPhail, A.N. *Hospital and Community* (Oxford University Press, London, 1954).

Fox, J. *et al Working Paper No. 18,* ESRC *Workshop on Health and Unemployment* (Oct. 26th, 1984).

Freidson, E. *Profession of Medicine* (Dodd, Mead & Co., New York, 1975).

Freidson, E. 'Comment on McKinley' in *International Journal of Health Services* (Vol. 7, No. 3, pp.485-86, 1977).

Friedman, M. and Rosenman, R.H. 'Association of specific overt behaviour pattern with blood and cardiovascular findings'. *Journal of the American Medical Association,* 169, 1286-1296, 1959.

Garfinkel, H. *Studies in Ethnomethodology* (Prentice Hall, Englewood Cliffs, 1967).

Gerhardt, U. 'Coping and Social Action' in *Sociology of Health and Illness* (Vol. 1, No. 2, 1979).

Goffman, E. *Asylums, Essays on the Social Situations of Mental Patients and Other*

Inmates (Doubleday Anchor, New York, 1961).

Hall, M.H. *et al* 'Is Routine Ante-Natal Care Worthwhile?' *The Lancet* July 1980, 78-80.

Hinkle, L.E. 'The Concept of Stress in the Biological and Social Sciences' in *Science, Medicine and Man* (Vol. 1, 31-48, 1973).

Hinkle L.E. and Wolff H.G. 'The nature of man's adaptation to his total environment and the relation of this to illness' *Archives of Internal Medicine*, No. 22, 1957.

Holmes, T.H. and Rahe, R.H. 'The Social Readjustment Rating Scale' in *The Journal of Psychosomatic Research* (11, 213-18, 1967).

Illich, I. *Medical Nemesis* (Bantam Books, New York, 1977).

Illsley, R. 'Social Class Selection and Class Differences in Relation to Stillbirths' in *The British Medical Journal* (ii, 1520, 1955).

Lazarus, R. *Psychological Stress and the Coping Process* (McGraw Hill, New York, 1966).

Rees, W. and Lutkins, S. 'Mortality and Bereavement' *British Medical Journal* 1967, 4, 13-16.

McKeown, T. *The Modern Rise of Population* (Edward Arnold, London, 1976).

McKeown, T. *The Role of Medicine: Dream, Mirage or Nemesis?* (The Nuffield Provincial Hospitals Trust, London, 1976).

McKinley, J. 'The Business of Good Doctoring or Doctoring as Good Business: Reflections on Freidson's View of the Medical Game' in *International Journal of Health Services* (Vol. 7, No. 3, 459-83, 1977).

McNeill, W., *Plagues and Peoples* (Doubleday, New York, 1976).

Marmott, M.G. *Social Inequalities in Mortality - The Social Environment* (Dept. of Epidemiology, London School of Hygiene, 1982).

Millman, M. *The Unkindest Cut* (Morrow, New York, 1977).

Mishra, R. *Society and Social Policy: Theoretical Perspectives on Welfare* (Macmillan, London 1977).

Navarro, V. *Medicine under Capitalism* (Croom Helm, London, 1976).

OPCS *Longitudinal Study: Socio-demographic mortality differences, 1971-75*. Fox A.J. and Goldblatt P.O. (HMSO, London, 1982)

OPCS *Trends in Mortality* (HMSO, London, 1978).

OPCS *General Household Survey, 1974* (HMSO, London, 1976).

OPCS *Demographic Review, 1977* (HMSO, London, 1978).

OPCS *Occupational Mortality, 1970-72* (HMSO, London, 1978).

Parsons, T. *The Social System* (The Free Press, Glencoe, Illionois, 1951).

Parsons, T. 'The sick role and the role of the physician reconsidered' in *Millbank Memorial Fund Quarterly* (53: 257-78, 1975).

Selye, H. *The Stress of Life* (McGraw Hill, New York, 1956).

Stern, J. *Unemployment and its impact on Morbidity and Mortality* (Discussion Paper No. 93, Centre for Labour Economics, L.S.E.)

Stern, J. 'Social Mobility and the Interpretation of Social Class Mortality Differences' *Journal of Social Policy*, 1981.

Szasz, T. and Hollander, M. 'A contribution to the philosophy of medicine: the basic model of the doctor-patient relationship' in *Archives of Internal Medicine* (97: 585-92, 1956).

Totman, R. *The Social Causes of Illness* (Souvenir Press, London 1979).

Winter, J. 'Aspects of the Impact of the First World War on Infant Mortality in Britain' *Journal of European Economic History* 1982, Vol. 11, 713-738.

Wirth L. 'Urbanism As a Way of Life' *American Sociological Review* 1938, 44, 1-24.

Wrigley, A. and Scofield, R. *The Population History of England 1450-1870* (Cambridge University Press, Cambridge 1981).

Name Index

Subject Index